COMPREHENSIVE
Graphic
Arts

COMPREHENSIVE
Graphic Arts

Dr. Ervin A. Dennis
University of Northern Iowa

Dr. John D. Jenkins
Eastern Kentucky University

HOWARD W. SAMS & CO., INC.
INDIANAPOLIS · KANSAS CITY · NEW YORK

FOREWORD

Comprehensive Graphic Arts is a recent title to be added to Howard W. Sams & Co., Inc. publications in industrial education. This series of textbooks is designed to cover the broad fields in industrial, career, and occupational education.

Graphic arts education has needed a comprehensive publication for several years and we fully believe this volume will fill the gap. It is the most composite publication of its kind.

The book is essentially a basic text designed for a full year of graphic arts instruction at the secondary school level or for a post-high school program in a technical institution. The most recent and reliable information is provided concerning the many facets of graphic arts technology. The student is provided an opportunity to develop interesting and challenging activities through laboratory experiences related to the numerous theories and technical instruction presented.

This text is profusely illustrated with more than 1000 photographs and descriptive drawings. As in the other Sams publications, four colors are used to indicate and emphasize significant points and headings and to accent direction and action in the illustrations.

The authors and publisher know that this book will develop student interest and enlarge the concept of the rapidly expanding technological area of graphic arts.

DR. CLAUDE RIETH
INDIANA STATE UNIVERSITY

PREFACE

Comprehensive Graphic Arts has been designed by the authors to provide a full appreciation and recognition of the graphic arts technical areas of industry. This volume has been produced primarily as a graphic arts text for use at all levels of instruction.

The book acquaints readers with the unique technological aspects of the various graphic arts processes, the interrelationships among these areas, and other significant topics essential to successful performance and understanding of this communications area. It is organized into sections, or areas, of graphic arts, each section containing a number of relevant units. The first unit of each section provides a brief introduction to that area; the last one presents learning experiences through discussion topics and meaningful activities. These assist the reader in ascertaining whether or not he has learned the preceding material.

The profusely illustrated text uses color to emphasize information which assists in understanding movement and direction of the various illustrated processes. Important topics are treated and discussed basically, and if the reader desires a more detailed coverage of any of them, he should seek and examine appropriate resource material. Performance directions enable the person using this text to follow explicit processes in sequential numerical order.

Section 1 defines graphic arts and presents an overview of this significant and growing industrial technology. Sections 2 and 3 pertain to useful design and layout which are so important to all graphic reproduction. Sections 4, 5, and 6 explain and illustrate the several methods of producing type composition. Proofing and composition paste-up for camera-ready copy are also discussed at length. Section 7 introduces the area of photoconversion, which involves use of the process camera, films, and chemicals for high-contrast photography.

The techniques involved in preparing image carriers and the operation of image-transfer devices for the four major printing methods of letterpress, lithography, gravure, and screen printing are described in Sections 8 through 15. Section 16 deals with the area of continuous-tone photography. Section 17 reviews several office duplicating methods.

Section 18 outlines and describes what is done to the printed sheets after they leave the press. Binding methods are discussed in step-by-step detail. The processes of manufacture and the several kinds of basic raw materials, such as paper and ink, are reviewed in Sections 19 and 20.

Section 21 informs graphic arts students of a few of the many legal aspects in reproducing printed material. The student is encouraged to examine seriously Section 22 for the possibility of discovering a career.

Appreciation is extended to the many companies, corporations, and associations which provided photographs, drawings, and technical assistance in the preparation of this volume. Credit is given for each illustration obtained in this manner. Special recognition is given Dr. Darrell Smith, California State College, California, Pennsylvania, for his quality illustrative production and for his understanding and appreciation of the graphic arts field. Misses LaVada Dennis and Jerry Ann Jenkins are given credit for their patience, understanding, and help during the initial preparation of this material, and thanks goes to Mrs. Virginia Groneman for assistance in preparing the manuscript. Acknowledgment is due Dr. Chris H. Groneman for his encouragement and coordination efforts. Appreciation is also extended to Dr. Claude Rieth for his critical review of the entire manuscript.

ERVIN A. DENNIS
JOHN D. JENKINS

Cover photo: Courtesy of Harris—Intertype Corporation
The press is a Harris 125 sheet-fed offset press.

CONTENTS

A grocery store contains a wide
array of food packaging, all a product of the graphic arts industry.

UNIT 1
INTRODUCTION TO GRAPHIC ARTS

Graphic arts is first of all a communicative art. It is part of graphic communications, which deal with all industries, arts, and processes that produce a message with visible images on varied surfaces. It is also an important means of preserving art and is an essential part of visual communication, embodying a full range of aesthetic ingredients. A high degree of craftsmanship, mechanical aptitude, and a fine sense for the use of materials are required to accomplish this visual balance in a serious professional manner.

THE PURPOSE OF GRAPHIC ARTS

The primary purpose of the graphic arts is to create and produce products that will communicate visually. Some products of the industry do not necessarily communicate by words or pictures, but serve a functional purpose. These include paper bags and towels, dinner napkins, and plain paper.

Graphic arts communication materials are usually two-dimensional in nature (length and width), but three-dimensional materials are available and may soon constitute a sizable share of the many graphic forms.

Visual images such as reading matter, photographs, colored illustrations, and the like are on the products that we purchase (Fig. 1-1), and in newsstands throughout our cities (Fig. 1-2). Studies reveal that man learns 80 percent of what he knows through his eyes. This figure represents the strong impact of an industry that is concerned with the production of visual images.

Fig. 1-1. Just one sampling of the many graphic arts products used today.

Fig. 1-2. Magazines are a product which entertains, informs, and disseminates information.

THE INFLUENCE OF GRAPHIC ARTS

The information explosion has accelerated the output of both hard-cover and paperback books (Fig. 1-3), as well as magazines and technical journals. The industrial boom has also created markets for advertising and promotional copy, brochures, catalogs, and dictionaries. The printed sheet (graphic reproduction) has never in history had a place more prominent than it has today. Our culture relies to a high degree on graphic arts.

Fig. 1-4. Playing cards were one of the first products of the graphic arts.

Graphic arts industry products are the only means of permanent mass communication. Visual materials are available to most people, and any graphic product can be read and permanently stored for retrieval at a later date. Graphic arts products are an important force in the world scene.

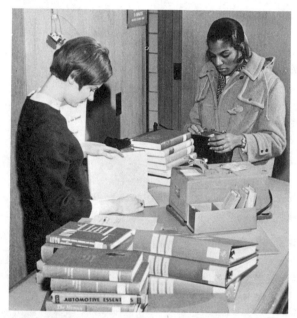

Fig. 1-3. Books are treasures. Without the graphic arts there would be few of them.

Objects used for recreation, such as playing cards (Fig. 1-4), were among the first graphic arts products. According to some authorities, the earliest form of visual image or graphic art was branding (Fig. 1-5). This means of identification was used as early as 2000 B.C. Tombs in Egypt show ancient brands and illustrations of the process of branding. There is biblical evidence that Jacob, the great herdsman, branded his stock. The Romans, Greeks, and Chinese marked their animals and even their slaves by branding. The first branding of cattle in America was done by Hernando Cortes, conqueror of Mexico.

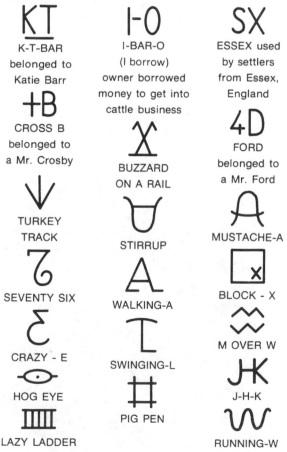

Fig. 1-5. Branding is one of the oldest forms of the graphic arts.

UNIT 2
THE SCOPE OF GRAPHIC ARTS

Graphic arts as a method of communication exists wherever there is civilization. Man must have graphic materials to assist him in his daily life. Have you ever gone through an entire day without coming into direct contact with some type of printed material, such as a newspaper, book, magazine, advertisement, clothes label, or letter? If you have had this experience, wasn't it a lonesome day?

A current phenomenon of the business-industry world is the computer and its impact on life. The graphic arts industry was quick to recognize the value of this new concept and the computer plays a major role in nearly all phases of the industry (Fig. 2-1). This book was typeset by the high-speed Linotron 505, a photographic composition system that includes a computer. The Linotron 505 was designed and produced by the builder of the original linotype machine, the Mergenthaler Company.

A BUSINESS ENTERPRISE

Several types of business enterprises make up the total graphic arts industry. Of these, the commercial printing plants and newspapers are the most common. Commercial printing plants produce all types of printed materials, from simple letterheads and business forms to complicated advertis-

Fig. 2-2. Tons of paper in sheet and roll form are consumed each year. (The Mead Corp.)

ing materials and books. Newspapers are available at newsstands and at stores throughout the nation, and millions of them are delivered to homes every day. Printed materials inform and entertain us nearly every day of our lives.

Paper is a commodity, or useful material. Paper manufacturers are located all over the United States and produce the tons of paper consumed each year (Fig. 2-2).

Another enterprise is *ink* manufacturing. Without this image-producing material or medium, there would be no way to relay information on paper and a variety of other solid materials.

Fig. 2-1. Computers are used throughout the business-industry world, and the graphic arts industry is no exception with equipment like the Linotron 505. (Alexander Typesetting Co.)

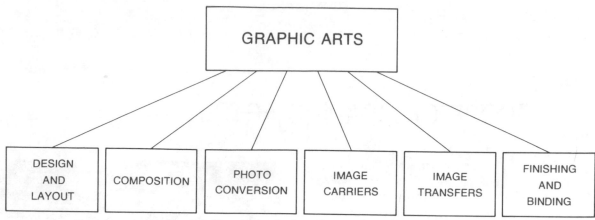

Fig. 2-3. The six production phases of graphic arts.

Equipment and *chemical* manufacturers are parts of the total graphic arts industry. Without them there would be no machines to produce printed materials and no raw materials from which printed matter is made.

DIVISIONS OF GRAPHIC ARTS

The production phases of graphic arts can be divided into six areas (Fig. 2-3). Commercial printing plants do not always identify these six production areas by name, but in most situations it is necessary for printed jobs to pass from one phase to another.

Design and *layout.* Planning graphic materials for multiple reproduction is the first and most important step in producing a graphic arts product. Creativity, a skilled hand, and a knowledge of the basic reproduction methods are needed by the design and layout artist (Fig. 2-4). The artist must also have a knowledge of design and color principles, characteristics of type, and layout procedures before mastering this area of graphic arts.

Composition. Assembly of alphabetical characters into usable and meaningful form is the second production phase of graphic arts. Several different methods of composing type permit a wide choice of sizes and styles. Sophisticated equipment has been developed to help the compositor prepare type composition (Fig. 2-5).

Photo conversion. Photo conversion encompasses the processes by which light-sensitive materials capture images, whether

Fig. 2-4. A design and layout artist completing plans for a company brochure. An understanding of the customer's needs is most important.

Fig. 2-5. A compositor preparing type (composition) by using two tape-controlled, automatic, hot-metal, type-composing machines. (Intertype Co.)

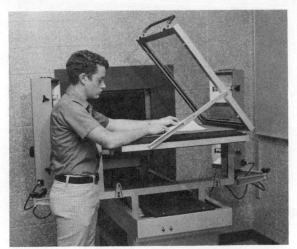

Fig. 2-6. A camera operator places copy in the copyboard of a process camera. (nuArc Company, Inc.)

Fig. 2-8. Skilled pressmen prepare printed copies that will soon reach the public. (The Miehle Co.)

they are on paper or film. Cameras, lights, light-sensitive film and paper, and chemicals are the items of equipment and materials that are used within this production area. The darkroom is the work center in which the photographic technician completes his phase of work (Fig. 2-6).

Image carriers. These are the devices which carry the images or designs from the photographic film to the press and ultimately reproduce multiple copies. *Plates, cuts,* and *printing screens* are common terms used throughout industry to name these devices.

Research specialists constantly conduct tests and experiment with new processes, methods, and equipment. Several new

image carriers have been developed in recent years (Fig. 2-7).

Image transfer. Within this area the operation procedures of actual printing take place. Of the six production areas of the graphic arts this is the only area where actual printing is done. Machines containing image carriers prepared in the previous production phase are used to print images on many kinds of receptors, or materials and surfaces such as paper, cloth, metal, glass, wood, etc. (Fig. 2-8). Skilled personnel are needed to operate the sophisticated image transfer machines.

Finishing and *binding.* After the printed copies have been produced by one of the image transfer methods, the area of finish-

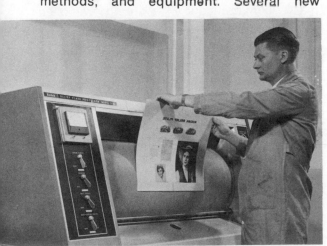

Fig. 2-7. A research specialist conducts tests on a new image carrier. (Eastman Kodak Co.)

Fig. 2-9. Printed sheets are gathered and bound, ready for customer use. (General Binding Corp.)

ing and binding is involved. Paper must be folded, cut, perforated, drilled, punched with holes, gathered, and bound in one of several ways (Fig. 2-9).

Once the product has passed through the finishing and binding phase, it is ready to be distributed to the customer. This book, in fact, has been prepared according to the production phases just presented.

Specialties. Within larger communities, graphic arts business establishments cater to certain specialties of manufacturing or production phases. These specialty houses deal strictly with design and layout, composition, or photoconversion. They are needed because some commercial printers do not have a means of composing type and must subcontract a type composition job to a composition specialty house. Specialty houses increase in popularity as the complexity of the graphic arts industry increases.

UNIT 3
CULTURAL CONTRIBUTIONS OF GRAPHIC ARTS

Throughout the centuries communication, products of the graphic arts have contributed significantly to cultural development. In his desire to communicate with others, man began with gestures and simple sounds. These, however, limited him to communication within a small geographical area. He had to discover the means to share knowledge with posterity before he could advance his way of life. Graphic forms evolved slowly. Approximately 2500 B.C. the first simple alphabet was used (refer to Unit 8). This became the link between the past, present, and future.

EARLY SIGNIFICANT EVENTS

Numerous events through the centuries contributed to cultural development. In A.D. 105 Ts'ai Lun, a Chienese, invented paper. Wood blocks were first used for communication by the Japanese in A.D. 770. Approximately 100 years later the Chinese produced the first book, *The Diamond Sutra.* The first movable type was cast in A.D. 1100 by the Chinese. This type consisted of reusable symbols or characters which were cast in earthenware.

The Chinese secrets were well kept, and it was not until about 1450 that Johann Gutenberg of Germany developed reusable, movable *metal* type. These type characters were cast individually and could be assembled into any order desired. Gutenberg's invention made it possible for man to advance in his cultural development over the centuries. Other events promoted the recording of man's thoughts and desires but none compare to the invention of Gutenberg, which made possible the development of mass communication. Printing removed man from the Dark Ages of ignorance and raised him into the light of knowledge.

SIGNIFICANT UNITED STATES EVENTS

The first printing press in the United States was set up near Boston, Massachusetts, in the year 1638, to print materials for Harvard University (then in its third year). The printer, Matthew Daye, produced the first book printed in the colonies, *The Whole Book of Psalms.*

Fifty years later, William Bradford, a Quaker living in Philadelphia, Pennsylvania, started the second printing shop in America. In 1690 Bradford also helped found America's first paper mill, the Rittenhouse Mill, which was also located in Philadelphia. Soon other printing shops were established, most of them situated in seaport cities.

THE BEGINNING OF NEWSPAPERS

By the early 1700s printers had developed a very annoying habit. They kept starting newspapers, and their newspapers kept starting controversies.

Among the earliest of the "bad boy" printer-journalists was James Franklin. His paper, the *New England Courant,* proved to be quite a departure from what British authorities considered acceptable journalism. In 1721 he strayed so far from the *acceptable* that he was put in a Boston prison for a month. He served his time, then started a controversial paper again. Within a year he was banned from publishing. He then decided to have the paper published under the name of a sixteen-year-old apprentice, his brother Benjamin.

To avoid the criticism of having a paper published by a lowly apprentice, James tore up Benjamin's apprenticeship agreement, which had five more years to run, and in its place they signed a private agreement to continue Benjamin's indenture. However, after a few quarrelsome months Ben Franklin left for New York and then went on to Philadelphia, where he became the most famous printer of all.

MAN AND MACHINE

In early Colonial days type was composed by hand (Fig. 3-1). In the 1880s an American-born German named Ottmar Mergenthaler introduced the first successful typesetting machine. The editorial page of the *New York Tribune* of July 3, 1886 was composed on Mergenthaler's machine. It revolutionized the graphic arts industry. Since this invention, machines have been perfected to produce hundreds of characters per second (Fig. 3-2), such as Mergenthaler's Linotron 505 that set this book.

One of the most successful early metal presses was made in London, England in 1838 (Fig. 3-3). It was used in the first printing of the *Kent Times* Kent, England in the year 1860.

Fig. 3-1. A typical eighteenth-century composing room. (Diderot's Encyclopedia, Courtesy Colonial Williamsburg)

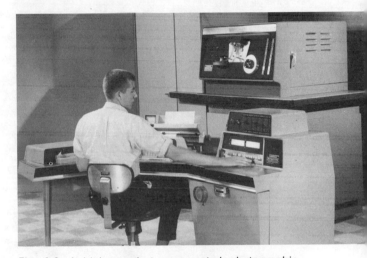

Fig. 3-2. A high-speed, tape-operated photographic composing system. (Harris Intertype Corp.)

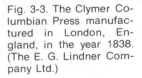

Fig. 3-3. The Clymer Columbian Press manufactured in London, England, in the year 1838. (The E. G. Lindner Company Ltd.)

Research and technical development improved the quality and speed of printing machines. Today giant printing presses produce thousands of high-quality copies per hour (Fig. 3-4).

The first paper-making machine was invented by Nicolas Louis Robert in the year 1798 (Fig. 3-5). A commercial model was developed in the early 1880s by the Fourdrinier brothers of England. The same continuous-wire principle used in the first machine is still basic to today's modern paper-making machines.

The quality and speed of graphic communication methods and devices have constantly improved. On October 17, 1967 a full-size newspaper front page was sent by satellite, telephone wire, and underground cable nearly 5,000 miles from London, England to San Juan, Puerto Rico in less than fifteen minutes. Light, electronic signals, and photographic film were key factors in this demonstration of scientific development. The information sent was graphic copy that was recorded on photographic film at the receiving end. The film was then used to prepare the image carrier or printing plate for the newspaper press. The newspaper front page appeared simultaneously in London, England and San Juan, Puerto Rico.

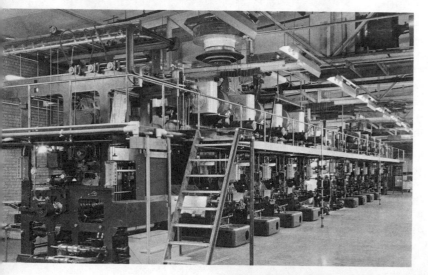

Fig. 3-4. A multistory press used to produce thousands of printed sheets per hour. (Brown and Bigelow)

Fig. 3-5. A model of the first paper-making machine, invented in 1798 by Nicolas-Louis Robert of France and developed by the Fourdrinier Brothers of England. (Dard Hunter Paper Museum)

UNIT 4
SIZE OF THE INDUSTRY

The graphic arts industries produce growth because of their central role in the dissemination of knowledge through education and communication. The changes and expansion within the industry are reflected in (1) the products, (2) the methods of production, (3) the speed and quality of production, and (4) the type of people who are needed to do the jobs efficiently and with imagination.

The industry has many small companies in addition to a significant number of large ones. There are over 40,000 individual commercial graphic arts facilities in the United States and they are among the most widely distributed type of industrial activity. Geographic concentration of printing facilities is in proportion to population density and industrial development, but there are few counties in the United States that do not have a newspaper or a commercial printing plant. There are also many in-plant or job shops. These may be part of any large non-printing firm and will do only the printing for that firm.

EMPLOYMENT

The graphic arts industry has very stable employment with over one million employees working in all aspects of the industry. In the past decade the total employment has shown a yearly growth of 1½% per year. There remains a shortage of qualified management personnel and skilled production workers.

The wages and salaries of graphic arts employees tend to be higher than in most manufacturing industries. This is due to the shortage of skilled personnel and to the

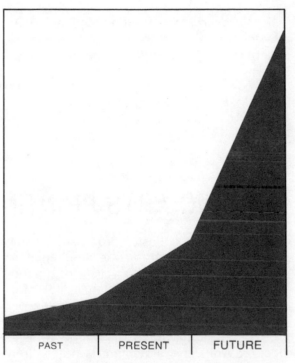

Fig. 4-1. The increasing need and production of printed products.

level of skills necessary to participate in this highly technical industry.

INDUSTRY GROWTH

The graphic arts industry is highly competitive, and this has contributed to its growth. The individual production plants compete not only with others in their own geographical areas but also with those in all areas of the United States, and even in foreign markets. This has resulted in a continuous growth pattern, and predictions for the future indicate a continued rapid rise in the production and consumption of printed materials (Fig. 4-1).

In a recent ranking of all United States industry, graphic arts is seventh in payroll, eighth in value added, and eleventh in product value. In an overall average it is ranked within the top ten major manufacturing industries in the United States.

GOVERNMENT PRINTING OFFICE

The Government Printing Office (GPO), Washington, D.C., is the largest single printing plant in the world. It operates on an around-the-clock basis and employs approximately 7,500 people. The GPO has extensive facilities for producing printed materials and processes approximately 24,000 separate printing orders per year.

The GPO is responsible for printing materials for Congress, the Executive Office, the Judiciary (other than the Supreme Court of the United States), and every executive department and independent office of the Government. Since it is impossible for the GPO to print all materials requested, work is often completed outside by private graphic arts commercial plants.

UNIT 5
GRAPHIC ARTS PRINTING PROCESSES

There are six basic processes which transfer an image from one substance or material to another: (1) relief, (2) planographic, (3) intaglio, (4) stencil, (5) photographic, and (6) electrostatic. They are categorized according to the type of surface from or through which the image transfer occurs. While this statement is not entirely descriptive, it helps separate each of these six printing methods in use. The first four methods have been used for years; the last two are relatively new and much work and research remains to make them feasible for high-production graphic arts requirements.

RELIEF

The *relief* image transfer method (Fig. 5-1) is based upon the principle that when ink is applied to a raised surface and a receptor or material (commonly paper) is placed against that surface, image transfer takes place. The nonimage area is recessed, or below the image area, so that ink does not come in contact with areas where the image or print is not desired.

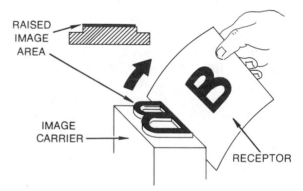

Fig. 5-1. The principle of the relief image-transfer method.

Letterpress is a more common name for relief. This term is favored by the management and production personnel of the graphic arts industry in general. The letterpress image transfer method is several thousands of years old. The Chinese are credited with first using this principle in approximately A.D. 770 when they produced images from relief wooden blocks.

In about 1450 Johann Gutenberg of Germany invented and produced the first movable metal type. Each type character contained a separate letter and could therefore be assembled into any order needed to produce a printed graphic communication. The images on these movable metal characters were cast in relief as they still are today, and thus were capable of producing images via the relief image-transfer method. Common products of the letterpress relief principle include newspapers, books, magazines, and tickets.

PLANOGRAPHIC

Planographic image transfer (Fig. 5-2) produces an image from a smooth surface. A novice sometimes asks, "Why doesn't the entire image-carrier surface accept ink, instead of just a small area?" The principle involved is the chemical fact that oil and water do not mix.

A thin coating of water is placed over the entire image-carrier area, and the water adheres only to the nonimage area. Ink is applied to the entire image-carrier area, and adheres only where there is no water. The ink readily transfers to a receptor pressed to the image carrier. A small amount of water also transfers to the receptor but is not noticed by the naked eye.

The term *lithography* rather than *planographic* is used to identify this image-transfer method, even though it is not as descriptive. *Offset* is also used in place of the term *lithographic*. No one image-transfer process holds a patent on the offset principle. It can be and is applied to most of the other image-transfer processes.

Alois Senefelder of Germany is credited with the discovery of the lithographic printing method in the year 1796. He used a greased pencil to apply the image to a flat limestone surface. Then he wet the stone, inked the image, and pressed paper to its surface causing the image to be transferred. The offset-lithography press was invented near the beginning of the twentieth century and is used for modern-day lithographic image transfer. Newspapers, books, magazines, and general commercial printing are done by using this process as it is very versatile and allows the designer to be creative.

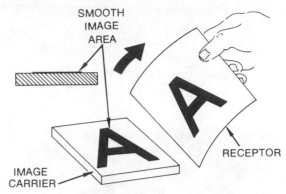

Fig. 5-2. The principle of the planographic image-transfer method.

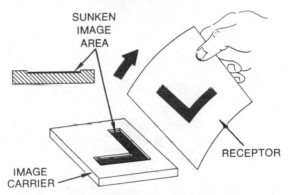

Fig. 5-3. The principle of the intaglio image-transfer method.

INTAGLIO

The *intaglio* image-transfer method (Fig. 5-3) works on the principle that the image is sunken, or below the nonimage area of the image carrier. Ink is applied to the entire surface of the image carrier, filling in the recessed image area, and is then removed from only the nonimage area by either scraping or wiping. The receptor is then pressed against the image carrier and the ink transfers.

Gravure is another term for intaglio. Gravure incorporates the use of photography and chemicals to prepare the image carrier for printing. Intaglio generally refers to the hand-prepared, below-surface image carriers.

The invention of the gravure image-transfer method is credited to Karl Kleitsch of Austria in the year 1879. The process developed rapidly and by 1905 there was a

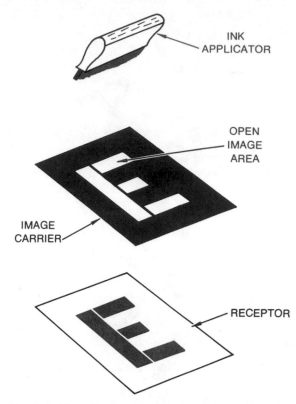

Fig. 5-4. The principle of the stencil image-transfer method.

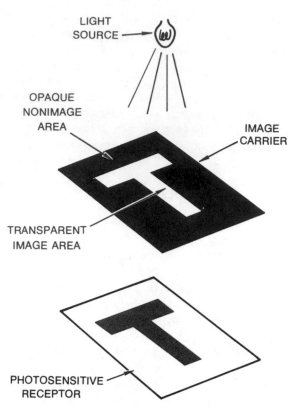

Fig. 5-5. The principle of the photographic image-transfer method.

gravure printing facility in New York City. A few years later the *New York Times* established its own gravure facility to produce portions of its newspaper. Common products of this type of printing are paper money, calendars, magazines, Sunday newspaper supplements, and a variety of food and other product packaging.

STENCIL

The *Stencil* image-transfer method (Fig. 5-4) uses the principle of forcing ink through an open image area. It works because the image area has been removed by one of several methods. Other names for this method are screen process, screen printing, and silk-screen printing. The term screen printing is the most correct and is in common use throughout the industry. It is replacing the reference to silk screen, although originally silk was the only material that was stretched in the frame. The silk held the image carrier, making possible

printed copies. Today other fabric screen materials such as nylon, polyester, and stainless steel are also used.

The stencil method is an old image transfer method. The Chinese and Egyptians experimented with stenciling. The Japanese used stenciling and screen printing procedures similar to those of today. The modern developments of this process really developed in the United States in the first decade of the twentieth century.

Screen printing has the advantage of being able to produce images on nearly any solid surface, material, or shape. Felt sports pennants were among the first items produced by this method. Other common products printed by this method are posters, bumper stickers, glass food containers, children's toys, electrical circuits, plastics and textiles.

PHOTOGRAPHIC

The *photographic* image-transfer method (Fig. 5-5) involves a light source, an image

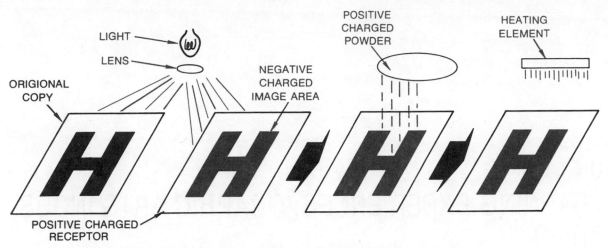

Fig. 5-6. The principle of the electrostatic image-transfer method.

carrier, and a photosensitive receptor. Photographic developing chemicals are also needed to make the image visible once the light has struck the photosensitive receptor through the image carrier.

The photographic principle of Image production is not used to the same extent as those of the other methods discussed, but research is being conducted and possibly mechanical means will be found of making this process feasible. The first attempt at photography took place in approximately 1802. Only a silhouette outline of the subject photographed was obtained, but in the years that followed the photographic principle was perfected, and in 1884 the first flexible film was patented. Before that time the light-sensitive coating was placed upon glass and required careful handling. Space-age materials and techniques surely will provide for widespread use.

ELECTROSTATIC

The *electrostatic* method of image transfer (Fig. 5-6) works upon the principle that *like* electrical charges repel and *unlike* charges attract. When projected onto a charged receptor, light will change polarity; when the positive-charged powder involved in this process is sprinkled over the sheet being printed, it adheres only to the negative-charged areas. After the powder is attracted to the image areas, it is then subjected to heat. This fuses the powder permanently to the sheet.

This process is still in its infancy; the first patent for electrostatic printing was issued in 1940. Many office copying machines are designed along this principle, but much research remains to be done before the electrostatic image-transfer method can be considered perfected.

UNIT 6
LEARNING EXPERIENCES: GRAPHIC ARTS INDUSTRIES

DISCUSSION TOPICS

1. Define graphic arts. What is the primary purpose of the graphic arts? In what ways does the world depend on graphic arts?

2. List some of the products of the graphic arts industry. Where can these products be found?

3. What has happened to the graphic arts industry in recent years? Give some projected future happenings within this mass communication industry.

4. Enumerate the various business enterprises that make up the total graphic arts industry. How does each of these contribute to the overall graphic arts industry?

5. Distinguish between the divisions of graphic arts. Describe the part that each division plays in the overall graphic arts industry. Why is there a need for specialty houses?

6. Explain how visual communication products of the graphic arts industry have contributed to the cultural development of people throughout the world. What are some of the significant events leading to the overall contributions? Cite specific events in the United States that have contributed to the cultural development of its people.

7. Explain the effects of *Man* and *Machine.* Why did man develop machinery?

Describe the effects of this machinery upon man.

8. Define growth industry. Why can the graphic arts industry be considered a growth industry?

9. Describe the general geographical location of the graphic arts industry. Identify the geographical area containing the largest concentration of graphic arts establishments.

10. How many people are now employed within the several facets of the industry? Can you determine why the industry has a very stable employment? How do the wages and salaries compare to those of other manufacturing industries? Does the length of the average workweek compare favorably or unfavorably to that of other industries? Why?

11. Overall, how does the graphic arts industry rank in size as compared to the other major manufacturing groups in the United States?

12. What is the largest single printing plant in the world? Identify its primary purpose. Is this plant capable of producing all of the work under its jurisdiction? If not, how is this work done?

13. Enumerate the six basic processes that are available to transfer an image from one substance to another. How are these image-transfer methods categorized?

ACTIVITIES

1. Without moving from where you are seated, look around and carefully list all products and materials that are the result of the graphic arts industry. Categorize these items as to whether they are reading material, packaging materials, or paper products.
2. Visit a commercial graphic arts printing plant. Attempt to locate the six production phases of the graphic arts—design and layout, composition, photoconversion, image carriers, image transfer, and finishing and binding. Ask the printing plant representative why each production phase is physically located where it is. Has it been changed recently?
3. Conduct some library research into the cultural development of the people of the United States and also of the rest of the world. Determine the role that graphic arts has had in this development. Discuss these contributions with a history teacher. Summarize your findings in a written paper.
4. Obtain an almanac. Look under the headings for printing and publishing and compare the current size rankings of the graphic arts industry with those of other manufacturing industries. Also obtain current industry reports that give the status of the manufacturing industry. Compare the graphic arts with the manufacturing industry in general and attempt to determine why it has the position that it does.
5. List and illustrate the six image transfer methods. Try not to use the illustrations contained within unit five. Use your imagination and other resource materials to visually present the processes of transferring an image from one surface to a receptor.

Looking through a typeface
specimen book.

UNIT 7
INTRODUCTION TO TYPEFACES

We begin the process of learning about typefaces as early as kindergarten, and even before. Typefaces are later related to words which we have already learned to speak and understand. In succeeding years we recognize and understand combinations of typefaces readily. We recognize that there are different typeface designs and realize that different meanings are attached to their usage. For example, an *Italic type* emphasizes and draws attention to a word or phrase.

Typefaces are the communication link between the author and reader because they take the place of the human voice. Without typefaces there would be a tremendous gap in the ability of civilized people to communicate effectively.

The twenty-six letters of our alphabet are the ingredients for typefaces. Each letter has a specific shape and designates a certain sound, and the design of each shape can be altered to make a specific typeface. The history of our alphabet is fascinating. See Unit 8, "Evolution of the Alphabet."

PSYCHOLOGY OF A TYPEFACE

The typeface is the printed record of the human voice. Some typefaces talk; others shout. Various typefaces are used to draw our attention; then after our attention is obtained, other type is used to talk to us. Some type makes us think or feel old; others have a new, modern look. These display a bold feeling and flow smoothly.

Some typefaces are designed to encourage the feeling of gaiety while others create a formal mood. Entertainment, closeness, negative reaction, ease of reading, and variety are all within the scope of the typeface. Most often type is used to talk to us and to relay the thoughts and ideas of the author. In this case ease of reading is an essential virtue.

Typefaces have texture in that they create a look or feeling in the same way that threads in cloth do. Typefaces react with the mind of the reader to convey specific information. A poem that colorfully describes the feelings that typefaces can cause is presented in Fig. 7-1.

CHOOSING A TYPEFACE

There are five important factors to consider when choosing a typeface: (1) legibility, (2) readability, (3) appropriateness, (4) reproducibility, and (5) practicality.

Legibility. Criteria for this factor include such questions as (1) can the typeface be seen easily? (2) Does it have a familiar shape and proper design for the use? (3) Can it be recognized at a distance and up close?

Readability. Pertinent questions for readability are (1) is the typeface easy for the eye to follow? (2) Can it be read for long periods of time without excessively tiring the eyes? (3) If designed for specific conditions, such as road signs are, can the letters be read easily, quickly, and efficiently, without excessive effort?

TYPEFACES HAVE FEELINGS

Some interesting aspects of types that abound
Are the various natures in which they are found,
Preserving in print our knowledge and lore,
They often reflect what their words have in store.

They're handsome in concept of pureness of form
And grotesquely mutant away from the norm;
They're easy to read in a functional way
And puzzling enough for a mystery play.

They're blatantly male, their muscles they flex
Or allure with the charm of the opposite sex.
They're raucous and wild and sober and mild;
And they're formally dressed and casually styled.

They're squat and they're tall, some fat and some
*   lean,*
And they're dull or they shine with a radiant sheen.
They're slanted and bowed and stand up erect
And they're happy and gay in garlands bedecked.

They're humble and proud, warmhearted and cold,
And they're weak and they're strong, and timid and
*   bold.*
They're rough as a tweed and sharp as a pin
And they're solid or open or textured within.

They're fresh as a spring and whiskered with age
And often burlesqued to enliven the page.
They're mellowed as wine and tempered like steel
And some of them have a spontaneous "feel."

Some seem to be moving with flashes of speed,
Or crouch in tense stillness awaiting your heed.
They're ribbon and rope and some have the fate
To be cut out like stencils on the side of a crate.

They're pictured as cuttings from branches of trees
And broken in sections to build as you please.
They're made up of swirls and wedges as well
To weave and embrace with an exotic spell.

Typefaces have feelings, that's plain to be seen
Even those missing—save their shadows, I mean.
From announcing a tea to swaying the mob,
There's a typeface designed to foster the job.

—Edwin W. Shaar

Fig. 7-1. Typefaces Have Feelings. A poem which describes the sensations created by the visual images.

Appropriateness. The typeface must be appropriate for the audience it is directed to and for the message it is meant to convey. The company that is sending the message must be well represented by the typeface as well as by the paper used; the photographs and art work must go along with the typeface.

Reproducibility. Reproducibility characteristics of typefaces are very important. Some typefaces do not reproduce well when used with certain image-transfer methods. For example, those with very narrow lines are not desired when the printed materials are produced by the gravure image-transfer method.

Practicality. A practical consideration in printing is to find out whether the typeface is available in the commercial establishment where the printed product is to be reproduced. Economy in using a certain typeface must also be considered because some types require more hand manipulation than others do.

TYPEFACE CLASSIFICATIONS

There are several hundred specific kinds of typefaces, each face having its own name. The majority of graphic arts people never learn to recognize all of these types by their actual names, but they are capable of placing most kinds into a specific classification.

Classification systems have been offered by graphic personnel such as typographers who work with typefaces, designers, production men, and others interested in typography. Some of these experts have identified only two or three classes of type face designs. Others have discussed a dozen classes or more. Many graphic arts prople agree upon six major typeface classifications: (1) *text*, (2) *Roman*, (3) *sans serif*, (4) *square serif*, (5) *script*, and (6) *novelty*. Examples and specific details of each classification are presented in Units 12 through 16.

UNIT 8
EVOLUTION OF THE ALPHABET

A level of civilization depends very largely upon how easily and permanently written messages can be duplicated and communicated. Spoken language extended man's ability to communicate and made his meanings more precise, but for many years the perpetuation of knowledge depended entirely upon memory. Words change in meaning and factual information can easily become distorted after it has been repeated several times.

Fig. 8-1. Early cave drawings showing animals without action.

VISUAL COMMUNICATION

A written, visible language took the place of memory. Man began visual communication in many ways. Twigs were broken to form pointers, marks were made on tree trunks, and piles of rocks indicated something had happened. The question was, what?

The most important stage in early written communication came when men learned to draw pictures to represent things they had seen and to express their ideas. These first drawings or writings (Fig. 8-1) were done on walls of caves, man's first home.

The next important development in the history of writing was that of showing action within drawings (Fig. 8-2). American Indians developed a system of picture writings that could be used to describe many activities. One of the more famous picture writings (Fig. 8-3) tells of a man's leaving home and taking his canoe to travel ten days to a friend's home. Together they travel in their canoe to the hunting area. They stalk their prey with bows and arrows and are successful in their kill. They then travel homeward, taking the amount of time indicated by the number of fingers shown.

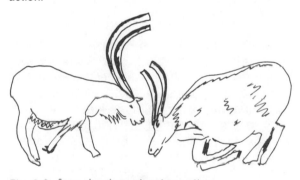

Fig. 8-2. Cave drawings showing action.

Fig. 8-3. Picture writing as developed by the American Indian.

APPROACHING AN ALPHABET

A system containing several hundred signs and small pictures was developed by the ancient Egyptians. These signs (pictures) stood for full words or for symbols, but some also stood for sounds. When these signs were combined, a distinct form of communication was possible. By studying the example of Egyptian *hieroglyphics* (picture script) shown in Fig. 8-4, it can be seen that this form of written communication is rather precise and permanent. It was, however, slightly clumsy and time consuming.

In Fig. 8-4 the name Cleopatra (Kleopatra) was phonetically spelled out, and idea pictures were used for the concept words of *divine* add *queen.* To spell out these two words the Egyptians would have had to use a true alphabet, but they never reached this stage of development.

THE REAL ALPHABET

Most scholars give the *Phoenicians* credit for taking the last step toward a writing system without pictures or general symbols. It is not entirely clear how or from whom the Phoenicians obtained their ideas for each alphabetical character. They leaned heavily on the beginnings of alphabets that were being developed by the other peoples around them, and gradually evolved a twenty-two character alphabet which greatly assisted them in their energetic trade and travel civilization. In approximately 1000 B.C. their alphabet was in full use.

After the Phoenicians, the *Greeks* were the first people to make significant cultural contributions and to use the alphabet. The Greeks used nineteen characters, all representing consonants. They wrote entirely in consonants and it was the decision of the reader if and where a vowel sound was needed. This great cultural civilization perfected its alphabetical system in approximately 600 B.C.

The *Romans* also needed a sophisticated system of writing. This civilization adapted to its needs those elements developed by

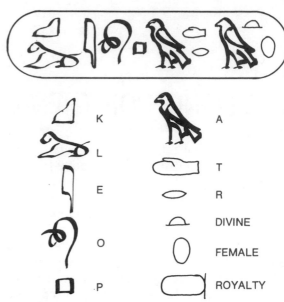

Fig. 8-4. Egyptian hieroglyphics. Translated it says *Cleopatra.*

others, and thus borrowed as much of the Grecian alphabet as desired. The Roman alphabet of twenty-three characters was perfected around 114 A.D.

The study and comparison of each alphabetical character is an interesting experience. The first three letters of the alphabet are shown in Figs. 8-5, 8-6, and 8-7. The letter *A* (Fig. 8-5) originally represented the head of an ox. Food was the most important thing to the Phoenicians, and the use of the oxhead as an outline for their letter *Aleph* is not surprising. The Greeks changed the symbol and called it *Alpha.* The Romans redesigned the letter, giving it the appearance and sound to which we are accustomed, and called it *A.*

The second most important thing to the Phoenicians was their home or shelter. Their symbol for the letter *B* represented the shape of a shelter (Fig. 8-6). This letter was termed *Beth.* The Greeks called it *Beta;* the Romans borrowed the character, gave it round and graceful strokes, and called it *B.*

The third letter originally represented the camel, an important means of travel for the Phoenicians. The symbol represented the head and neck of a camel (Fig. 8-7), and was named *Gimel.* The Greeks turned the character around and called it *Gamma;* the

PHOENICIAN
"ALEPH"

PHOENICIAN
"BETH"

PHOENICIAN
"GIMEL"

GREEK
"ALPHA"

GREEK
"BETA"

GREEK
"GAMMA"

ROMAN "A"

ROMAN "B"

ROMAN "C"

Fig. 8-5. The development of the present-day letter *A*.

Fig. 8-6. The development of the present-day letter *B*.

Fig. 8-7. The development of the present-day letter *C*.

Romans borrowed the basic symbol, gave it a graceful curve, and called it *C*.

Each letter of our present-day alphabet of twenty-six characters has a similar interesting history. It took several hundred years to fully develop each symbol.

THE TWENTY-SIX LETTERS

The word "alphabet" comes from the first two letters of the Greek alphabet, *Alpha* and *Beta*. The capital or uppercase letters were the only forms used for centuries. The lowercase or small letters were developed by scribes, writers, and scholars as they copied manuscripts and books, since capital letters were difficult to produce at a rapid speed and took up too much space.

The alphabet used today is far from perfect, but it has served man well in helping him communicate with his fellow men, now and into the future. A poem that commemorates the alphabet is shown in Fig. 8-8.

ALPHA-BETA

The power potential of words took a surge
When means to record them began to emerge.
Were it not for symbols of speech taking shape
Man would have continued a glorified ape.

Not fire, not wheel, nor riding a horse—
'Twas letters that fixed him on civilized course.
Their import forever will always remain
Commingled as one with his God-given brain.

As learning progressed new ideas gave effect
Building brick upon brick toward high intellect.
Great things to follow were destined to stem
From letters with meanings pictured in them.

Those twenty-six letters of our alphabet
Have truly evolved a remarkable set.
From Semite to Greek to Roman they came
Improving in form while extending their fame.

They're written and drawn and chiseled in stone—
Ensconced in décor or shown smartly alone.
They're beamed onto film and molded in lead
To march into print calling out to be read.

What bountiful blessings to mankind were brought
By way of these symbols our ancestors wrought.
O, letters sublime, you're the tool that unlocks
More valuable treasure than the key to Fort Knox.

They teach us and guide us, they herald our wares
And bring us the Scriptures that wash away cares.
So don't sell them short—they're the greatest by
*   far—*
For they're made us and keep us whatever we are!

Omega?

Today we must use them with wisdom and prayer
To mend world relations and ever beware,
Lest all that we've savored spews up with aplomb
In the belch of our malconceived nuclear bomb!
*   —Edwin W. Shaar*

Fig. 8-8. A poem to commemorate the alphabet. (Inland Printer/American Lithographer)

A NEW SYMBOL

The present alphabet, numbering system, and several punctuation marks have been used for centuries. In 1967 a new punctuation mark appeared (Fig. 8-9). It is called the

Fig. 8-9. The newest punctuation mark, the *Interbang*.

interabang and is a combination of an exclamation point and a question mark. It is an interrogative exclamation mark used to end a question full of excitement. It makes a statement and asks a question simultaneously. Time will tell whether it increases the effective communication of already-existing punctuation marks.

UNIT 9
DEVELOPMENT OF A TYPEFACE

There are many typefaces. Some are used over and over in available publications and others gather dust in the typecases of commercial graphic arts plants. Even though many typefaces exist, there are new ones created each year. Several manufacturers of type composition equipment sponsor annual type-styling contests. This constantly encourages the professional designer and also the novice to create new type designs.

TYPEFACE DESIGN

A purpose or reason must be established before a new typeface is designed. As noted in Unit 7, a type must have legibility and readability. These two requirements must be uppermost in the mind of the designer during the creative process. Type is to be seen and read, and if it cannot be interpreted it has no value.

Typefaces must also be designed for use with a specific composition system. Some composing methods are limited to the production of certain type designs, while others are capable of producing nearly all styles. The reproduction method must also be considered when preparing a new type design.

The continuity among the twenty-six letters and several auxiliary characters must be great enough to indicate that each one belongs to the next. Without this continuity it would be difficult to read text matter.

CREATING THE FACE

A type designer must begin at the drawing board (Fig. 9-1). He may begin designing with two basic letters, lowercase *n* and *o*. These contain nearly all the strokes present in the other twenty-four letters of the alpha-

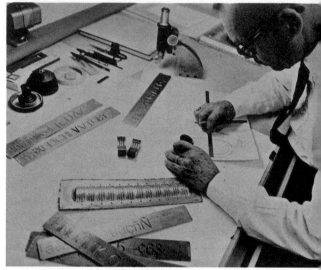

Fig. 9-1. A type designer at work. (Varityper Corp.)

bet. After the designer is satisfied with these two letters, he can then develop the remaining ones, including uppercase (capitals), basing each character upon his original design of the *n* and *o*. The entire process of producing an entirely new typeface can take a period of time ranging from weeks to months.

FOUNDRY TYPE PRODUCTION

The production of foundry type is the oldest of the mechanical type-production methods. It is well to mention, however, that there are other type composition systems in use throughout the world (see Section 4).

Foundry type characters have been cast in a metal alloy of lead, tin, and antimony. They are hand assembled to make up a headline or paragraph that is used for reproduction.

Fig. 9-2. A designer adding the final touches to a new typeface. (American Type Founders)

TYPEFACE DEVELOPMENT

The typeface is *designed* (Fig. 9-2). The finished drawing can be any size convenient to the designer, although most designers prefer working with a capital letter height of approximately two inches.

The original artwork is *photographed* (Fig. 9-3). A film negative of the original artwork is made. Depending upon the original, the negative image can be enlarged or reduced in size by use of the camera.

The *pattern plates* are produced (Fig. 9-4). Film obtained from the previous step is now used to make the pattern plate. The photosensitive metal plate is exposed by placing the film upon the plate and subjecting it to bright lights. The nonimage area is then etched or removed with acid to a depth of approximately 0.007 inch.

Using a special engraving machine (pantograph, Fig. 9-5), a *brass matrix* (mold or die) is engraved. The matrix can be made large or small, depending upon the type size needed.

The matrix is *fitted* to insure proper character alignment (Fig. 9-6). This process places the engraved matrix under a highly accurate microscope equipped with a grinding attachment. After the brass matrix is perfected, it is chrome plated to increase wearability.

The matrix is placed into a *casting machine*. Molten metal under high pressure is

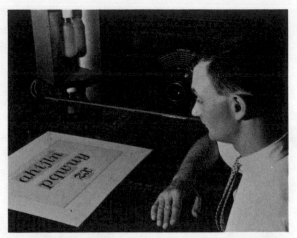

Fig. 9-3. The original artwork being photographed and enlarged or reduced to the proper working size. (American Type Founders)

Fig. 9-4. Pattern plates of each character—capital letters, small letters, numbers, and punctuation marks.

Fig. 9-5. An engraving machine used to produce the type matrix. (American Type Founders)

Fig. 9-6. Fitting the matrix to insure proper character alignment. (American Type Founders)

Fig. 9-7. The ejection area of a foundry type-casting machine. (American Type Founders)

Fig. 9-8. An early hand crank type-casting machine that was designed and built in America. (Dard Hunter Paper Museum, The Institute fo Paper Chemistry, Appleton, Wisconsin)

forced into the mold (matrix). After the mold and type are water cooled, they are automatically ejected from the casting unit as shown in Fig. 9-7.

This entire operation is done automatically in modern machines, but early type casters poured the molten metal into the mold and allowed it to cool naturally. It was time consuming, and production of the thousands of characters was a difficult task. Fig. 9-8 shows an early hand-operated type-casting machine developed in America. It produced many more type characters than were produced by the hand method.

A *final inspection* takes place (Fig. 9-9) after the type character has been cast and trimmed of excess metal. It is essential that each character be produced with exacting accuracy or it has no value. After inspection the type characters are packaged and shipped to the customers.

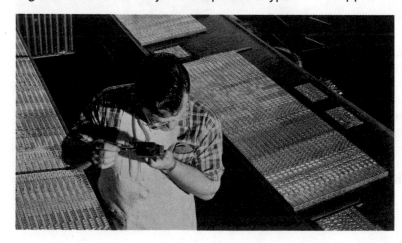

Fig. 9-9. Making the final inspection of the cast characters. (American Type Founders)

UNIT 10
CHARACTERISTICS OF TYPEFACES

It is necessary to know the several parts of the letters to distinguish the many kinds of type. Study the several typeface parts shown in Fig. 10-1.

Thick strokes are the wide parts of a letter; they are either vertical, diagonal, or horizontal.

Thin stokes are the narrow parts of a letter; they, too, are either vertical, diagonal, or horizontal.

Serifs are the little extra strokes at the end of the main character strokes in many kinds of type. They serve to finish the stroke. All type, however, does not contain serifs.

The *ascender* is the top portion of the vertical stroke that extends above the main letter, such as in b, d, f, h, and k.

The *counter* is the central area of letters that have no image. This area can be completely enclosed, as in the letter *b,* or partially enclosed, as in *n.*

The *bowl* is the loop, or rounded portion of a letter, such as in *p* and *c.*

The *descender* is the portion of the vertical stroke which extends below the main portion of the letter, as in *p* and *q.*

DISTINGUISHING CHARACTERISTICS

Knowing the six basic classifications of type and being able to classify any one specific kind of type are essential. One way to distinguish type classifications is through the shape of the serifs. As one studies some of the many kinds of type, it is seen that there are serifs of all sizes, shapes, and forms (Fig. 10-2).

Serifs were originally placed on letters because of the instruments used. The early Romans developed the Roman letter; this contained serifs because of the types of chisels used to cut the letters into their architectural structures. Early scribes and monks developed certain types of serifs through the use of quills and pens. Other serif designs resulted from brushes which left peculiar ending strokes. Today serifs are an important part of the designs of letters, although there is a group of letters that does not contain serifs. This group is classified as *sans serif.*

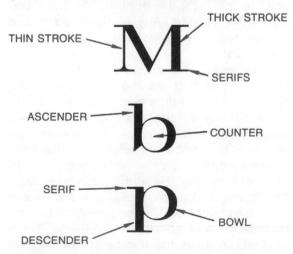

Fig. 10-1. The typeface parts.

THIN STROKE — THICK STROKE — SERIFS — ASCENDER — COUNTER — SERIF — BOWL — DESCENDER

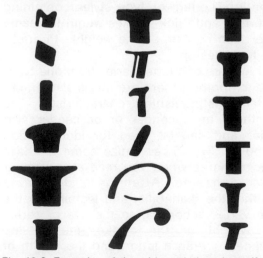

Fig. 10-2. Examples of the wide variations in serifs.

LIGHT   MEDIUM   BOLD   EXTRABOLD   ULTRABOLD

Fig. 10-3. Five common typeface weights.

Century Nova Italic Series 721

CAPITALS	*ABCDEFGHIJKLMNOPQRSTUVWXYZ*
LOWERCASE	*abcdefghijklmnopqrstuvwxyzffffiffifflfl*
PUNCTUATION	*$ \$ ¢ £ % . : , ; - - - - · ( ) ? ! [ ] ' ' " " * &*
FIGURES	*1234567890*

Fig. 10-4. A complete font of type. (American Type Founders)

The weight of the various typefaces also helps to distinguish specific kinds of type (Fig. 10-3). The five common letter weights are (1) light, (2) medium, (3) bold, (4) extrabold, and (5) ultrabold. The first two weights are for normal reading; the last three are used in headline and poster work to attract attention. Letters or type styles containing both thin and thick strokes within the same letter also contain stroke weights throughout their design.

Thickness of a letter varies from one typeface to another; therefore this is also an important distinguishing characteristic. The length of an ascender or descender also varies and can be used for identification purposes. Try to recognize some of these special marks when you read a newspaper or a magazine. Attempt to determine whether the readability and legibility of the type varies according to the use of serifs, the weight of the stroke, the varying thickness within a letter, and the length of ascenders and descenders.

A FONT OF TYPE

A *font* is an assortment of type of any one kind, style, and size (Fig. 10-4). Complete type fonts are divided into four subdivisions: (1) the capital part, (2) the lowercase or letter part, (3) the punctuation part, and (4) the figure part. Any of these parts can be purchased separately or as a unit in an entire font.

The number of characters in a font of type varies, depending on the kind, style, and size of the type. Fonts available for use with hand or hot composition are purchased, based on specific schemes. Samples of type shown in type books or catalogs contain the scheme information for each style (Fig. 10-5). Note that with 18-point type, fifteen capital *A's,* twenty-five lowercase *a's,* and twelve *1's* are obtained with one font. With this information, it is possible to refer to Table 10-1 which gives the number of characters for each letter, punctuation mark, or figure.

Whedons Gothic Outline 722

18 pt. shown

PACK MY BOX WITH FIVE DOZE
pack my box with five doze 123

18pt	15A	25a	12-1	36pt	8A	11a	7-1	60pt	4A	6a	4-1
24pt	12A	17a	10-1	42pt	6A	9a	6-1	72pt	4A	4a	5-1
30pt	10A	14a	8-1	48pt	5A	8a	5-1				

Fig. 10-5. A typical fonting scheme for one kind and style of type. (American Type Founders)

To use the table, refer to the number of capital *A's* in the type font shown in Fig. 10-5—18 point. Fifteen *A's* are indicated; note that several other letters come in the same quantity. Six characters of capital *B, W,* and *Y* aae obtained, and ten of *C* and *L.* In this same font, twenty-five lowercase *a's* are obtained; it is therefore necessary to move to the portion of the table under lowercase, and over to the column headed with the number 25. It is then possible to see how many characters of each letter are obtained. In Table 10-1 it is seen that twelve number

1's are obtained; therefore it is again necessary to move to the third portion of the table, entitled "figures," and over to the column headed with the number 12.

It is seen that a larger number of *e's*, whether capital or lowercase, is obtained than of any other letter. This is because *e* is the most common letter used in the English alphabet.

The number of characters in a font of type varies, depending on the frequency of use in normal writing. A quick character count of the letters used to make up words will reveal that certain letters are used more often than others. There is little need, therefore, to have an equal number of characters in a font of type.

A TYPE SERIES

A *type series* consists of the several sizes of one kind and style of type available (Fig. 10-6). The *Americana* typeface, for exam-

Table 10-1. Approximate Character Quantity Per Font

CAPITALS

A I N O R S T . ,	3	4	5	6	7	8	9	10	11	12	13	14	15	16	17	18	19	20	21	22	23	24	25	26	27	28	29	30	31	32	33
B W Y	2	2	2	3	3	3	4	4	4	5	5	6	6	7	7	8	8	8	8	9	9	10	10	11	11	11	11	12	12	13	13
C L	2	3	4	4	5	5	6	7	7	8	9	9	10	11	12	12	13	13	14	15	16	16	17	18	19	19	20	20	21	21	22
D H M P U	2	2	3	4	4	5	5	6	7	7	8	8	8	9	10	10	11	11	12	12	13	13	13	14	15	15	16	16	17	17	18
E	4	5	6	8	9	10	11	12	13	14	16	17	18	19	21	22	23	24	26	27	28	29	30	32	33	34	35	36	38	39	40
F G '	2	2	3	3	3	4	4	5	5	6	6	7	7	8	8	9	9	9	10	10	11	11	12	12	13	13	14	14	15	15	16
J K V -	2	2	2	3	3	3	4	4	4	4	5	5	5	5	6	6	6	6	7	7	7	7	8	8	8	8	8	8	9	9	9
Q X Z & : ; ! ?	1	1	1	2	2	2	2	3	3	3	3	3	3	4	4	4	4	4	4	5	5	5	5	5	5	5	6	6	6	6	6

LOWERCASE

a i n o r s t	3	4	5	6	7	8	9	10	11	12	13	14	15	16	17	18	19	20	21	22	23	24	25	26	27	28	29	30	31	32	33
b g p w y	2	2	2	3	3	3	4	4	5	5	5	6	6	7	7	8	8	8	9	9	10	10	10	11	11	11	12	12	13	13	14
c f m u	2	2	3	4	4	5	5	6	6	7	7	8	8	9	9	10	10	11	11	12	12	13	13	14	15	15	16	16	17	17	18
d	2	3	3	4	4	5	6	7	8	8	9	9	9	10	11	11	12	12	13	13	14	14	15	16	17	17	18	18	19	19	20
e	4	5	6	8	9	10	12	13	14	16	17	19	20	21	23	24	25	27	28	29	30	32	33	35	36	37	38	40	41	43	44
h l	2	3	4	4	5	5	6	7	8	8	9	9	10	11	12	12	13	13	14	15	16	16	17	18	19	19	20	20	21	21	22
j k v	2	2	2	2	3	3	3	4	4	4	5	5	5	5	6	6	6	6	7	7	7	7'	8	8	8	8	8	8	9	9	9
q x z	1	1	1	2	2	2	2	3	3	3	3	4	4	4	4	4	4	5	5	5	5	5	5	6	6	6	6	6	6	6	6
. ,	2	2	3	4	4	5	5	6	6	7	7	8	8	9	9	10	10	11	11	12	12	13	13	14	14	15	15	16	16	17	17
. /	1	1	1	1	2	2	2	2	2	3	3	3	3	3	3	3	3	3	3	3	4	4	4	4	4	4	4	4	4	5	5
fl ffi ffl : ; ! ?	1	1	1	1	1	1	1	1	1	2	2	2	2	2	2	2	2	2	2	3	3	3	3	3	3	3	3	3	3	3	3
fi ff	2	2	2	2	2	2	2	2	3	3	3	3	3	3	3	3	3	3	4	4	4	4	4	4	4	4	4	4	4	4	4
'	1	1	1	2	2	2	2	3	3	3	3	4	4	4	4	4	4	4	5	5	5	5	5	5	5	5	6	6	6	6	6

FIGURES

Char																															
1	3	4	5	6	7	8	9	10	11	12	13	14	15	16	17	18	19	20	21	22	23	24	25	26	27	28	29	30	31	32	33
2 3 4 5 6 7 8 9 $,	2	3	4	4	5	6	7	8	9	10	11	11	12	12	13	13	14	15	16	18	19	19	20	21	22	23	24	25	26	27	28
0	3	5	6	7	8	10	11	12	13	15	17	17	18	19	20	21	22	24	26	28	29	29	30	31	32	34	35	36	37	38	39
-	2	2	2	2	3	3	3	4	4	4	4	5	5	5	5	6	6	6	6	7	7	7	7	8	8	8	8	8	8	9	9

72 POINT

HSMOUEA
hsmoueak

60 POINT

HSMOUEAK
hsmoueakfg

48 POINT

HSMOUEAKFG
hsmoueakfgdtjb

36 POINT   HSMOUEA   hsmoue

30 POINT   HSMOUEAKF   hsmoueak

24 POINT   HSMOUEAKFGD   hsmoueakfg

18 POINT   HSMOUEAKFGDTJBP   hsmoueakfgdtjbp

14 POINT   HSMOUEAKFGDTJBPRLZYN   hsmoueakfgdtjbprlzyn

12 POINT   HSMOUEAKFGDTJBPRLZYNICQV   hsmoueakfgdtjbprlzynicq

10 POINT   HSMOUEAKFGDTJBPRLZYNICQVXW   hsmoueakfgdtjbprlzynicqvxwl

Fig. 10-6. *Americana* type series, 10 point through 72 point. (American Type Founders)

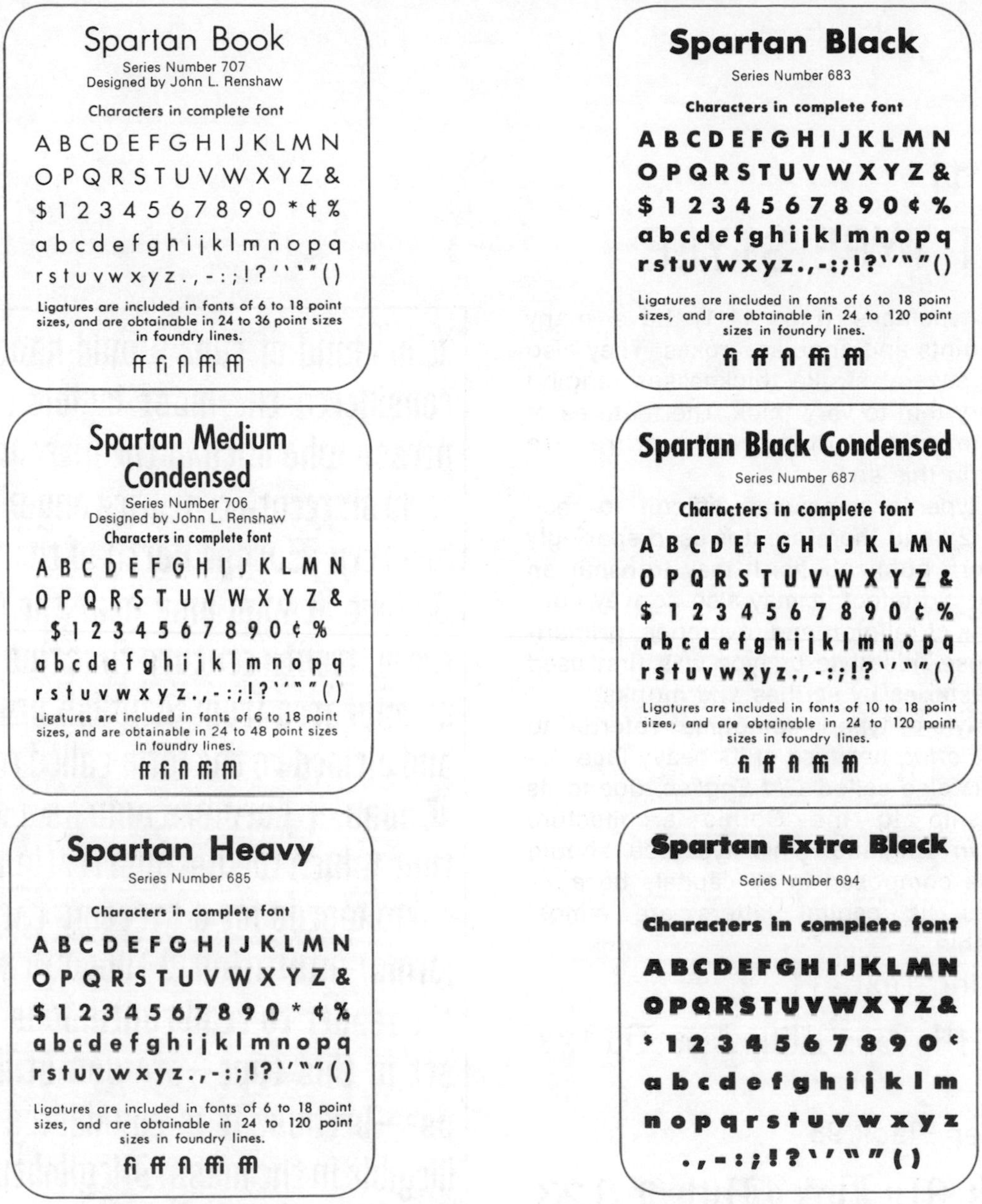

Spartan Book
Series Number 707
Designed by John L. Renshaw

Characters in complete font

A B C D E F G H I J K L M N
O P Q R S T U V W X Y Z &
$ 1 2 3 4 5 6 7 8 9 0 * ¢ %
a b c d e f g h i j k l m n o p q
r s t u v w x y z . , - : ; ! ? ' ` " " ( )

Ligatures are included in fonts of 6 to 18 point
sizes, and are obtainable in 24 to 36 point sizes
in foundry lines.

ff fi fl ffi ffl

Spartan Black
Series Number 683

Characters in complete font

A B C D E F G H I J K L M N
O P Q R S T U V W X Y Z &
$ 1 2 3 4 5 6 7 8 9 0 ¢ %
a b c d e f g h i j k l m n o p q
r s t u v w x y z . , - : ; ! ? ' ` " " ( )

Ligatures are included in fonts of 6 to 18 point
sizes, and are obtainable in 24 to 120 point
sizes in foundry lines.

fi ff fl ffi ffl

Spartan Medium Condensed
Series Number 706
Designed by John L. Renshaw
Characters in complete font

A B C D E F G H I J K L M N
O P Q R S T U V W X Y Z &
$ 1 2 3 4 5 6 7 8 9 0 ¢ %
a b c d e f g h i j k l m n o p q
r s t u v w x y z . , - : ; ! ? ' ` " " ( )

Ligatures are included in fonts of 6 to 18 point
sizes, and are obtainable in 24 to 48 point sizes
In foundry lines.

ff fi fl ffi ffl

Spartan Black Condensed
Series Number 687

Characters in complete font

A B C D E F G H I J K L M N
O P Q R S T U V W X Y Z &
$ 1 2 3 4 5 6 7 8 9 0 ¢ %
a b c d e f g h i j k l m n o p q
r s t u v w x y z . , - : ; ! ? ' ` " " ( )

Ligatures are included in fonts of 10 to 18 point
sizes, and are obtainable in 24 to 120 point
sizes in foundry lines.

fi ff fl ffi ffl

Spartan Heavy
Series Number 685

Characters in complete font

A B C D E F G H I J K L M N
O P Q R S T U V W X Y Z &
$ 1 2 3 4 5 6 7 8 9 0 * ¢ %
a b c d e f g h i j k l m n o p q
r s t u v w x y z . , - : ; ! ? ' " " ( )

Ligatures are included in fonts of 6 to 18 point
sizes, and are obtainable in 24 to 120 point
sizes in foundry lines.

fi ff fl ffi ffl

Spartan Extra Black
Series Number 694

Characters in complete font

A B C D E F G H I J K L M N
O P Q R S T U V W X Y Z &
$ 1 2 3 4 5 6 7 8 9 0 ¢
a b c d e f g h i j k l m
n o p q r s t u v w x y z
. , - : ; ! ? ' " " ( )

Fig. 10-7. Examples of the *Spartan* family of type. (American Type Founders)

ple, is available in eleven different sizes, or in a series ranging from 10 point through 72 point. Some typefaces are available only in 18 through 36 point, or in some other combination. Type sizes are produced to be used; therefore, only those sizes commonly used in any one kind are produced.

A FAMILY OF TYPE

A family of type contains several different styles under the same basic name (Fig. 10-7). A style refers to the specific appearance of one kind. The Spartan family (Fig. 10-7) contains eleven different styles of type. These range from the standard book face to the extra black face, but each face contains the same basic design, except for the weight, angle, or space allotted to each character. Type families have been designed so that different face styles can be used together while still retaining harmonious design.

UNIT 11
TEXT TYPE STYLE

Text typefaces (Fig. 11-1) have many sharp points and angular strokes. They also contain several stroke thicknesses ranging from very thin to very thick. The features of characteristic Gothic architecture are present in this style.

Text type is somewhat difficult to read (Fig. 11-2), and therefore it is used sparingly in modern publications. It may transmit an aging or old effect. It may also convey connotations of religion and reverence, primarily because this style of type was first used in monasteries by scribes and monks.

This style of type is sometimes referred to as *Blackletter,* because of its heavy face design. It is also called *Old English,* due to its relationship to the Gothic architecture period in England. This typeface should never be composed in all capitals because some of its capital letters are almost unreadable.

Wedding Text 414

Pack My Box With Five Do 123

Cloister Black 98

Pack My Box With F 123

Engravers Text 541

Pack My Box With Five Doz 1234

Engravers Old English 148

Pack My Box With Fiv 123

Fig. 11-1. A sample of text typefaces. (American Type Founders)

This kind of type would have been considered the most legible to any person who lived in the fifteenth and early sixteenth centuries anywhere in western Europe north of the Alps. In fact, it was only near the end of the sixteenth century that this letter disappeared from English printing, and yielded to the form called roman. Today, it survives only as a quaint type which we use discreetly to set a few words for a greeting card or a formal invitation. Nobody expects the reader to read continuous prose set in this type—are you still with us?—because it is considered to be illegible in the mass. Illegibility does not mean that it cannot be read, but rather that it cannot be read easily; the eye and the mind become fatigued with the effort involved in trying to identify the letters whose forms are unfamiliar to us today.

Fig. 11-2. A paragraph composed in the text typeface. Can you read it? (West Virginia Pulp and Paper Co.)

USES

Text typefaces are commonly used by churches and for formal announcements and invitations to weddings, graduations, and receptions. Greeting cards often contain text typefaces, as do cards concerned with religious holidays such as Christmas, Easter, and other holy occasions.

HISTORICAL HIGHLIGHTS

Text type was originated by the ancient scribes who copied religious works by hand. Because of the flat shape of the marking instrument that was available during the early eras, narrow, thick lines and angular strokes resulted. The Gothic style of architecture also influenced the design of this type.

Examples of text type style have been found which date back to 700 A.D. Gutenberg, originator of movable metal type, used this type style to cast his first characters, making text style the oldest cast-metal type in the world. Almost without exception, the early bibles that were typeset used this style of type.

UNIT 12
ROMAN TYPE STYLE

The most distinguishing characteristics of Roman typefaces (Fig. 12-1) are the many shaped serifs and the thin and thick strokes. These typefaces can easily be distinguished from the other five classifications because of the use of many serifs. Serifs are either angular, rounded, rectangular, or a combination of all three shapes. Because of the serif shape, the Roman classification is subdivided into three divisions: (1) oldstyle faces (Fig. 12-1), (2) modern (Fig. 12-2), and (3) transitional (Fig. 12-3).

Oldstyle faces (Fig. 12-1) contain serifs that are rounded at the ends. The contrast between the thick and thin strokes is only moderate, giving the appearance of a pleasant face weight.

Modern Roman type (Fig. 12-2) has the most extreme contrast between the thin and thick strokes. A bright and shadowed effect results. The serifs are generally straight, thin, and somewhat rectangular, except for some rounding at the corners. The ascenders and descenders of the face style are generally quite long; the counters of the letters are large, providing easy reading.

Transitional Roman type style (Fig. 12-3) is a combination of the old and modern. The contrast between the thin and thick strokes

Caslon No. 540-233

PACK MY BOX WITH
Pack my box with five d 123

Century Schoolbook 454

PACK MY BOX WITH FI
Pack my box with five 123

Cooper Black Italic 1592

PACK MY BOX WITH
Pack my box with 123

Goudy Bold Italic 464

PACK MY BOX WITH
Pack my box with five   123

Fig. 12-1. Oldstyle Roman typefaces. (American Type Founders)

is not as great as in modern Roman type. The serifs are relatively long and contain smooth, rounded curves.

Craw Modern Bold 716

PACK MY BOX
Pack my bo   123

Onyx 661

PACK MY BOX WITH FIVE DOZEN JUG
Pack my box with five dozen jugs 12345

Bodoni Bold 24

PACK MY BOX WITH FIV
Pack my box with five   123

Bernhard Modern Italic 669

PACK MY BOX WITH FIVE
Pack my box with five dozen 123

Fig. 12-2. Modern Roman typefaces. (American Type Founders)

Whitin Black Condensed 30

PACK MY BOX WITH F
Pack my box with fiv 123

Baskerville Roman 15

PACK MY BOX WITH FI
Pack my box with five d   123

Whitehall 566

PACK MY BOX WITH FIV
Pack my box with five d   123

Bulmer Roman 497

PACK MY BOX WITH FIVE
Pack my box with five doze   123

Fig. 12-3. Transitional Roman typefaces. (American Type Founders)

All Roman type styles are very legible and look good when used in large amounts. The typefaces possess dignity and can be read with ease. Design of the serifs tends to lead the eye from one letter to another and from word to word. This reduces the amount of eye strain when reading. The shapes of the capital letters are such that each one is easily distinguishable. Because of this, Roman typefaces can be composed in all capitals without producing unreadable material.

Typefaces containing a slight forward angle are called *italic*. Italic faces are designed for use with normal letters that generally contain vertical strokes. This makes the italic letter stand out, commanding attention. *Note that this line of type is in italic face, making it stand out from the other copy.*

USES

The bulk of reading material contained in newspapers, books, and magazines is composed with Roman typefaces. Because of the high readability level of this face, few other type styles have challenged Roman faces.

HISTORICAL HIGHLIGHTS

Roman type was first created in the fifteenth century by a Frenchman named Nicholas Jenson. He became interested in the art of producing graphic images and traveled to Venice, Italy to learn the new art of printing. As a typeface designer he created his distinctive Venetian typeface, and in approximately 1470 he reproduced nearly 100 books in this face. Because of his work, Jenson is considered the world's first great type designer.

Many other type designers, such as Claude Garamond of France, William Caslon of England, and Giambattista Bodoni of Italy, began developing their variations of the Roman typefaces. Their typefaces have been used throughout the years. Caslon typefaces were extremely popular in the early printed materials of the United States. The Declaration of Independence was first composed in Caslon type, as was Ben Franklin's *Pennsylvania Gazette*. Roman typefaces are now designed and prepared for machine use, but none can yet compare to the faces that were designed and used during the fifteenth through the eighteenth centuries.

UNIT 13
SANS-SERIF TYPE STYLE

The French word *sans,* meaning without, defines the sans-serif typeface classification (Fig. 13-1). Sans-serif type contains no serifs. Because the strokes of the letters are all of the same weight or thickness, they are quite monotone. Some contain a slight variation, but the true sans-serif has none.

Sans-serif letters are the simplest and most primitive of all styles. Very direct and abrupt strokes are characteristic. Because the letters are designed with simplicity, the capitals are easily distinguishable. This allows sans-serif to be composed in all capitals, and gives the typeface a tremendous amount of power that is used to good advantage in many kinds of printed material.

Several sans-serif faces contain italic styles as shown in Fig. 13-1. As in the Roman faces, these italic styles are used for emphasis and variety.

USES

Sans-serif types are being used, to a greater degree, in place of the Roman typefaces faces in books, magazines, and newspapers. With proper spacing this type classification is often used where there is a great amount of copy. This book is typeset with a modern sans-serif type called Helvetica.

Sans-serif types are also used a great deal with advertising material, visiting and business cards, and personal and business stationery. The clear-cut design of the letters gives a modern appearance, which is a desired characteristic of these kinds of printed products.

HISTORICAL HIGHLIGHTS

Sans-serif type is a product of the twentieth century, although the Greeks first used this letter style in identifying their architectural structures during the fourth century B.C. Paul Renner, a German type designer, designed a sans-serif typeface in 1927 and it has become very popular.

The name Gothic is sometimes attached to the monotone sans-serif letter. However, this term is considered a misnomer because the real meaning of Gothic denotes a very ornamental appearance. The text-type classification is nearer to Gothic style.

Univers 75
PACK MY BOX WITH FIVE
Pack my box with five 123

News Gothic 338
PACK MY BOX WITH FIVE D
Pack my box with five 123

Headline Gothic 650
PACK MY BOX WI 123

Huxley Vertical 596
PACK MY BOX WITH FIVE DOZEN JUGS 12345

Spartan Heavy Italic 686
PACK MY BOX WITH FIVE
Pack my box with five d 123

Lydian Bold Italic 674
PACK MY BOX WITH FIVE D
Pack my box with five do 123

Fig. 13-1. A sample of sans-serif typefaces. (American Type Founders)

34   *Type Styles*

UNIT 14
SQUARE-SERIF TYPE STYLE

Square-serif typefaces (Fig. 14-1) are somewhat of a cross between the Roman and the sans-serif classifications. The presence of many serifs, although very rectangular in shape, relates square-serif to Roman. The monotone strokes of the letters resemble the sans-serif types.

Tower 587
PACK MY BOX WITH FIVE DOZEN JU
Pack my box with five dozen jugs 1234
Stymie Medium 552
PACK MY BOX WITH F
Pack my box with f 123
Stymie Bold Italic 561
PACK MY BOX WIT
Pack my box with 123
Hellenic Wide
PACK MY B
Pack my 123
Barnum
PACK MY BOX WITH FIVE DOZE
Pack my box with five dozen 123
Trylon
PACK MY BOX WITH FIVE DOZEN JUG
Pack my box with five dozen jugs 1234

Fig. 14-1. Square-serif typefaces. (American Type Founders)

Square-serif types are designed with a pure geometrical look. For example, a compass can be used to construct the letter O in most square-serif types because it is a perfect circle. All of the letters can be constructed by using three instruments: the T-square, triangle, and compass. The typeface is open and because of this it is very readable and legible.

There are only a few square-serif typefaces, as compared to the many Roman types; but with most square-serif types there is a companion italic style. This is used for emphasis. The three previously named typeface classifications are the only ones that do contain italic type—Roman, sans-serif, and square-serif.

USES

Square-serif types have limited usage in newspapers, books, and magazines where large amounts of copy must be read. The geometrical structure of the letters limits rapid reading. However, the type tends to draw attention, or in some cases shout at the reader. It is good for advertisements, newspaper headlines, letterheads, and some invitational items.

HISTORICAL HIGHLIGHTS

Square-serif type style first appeared in type books in the early nineteenth century, but it did not become popular until it was made more modern by Heinrich Jost of Germany. This designer created a modern square-serif face in 1931. Since that time the typefaces with rectangular serifs have become quite popular.

UNIT 15
SCRIPT TYPE STYLE

Script type resembles handwriting or hand lettering containing thin and thick strokes. These variances result from pen-point designs and the natural pressure differences that are exerted in normal penmanship.

There are two divisions of script types: (1) those styles with letters that join (Fig. 15-1), and (2) those that do not join (Fig. 15-2). The types that do not join are sometimes called *cursive* letters.

Some script faces have a fragile, handwritten, feminine appearance. Most of the faces tend to slant forward at approximately 22 degrees. Upon studying the design of the capital letters, it is obvious that script styles should never be composed in all capitals. They would be nearly impossible to read.

USES

Script types are very popular for use in advertisements, announcements, and invitations. Greeting cards are also composed with script because it gives a personal, handwritten feeling.

HISTORICAL HIGHLIGHTS

The ancient scribes and monks are given credit for developing the script type style. It came into use in Europe during the Georgian Period (1740-1830).

Bank Script 1540

Pack My Box With Five 123

Brush 689

Pack My Box With Five 123

Kaufmann Script 652

Pack My Box With Five Doz 123

Typo Script 399

Pack My Box With Five Dozen Ju 1234

Commercial Script 107

Pack My Box With Five 123

Fig. 15-1. Joining script typefaces. (American Type Founders)

Bernhard Tango 582

PACK MY BOX WITH FIV
Pack my box with five dozen j 123

Keynote 579

Pack My Box With Five D 123

Grayda 678

Pack My Box With Five Dozen Ju 123

Liberty 511

Pack My Box With Five Doze 123

Park Avenue 577

Pack My Box With Five Do 123

Fig. 15-2. Nonjoining script typefaces. (American Type Founders)

UNIT 16
NOVELTY TYPE STYLE

The Novelty type classification contains those types that cannot be fitted into the five previously named classifications. This classification is a catch all. Novelty types can be divided into conservative novelty faces (Fig. 16-1), and contemporary novelty faces (Fig. 16-2).

Conservative faces are in general those containing some alterations of one of the other type styles. Shading, outlining, uneven letters, and unique serif designs are a few characteristics. *Contemporary* faces are those made to resemble the meaning of the word or the content of a specific article. Almost any look can be given to this typeface.

A specific characteristic of novelty typefaces is that each face has individuality and the ability to be very expressive. These faces cannot come under a blanket rule as to whether or not they can be composed in all capitals, because each specific style has different characteristics. Decisions as to composition therefore rest upon the typeface design and the discretion and originality of the typographer or the layout artist.

USES

The ability of the Novelty type style to be very expressive gives it the special quality needed for use in trade names of companies. A graphic artist assigned to design a trade name or an identification symbol for a company can create any new typeface appropriate to the situation. Anything he prepares is considered a novelty face.

There are standard novelty typefaces shown in Fig's. 16-1 and 16-2 and these are used for advertising material. They attract attention, shout to people, and serve their purpose well in promoting a product or a service.

HISTORICAL HIGHLIGHTS

The Novelty typeface classification has the distinction of being the only one developed in the United States of America. This development began during the period immediately following World War I. There was need for new and modernistic typefaces following the war years, because American business and industry were capable of producing products and materials but the American public had no desire to buy. Novelty typefaces were designed to command the attention of the people and to high pressure them by visual means into purchasing the products.

Copperplate Gothic Bold 132

PACK MY BO 123

Balloon Extrabold 677

PACK MY BOX WITH F   123

Engravers Shaded 151

PACK   M 123

Cheltenham Bold Outline 75

PACK MY BOX WITH FI

Dom Casual 696

PACK MY BOX WITH FIVE DOZEN JU

Fig. 16-1. Conservative novelty typefaces.

ABCDEFGHIJKLMN

A B C D E F G H I

ABCDEFGHIJKL

ABCDE   *ABCDE*

Fig. 16-2. Contemporary novelty typefaces.

UNIT 17
LEARNING EXPERIENCES: TYPE STYLES

DISCUSSION TOPICS

1. What is the purpose of the typeface or of a combination of typefaces? Of what importance is the alphabet to the typeface?

2. Describe typeface psychology. Why is it important that we learn to recognize and understand typefaces?

3. List the five important factors to consider when choosing a typeface. Explain what is meant by each one of these factors.

4. Why was there need for a written form of visual communication? What were some of the forms of nonverbal communication prior to the development of the alphabet?

5. What were three stages in the development of picture drawings? Cite the advantages and disadvantages of each of these three methods of graphic communications.

6. Identify the written communications system that was developed by the Egyptians. How did this system improve communications? Discuss the advantages and disadvantages of this system.

7. Who has been given credit for the actual development of the alphabet? Why did these people need an alphabet? When was their alphabet in use?

8. Name the two groups of people who borrowed, adapted, and refined the original alphabet. How many characters were contained in each of their alphabets? Are these alphabets still in use today?

9. Describe the development of the first three letters in our modern-day alphabet. Tell how each letter originated, giving reasons why each representation may have been chosen.

10. Where does the word "alphabet" come from? In what time span was the alphabet created and developed? Were the small letters and capital letters developed at the same time?

11. What is the newest symbol used in our present day alphabetical communication? Tell why and how this new symbol was formed.

12. Why is there a need for new typefaces to be designed? Who is generally involved with the development of a new typeface?

13. What two letters are commonly designed first by the typeface designer when he is creating a new face? Why are these two characters generally chosen? Does the development of a new typeface take very long?

14. List the basic steps necessary in the production of foundry type. Why is it essential that quality control be practiced throughout the production phase? Name the machine that is used to prepare the brass matrix.

15. Identify the major parts of a piece of foundry type. Why is it desirable to have a basic knowledge of these parts?

16. Cite the distinguishing characteristics of typefaces. Identify the typeface part that generally gives the greatest assistance

in specifically identifying the typeface. Do all typefaces contain this part?

17. Define a type font, a type series, and a type family. How are they related to each other?

18. List the identifying characteristics of the text type style. What are the general uses of this type style? Describe the historical development of this type style.

19. List the identifying characteristics of the Roman type style. What are the general uses of this type style? Describe the historical development of this type style.

20. List the identifying characteristics of the sans-serif type style. What are the general uses of this type style? Describe the historical development of this type style.

21. List the identifying characteristics of the square-serif type style. What are the general uses of this type style? Describe the historical development of this type style.

22. List the identifying characteristics of the script type style. What are the general uses of this type style? Describe the historical development of this type style.

23. List the identifying characteristics of the Novelty type style. What are the general uses of this type style? Describe the historical development of this type style.

ACTIVITIES

1. Obtain printed examples of several different type styles. Group the printed examples according to the significant characteristics of the typefaces. Have several of your friends and instructors study the type styles and give their impressions as to how the typeface makes them feel. Take careful note of the reactions of each person and after collecting several opinions attempt to analyze the comments. Note whether or not there are similarities of impressions concerning each typeface.

2. From your school or city library obtain several books dealing with the development of the alphabet. Read how each of our twenty-six letters was developed. Prepare a written paper on the development of the alphabet.

3. Sketch an original typeface design. Begin by identifying a purpose for the typeface and keep continuity among all of the letters. Subject your new typeface to criticism by your friends and teachers. Make refinements based upon these criticisms. Reproduce several copies of your alphabet via the offset-lithography printing process.

4. Obtain a type catalogue. Identify the minimum and maximum type sizes available for a specific kind of type. Obtain a complete series of type. Study these sizes and learn to recognize them in finished form.

5. Locate printed examples of each of the six typeface classifications. Clip these samples from outdated or unwanted publications and glue them to sheets of paper—one for each type classification. Obtain different sizes and specific typefaces within each classification. Compare each specific type style with each basic type classification.

The printed page can live forever.

This is a spread from the Gutenberg bible, the world's first book printed from movable type.

The Gutenberg bible came off the press in 1455. Some 47 copies are still in existence today.

A message in print is not like a message in time.

A message in time will last for 10, 20, 30 or 60 seconds. Like a stroke of lightning, a message in time lives gloriously for a moment and then dies.

A message in print can die just as fast. On the other hand, a message in print can be read for 10 minutes, can be taken to the store a week later or perhaps saved for several lifetimes like this bible.

If you have something important to say, your message will last longer if you put it in print.

Your message in print will live as long as it is relevant to the needs and interests of your marketplace.

Your message in print can live forever.

A design and layout artist at work.

UNIT 18
THE VALUE OF PLANNING, DESIGNING, AND LAYOUT

A printed product or job must be well planned. The combination of ideas used in planning and designing the product is called a *layout*. It can be defined as the arrangement of all the units or elements into a printed usable format. These units or elements include the heading, subheading, text matter, illustrations, and photographs. The preparation of a complete set of layouts requires thumbnail sketches, a rough layout, and a comprehensive layout (Fig. 18-1). A definite predetermined plan is very necessary.

THE VALUES OF GOOD PLANNING

Graphic planning allows the designer to review and revise his thoughts. Printed work is often completed in less time and every person that performs a mechanical function leading to the final product knows his job. Questions are kept to a minimum.

Spelling, wording, and placement of material must be accurate, otherwise the final product will have little value. The specifications of the buyer of the printed material

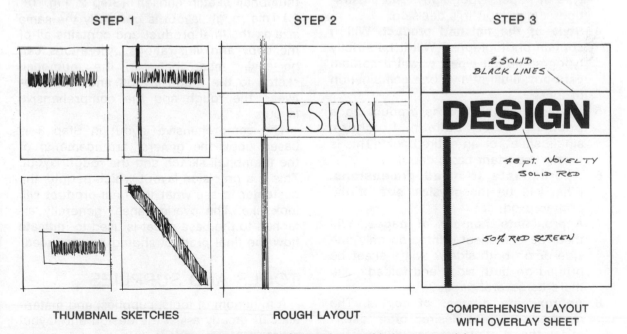

STEP 1   STEP 2   STEP 3

DESIGN

2 SOLID BLACK LINES

DESIGN

48 pt. NOVELTY SOLID RED

50% RED SCREEN

THUMBNAIL SKETCHES   ROUGH LAYOUT   COMPREHENSIVE LAYOUT WITH OVERLAY SHEET

Fig. 18-1. The sequence of preparing graphic layout materials.

must be accurately met. A high-quality final product will result and the buyer, the graphic arts commercial printing plant management, and the skilled workers will be satisfied that their work fulfills a particular requirement.

PRELAYOUT PLANNING

A prelayout planning form should be completed to help formulate the ideas of the person who is originating the printed job. Each of the following twelve questions or items should be listed on the form and must be well thought out. The answers should be recorded for reference during the layout preparation.

1. **Objective of the product.** What is the purpose of the finished product? Why do it?
2. **Designated group.** Will the printed material be for personal use, for students, for parents, or for some other group? The design approach would be different for each.
3. **Personality of the product.** Should it be sophisticated, gaudy, dignified, humorous, or have some other quality? The type of paper, typography, and illustrations depend on this decision.
4. **Style of the finished product.** Will it contain photographs? Will it be strictly typographic (all type), or will it contain cartoons, illustrations, or a combination of these?
5. **Layout format.** Will the product be a booklet, folder, bulletin, brochure, single sheet, or an entire book? This is a very important basic decision.
6. **Approximate trimmed dimensions.** What will be the physical size of the printed product?
7. **Approximate number of pages.** Will there be one sheet printed on only one side or on both sides? Will a sheet be printed on both sides and folded? Will there be several pages?
8. **Approximate number of copies.** The number of copies desired often determines the printing process used.
9. **Finishing and binding requirements.** Will the printed sheets from the press or duplicator need to be trimmed, folded, scored, or bound together by one of several methods?
10. **Layouts required.** Does the customer require thumbnail sketches, a rough layout, and a comprehensive layout?
11. **Estimated hours for completion.** How long will it take to complete the entire job? The answer to this question will depend on the answers to the ten previous questions, and will assist in making a cost estimate.
12. **Approximate date of completion.** This involves consideration of the time available per day, and the number of hours or days required.

LAYOUT PROCEDURE

The sequence for preparing graphic layout materials is shown in Fig. 18-1. Several thumbnail sketches are usually proposed, as indicated in Step 1 of this figure. The selection of one of the thumbnail sketches is made by the person who is ordering the product.

The rough layout is made up of the thumbnail sketch chosen. (Step 2, Fig. 18-1.) This rough layout is generally the same size as the final product and contains all of the copy and illustrations. Alterations can be easily made between the thumbnail sketch to the rough layout, and again between the rough and the comprehensive layouts.

The comprehensive layout in Step 3 is based upon the general arrangements of the thumbnail sketch and the rough layout. This is a precision layout which permits the customer to see what the final product will look like. The overlay sheet generally attached to the base sheet is used to indicate how the final product should be produced.

TOOLS AND SUPPLIES

A minimum of tools, supplies, and materials can greatly assist the design and layout artist. Not necessary but helpful are a draftsman's drawing board, a triangle, and a T-square; necessary for layout are paper, pencil, straight edge, and a table top.

Other items that are helpful are a line gauge or measuring device of some kind, an eraser, several pencils of various colors, rubber cement, and pads of drawing, tracing, and grid paper. Additional useful items are type sample catalogs, an illustrator's art book, samples of papers, and an ink sample catalog.

DESIGN AND LAYOUT CONSIDERATIONS

1. Planning is important.
2. Design and layout are essential to obtain a quality finished product.
3. Make it readable. A printed product is designed to give information.
4. A layout is a blueprint, a master plan.
5. Compose the final product in pencil; then compose it with type, illustrations, and photographs.
6. Simplicity is important.
7. Knowledge of type and typography is necessary.
8. The point system must be understood.
9. Basic design principles must be understood.
10. Knowledge of color and its effect on people are important.

UNIT 19
THE POINT AND METRIC MEASUREMENT SYSTEMS

Points and *picas* are the base of the measurement system used for type composition. It is important to become very familiar with these basic units of measure in Table 19-1. The inch has been divided into approximately 72 parts, called *points*. Twelve points equal one *pica* and six picas equal approximately one inch.

A measurement commonly used in the newspaper phase of the graphic arts industry is the *agate*. This unit equals exactly 5½ points. The agate measure is not commonly used in commercial printing firms.

Points and picas are not always used for measuring; therefore Table 19-2 can help convert from picas to inches.

The *line gauge* shown in Fig. 19-1 is used to determine point and pica measurements. It is marked with picas on the left side and inches or agates on the right side. It is a useful tool for the graphic arts production worker as well as for the estimator and designer.

Table 19-1 Graphic arts basic units of measure		
1 inch	=	72 points (approximate)
12 points	=	1 pica (exactly)
6 picas	=	1 inch (approximate)
5½ points	=	1 agate (exactly)

HISTORICAL HIGHLIGHTS

In about 1737 Simon-Pierre Fournier of France developed a system of measurement for the common type sizes and for other graphic arts measurement. In approximately 1770 two men, Francois and Firman Didot, amended the Fournier point system and in 1879 the Europe Type Founders Congress adopted their system.

The Anglo-American Point System was adopted in 1886 by the U. S. Type Founders Association. This system met with much criticism, but was not changed from the value of 1 point = 0.01384 inch. The Euro-

Table 19-2 Conversion of picas to inches

Picas	Inches	Picas	Inches	Picas	Inches	Picas	Inches
1	.166	26	4.316	51	8.466	76	12.616
2	.332	27	4.482	52	8.632	77	12.782
3	.498	28	4.648	53	8.798	78	12.948
4	.664	29	4.814	54	8.964	79	13.114
5	.830	30	4.980	55	9.130	80	13.280
6	.996	31	5.146	56	9.296	81	13.446
7	1.162	32	5.312	57	9.462	82	13.612
8	1.328	33	5.478	58	9.628	83	13.778
9	1.494	34	5.644	59	9.794	84	13.944
10	1.660	35	5.810	60	9.960	85	14.110
11	1.826	36	5.976	61	10.126	86	14.276
12	1.992	37	6.142	62	10.292	87	14.442
13	2.158	38	6.308	63	10.458	88	14.608
14	2.324	39	6.474	64	10.624	89	14.774
15	2.490	40	6.640	65	10.790	90	14.940
16	2.656	41	6.806	66	10.956	91	15.106
17	2.822	42	6.972	67	11.122	92	15.272
18	2.988	43	7.138	68	11.288	93	15.438
19	3.154	44	7.304	69	11.454	94	15.604
20	3.320	45	7.470	70	11.620	95	15.770
21	3.486	46	7.636	71	11.786	96	15.936
22	3.652	47	7.802	72	11.952	97	16.102
23	3.818	48	7.968	73	12.118	98	16.268
24	3.984	49	8.134	74	12.284	99	16.434
25	4.150	50	8.300	75	12.450	100	16.600

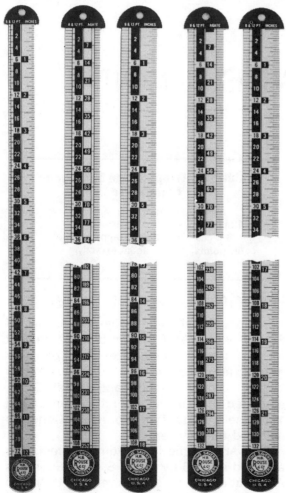

Fig. 19-1. Styles of line gauges used in graphic arts. (H. B. Rouse & Co.)

pean system has a slightly larger point value of 1 point = 0.01483 inch. Some equipment that is manufactured in the United States for use in Europe must therefore have certain different specifications to be useful with the European measurement system, and vice versa.

COMMON TYPE SIZES

Type that is used in books, magazines, newspapers, and other materials is measured in *points.* The typeface that you are reading at this moment has a specific point size. It is 10 point. Type size is determined by measuring from the top of the ascender of a tall letter such as capitals or f, b, d, and 1 to the bottom of the descender of letters like y, p, q, and g (Fig. 19-2).

Type that is cast on metal is measured by the type-body size (Fig. 19-3). No one letter in the alphabet is as large or high as the point size designation.

The common sizes of type range from six point through 72 point. Larger sizes are

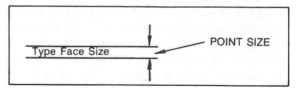

Fig. 19-2. The method of measuring the size of a type face.

available for headlines and posters, but are generally obtained from specialty houses. Because of the various mechanical and photographic methods of producing type as discussed in Section 4, it is possible to obtain any size of type desired. Examples of the traditional type sizes are shown in Fig. 19-4.

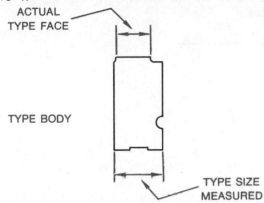

Fig. 19-3. The method of measuring foundry type.

THE METRIC SYSTEM

The metric system was conceived as a measurement system to the base ten; that is, the units of the system and their multiples and submultiples are related to each other by simple factors of ten. This is a great convenience because it conforms to our common system for numerical notation, which is also a base ten system. To convert between units and their multiples and submultiples, it is therefore not necessary to go through a difficult multiplication or division process, but simply to shift the decimal point.

For example, multiplying 1 pound, 9 ounces by 10 entails reducing the two units of measurement to one—25 ounces. Multiplying 25 ounces by 10 results in 250 ounces; this is then reconverted into pounds and ounces. To multiply 1.9 kilograms by 10, the decimal point is moved one place to the right, thus giving the product of 19 kilograms; this is an almost instantaneous computation.

In The Modernized Metric System, six base units of measurement are utilized in all but a few countries throughout the world.

6 PT.
THE EARLY PRINTERS CAST THEIR OWN TYPES, MADE INK
They instructed some local blacksmith to make the iron frames

8 PT.
THE EARLY PRINTERS CAST THEIR OWN TYPES AND
They instructed some local blacksmith to make the iron

10 PT.
THE EARLY PRINTERS CAST THEIR TYPES
They instructed the local blacksmith to make

12 PT.
THE EARLY PRINTER CAST blacksmith

14 PT.
THE EARLY PRINTERS instructed

16 PT.
THE EARLY printers cast their

18 PT.
THE EARLY printers came

24 PT.
BRAZIL and countries

30 PT.
JADE varies into

36 PT.
KNIGHTS us

42 PT.
SOME xylo

48 PT.
FINE quali

60 PT.
WHILE a

72 PT.
THE pri

Fig. 19-4. The traditional type sizes. (American Type Founders)

The United States has conducted a considerable amount of study and research to determine if this system should be adopted. Results from business and industry indicate a favorable reaction; therefore the United States will now begin the conversion process since necessary legislation was passed. Complete conversion will eventually take place during the 1980s.

The graphic arts industry is presently using some metric measure (Unit 53) and with some equipment (Unit 32), but the change will be slow until a concentrated effort is conducted. The point system will very likely continue to be used to measure typefaces, as it would be difficult to adopt the metric system to the existing standard type sizes.

UNIT 20
DESIGN PRINCIPLES

Basic design principles must be understood before preparing a set of layouts, although only a few considerations are suitable for the designer for use in preparing a graphic two-dimensional layout. Four of the most important considerations reviewed in this unit are (1) page proportion, (2) balance, (3) contrast, and (4) unity. Space is also discussed, because without it there would be little or no need for the four basic considerations.

SPACE

Space has little value until something is done with it, or something happens to it. A designer in the graphic arts area is concerned with the two dimensions of length and width. A blank space (Fig. 20-1), whether it is on a billboard, poster, page of a newspaper, book, or even a portion of a page, is always ready to accept graphic elements. Before placing these elements in a given space the content for the space must be considered, and then arranged according to the four basic design considerations. A well-designed space (Fig. 20-2) will be noticed and will serve the purpose for which it was intended.

PAGE PROPORTION

Page proportion is important to all two-dimensional graphic materials. One of the first decisions a designer makes is in selecting the most functional and attractive plan for the page. The basis for this selection depends on the amount of copy to be placed on the page and also upon the intended use of the material being prepared.

Several page proportions used in education, business, and industry are illustrated in Fig. 20-3. Index file cards have proportions of 3 x 5, 4 x 6, and 5 x 8 inches. Photographic enlargements are usually 5 x 7 or 8 x 10 inches. The proportion upon which the business world operates is 8½ x 11 inches. By placing all of the proportions against the same horizontal and vertical axes, it is possible to observe their relationship. By drawing diagonal lines through the bottom left and top right corners of each proportion, one can see that they vary.

The page proportion selected for the particular graphic layout can be reduced or enlarged by the diagonal-line method (Fig. 20-4). When the diagonal line is drawn through the intersection of the horizontal and vertical axes and extended through the opposite

Fig. 20-1. A blank space ready to accept the graphic elements.

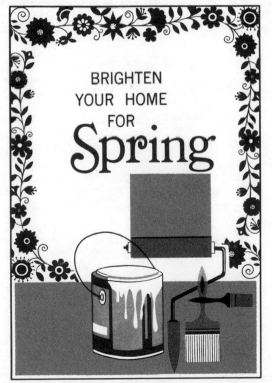

Fig. 20-2. This space has been used for important graphic elements.

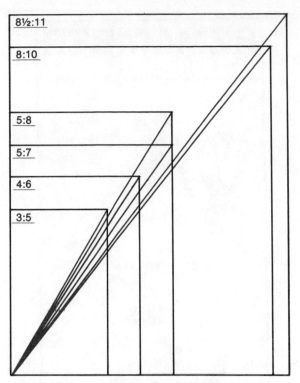

Fig. 20-3. Common page proportions. The diagonal lines emphasize the relationships among the proportions.

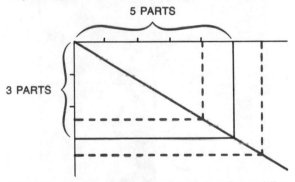

Fig. 20-4. The proportion 3″ x 5″ and the diagonal-line method of enlarging and reducing.

corner, one can select any width of page desired, either smaller or larger than the original proportion measurement. The new width is selected and a perpendicular line is drawn from the horizontal axis to the diagonal line. A horizontal line is extended from the point of intersection to the vertical axis.

The 3 x 5-inch page proportion was used by the ancient Greek architects. They followed this ratio in designing the magnificent structures that have endured through

Fig. 20-5. Formal balance. Graphic elements are equally balanced on each side of the center line. (Dynamic Graphic, Inc.)

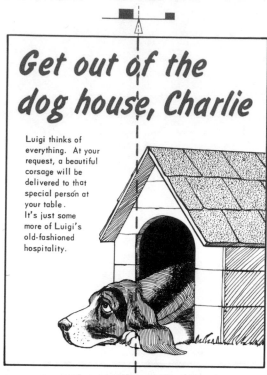

Fig. 20-6. Informal balance. Graphic elements are unequally balanced on each side of the center line. (Dynamic Graphics, Inc.)

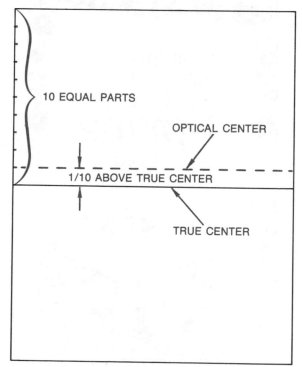

Fig. 20-7. The relationship between the optical center and the true center of a page.

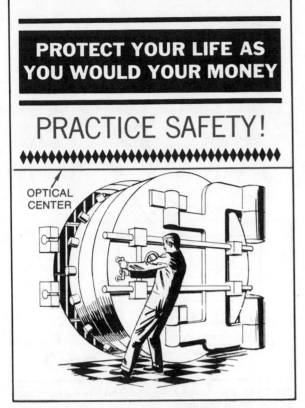

PROTECT YOUR LIFE AS
YOU WOULD YOUR MONEY

PRACTICE SAFETY!

◆◆◆◆◆◆◆◆◆◆◆◆◆◆◆◆◆◆◆◆◆◆◆◆◆◆◆◆◆◆

OPTICAL
CENTER

Fig. 20-8. Graphic elements positioned according to the optical center. (Dynamic Graphics, Inc.)

the ages. Some designers refer to this proportion as the Golden Rectangle.

The square, or that page with equal width and height, is not usually used for two-dimensional graphic materials. It is uninteresting to the eye because it does not suggest movement or change.

BALANCE

There are two kinds of balance: *formal* (Fig. 20-5), and *informal* (Fig. 20-6). With formal balance the elements of the page are centered horizontally and an equal amount of each major unit is placed on either side of the imaginary center line. Informal balance has graphic elements unequally placed. Note in Fig. 20-6 that the page looks balanced, but that the graphic elements are not placed according to the imaginary center line. This style is more modern and is used extensively in advertising.

Another consideration is to place the elements of a page in the proper vertical position. They should be arranged according to the *optical center,* which is the imaginary center line slightly above the true vertical center of a page. It is normally one-tenth of the distance from the true center to the top of the page (Fig. 20-7). If elements are placed according to true center they will appear to be far below the center of the page. For proper viewing the optical center serves as the positioning guide (Fig. 20-8).

CONTRAST

Contrast is the accentuation of an element in the copy. It can be a word, a series of words, or an illustration. Several ways of emphasizing words are shown in Fig. 20-9.

Twelve ways to emphasize with type.
1.   Change the size.
Twelve ways to EMPHASIZE with type.
2.   Use capital letter.
Twelve ways to EMPHASIZE with type.
3.   Use small capital letters.
Twelve ways to *emphasize* with type.
4.   Use italic type.
Twelve ways to ●mphasize with type.
5.   Use a different kind of type.
Twelve ways to **emphasize** with type.
6.   Change the face.
Twelve ways to emphasize with type.
7.   Underline the word or words.
Twelve ways to ➔ emphasize with type.
8.   Use eye directing symbols.
Twelve ways to emphasize with type.
9.   Alter the position.
Twelve ways to emphasize with type.
10.   Enclose the word(s) with lines.
Twelve ways to emphasize with type.
11.   Use color when possible.
Twelve ways to emphasize with type.
12.   Create reverse type.

Fig. 20-9. Methods of emphasizing words with type.

Fig. 20-10. A layout with good unity among the elements of the page. (Dynamic Graphics, Inc.)

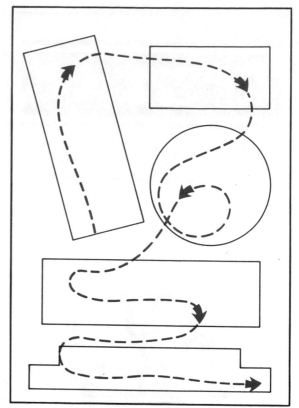

Fig. 20-11. Eye movement is obtained when a page such as Fig. 20-10 has unity.

A general criterion is, "All display is no display." If all elements of the page are large, bold, underlined, or in color they would not indicate change; therefore no specific item would be noticed.

UNITY

Unity ties together the graphic elements of a two-dimensional layout. Elements should not appear crowded, but should have a "oneness" or a look of belonging together. Illustrations and type must be compatible and arranged in an order that compliments each single element (Fig. 20-10).

Eye movement is obtained with good unity. Normally the eye enters a page at the upper left-hand corner, proceeds across the page and down to the lower left-hand corner, and out of the page at the lower right-hand corner. Fig. 20-11 illustrates typical eye movement on the layout shown in Fig. 20-10. All professional layouts must be planned to have eye movement, otherwise portions of the page might go unnoticed altogether.

UNIT 21
COLOR PRINCIPLES

Color is everywhere; in clothes, food, homes, automobiles, nature, and nearly everything else. What would the world be like without color? Color is one of the most valuable assets people have, because everyone uses and benefits from it whether or not he is aware of it. Color in the graphic arts makes the products interesting and challenging, and a designer of two-dimensional graphic materials must become very familiar with the principles of color.

THE COLOR WHEEL

The color wheel in Fig. 21-1 is a useful tool to the graphic arts designer. It gives ready reference to the several common colors and shows the relationships among them. Experienced designers use color wheels that contain additional colors, but for normal design work a wheel such as the one illustrated is sufficient.

Three *primary* colors produce all pigment colors. These are yellow, red, and blue (Fig. 21-2). These three cannot be formed by mixing other colors, but other colors result when these three are mixed.

Secondary colors (Fig. 21-3) are obtained by mixing equal amounts of two primary ones. They are green made by mixing yellow and blue; violet made by mixing red and blue; and orange made by mixing red and yellow.

Intermediate colors (Fig. 21-4) result when equal amounts of one primary color and an adjacent secondary color are mixed.

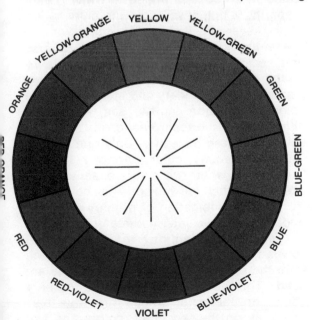

Fig. 21-1. Pigment colors of the color wheel.

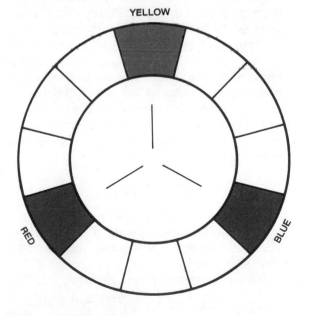

Fig. 21-2. Primary colors.

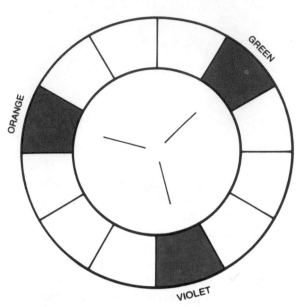

Fig. 21-3. Secondary colors.

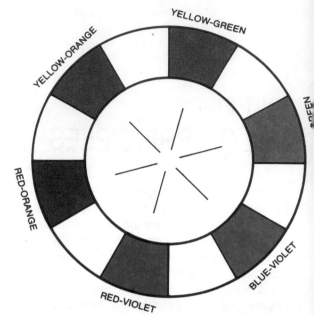

Fig. 21-4. Intermediate colors.

These are yellow-green, blue-green, blue-violet, red-violet, red-orange, and yellow-orange. Note that the primary color is given first to denote the dominance or power of the primary colors.

Eye response which is created by white and black cannot be considered as color sensation. Science defines *white* as the presence of all colors; *black* is the absence of them as shown in Fig. 21-5. Objects that appear white to the eye are reflecting almost all light reaching the surface, combining the primary colors and forming the white-eye sensation. The black-eye sensation results because the material or object absorbs almost all of the light and does not reflect any of the light rays. To simplify communication in the graphic arts, however, white and black are referred to as colors.

COLOR HARMONY

There are four color harmonies obtained by combining colors from a color wheel: monochromatic, analogous, complementary, and triadic.

Monochromatic color harmony in Fig. 21-6 is obtained by combining a color and a shade or tint of the same color. A *shade* results when black is added; a *tint* is ob-

Fig. 21-5. White—the presence of all colors; black—the absence of all colors.

tained when color is added to white. When preparing a tint, always add the color to the white; never add the white to the color.

Analogous color harmony in Fig. 21-7 is obtained by combining two adjacent colors on the color wheel. A primary and an intermediate or a secondary and an intermediate color combination can be used. Analogous differs from monochromatic in that two colors are used instead of only one.

Complementary color harmony in Fig. 21-8 results when two colors exactly opposite each other are mixed. This color harmony is a combination of primary and secondary, or of two intermediate colors.

Triadic color harmony in Fig. 21-9 involves three colors. Any three colors which form the point of an equilateral triangle are used. The position of the three primary colors on the color wheel form this harmony, as do the secondary colors and two combinations of intermediate ones.

Fig. 21-6. Monochromatic color harmony.

Fig. 21-7. Analogous color harmony.

Fig. 21-8. Complementary color harmony.

Fig. 21-9. Triadic color harmony.

It is important to remember that each color of any one of the four color harmonies cannot be used in the same intensity or amount. One color should dominate the combination used in any two-dimensional graphic layout. Study examples of the four harmonies and note the relationships.

PSYCHOLOGY OF COLOR

Colors are described as *warm* or *cool.* Yellow, orange, and red are considered warm, reminding one of heat. Green, blue, and violet are cool, the colors of nature; green, the color of grass; blue, the color of water; and violet, the feeling of night or darkness. The selection of colors is important when designing two-dimensional graphic materials. Human emotions are also often affected by them. Warm colors excite and create a higher pulse rate. Cool ones tend to be quieting.

MODERN USE OF COLOR

The identification of objects and situations is easily controlled with color. Red usually indicates danger; green means that all is going well and one can proceed. Examples of these are the red and green used in street and highway intersection lights. Color and the use of it cannot be overemphasized. To use it effectively in two-dimensional graphic material, choose colors with utmost care.

UNIT 22
THUMBNAIL SKETCHES

Thumbnail sketches are simple idea sketches which help both the designer and economic growth and explosive expansion of the planned product in many ways to obtain an attractive, acceptable final result. The purchaser can see the ideas and choose the layout which he prefers.

Thumbnail sketches serve three primary purposes: They (1) graphically preserve ideas, (2) visually portray ideas, and (3) compare two or more ideas visually.

Preparation of these sketches should begin immediately after the desired product has been selected and after completion of the prelayout planning sheet (Fig. 18-1). Copy selection precedes thumbnails; therefore, one of the responsibilities of the designer is to obtain the copy that will appear on the final product. The originator of the planned printed product should have this information available.

METHOD OF PREPARATION

1. Prepare the prelayout planning sheet and list the copy.
2. Choose the final size of the printed product and plan to sketch the thumbnails 1/4 size.
3. Select copy elements needing emphasis. Block and shade areas of space in the approximate position that each element is desired. The space given should be a representation of the desired final size.
4. Use straight lines to represent type that is 12 points or smaller in size. Do not use lettering for either the large or small type.
5. Outline the space for illustrations or photographs. Within this space, sketch the illustrations or content of the photograph. This permits another person studying the sketches to obtain a basic idea of the content. Detail is not needed for thumbnail-sketch illustrations or photographs.

It is important to sketch several ideas from which a final selection can be made. Prepare as many thumbnail sketches as you have ideas. Skilled designers prepare at least four of any copy given to them. It is sometimes difficult for the beginner to visualize a large number of possibilities.

Figs. 22-1 and 22-2 are examples of thumbnail sketches. The copy for Fig. 22-1 is as follows:

Baseball
Support Little League
Every Saturday 9:00 a.m. Valley Park
Sponsored by: City Council

Study the copy. Note various positions or locations in which copy elements could be placed for each of the four thumbnail sketches.

Copy listed for Fig. 22-2 includes:

Summer Clothes Drive
April 8
We Need Clothes
Please Contribute
Bring Clothes to Main Lounges of the Dorms, 7:00 to 9:00 p.m.

Note that only the word content is listed. In most situations it is the responsibility of the designer to select an illustration, if one is desired, to help relay the message to the reader. With each of the four thumbnail sketches, a different illustration was used.

Thumbnail sketches are extremely important. They serve as the foundation for the final usable printed material.

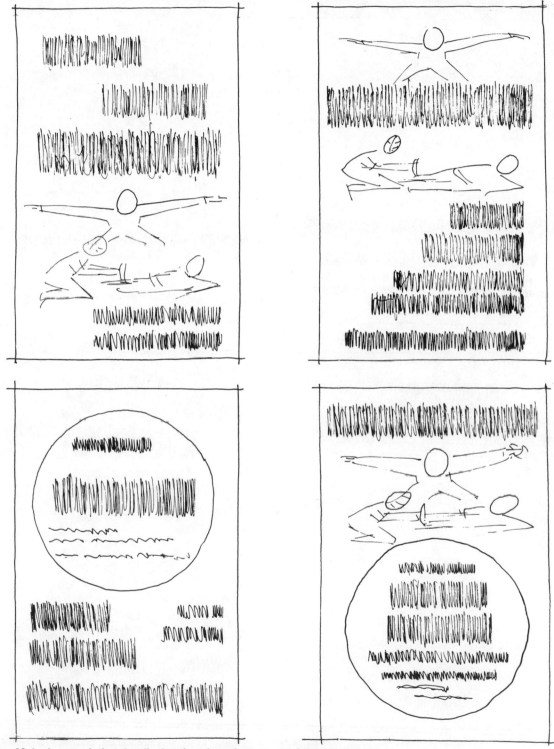

Fig. 22-1. A set of thumbnail sketches based upon predetermined copy.

Fig. 22-2. A set of thumbnail sketches. Note that each sketch contains a different illustration, but has provision for the same copy.

UNIT 23
THE ROUGH LAYOUT

The second major step in layout procedure is the preparation of a rough layout. The *rough* is an improvement or refinement of a thumbnail sketch, or even a combination of two or more.

Purposes of a rough layout are to (1) force a selection of one of the several sketched ideas, (2) begin refining a specific idea, and (3) provide a tangible item that can be studied and changed. Actually, a rough layout can be considered a prefinal product.

METHOD OF PREPARATION

1. Study the several thumbnail sketches that have been prepared.
2. Select the one that best presents the content of the final two-dimensional product. Selection is made by the designer and/or the purchaser.
3. Obtain a sheet of paper that will allow the layout to be drawn full size.
4. Block or outline the area that will be devoted to type and illustrations according to the thumbnail or combinations of them selected (Fig. 23-1).
5. Add type to the rectangular outlined areas, based upon the copy. Straight lines signify 12-point type and smaller.
6. Sketch the illustrations within the outlined areas (Fig. 23-2). They should be of a higher quality and contain more detail than a thumbnail-sketch illustration. The rough layout should reasonably resemble the finished product.
7. Study the rough layout; make additions or changes. Consult the purchaser of the final product as this gives him the opportunity to suggest necessary changes.

As noted in the previous procedural steps, it is possible to combine two or more thumbnail sketches to obtain the basic appearance for a rough layout. An example of such a combination is shown in Fig. 23-3. This rough is based upon two thumbnail sketches (A and D) in Fig. 22-2. Study these two figures to see how the combined rough layout was made.

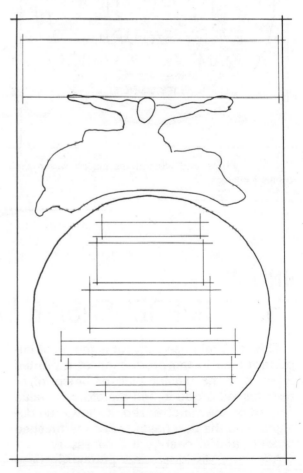

Fig. 23-1. Beginning a rough layout based upon thumbnail sketch *D* in Fig. 22-1.

Fig. 23-2. Words and illustrations placed within the outlined areas.

Fig. 23-3. A rough layout based upon two thumbnail sketches—Fig. 22-2, *A* and *B*.

UNIT 24
THE COMPREHENSIVE LAYOUT

The comprehensive layout is the most important step in the production of a printed work. It is the master plan or blueprint of the finished product, and therefore its value cannot be overemphasized. It allows the designer and the purchaser to see the finished product and to change it if necessary.

After the designer and purchaser have made all necessary decisions, the comprehensive layout will contain all information needed to complete the printed product. It will guide specialists who will produce the final product.

STEPS OF PREPARATION

1. Study the rough layout similar to those in Unit 23.
2. If the complete material is to be multiple colored, choose the colors and the

content for each. Use colored pencils to represent the color of each element.

3. Letter all type in the exact position desired. Make the type look like the actual kind. Study Fig. 24-1 for the first three procedural steps.

4. Lines should be used to designate the correct position, even if the layout contains 12-point type or smaller. However, the typewritten copy should also be attached.

5. Draw the illustrations carefully in the correct positions.

6. Block the space for the photographs, if they are used, and attach the glossy print if it is available. If the photographs have not yet been taken, give directions as to the content and where

the subject or photograph contents can be obtained.

7. Prepare an overlay sheet after all content has been placed on the layout.

8. Thoroughly review the layout. Be certain that you have included all copy and given full production information on the overlay sheet. For detailed instructions on how an overlay sheet should be prepared, study the following seven steps.

CONTENT OF THE OVERLAY SHEET

The overlay sheet should contain all information necessary to complete the finished product. This sheet is valuable to the production personnel who must produce the product. Use of the overlay sheet permits the designer to keep the layout free of instructions that hamper a view.

1. Itemize the kind, size, and style of type for each group or element of the layout.

2. Indicate the type position if specific margins or line lengths are desired. It is often possible for the compositor to measure the position of the words or lines from the layout.

3. Give specific information relating to the illustrations and/or photographs. These should include information as to where the camera-ready illustration copy is available and where the photograph can be obtained.

4. List the color or colors of ink. If the entire product is pronted in one color, mention this only once. If several colors are used it is advisable to pinpoint them to the various elements of the job.

5. Indicate the paper as to kind, finish, weight, and size.

6. List the number of finished copies desired.

7. If possible, note the reproduction process. Sometimes this information is not the responsibility of the design specialist but that of the foreman for the production department.

Fig. 24-1. The first three steps of a comprehensive layout have been completed, based upon the rough layout in Fig. 23-2.

The importance of the overlay sheet cannot be overemphasized. The quality of work of the entire comprehensive layout is very important, but if the overlay sheet is not prepared correctly a quality final product will not result. Study the overlay sheet for Fig. 24-2. It contains the information that should be listed. Note the manner and order in which these data are listed.

Normally the thumbnail sketches, rough layout, and comprehensive layout are completed for a set of layouts. However, sometimes the purchaser of the printed product desires to see a finished or final layout. This layout is also called a *mechanical,* and it can be used as camera-ready copy. It contains the actual illustrations or photographs used, and also has proofs of the type that has already been composed. The purchaser can then see exactly how the final product will look. In many instances this finished or final layout is not produced because it is expensive.

Study the complete set of layouts, from the thumbnail sketches, to the rough layout, to the comprehensive, to the finished or final one (Figs. 24-3 through 24-6). Note how the theme or basic idea was carried from the thumbnail sketches to the final layout.

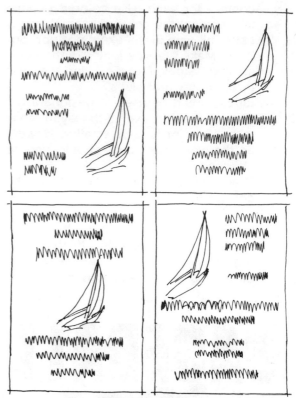

Fig. 24-3. Thumbnail sketches, the first important step in two-dimensional graphic layout.

Fig. 24-2. A completed comprehensive layout, based upon the rough layout in Fig. 23-3. Point sizes are larger than shown.

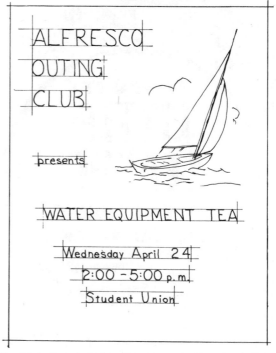

Fig. 24-4. Rough layout, the second step in two-dimensional graphic layout.

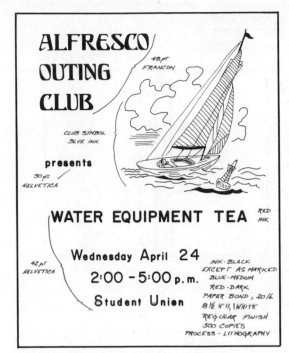

Fig. 24-5. Comprehensive layout, the third step in two-dimensional graphic layout (point sizes are larger than shown).

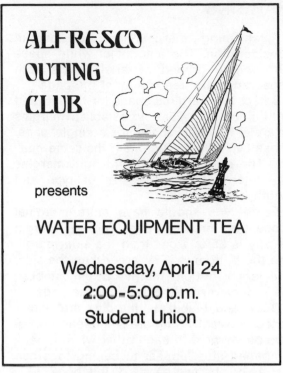

Fig. 24-6. A finished or final layout. It is also called a *mechanical*, and can be used for camera-ready copy.

DESIGN PRINCIPLES REVIEWED

During the preparation of the layout it is important to constantly consider the four basic design principles discussed in Unit 20. When the comprehensive layout has been completed, check it very closely with basic design principles of *page proportion, balance, contrast,* and *unity.* Persons other than those who requested or worked on the layouts should be consulted for their unbiased review.

During the process of preparing the series of layouts needed for the completion of a printed product, changes are constantly made to produce a final quality product. The only way to prepare the final product is to compose it in pencil through the design and layout process, then closely study it before the mechanical operations start.

Customer conferences can result in many changes being made to meet his needs.

UNIT 25
PAGE AND SIGNATURE LAYOUT

A page for a book, magazine, newspaper, or other printed material should be designed for easy reading. The eye should enter the page at the upper left-hand corner and follow the lines of the text material and illustrations without encountering difficulty. Pages of printed matter should produce an interesting effect, and design principles must be considered when preparing page and signature layouts.

MARGINS

Establishing margins requires careful consideration. The amount of white space surrounding printed material effects both appearance and readability of the page.

Select the marginal space for the left and right sides (Fig. 25-1) to establish margins or areas of white space for a single page. These two sides will contain the same margin. The size of the left and right margins are determined by the size of type and length of lines.

Large type should have more marginal space than smaller sizes. The top margin usually is 25% larger than the side margin and the bottom is 75% larger than the side. The larger bottom margin helps establish the proper vertical balance for the page.

Book and magazine margins are established differently than are single-page ones. Two pages next to each other when a book is opened must appear to belong together, just as do the two pages of this book.

The size of the outside margin is arbitrary. It is based, generally, upon the type size and the length of lines. The inside margin is ½ the width of the outside one; but when the two inside margins are combined they equal the same amount of space as the outside

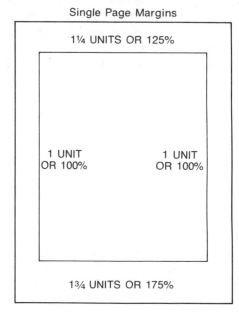

Fig. 25-1. Margins for a single page.

Single Page Margins

1¼ UNITS OR 125%

1 UNIT OR 100%   1 UNIT OR 100%

1¾ UNITS OR 175%

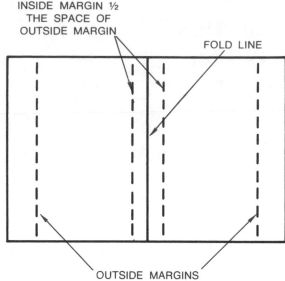

INSIDE MARGIN ½ THE SPACE OF OUTSIDE MARGIN

FOLD LINE

OUTSIDE MARGINS

Fig. 25-2. Book margins. Establish outside margins, then inside ones.

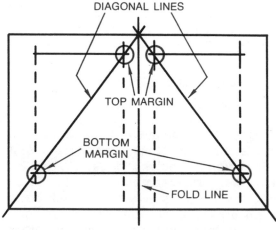

DIAGONAL LINES

TOP MARGIN

BOTTOM MARGIN

FOLD LINE

Fig. 25-3. Book margins. Establish top and then bottom margins.

ones. The three vertical margins are therefore equal and have a balanced appearance as shown in Fig. 25-2.

Figure 25-3 shows how to establish top and bottom margins. Draw diagonal lines from the upper inside corner to the lower outside corner of each page. The intersecting points of the diagonal line and the vertical side marginal lines establish the top and bottom margins. Draw solid marginal lines for each page. Note how the two areas in Fig. 25-4 that are to contain the reading material appear to belong together. Also note their balanced appearance.

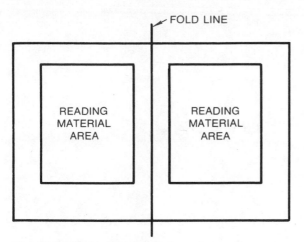

Fig. 25-4. Book margins. Balanced margins give a pleasing and readable page.

DUMMY LAYOUT

A dummy layout is a folded representation of the finished booklet, pamphlet, or any other multiple-page printed product. It serves to give the general layout or content of the key pages.

The main purpose of the dummy is to establish the page locations for a *signature,* or section, of a book. A signature is a large sheet of paper that contains several pages folded to the size of one individual page. The normal signature has a page count of four, eight, sixteen, thirty-two, or sixty-four.

The method of determining the page location for a four-page signature is very simple (Fig. 25-5). Fold a sheet of paper in half and number the pages 1 through 4. The sheet can then be opened and the page-location relationship is established.

To obtain the page location for an eight-page signature (Fig. 25-6), fold a sheet in half twice. Number the pages 1 through 8 in the lower right- and left-hand corners. The uniformity of page numbering will assist the production personnel in preparing the final printed copy. Open the folded sheet which is now called a signature and note the relationship of the various pages.

A four-page signature, printed on one side only, is a sheet of paper folded in half twice (Fig. 25-6). This type of fold and signature is common for greeting cards.

Note the page numbering in the center top of each page.

In addition to page numbering, the content of a dummy should include indications of the headings and illustrations, or topics of each key page. It is good practice to list the content for each page. This insures identification needed for the several mechanical functions to complete the final product.

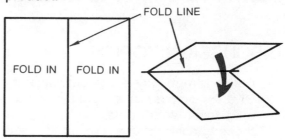

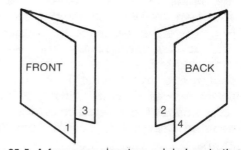

Fig. 25-5. A four-page signature printed on both sides.

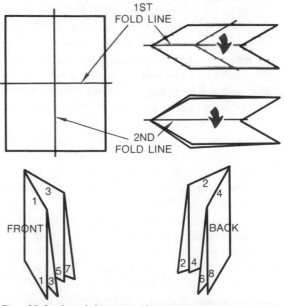

Fig. 25-6. An eight-page signature printed on both sides; or a four-page greeting card printed on one side.

UNIT 26
LEARNING EXPERIENCES: PLANNING, DESIGNING, AND LAYOUT

DISCUSSION TOPICS

1. Define layout. Why is a layout valuable?
2. Give the purpose of the prelayout planning sheet. What value does it have for the originator of the printed job and other people who are connected with the planning and layout stages? Develop your own prelayout planning sheet.
3. Enumerate the sequence for preparing graphic arts layouts. List the several tools and supplies that are used by the design and layout artist in preparing a set of layouts. Cite the primary point to remember of those listed under the subheading *Design and Layout* Considerations.
4. Name the standard measurement system used in the graphic arts. Why is it important to become familiar with this basic system of measurement? What advantage, if any, does this system have over the linear-inch system?
5. Define line gauge. Tell basically how it is constructed and list the markings that are commonly placed upon it.
6. Explain the historical background of the measurement system used within the graphic arts. Is this system very old? Is this measurement system consistent throughout the world?
7. Discuss the value of using the metric system as compared to the linear-inch system. List the common metric measurements in one column, then, list the linear-inch counterpart in another column. Study these two columns until you are familiar with the metric system.
8. Enumerate the several common type sizes that are in use today. Be sure to identify these according to the standard measurement system used in the graphic arts. Is it possible to obtain type sizes other than the common listed sizes? If so, what are they?
9. Does space have value? Why? How can space serve the purpose for which it is intended? Cite the two dimensions of space that concern a designer.
10. List the four important principles of graphic design. Explain the underlying basis for each.
11. Where is color? Why is color a valuable asset to people? Does color have a place in the graphic arts? Why?
12. Explain the value of the color wheel to the graphic arts designer. What three colors are responsible for producing all other pigment colors? What significance do these three colors have?
13. List the three secondary colors. How are these colors formed? List the intermediate colors. How are these formed?
14. What is color harmony? Enumerate the four common color harmonies. How are these obtained?
15. How does color affect us? Cite several uses of color in our modern world. Study and report on the color scheme of this room.
16. Define a thumbnail sketch. When should thumbnail sketches be prepared? Explain the general method of preparing thumbnail sketches.

17. Define a rough layout. List the specific purposes of the rough layout. Explain the general method of preparing a rough layout.
18. Define a comprehensive layout. Cite the several purposes and explain the general preparation of a comprehensive layout.
19. Give the purpose of the overlay sheet of a comprehensive layout. Enumerate the several items of information that should be included on the overlay sheet. How important is the overlay sheet?
20. Identify the layout that is sometimes prepared after the preparation of the comprehensive layout. Specifically, what value does this layout have? How is this layout prepared?
21. Why must the margins be given careful consideration when preparing layouts for a book, magazine, newspaper, or other printed matter? Explain the method of determining the margin sizes for each of the four sides of a page. Should the type-page size be considered?
22. Define a dummy layout. What is the main purpose of the dummy? How can page location be determined for a book, magazine, or other multiple-page printed product?

ACTIVITIES

1. Complete an entire set of layouts for a poster advertising a future sporting event in your school. Prepare the pre-planning layout sheet, four thumbnail sketches, one rough layout, and one comprehensive layout. Be sure to include the overlay sheet on the comprehensive layout.
2. Obtain several printed samples of advertising brochures. Examine them closely and determine whether the space was used in the most effective manner. Consider the four principles of design and determine whether each design principle—page proportion, balance, contrast, and unity—was considered in the. brochures. Identify areas of the layout of the brochures that could have been improved.
3. Prepare a color wheel. Use water paints and mix them to match the proper secondary and intermediate colors. Also show examples of the four common color harmonies.
4. Prepare a dummy for a sixteen-page booklet. Identify each page by number and also calculate and rule in the margins for each of the sixteen pages.

Composing type with
a tape-operated impact
(strike-on) machine.

UNIT 27
INTRODUCTION TO COMPOSITION

Composition and *typesetting* are words that refer to the processes of setting, preparing, and arranging type. Composition is the act of producing symbols to communicate thoughts and ideas to someone else. The letters, words, sentences, and paragraphs that you are reading now have been composed by one of several methods.

METHODS OF COMPOSITION

There are two general basic classifications, or methods, of composition: hot and cold. In *hot* composition molten metal is cast to form the letter (symbol) or the entire line of type. From a hot composition type form, printed copies can be produced or proofs pulled so that photographic negatives can be made.

Cold composition refers to nonhot metal typesetting and is accomplished in several ways. Machines that place an image on paper using pressure action are called *impact devices.* Other machines that place an image on paper through photographic means are termed *photocomposers.* A third method is that of *dry transfer.* In this, the preprinted letters are fastened into place by hand in preparation for the camera.

IMPORTANCE OF QUALITY AND SPEED

The age of automation has had a tremendous effect on composition methods. Electronics has influenced the area of composition by use of computers and coded tape-control equipment for automatic operations.

Photography also plays a large part in many of the latest machines used in the graphic arts industry.

The need for quality and speed has led to the development of sophisticated machinery for the composition of words. When combined, words form the thoughts of man and have more power than the combined military fire power of all the countries in the world. This book was typeset by the fully automatic, tape-controlled, high-speed, photocomposition *Linotron 505.*

HISTORICAL NOTES

In about 1450 Johann Gutenberg of Germany first invented a practical method for composing individual letters into words. He devoted his entire life to the invention of movable metal type. Before that date entire

Fig. 27-1. A ticket-printer set manufactured before the Civil War. (Mable Tainter Literary Library and Educational Society)

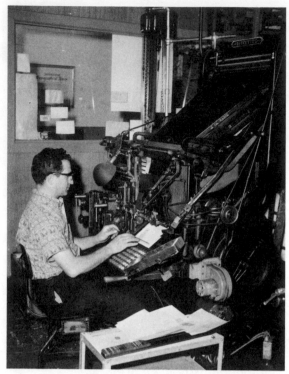

Fig. 27-2. An early slug-casting composing machine. (St. Paul Dispatch-Pioneer Press)

pages of type were cut by hand, in reverse, on blocks of wood. By casting individual letters Gutenberg was able to compose, print, and reuse the type, which, unlike the wood block, did not have to be thrown away.

An early ticket printer is shown in Fig. 27-1. Because of its size, the box of small type characters and the printing *palet* (which held the type while printing) could be transported easily from place to place.

Mechanical composition was not developed until four centuries after Gutenberg's invention. In 1884 Ottmar Mergenthaler, also of Germany, introduced a machine called a slug caster that could cast a complete line of type. This machine, called a *linotype,* was put into practical use in about 1886. Fig. 27-2 shows an early slug-casting machine that was manufactured in 1913. Note its similarity to today's counterpart of this early machine, shown in Fig. 27-3. There are only three major differences between the two: (1) operating speed, (2) a coded tape attachment, and (3) the streamlined appearance.

At the close of World War II another major development took place in composition. A machine was developed that produced type by photographic means. This revolutionized graphic arts industry. In modern industry, not only photography, but also electronics and computors are combined to produce type. A striking example of a modern composing machine is shown in Fig. 27-4.

Fig. 27-3. A modern slug-casting composing machine. (Intertype Corp.)

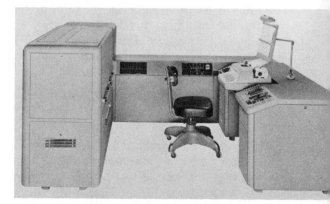

Fig. 27-4. A phototypesetting complex. (Photon, Inc.)

UNIT 28
FOUNDRY TYPE COMPOSITION

Foundry type composition is a good example of one fundamental process of reproduction. While it is not used for production as much as it was from the fifteenth through the nineteenth centuries, specialty jobs, such as letterheads and visiting cards, still require the versatility and exactness of hand-set type.

letters, capital or uppercase letters, numbers, punctuation points, and word-spacing materials. Typecases are stored in banks or cabinets (Fig. 28-2). They are placed on top of the bank while composing or making up type. The lay or arrangement of the case should be studied and learned before beginning to compose type.

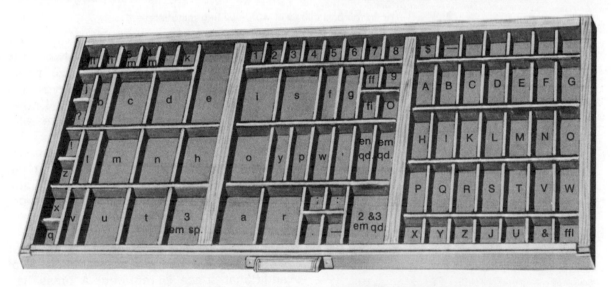

Fig. 28-1 The lay or arrangement of the California job case.

CALIFORNIA JOB CASE

The *California job case,* shown in Fig. 28-1, is a basic storage and retrieval system for foundry type. The case or drawer measures approximately 1 x 16 x 32 inches and it contains 89 individual compartments. Storage is provided for small or lower case

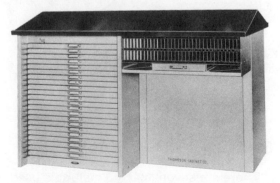

Fig. 28-2. Typecase storage and work area, called a *blank.* (Thompson Cabinet Co.)

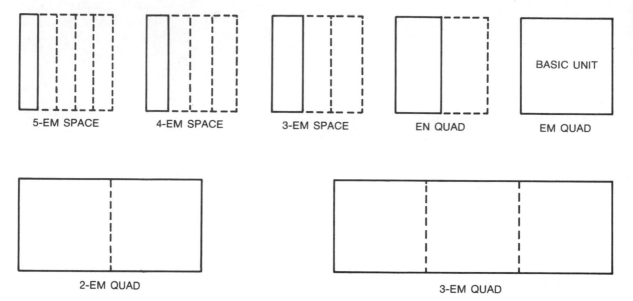

Fig. 28-3. The seven basic sizes of word-spacing materials.

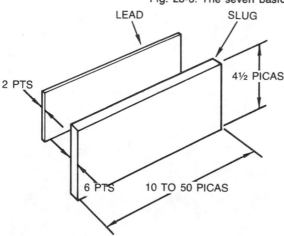

Fig. 28-4. Line-spacing materials.

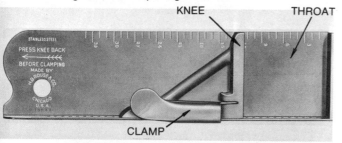

Fig. 28-5. A composing stick. (H. B. Rouse Co.)

SPACING MATERIALS

There are seven spacing materials used to provide word spacings (Fig. 28-3). These word-spacing materials are sized for use with matching type sizes. The unit, or *em quad,* is the basic spacing; it is always the square of the particular type size being used. For example: with 12-point type, the em quad is 12 points x 12 points. All other spaces and quads have a direct size relationship to the em quad.

The *en quad* is ½ the width of an em quad. A 3-em space is ⅓ the width of an em quad, a 4-em space is ¼ of the width and a 5-em space is 1/5 of the width. The 2-em quad is twice the width of the em quad; the 3-em quad is three times as wide.

Hair spaces or thin spacers are used for word spacing when a very small amount of additional space is required. A brass hair space is 1 point in thickness; a copper hair space is ½ point.

Line spacing material consists of two major thicknesses (Fig. 28-4). The *slug* is commonly 6-points thick and can be cut to any pica length. A *lead* is generally 2-points thick and can also be cut to any pica length.

COMPOSING STICK AND GALLEY

The *composing stick* (Fig. 28-5) is a device in which foundry type is composed or set up. The stick is approximately 2 inches wide and is adjustable in pica and half-pica lengths. A common maximum length for a composing stick is 34 picas.

A *galley* is used for type storage and form make-up (Fig. 28-6). Several gallies can be stored in a galley cabinet shown in Fig. 28-7.

COMPOSING TYPE

Foundry type composition is not difficult, but it must be done with care. Knowledge of the lay of the typecase and the point system of measurement discussed in Unit 19 are essential to good composition. Follow these procedural steps closely for a successful foundry type composition experience.

1. Place the typecase on top of a bank. Be sure the case is positioned above the lip of the slanting top so that it will not slide to the floor.
2. Select a composing stick and adjust it to the desired length of line. Hold the composing stick in the palm of the left hand, with the thumb extending into the open throat (Fig. 28-8).
3. Place a slug in the stick. Slugs and leads should be slightly shorter than the line length to eliminate binding in the stick.
4. Insert the first letter of the first word in the lower left corner of the stick as shown in Fig. 28-9. Be sure that the nick on the type is toward the open side or scale of the composing stick. Type in the stick is read upside down but always from left to right.
5. Continue composing the remaining letters of the first word.
6. Insert a 3-em space which is the common word spacing between words composed in small letters (Fig. 28-3). An en quad should be used between words composed in all capital letters. Continue composing in the same manner until there is no space left to compose another word.
7. *Justify* (space the line to the correct length) by placing necessary spaces and quads to make the line snug.

Fig. 28-6. A galley, used for typeform storage and make-up. (Thompson Cabinet Co.)

Fig. 28-7. A galley storage cabinet. (Thompson Cabinet Co.)

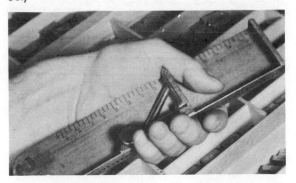

Fig. 28-8. The correct way to hold a composing stick.

When the line can be pushed away from the back of the stick and stand alone, it is properly justified.

8. Insert a lead or slug into the stick. The one chosen depends upon the amount of space desired between the lines. Sometimes two leads or a lead-slug combination are used.

9. Continue composing lines in the same manner. Carefully justify each line, as all lines must be the same length to be properly held in the printing press.

DUMPING AND TYING

When the composing stick is full or when the necessary lines have been composed, the type must be removed (dumped) from the stick and tied with string. The operations should be done with care to reduce the chances of spilling the type which is called making *pi*.

1. Insert a *slug* against the last line that was composed in the stick. This gives support to the line and to the entire typeform.
2. Place a galley on top of the bank.
3. Position the composing stick inside the galley.
4. Grasp the lines of type (typeform) as shown in Fig. 28-10 and push from the stick.
5. Slide the typeform against the corner of the galley as shown in Fig. 28-11.
6. Tie the typeform in a clockwise direction (Fig. 28-11). Wrap the string around the form six or seven times and secure it with a printer's knot, as illustrated in Fig. 28-12.
7. The proofing operation is the next step and is discussed in Section 5, Unit 36.

DISTRIBUTING TYPE

The individual letters and spaces must be returned to the proper locations after the typeform has been proofed or printed. It is essential that care be taken to restore all materials—type characters, spaces, quads, leads, and slugs—to their correct locations.

1. Place the galley, with the typeform and the typecase on top of the bank.
2. Position the typeform with the nicks away from you and untie it. Use care not to pi the form while removing the string.
3. Position two or three lines of type in the left hand as in Fig. 28-13. Squeeze the lines tightly on all four sides and

Fig. 28-9. Composing lines of foundry type.

Fig. 28-10. Removing lines of type from the composing stick.

Fig. 28-11. Tying a typeform.

lift carefully. Place the lines in the left hand between the thumb and middle finger with the index finger supporting the bottom slug.

4. Remove the top slug and begin on the right side by grasping a complete word between the thumb and index finger of the right hand also as in Fig. 28-13.

5. Distribute the letters and spacing in their proper locations in the case by carefully dropping one character at a time. This operation takes practice; do not become discouraged if you have trouble dropping only one character.
6. Restore all other materials to their correct locations—leads, slugs, galley, string, and typecase.

Fig. 28-12. A tied typeform. Note the printer's knot.

Fig. 28-13. Distributing type back into the typecase.

UNIT 29
HOT-METAL COMPOSITION

Hot-metal composition is the traditional method of setting type by mechanical means. Hot-metal machines have been the backbone of the composition function of the graphic arts industry since the latter part of the nineteenth century. Composition machines in the *hot* category are those that use molten metal to cast letters into complete lines called *slugs* or into individual characters of type.

LINE CASTING

Line- or slug-casting machines are controlled by either a punched tape (Fig. 29-1) or a keyboard (Fig. 29-2). They can be equipped to handle both a punched tape and a keyboard, as shown in Fig. 29-2. Because many controls are needed to regulate the functions performed, it takes an opera-

Fig. 29-1. A tape-controlled, slug-casting machine. (Intertype Co.)

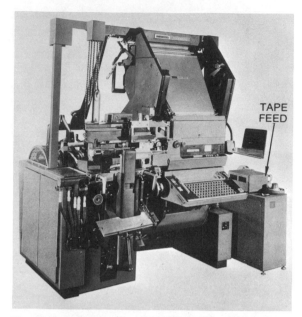

TAPE
FEED

Fig. 29-2. A slug-casting machine with dual keyboard and tape control. (Mergenthaler Linotype Co.)

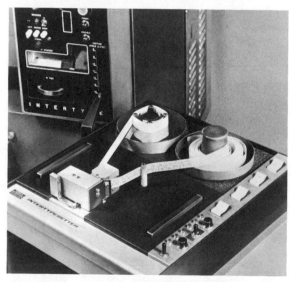

Fig. 29-3. The control panel and tape reader of a slug-casting machine. (Intertype Co.)

Fig. 29-4. A matrix or mold used in a circulating matrix line-casting machine. (Intertype Co.)

Fig. 29-5. A slug from a circulating matrix line-casting machine. (Mergenthaler Linotype Co.)

Fig. 29-6. A slug-casting machine used for display composition, shown with storage cases. (Ludlow Typograph Co.)

tor several years of practice to become proficient. Fig. 29-3 illustrates a control panel and tape reader of a slug-casting machine.

Slug-casting machines work on the principle of the circulating matrix. A matrix or mold, seen in Fig. 29-4, can be used over and over to produce letters. At the touch of a key or at the direction of a control tape, matrices are released from a magazine (ma-

trix storage case). When the matrices for one line are assembled, the line is automatically justified and an entire slug of type can be cast (Fig. 29-5).

After the casting procedure, matrices are returned automatically to the magazine for reuse. Each size, kind, and style of type has its own magazine. Modern keyboard- and tape-controlled slug casters can produce fourteen newspaper lines per minute.

SEMIAUTOMATIC SLUG CASTER

Another slug-casting system called *Ludlow* is a semiautomatic method that combines both hand and machine functions. This method is used primarily for display composition requiring large letters. The machine assembly consists of a casting device and matrix storage cases shown in Fig. 29-6. Correct reading letters are recessed into brass to form the mold or matrix. These matrices are gathered by hand, placed into the casting device, and a slug is cast like those in Fig. 29-7. Type sizes range from 4 to 96 points.

The basic procedure for the operation of the *Ludlow* is carried out in the following five steps.

1. Gather the matrices from the matrix case (Fig. 29-8).
2. Place the matrices in the specially designed composing stick (Fig. 29-9).
3. Tighten the matrices in the composing stick and place them into the casting position (Fig. 29-10).
4. Cast as many slugs as needed from the one assemblage of matrices.
5. Assemble the slugs into a form for proofing or printing on a press, as shown in Fig. 29-11.

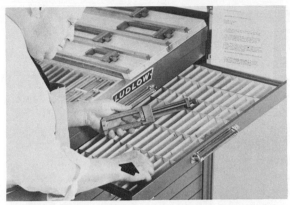

Fig. 29-8. Gathering matrices from a case. (Ludlow Typograph Co.)

Fig. 29-9. Placing matrices in the composing stick. (Ludlow Typograph Co.)

Fig. 29-10. Tightening the composing stick prior to casting the slug. (Ludlow Typograph Co.)

Fig. 29-7. Matrices or molds and a slug of display type. (Ludlow Tyopgraph Co.)

Fig. 29-11. Slugs of display type being assembled in a multiple form. (Ludlow Typograph Co.)

SINGLE-CHARACTER CASTING

A system that produces single characters of type called *Monotype* consists of two machines: the tape-producing keyboard (Fig. 29-12) and the casting machine (Fig. 29-13). The keyboard operator presses the keys of the keyboard unit, which perforates a coded paper tape. The coded tape is then fed into the casting unit which molds single characters of type, similar to hand-set type. This hot-type system produces high-quality type, which makes it ideal for setting complicated tabular matter such as financial statements and charts.

LINE SPACING CASTING

Unit 28, *Foundry Type Composition*, showed how leads and slugs are used for line spacing. An *Elrod* machine that produces leads and slugs (strip material) is pictured in Fig. 29-14. This machine produces a continuous strip of metal from 1 through 36 points in thickness.

Molten metal is fed into the mold, where it is cast, solidified under pressure, and ejected from the machine in a continuous strip. This is the principle of *extrusion*. Most commercial graphic arts companies that use hot-composition methods have a strip-making machine of this kind.

Fig. 29-13. A single-character casting machine. (Lanston Monotype Co.)

Fig. 29-12. Tape-producing keyboard unit of a single-character casting machine. (Lanston Monotype Co.)

Fig. 29-14. A casting machine (Elrod) that produces leads and slugs. (Ludlow Typograph Co.)

UNIT 30
IMPACT COMPOSITION

Impact or strike-on composition machines are either keyboard or tape operated and they are manual, semiautomatic, or entirely automatic in justifying the copy. There are machines with fixed styles of type and those on which the type styles and sizes can be changed. Impact composing machines use the principle of forming an image by striking the paper with a key containing a character. A common machine, the typewriter, utilizes the impact principle.

REGULAR TYPEWRITER

The first typewriters were made during the first half of the nineteenth century; however, they proved impractical. In 1867 the first practical typewriter (Fig. 30-1) was designed and built by Christopher L. Sholes, Carlos Glidden, and S. W. Soulé of Milwaukee, Wisconsin. These inventers patented the machine in 1868 and placed it on the market in 1874.

Fig. 30-1. One of the first typewriters to be built and demonstrated for the public. (Remington Office Machines)

The typewriter is valuable to the business world and to those who desire to compose economically. Regular typewriters have the disadvantage of not producing print that looks like printer's type, not being able to change type styles, and leaving too much white space between some letters. It is not easy to justify typewriter copy flush left and flush right. There are typewriters, however, that make this possible.

Advantages overrule the disadvantages: composition by typewriter is economical because most persons have access to one, no skilled operators are needed, and type sizes can be reduced or enlarged with a camera to fit any purpose. When typed copy has been reduced to 75% (25% smaller than original size) it reads much better (Fig. 30-2). Enlarged to 125% (25% larger than original size) it loses some quality but is still very usable (Fig.30-3).

JUSTIFYING LEFT AND RIGHT MARGINS

Standard typewriters can be used to prepare composition with flush left and right margins. Follow these ten steps to obtain clean and quality copy.

The guide lines for printed communications of the future seem to be very well drawn. At one point in history, man worked from sun to sun; there was no time to think of self improvement or even the operation he was part of. Automation has freed us from humdrum, repetitious, back breaking chores, and man is free to spend more time learning and improving.

Fig. 30-2. Typewritten copy reduced to 75% of original size.

The guide lines for printed communications of the future seem to be very well drawn. At one point in history, man worked from sun to sun; there was no time to think of self improvement or even the operation he was part of. Automation has freed us from humdrum, repetitious, back breaking chores, and man is free to spend more time learning and improving.

Fig. 30-3. Typewritten copy enlarged to 125% of original size.

The guide lines for printed communications of the future1234 seem to be very well drawn. At1 one point in history, man worked from sun to sun; there was no123

Fig. 30-4. The largest number indicates the spaces that must be made up on retyping.

1. Set margins.
2. Begin typing copy.
3. Stop with a complete or divided word as near the desired right hand margin as possible.
4. If the line is short (Fig. 30-4), type consecutive numbers until the margin is reached. If the line is over the right margin by more than 3 spaces it may be difficult to reduce the space between the words.
5. Type the entire copy, following Step 4 (Fig. 30-5).
6. Place a new ribbon on the typewriter or use a typewriter with a carbon ribbon to give a sharp, black image. A good image is needed when a photographic negative will be made from the copy.
7. Begin retyping the copy on clean paper.
8. On lines that are short, add as many additional word spaces as the highest number typed on the first typed copy. Add an additional space between words that have tall letters at the end of one word, and at the beginning of the next one. Example: long high
9. Make up space on lines that went over the desired margin. Put half-spaces be-

The guide lines for printed communications of the future12 seem to be very well drawn. At one point in history, man worked from sun to sun; there was no1 time to think of self improvement or even the operation he1 was part of. Automation has12 freed us from humdrum, repe-12 titious, back breaking chores, and man is free to spend more1 time learning and improving.12 I have been told that 75 per-1 cent of all the scientists who have lived in the history of12 the world are alive and working today. A new generation is123 coming along and they are extrem ly sharp. They are not going1 to be content with tradition.1 They are being trained to study problems and meet new objec-12 tives; to find better systems1 and not copy what has been done.

Fig. 30-5. A page of copy after the first typing.

tween words that have short letters at the end of one word and at the beginning of the next. Example: little short

10. Retype the entire copy, following the procedure outlined in Steps 8 and 9 (Fig. 30-6).

PROPORTIONAL SPACING TYPEWRITERS

More aesthetic or artistic quality is obtained with special proportional spacing typewriters like the one shown in Fig. 30-7. A typewriter of this kind delegates to each letter an amount of space relative to its natural width. It is electrically powered and has such standard electric typewriter features as push-button carriage return, automatic repeat keys, and choice of several typefaces. The typeface, though, must be specified when the machine is purchased.

The guide lines for printed communications of the future seem to be very well drawn. At one point in history, man worked from sun to sun; there was no time to think of self improvement or even the operation he was part of. Automation has freed us from humdrum, repetitious, back breaking chores, and man is free to spend more time learning and improving. I have been told that 75 percent of all the scientists who have lived in the history of the world are alive and working today. A new generation is coming along and they are extremly sharp. They are not going to be content with tradition. They are being trained to study problems and meet new objectives; to find better systems and not copy what has been done.

Fig. 30-6. Justified copy after the second typing.

Fig. 30-7. A proportional spacing typewriter. (International Business Machines Corp.)

Double typing and manual insertion of space are necessary to create justified copy (Fig. 30-8). Note the improved readability of the copy because the appropriate space has been allotted to each letter.

INTERCHANGEABLE TYPEFACE COMPOSERS

James B. Hammone, a correspondent during the Civil War, is credited with developing the first typewriter-like machine with interchangeable typefaces. In 1881 he produced the first commerical model shown in Fig. 30-9. Woodrow Wilson was one of the first persons to use this machine and while President of the United States he prepared the historic document entitled *Fourteen Points* on this new invention.

Interchangeable typeface composers manufactured at the present time are very sophisticated in operation. The operator must still type the copy twice with two common machines like the ones shown in Figs. 30-10 and 30-11. However, during the second typing the machine automatically adds the proper space between the words to end the copy exactly on the margin.

Anyone who types can quickly learn to use these machines. Nearly all type styles and sizes up to 12 point are available. Letters of foreign languages, including ancient Greek, and mathematical symbols are available.

The guide lines for printed communications of the future seem to be very well drawn. At one point in history, man worked from sun to sun; there was no time to think of self improvement or even the operation he was part of. Automation has freed us from humdrum, repetitions, back breaking chores, and man is free to spend more time learning and improving. I have been told that 75 percent of all the scientists who have lived in the history of the world are alive and working today. A new generation is coming along and they are not going to be content with tradition. They are being trained to study problems and meet new objectives; to find better systems and not copy what has been done. "Sputnik put a new emphasis on learning. More leisure time is not as important as more knowledge and understanding.

The guide lines for printed communications of the future seem to be very well drawn. At one point in history, man worked from sun to sun; there was no time to think of self improvement or even the operation he was part of. Automation has freed us from humdrum, repetitions, back breaking chores, and man is free to spend more time learning and improving. I have been told that 75 percent of all the scientists who have lived in the history of the world are alive and working today. A new generation is coming along and they are not going to be content with tradition. They are being trained to study problems and meet new objectives; to find better systems and not copy what has been done. "Sputnik" put a new emphasis on learning. More leisure time is not as important as more knowledge and understanding.

Fig. 30-8. Unjustified and justified copy from a proportional-spacing typewriter.

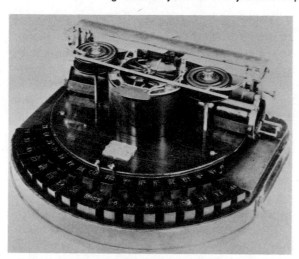

Fig. 30-9. The first impact machine with interchangeable typefaces. (Varityper Corp.)

Fig. 30-10. An interchangeable face, semiautomatic composer. Note the type fonts in the lower right corner. (Varityper Corp.)

There are systems that require only one typing since they set justified copy automatically from coded tape produced as a by-product of the first typing. One typical composing machine consists of two units, a *recorder* and a *reproducer*, both electrically operated (Fig. 30-12). Copy is typed on the recorder, which simultaneously produces an unjustified proofreading copy and a punched paper tape. The reproducer is then used to read the tape and set justified copy at the rate of 100 words a minute. Thirteen typefaces from 8 to 14 point are available.

Another system is the completely automatic line-justification system. It has one or more recorders, a tape reader, a control station console, and a composer (Fig. 30-13).

Fig. 30-11. This semiautomatic composer has the basic typewriter keyboard. Note the ball-like type fonts in the lower left corner. (International Business Machines Corp.)

During typing, all machine functions are recorded on magnetic tape which is then placed in the tape-reading unit. The operator chooses a type font, sets controls on the control panel, and the composer unit sets camera-ready copy at speeds of 14 characters per second.

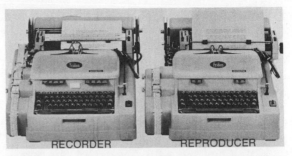

Fig. 30-12. An automatic-impact composer, consisting of two units, that uses punched coded tape. (Friden, Inc.)

Fig. 30-13. An automatic-impact composer that uses a coded magnetic tape. (International Business Machines Corp.)

UNIT 31

DRY-TRANSFER AND HAND-MECHANICAL COMPOSITION

Dry-transfer and hand-mechanical composition methods are not designed for a high rate of production. They are intended for use by specialty job printers and in-plant reproduction departments of manufacturing industries and business establishments.

Dry-transfer type and symbols are pre-printed and attached to a clear plastic or translucent paper carrier. A wax-like adhesive is applied to the back side of the type and symbols. Engineering drawings, maps, charts, newsletter headlines, and advertising brochures are some of the printed materials produced by the dry-transfer method.

Hand-mechanical composition utilizes a device that assists an operator in producing type of many sizes and styles, yet is available at a small cost as compared to impact and photographic composition machines. This composition method is mainly used to produce display material such as headlines and advertisements.

DRY-TRANSFER MATERIALS

Several dry-transfer materials, such as complete alphabets and punctuation marks of many sizes and styles (Fig. 31-1), are available for this method of composition. Symbols (Fig. 31-2), borders (Fig. 31-3), and background textures (Fig. 31-4) are examples of additional materials available.

DRY-TRANSFER COMPOSITION

Quality composition by this method can be achieved with little or no previous expe-

rience. Important considerations are neatness and attention to the following procedural steps.

1. Draw light blue guidelines on the copy sheet. Light blue lines will not photograph, thereby causing no unwanted lines on the film negative (see Sections 6 and 7).
2. Remove the protective backing sheet of an alphabet sheet. It is recommended, though, that the backing sheet be removed only from the area of the selected letters. The adhesive will stay cleaner when protected.
3. Position the selected letters on the guidelines of the copy sheet as shown in Fig. 31-5.

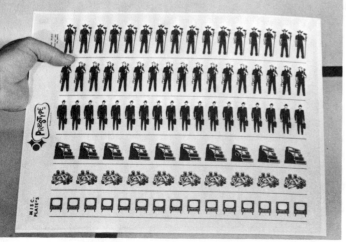

Fig. 31-1. Alphabets, punctuation marks, and numbers.

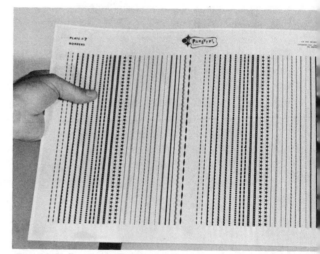

Fig. 31-3. Borders. (Prestype, Inc.)

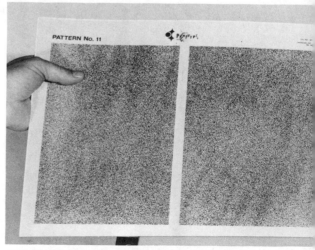

Fig. 31-2. Symbols. (Prestype, Inc.)

Fig. 31-4. Background patterns and textures.

4. Rub the area to be transferred with a blunt instrument (Fig. 31-6). A dowel, ball-point pen, or a pencil, will work as a rubbing instrument. Be careful to rub only the area that you wish transferred.

5. Lift the carrier sheet from the copy sheet (Fig. 31-7). If burnished correctly the entire letter will adhere to the copy sheet.

6. Permanency results from using a protective backing sheet as a shield and burnishing the entire copy area (Fig. 31-8). Additional protection to the image face is obtained by applying a clear spray. This technique can be used when the dry-transfer materials are used directly on a poster.

7. Special effects can be created by using a background pattern. Draw guidelines to outline area to be covered as shown in Fig. 31-9.

8. Lay the background pattern down and burnish only the area to be textured.

9. Cut on guidelines and lift the unwanted pattern from the copy sheet (Fig. 31-10).

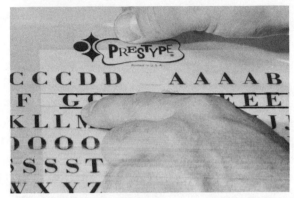

Fig. 31-5. Position the letter on the copy sheet.

Fig. 31-6. Rub the area to be transferred.

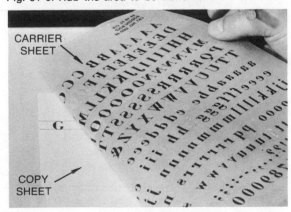

Fig. 31-8. Extra burnishing increases permanency.

Fig. 31-9. Special-effect guidelines.

Fig. 31-10. Completion of background effect.

HAND-MECHANICAL COMPOSITION

The mechanical equipment needed to compose type is (1) the spacing and guiding mechanism, (2) the matrix or mat, (3) the inking pen, and (4) a composing table or drawing board (Fig. 31-11). Almost any size and style of type can be produced with a minimum of practice.

Fig. 31-11. A mechanical composition unit. (Varigraph, Inc.)

UNIT 32
PHOTOGRAPHIC COMPOSITION

Phototypesetting methods use the basic principle of sending a beam of light through a transparent image which is on an opaque background. This projects a positive image on light-sensitive paper or film (Fig. 32-1). By using photographic devices, images can be created with dense opacity (not transparent), with very sharp line edges, and without voids or vacant spaces within the image area.

During the early 1940's the first phototypesetting device was conceived in the cellar of a French home during the Nazi occupation. Since then many developments have taken place to make photographic composition very valuable to the graphic arts industry.

DISPLAY PHOTOTYPESETTERS

Display phototypesetters vary widely in size, speed, design, and flexibility. Most of the machines are manually operated, using a contact principle to produce the image. Two machines of this kind are shown in Figs. 32-2 and 32-3. The second machine uses the projection method of image production. It is capable of producing type from 18 to 144 points.

Some machines have such automatic features as type sizes ranging from 30 to 120 point, special lenses, automatic letter fitting and spacing, precise line-advance control, and even photographic development of the paper or film. A typical direct-keyboard machine in this category is portrayed in Fig. 32-4. A high-speed tape-operated two-unit system is shown in Figs. 32-5 and 32-6.

The machine in Fig. 32-5 produces a punched tape that is used with photocomposition unit shown in Fig. 32-6. The tape from the keyboard unit is placed onto the reader of the photocomposition unit and the machine functions are directed by the tape. Composition units of this kind are mainly used for producing very large quantities of material.

THE DISPLAY PHOTOCOMPOSITION MACHINE

Proper preparation and operation of the display photocomposition machine (Fig. 32-7) is necessary if quality results are expected. Study the parts and their uses before attempting to operate the photocomposition machine.

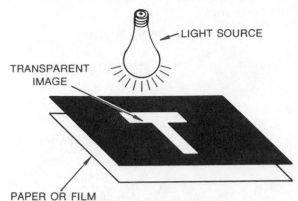
Fig. 32-1. The basic principle of phototypesetting.

Fig. 32-2. A manual display-composing machine that uses the contact method of image production. (Alphatype Filmotype Sales)

Fig. 32-3. A manual display-composing machine that uses the projection method of image production. (Visual Graphics Corp.)

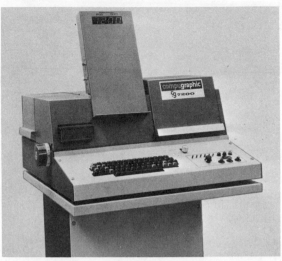
Fig. 32-4. A keyboard operated phototypesetting unit designed for fast, accurate production of top-quality display lines. (Compugraphic Corp.)

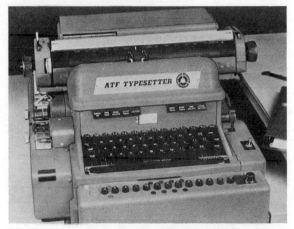
Fig. 32-5. Tape-producing keyboard unit compatable with a tape-driven display composition unit. (American Type Founders)

Fig. 32-6. A tape-driven display composition unit. (American Type Founders)

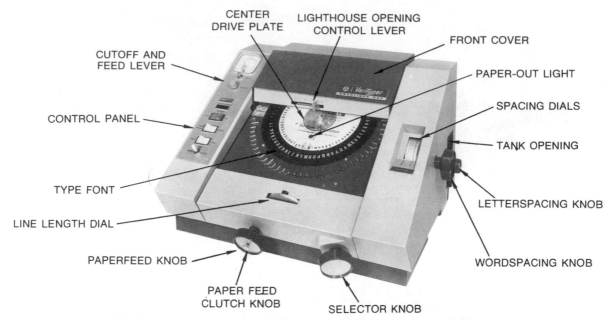

CENTER DRIVE PLATE
LIGHTHOUSE OPENING CONTROL LEVER
FRONT COVER
CUTOFF AND FEED LEVER
PAPER-OUT LIGHT
CONTROL PANEL
SPACING DIALS
TANK OPENING
TYPE FONT
LETTERSPACING KNOB
LINE LENGTH DIAL
PAPERFEED KNOB
WORDSPACING KNOB
PAPER FEED CLUTCH KNOB
SELECTOR KNOB

Fig. 32-7. A display photocomposition machine. (Varityper Typesetting Systems)

PARTS AND USES

Control panel (Fig. 32-8). Exposurminder —a visual representation of the lighthouse lamp current. It enables the operator to set the light intensity at the exact setting for proper character density. Read Button— Used when setting the exposurminder and at any other time to check the voltage supply entering the machine. Adjust Knob—

Fig. 32-8. Control panel. (Varityper Typesetting Systems)

Used to set the exposurminder at the desired exposure light setting. Turning the knob counterclockwise will reduce current flow through the meter, moving the meter needle toward the left side of the scale marked *lighter.* Turning the knob clockwise will increase current flow. Increasing or decreasing current flow will increase or decrease the exposure light's intensity. Indicator lights—The amber developing light goes on a few seconds after the cutoff and feed lever is raised, and indicates that the exposed strip has engaged the tank drive sprocket and is on the way through the developing tank. Switches—The off-on switch will turn the machine on when moved to the appropriate marking. When copy is composed only for the purpose of determining the length of the line on the line-length dial, the print-nonprint switch is moved to the nonprint position to keep the exposure light from operating. At all other times during composition the switch must be set in the print position. The font switch is used to set the machine for full- or half-font operation, depending on the type font being used. All type fonts are marked to indicate at which setting they are to be used. The print-space switch is moved to the left to print and to the right to space between words.

Type Font. (Fig. 32-9) These are made of clear, durable plastic to which is laminated the photographic negative of type. These discs are easily inserted and removed from the machine, and many styles and sizes of type are available.

Cutoff and Feed Lever. After composition has been completed, the cutoff and feed lever is raised to cut the exposed strip and feed it into the developing tank.

Paper Out Light. When the paper out light goes on, it indicates that the end of the roll of paper has been reached. Complete the word being printed and develop the strip, then install a new roll of paper.

Lighthouse Opening Control Lever (Fig. 32-10). This control lever is used to adjust the lighthouse opening to accommodate the size of the characters on the type font being used. This size designation is indicated in all type fonts.

Line Length Dial (Fig. 32-11). It indicates the amount of paper being advanced during printing and registers the cumulative total in inches on the top scale and picas on the bottom scale. The dial can be reset to zero by turning it in either direction. Manual operation of the dial does not feed paper.

Character Selector Knob. It can position the character to be printed within the type-indexing circle.

Paper Feed Knob and Clutch. The knob is used to advance paper manually and can be turned in a clockwise direction pictured in Fig. 32-16. The keyboard console to engage and disengage the paper feed mechanism. During printing, the feed clutch knob must be pushed in so that paper feed can take place.

Wordspacing Dial and Knob (Fig. 32-12). The wordspacing knob is used to set the wordspacing dial for the point size of the type font being used, so that the proper amount of paper will be fed between words.

Letterspacing Dial and Knob (Fig. 32-12). It is used to set the letterspacing dial which determines the amount of space between characters. The normal setting for all type fonts is zero. This setting can be increased or decreased when copyfitting or to obtain special effects.

Fig. 32-9. A photographic film font used in the machine shown in Fig. 32-7. (Varityper Typesetting Systems)

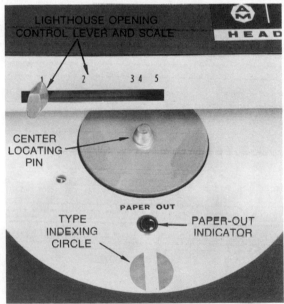

Fig. 32-10. Lighthouse opening and type font controls. (Varityper Typesetting Systems)

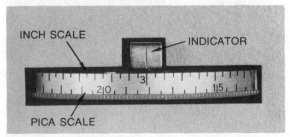

Fig. 32-11. Line length dial. (Varityper Typesetting Systems)

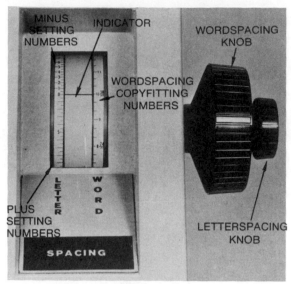

Fig. 32-12. Word and letterspacing controls. (Varityper Typesetting Systems)

Fig. 32-13. A typical tape-producing keyboard machine. (Intertype Co.)

Fig. 32-14. A first-generation phototypesetting machine with a keyboard. (Intertype Co.)

TEXT PHOTOTYPESETTERS

Most text phototypesetters are operated automatically from coded tape. A typical tape-producing keyboard machine is illustrated in Fig. 32-13. Several keyboard units are needed to produce sufficient tape to keep one high-speed phototypesetter operating at full capacity.

Not all text phototypesetting machines require a coded tape for operation. Fig. 32-14 shows a first-generation machine that contains a keyboard unit, which operates in much the same way as the slug-casting machine described in Unit 29. It uses the circulating-matrix principle, but instead of having a character mold on the edge, each matrix has a character on the negative film embedded in its side (Fig. 32-15). Characters are photographed one at a time.

A phototypesetting machine, consisting of a keyboard console and a print-out unit, is pictured in Fig. 32-16. The keyboard console produces a readable proof copy and also a perforated tape to operate the print-out unit automatically. The photographic print-out unit exposes text type at a rate of 20 characters a second, or 22 newspaper lines per minute. An advanced unit (Fig. 32-17) is capable of producing 150 lines per minute. Composition speeds are being increased each year with new models.

Under program control, the machine in Fig. 32-17 is capable of producing 600 characters a second from a computerized tape. A cathode ray tube (CRT) is used in its electronic character-generating system (Fig. 32-18). With this machine it is possible to ex-

Fig. 32-15. A matrix (pattern) used by the phototypesetter in Fig. 32-18. (Intertype Co.)

Fig. 32-16. A phototypesetter consisting of a keyboard console and a print-out unit. (Intertype Co.)

Fig. 32-17. A CRT phototypesetter capable of producing 600 characters a second.

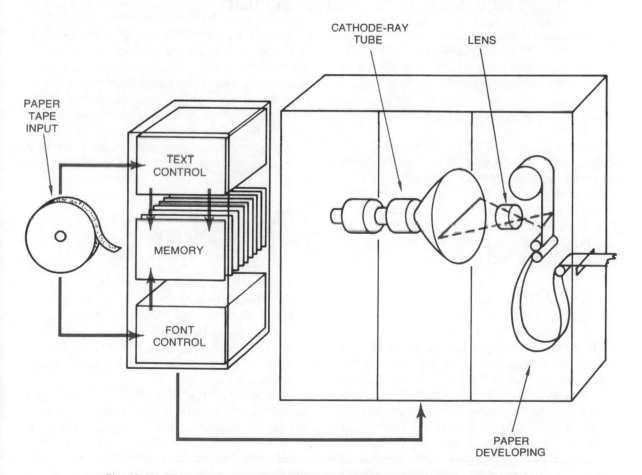

Fig. 32-18. The operating principle of the CRT phototypesetter shown in Fig. 32-21.
(Radio Corporation of America)

pand, enlarge, compress, or oblique characters; change fonts within a line; add foreign accent marks; and vary line lengths. Characters are produced on film or paper as shown in Fig. 32-19.

Third-generation CRT composing units are capable of producing up to 10,000 characters per second. A typical system exposes an entire page of type at one time. Characters are flicked across the face of a cathode ray tube, positioned where they will appear on the page, then recorded on film.

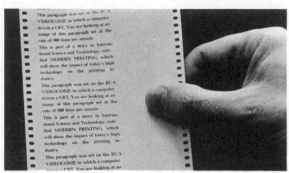

Fig. 32-19. A justified column of copy from a high-speed CRT phototypesetter.

UNIT 33
COMPUTER-AIDED COMPOSITION

Computer-aided composition has generated much interest in the graphic arts industry throughout the world. The computer has a tremendous capacity for information storage and retrieval. This fact has brought about a changing world of graphic arts performance.

There is a great need to record all worthwhile information and make it available wherever and whenever it can be helpful. *Time* is the key word in industry and time is especially vital within the graphic arts. The computer has entered the area of composition for the expressed purpose of reducing the time factor.

THE COMPUTER IN GRAPHIC ARTS

The idea of the digital computer was conceived as early as 1835, but the concept was 100 years ahead of its time. People would not accept such a revolutionary device and it was not built. However, in 1944 Howard Aiken, a professor at Harvard University, finally built a machine of the kind envisioned in 1835. Since then many have been built. Each new computer has improved electronic components of smaller size.

In 1962 the graphic arts industry capitalized upon the ability of the computer to store instructions. The computer was successfully used in speeding up the typesetting function. In the decade before 1962 much use had been made of computers in accounting and record keeping. In recent years computers have established their vital role within the composition function of the graphic arts.

COMPUTERS AND SERVICEABILITY

Computers *accept* information or data in the form of coded mathematical equivalents; they *process* it in accordance with predetermined instructions in the form of coded mathematical equivalents; and then *output* the information on tape. The output is also in the form of coded mathematical equivalents.

Instructions for the machine can be stored on magnetic tape, disks, magnetic drums, or magnetic cords. Typesetting consists of sorting, updating, correcting, and otherwise changing materials. The computer is ideal for this work when it is run by competent operators.

The digital computer is the kind used in composition and is designed for special-purpose and general-purpose utilization. The general-purpose computer (Fig. 33-1) is the more expensive one, but it can accomplish many kinds of work. It is used not only for composition purposes but also for scheduling, accounting, and preparing payrolls. Special-purpose computers, designed only for composition, are more economical in cost, but have limited use.

Two of the primary purposes of the computer are to justify lines of type (make each line the same length), and to hyphenate

Fig. 33-1. A general purpose computer. (International Business Machines Corp.)

words when necessary. Much difficulty has been encountered in programming the computer to hyphenate English words correctly. There are two systems of computerized hyphenation that are presently used. The first method is to store in the computer thousands of words that have been correctly hyphenated according to a dictionary. The second method is to store the basic rules of hyphenation in the computer and allow the computer to select the correct hyphenation, based upon the appropriate rule. Neither method is foolproof, but it appears that the second method is being more widely used. A computer does not think; it merely examines one thing at a time in accordance with instructions placed into it by the builders and operators.

THE COMPUTER AND PREPARING COMPOSITION

Figure 33-2 illustrates the position of the computer in preparing hot or cold composition. Note that it plays only one part in the complete procedure for composing type automatically.

1. An author writes and edits the copy.
2. The copy is typed and perforated tape is prepared using a keyboard unit as shown in Fig. 33-3.

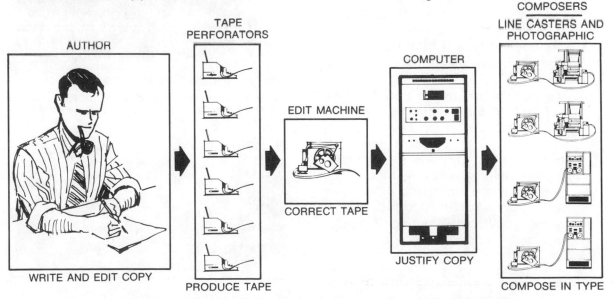

Fig. 33-2. The position of the computer in the computer-aided composition procedure.

Fig. 33-3. A computer input-mixer keyboard. (Automix Keyboards, Inc.)

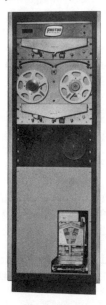

Fig. 33-4. A high-speed tape-correcting machine. (Photon, Inc.)

Fig. 33-5. A special-purpose computer used for both hot and cold composing machines. (Mergenthaler Linotype Co.)

Fig. 33-6. A special-purpose computer designed for use with hot-composition casters only. (International Business Machines Corp.)

Fig. 33-7. A photographic composing unit that accepts computer-prepared tape. (Photon, Inc.)

3. The author proofs the copy and designates all needed corrections.
4. The original type is then corrected by using a high-speed tape-correcting machine (Fig. 33-4).
5. The tape is fed into a computer (Figs. 33-5 and 33-6). It reads the tape and determines how many words can be contained in a predetermined line length. If words need to be hyphenated, the computer will select the proper place for the word division. The computer also prepares a new tape with all of the additional information needed for proper justification of lines.
6. The tape from the computer is then fed into a composing unit. This unit can be either the photographic kind (Fig. 33-7), or the line casting variety

(Fig. 33-8). From this point, the photographic copy and the slugs of type are handled in the conventional manner.

Fig. 33-8. A line-casting composing unit that accepts computer-prepared tape. (Intertype Co.)

MAKING FULL USE OF THE COMPUTER

The purpose of a computer is to save time. It measures time in milliseconds (thousands), microseconds (millions), and in nanoseconds (billions). A nanosecond is to a second as a second is to thirty years.

In order to save time, steps on either side of the computer step of composition preparation must be organized and controlled precisely. Modern practice has a large computer located in a central geographical area. Newspapers and commercial graphic arts establishments within that area make use of the one computer with great efficiency. Each establishment will have all components necessary to develop tape and to accept tape from the computer. By having one central computer, the cost factor of composition is greatly reduced.

UNIT 34
LEARNING EXPERIENCES: COMPOSITION METHODS

DISCUSSION TOPICS

1. Define the term composition as used in the graphic arts. Identify the central purpose of composition.
2. Name the two general classifications or methods of composition. Why have these two methods been identified by these names?
3. Who has been given credit for first developing a practical method for composing individual metal characters into words? How were pages of type produced prior to this invention? What im-

pact do you think this composition method had upon the civilized peoples of the world?
4. When did mechanical composition finally come about? Who was given credit for the development of the first practical mechanical composition machine? What was the name given to this machine? Cite the major differences between today's modern composition machines of the same type and the first one to be developed.
5. During what years was foundry type in major use? To what extent is this meth-

od of composition still in use in commercial establishments today? Why is this method of composition taught in schools offering graphic arts courses?

6. Identify the basic purpose of the California job case. Explain the general lay of the case. List the seven wordspacing materials found in the California job case.

7. Identify the basic unit of word spacing. Describe the shape and the size variations of this unit of spacing. Compare the other six word-spacing materials found in the California job case to the basic unit of word spacing. Name the two hair spaces. Give their specific uses.

8. How are lines of type spaced in foundry type composition? Name the two line-spacing materials and give the thicknesses of each.

9. What is the use of the composing stick? Describe a composing stick and name the various parts. How should the composing stick be held? Identify the purpose of the galley.

10. Explain the procedure for composing a line of foundry type. Define justification. Why is it important to have a properly justified line?

11. Describe the procedure for dumping, typing, and distributing foundry type. Why is it important to handle the line of type with care while completing these three operations? Specifically, why is it very important to properly distribute the individual characters of type into their proper locations in the California job case?

12. Identify the two methods of hot-metal composition. Explain the mechanical operation principle of each of these two systems. Name the machine used to produce leads and slugs. Upon what principle does this machine produce line-spacing materials?

13. List the four methods of cold composition. Which of these four methods are used extensively in commercial graphic arts concerns? What use is made of the other two cold-composition methods?

14. How can the regular typewriter be considered a composition machine? Under what specific category of composition can it be included? Mention the primary advantage of the proportional-spacing typewriter.

15. Compare the value of the standard impact-composing machine with the standard typewriter. List the advantages and disadvantages of this style of composing machine. Name the additional system that has been added to impact composing machines that make them extremely fast and accurate. How has the use of magnetic tape been incorporated into the functions of impact composing machines?

16. Describe the procedure for using dry-transfer type and symbols. List the major uses of this method of composition. Name the various categories of dry-transfer materials. Outline the procedure for using dry-transfer materials.

17. Define hand-mechanical composition. What use is made of this method and what tools or devices are needed to prepare mechanical composition? Outline the method of using a mechanical composing machine.

18. Give the basic principle of the photo-typesetting method. List the advantages of this method over other composing methods. When was the first phototype-setting device developed?

19. Name the two categories of photocomposition machines. What place does each of the two photocomposition-style machines have in the area of composition? Can program control be used for both methods?

20. What is the underlying purpose of using the computer in the area of composition? In what year was the idea for a computer first conceived? Why did the computer receive little attention until World War II? In what year was the computer first used in the graphic arts industry?

21. List the functions completed by the computer in the area of composition. Why can the computer be used for such

operations? In what position (location) in the process of composing type is the computer used? Does this electronic device replace or supplement skilled people? What advantage is there to a computer being located in a central geographic area?

ACTIVITIES

1. Gather several printed materials and closely inspect each of them. Attempt to determine which method of composition was used to compose the type for each printed item. Compare the quality and readability of each method and discuss the cost of producing type by each method.
2. Compose several lines of foundry type from any given copy. Use various sizes of type and carefully justify each line. Have your work critiqued and then carefully distribute the type back into the type cases.
3. Visit several commercial graphic arts plants and study their composing department. Carefully record the kinds of composing machines that each com-

pany has and categorize these machines according to the information presented in this section. Also study the operating principle of each machine so that you may have a better understanding of how the several machines work. Choose one machine and write a complete description of its operation.

4. Using a typewriter, compose several paragraphs flush left and flush right. Type or compose several lines to give you sufficient practice in extending or reducing the length of lines as needed. If a proportional-spacing typewriter is available, compose the same material used for the regular typewriter and then compare the aesthetic qualities of the copy resulting from each method. Repeat this process if an interchangeable typeface composer is also available.
5. Compose some headlines by the dry-transfer, mechanical, and photographic composition methods. Compose the same headlines with each method and compare the results and quality of each method. Which of these methods has the greatest potential? Identify the advantages and disadvantages of each method.

Making proofs and proof-
reading are necessary
in graphic arts.

UNIT 35

INTRODUCTION TO PROOFING AND PROOFREADING

Proofing and proofreading are two important steps In preparing composition. Before composition can be used to reproduce multiple copies of graphic images, it must be proofed and *proofread* with utmost care. Nothing is more annoying to a publisher and a reader than to discover several misspelled words in a newspaper, magazine, or book.

Proofing requires the skill of a proofpress operator, as the quality of a proof depends on his ability and careful attention to detail. Basically, there are two kinds of proofs: (1) the reading proof, and (2) the reproduction proof. The reading proof is made from hot or cold composition and it is used in checking for errors. A reproduction proof is processed after all corrections have been made in the composition. It is used to reproduce multiple copies.

Proofreading is an ancient profession developed long before the advent of movable metal type. Ancient scribes used proofreaders to detect errors in their copy. After books were produced by movable-metal type, proofreading became even more important. In some of the early printed books, though, there is very little evidence that proofreading was done. The first edition of Shakespeare contained no fewer than 20,-000 misspelled words.

Proofreading is actually the closest link between the composing room and the customer. Educated and skilled proofreaders are needed to insure final correctness of the printed product. Large graphic arts companies employ several proofreaders to correct and improve daily newspapers, monthly magazines, or school textbooks (Fig. 35-1).

The proofreading function has changed very little over the years. Highly mechanized and automated pieces of machinery have not been able to replace the proofreader—the human element. Composition proofs still must be read and compared to the original manuscript, and no machine at this time is capable of this kind of work.

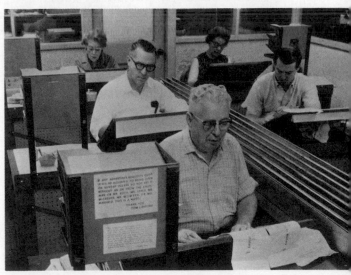

Fig. 35-1. Proofreaders at work in a large daily newspaper plant. (St. Paul Dispatch and Pioneer Press)

UNIT 36
PROOF PRESSES

There are several types of proof presses, each having specific uses and capabilities. Some are hand operated; others are power operated. Some closely resemble and simulate actual printing press conditions.

LETTERPRESS PROOF PRESSES

Proof presses which reproduce copy from a relief image are the most common kind. These basic machines are used in most commercial establishments.

Hand-operated proof presses are small and inexpensive. They are designed to make reading proofs, as shown in Fig. 36-1. Their use is limited because they cannot be adjusted.

A standard proof press with adjustable packing on the impression cylinder is shown in Fig. 36-2. This press has the advantage of having grippers or finger-like devices which hold the paper securely to the impression cylinder while the proof is being taken.

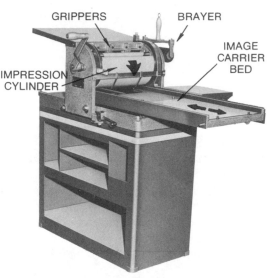

Fig. 36-2. A standard proof press with adjustable packing. (The Challenge Machinery Co.)

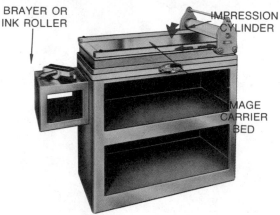

Fig. 36-1. A small, inexpensive proof press. (The Challenge Machinery Co.)

Fig. 36-3. Power ink distribution and automatic washup are features of this hand-operated proof press. (Vandercook & Sons, Inc.)

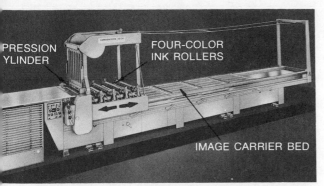

Fig. 36-4. A power-operated proof press for four-color proofing. (Vandercook & Sons, Inc.)

Power-operated proof presses like the one shown in Fig. 36-3 contain power-operated ink rollers which ink the type prior to taking the proof. Grippers on the cylinder hold the paper securely while the cylinder is rolled over the type by turning the hand crank. These presses are considered to be reproduction proof presses because they reproduce proofs of very high quality for photographic purposes.

Another kind of proof press is one designed to proof image carriers or plates prior to placing them on a press for high-speed reproduction. A four-color proof press (Fig. 36-4) is capable of pulling proofs for four-color reproduction. The operator places four image carriers on the press, one for each color. In one pass of the press a sheet of paper receives ink from each image carrier to make proofs of the four-color reproduction. Usually the first image carrier contains the yellow copy; the second, red; the third, blue; and the fourth, black. The purpose of taking four-color proofs is to inspect the quality of the image carriers and to make necessary corrections.

LITHOGRAPHIC PROOF PRESSES

Lithographic (offset-lithography) proof presses are designed to simulate the production press sequence of dampening, inking, and printing (Fig. 36-5). The lithographic principle that ink and water do not mix is the basis for this procedure.

The image carrier is attached to the proof press and the dampened rollers are rolled

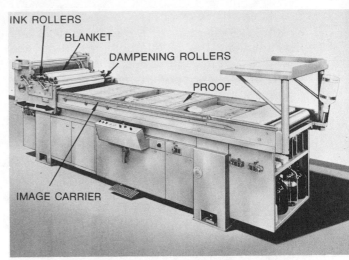

Fig. 36-5. A flat-bed, one-color offset-lithography proof press. (Vandercook & Sons, Inc.)

Fig. 36-6. A rotary, four-color, offset-lithography, proof press. (Vandercook & Sons, Inc.)

over the carrier to place water on the non-image areas. The ink rollers then are rolled over the image carrier to ink the image areas. The rubber blanket cylinder immediately follows the ink rollers. It picks up the ink from the image carrier and deposits it onto the paper in the next revolution. After the proof is taken, the operator inspects it and determines whether the image carrier needs correction.

A rotary four-color offset-lithography proof press is shown in Fig. 36-6. This one simulates actual production press sequence and operating conditions. Each of the four image carriers contains the image area for one of the four colors used in four-color reproductions. These are the same as in letterpress reproduction: yellow, red, blue, and black. If corrections are needed on the image carriers they can be made before the image carriers are placed on a high-speed production press.

GRAVURE PROOF PRESSES

Gravure proof presses are designed to produce an image that has been etched into the surface of the image carrier. The proof press shown in Fig. 36-7 pulls a proof of a flat gravure image carrier.

Most reproductions made by the gravure reproduction process are produced from cylinders. Before a cylinder is placed onto a high-speed production press, a proof is taken to insure the correctness and quality of the gravure cylinder. A proof press designed for a gravure cylinder (Fig. 36-8) must simulate actual production presses.

The cylinder turns in a vat or pan of ink and the doctor blade removes the ink from the nonimage area. As the paper travels between the impression cylinder and the gravure image carrier cylinder, the ink is transferred from the tiny wells of the cylinder to the paper. As in letterpress and lithographic processes, the proofs are inspected. If corrections are needed, cylinder inaccuracies can be corrected before being placed on a reproduction press.

GRIPPERS

IMPRESSION CYLINDER

DOCTOR BLADE

IMAGE CARRIER BED

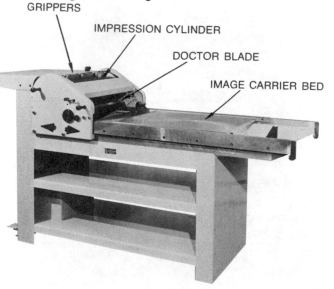

IMAGE CARRIER
CYLINDER   INK PAN   IMPRESSION   DOCTOR
                                   CYLINDER   BLADE

Fig. 36-7. A proof press designed to proof flat gravure image carriers. (C and G Machine Co.)

Fig. 36-8. A gravure-cylinder proof press. (The John C. Motter Printing Press Co.)

UNIT 37
TAKING THE PROOF

Proper proof press operation is an important aspect in obtaining usable proofs for reading or for reproduction. Image carriers or prepared plates are often proofed before being placed on a press. This is done to insure a properly made plate.

READING PROOFS

Reading proofs are used for proofreading the copy and to identify errors in spelling and grammar. Proper spacing of lines, paragraphs, and full pages can also be determined. The following procedure illustrates the techniques utilized in proofing a typeform.

1. Position the typeform on the proof press bed (Fig. 37-1). Be sure the typeform is tied securely and slid into the corner of a galley.
2. Distribute proofing ink on the ink plate of the proof press with an ink brayer as shown In Fig. 37-2.

3. Ink the typeform (Fig. 37-3). Roll the brayer over the form two or three times, but do not ink the form excessively. Too much ink makes a poor proof.

Fig. 37-2. Distributing ink on the ink plate.

Fig. 37-1. The proper position of the typeform.

Fig. 37-3. Inking the typeform with the brayer.

4. Lay proofing paper carefully on the typeform (Fig. 37-4).
5. Roll the cylinder gently over the paper and the typeform (Fig. 37-5). Pressure causes the ink to transfer from the typeform to the paper.
6. Strip (remove) the paper from the typeform.
7. Remove the galley and typeform from the proof press.
8. Wash the face of the type (Fig. 37-6).
9. Proofread the proof. Follow the procedures as outlined in Unit 38. If corrections are needed, make the typeform changes by following instructions in Unit 39.

Fig. 37-6. Washing the typeform.

REPRODUCTION PROOFS

Reproduction proofs are made from a typeform for the purpose of photographic reproduction. They are taken after the reading proofs have been made, proofread, and corrected. These proofs must be of very high quality; a skilled operator is therefore essential to obtain quality results. Besides the operator, seven other equally important elements should be stressed. These elements are essential if high quality reproduction proofs are to be made.

1. A precision proof press that is well designed and equipped.
2. A typeform that is as accurate and flawless as a skilled compositor can make it.
3. High-quality paper made especially for reproduction proofs.
4. High-quality ink.
5. Clean and accurate ink rollers.
6. Proper cylinder packing and tympan.
7. Proper solvent to remove ink from the typeform and rollers.

Reproduction proofs are made in a similar manner to that for producing reading proofs, but there are some exceptions. Follow this step-by-step procedure to obtain high-quality proofs.

1. Lock up the typeform in the chase, as shown in Unit 77.

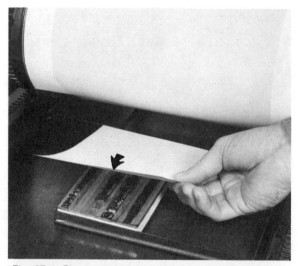

Fig. 37-4. Placing the proofing paper on the typeform.

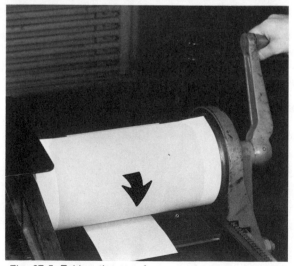

Fig. 37-5. Taking the proof.

Fig. 37-7. Securing the typeform with the lock-up bar.

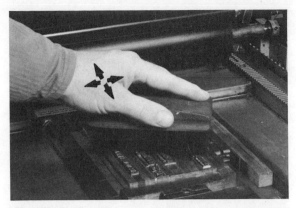

Fig. 37-8. Carefully brushing the typeform to remove dirt particles.

2. Position the locked-up typeform in the bed of the proof press. Secure it with the lock-up bar as shown in Fig. 37-7.

3. Clean the type with a rapid-drying type wash. Thoroughly brush the typeform with a standard type-brush to remove any particles of lint or fuzz (Fig. 37-8).

Fig. 37-9. Attaching a sheet of reproduction paper under the grippers.

4. Ink the form. If a hand brayer is used, exercise great care to apply the correct amount of ink. High-quality reproduction proof presses will contain an automatic inking system, thereby eliminating inking the typeform prior to attaching the proofing paper.

5. Attach a sheet of reproduction paper under the cylinder grippers (Fig. 37-9).

6. Roll the cylinder carefully over the typeform.

7. Remove the paper from the grippers (Fig. 37-10).

8. Inspect the proof thoroughly with a magnifying glass. If defects in the image are seen, correct the problem and pull another proof.

9. Make sure that the proof is of high quality. Allow it to dry thoroughly before additional handling.

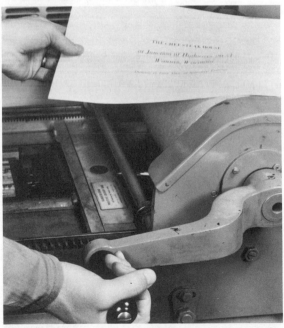

Fig. 37-10. Removing the reproduction proof from the proof press.

IMAGE CARRIER PROOFS

Image carrier proofs are made for reading purposes, but they must also be of highest quality. Letterpress image carriers or plates are proofed in a manner similar to that of proofing the reading proofs described earlier in this unit. Offset-lithography plates and gravure cylinders are attached to proof presses and proofs are made to assure the quality of the printing plate.

Image carriers for multiple-color reproductions must be checked very carefully to see that the colors balance when the printing operation takes place. If flaws are discovered in one or more of the plates, corrections can be made before the plates are put into production. This saves much press time and assures a higher quality of printed product.

UNIT 38
PROOFREADING PROCEDURES

Proofreading, if possible, should be done by two people: a *copyholder* and a *proofreader.* The copyholder does just what the name implies; he holds the copy and reads aloud to the proofreader. The proofreader watches closely the reading proof and marks necessary corrections.

The objective of the proofreader is to discover errors and mark them for correction. He does not read the proof for pleasure or for specific information. He must see every letter, number, and punctuation mark on the proof. He must also note the word, line, and paragraph spacings.

The function of the copyholder is to read carefully the original manuscript to the proofreader. He must learn to read distinctly and without error, and at a speed at which the proofreader can accomplish his task. Accuracy is a must; speed is only an added asset.

There are many commercial firms that do not use a copyholder. In these instances, the proofreader carefully checks the manuscript copy against the proof. This is somewhat more time consuming but may offset the cost of using two persons.

QUALIFICATIONS OF PROOFREADERS AND COPYHOLDERS

Through education and extensive training, the proofreader must be able to read, hear and spell well; his reactions must be quick, and he must have concentration and a good knowledge of grammar.

The copyholder should also have a good education in order to be able to read accurately, distinctly, and rapidly; he should also have patience and be willing to follow directions.

PROOFREADER'S MARKS

Proofreader's marks are the shorthand used by the person reading proofs (Fig. 38-1). Their use shortens the necessary explanations of errors in the composition. All marks made by the proofreader must be legible so that the compositor can make the necessary corrections in the composition. Learning and using the standard marks will improve efficiency in proofreading.

PROOFREADING MARKS

Meaning	Mark	Example
Dele, or delete, take out	ℐ	We are crafts¢men printers.
Insert space	#	We arecraftsmen printers.
Turn over	9	We a̲re craftsmen printers.
Close up, no space	⌒	We are craftsmen print⌒ers.
Insert apostrophe where indicated	∜	We are printers‸craftsmen.
Character of wrong size or style, wrong font	wf	We are crafts**m**en printers.
Put in lower case	lc	We are craftsmen <u>PRINTERS.</u>
Reset in bold face	bf	We are <u>craftsmen</u> printers.
Put in italic type	ital	We are <u>are</u> craftsmen printers.
Let it stand; ignore marks above dots	stet	We are craftsmen ~~printers.~~
Defective letter	✗	We are c̲raftsmen printers.
Make paragraph	¶	printers. [We are craftsmen
No paragraph	no ¶	printers.⌒ We are craftsmen printers.
Insert period	⊙	We are craftsmen printers‸
Carry to the left	L L	We are craftsmen printers.
Carry to the right	⌐	We⌐are craftsmen printers.
Lower to place indicated	⊔	⌊We are craftsmen printers.⌋
Raise to place indicated	⊓	⌈We are craftsmen printers.⌉
Transpose	tr	We are craftsmen printesr
Insert hyphen	/=/	We are craftsmen‸printers.
Put in small capitals	sc	We are <u>craftsmen printers.</u>
Insert comma	‸	Yes‸ we are craftsmen printers.
Query to author	are?	We‸craftsmen printers.
Spell out words marked with a circle	spellout	We are 2nd to none.
Push down space	⊥	We⊥are craftsmen printers.
Space more evenly	eq #	We‸are‸craftsmen printers.
Indent 1 em	▢	We‸are craftsmen printers.
Indent 2 ems	▭	We are craftsmen printers
1-em dash	/em/	We are craftsmen printers‸
2-em dash	/em/	We are craftsmen printers.
En dash	/n/	We are craftsmen printers.
Straighten alignment	=	we are craftsmen printers.
Enclose in quotation marks	⌣" "	‸We are craftsmen printers.‸
Put in roman type	rom	We *are* craftsmen printers.
Words are omitted from, or in, copy	out see copy	We‸printers.
Put in capitals as indicated	caps	We are craftsmen <u>printers.</u>

Fig. 38-1.

UNIT 39
CORRECTING COMPOSITION

Correcting composition is time consuming and costly. The composition must be made free of errors after the proofs are read by the proofreader and copyholder. This takes up a large amount of the time required for the original manuscript to reach the press. There are special correcting techniques for each of the six composition methods discussed in Section 4. They are used to shorten the time needed to correct the composition.

FOUNDRY TYPE COMPOSITION

Individaul characters: If letters are the same set width, change character for character. If letters are a different set width, place the entire line in the composing stick. Spacing material must be removed, the character changed (Fig. 39-1), and the line rejustified. *Complete words:* Follow the same procedure used to correct individual characters. *Complete lines:* Compose the correct line the exact length as the incorrect one. Exchange the correct line for the incorrect one in the typeform (Fig. 39-2). *Complete paragraphs:* Follow the same procedure used to correct complete lines. *Space:* To change word spacing, place the line in the composing stick. Remove a quad from the end of the line. Make the spacing change, and then rejustify the line. To change line spacing, insert or remove leads and slugs as necessary while the form is in the galley.

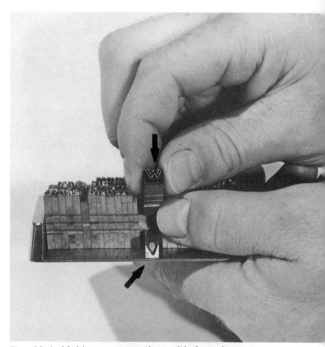

Fig. 39-1. Making a correction with foundry type.

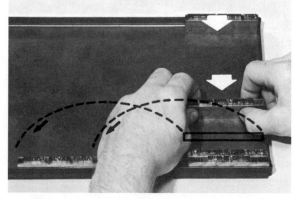

Fig. 39-2. Exchanging a corrected line of type for an incorrect one in a typeform.

HOT-METAL COMPOSITION

Individual characters: To change one character, a complete new line is made on a slug-casting machine. In composition produced from a single-character casting machine, a correction is made in a manner similar to that for correcting foundry type composition. *Complete words:* Follow the same procedure as for correcting individual characters. *Complete lines:* With slugs, cast a correct slug and exchange it for the incorrect one (Fig. 39-3). With single characters, a new coded paper tape is produced. The line is cast, and the incorrect line is replaced with the correct one. *Complete paragraphs:* with slugs of type, the necessary lines are cast and exchanged for the incorrect paragraph (Fig. 39-4). *Space:* To change word spacing, cast a new line to replace the incorrect one. To change line spacing, insert or remove leads and slugs as necessary while the form is in a galley.

Fig. 39-3. Exchanging a corrected slug of type for an incorrect one.

Fig. 39-4. Exchanging a complete paragraph.

IMPACT COMPOSITION

Individual characters: These generally are not corrected separately. *Complete words:*

1. Compose the corrected word on a sheet of paper.
2. Tape the sheet to a light table (a glass-topped box with a light underneath).
3. Lay the original composition, in register, over the corrected word. Tape it to the glass.
4. Using an artist's knife, cut a rectangular box around the incorrect word (Fig. 39-5). Be sure to cut through both sheets of paper.
5. Remove the original composition sheet from the light table. Turn the sheet over.
6. Fit the corrected word into position. Attach it with transparent tape as shown in Fig. 39-6.

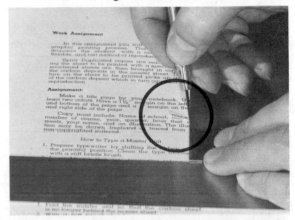

Fig. 39-5. Cutting a rectangular box around an incorrect word.

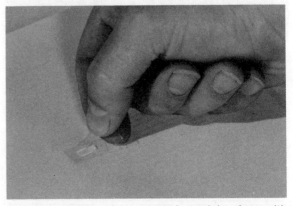

Fig. 39-6. Holding the corrected word in place with transparent tape.

Complete lines: Follow the same procedure as for correcting complete words. *Complete paragraphs:* Follow the same procedure as for correcting complete words. A second method is to paste the correction over the error by trimming the corrected paragraph closely. Apply adhesive, then lay in proper register over the original position. Do not use an excessive amount of adhesive. *Space:* Generally, the copy must be composed again because it is difficult to change the amount of space between lines. To alter space between paragraphs, cut them apart. Fasten them to another sheet of paper, leaving the desired space.

DRY-TRANSFER AND HAND-MECHANICAL COMPOSITION

Dry-transfer letters are removed with a soft rubber eraser (Fig. 39-7). Once removed the letter cannot be reused; a new letter must therefore be selected.

Hand-mechanically produced letters can be removed using standard erasure techniques; however, the surface of the paper is damaged. Because of the roughened surface it is difficult to ink in the same area

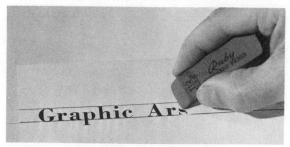

Fig. 39-7. Removing a dry-transfer letter with a rubber eraser.

again. Therefore, if an error has been made it is recommended that the entire word or line be composed again.

PHOTOGRAPHIC COMPOSITION

Composition produced with display phototypesetters is not often corrected in the conventional manner. Time can be saved if the entire display word or line is re-composed.

Composition produced with text phototypesetters on paper is corrected in the same manner as impact composition. Composition produced on film is also corrected with a similar method to that used for correcting composition produced on paper.

UNIT 40
LEARNING EXPERIENCES: PROOFING AND PROOFREADING
DISCUSSION TOPICS

1. Why are proofing and proofreading two very important aspects in preparing composition? Name the two kinds of proofs. Describe the purpose of each proof.

2. Cite the earliest usage of proofreading. Was and is proofreading always carefully done?

3. List the several types of letterpress proof presses. Which of these proof presses can be used for producing reading proofs and which ones are capable of producing reproduction proofs? Describe the operation of a four-color letterpress proof press. Discuss the differences between proof and repro presses.

4. Explain the principle of a lithographic proofpress. How is the image transferred from the image carrier to the paper? Identify the purpose of the lithographic image carrier. How does the gravure proofpress differ from the lithographic proofpress?

5. Briefly explain the procedure for *pulling* a reading proof. Identify the tool used to place a coating of ink upon the type-form prior to pulling the proof. How many times should the cylinder of the proofpress be rolled over the paper when pulling the proof?

6. Enumerate the seven important elements, besides a skilled operator, that are needed when pulling reproduction proofs. Cite the differences between pulling a reproduction proof and pulling a reading proof.

7. Is there a need for two people to proofread? List the qualifications of the proofreader and the copyholder.

8. Cite the primary purpose of proofreader's marks. Where are proofreader's marks placed? List the marginal marks for each of the following: missing period, missing parentheses, delete, indent, transpose letters, close-up space, wrong font, and query to author.

9. How are corrections made in foundry-type composition when the new type character has the same set width as the incorrect type character? When the new type character has a different set width than the incorrect type character? What procedure is used to make changes in the line spacing?

10. Compare the procedures necessary to make corrections in hot-metal and impact composition according to the following categories: individual characters, complete words, complete lines, complete paragraphs, and space.

11. Explain the basic methods used to correct dry-transfer and hand-mechanical composition, photographic composition, and computer-aided composition. Why is it wise to have an error-free tape to feed into a computer? How is the error-free tape obtained?

ACTIVITIES

1. Obtain the current issue of your daily newspaper and read each article on the front page. Indicate the composition errors according to the proofreader's marks listed in Unit 38. Tabulate the errors on a separate sheet of paper under the headings *punctuation, delete, insert, paragraphing, position, spacing, style of type,* and *miscellaneous.* Repeat this for an entire week and then carefully compare the total number of errors found during the week. On which days were there more errors and less errors? Repeat this procedure with another newspaper or one of your favorite journals. One week later. Compare the two tabulations and report on your analysis.

2. Obtain a galley of foundry type composition or hot-type machine-set composition. Prepare a reading proof and a reproduction proof of the type. Compare the results of the two different proofs. Select a fellow classmate and proofread the reading proof, using the original hand-written or typed copy. Take turns being the proofreader and copyholder. Be sure to use the proper proofreading marks when errors in the composition are discovered. Use any color for marking. Be sure it is different than the color of the copy, and is eraseable.

3. Obtain several different kinds of letterpress image carriers (Section 8). Proof these several image carriers and carefully inspect them for flaws or errors. Note the differences in proofing image carriers and typeforms.

4. Visit a daily newspaper plant. If possible, make arrangements to spend some time with the proofreaders. If it is permitted, sit down and observe them at work. Note how the copyholder and proofreader work together, and also how the proofreaders indicate errors that they have found. Also observe how the proofs reach the proofreader and what happens to the proofs once the proofreader has finished with them. Prepare a written report on your visit.

This artist is completing an ink
drawing illustration.

UNIT 41
INTRODUCTION TO COPY PREPARATION

Much of today's visual material is printed from image carriers (Sections 8, 12, 14, and 15) that were prepared with photographic techniques. Before the photography for the image carrier can be prepared, it is necessary to prepare copy. *Copy* is that which accurately represents what is to be printed, with each element in the exact position it will be when printed. The location of the elements is usually determined by the layout as discussed in Section 3. Type matter and illustrations are the two kinds of elements found in copy.

Type Matter. The letters which form the words make up the type matter in a piece of copy. As explained in Section 4, type matter is prepared by several different methods. You should be thoroughly familiar with each method.

Illustrations. Illustrations are the elements of copy other than type matter that produce a visual image, thought, or concept. Some common examples of illustrations are photographs, drawings, sketches, and paintings. Several specific examples of illustrations are shown in Unit 43.

This section deals with the methods of transforming a layout into material to be photographed for printing. This function is performed by an artist. It should be realized that the artist does many other things besides prepare copy. He may also purchase the printing material or even do the printing.

When copy is prepared, the artist must be aware of the suggestions made by the customer or person who prepares the layout and of the methods to be used to produce the printed material. In other words, the artist must consider and be knowledgeable about the desires of the customer and the methods to be used by the printing plant. The artist must know how the printed item will be used, who will use it, what printing process and what color paper and ink will be used to print the material. He must also consider the emotional feeling (quiet, bold, serious, etc.) to be conveyed, and the time schedule for artwork completion. Fig. 41-1 shows a piece of copy with illustrations and type matter in place.

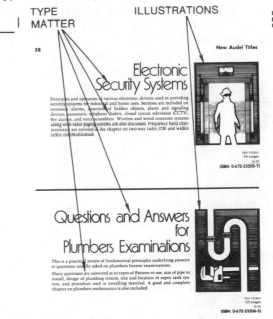

Fig. 41-1. Piece of copy that is ready to be photographed for printing. This piece of copy has both type matter and illustrations.

UNIT 42

EQUIPMENT AND MATERIALS FOR COPY PREPARATION

Equipment and materials used for copy preparation are second in importance only to the skill of the person preparing the copy. Without a thorough knowledge of equipment and materials and how to use them, the artist cannot express his creative ideas.

Copy should be prepared by placing either black or red on a white background. However, this is not always true when preparing copy for multicolor printing. Any method used to place black or red on the white background is satisfactory if it produces the desired results. Black on white is most commonly used.

A list of equipment and materials for copy preparation could be endless. The artist should be seeking new methods to produce copy constantly.

BACKGROUND FOR THE COPY

White paper or board is used most frequently as a background for copy preparation. Not all papers or boards are suitable, however, for all kinds of copy preparation. The artist must give serious consideration to the material he selects. If improper or poor materials are used, the result is unsatisfactory copy.

Color. Additives such as dyes are often blended into paper to make it appear whiter. However, they sometimes make the paper or board undesirable for copy preparation. Only recommended papers or papers which through tests have been proven satisfactory for copy preparation should be used.

Weight. Many different weights of paper and board are used for copy preparation. In general, it is desirable to use the heaviest possible paper because it is easier to handle and is not affected by moisture as are thinner papers. Copy is often prepared on lightweight paper and then later attached to heavier paper.

Surface. The effect desired by the person preparing copy should determine the type of paper surface selected. Different effects can be obtained from papers having unusual textured surfaces. One should be aware of how different drawing mediums, such as inks and pencils, react on various surfaces.

Layout sheets. Layout sheets are preprinted sheets of paper or board that are used to prepare copy. These are available in a variety of sizes and weights. Layout sheets have graduations printed on the borders and are useful for making rapid measurements without using a ruler, T-square, or triangle.

DRAWING EQUIPMENT AND INSTRUMENTS

Drawing instruments are often used for drawing both guide lines and actual copy lines. The artist should have a complete set of drawing instruments to use in copy preparation.

Drawing boards. A good drawing board of sufficient size is essential for copy preparation. Sometimes the surface of a drawing *table* is substituted for the drawing *board.*

T-squares and triangles. When a drawing board is used, a T-square is needed (Fig.

42-1). Care should be taken to protect the drawing edges and alignment of the head and blade of the T-square. Triangles are essential for drawing accurate vertical and diagonal lines when using a T-square (Fig. 42-2). An adjustable triangle is frequently useful (Fig. 42-3). A drawing machine, sometimes used when the artist works on a drawing table, is shown in Fig. 42-4.

Drawing instruments. A set of drawing instruments (Fig. 42-5) is needed to draw arcs and circles as well as straight lines. A set should include compasses, dividers, and ruling pens.

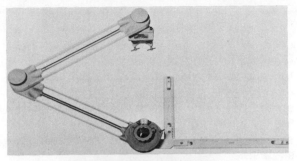

Fig. 42-4. A drawing machine. (Bruning)

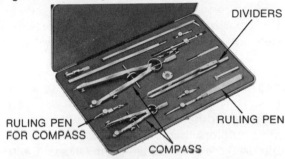

Fig. 42-5. A set of drawing instruments. (Frederic Post Co.)

Fig. 42-1. A typical T-square. (Frederic Post Co.)

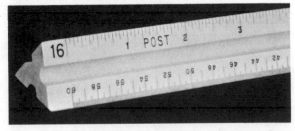

Fig. 42-6. A scale used for measuring. (Frederic Post Co.)

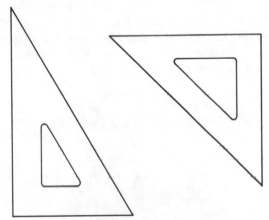

Fig. 42-2. 45° and 30°-60°-90° triangles.

Fig. 42-7. Several different-shaped French curves.

Rules and scales. Accurate rules and scales are necessary for precise drawings. The artist should be able to make measurements as small as $\frac{1}{16}$ inch (Fig. 42-6). Sometimes it is also necessary to measure $\frac{1}{10}$ to $\frac{1}{20}$ inch, or in points or picas.

Drawing curves. Drawing curves are manufactured shapes that assist in rendering irregular curves. The most common are called French curves, shown in Fig. 42-7. An adjustable curve may also be used.

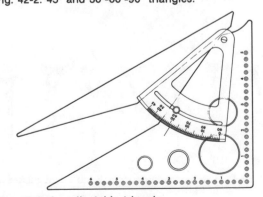

Fig. 42-3. An adjustable triangle.

Pencils. Pencils are used to make guide lines, notes, and sketches. Blue pencils are used to make guide lines and notes. The reason for using blue is that blue is photographed as though it were white, and therefore the guide lines do not have to be erased. Use only light blue pencils, making the lines very light. Almost any kind of black standard grade pencil can be used for sketching.

Inking pens. Inking pens are classified into two groups: those used to draw precise lines, and those used to do freehand inking.

Ruling pens in drawing sets are one type used to draw precise straight or curved lines. They are adjustable to permit drawing different widths of lines. Some ruling pens with predetermined point size are also available for drawing exact-width lines. Each point draws only one width. Fig. 42-8 shows a typical set of ruling pens and the width of line that can be drawn with each point.

Examples of pen points used for freehand lettering are seen in Figs. 42-9 and 42-10. The points are placed in pen holders when making illustrations or doing lettering. Fig. 42-11 shows a penholder to be used with the pen points seen in Figs. 42-9 and 42-10.

Paint brushes. Small paint brushes used by artists are other items in addition to pens. With them an artist fills in large areas or creates special effects. A good-quality black drawing ink should be used.

AIRBRUSH

The airbrush (Fig. 42-12) is a useful tool. It is much like a small conventional spray gun in that it sprays paint or ink. It is used to make illustrations and to touch up or make alterations and eliminate errors in photographs and other types of illustrations.

A variation of the airbrush is the *aireraser.* This instrument removes unwanted areas in copy. Fig. 42-13 shows the use of this aid.

TAPE, WAXING MACHINE, AND RUBBER CEMENT

Double-surface tape, wax, and rubber cement are used to paste up copy. This process attaches elements of copy onto the main copy.

Double-surface tape. Adhesive is on both sides of the core material, which is usually paper, like masking tape, or cellophane. Placing the tape on one side of one of the elements of copy enables it to be attached permanently to support the entire piece of copy (Fig. 42-14).

Waxing machine. Wax is applied to the back of an element of copy by a waxing machine (Fig. 42-15). The wax serves as an adhesive to attach the element to the copy support. One of the significant advantages of wax is that the element can be removed at any time without damaging the copy support or element.

Rubber cement. Rubber cement is another material used to paste up elements of copy to the main copy support. It should be applied to both the element and the copy-support material, then allowed to dry before attaching the two pieces (Fig. 42-16).

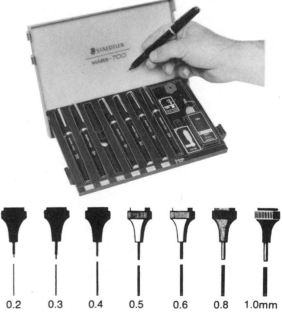

0.2   0.3   0.4   0.5   0.6   0.8   1.0mm

Fig. 42-8. A set of ruling pens. Each point makes a different-width line.

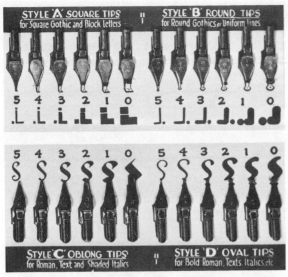

Fig. 42-9. Pen points used for lettering and making freehand sketches. (Hunt Manufacturing Co.)

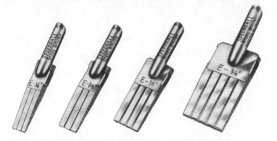

Fig. 42-10. Pen points that are used like brushes. (Hunt Manufacturing Co.)

Fig. 42-11. A pen holder.

Fig. 42-12. An airbrush. (Paasche Airbrush Co.)

Fig. 42-13. An aireraser. (Paasche Airbrush Co.)

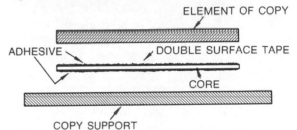

Fig. 42-14. Showing how double-surface tape attaches copy elements to the support.

Fig. 42-15. A wax-coating machine. (The M. P. Goodkin Co.)

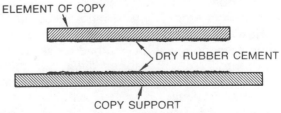

Fig. 42-16. How rubber cement is used to attach elements of copy to the copy support.

OTHER ITEMS FOR COPY PREPARATION

Paints. Both tempera and water-color paints are used frequently for needed effects in copy preparation.

Charcoal or chalk. These are used in sketching. Black is the color most often used to prepare black-and-white copy.

Masking film. Masking film is used for a variety of purposes in both single-color and multicolor copy preparation. Fig. 42-17 shows the structure of masking film. It has a transparent or translucent base with red gelatin or plastic film on one side. The gelatin or plastic film can be removed as necessary. Use of this film is discussed later.

Knives. Knives are used to cut copy to size and shape. They are also used to cut masking film (Fig. 42-18). Scissors may also be used to cut copy to shape and size.

Many additional pieces of equipment and materials are available; those listed above are the necessary and basic ones most frequently used for copy preparation.

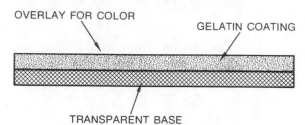

Fig. 42-17. The structure of masking film.

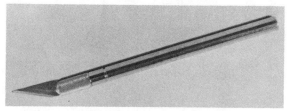

Fig. 42-18. A knife used for copy preparation.

UNIT 43
KINDS OF COPY

Anything that can be visualized or seen can be potentially photographed for printing. Because of this, it is difficult to classify different kinds of copy. The purpose of this unit is to present several kinds of copy so that you will recognize common characteristics and differences.

The most logical classification is *line* and *continuous-tone* copy. These two categories are appropriate because they determine the photographic method to be used. Line copy is photographed differently than is continuous-tone. It is assumed in this unit that the copy will be printed with black ink on white paper, however each kind could be printed with other colors and combinations of ink on several colors of paper.

Illustrations, both line and continuous-tone, should be used when they add clarity or increase interest in a printed item. In many situations, illustrations express ideas or concepts much better than words, and frequently require less space than the printed explanation.

LINE COPY

Line copy has no shades of gray. The image is produced for the copy by contrasting black areas with white ones. The following examples are kinds that are referred to and treated photographically as line copy.

Type matter. Letters and symbols, as used in this book, are considered to be line copy. It is prepared by any of the methods discussed in Section 4.

Inked drawings. Drawings shown in Figs. 43-1 and 43-2 are examples of line copy. It is prepared by merely drawing on white paper with black ink. It is important that the ink be true black not gray. Frequently blue guide lines are drawn. They photograph as though they were white, and therefore do not have to be erased before process photography.

Fig. 43-2. Line drawing made with pen and ink.

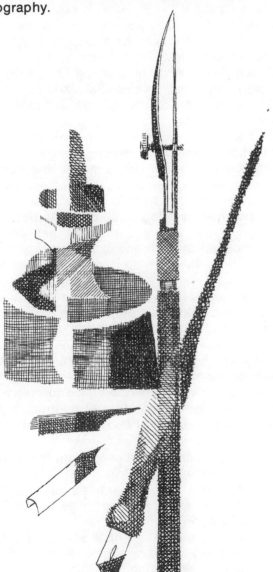

Fig. 43-1. Line drawing made with pen and ink.

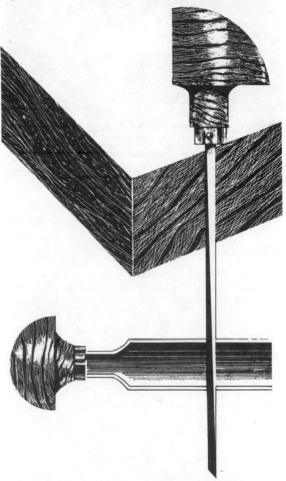

Fig. 43-3. An illustration using the scratch-board technique. (Kimberly-Clark Corp.)

Scratch board. Scratch board (Fig. 43-3) is a piece of drawing board that has been coated with a chalky substance. India ink is applied to a portion, or sometimes the entire surface. The artist scratches lines in the surface having the inked areas and exposes the white surface.

Fig. 43-4. A reproduction of a wood-block cut. (Nekoosa-Edwards Paper Co.)

Fig. 43-5. A silver point drawing. (Nekoosa-Edwards Paper Co.)

Block prints. Fig. 43-4 is an example of a print from a wood cut. The design was cut from a piece of wood so that the image or part of the design to be printed was higher than the remaining part of the block. The block was then printed on a rough-textured piece of paper to achieve the textured effect. Notice also that parts of the wood, other than the image area, were not cut away. This gave more interest, and actually gives the illusion of movement.

Silverpoint drawing. The silverpoint technique illustrated in Fig. 43-5 is not as typical a method for producing line copy as are the others. It is, however, an example of one of the unusual items that confront a printer. Silverpoint is done by drawing lines with a silverpoint pencil on a special kind of paper. The image is actually minute deposits of silver on paper.

Reversal. A reversal has the same characteristics as any other kind of line copy. The difference between conventional line copy and a reversal line copy is that selected areas are reproduced in white, instead of black (when printing black on white paper). In Fig. 43-6 the type material has been reproduced as white instead of black.

Copy for this method can be prepared in reverse. In Fig. 43-7, everything is made black, except the type material. In this situation, the black background of the truck was drawn on illustration board with ink. White letters were then applied over the drawing. If lighter-weight paper were used, the moisture of the ink would have caused it to curl.

A more common method used to prepare reversal copy is the *overlay* method. Fig. 43-8 shows a piece of copy prepared in this manner. Procedure is as follows:

1. Make a drawing of everything that is to be printed (Fig. 43-9).
2. Attach a piece of tracing paper (the overlay sheet) to one edge of the illustration board.
3. Attach the letters (that will appear in reverse) in the proper location on the overlay sheet (Fig. 43-10).
4. Make register marks on both the illustration board and the overlay sheet. The register marks must be aligned.

Fig. 43-6. A print of the art shown in Fig. 43-7.

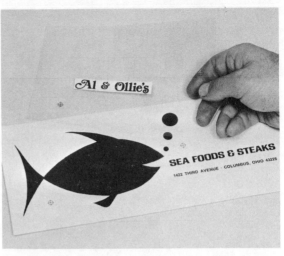

Fig. 43-9. Display type and art for each part of the reversal copy.

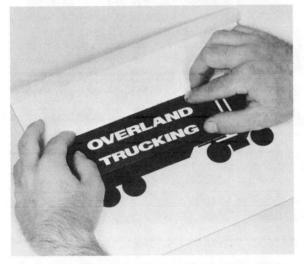

Fig. 43-7. Art copy ready for use with type being applied for direct reversal.

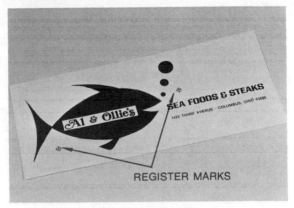

Fig. 43-10. The overlay portion properly located over the portion that will be printed in black.

Fig. 43-8. A reversal that was prepared by using the overlay method.

Screened tints. Screened tints are backgrounds that are composed of many evenly-spaced dots. Other patterns are also available. They come in dry-transfer material as discussed in Unit 31, and on acetate film base. Dry-transfer material is applied directly to the copy before it is photographed. Tints on acetate film sheets are placed underneath the negatives before making the printing plates.

Tints can be obtained in several densities (percentage of light that passes through the tint), and in many screen sizes, such as 65-line, and 85-line (Fig. 43-11). Fig. 43-12 shows a print in contrast, with and without the use of a tint. Fig. 43-13 shows how tints can be used to add emphasis to certain portions of a printed form. Only enough tint should be used to obtain the desired effect. Too much tint destroys this effect.

150 LINE	5	10	20	30	40	50	60	70	80 90
133 LINE	5	10	20	30	40	50	60	70	80 90
120 LINE	5	10	20	30	40	50	60	70	80 90
110 LINE	5	10	20	30	40	50	60	70	80 90
100 LINE	5	10	20	30	40	50	60	70	80 90
85 LINE	5	10	20	30	40	50	60	70	80 90
65 LINE	5	10	20	30	40	50	60	70	80 90

ByCHROME PERCENTAGE-CALIBRATED SCREEN TINTS (Stable base)

Fig. 43-11. An example of screened tints. (ByChrome Co., Inc.)

TINTS ADD "VALUE" TO YOUR PRINTING

normal line copy

An acetate overlay was prepared to add a tint block to this illustration, then screened with a 150-C tint and "double-burned" onto the plate (shown at right).

LITHOGRAPHY

... with screen tints added

The "shadow" effect on the word "lithography" was easily prepared by stripping a second line negative (screened with a 150-C tint) slightly out of register with the solid type.

LITHOGRAPHY

Fig. 43-12. Screened tints used to emphasize a specific area of a piece of copy.

STOCK REQUEST

o. of Sheets_____SIZE:_____

IND_____

T._____COLOR_____

UT_____OUT, TO PRESS SIZE_____

NEEDED:DAY_____HOUR_____

PECIAL STOCK: FROM_____

O# _____DAY NEEDED_____

SPECIAL INK REQUEST

Fig. 43-13. Tints used to emphasize certain portions of a typeform.

Fig. 43-14. A portion of a photograph magnified to show the dot formation of a halftone.

CONTINUOUS-TONE COPY

Copy that has intermediate tones of gray, from black to white, is considered to be *continuous-tone* copy. It is broken up into a dot formation to produce a *halftone* (Fig. 43-14). Each of the following examples of continuous-tone copy will be printed as halftones.

Photographs. The most common kind of continuous-tone copy is a photograph because it is one of the easiest to obtain. A photograph is the result of an image produced by a camera. It has gradations of tone (shades of gray) between black and white. There are exceptions to this designation, but it suitably defines continuous-tone photographs. Glossy photographs produce the best results when reproduced.

Photographs are printed in many different ways. Fig. 43-15 is an example of a *rectangular* photograph printed in much the same shape as it was received from the photographer.

Fig. 43-16 shows an *outline* photograph. Certain parts of the original are eliminated by artists or process photographers (those who prepare negatives for printing), to produce this effect from a normal photograph. Using a red masking film is one technique that produces printed outline photographs. Fig. 43-17 shows a photograph with a mask attached.

Fig. 43-15. A rectangular photograph.

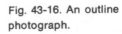

Fig. 43-16. An outline photograph.

Fig. 43-17. A masking sheet being placed on the photograph used in Fig. 43-16. This will be carefully placed over the image on the photograph.

Pencil or charcoal drawings. Pencil or charcoal drawings and sketches are treated as continuous-outline copy if the variation in shades is to be reproduced faithfully. Fig. 43-18 is a pencil sketch. Figs. 43-19 and 43-20 are sketches done with charcoal. Chalk is sometimes used in place of charcoal.

Fig. 43-18. A pencil sketch. (Nekoosa-Edwards Paper Co.)

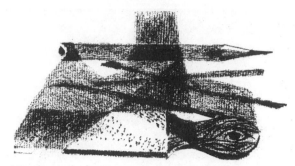

Fig. 43-19. A charcoal sketch. (Kimberly-Clark Corp.)

Fig. 43-20. A charcoal sketch. (Nekoosa-Edwards Paper Co.)

Fig. 43-21. An airbrush rendering. (Nekoosa-Edward Paper Co.)

Airbrush renderings. The illustration in Fig. 43-21 was done with an airbrush. This artwork often resembles the effects produced by photographs. Airbrush techniques are often used to touch up photographs (eliminate unsightly parts). Often more detail is produced than shown in a photograph.

Wash drawings. A wash drawing is a rendering or painting made with water colors, ink wash, or lamp black solution, using a pen or brush. A diluted solution produces desired grays. See Fig. 43-22.

COMBINATIONS

Combinations refer to combining line and continuous-tone copy into one printed image. Such a technique often gives sufficient variety to the printed item to make it more interesting than if only a line drawing or a piece of continuous-tone copy had been used. Fig. 43-23 shows a combination in which the continuous-tone copy (a wash drawing) is used as the background.

The examples given are the ones most commonly used to produce continuous-tone copy. This should not be considered an exhaustive list, however. Each piece of copy should be considered carefully to determine if it should be treated either as continuous-tone or line.

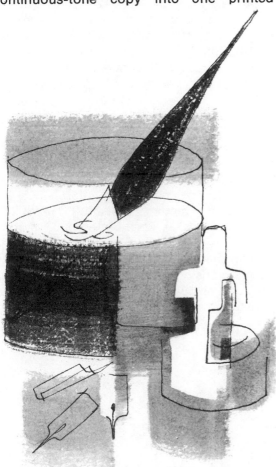

Fig. 43-22. A wash drawing. (Kimberly-Clark Corp.)

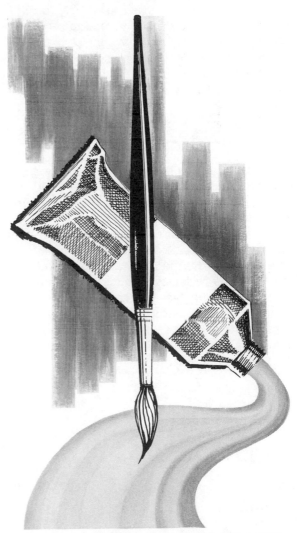

Fig. 43-23. A combination of line and halftone copy.

UNIT 44
COPY CONSIDERATIONS

Handling and preparing copy for process photography is of great concern to the customer and the printer. The quality of the printed material is largely dependent upon the conditions of the copy received by the photographer. The cost of printed material can be kept at a minimum if certain precautions are taken when preparing and handling copy.

SIZE OF THE COPY

Copy should be prepared larger, as a general rule, than the desired printed product. Rarely is it wise to prepare copy smaller than the size of the printed item.

If copy is prepared larger than the finished printing size, it will be reduced or made smaller by the photographer. Such reduction in size tends to make any errors or poor line quality less noticeable. It is not advisable to make large reductions, because type matter and illustrations are sometimes distorted and thin lines often become too thin for quality printing.

When possible, make the copy size sufficiently large so that the reduction will be no more than ⅓ smaller than the original. This means that if the final piece of copy is to be 8 to 9 inches in length, the original should be no more than 12 inches.

The opposite is true when copy is prepared smaller than the size of the finished printed material. In many cases, errors or poor line quality that are not visible on the original are quite obvious when copy is enlarged. Fig. 44-1 illustrates some of the effects of enlargement and reduction of typewritten copy.

Another consideration of enlarging or reducing copy is that both dimensions are equally affected. If a piece is 8 inches x 10 inches and the desired reduction is 50% the final printed material will be 4 inches x 5 inches (Fig. 44-2). The printed copy is actually ¼ the size of the original copy. The person preparing copy should be aware of both dimensions. This significant change in both dimensions is a valuable tool when copyfitting problems arise.

25% This copy was prepared by a typewriter.

50% This copy was prepared by a typewriter.

75% This copy was prepared by a typewriter.

100% This copy was prepared by a typewriter.

125% This copy was prepared by a typewriter.

150% This copy was prepared by a typewriter.

175% This copy was prepared by a typewri

Fig. 44-1. Typewritten lines enlarged and reduced.

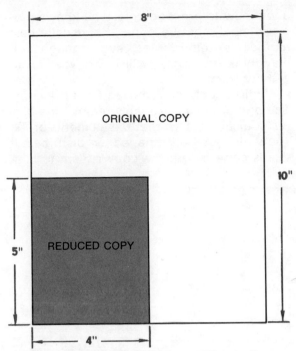

Fig. 44-2. Size comparisons after a 50% reduction.

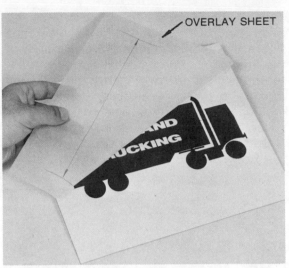

Fig. 44-3. Illustration with overlay sheet.

PROTECTING COPY

Almost as important as preparing copy is protecting it until it is photographed. Much time, effort, and expense are wasted when copy is damaged, soiled, or destroyed before it can be used.

All copy should have a protective *overlay sheet* attached to one edge (Fig. 44-3). It can be either tissue (tracing) paper or bond paper, and is usually attached with either tape or rubber cement. The overlay sheet is also often used as a place to make notes to the photographer or the printer.

Copy should be transported and stored so that it will not curl, fold, or tear. A convenient storage and mailing technique is to place the copy in a large envelope. The envelope should be clearly marked with notations to describe the piece of copy, the person for whom the copy was prepared, and the name of the person who prepared the copy.

Special attention should be given to handling photographs. It is best to mount them on heavy mounting board when possible. Never make marks on either side of a photograph, except in the borders. If notes must accompany a photograph, place them on a separate sheet of paper. Attach this sheet of notes to the photograph.

Always handle copy so that dirt or smudges will not get onto it. Handling copy by the edges will prevent fingerprints from getting on the image areas. Try to keep your hands very clean when working with copy, and never have food or drinks around the places where copy is being prepared or used. Many companies have extremely strict rules of cleanliness which must be observed when preparing and working with copy.

CHECKING THE FINAL COPY

Because the final printed material can be no better than the copy, it is extremely important that all copy be thoroughly checked before it is sent to the photographer. Many companies have a systematic procedure for making final checks on copy. The procedure usually requires that the copy be examined by someone other than the person who prepared it.

The copy should be carefully checked for accuracy. Type matter should be proofread, examined for image damage, and studied for completeness. All lines for both type matter and illustrations should be straight and parallel when appropriate. It is especially important to check for accuracy with paste-up copy because it is quite easy to paste up elements which are not straight and parallel.

All of the elements of the copy must be in proper location to the other elements. The artist should compare the layout with the final copy. When elements such as photographs or large drawings are not attached directly to the copy, be sure that they are included and that their position is properly noted on the copy.

Be sure all notes and instructions are on the copy. The printer will have questions about how to proceed unless he knows precisely what must be done. It is usually best to include some notes, even though you may think the printer will know what to do without them.

All dirt should be removed from the copy. The printer would probably remove the dirt, but you can be sure that the elements of the copy will not be damaged or disturbed if this is done before the copy is sent to him.

UNIT 45
CROPPING, SCALING, AND REGISTER MARKS

Illustrations are usually *cropped* (selecting only the area to be printed) and *scaled* (proportioned) before the copy is sent to the photographer or printer. *Register marks* are also frequently attached to the copy. These adjust and align sheets to correspond exactly when accuracy is desired. These procedures help the photographer and printer know exactly what must be done to the copy.

CROPPING

It is not necessary to print an entire photograph or illustration in most situations. Many times the printed item is improved because photographs have been carefully cropped. Cropping identifies the areas that will be printed. Unless these parts or areas are identified, the entire photograph or illustration will be reproduced.

Selecting the area to be cropped. The artist should select carefully the area of a photograph that is to be printed. Only those parts that illustrate the idea being conveyed should be used in the printed material. The area outlined in Fig. 45-1 has been selected as that to be used.

AREA TO BE PRINTED

Fig. 45-1. A total photo showing the area to be printed. (Caterpillar Tractor Co.)

Making crop marks. Crop marks can be made on the borders of a photograph. They should be placed on all four sides (Fig. 45-2). Either ink or a grease pencil is used as the marking instrument. Never mark on the image area of a photograph.

Crop marks can also be made by using an overlay sheet (Fig. 45-3). Notice that in both Figs. 45-1 and 45-2 the size of one of the two dimensions has been clearly marked. From this, the photographer determines the exact reduction or enlargement.

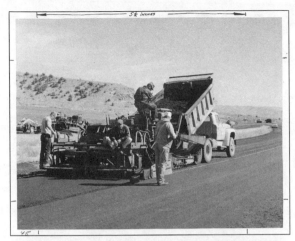

Fig. 45-2. Photograph with crop marks on the borders.

Fig. 45-3. Photograph with crop marks on an overlay.

SCALING COPY

Copy must be prepared to fit the size of the sheet, or the space on which it will be printed. The artist then prepares the copy in proportion to the final printed size. He can use any of the following methods to determine the size.

Proportioned rule method. Proportional rules are tools that determine the reduction or enlargement of copy. Using a proportional rule is probably the most simple and accurate method.

Fig. 45-4 shows a proportional rule having two scales. The outside one is for reproduction size; the inside one, for the original size. Following is the procedure for using this rule:

1. Determine the actual length of the copy. Width could be used instead of the length.
2. Locate this number on the inside scale.
3. Determine the length that the copy will

Fig. 45-4. A typical proportional scale.

be when it is printed. Width would be used when width is used in step 1.
4. Locate this number on the outside wheel.
5. Rotate the two wheels until the numbers are next to each other.
6. Read the number in the opening marked *percentage* on the proportional rule.

The number read in the window will be the reproduction percentage to be used for photographing the copy. The other dimension can also be read at this time. This is done by finding the other dimension of the copy on the wheel marked *original* size. The reproduction size or dimension can be read from the mark next to it on the reproduction size scale.

Mathematical formula technique. When no proportional rule is available, the following formula may be used to calculate reductions or enlargements:

$$\frac{WO}{HO} = \frac{we}{he}$$

when:

WO = width of the original copy
HO = height of the original copy
we = width of the enlargement or reduction
he = height of the enlargement or reduction

The formula is used for a problem such as: An 8 x 10 inches photograph is to be reproduced to fit into a space width of 3.5 inches. By substituting into the formula the height of the reproduction size, calculate:

$$\frac{8}{10} = \frac{3.5}{he}$$

$$8he = 35$$

$$he = \frac{35}{8}$$

$$he = 4.375 \text{ inches}$$

Diagonal line technique. A third method is sometimes used to determine copy size. It takes more time and gives only an approximate answer.

1. Draw a rectangle exactly the same size as the original copy (Fig. 45-5).
2. Mark the corners with letters *W, X, Y,* and *Z* (Fig. 45-5).
3. Extend a line from point *W* through *Y* and beyond.
4. From point *W* measure either the width or length of the reproduction size of the copy.
5. Draw a horizontal or vertical line until it intersects the diagonal line *WY* at point *A.*
6. Make a vertical or horizontal line from point *A* until it meets extended line *WX* at *B,* or extended line *WZ* at *C.*
7. Distance *WB* or *WC* can be measured to determine the unknown dimension.

To apply this method, assume that a piece of copy is to be reproduced in final printing to 9 x 12 inches. The artist would like to make the original copy with a height of 15 inches. Using the diagonal line technique, what size would he make the width of the original copy? The answer is 11.25 inches.

SPECIFYING REDUCTION AND ENLARGEMENT SIZE

Many methods can be used to provide this information. It is extremely important that the artist and the printer understand each other so that errors will not occur.

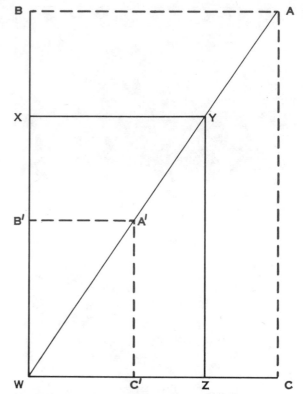

Fig. 45-5. The layout for the diagonal method of scaling copy.

The most common method used to specify reductions or enlargements for the printer is by the height or width of the reproduction size of the copy in inches, picas, or centimeters. The marking should be done on the margins of the copy or overlay sheet.

Another method gives specifications in terms of a percentage. For example, if the width of the original copy is 8 inches and it is to be reproduced so that it is 6 inches wide, the correct percentage to indicate on the copy is 75%. If the copy were to be reproduced the same size as the original (8 inches), the correct notation would be *same size,* or 100%. If the copy were to be reproduced to 10 inches, the notation would be 125%.

Greater confusion can occur when specifying the size of copy if the percentage technique is used than to use the exact measurement method. Many artists use both methods to eliminate errors. Regardless of the method used, it is important that the cameraman and printer know the precise size of the final reproduction.

Register marks are identification marks. They are used when two or more elements of a piece of copy are to be photographed and/or printed separately, but on the same sheet of paper. Register marks are used extensively in multicolor printing.

Fig. 45-6 shows several kinds of preprinted register marks that can be attached directly to the elements of copy. Register marks can also be drawn on the elements of copy by the artist.

Register marks should be placed on the base element at two to four points as shown in Fig. 45-7. When an overlay is added, place the register marks on the overlay so that they are directly over the ones on the base element (Fig. 45-8).

If the printing is in *register,* the marks will print on top of each other as shown in Fig. 45-9. When the register marks do not line up with each other, they are out of register and appear as shown in Fig. 45-10.

Fig. 45-6. Register marks.

 AMOS AIRLINES

Fig. 45-7. Base element with register marks in place.

TIMELINE FIELD
LIGHTHOUSE, KENTUCKY, 44391

Fig. 45-8. Overlay for the base element in Fig. 45-7 with register marks in place.

 AMOS AIRLINES

TIMELINE FIELD
LIGHTHOUSE, KENTUCKY, 44391

Fig. 45-9. Base element and overlay printed *in* register.

 AMOS AIRLINES
TIMELINE FIELD
LIGHTHOUSE, KENTUCKY, 44391

Fig. 45-10. Base element and overlay printed *out* of register.

UNIT 46
MAKING THE PASTE-UP

Copy for photographic reproduction is prepared in several ways. Each element can be prepared and photographed separately and the negatives later brought together during the stripping stages or preparation for making the plate. A more economical method, however, is to place as many elements as possible on a base, and photograph them at the same time. This is often done by using the *paste-up* technique.

The paste-up technique attaches the elements to be printed in the proper location on a suitable base. The paste-up is then used as the copy to make the photographic negative. This unit explains the procedure and considerations for making a paste-up.

DETERMINING THE SIZE OF THE BASE

The person who usually makes the paste-up is an artist who works from a comprehensive layout, or at least from a sketch that shows the proper location of each element and the size of the final reproduction. He determines whether the copy will be prepared *smaller,* the *same size,* or *larger* than the final reproduction size. Copy is most often prepared the same size, or slightly larger, than the final reproduction size. If the reproduction size of a piece of printed material is to be 5½ x 8½ inches, and the artist decides to prepare the copy so that the photographer will make a ⅔ reduction, he must prepare the copy so that when the ⅔ reproduction is made, the resulting negative will be 5½ x 8½ inches. In this instance, the *copy* would be 8½ x 12¾ inches.

SECURING THE ELEMENTS FOR THE PASTE-UP

The next step in preparing a paste-up is to obtain the elements to be used in it. These consist of type material, drawings, and sometimes prescreened photographs. Each must also be proportionate to the final reproduction size. Using the same ⅔ reproduction size, the type material for the paste-up would be prepared with 18 point type if the desired size of the type material to be printed were 12 points.

Illustrations would be prepared proportionately. Drawings can be made directly on the base material, or on another material and then attached to the paste-up base. Frequently, illustrations are prepared to a size that is *not* proportionate to the paste-up size, and the artist then makes a note in black pencil or ink to indicate the precise location of the illustration. He also identifies the specific illustration for that position.

TREATMENT OF PHOTOGRAPHS ON COPY

Photographs, and other continuous-tone copy, must be photographed separately from line copy. Because of this, glossy or original photographs are not placed directly on the paste-up. Three methods are usually employed to locate photographs on copy or paste-ups: (1) The block method, (2) the outline method, and (3) the halftone-print method. Before any of these methods can be used, the photograph should be cropped for the size it will be on the copy. *Block method.* This consists of placing a piece of black or red material on the paste-up. This should be exactly the shape of the photograph when printed. It also must be proportionate to the final reproduction size (Fig. 46-1). If a paste-up is prepared the same size as the final reproduction (100%), a block of 2 x 3 inches would be placed in the exact location where a 2 x 3 inches photograph will be positioned.

Separate negatives are made of the paste-up and the photograph. The block often referred to as a window will be a clean, clear spot on the negative of the paste-up. The halftone negative of the photograph is then taped behind the clear block on the paste-up negative to make the printing plate. This method is quite economical because it saves time in combining the halftone negative with the line negative.

Outline method. The outline method is similar to that of the block, except that the location of the photograph is marked by four lines, instead of a solid block (Fig. 46-2). When the two negatives are prepared, a hole is cut into the paste-up negative where the lines were drawn. The halftone negative and the paste-up are then taped together. This method takes more time and is therefore more costly, but has some distinct advantages over the block method.

Halftone print method. To use the halftone print method, a halftone negative is made to the size required on the copy or paste-up. A photographic contact print is then made of the halftone negative. The halftone print is pasted directly on the paste-up. The entire paste-up can then be photographed as line copy. This method is very useful when a single negative is required, but should be used only when the copy will be photographed at 100%. The *dot formation* of the halftone negative will be distorted if it is enlarged or reduced. It should also be noted that every photographic step away from an original results in a small loss of detail. Because of this, the final reproduction is often slightly inferior to that obtained by the other methods.

ATTACHING THE ELEMENTS

Several techniques are used to paste-up or attach elements to the base of a piece of copy. Three common satisfactory ones are (1) waxing, (2) taping, and (3) cementing.

Waxing. A waxing machine is required for this method. It is desirable because of the speed of preparation and cleanliness of the finished paste-up. Each element can also be removed at a later date for use on another paste-up.

The procedure for attaching elements to the paste-up with wax is quite simple. Elements are fed into the rollers of the waxing machine where wax is applied to the back. They are then placed into the proper position on the base, and pressed with a clean hand or a burnisher (a tool used to apply pressure). Be sure that the elements are properly located on the base.

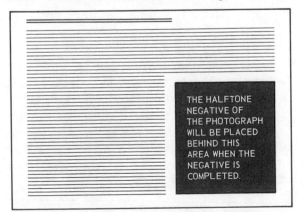

Fig. 46-1. Place a solid red or black image on the paste-up where the photograph will appear.

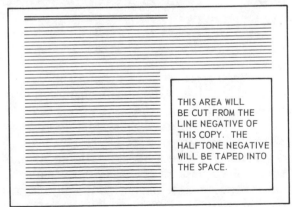

Fig. 46-2. Outlines of the photo drawn on the paste-up help identify where the halftone will be attached on the negative.

Taping. Double-surface tape has adhesive on both sides of a core material. The tape is applied to the back of the element which is then put in the correct position on the base (Fig. 46-3). Place the element in the exact location the first time, because it is difficult to remove it from the base without damage. Small marks or corners can be used as a locating aid.

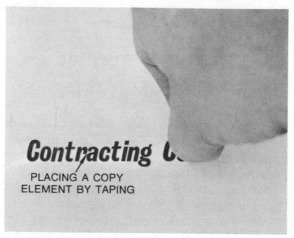

PLACING A COPY
ELEMENT BY TAPING

Fig. 46-3. The element is placed into position after the double-surface tape is applied to the back of the element.

Cementing. Rubber cement is the most common and best type of cement for making paste-ups. It is applied to both the back of the element and to the position on the base where the element will be located (Fig. 46-4). When the cement on both the element and the base is dry, the element is positioned. Rub off excess rubber cement around the element.

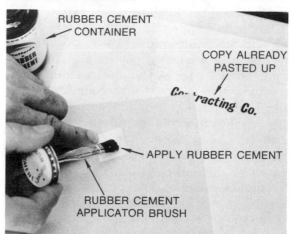

RUBBER CEMENT
CONTAINER

COPY ALREADY
PASTED UP

APPLY RUBBER CEMENT

RUBBER CEMENT
APPLICATOR BRUSH

Fig. 46-4. Apply rubber cement to the paste-up base and back of the element. When both surfaces are tacky, position the element properly the first time.

UNIT 47
COPY DIVISION FOR MULTICOLOR REPRODUCTION

Multicolor printing, using more than one color of ink, has become increasingly more popular in recent years. This is primarily due to the improved materials and machines which are now available. The use of color adds interest to the printed items, emphasizes important parts, and makes illustrations more realistic. More skill and attention to detail is required to prepare copy for multicolor printing than to prepare copy for single-color printing. The copy must be prepared so that each printing operation will be done properly and accurately. Copy for multicolor printing is classified as either *process-color* or *mechanical-color*. Sometimes both kinds of copy are used to produce a single printed product.

PROCESS-COLOR COPY

Process-color printing produces full-color illustrations, such as color photographs, transparencies (similar to 35mm slides), and color paintings. Each full-color illustration is photographed using filters on the process camera to produce three or four separate halftone negatives or positives of one color each. These separate single-color negatives are called *color separations.*

Each of the three or four halftone or single-color negative or positive is used to produce an image carrier which will print a single but different primary-color or black ink. Primary printing ink colors are *yellow, magenta* (red), and *cyan* (blue). The colors blend with each other when printed and produce a print that looks like the original copy. Each single-color negative or positive is referred to as a *color printer* (yellow printer, cyan printer, etc). Examples of process-color prints are shown in the color pages of this book.

The two classifications of copy used for process-color are reflection copy, and transmission copy. *Reflection* copy is photographed by reflecting light from the surface of the illustration to the camera (Fig. 47-1). Examples are reproductions of oil paintings, water colors, and color photographs. *Transmission* copy is photographed by passing light through the copy (Fig. 47-2). Transparencies like 35mm slides are typical.

The artist usually supplies the printing company with the illustrations. The photographer makes the process-color separation negatives for printing. The artist also gives the printing company the typeset copy in which the color illustrations will be used. This is similar to the block or outline methods discussed in Unit 46.

When the halftone negatives are prepared, the screen angle is different for each color printer (negative or positive). Screen angles for a set of four process-color negatives are 45° for the black printer, 75° for the magenta printer, 90° for the yellow printer, and 105° for the cyan printer. If only three colors are to be printed, the screen angles are 45° (cyan), 75° (magenta), and 105° (yellow). An undesirable *moiré pattern* (Fig. 47-3) will result if the correct screen angles are not used.

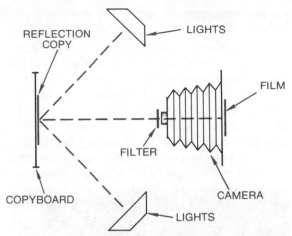

Fig. 47-1. Light is reflected from the surface of reflection copy through a filter and into the camera to expose the film.

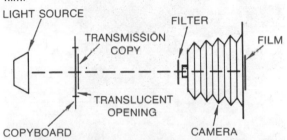

Fig. 47-2. Light passes through the transmission copy, a filter, and into the camera to expose the film.

Fig. 47-3. A *moiré* pattern results when two or more screens are printed over each other if the screen angles are incorrect.

DUOTONES

A duotone is an illustration printed in only two colors. It is usually printed in one dark color, such as dark blue or black, and one lighter color. Duotones are most commonly produced by printing two halftone negatives of the same illustration (usually a photograph) on top of each other. Both halftones are produced from the same illustration, but have slightly differing tonal ranges.

Fig. 47-4. A duotone is a photograph printed in two colors. (Lithographers and Photoengravers International Union)

Fig. 47-5. The light color of a duotone print. (Lithographers and Photoengravers International Union)

Fig. 47-6. The dark color of a duotone print. (Lithographers and Photoengravers International Union)

A duotone is shown in Fig. 47-4. The light color printer is pictured in Fig. 47-5; the darker one in Fig. 47-6. The screen angles of each halftone must be different to prevent a moiré pattern. One angle is 45° for the dark printer; 75° for the lighter one.

MECHANICAL-COLOR COPY

Copy prepared by an artist so that certain portions will print in one color, and other parts in another, is considered to be *mechanical-color* copy. The images might require that the colors overlap each other, or at least butt or touch. The desired effect to be obtained in a printed item determines the technique used. The details for preparing the copy vary with the artist and are often determined by the desires of the printer. Regardless of the technique used to prepare mechanical-color copy, all of the images must be either black-and-white, or red-and-white.

Masking. People use the masking technique to prepare copy when none of the colors overlap or butt. A single piece of copy is prepared as though the item would be printed in a single color (Fig. 47-7). Notes should be attached to the copy to indicate which parts are to be printed in a particular color. The copy is photographed

Fig. 47-7. Copy which can be used to make a multicolor print using the masking technique.

1227 Fifth Avenue   Columbus, Ohio 43234

Fig. 47-8. The portion of Fig. 47-7 copy selected to prepare the first image carrier.

Fig. 47-9. The areas selected to print the second color.

VICTORY HOUSE FURNITURE
1227 Fifth Avenue   Columbus, Ohio 43234

Fig. 47-10. A print of Fig. 47-7 with the two colors in register.

only once. After the negative is complete, all of the areas to be printed in one color are *masked off* (images are covered to prevent light from exposing the image carrier). Masking is usually done with lithographic tape or a masking sheet (goldenrod). This leaves all of the areas to be printed in the second color, clear on the negative.

The masked negative is used to prepare the image carrier. An example of the first image carrier after printing is shown in Fig. 47-8. After it is prepared, the masking material is removed from the negative. The second image carrier is masked off by blocking out the image areas which appeared on the first. A print of the second image carrier is shown in Fig. 47-9. When two image carriers are printed in register (images in correct relation to each other), the copy appears as illustrated in Fig. 47-10.

Overlays. This technique is used when one color must overlap one of the other colors. The image for each color is placed on a different sheet of paper. One color (usually the black image) is located on a piece of heavy illustration board.

A piece of acetate or tracing paper is attached to the base for each additional color

to be printed. The artwork for the overlays must be perfectly matched, or be keyed to the image on the base material. Register marks are placed on the base and the overlays to insure accurate printing of the image. All images on the base and overlays must be prepared in either black-and-white, or red-and-white.

Key line. The key-line technique of copy preparation is often used when two or more colors are to butt or be adjacent. It produces a very accurate print. The colors should overlap slightly to avoid undesirable space between the images. Most artists prefer the key-line method because small and precise overlaps are difficult to draw when using the overlay technique.

A single drawing of all images to be printed is prepared in black-and-white. A narrow line, the width of the overlap, is drawn where the colors touch. This line is the *key line.* The areas to be printed are not completely filled with ink (Fig. 47-11). Fuzzy edges are made to indicate to the printer that the illustration is not complete. Notes are placed on the copy, or on an overlay sheet, to indicate which images will be printed in each color.

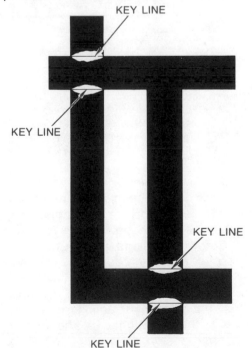

Fig. 47-11. An example of key-line copy.

Multiple negatives are made of the copy (the same number of negatives as colors which will be printed). If two colors are required, there will be two negatives. One will be used to prepare the image carrier for one color; the second, for the second color. Each will require additional preparation before the image carrier can be made.

The following steps indicate the procedure to prepare the negatives for making image carriers:

1. Obtain the negative to be used to print the first color.
2. Opaque the area which is to be printed with the second color. See Units 90 and 93.
3. Permit the opaqued negative to dry.
4. Turn the negative over so that the emulsion side is up.
5. Scratch away the emulsion carefully to the separation line. Be sure to remove all of the emulsion.
6. Follow the same procedure to prepare the negative for the second color, except that the areas which were clear in the first negative will be opaqued in the second one.

Fig. 47-12. A two-color print of the Fig. 47-11 key-line copy.

A print of Fig. 47-11 is shown in Fig. 47-12. Note that when the two colors to be printed are black, and a second color, they are not always butted. The black often overlaps the second color completely.

UNIT 48
NOTES AND INSTRUCTIONS TO THE PRINTER

Notes and instructions should accompany each piece of copy. The instructions should be complete, but as brief as possible. They must include all of the information required by the photographer and printer to either photograph or print the copy. The notes can be made by the artist, the customer (the person purchasing the printing), the photographer, the printer, or anyone else concerned with the production of the printed material. The customer is responsible for describing how the material should appear when printed. The printer must be sure that the notes and instructions are complete enough for all of the people who will handle the copy at a later time. Much of this kind of information can be obtained by the printer at his meeting with the customer. There are no standard procedures that are followed throughout the graphic arts industry, but in general similar information is required by all printers. Two kinds of information usually accompany copy: personal data and technical and production data.

PERSONAL DATA

Personal data is information about the persons involved in the printing (the customer and the artist). The following items are necessary:

1. Name of the customer.
2. Address and telephone number of the customer.
3. Name, address, and telephone number of the person who will answer questions about the copy.
4. Place of delivery of the final printed material. Note that items 1 and 2 are not always the same as items 3 and 4.

Many customers, artists, or advertising agencies include the information mentioned for items 3 and 4 as standard procedure. The photographer and printer can often save time if they obtain this information for each job that comes into the printing plant.

TECHNICAL AND PRODUCTION DATA

Technical and production data include information necessary to transform the copy into printed material. The amount and kind of information that accompanies a piece of copy vary considerably. Because of this, different instructions must be written for nearly every piece. Following are examples of items that should be included on the copy:

1. Size of the final reproductions.
2. Special photographic treatment (reversals, drop-outs, etc.).

3. Location of photographs and drawings (when separate from the composed type matter).
4. Kind of paper stock to be used.
5. Color(s) of ink.
6. Finishing operations (padding, collating, packaging, etc.)

Items other than the ones listed above are needed quite frequently. Any information required to produce the material should be listed.

METHODS OF MAKING NOTES AND INSTRUCTIONS

Three methods are used to make notes to accompany copy through the printing processes. In actual practice these methods are often combined.

1. Notes are made directly on the copy.
2. Notes are attached to the copy.
3. Notes are made on the envelope in which the copy is placed.

Notes made directly on the copy are usually the most explanatory, because they cannot be separated from the copy. This procedure is used most often when the notes are brief and will not interfere with the image to be photographed (Fig. 48-1). Notes placed directly on the copy should be done with a *light blue* pencil.

Attaching notes to the copy is used when several informational items must be attached, or when there is no room on the copy to make comments. The overlay method (Fig. 48-2) is often used because the

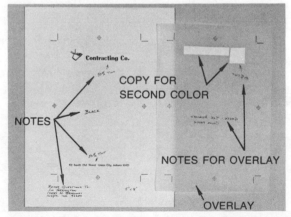

Fig. 48-1. Notes are directly on the copy in light blue pencil. The overlay sheet contains additional copy for the second color.

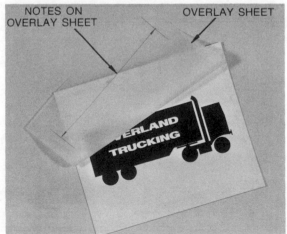

Fig. 48-2. Notes made on the overlay sheet.

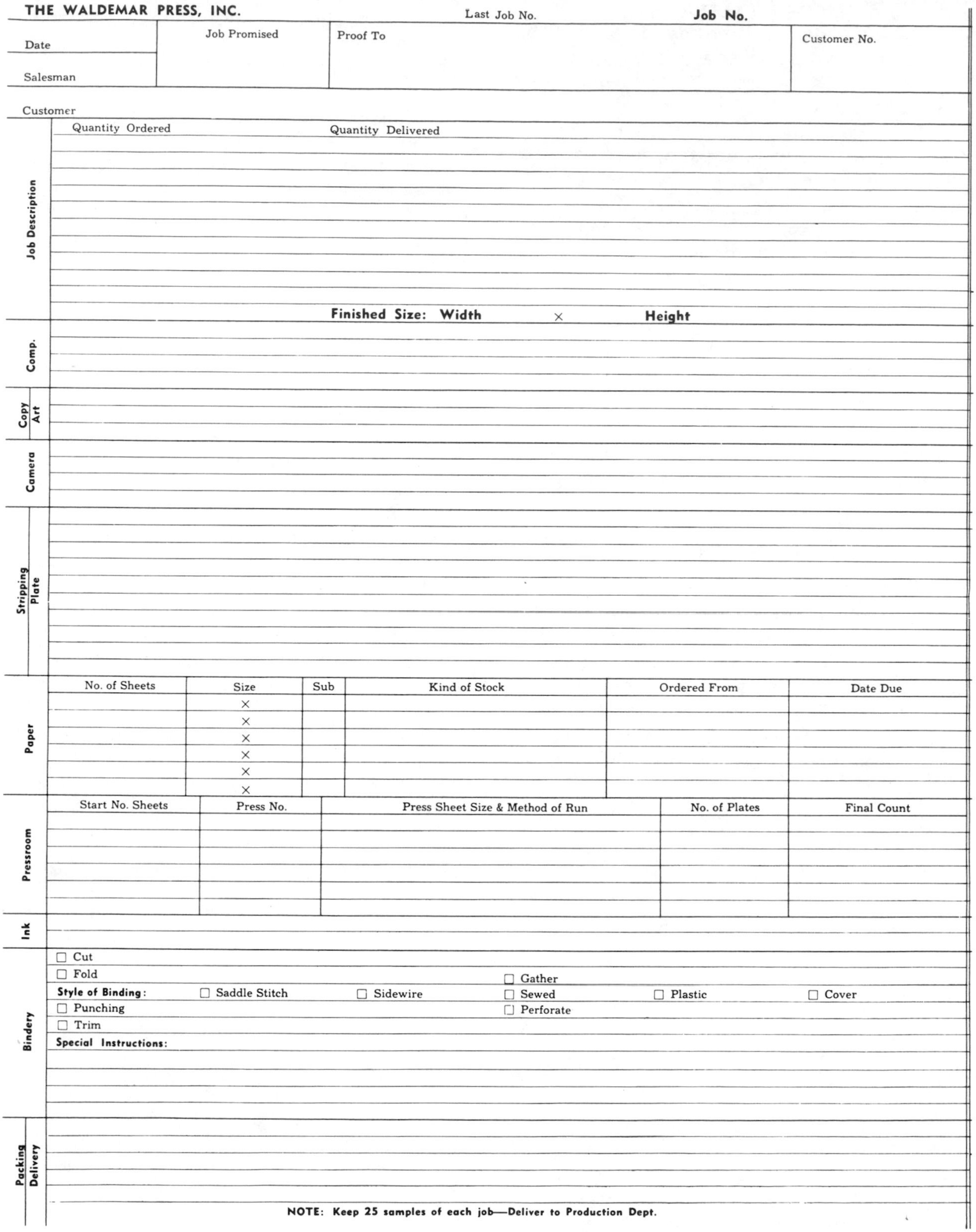

THE WALDEMAR PRESS, INC.			Last Job No.		**Job No.**	
Date	Job Promised	Proof To				Customer No.
Salesman						

Customer

Job Description

Quantity Ordered		Quantity Delivered				

Finished Size: Width   ×   Height

Comp.

Copy Art

Camera

Stripping Plate

Paper

No. of Sheets	Size	Sub	Kind of Stock	Ordered From	Date Due
	×				
	×				
	×				
	×				
	×				
	×				

Pressroom

Start No. Sheets	Press No.	Press Sheet Size & Method of Run	No. of Plates	Final Count

Ink

Bindery

☐ Cut
☐ Fold   ☐ Gather
Style of Binding: ☐ Saddle Stitch ☐ Sidewire ☐ Sewed ☐ Plastic ☐ Cover
☐ Punching   ☐ Perforate
☐ Trim
Special Instructions:

Packing Delivery

NOTE: Keep 25 samples of each job—Deliver to Production Dept.

Fig. 48-3. Typical job ticket.

notes are close to the copy and the overlay protects the copy. Instructions are also frequently attached to the back of the copy.

Some companies prefer to place copy in large envelopes. The envelope protects the copy and is a place where information about the printing of the copy can be recorded. All items required (negatives, flats, and plates) can be placed in the envelope when finished. Fig. 48-3 shows the information included on an envelope or a job ticket. There are places on the job ticket for more information than will be used for a single printing job. Therefore, a job ticket can be used for all types of printing jobs that come into the printing plant. Quite frequently notes are written on the back of the job ticket. If an envelope is used, notes are often inserted into it because there is not always sufficient space on the outside.

UNIT 49

LEARNING EXPERIENCES: COPY PREPARATION FOR PROCESS PHOTOGRAPHY

DISCUSSION TOPICS

1. Define copy preparation. Give the meaning of the term—elements.
2. What are the two main kinds of elements included in copy? Explain each kind.
3. List some of the items which must be considered by the artist when preparing copy.
4. Name the color of the base on which copy should be prepared. What are some of the considerations that should be made when selecting the base?
5. Identify the two most appropriate colors to place on the base when preparing copy for process photography.
6. Make a list of the common tools used to prepare copy for process photography.
7. What kinds of pencils are needed by the artist when preparing copy? Give some methods of applying ink to the copy.
8. List three methods of attaching elements to the base material. What are the advantages and disadvantages of each?
9. Distinguish between line and continuous-tone copy. Give specific examples of each.
10. How does a *reversal* differ from regular line copy? Explain some uses of screened tints.
11. Briefly describe how continuous-tone copy is printed. Why is this method necessary?
12. Should the copy be prepared larger or smaller than the desired printed size? Explain the reason for your answer.
13. Why is it not advisable to prepare the copy much larger than the final printed size? Give some reasons for your answer.
14. How should copy be protected? Name some reasons for protecting copy.
15. List the procedure for checking copy.

16. What is the purpose of cropping? How and where should crop marks be made on the photograph?
17. Define the term *scaling* as it is used for preparing copy for process photography.
18. Give three methods used to scale copy. Explain each in detail.
19. Name two methods of specifying the amount of enlargement or reduction which copy is to receive. Why is it important that the printer be aware of the amount of enlargement or reduction when he receives the copy?
20. What are register marks? Give the purpose of register marks. Name some examples of how and where register marks are used.
21. Describe the *paste-up* technique for preparing copy. Why is this method popular and frequently used?
22. Explain what the artist must consider when preparing the base material for a paste-up. What are some considerations concerning the elements to be placed on the base? How are illustrations prepared for a paste-up?
23. Give three methods of preparing a paste-up so that photographs can be used. Describe each method.
24. Name and describe three techniques used to attach elements to the base when making a paste-up.
25. Identify some reasons why material is printed in multiple colors.
26. What are two classifications of copy prepared for color reproduction?
27. Define *process-color copy* and give examples. Explain briefly how process-color copy is reproduced.
28. Name two different kinds of process-color copy. How do the two kinds of process-color copy differ? Give examples of each kind of copy.
29. What are the four colors of ink commonly used to print process-color copy? Give the screen angles for a set of four process-color negatives and give the ink color associated with each angle. List the screen angles and ink colors for a set of three process-color negatives.
30. What is the name for the undesirable pattern produced if the screen angles are not correct when printing the process negatives?
31. Describe a *duotone.* What are the colors usually used to print a duotone? Give the screen angles usually used to print a duotone.
32. How does mechanical-color copy differ from process-color copy? What colors should be used to prepare mechanical copy?
33. Explain the *masking* technique for preparing mechanical color copy. When would this method be the most effective and efficient way to prepare copy?
34. Describe the *overlay* technique for preparing multiple-color copy. What are some materials that are used for the overlays? Give examples of situations when it would be most appropriate to use overlay copy.
35. What is meant by *key-line* copy? Give the specific procedure for preparing key-line copy. When would it be most appropriate to prepare key-line copy? Explain the procedure for preparing key-line copy for printing.
36. Give some of the items usually included as personal data on copy.
37. Itemize the technical and production information commonly provided on copy for process photography.
38. Explain three methods for making notes on copy.

ACTIVITIES

1. Collect printed materials which illustrate several different kinds of copy preparation. Identify how the copy was prepared for printing.
2. Prepare paste-ups, using as many as possible of the different kinds of elements and methods of attaching the elements to the base.
3. Obtain a proportionate rule and solve the following problem. If copy is to be printed on 8½ x 11 inch paper with a

1-inch border around the copy, what should the size of the copy image be if the copy will be reduced by 25%? (Copy will be printed at 75% of the original size.)

4. Prepare a piece of copy using the keyline technique of multiple-color copy preparation.

5. Obtain two halftone screens, two halftone negatives, or two screen tints. Place one on top of the other and turn them from side to side. Observe the pattern that is produced and describe it on paper. Try to determine the points where the pattern is least obvious and most obvious, and record both.

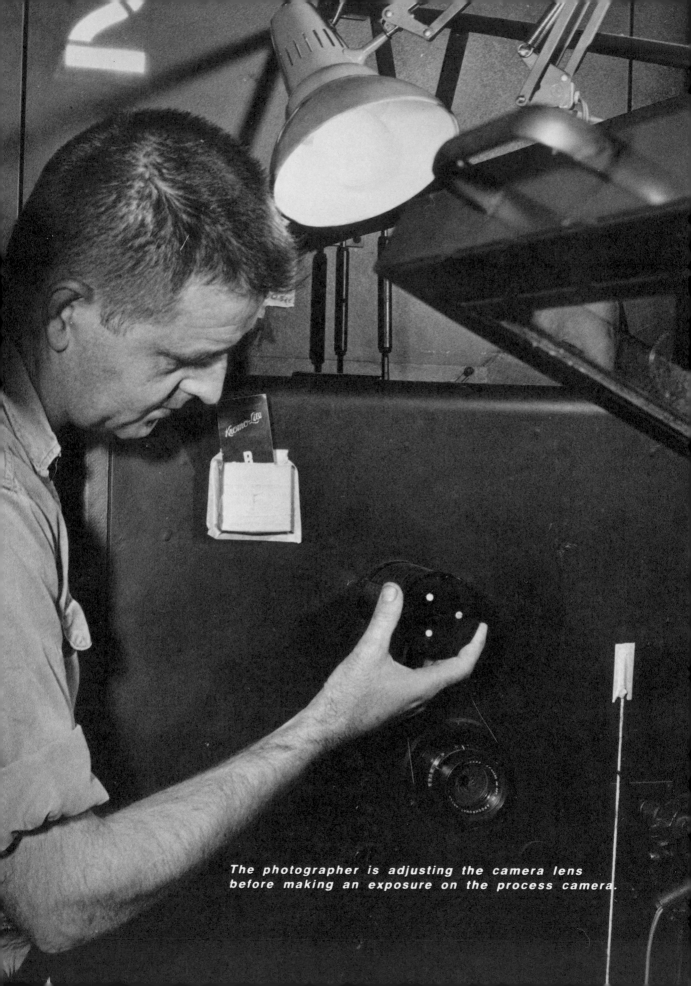

The photographer is adjusting the camera lens
before making an exposure on the process camera.

UNIT 50
INTRODUCTION TO PROCESS CAMERAS AND DARKROOM PROCEDURES

It is difficult to find a printed article that has not, in part, been produced through the use of a *process camera*. While photography dates back to the early 1800s, its application to the graphic arts is a twentieth-century development. The photographic process has made printing much more flexible than it was years ago.

Process cameras are those used to reproduce flat copy. They make precise enlargements, reductions, and same-size reproductions. Cameras have several precision components which must be protected and handled with extreme care.

PARTS OF A CAMERA

Process cameras, regardless of the kind or manufacturer, have the same basic parts: (1) lens, (2) bellows (lens extension), (3) camera back (film holder), (4) copyboard (copy holder), and (5) lights. There are many other parts and attachments, some of which will be mentioned later. Fig. 50-1 shows a typical process camera with some of the parts identified. This is a *horizontal camera* and will be used for discussion purposes throughout this unit. It will also be compared to other kinds of cameras later.

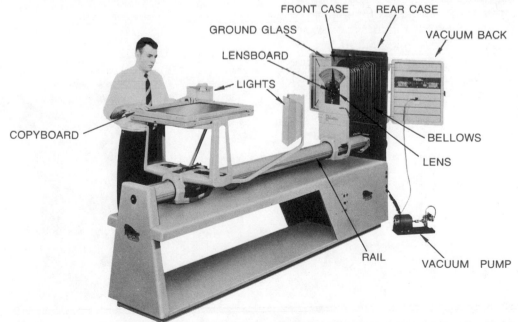

Fig. 50-1. A horizontal process camera. (Robertson Photo-Mechanix, Inc.)

143

Lens. The lens is the most precise and costly part of a process camera. The quality of the negative is largely dependent upon the quality of the lens. It consists of several glass elements, and a diaphragm, or iris, (Fig. 50-2). These are enclosed in a case called a lens barrel. Two typical lenses used are illustrated in Fig. 50-3.

The diaphragm regulates the amount of light entering the camera. An arrangement of metal leaves or blades mesh to make a circular opening called the *aperture opening* for light to pass through (Fig. 50-4). The diaphragm is opened or closed by turning a ring or collar on the outside of the lens barrel. (Fig. 50-3).

The numbers on the collar refer to the size of the diaphragm opening. They are called *f-stops* (see Fig. 50-3). Some common diaphragm f-stop numbers are f/8, f/11, f/16, f/22, and f/32. The larger the f-stop number, the smaller the diaphragm opening: f/16 is smaller than f/11. Each larger f-stop number reduces the size of the aperture opening by ½. The number f/16 has twice the aperture opening as f/22, allowing twice the amount of light to enter.

Enlargements and reductions require that the lens and copyboard be moved either closer or farther apart. When this is done, an adjustment must be made in the aperture opening by changing the diaphragm setting. Many cameras have a manual diaphragm control which, in turn, adjusts the aperture opening (Fig. 50-5). This maintains constant exposure light.

Fig. 50-3. Two typical lenses for process cameras. (Goerz Optical Company, Inc.)

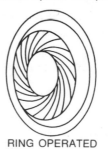

Fig. 50-4. A lens diaphragm. (Goerz Optical Company, Inc.)

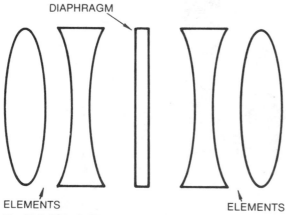

Fig. 50-2. The elements and diaphragm of a lens. (Goerz Optical Company, Inc.)

Fig. 50-5. A manual diaphragm control. (nuArc Company, Inc.)

The lens unit is attached to a *lensboard,* which, in turn, is fastened to the *front case* (Fig. 50-1). The front case can be moved either forward or backward to make adjustments for enlargements or reductions.

The lens should be protected at all times. A lens cap should be placed over the lens when the camera is not in use to prevent dust from settling on it. Examine the lens frequently for dust or dirt because they can cause flaws on the negative. Fan the lens with a sheet of paper to remove dust. If this does not work, use lens cleaner and a piece of commercial lens tissue. Never use plain household tissue or cloth because they may contain abrasive particles that could scratch the lens. Never touch the lens surface with the fingers, as acid in perspiration can etch or eat away the lens surface. Always consult a knowledgeable authority before cleaning a lens.

Shutter. A shutter is included on the front case of most cameras. It is behind the lens and inside the bellows (Fig. 50-6). The shutters on most cameras open electrically and are connected to a *timer* (Fig. 50-7). The timer opens and shuts the lens so that light can pass through the lens for a specific amount of time. Sometimes the camera lights are also connected to the timer. More often, however, the lights are turned on manually.

Bellows. The bellows provides a light-tight closure between the front case and where the film is held, the camera back. The bellows is made of cloth or similar material, which stretches or compresses when adjustments are made to the camera for enlargements or reductions. A bellows is easily punctured. It should be protected from sharp objects and inspected every six months to be certain it is light-tight and permits no light to enter the camera.

Camera back. The camera back, which holds the film in the camera, is behind the lens and bellows. The most popular kind in use is the *vacuum back.* This is actually a swinging door with holes on the plate surface that holds the film (Fig. 50-8). There is a vacuum chamber behind the plate, and a vacuum pump is attached to the vacuum

Fig. 50-6. A shutter. (nuArc Company, Inc.)

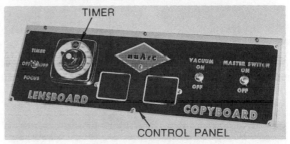
Fig. 50-7. A control panel and timer. (nuArc Company, Inc.)

Fig. 50-8. A vacuum back. (nuArc Company, Inc.)

chamber. The film is placed in the correct position and held by the vacuum. The vacuum back opens to place film on the camera back and closes to make the exposure.

Most cameras also have a ground-glass back to check the focus of the camera (Fig. 50-9). The ground glass is placed into position exactly where the film will be located. When the camera lights are turned on and the lens is opened, the image from the copy is visible on the ground glass. The cameraman can check for focus, sharpness of image and see if the copy has been properly placed on the copyboard.

Fig. 50-9. A ground-glass focusing back. (nuArc Company, Inc.)

Copyboard. Copy is held in place by the copyboard, which is attached to the same rail or track as the front case (Fig. 50-10). Most copyboards consist of a frame with a spring-loaded back or foam cushion. The pad is covered with a glass lid that covers the copy and locks into place. The center of the copyboard is in line with the center of the camera back. It moves either forward or backward on the rail or track to make adjustments.

Lights. Three kinds of lights most often used on process cameras are incandescent, arc, and quartz. Each has advantages and disadvantages. Incandescent lamps are the least expensive and are quite adequate for black-and-white work, but as the bulbs age, they become dim. Arc lamps are excellent for both color and black-and-white work, but it is difficult to maintain a constant light with them, as the elements wear out. The quartz systems are probably the most satisfactory because they produce light that is usable for both color and black-and-white, and a very constant light can be maintained. The lights are usually held on the copyboard frame and can be adjusted to different angles (Fig. 50-11).

Darkroom. The darkroom is a room which can be made completely dark. It is used to process photographic materials. Due to the nature of the work done in the darkroom, special tools, equipment, procedures, and layout will be discussed in the following units.

Fig. 50-10. A camera copyboard. (nuArc Company, Inc.)

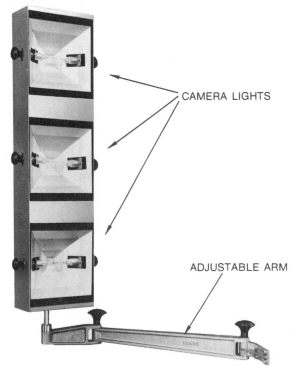

Fig. 50-11. Camera lights. (nuArc Company, Inc.)

UNIT 51
CLASSIFICATIONS OF PROCESS CAMERAS

Process cameras can be classified in many categories. Two designations which are most commonly used are discussed in this unit. The first is concerned with where the cameras are placed in the printing plant. The second defines cameras according to their construction.

GALLERY AND DARKROOM CAMERAS

Some cameras are constructed for use in a room with normal lighting; some are designed for use in a darkroom; others can be used in either area. Parts of cameras differ, depending on where the camera is used. Each camera also has advantages and disadvantages.

Gallery cameras. Process cameras used or located entirely in normally lighted rooms are called gallery cameras. They are not used too frequently because it is somewhat inconvenient to make negatives with them. Film must be loaded into the film holder in the darkroom. It is then transported to the camera in the lighted room. After the exposure (picture taken), the film holder is removed from the camera and brought back to the darkroom for developing, which makes this process time consuming. A gallery camera usually has a shutter to control the amount of light that enters it plus most of the other features of any quality camera. The primary advantage of a gallery camera is that no valuable darkroom space is occupied.

Darkroom cameras. Darkroom process cameras are located and used in the darkroom. Sometimes the entire camera is placed in this area. In other situations, only the rear case is in the darkroom; the re-

mainder is placed in the lighted room. As illustrated in Fig. 51-1, the camera is installed through the wall. The darkroom camera is the most popular because film can be loaded and unloaded directly in the darkroom.

When the camera is placed entirely in the darkroom, exposures cannot be made while the film is being developed, because light would ruin it. Sometimes a camera is placed in a separate, adjacent darkroom and used only for making exposures.

The most satisfactory darkroom arrangement is to have only the rear case of the camera in the darkroom. The film is loaded into the camera in the darkroom and exposures are made while developing is being done. The exposure lights are located in the light room. The principle disadvantage in this method is that the cameraman must leave the darkroom to change the copy out in front. This problem can be overcome if one person changes the copy in the light room while another makes the exposure in the darkroom.

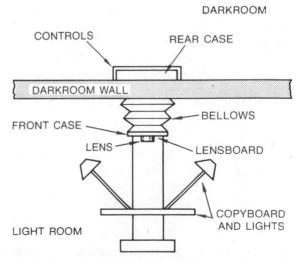

Fig. 51-1. A darkroom camera with the rear case in the darkroom.

LINE OF EXPOSURE

Fig. 51-2. A horizontal camera. (Robertson Photo-Mechanix, Inc.)

HORIZONTAL AND VERTICAL CAMERAS

Cameras are also classified by the structure or direction in which the exposure is made. There are both horizontal and vertical cameras. Most photographic departments have the horizontal darkroom type. Both cameras have essentially the same basic parts.

Horizontal cameras. This type takes pictures in a horizontal position. If a line were drawn through the center of the copyboard, lens, and film holder, it would be a horizontal one as shown in Fig. 51-2. Horizontal cameras are made so that part is in the light room and part in the darkroom. The rear case with film holder and controls is placed in the darkroom, permitting film loading in this area. The remainder with front case, lensboard, and copyboard extends into the light room where copy is loaded. Because the required lighting for exposures is produced in the light room, negatives can be made without interrupting the developing process in the darkroom. This arrangement

LINE OF EXPOSURE

Fig. 51-3. A vertical camera. (Robertson Photo-Mechanix, Inc.)

requires very little darkroom space.

Horizontal cameras can be placed entirely within a darkroom, but there are disadvantages. As with all darkroom cameras, negatives cannot be developed while exposures are being made and considerable darkroom space is taken up with the entire camera.

Vertical Cameras. The negative film is in a horizontal position on a vertical process camera (Fig. 51-3). The copyboard is at the bottom of the camera and the film holder is at the top. This type of camera must be used entirely in the darkroom or entirely in a light room. Most are used in the darkroom be-cause this makes film loading easier. When the vertical camera is used in the darkroom, it is not necessary to use a shutter. The camera lights are connected to the timer. The time the lights are on serves the same purpose as the shutter. The copyboard lights prevent film from being developed when the vertical camera is used in a dark-room. An advantage of this camera is that it requires less floor space. However, its physical size limits the size of copy, en-largements, and reductions. Another disad-vantage is that the photographer must bend over each time he changes copy.

UNIT 52
FILMS AND CHEMICALS FOR PROCESS PHOTOGRAPHY

Many printing processes require that copy be photographed before it can be repro-duced or printed. With cameras, pho-tographic films and chemicals are used for this purpose. Film is exposed or the picture taken while it is held in a camera or contact frame. After the exposure is made, the film must be processed in certain chemicals. This is called *developing.*

There are many films and chemicals avail-able for photographic reproduction. This unit is concerned only with films and chemi-cals that are normally used for process pho-tography. Each person should also consult film manufacturers' representatives for an-swers to specific questions.

STRUCTURE OF FILM

The basic parts of a piece of film are base (support), and emulsion (the light-sensitive coating). The other parts or elements of a film are shown in Fig. 52-1.

Base. The base supports the light-sensi-tive emulsion. The material may be translu-cent, permitting some light to pass through. Most film bases, however, are transparent, or clear like glass. Film can be purchased with many kinds of base materials. These are polyester, acetate, glass, and paper. Until recently, acetate was the most fre-quently used, but polyester has become popular because it has more dimensional stability.

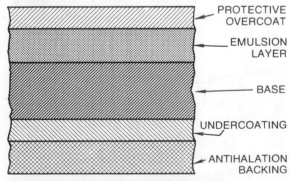

PROTECTIVE OVERCOAT

EMULSION LAYER

BASE

UNDERCOATING

ANTIHALATION BACKING

Fig. 52-1. Cross section of a piece of film.

Bases come in several thicknesses. A standard thickness is about 0.005 inch. Film of 0.0035 inch would be considered thin-base film. That of approximately 0.007 inch is thick-base film. All film must be able to withstand the effects of chemicals and handling.

Emulsion. The emulsion is light-sensitive material suspended in a clear gelatin which is coated on one side of the base as shown in Fig. 52-1. Without emulsion no image could be formed. Light-sensitive materials most often used in emulsions are *silver halides.* When silver halides are developed after having been exposed to light, they turn black to form the image on the piece of film.

Overcoat. A protective overcoat is applied to the emulsion side of the film. It is a thin layer of clear gelatin. This protects the emulsion from abrasion and scratching during handling.

Antihalation. Antihalation backing is a dye applied to the base side opposite the emulsion. During exposure, it is possible for the light reflected from the copy to completely penetrate the emulsion. Should this happen, the light could reflect to the film and cause secondary exposures where undesired. The dye or antihalation back absorbs all of the light that passes through the emulsion. This prevents the light from reflecting back into the emulsion (Fig. 52-2) The dye is removed from the film during the developing process.

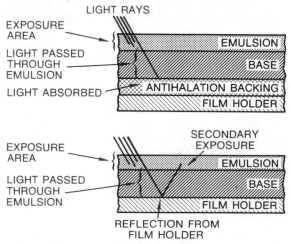

Fig. 52-2. Effects of light on film with and without antihalation backing.

Anticurl. Many films have an anticurl coating. The purpose is to counteract the curling tendency.

KINDS OF FILM

Panchromatic and orthochromatic are the two main kinds of film used for process photography. Both must produce high-contrast negatives (either black or clear). The most widely used is orthochromatic film.

Panchromatic film. This type is sensitive to all colors of light, including red. It is used primarily for photographing copy that consists of several colors. Panchromatic films must be handled in total darkness. Even though certain types can be developed with a dark green light, it is safer to develop them in total darkness.

Orthochromatic film. This film is sensitive to blue, green, and yellow; it is insensitive to red light. Light blue guidelines can be used on copy without having to be erased, since these lines are not recorded on orthochromatic film. This film can also be handled under red light because red has no effect on it.

HANDLING FILM

Film is extremely delicate and highly sensitive. It must be handled with care. Possible causes of damage are high temperature and humidity, harmful gases, pressure, and abusive handling.

Temperature and humidity. Best temperature range for film storage is from 68° F. to 75° F. Desirable humidity ranges from 40 to 50 percent. Loss in film sensitivity can result if these conditions are not maintained. Unopened packages are frequently stored under refrigeration, but the film must be returned to room temperature before use. Store film where it is not near any source of heat or high humidity.

Pressure. Pressure resulting from film packages being stacked on each other or from damaged packages can cause fogging. Fogging causes the clear areas to turn dark more easily when developed. Pressure also

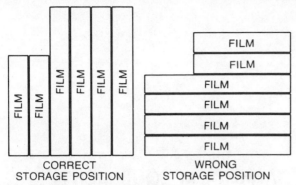

CORRECT
STORAGE POSITION

WRONG
STORAGE POSITION

Fig. 52-3. Film storage position.

causes scratches on film surfaces. Store packages in a vertical position as shown in Fig. 52-3.

Handling. Film should be handled by the edges. Fingerprints can ruin a piece of film. This is especially true in warm summer months when hands are moist. Always be sure that hands are dry, clean, and free of processing chemicals before handling film.

When film must be laid down for an activity such as cutting, be sure that the surface where it is placed is clean and dry. Always lay the film down with the base side against the surface. This prevents damage to the emulsion.

Avoid sliding pieces of film over each other, as this causes static electricity. Sparks caused by static electricity will pre-expose the film.

Probably the most important precaution when handling film is to keep the package closed. If a light is accidentally turned on while it is open, an expensive package of film can be ruined.

CHEMICALS

Exposed film has a latent or invisible image. This refers to the areas that have been exposed by light. The latent image cannot be seen, and the purpose of the chemicals is to make it visible.

The three main solutions for processing film to produce a negative or film positive are developer solution, rinse bath, and fixing solution. Manufacturers recommend specific chemicals to be used with particu-

lar films. Follow the directions of the film manufacturer.

Developer. Exposed film is first placed into the developer solution. This solution penetrates the gelatin and changes the latent image or exposed areas from silver salts to black metallic silver. Developer is an alkaline, or basic, chemical solution.

Developer is made up of several chemical agents, each with a specific purpose. The main reducing or developing agent is hydroquinone. This chemical turns the exposed silver salts to black metallic silver.

Chemicals such as *accelerators* speed up developing, *buffers* control activity of the accelerator, *restrainers* retard the speed of developing, and *preservatives* lengthen the life of the developer. These chemicals are included in many developer solutions.

Most developers for orthochromatic process film are made in two parts—Part A and Part B. These parts are prepared and stored separately. They are mixed to make one solution immediately before developing the film. The mixture lasts only a short time (thirty minutes to an hour) after mixing. It becomes exhausted and ineffective after developing only a few pieces of film.

Rinse bath. The rinse bath, also called *stop bath,* stops the developing action of the developer. A very weak acetic acid and water solution is used. Plain water will work, but the action is slower. The stop bath also removes the developer from the film and protects the fixing solution from contamination.

Fixing solution. The fixing solution, called the *fixer* or *hypo,* removes the undeveloped silver salts and cleans the film. The main ingredient is sodium thiosulfate. Acetic acid is also added to the fixer to remove any remaining alkaline developer. Some fixers contain a chemical to harden the emulsion which remains after developing. After the film has been *fixed,* it is no longer sensitive to light and is safe in any light. The fixer must be thoroughly washed from the negative with clean water before the negative is dried.

UNIT 53
DARKROOMS

A darkroom does not have to be elaborate and contain expensive or complicated equipment to be an efficient and effective place in which to work. It must be arranged, however, so that it can be kept clean, neat, and safe. Fig. 53-1 illustrates a well-organized darkroom. Equipment and utensils in the darkroom are used to process photographic materials. Extremely sophisticated and expensive equipment is available, but generally the accuracy with which the photographer must work determines the quality of the equipment and utensils.

Fig. 53-1. An efficiently arranged darkroom. (Eastman Kodak Co.)

Fig. 53-2. Fiberglass developing sink. (nuArc Co.)

DARKROOM EQUIPMENT

Darkroom sinks are a source of fresh running water and provide a place to hold the developing trays and to dispose of used chemicals. They are made primarily of fiberglass or stainless steel (Figs. 53-2 and 53-3). Stainless steel sinks are more rigid and easy to clean, and are unaffected by water or chemicals. A temperature-controlled sink is pictured in Fig. 53-4. The refrigerated storage cabinet is located beneath the sink for storage of chemicals and film.

Water Mixers. Fig. 53-5 shows a mixer that is capable of mixing water to temperatures accurate to within $\pm\frac{1}{2}°F$. The mixer shown in Fig. 53-6 is accurate to within $\pm\frac{1}{4}°F$. Water mixers are frequently used to provide a constant supply of circulating water around processing trays.

Processing trays hold the chemicals during the developing process. At least three are required: (1) for the developer solution,

Fig. 53-3. Stainless steel sink. (Leedal, Inc.)

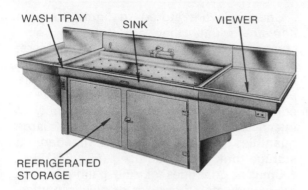

Fig. 53-4. Temperature-controlled sink. (Leedal, Inc.)

Fig. 53-5. Water mixer that is accurate to ±½°F. (Leedal, Inc.)

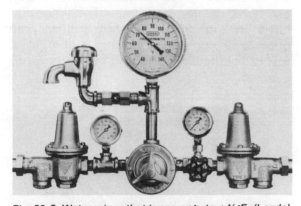

Fig. 53-6. Water mixer that is accurate to ±¼°F. (Leedal, Inc.)

Fig. 53-7. Stainless steel processing tray. (Leedal, Inc.)

Fig. 53-8. Safelights (nuArc Co.)

(2) for the stop bath, and (3) for the fixer or hypo solution. The tray should be slightly larger than the material being processed. If the tray is too large, expensive chemicals will be wasted. Trays are made from plastic, hard rubber, fiberglas, and stainless steel (Fig. 56-7).

Thermometers are precise, delicate instruments used to process photographic materials. They come in many sizes and degrees of accuracy. Photographers often keep two in the darkroom and check the accuracy of one against the other.

Safelights are usually found in darkrooms, because some film, such as orthochromatic, can be handled in red light. Safelights are located where most of the developing activity occurs, such as over the sink or near the film storage areas. They are built to be plugged directly into a wall receptacle, attached to a wall, or hung from the ceiling (Fig. 53-8). Some photographers use only red light bulbs; however, this practice is not suggested. Safelights with correct wattage bulbs should be used in the darkroom.

Utensils used for mixing, pouring, and measuring are needed. The utensils commonly found in a darkroom are graduates, beakers, pails, and funnels. The material of the utensils should not contaminate the chemicals. Glass, plastic, and stainless steel are satisfactory.

Fig. 53-9. Stainless steel graduate. (Leedal, Inc.)

Fig. 53-10. Stainless steel beaker. (Leedal, Inc.)

Fig. 53-11. Stainless steel pail. (Leedal, Inc.)

Fig. 53-12. Funnel. (Leedal, Inc.)

Fig. 53-13. Stainless steel chemical storage tank. (Leedal, Inc.)

Chemicals are stored in liquid form in *containers* until they are needed. Some chemicals are purchased in containers; others are in powder form and must be mixed into liquid form before they are placed in containers. The kind and size of container used depends on the quantity of chemicals used in the darkroom. If large quantities of chemicals are needed, a storage tank should be used (Fig. 53-13).

Smaller quantities of one gallon or less are usually stored in glass or plastic bottles. All containers should be clearly labeled to describe the contents. Some photographers even like to place additional instructions on the bottles or containers. It is also wise to have full duplicate containers of each chemical to prevent running out at a crucial time. Containers should be such that they prevent air from reaching the chemicals. It is also important that direct light does not come into contact with the chemicals.

Timers are essential in the darkroom. The one shown in Fig. 53-14 has a large, luminous face which is easily seen in the dark. There is a buzzer to indicate lapse of time. Darkroom equipment, such as an enlarger, can be controlled by a timer. The timer pictured in Fig. 53-15 is used primarily to operate or control darkroom equipment. It resets itself after the specific time has elapsed.

Graduates are commonly used to measure quantities of chemicals. They are usually calibrated in both ounces and cubic centimeters (Fig. 53-9).

Beakers and *pails* are used primarily for mixing chemicals. Beakers have a smaller capacity (usually one gallon or less) than pails (Fig. 53-10). Pails are used to mix larger quantities like three to five gallons of chemicals (Fig. 53-11).

Funnels. Funnels (Fig. 53-12) make it easier to pour chemicals into storage bottles with small openings.

Fig. 53-14. Darkroom timer. (Dimco)

Fig. 53-15. Equipment control timer. (Industrial Timer Corp.)

Contact printers are used to make same-size reproductions. These printers can be made on either film or photographic paper. The negative or film positive is placed on the glass (Fig. 53-16). The photographic material (paper or film) is placed on the negative, and the lid is closed. The vacuum blanket forces the negative and the material on which the reproduction is being made into tight contact. The lights, located in the lower part of the printer, are turned on for a specific amount of time. The photographic material is then removed and developed.

The *light source* shown in Fig. 53-17 is used to expose contact prints. It is used with a printing frame which is usually a contact vacuum frame. The lamp is located over the printing frame; the transformer governs the intensity or brightness of the light.

Inspection lights (Fig. 53-18) are found in many darkrooms. The lights are used to examine negatives and film positives during the development process. They are equipped with ortho-safe and white lights.

Many other pieces of equipment and utensils are used in darkrooms, but most are for special purposes and are not absolutely essential. The photographer must determine the equipment and utensils required to achieve the desired results. It must be remembered that equipment is of little value unless the photographer is able to use it properly.

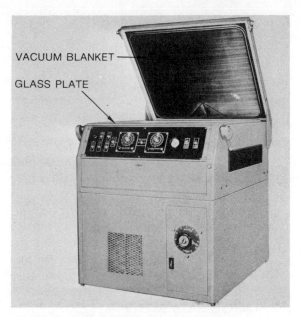

VACUUM BLANKET

GLASS PLATE

Fig. 53-16. Contact printer. (Colight, Inc.)

Fig. 53-17. Light source for contact printing. (nuArc Co.)

Fig. 53-18. Inspection lights. (nuArc Co.)

DARKROOM ARRANGEMENTS

Darkrooms are usually set up according to the preference of the photographer, but there are some features common to all arrangements. A well-planned darkroom should have the following features:

1. It should be completely light-tight.
2. The size and shape should accomodate the equipment and provide work space without being overcrowded.
3. There should be a door or light trap arrangement which permits people to enter and leave without disturbing the activities in progress in the darkroom.
4. There should be a sink with fresh running water, preferably hot and cold with a temperature control.
5. A system of supplying fresh, clean air is essential. An air conditioner that maintains a constant temperature and humidity is ideal.
6. Sufficient electrical outlets to safely accomodate the darkroom equipment are necessary.
7. There should be ample space for storage.
8. There should be a white-light source for use when cleaning up or preparing the darkroom.

Making the darkroom light-tight. A darkroom must be dark. If even a small amount of light enters the room, the photographic film or paper will be ruined. There must be constant inspection for possible light leaks and some photographers do this daily. Inspection includes looking for cracks in walls, space around doors, and places where objects or utilities pass through the walls. These all are potential trouble areas.

Darkroom plans. There are nearly as many darkroom plans and arrangements as there are darkrooms. Many times, however, the photographer has no control over these. Reasons for a particular plan may include the size and space available, location of electrical outlets, water supply, equipment required, and placement and design of the entrances.

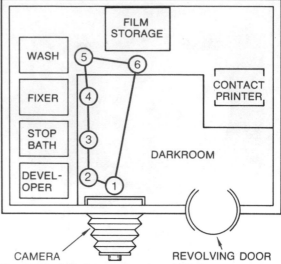

Fig. 53-19. A darkroom showing work-flow.

Work flow. The photographer should strive to arrange the darkroom to secure an efficient work-flow pattern. This means the direction and distance between sequential steps of a process or procedure (Fig. 53-19).

Storage and work space. Not all of the space in the darkroom should be consumed with equipment. Space is also needed for storage of film, chemicals, utensils, and other required materials. A flat work space is needed for cutting paper or film, organizing copy, and placing equipment.

Electrical outlets. Electrical outlets should be placed about every five feet around the darkroom. There should also be several circuits to prevent overloading of any single circuit.

Darkroom doors. Darkroom doors must prevent light from entering when work is in progress. The most desirable types permit persons to enter and leave the darkroom while work is being done. Each has advantages and limitations.

The *light trap* is a common method of providing for entrance and exit from a darkroom. The light trap involves two or more passages which must be passed through in order to get from the lighted room into the darkroom (Fig. 53-20). Walls of the light trap are painted black to absorb as much light as possible. Curtains are sometimes placed in the light trap to further reduce the amount of light. Disadvantages are that this

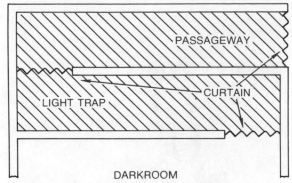

Fig. 53-20. A light trap.

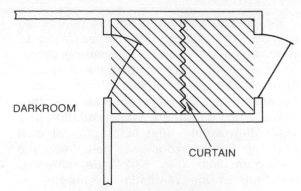

Fig. 53-21. Double doors for a darkroom.

type of darkroom door consumes considerable space and requires more time to enter and leave. Moreover, the passageways are often quite narrow, and it is difficult to move equipment in and out.

Double doors are used for some darkrooms. The effect is much like that of the common light trap, but allows more space (Fig. 53-21).

Revolving doors are quite effective for darkrooms (Fig. 53-22). They consist of two cylinders, the smaller-diameter one fitting into the larger (Fig. 53-23).

MULTIPLE DARKROOMS

There are at least three kinds of activities performed in darkrooms. They are: (1) processing photographic materials in total darkness, (2) processing photographic materials in red light, and (3) exposing photographic materials with white light. If there is only one darkroom, it is impossible for all three activities to be done at the same time. Many printing plants have divided their darkroom space into several darkrooms so that all activities can be done at the same time. These darkrooms are usually placed adjacent to each other.

DARKROOM CLEANLINESS

Dirt and dust cause some of the greatest problems in the darkroom. A good photographer is constantly trying to eliminate dirt within the darkroom. Dirt and dust can enter from the outside or be formed by dried chemicals in the darkroom.

Fig. 53-22. Revolving darkroom door. (Consolidated International Corp.)

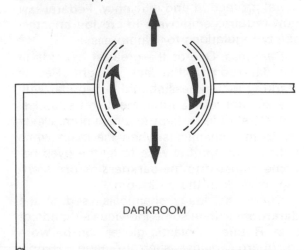

Fig. 53-23. Plan view of a two-opening, revolving, darkroom door.

Keeping a darkroom clean is a continuing process and attention should be given to the problem daily. To make cleaning easier, keep as much equipment off the darkroom floor as possible. Mop the floor frequently, because it collects more dirt than any other place in the darkroom. The installation of a ventilation system that helps control dust entering the darkroom will help keep the darkroom clean (Fig. 53-24). Be sure that the filter in the ventilation system is replaced or cleaned frequently. Fill all light leaks in the darkroom, because dirt and dust can enter spaces that are large enough to permit even small amounts of light to enter. All surfaces should be washed before starting any darkroom work and after finishing work, and it is often necessary to wash the surfaces several times during the work session. Clean up spilled chemicals immedi-

Fig. 53-24. Darkroom ventilator.

ately even if the spill does not interfere with your work at that time.

Most good photographers adhere to a regular routine for darkroom cleanup. Such a routine accounts for items to be cleaned when they *should* be cleaned. Your attitude toward cleanliness will pay many benefits in quality photographic work.

UNIT 54
SAFETY IN THE DARKROOM

Major safety considerations when working in a darkroom include the following points. Observe these at all times for personal protection and efficiency. Federal law now requires employers to provide effective safety regulations for employees.

Darkness. One of the greatest hazards in the darkroom is the lack of light. People working in darkness should be familiar with the location of the equipment and supplies. Activity should be kept to a minimum. Never try to mix chemicals when the main white light is not on. It is wise to let the eyes become adjusted to the darkness before starting to work in the darkroom.

Chemicals. Many chemicals used in the darkroom irritate some individuals' hands or skin. Rubber or plastic gloves can be worn to guard against such irritation. Handle chemicals with care to prevent splashing them into the eyes. Always wash hands

thoroughly as soon as possible after having had them in chemicals.

Moisture. Always clean up moisture from the floors and working surfaces. A moist floor can cause slipping and serious falls. The chance of electrical shock is increased when moisture is present.

Chemical storage. Chemicals should be stored in safe containers where they can be easily reached. Plastic or stainless steel containers are preferred over glass ones because they will not break as easily. Plastic ones are also lighter and easier to handle.

Electrical equipment. All electrical items in the darkroom should be grounded according to the specifications of the manufacturer. Never place electrical equipment near moisture, or where moisture can get into it. *Never* handle electrical equipment when your hands are in liquids, or even when they are wet.

UNIT 55
EXPOSING AND DEVELOPING A LINE NEGATIVE

A *line negative* is a reproduction of line copy. It is produced on film (usually orthochromatic) and is a reversal of line copy. A negative is black in the areas that correspond to the white areas of the copy (Fig. 55-1).

The process of making a line negative consists of exposing the film in a camera and then developing it. The major steps are preparing the darkroom, adjusting the camera, placing the copy in the copyboard, locating the film, developing the film, and cleaning up.

PREPARE THE DARKROOM

Before work is done, the photographer must prepare the darkroom. This activity should be done with the white light turned on. It includes attention to many items.

Surfaces. All dust and dirt must be cleaned from the working surfaces and from the darkroom utensils. Dust can cause pinholes (small holes in the emulsion of the negative). Clean the copyboard and the film holder (vacuum back). Examine the lens of the camera to be certain it is clean. If it is kept covered with a lens cap, it will not require cleaning too frequently. Clean the entire darkroom and camera with a vacuum cleaner periodically. If possible, it should be done weekly.

Sink and chemicals. Place the trays in the sink. They should be slightly larger than the film that will be developed. At least four trays are required: one for the developer, one for the stop bath, one for the fixer, and one for washing. If a sink has a film-washing area, only three trays will be needed. The wash tray should have a supply of fresh running water.

Fig. 55-1. A line negative made from line copy. (Eastman Kodak Co.)

Arrangement of trays. The trays should be arranged so that the film being processed can be moved from the left to the right or vice-versa without having to move it over another tray. The developer tray should be closest to the camera to eliminate extra movement. The sequence of tray placement should be (1) developer, (2) stop bath, (3) fixer, and (4) wash. Fig. 55-2 shows the proper order.

Developer tray. Developer is prepared by mixing amounts of *Part A* and *Part B* just before developing the film. As mentioned in Unit 52, developers have a very short period of usefulness once they have been mixed. Because of this, actual mixing of the two parts should be delayed as long as possible.

To insure that the photographer has the maximum amount of time to use the developer, he should follow a simple procedure. Measure the correct amount of Part *A* of the developer in a graduate and pour it into the developer tray. Clean out the graduate with water and measure the same amount of Part *B*. Do not pour the quantity of Part *B* into the tray until you are ready to develop the first piece of film. The developer should be discarded after about one hour of use, or after four or five pieces of film have been

Fig. 55-2. The proper sequence of trays for developing

developed, or when work in the darkroom is completed.

Stop-bath tray. Stop baths can be either clear water or a solution made up of 8 ounces of 28 percent glacial acetic acid with 1 gallon of water. Stop bath liquid should be discarded each time new developer is mixed. *Note:* Glacial acetic acid can cause serious irritation to skin and eyes. Avoid contact with it, and always flush the exposed areas with water immediately if contact is made.

Fixer tray. Fill the fixer tray about ½ to ⅔ full with fixer or hypo. Fixer lasts much longer than the other chemicals. Discard it only when it does not clear (remove the milky, undeveloped areas) the film in approximately 1½ minutes.

Temperature. Place the overflow standpipe (Fig. 55-3) into the sink. Turn on the water to the desired temperature. Permit the water to circulate throughout the development process to maintain an even temperature of the developing solutions.

ADJUST THE CAMERA

Basic camera adjustments are the settings of *time, lens,* and *enlargement* or *reduction.* To insure accuracy, all adjustments should be made while the darkroom white light is on.

Identifying the basic exposure time. Before a line negative can be made, the photographer must establish the limits of the materials and equipment being used. By doing this, the basic exposure time can be established. Variables to be controlled are (1) kind of film, (2) developer, (3) temperature, (4) time, (5) condition of the copy, (6)

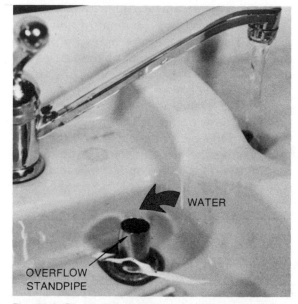

Fig. 55-3. The height of the overflow standpipe determines the depth of the water.

camera lens, (7) f-stop, (8) lighting, and (9) enlargement or reduction of the copy. The photographer attempts to control all of the variables except the kind of film. The following procedure can be used to establish the basic exposure time:

1. Obtain copy with clean, black lines. Try to have both fine and heavy lines.
2. Prepare the darkroom as described above, with the developer temperature from 68° to 72° F. Refer to the instructions of the film manufacturer.
3. Adjust the camera to the same size as the copy or 100%.
4. Place the copy in the center of the copyboard (Fig. 55-4).
5. Place a *cameraman's sensitivity guide* on the copy as near to the center as possible (Fig. 55-5).

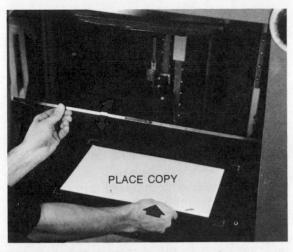

Fig. 55-4. Placing copy on the copyboard.

Fig. 55-5. Camerman's sensitivity guide.

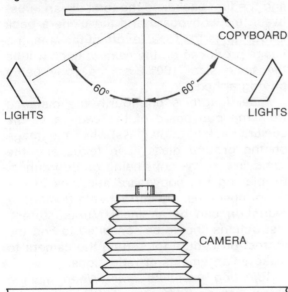

Fig. 55-6. Proper angles for camera lights.

Fig. 55-7. Placing film on the vacuum back.

Fig. 55-8. Camerman's sensitivity guide developed to a number 4 step.

6. Adjust the camera lights, if possible to an angle of 30° with the copyboard (60° with the lens axis). See Fig. 55-6. This angle of light achieves more uniform lighting than an angle of 45°; the angle used by some camera operators.

7. Set the timer to approximately the time necessary for a normal exposure. Consult your instructor or the film instruction sheet for an idea of the correct time.

8. Adjust the lens to about ½ the number of f–stops. If they range from f/8 through f/32, set the lens at f/16.

9. Turn off the white light. Turn on the safelights.

10. Obtain a piece of film of the correct size; turn on the vacuum film holder and place the film on the vacuum back so that it will receive the image from the copy on the copyboard (Fig. 55-7).

11. Turn on the camera and make the proper exposure.

12. Place the exposed film in a light-tight container. An old film box is usually satisfactory.

13. Set the camera time for *twice* the original exposure.

14. Obtain another piece of film and cut one corner off the piece.

15. Make the *second* exposure.

16. Make a *third* exposure that is ½ the original one. Cut two corners off this piece of film.

17. Develop all three pieces of film at the same time. Use the time-temperature method explained later in this unit.

18. Examine the three negatives to identify the one that has most nearly been developed to number 4 on the sensitivity guide. The number 4 step appears black with little black specks in the number 5 step when the film is properly developed to the number 4 step (Fig. 55-8).

19. More accurate test exposures may be obtained in a second effort by using smaller second intervals, following the above-outlined procedure.
20. When the correct exposure time has been determined, record it for further reference.

The above steps should be repeated each time one of the variables changes. If the camera has incandescent lights, repeat the procedure monthly because the bulb strength reduces with time.

Identifying the basic f–stop. The basic f–stop is the f/number that yields a negative that is as nearly like the original copy as possible. Only minimum loss of detail should occur at this f–stop.

Each lens has a best f/number for photographic reproduction. The number varies from camera to camera, but is generally near the middle of the f/numbers on the lens. When the lens is moved one stop, exposure time must be either doubled or halved. When the lens is moved to a number larger by one (smaller opening), the basic exposure time is doubled. If moved to an f/number smaller by one (larger opening), the time must be reduced by one half.

A procedure similar to the one used to identify the basic exposure time is used to determine the basic f–stop:

1. Prepare the darkroom as usual.
2. Adjust the camera and lights as before.
3. Place a piece of copy, similar to the one described earlier, in the center of the copyboard.
4. Set the lens to f/8 and determine the exposure time.
5. Set the timer.
6. Make the exposure.
7. Make other exposures at several of the other f–stops on the lens. Be sure to cut off corners to identify the pieces of film after development.
8. Develop all pieces of film by the time-temperature method described later in this unit.

Examine the film after it is developed. The piece with the sharpest image will identify the most satisfactory f/number for the lens.

Do not be too surprised if little difference can be observed. Often the negative must be magnified before differences can be identified.

Enlargements and reductions. Quite frequently line copy is reduced or enlarged so that the image on the negative is either smaller or larger than the original copy. Most process cameras have gauges for adjusting them to the desired enlargement or reduction. Process cameras are made so that the lens and copyboard can be moved to different positions. The film back is also adjustable on some cameras. The lens moves by expanding or compressing the bellows so that the distance between the lens and the film back is variable.

When the distance between the copyboard and the center of the lens is equal to the distance between the center of the lens and the film back, and the total distance between the copyboard and the camera back is four times the *focal length* of the lens, the image produced on the camera back will be the same size (100%) as the copy being photographed.

Focal length is one-fourth the distance from the copyboard of the camera to the camera back (ground glass) when the image on the ground glass is in focus and the same size as the copy being photographed. By placing the copyboard and lens in different positions, the correct enlargement or reduction can be attained. Manufacturers' instructions should be consulted to find the correct procedure for setting the camera to make enlargements or reductions.

Adjusting exposure time. When making same-size or 100% reproductions, use the exposure time which has been determined by the above procedure. The kind of camera in your darkroom will determine the method to be used to compute new exposure times for enlargements and reductions.

1. The following formula should be used to compute enlargements or reductions when the distance between the copyboard and the copyboard lights remains the same as the distance for a same-size reproduction. The formula is:

$$NT = BE \times EF$$

when;

NT = the new exposure time for the enlargement or reduction,

BE = basic exposure time used to make a same-size reproduction,

EF = exposure factor.

The exposure factor is determined by using the following formula:

$$EF = \frac{(ER + 1)^2}{4}$$

when ER = percentage of enlargement or reduction. Example: Suppose a 75% exposure is to be made of a piece of copy. The basic exposure time is 30 seconds. What is the new exposure time?

First compute EF:

$$EF = \frac{(.75 + 1)^2}{4}$$

$$= \frac{(1.75)(1.75)}{4}$$

$$= 0.77$$

The new exposure time is found by using the formula:

$$NT = BE \times EF$$
$$= 30 \text{ sec.} \times 0.77$$
$$= 23.10 \text{ seconds}$$

The new exposure time is 23 seconds.

2. On some cameras, the lights are not attached to the copyboard. When they are not attached, the distance between the light and the copyboard changes when enlargement or reductions are made. If your camera is of this type, the following formula should be used to obtain the accurate exposure time for an enlargement or reduction:

$$\frac{OT}{(OD)^2} = \frac{NT}{(ND)^2}$$

when;

OT = old exposure time (time obtained from formula #1).

NT = new exposure time,

OD = old distance of the lights to the copyboard,

ND = new distance of the lights to the copyboard.

Example: Assume the distance of lights from the copyboard for the basic exposure (100%) to be 15 inches. The new adjustment requires 20 inches between the copyboard and lights. If the original calculated exposure time is 23 seconds, what is the new exposure time?

$$\frac{OT}{(OD)^2} = \frac{NT}{(ND)^2}$$

$$\frac{23}{15^2} = \frac{NT}{20^2}$$

$$225NT = 23 \times 400$$

$$NT = 40.8 \text{ seconds}$$

To be even more precise, the photographer could make an exposure correction to account for the change in the angle of the lights with the copyboard. The calculations for angle change are quite complicated and will not be treated in this book. If you are concerned with the problem, ask a competent authority to identify sources which explain the procedure.

PLACE THE COPY ON THE COPYBOARD

The exposure will be easier and more accurate if copy is properly placed on the copyboard. Most copyboards have targets (guidelines) to assist the photographer in placing the copy in the center (Fig. 55-9).

The guidelines on the vacuum back usually correspond to those on the copyboard. If the copy is located in the center of the vacuum back, the image will be on the negative after development.

The lens inverts the image on the copyboard. The image will therefore be upside down on the ground glass when compared with the copy on the copyboard. If the copy is placed upside down on the copyboard, the image appears rightside up on the ground glass.

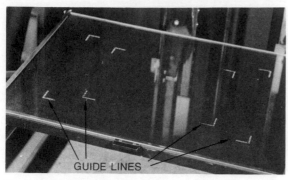

Fig. 55-9. Copyboard guide lines.

LOCATE THE FILM

The film must be located on the vacuum back of the camera so that it will receive the image of the copy on the copyboard. Place the film on the vacuum back while the white light is out.

The *emulsion side* of the film should be toward the copyboard; the base side toward the vacuum back. The emulsion side of film is lighter in color than the base side. If orthochromatic film is used, the emulsion side can be identified by holding the film so that the red safelight reflects on it. It is easy to see the lightest (emulsion) side, which goes toward the copyboard.

An alternate way to find the base side of film is to hold the edge toward the safelight. The emulsion side has a duller finish than does the base side. The photographer can use either method to identify the emulsion side, but it is important to remember that the emulsion side is placed toward the copyboard.

DEVELOP THE FILM

The film has a *latent image* of the copy after it has been exposed. The latent image cannot be seen, but the structure of the emulsion has been changed where the light has exposed the film. The development process changes the latent image to a *visible* one.

Development procedure consists of passing the film through three solutions in a specific sequence: (1) developer solution, (2) stop bath, and (3) fixer.

There are several film development methods, but the three most common methods are: (1) time-temperature, (2) visual inspection, and (3) gray scale.

The *time-temperature* method requires that the photographer develop film for a specific length of time in a developer of a precise temperature. This is recommended by most film manufacturers. The technical data sheets for the film used should be consulted for time and temperature. For those persons who cannot control temperature accurately, the method is somewhat unsatisfactory. Variations also occur because of the short life of the developer.

The *inspection* method is used frequently by experienced photographers. It requires that the film be observed while it is being developed. The photographer must determine when development is completed by observing both sides of the film as the process takes place. The emulsion side will get black first. When the base side is as dark as the emulsion side, the film is developed.

The *gray scale* method of developing film is probably the most satisfactory. It is possible to obtain uniform negatives when there are variations in chemical temperature, chemical contamination, and exposure time.

The gray scale (cameraman's sensitivity guide) is placed on the copy (Fig. 55-10) as near to the center as possible. When it cannot be centered on the copy, it should be placed along the side of the copy (Fig. 55-11). The results will be the same.

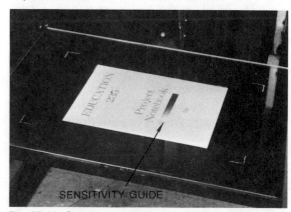

Fig. 55-10. Sensitivity guide placed within the copy.

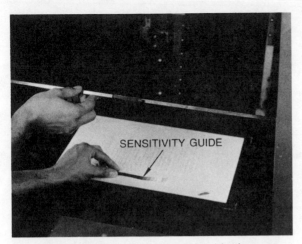

Fig. 55-11. Sensitivity guide placed beside the copy.

Fig. 55-12. A photographer plunging exposed film into the developer.

When the film is developed, the number 4 step should be black, and there should be little black specks in the number 5 step (see Fig. 56-8). The photographer should look at the sensitivity guide rather than at the image on the film. It is recommended that the same conditions used to make the test negatives should also be used for these negatives. When extremely fine line copy is photographed, it is sometimes necessary to develop the negative to the number 3 step. A negative developed to a number 3 is black, with little black specks in the number 4 step.

The development process. The development technique is a variable that affects the consistency and quality of negatives. It is important that the photographer establish a consistent and accurate pattern of film development. He should attempt to develop each piece of film in exactly the same way.

After the film has been exposed, it should be plunged directly into the developer solution as in Fig. 55-12. The emulsion side should be up. It is important that the entire piece of film be covered with developer as quickly as possible. If one portion is not coated with developer, the development of that part of the film will be retarded. The following steps are used by many photographers.

1. Grasp the piece of film by the corner.
2. Lift the front of the developer tray until the developer flows to the back of the tray.
3. Plunge the edge of the film into the developer.
4. Drop the front of the tray as the film is plunged into the liquid. This permits the developer to flow quickly over the entire piece.
5. Begin immediate agitation or movement, and continue until the film is developed. Do not agitate in only one direction because it might cause overdevelopment of one portion of the negative. Alternate lifting the tray corners randomly so that all parts of the negative receive fresh developer (Fig. 55-13).
6. When the film is developed, transfer it quickly to the stop bath. If too much time elapses between the development and the stop bath, the process continues and overdevelops the film.
7. Let the negative remain in the stop bath for approximately one minute. The ex-

Fig. 55-13. Agitating film during development.

posed portions will be black; the unexposed ones will appear milky.
8. Remove the negative from the stop bath and allow the solution to drip from it.
9. Place the film into the fixer and let it remain about 5 minutes. The milkiness should leave after about 1½ to 2 minutes.

10. Wash the negative in clean running water for at least 10 minutes after it is fully fixed. It is better to wash it too much than not enough. If the film is insufficiently washed, a residue will form on it after it is dry.
11. Squeegee the water off the washed film.
12. Hang it in a dust-free place to dry.

UNIT 56
EXPOSURE CALCULATIONS FOR A HALFTONE NEGATIVE

Halftones are reproductions made from continuous-tone copy. They consist of several shades of gray, from black to white. Refer to Unit 43 for examples of continuous-tone copy.

PRINTING CONTINUOUS-TONE COPY

Printing presses do not print more than one shade of a color at a time. If there is black ink on the press, everything will be printed black. It is impossible to print gray and black with a single printing on a press that has been inked with black ink. The picture in Fig. 56-1, however, appears to have black areas and several shades of gray.

An optical illusion is produced by breaking the copy into many small dots. Each dot is printed black; there are no gray dots. In Fig. 56-2 there are small black dots with large white areas around them. There are also several small white dots with large black areas around them. When the picture is observed from a distance, the dots seem to blend to form shades of gray. The areas around white dots appear to be darker than those white areas with black dots.

Fig. 56-1. A typical photograph printed as a halftone.

METHODS OF PRODUCING HALFTONE DOTS

Continuous-tone copy is broken into dots by using one of three methods: (1) the glass halftone screen, (2) the contact screen, and (3) *Autoscreen* film. The first two methods

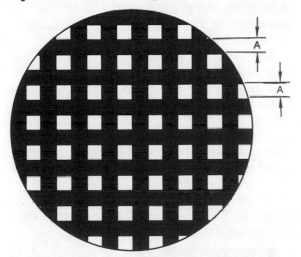

Fig. 56-2. Halftone dots magnified.

Fig. 56-4. Enlarged view of a contact screen.

The glass screen is held a short, but precise, distance from the film. Each small opening serves as an individual lens. When *intense* light passes through the openings, it spreads out and produces large dark areas with small, clear dots. When *dim* light is used, black dots with large clear areas are produced. It is useful to remember that a negative is a reversal of the final print. Black areas on the negative do not print; clear areas do.

Glass screens are expensive and require a rather complicated procedure to produce a halftone negative. They can be obtained with several spacings of lines. The more coarse ruling, such as 65 lines per inch, is primarily used for newspapers or crude kinds of printing. A finer ruling, such as 133 lines per inch, is used for better quality printing, usually on smooth, coated paper.

Contact screens. The majority of halftone negatives produced today are made by using contact screens. These have vignetted (shaded) dots on a flexible, but stable, base (Fig. 56-4). This type of dot is nearly clear in the center, and becomes progressively darker away from the center.

When light with little intensity contacts the screen, it passes only through the clear areas, or through very little of the darker parts. High-intensity light penetrates more of the dark area of the dots and makes the negative darker in these areas.

Fig. 56-3. Enlarged pattern of a glass halftone screen.

utilize a screen in front of the film in a camera; the third is done directly on a special film labeled *Autoscreen Ortho Film.*

Glass screens. The first efficient and effective method to produce halftone negatives used a glass halftone screen. This consists of two pieces of glass bonded together with parallel lines etched into each. The lines are filled with an opaque material. The two pieces are cemented together so that the lines are at right angles to each other. The final screen has many small, clear openings (Fig. 56-3).

Contact screens are much less expensive than glass ones and are much easier to use. Both magenta (purplish-red) and gray screens are available. They come in several sizes and rulings, ranging from 65 to 200 lines per inch. Contact screens must be handled with extreme care because they can be easily scratched or spotted.

Autoscreen film. Autoscreen film has a screen, or grid, built into the film. Halftone negatives are produced without any screen in front of the film. This type of film has an emulsion that is not uniform on the entire piece (unlike regular film). There are thousands of small, light-sensitive areas. Weak reflections from the dark areas of the original copy expose only the most sensitive portions of the film. Strong reflections, resulting from the middle tones and highlights (lightest areas of the copy), expose more of the light-sensitive areas and create larger black ones.

Autoscreen film is available only in rulings of 133 lines per inch. It is possible to obtain coarser or larger dots by enlarging the negative. It requires shorter exposures, and halftone negatives are made without a vacuum back (to hold a contact screen over the film) or a frame (to hold a glass halftone screen in front of the film).

NATURE OF CONTINUOUS-TONE COPY

Continuous-tone copy consists of many shades of gray, including white and black. The lightest tones are called *highlights.* The darkest tones are *shadows.* Gray tones are termed *middle tones.* Characteristics of this type of copy include dark highlights and light shadows, light highlights and faint shadows, dark highlights and dark shadows, or even white highlights and black shadows and a full range of middle tones.

Printing processes are not capable of reproducing a complete tonal range, which is distribution of tones from black to white, including all of the middle tones. If a piece of copy has tones ranging from 0.00 (white) to 2.00 (black), the tonal range will be 2.00 (highlight subtracted from the shadow).

Depending on all conditions, a printer might print a tonal range of 1.30. If this were the case, it would be difficult to faithfully reproduce detail in both the highlight and shadow areas at the same time. Such a problem is overcome by compressing the tonal range.

COMPUTING HALFTONE NEGATIVE EXPOSURES

The *Kodak Graphic Arts Exposure Computer* is an example of a device used by process photographers to obtain the best exposure for continuous-tone copy, regardless of the tonal range. It is used to calculate exposures for negatives made with contact screens or *Autoscreen* film. The primary parts of the computer are the *Reflection Density Guide* and the *Exposure Computer* (Fig. 56-5). An exposure computer must be available for figuring out the best exposure for many different situations.

The exposure computer is calibrated, by test negatives, to the specific conditions and equipment in the printing plant and darkroom. It can then be used without change until these factors alter. Some conditions to be controlled for the test exposure and all succeeding ones based on it are the camera lens, screen, lighting, film, type of developer, temperature, development time, and agitation of the developer. When any of these change, the calibration procedure must be repeated.

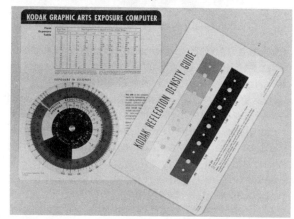

Fig. 56-5. Exposure computer and reflection density guide.

CALIBRATING THE COMPUTER

The exposure computer is calibrated by making a two-part test negative. The first part calibrates the *main* exposure; the second, the *flash* exposure. The following procedure gives accurate results.

To make the main exposure on the test negative:

1. Place the reflection density guide on the copyboard of the camera as shown in Fig. 56-6.
2. Adjust the camera to make the same-size reproduction (100%).
3. Adjust the lens opening to f/16.
4. Place an 8 x 10-inch piece of film (or larger) on the vacuum back of the camera. The white light must be off.
5. Cover the film with a contact screen.
6. Cover a 1-inch wide strip on one edge of the film, using opaque card stock.
7. Make an exposure of the reflection density guide through the camera lens. The exposure time should be 10 to 12 times longer than a normal line exposure.

Make the flash exposure on the test negative.

1. Set up a lamp for flashing the negative. A satisfactory arrangement is a safelamp with a Wratten Series 00 filter and a 7½-watt frosted bulb. Place it 6 to 8 feet from the camera back (Fig. 56-7).
2. Cover the portion of the film that received the main exposure. Move the piece of card stock down about ½ inch for each flash and count the number of flash exposures for later reference (Fig. 56-7).

Process the test negative.

1. Set up the chemicals as for making a line negative.
2. Check the developer temperature for 68° F. A different temperature can be used, but all future halftone negatives must be developed at the temperature used for the test piece.
3. Develop the test for 2¾ minutes with continuous agitation.

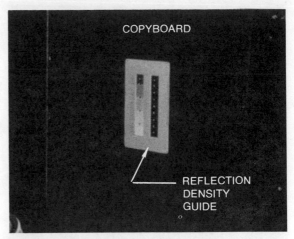

Fig. 56-6. Reflection density guide on the camera copyboard.

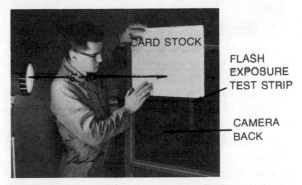

Fig. 56-7. Photographer making test flash exposures. (Eastman Kodak Co.)

Examine the test negative.

1. Place the dry test negative on a clean light table.
2. Use either a linen tester or a magnifying glass to examine the portion of the test negative that contains the reflection density guide.
3. Examine the highlight end of the gray scale (lightest portion), which is the darkest part of the test piece. No dots should appear in the 0.00 step of the gray scale. If there are dots, make the negative again, using a longer exposure.
4. Identify the step which has the most normal highlight dots. In Fig. 56-8, step 0.20 has these dots.
5. Examine the shadow dots. There should be none in the 2.00 step. If there are, make a new negative with a shorter exposure.

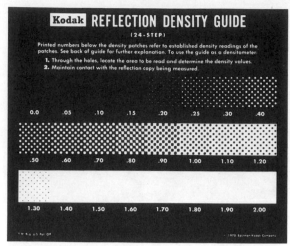

Fig. 56-8. Test negative of a reflection density guide. This is what should be seen when examining the test negative. (Eastman Kodak Co.)

6. Identify the step which produces a good shadow dot. In Fig. 56-8, step 1.30 gives the best one.
7. The difference between the best highlight dot and the best shadow dot is the *basic density range*. In Fig. 56-8, this is 1.30 minus 0.20 = 1.10.

Note that often the best dots for highlights and shadows may occur between steps. When this happens, estimate the correct density.

Set the computer.

1. Rotate the dials on the computer so that the same-size magnification (100%) is next to the lens aperture opening number of f/16 (Fig. 56-9).
2. Hold the bottom dial of the computer in place. Rotate the top red dial so that the highlight density value is next to the exposure time of the main exposure of the test negative. Fig. 56-10 shows that the density value of 0.20 is next to the time of 20 seconds.
3. Tape the two dials together. The computer is now calibrated and ready to use.

Determine the basic flash exposure.

1. Examine the edge of the test negative where the flash exposures were made.
2. Identify the exposure that produced the most normal shadow dot. Compare the best shadow dot from the gray scale with the flash exposure.

LENS OPENING & MAGNIFICATION

Fig. 56-9. Magnification and lens opening set next to each other. (Eastman Kodak Co.)

EXPOSURE TIME & HIGHLIGHT DENSITY

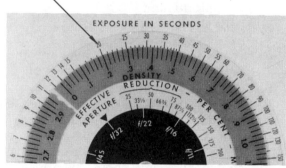

Fig. 56-10. Test exposure highlight density placed next to the time required to make the test exposure. (Eastman Kodak Co.)

3. Note the exposure time required to produce this dot formation. It is the *basic flash exposure.*

USING THE COMPUTER

The test exposure settings have established the working conditions for making halftone negatives with the *Kodak Graphic Arts Exposure Computer.* It can be used without change as long as the conditions of the test negatives are not altered. Use the following procedure to calculate exposure times for making halftone negatives on the process camera.

Determine the copy density range.

1. Examine the piece of copy to identify the highlight and shadow areas. Highlights are the lightest areas, shadows are the darkest.
2. Place the reflection density guide over the copy (Fig. 56-11). Compare the

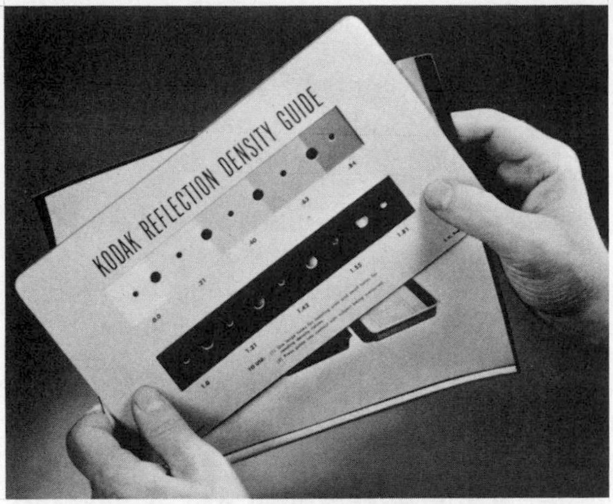

Fig. 56-11. Comparing the reflection density guide to a photograph. (Eastman Kodak Co.)

gray scale with the copy. Record the values.

3. Subtract the highlight density from the shadow density. This value is called the *copy density range.*

Determine the main exposure.

1. Rotate the dials of the computer until the magnification or reduction is opposite the lens opening to be used for the main through-the-lens exposure.
2. Identify the highlight density value obtained from the copy.
3. Read the number that is next to the highlight density. It will be the main exposure time in seconds.

Determine the flash exposure.

1. Subtract the basic density range, obtained from the test negative, from the copy density range. This value is the excess density range.
2. Locate this value on the top row of the Flash Exposure Table above the exposure computer (Fig. 56-12).
3. Identify the basic flash exposure in the left column (Fig. 56-13) of the Flash Exposure Table. This is the value obtained from the flash exposure of the test negative.
4. Read down from the Excess Density Range value and to the right from the Basic Flash Exposure value. This number is the *flash exposure* for the particular piece of continuous-tone copy.

Flash Exposure Table

Basic Flash Exposure in Seconds*	Flash Exposure Times in Seconds for Excess Density Range								
	0	0.1	0.2	0.3	0.4	0.5	0.6	0.8	1.0
16	0	3½	6	8	9½	11	12	13½	14½
18	0	4	7	9	11	12	13½	15	16
20	0	4	7½	10	12	13½	15	17	18
22	0	4½	8½	11	13	15	16½	18½	20
24	0	5	9	12	14½	16	18	20	22
26	0	5½	10	13	15½	17½	19½	22	23½
28	0	6	10½	14	17	19	21	23½	25
30	0	6½	11	15	18	20½	22½	25	27
35	0	7	13	18	21	24	26	29	32
40	0	8	15	20	24	27	30	34	36
45	0	10	17	23	27	31	34	38	41
50	0	11	19	25	30	34	38	42	45
55	0	12	20	27	33	37	41	46	50
60	0	13	22	30	36	41	45	50	55
70	0	15	26	35	42	48	53	59	63
80	0	17	30	40	48	54	60	67	72

*Flashing-lamp arrangements which give basic flash exposures of less than 16 seconds are not recommended unless accurate timing devices are used, in which case this table can be expanded easily. For example, the times for 14 seconds' basic flash would be ½ those in the 28-second row; the times for 10 seconds' basic flash, ½ those in the 20-second row, etc.

Fig. 56-12. Excess density range values are on the flash exposure table.

Flash Exposure Table

Basic Flash Exposure in Seconds*	Flash Exposure Times in Seconds for Excess Density Range								
	0	0.1	0.2	0.3	0.4	0.5	0.6	0.8	1.0
16	0	3½	6	8	9½	11	12	13½	14½
18	0	4	7	9	11	12	13½	15	16
20	0	4	7½	10	12	13½	15	17	18
22	0	4½	8½	11	13	15	16½	18½	20
24	0	5	9	12	14½	16	18	20	22
26	0	5½	10	13	15½	17½	19½	22	23½
28	0	6	10½	14	17	19	21	23½	25
30	0	6½	11	15	18	20½	22½	25	27
35	0	7	13	18	21	24	26	29	32
40	0	8	15	20	24	27	30	34	36
45	0	10	17	23	27	31	34	38	41
50	0	11	19	25	30	34	38	42	45
55	0	12	20	27	33	37	41	46	50
60	0	13	22	30	36	41	45	50	55
70	0	15	26	35	42	48	58	59	63
80	0	17	30	40	48	54	60	67	72

*Flashing-lamp arrangements which give basic flash exposures of less than 16 seconds are not recommended unless accurate timing devices are used, in which case this table can be expanded easily. For example, the times for 14 seconds' basic flash would be ½ those in the 28-second row; the times for 10 seconds' basic flash, ½ those in the 20-second row, etc.

Fig. 56-13. Basic flash exposure is located on the flash exposure table.

EXAMPLES

Some examples are given of ways that the computer can be used to calculate exposure times for making halftone negatives. Study each one carefully and make the calculations for the *main* and *flash* exposure for each example.

Standardization of the computer. Assume that a test exposure of the reflection density guide revealed the following: (1) the best highlight dot was found in step 0.20, (2) the best shadow area dot was identified in step 1.40, (3) the basic density range is 1.40 minus 0.20 or 1.20, (4) the test exposure of the reflection density guide was made for 30 seconds with a lens opening of f/16 and a 100% magnification, and (5) the basic flash exposure was found to be 35 seconds.

Example 1.

A photograph was compared with the reflection density guide and the highlight was 0.25 and the shadow density was 1.40. The lens opening for the exposure was to be f/16 and the magnification was to be 100%. Assume that the photograph is to be printed so that the highlights appear to have a 0.00 highlight density.

Findings:

Main exposure time	34	seconds
Shadow density	1.40	
Highlight density	0.25	
Copy density range	1.15	
Basic density range	1.20	
Excess density range	-0.05	
Flash Exposure Time	0.00	seconds

The main exposure time was calculated by rotating the dials until the lens opening (f/16) was next to the magnification (100%). Exposure time was the number, in seconds, that is next to the highlight density of 0.25. In this case the exposure time was about 34 seconds.

The flash exposure time was found by computing the excess density range or the difference between the basic density range and the copy density range. This meant that the density range of this piece of copy was well within the limitations of the equipment and conditions. Therefore, *no* flash exposure was required to produce the dot formation in all of the areas of the photograph.

Example 2.

A piece of continuous-tone copy has a highlight density of 0.00 and a shadow density of 1.70. If the exposure is to be made with a lens opening of f/16 and a magnification of 100%, what are the exposure times?

Findings:

Main exposure time	19	seconds
Shadow density	1.70	
Highlight density	0.00	
Copy density range	1.70	
Basic density range	1.20	
Excess density range	0.50	
Flash exposure time	24	seconds

The main exposure time was calculated in exactly the same way as for Example 1, except that the highlight was 0.00 and was used instead of 0.25. If the highlight had been 0.15, the main exposure time would have been about 26.5 seconds.

The excess density range was found to be 0.05 for Example 2. This meant 0.50 distance of the copy density range would contain no dots if only one or the main exposure was made. By making a flash exposure of 24 seconds the copy density range was compressed so that detail would appear in shadow areas.

The flash exposure time was obtained by reading across from the left column (basic flash exposure in seconds), and down from the top row (flash exposure time in seconds for excess density range).

Example 3.

Use the same piece of copy as was used in Example 2, but with a lens opening of f/11 and a magnification of 150%.

The *new main exposure* time was found by rotating the dials until f/11 was next to 150%. The time next to 0.00 density is the new exposure. Because the excess density range remained the same, the flash exposure time remained unchanged.

Calculating exposure times for Autoscreen film. The exposure computer can also be used to compute halftone exposure times for *Kodalith Autoscreen* film. The computer is calibrated in exactly the same procedure as was used for contact screen halftone negatives, except that no screen is used and an *OA* filter is used in the flashing lamp. Exposure time will be somewhat less than that for halftones made with contact screens.

UNIT 57
EXPOSING AND DEVELOPING A HALFTONE NEGATIVE

The process of exposing and developing halftone negatives is quite different than working with line negatives. Photographers must give much more attention to the details or there will be a loss of valuable time and materials. While most people agree that photographs add interest to printed material, poorly produced halftones will significantly reduce the value of the printed item. For the purposes of this unit, it is assumed that halftone negatives will be produced by using a contact screen.

DETERMINE THE EXPOSURE TIMES

Exposure times, which will be used to photograph the halftones, can be determined in a lighted room. In fact, it is best to determine the essential exposure information for all photographs before entering the darkroom. These calculations should be written on a piece of paper and attached to the photograph. The information that should be determined for the exposure includes the magnification, highlight exposure, flash exposure, and lens opening (not needed when a photographer uses a constant lens opening).

Unit 56 was concerned with standardizing the *Kodak Graphic Arts Exposure Computer* so that it can be used to achieve consistent results. Once the computer has been accurately calibrated, it is quite simple to determine exposure times for making a halftone from continuous-tone copy. The beginner should review the procedure used to calibrate the computer in Unit 56.

The photographer should examine the copy to identify the highlight areas and the shadow areas. Remember that the lightest areas of the copy are the highlight areas and the darkest areas are the shadow areas. Highlight and shadow areas are identified in the photograph in Fig. 57-1.

Compare the reflection density guide with the areas identified as highlights and shadows as shown in Fig. 57-2. This comparison should permit you to determine the exact density (lightness or darkness) of the highlight and shadow. The number next to the area that corresponds to the density of each should be recorded.

When the copy has been compared with the guide, the photographer should determine the enlargement or reduction of the copy. This specification is often given by the customer, but the photographer will often

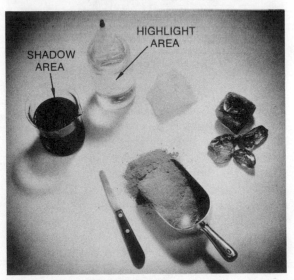

Fig. 57-1. A typical photograph.

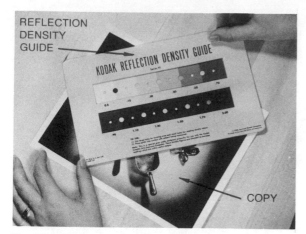

Fig. 57-2. Compare the guide to the photograph to get the highlight and shadow densities.

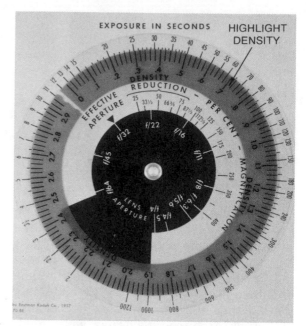

Fig. 57-4. Highlight density found from the copy.

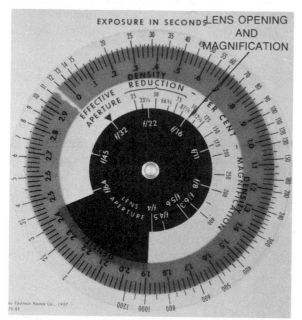

Fig. 57-3. Proper lens opening and magnification in position.

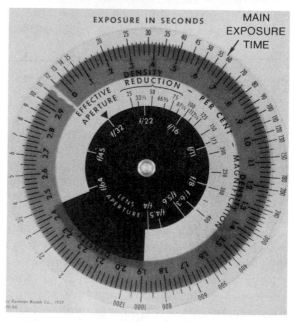

Fig. 57-5. Main exposure time is across from the highlight density.

have to make the calculation. The lens opening that will be used to make the exposure should also be noted.

The actual exposure times are found by using the *Kodak Graphic Arts Exposure Computer.* The lens opening for the exposure should be placed next to the magnification on the circular scale of the computer (Fig. 57-3). For example, you will note that the lens opening of f/16 is next to the magnification of 100%. The highlight density determined by comparison with the reflection density guide can be found on the

scale as indicated in Fig. 57-4. The main exposure time is read from the outside scale (Fig. 57-5). The *highlight exposure time* is found by reading the number of seconds adjacent to the highlight density of the copy. If the highlight density on the photograph in Fig. 57-1 was 0.10, the highlight exposure time would be 60 seconds.

BASIC FLASH EXPOSURE COLUMN

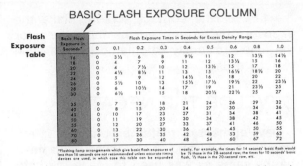

Fig. 57-6. Locate the basic flash exposure in this column.

EXCESS DENSITY RANGE FACTORS

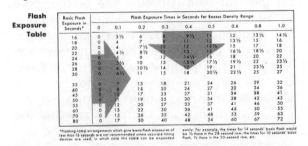

Fig. 57-7. Locate the excess density range in this row.

Fig. 57-8. Read across from the basic flash exposure column and down from the excess density range row.

The flash exposure time is also calculated from the Flash Exposure Table located at the top of the computer. Determine the *excess density range* (copy density minus the basic density range) as described in Unit 56. Locate the basic flash exposure time, determined by calibrating the computer, in the left column of the table (Fig. 57-6). Find the excess density range on the top row of the table (Fig. 57-7). Identify the flash exposure by reading down from the excess density range row and to the right from the basic flash exposure column (Fig. 57-8). If the basic flash exposure time was 35 seconds and the excess density range was 0.40, the correct flash exposure will be 21 seconds.

PREPARING THE DARKROOM

The darkroom must be prepared to precisely duplicate the conditions used to calibrate the exposure computer. If some of the conditions are different, the resulting negatives will not be accurate. Arrange the process trays as usual. Prepare the developer so that it has exactly the same temperature as was used to make the test negative. Time can be saved by keeping a quantity of developer at the correct temperature, because the developer should be changed more frequently for halftone negatives than for line negatives. The trays for the stop bath, fixer, and wash should also be prepared at this time. Most photographers keep a thermometer in the developer at all times so that they can constantly see whether the temperature is correct.

PREPARE THE CAMERA

Preparing the camera for making halftone negatives is similar to the procedure used for making line negatives. Special attention must be given to cleanliness. Dirt causes pinholes on negatives and pinholes on halftone negatives are much more difficult to work with than those on line negatives. The copyboard, timer, lens opening, and light angles should be checked to be sure that they are properly adjusted. When the camera is clean and properly adjusted, place the copy into the copyboard as was done for a line negative. Be sure to place a cameraman's sensitive guide (gray scale) next to the copy.

SET UP THE FLASHING LAMP

The setup for the flashing lamp must be the same as was used to make the flash exposure for calibrating the exposure computer (Unit 56). An *00* filter should be used when making halftones using a contact screen, and an *OA* filter should be used with *Autoscreen* film. Be sure that the timer is set for the flash exposure determined by the computer. The photographer should also be sure that the flash lamp is accurately placed with respect to the camera back.

MAKE THE MAIN EXPOSURE

The main exposure is made with the dark-room safelight on. Place the piece of film on the vacuum back with the base (shiny or dark side) side against the vacuum back. The film must be the same kind of film that was used to make the test exposure discussed in Unit 56. When the film is in place, turn on the vacuum. Place the contact screen over the film so that the screen is against the emulsion side of the film. The screen should be at least one inch larger than the film on all sides. Be extremely careful to handle the screen so that no fingerprints are placed on it (Fig. 57-9). Smooth the screen over the film with a roller. Care should be taken not to scratch the screen. When the film and screen are in place, move the vacuum back into place and make the exposure.

MAKE THE FLASH EXPOSURE

Not all halftone negatives require a flash exposure. Only those negatives with a copy density range that exceeds the basic density range require flash exposure. Open the vacuum back of the camera but do not disturb

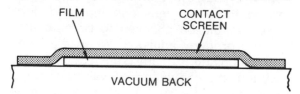

Fig. 57-9. Place the contact screen over the film.

the film or the contact screen. Make the exposure by turning on the flash lamp for the time previously calculated for the flash exposure time.

DEVELOP THE NEGATIVE

Development of halftone negatives is extremely critical and the process used must be the same as was used to make the halftone test exposures. The photographer should constantly try to standardize his procedure to achieve accuracy and consistency.

After the exposure has been made, carefully remove the contact screen and return it to its protective container. Turn off the vacuum and remove the exposed piece of film. Hold the film by the corners to prevent fingerprints from getting on the image portion of the film. Place the film in the developer for the same amount of time as used for the test strip. Be sure the temperature of the developer is accurate, and agitate the film continuously. Move the negative to the stop bath. Let the stop bath drip from the film before moving the negative to the fixer. Let the negative remain in the fixer for about five minutes before turning on the white darkroom light. Check to see that the film has cleared (the milky appearance disappeared). Permit the negative to wash in running water for at least 15 minutes. The excess water can be removed with a squeegee. Hang the negative in a dust-free area until it is completely dry.

UNIT 58
EXPOSING AND DEVELOPING *AUTOSCREEN* FILM

Halftone negatives can be produced without using a screen in front of the film. This is done by using *Kodalith Autoscreen Ortho Film.* The screen effect is manufactured into the emulsion of the film. The exposure is made exactly the same way as a halftone negative is made with a contact screen, except that no screen is used. Many photographers prefer to use this kind of film because they do not have to bother with a screen.

A *Kodak Graphic Arts Exposure Computer* must be calibrated for use with *Autoscreen* film to achieve consistency. As in making negatives with a contact screen, the conditions used to calibrate the computer must be duplicated when making a halftone negative with *Autoscreen* film.

MAKE THE EXPOSURE

The copy should be examined and compared with the reflection density guide to determine the highlight and shadow densities. Determine the main exposure (highlight exposure) and the flash exposure. Compute the flash exposure by determining the excess density range. This is the difference between the copy density range and the basic density range. Using the excess density range, determine the flash exposure for the halftone negative. The film should be held in the vacuum so that the base or shiny side of the film is against the vacuum back. The exposure and development procedure is exactly the same for *Autoscreen* film as was used to make a contact screen halftone. Fig. 58-1 shows a photographer developing a halftone negative in the darkroom.

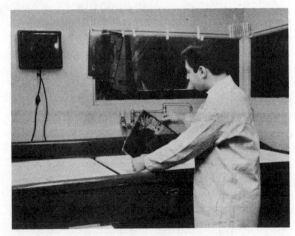

Fig. 58-1. A photographer processing a halftone negative in the darkroom. (nuArc Company, Inc.)

TONE REPRODUCTION

In comparing the process utilizing *Autoscreen Ortho Film* with most other methods of making halftones it will be found that the highlight contrast is higher and the shadow contrast lower. Most pictures require good highlight separation, and this film is made for the purpose of producing negatives with excellent highlight contrast. In the few instances where shadow detail is of utmost importance, conventional halftone methods are more satisfactory. For optimum negative quality with *Autoscreen Ortho Film,* the picture material should have good tone separation throughout the entire tonal range.

The film is designed for photolithography; contrast of the negatives is too high for use in the photoengraving process. It is primarily intended for copying black-and-white or colored photographs, paintings, continuous-tone sketchs, etc.

UNIT 59
MAKING A FILM POSITIVE

A film positive is the opposite of a film negative. The black areas of a film negative correspond to the white ones of the copy, and the clear ones of the negative represent the black areas of the copy (Fig. 59-1). A film positive is clear in the areas that correspond to the white areas of the copy, and black in the areas which represent the black ones of the copy (Fig. 59-2).

An easy way to produce a film positive is to make a contact print of a negative on a piece of film. The negative is held in tight contact with a piece of film by using a contact printer or contact printing frame (vacuum printing frame) and a light source (Fig. 59-3). A light source similar to the one shown in Fig. 59-4 is used to make the exposure.

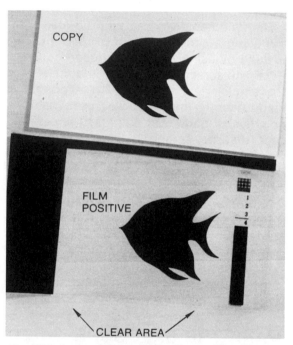

Fig. 59-2. A piece of copy and a film positive. The positive was made from the negative in Fig. 59-1.

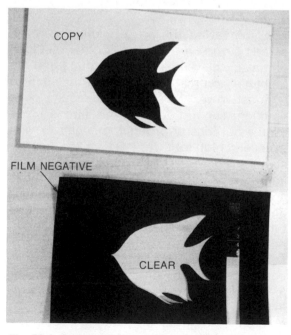

Fig. 59-1. A piece of copy and a negative of it.

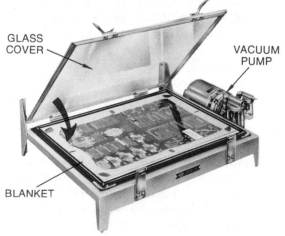

Fig. 59-3. A vacuum printing frame. The frame can be used for making printing plates as well as film positives.

Fig. 59-4. A point source light used to make a film positive.

MAKE THE FILM POSITIVE

A film positive is made from a film negative by making a contact print on a piece of film. The preparation for making a film positive is the same as for making a negative. All of the lights should be turned off except the darkroom safelights. Place a piece of film at least as large as the image on the rubber blanket of the printing frame. Some photographers place a heavy black piece of paper under the piece of film. The base side of the piece of film should be toward the rubber blanket. The film negative should be placed over the piece of film with the negative emulsion side against the film. Close the cover, turn on the vacuum, and make the exposure. After the exposure is made, the film should be developed as if it were a conventional line negative.

UNIT 60
PROCESS-COLOR REPRODUCTION

Process-color reproduction is created by producing an optical illusion for the observer. By printing three or four colors over each other, the viewer sees what appears to be a continuous-tone color print. What is actually seen are three of four colors which have been printed over each other. Fig. 60-1 illustrates how the combination of certain colors can produce other colors. In practice, magenta, cyan, and yellow are used to print process color prints. Black is often used in combination with these colors to add more detail to the print.

Process color printing is much more complicated than black-and-white halftone photography. It often requires equipment and materials usually not found in school or small graphic arts laboratories. New photographers are encouraged to attempt to make color separations and should not be-

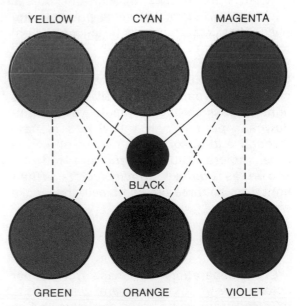

Fig. 60-1. By printing three colors, it is possible to produce other colors.

come discouraged if the quality of the results does not meet the standards of commercial prints. Manufacturers offer several excellent publications which will permit you to study the color separation procedure in much more detail.

COLOR

Objects appear to have color because the human eye is sensitive to various wavelengths of light. White light is said to contain all of the wavelengths of all light. It is believed to have the three primary light colors of blue, red, and green. When white light strikes an object, the object can absorb all of the light, reflect all of the light, or reflect certain wavelengths and absorb other wavelengths. If all of the white is absorbed, the object appears black. When all of the wavelengths are reflected (bounce off the surface), the object appears to be white. Those objects that absorb some of the light waves but reflect others appear to have the color of the combined wavelengths (colors) which are reflected. For example, in Fig. 60-2 the object has a red color because the other wavelengths (colors) are absorbed by the object and the wavelength for red is reflected from the object.

When light passes through an object, such as a window, the same principle applies. That is, certain rays of the white light are permitted to pass through. They are not absorbed. Those rays that do not pass through are absorbed by the material. A clear windowpane permits all of the white light to pass through, while a yellow windowpane permits only yellow rays to pass through and absorbs the rays of all of the other colors. Blue, green, and red are known as *additive primary colors*. When light from all three are combined, they make white.

COLOR SEPARATION

Color separations are made from either color *prints* or color *transparencies.* Light is reflected from color prints as shown in Fig. 60-3. Light is transmitted through the trans-

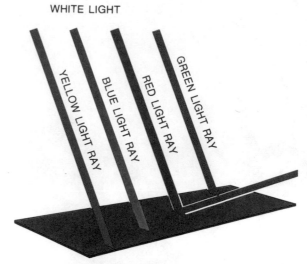

Fig. 60-2. The object *appears* to be red because red light rays are reflected from the surface and other light rays are absorbed by the object.

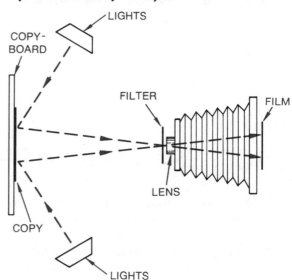

Fig. 60-3. Light is directed at the copy and is reflected toward the film.

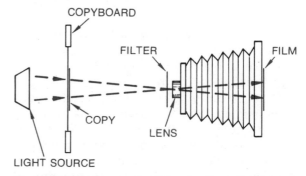

Fig. 60-4. Light passes through a transparency toward the lens and film.

parencies in Fig. 60-4. In either case, the light source used to make color separations must be very nearly the same as true white light.

The process used to make color separations is known as the *subtractive* method. The separation negative is produced by using *filters* which are the same as the additive primary colors of red, blue, and green. Filters work the same as the windowpane described earlier in the unit. When the red filter is placed in front of the camera or sometimes the enlarger lens, it permits all of the red rays of light to pass through the lens, but prevents the blue and the green rays from entering the camera. The separation negatives which are produced by the color-separation process are known as *printers*. There will be cyan, magenta, and yellow printers for *three-color process* printing. *Four-color process* printing requires the use of cyan, magenta, yellow, and black printers.

The *cyan printer* (color-separation negative) is made by placing a *red* filter between the copy and the film. This produces a negative that records all of the red light from the copy. That is, where the copy has red color, the corresponding part of the copy will be black on the negative. The parts of the copy that had red and blue will remain clear on the negative. Thus, when the negative is printed, it should be printed in cyan (a combination of blue and green).

When a *green* is used, the *magenta printer* is produced. The green filter permits only green rays of light to reach the film. Areas of the copy which have green in them pass through the filter, but the red and blue rays are absorbed by the filter. When the negative is developed, the black areas will correspond to the green areas of the copy. If a printing plate is made from the negative, everything will print except the green areas of the copy. The process has *subtracted* the green from the copy. The plate would print all of the areas which correspond to the *red* and *blue* areas of the copy (when red and blue are combined, magenta is formed).

The *yellow printer* is made by using a *blue filter*. The negative records all of the yellow

color on the copy. The red and blue colors do not reach the film. When the film for the yellow printer is developed, the areas of the copy that had green will turn black on the film. The areas of the copy that have green and red will not affect the film and the film will appear to be clear in those areas.

If the copy has a white area, that area will be black on all of the separation negatives. Remember that white light contains all three colors: red, blue, and green. Because of this some light passes through all three filters and exposes all negatives.

In theory, the three printers described should be able to reproduce the same image as the copy. But because the inks used to print the separations are not precise, the gray and black areas appear to be brownish color. Most printers use a fourth printer to produce an image which more nearly approximates the copy. This is called the black printer. There are several methods which can be used to make the black printer. One method that is quite satisfactory and used by many photographers is the *three-filter method*. This method requires that a piece of film (the same kind used to make the other three printers) receive three separate exposures; one each through each of the filters. Each exposure can vary from 30 to 100 percent of the time used to produce the printer, but they usually correspond to the proportion of color in the copy. For example, if a piece of copy has red as the predominate color, the exposures through the green and blue filters will be longer than the exposure through the red filter. Remember that the printer produced by using the red filter will not print any red color. Since the black printer is intended to add detail and contrast, and the major portion of the original is red, the black should have predominant impact on the printers that reproduce the red in the print (magenta printer and yellow printer).

COLOR CORRECTION

If it were possible to obtain process printing inks that would faithfully reproduce the colors to be printed from the color separation, the print would look very much like the

Fig. 60-5. Typical color copy.

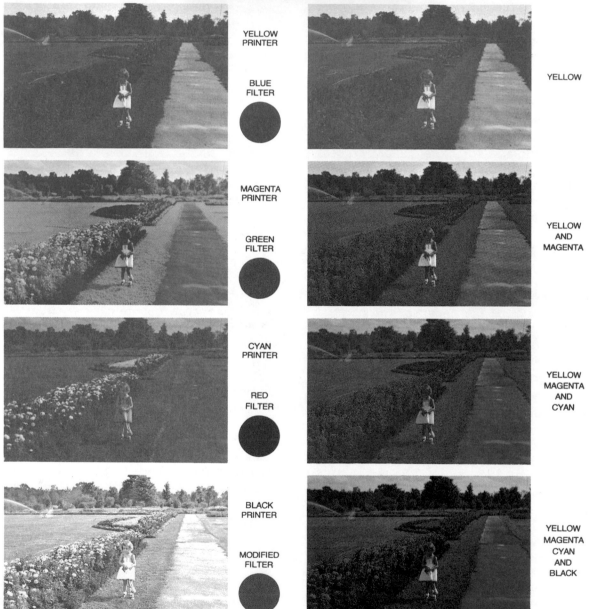

YELLOW
PRINTER

BLUE
FILTER

MAGENTA
PRINTER

GREEN
FILTER

CYAN
PRINTER

RED
FILTER

BLACK
PRINTER

MODIFIED
FILTER

YELLOW

YELLOW
AND
MAGENTA

YELLOW
MAGENTA
AND
CYAN

YELLOW
MAGENTA
CYAN
AND
BLACK

Fig. 60-6. Individual color separations or printers printed in the appropriate color.

Fig. 60-7. Progressive reproductions of the four printers.

original. Because of the impurities in the printing inks it is almost always necessary to correct the separation negatives. This is known as *color correction.*

Color correction can be done photographically or manually or both photographically and manually. It is also possible to electronically color-correct process-color negatives. The manual correcting processes most commonly used are called *dot etching* which is done to the color separations and *re-etching* which is done to the plates.

When color correction is done photographically, it is called *masking.* There are numerous methods used for masking. The student should study the various methods and select the one which is most feasible for the particular situation. Film manufacturers have masking systems which can be purchased to make the whole masking process much simpler. One such system is the *Kodak Tri Mask System.*

Color correcting is often considered to be the most difficult part of the color separation process. It also consumes considerable time and is therefore expensive. Unfortunately, masking will be necessary until it is possible to produce inks which are purer.

SCREENS FOR PROCESS COLOR

Each process color separation must be made into a halftone negative or positive before it is printed. This means that it must be screened. The most popular screening technique for color separations, as for black-and-white work, is to use the contact screen. Gray contact screens must be used to screen process negatives. Magenta screens would work the same as a filter.

It is also important that a screen with a different screen angle is used for each separation. This is necessary to reduce the *moiré* (wavy) pattern to a minimum. When *three-color process printing* is done, the cyan printer should be prepared with a screen angle of 45°, the magenta printer with a screen angle of 75°, and the yellow printer with an angle of 105°. The screen angles for

four-color process printing should be 45° for the black printer, 75° for the magenta printer, 90° for the yellow printer, and 105° for the cyan printer.

FILM FOR COLOR SEPARATIONS

Panchromatic film must be used to produce color separation negatives. This is because panchromatic film is sensitive to all colors. Orthochromatic film, used for making black-and-white halftone negatives, is insensitive to red light rays (reds react as though they were black). This prevents the photographer from obtaining faithful negatives. The use of panchromatic film causes additional darkroom problems because of the kind and intensity of light available. It is best to work in total darkness with panchromatic film.

The film should be processed by using the time-temperature method of development. Data sheets which accompany each package of film give more exact recommendations for processing film.

PROCESS-COLOR PRINTING

Process-color printing begins with an original piece of copy such as that shown in Fig. 60-5. The copy can be a painting, drawing, transparency, or color print. Paintings, drawings, and color prints are reflection copy (light strikes the copy and bounces back to the film). Transparencies are transmission copy (light passes through the copy).

The light from the copy passes through filters before reaching the film. This process of filtering produces three or four different negatives (printers). The negatives are screened to produce halftone negatives. Fig. 60-6 shows the four halftone negatives required to reproduce the original in Fig. 60-5. If each of these negatives is printed progressively, they will appear as shown in Fig. 60-7. When the negatives are printed progressively to yield the final print, they will look like the last element in Fig. 60-7.

UNIT 61
DIFFICULTIES AND ANSWERS IN WORKING WITH NEGATIVES

Process negatives should be examined after processing to be sure that the negatives do not contain defects. The examination should be done on an illuminator or light table. It is also good to have a magnifier available for closer examination. Defects in negatives must be identified so that poor negatives will not be printed and so that the cause of the defect can be corrected before making more negatives. A good quality negative should have black areas which are dense enough to prevent light from passing through, few or no pinholes in the dark areas, transparent areas which are clean and clear, and image edges which are as sharp as the original copy (proportionate to the original copy when enlargements or reductions are made).

Negative difficulties can result from several conditions. Some of the problem areas that should be examined when the photographer identifies faulty negatives are exposure procedures, development procedures, and darkroom cleanliness.

EXPOSURE PROCEDURES

If all procedures are accurate, a properly exposed negative should yield a print that looks exactly like the original copy. Fig. 61-1 shows a correctly exposed negative and a print of it. The print is the identical shape of the original, and it is proportionate throughout.

Underexposure. Fig. 61-2 shows an underexposed negative and a print from the negative. Notice that the printed image is quite different from that in Fig. 61-1. There are numerous ways to identify problems resulting from underexposure. The black areas are not as dense (opaque) as those of a normal negative when examined on a light table. Another common characteristic of an underexposed negative is that the image areas are thicker than those of a normal negative, as can be seen by comparing Figs. 61-1 and 61-2. It is sometimes difficult to distinguish between an underexposed negative and an underdeveloped negative.

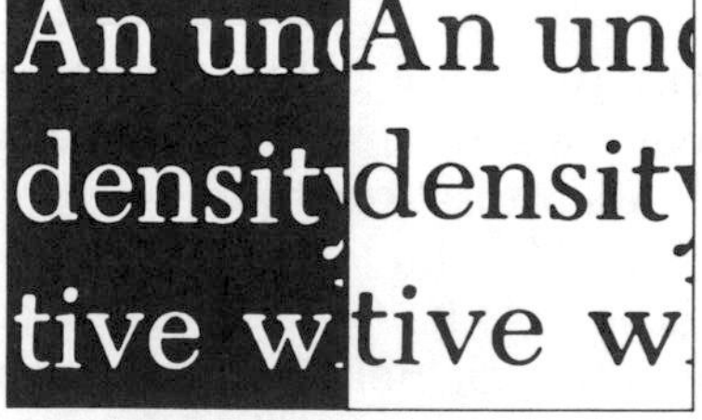

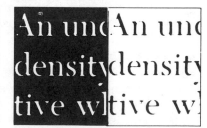

CORRECT EXPOSURE
This segment was exposed correctly. The negative areas are either clearly transparent or densely opaque. Edges are sharp, and detail proportions are true to the original.

Fig. 61-1. A print of a correctly exposed negative.

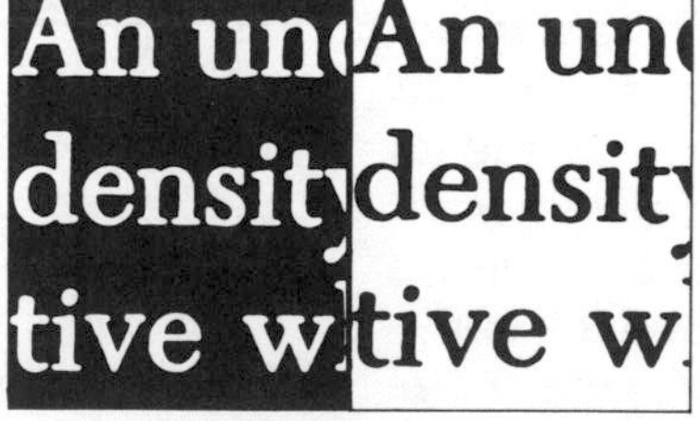

OVEREXPOSURE
This segment was overexposed. Although dense areas are opaque, density appears in some areas which should be clear. A positive made from a negative of this type shows loss of fine detail.

Fig. 61-2. A print of an underexposed negative.

UNDEREXPOSURE
This segment was underexposed. Although transparent areas are clear, the dark areas have low density. A positive made from a negative of this type shows thickening of all detail.

Fig. 61-3. A print of an overexposed negative.

Several circumstances could cause a photographer to obtain underexposed negatives. Some of the causes are faulty lighting with lights possibly aimed incorrectly, incorrect test exposure, inaccurately calculated exposure time, and improper lens adjustment.

Overexposure. Fig. 61-3 illustrates an overexposed negative and a print of the negative. The negative is very dense, but there is a loss of detail in the image areas. The fine line areas tend to close together on an overexposed negative. Some of the causes of overexposure are the direct opposite of the causes of underexposed negatives. That is, incorrect test exposures, incorrectly calculated exposure time, improperly adjusted light, and inaccurate lens opening are some of the possible causes of overexposure.

Accurate light placement is a critical item in properly exposing negatives. This is especially true when large pieces of copy are being photographed. It is possible on large negatives to overexpose one portion of the negative and underexpose another part.

Unfortunately, many photographers consistently produce negatives that are inaccurately exposed. A photographer should constantly make checks on negatives to be sure that they are accurately exposed. He should be especially sensitive to the placement of the lights; if the lights are incandescent, he should be aware of the brightness of the lights.

DEVELOPMENT PROCEDURES

Development problems are frequently the cause of faulty negatives, because there are so many variables that must be controlled. The three most common results of inaccurate development procedures are underdevelopment, overdevelopment, and fogging.

Underdevelopment. An underdeveloped negative is quite similar to an underexposed one. The image is thicker; the dark areas are not very dense. There are excessive pinholes (little clear dots) in the dense areas

of an underdeveloped negative. Some of the causes of underdevelopment are; developer which is too cool, insufficient development time, developer that is inaccurately formulated, and exhausted developer. This condition often causes film to appear brown in color. It is best not to exceed the limits of the developer, as recommended by the manufacturer.

Overdevelopment. An overdeveloped negative appears much like an overexposed one. There is loss of detail in the image areas, and the dark areas are very dense. Some of the causes of an overdeveloped negative are: developer that is too warm, too much development time, insufficient stop-bath time, developer is inaccurately formulated, and excessive agitation.

Fogging. Fogging results in a light coating of silver in the clear areas of a negative. It is usually caused by nonimage light striking the film or by improper development procedures. The results of fogging often resemble overdevelopment or overexposure. Some causes of fogging are: dirty lens, improper safelights, darkroom light leaks, exhausted fixer, and insufficient fixing time.

DARKROOM CLEANLINESS

Probably the greatest difficulties in negatives are pinholes. These are tiny, unwanted clear areas in the dense areas of the negative. While there are several reasons for pinholes, dust and dirt in the darkroom are the primary causes. Dirt and dust can accumulate quickly in a darkroom unless the photographer regularly cleans the area.

It should be remembered that dried chemicals and dust and dirt can produce pinholes. The photographer should clean the copyboard, vacuum back, developing trays, and any surface where the film will be placed before making a negative. The entire darkroom area, including the camera, should be cleaned frequently. Dust can be a particular problem when humidity is too low (air too dry) because the static electricity formed on the film will attract dust and dirt to it. Care should also be taken to see that the copy is as clean as possible.

UNIT 62
STANDARDIZING DARKROOM PROCEDURES

It is important to establish precise procedures to make an exposure, and then to duplicate them each time a negative is made. Probably the greatest single cause of poor or ruined exposures in the darkroom is failure to follow accurately established procedures. The photographer should be machine-like when processing photographic material in the darkroom. Many of these procedures have already been outlined in previous units.

The photographer must be thoroughly familiar with materials and equipment used to accomplish the particular results. Some of the areas which require control are calculating exposure time, preparing materials, preparing the darkroom for exposures, making exposures, processing exposed materials, and cleaning up.

CALCULATING EXPOSURE TIMES

The procedures for calculating various exposure times have been discussed in previous units. They should always be followed precisely because the data used were obtained from making test exposures. Conditions, such as materials and lighting, which prevailed at the time of the test exposure can change, however, and may render the test invalid. Because of this, a periodic check of a test exposure should be made to insure accurate data. A written record of the test data should be kept and made available.

PREPARING MATERIALS

Some materials used in the darkroom are prepared by the manufacturer, others are prepared by the photographer. These materials, like the developer, must be mixed in exactly the same way each time.

Preparation of materials can occur at two different times. First is when the photographer prepares the materials into bulk form, such as by mixing fixer salts with water to obtain fixer solution. The second time is when he prepares the chemicals for use in processing an exposure, as when he mixes Part *A* and Part *B* of the developer. In addition, procedures suggested by the manufacturer should be observed in storing materials.

PREPARING THE DARKROOM

Preparing the darkroom for exposures is extremely important if the activities are to be accomplished efficiently and accurately. The objective is to prepare everything while the room light is on so that no further preparation will be required after the lights are off. This procedure is nearly the same for all activities in the darkroom, and includes precleaning the darkroom, preparing the chemicals and darkroom sink (this varies with the different types of exposures), adjusting the temperature of the chemicals, locating the equipment for convenient use, and preparing and cleaning the camera and other equipment used for making the exposure.

MAKING EXPOSURES

Procedure for making an exposure should duplicate those conditions used in making the test exposure. Any deviations will cause imperfections in the resulting negatives and positives. The photographer should strive to establish the most efficient routine to conserve as much time as possible.

PROCESSING EXPOSED MATERIALS

Processing materials such as film or paper requires the most attention to established procedures because there are so many variables that must be controlled. These variables include developer mixture, development time, temperature, and agitation while developing.

The processing of photographic materials is so critical that many plants have installed expensive machines to do part or all of it. The machine shown in Fig. 62-1 is used for automatically processing film. After the

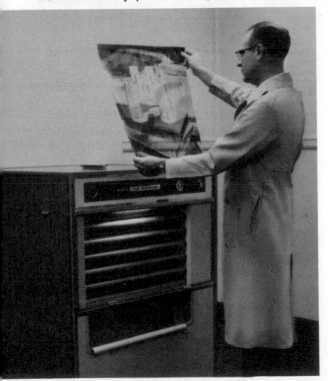

Fig. 62-1. Automatic film processor. (Eastman Kodak Co.)

Fig. 62-2. Mechanical tray rocker. (ByChrome Co.)

Fig. 62-3. Mechanical tray rocker submerged in water to control the developer temperature. (ByChrome Co.)

piece of film is exposed, it is fed into one end of the machine, and in a few minutes it comes out the other end completely processed and dry. These machines are useful in situations that require large production or more precise finished products than can be obtained from hand processing. The machine greatly reduces the chances for human errors in processing.

Fig. 62-2 illustrates an automatic agitation machine. It reduces the chance of poor negatives caused by inconsistent agitation by the photographer. Fig. 62-3 shows the mechanical tray rocker in operation in the darkroom.

CLEANING UP

Cleaning up consists of restoring the darkroom to an organized status and making the utensils ready for the next day. This includes replacing them in the specified storage locations. Photographers sometimes neglect this aspect of their work when they become rushed while meeting production schedules. The result is wasted time if exposures are ruined because of an unclean darkroom.

The darkroom should have a regularly scheduled general cleanup. Many photographers do this on the first day of each week. Dust, dirt, and other foreign matter that have accumulated during the weekend are then eliminated. A problem-free environment insures efficient work results.

UNIT 63

LEARNING EXPERIENCES: PROCESS CAMERA AND DARKROOM PROCEDURES

DISCUSSION TOPICS

1. List the basic parts of a process camera. Briefly describe each part. Which part of a process camera is the most costly?
2. Give another name for the diaphragm. What is the aperature opening? List some diaphragm f–stop numbers. Describe what happens when an f–stop is changed to the next smaller number.
3. How is the film held in most process cameras? Describe how the cameraman views the image to be photographed before the exposure is made.
4. Explain how a gallery camera differs from a darkroom camera. What are the advantages and disadvantages of each?
5. Describe the major differences between horizontal and vertical cameras. List the advantages and disadvantages of each.
6. What is the purpose of the *base* of a piece of film? Name some common materials used to make film bases. Which material is the most popular? How thick is thin-base film? Thick-base film?
7. Explain the purpose of the *emulsion* of a piece of film. What is the function of the *overcoat*? Why is the *antihalation* backing applied to the film? On which side of the film is the antihalation backing applied?
8. What are the two most common kinds of film used for process photography? How do the two kinds of film differ from each other? Which kind of film is most often used to make process negatives? What characteristics of orthochromatic film are advantageous to the photographer and artist? List some possible causes of damage to film.
9. Describe a latent image on film.
10. Identify the purpose of the *developer*. Why are most developers used for process photography made in two parts? What are the two purposes of the *rinse bath* (stop bath)? Describe two different kinds of commonly used stop baths. Give another name for the *fixer*. What is the primary purpose of the fixer?
11. List the features of a good darkroom sink. How does a water mixer assist the photographer? How many processing trays are needed to process or develop film? What are safelights? What is the

most common color for a safelight? With what kind of film should a safelight be used?

12. List the essential mixing, pouring, and measuring utensils required in a darkroom. Describe each.

13. Name the potential hazards of working in a darkroom. Identify some precautions which should be observed to prevent accidents in the darkroom.

14. What are some common kinds of darkroom doors? Give the advantages and disadvantages of each.

15. Where do light leaks most frequently occur in the darkroom? Give the procedure for identifying and repairing darkroom light leaks. What are some ways to keep the darkroom clean?

16. What kind of copy is used to make a line negative? How does a line negative differ from line copy? List the major steps required to make a line negative. Show how the trays should be arranged for making a line negative. Describe the special precautions that should be observed when preparing the developer tray.

17. List the basic camera adjustments for making a line negative.

18. Give the procedure for determining the basic exposure time for a line negative. Describe the cameraman's sensitivity guide. When a negative is developed to a number 4 step on the cameraman's sensitivity guide, how does it appear to the photographer? How often should the basic exposure time for line negatives be determined?

19. Describe the procedure for determining the basic f–stop for a camera. What is the purpose of determining the basic f–stop?

20. Define *focal length.* If the distance between the copyboard and the camera back is 40 inches, and the image on the camera back is in focus, what is the focal length of the camera lens?

21. Give the formula for computing line exposures when the lights remain the same distance from the copyboard. If a 130% exposure is to be made of a piece

of copy, and the basic exposure is 32 seconds, what is the new exposure time?

22. Write the formula for determining line exposure times when the distance of the lights from the copyboard change with enlargement-reduction camera settings. If the distance of the lights for determining the basic exposure were 18 inches from the copyboard, and the basic exposure time were 32 seconds, what is the new exposure time for a 75% exposure when the lights are 12 inches from the copyboard?

23. Explain how the copy should be placed on the copyboard. How does the image of the copy appear on the ground glass of the camera? Tell how the placement of the copy on the copyboard affects the placement of the film on the camera back.

24. Name three methods of developing film. What are the advantages and disadvantages of each?

25. Give the procedure for the development process of each of the methods in question 24.

26. What kind of copy is used to make halftone negatives? List some specific examples of kinds of copy that must be printed as halftones. Why is it necessary to make a halftone from these kinds of copy?

27. Describe the appearance of a print made from a halftone negative. Explain how the halftone print appears as though it had shades of gray.

28. Name and briefly describe the three methods used to produce halftone negatives. Which method is most commonly used? Identify two different kinds of contact screens.

29. Define the terms *highlights, shadows,* and *middle tones* with reference to continuous-tone copy. What is meant by *tonal range?*

30. Name the device used to determine halftone exposures. List the two main parts.

31. List the conditions which must be controlled in order to obtain consistent re-

sults when making halftone negatives.

32. List the procedures for making the main calibration exposure and the flash exposure.

33. What is the procedure required to process (develop) the test exposure?

34. When examining the test negative, what would be concluded if there would be small clear dots in the 0.00 step of the *Reflection Density Guide?* Define the term *basic density range.* What are the three primary items of information which should be obtained from the main exposure portion of the test negative?

35. Give the procedure for setting the *Graphic Arts Exposure Computer.*

36. How is the *basic flash exposure* determined from the test exposure?

37. What kinds of information, with reference to making halftone negatives, can be obtained from the *Graphic Arts Exposure Computer?*

38. Define the term *copy density range.* How is it determined?

39. Explain the procedure used to determine the *main exposure* for making a halftone negative from a piece of continuous-tone copy.

40. How is the *flash exposure* determined for a piece of continuous-tone copy? Define *excess density range.*

41. What are the differences in procedure for making halftone negatives using *Autoscreen* film and using a contact screen?

42. Explain the difference between a *film positive* and a *film negative.* What is the procedure for making a film positive?

43. List the qualities of a good negative. What are some of the main kinds of problems which cause negative difficulties? Identify the characteristics of an underexposed negative. What are some of the causes of underexposure? How does an overexposed negative differ from a normal negative?

44. Explain the meaning of the term *underdevelopment, overdevelopment,* and *fogging.* Give the causes of each. How can the cleanliness of a darkroom affect the quality of a negative?

45. Identify the darkroom procedures that should be standardized to achieve consistent-quality negatives.

ACTIVITIES

1. Examine the process camera in your laboratory and identify all of the parts on the camera. Learn how each part functions.

2. Cut a piece of orthochromatic film into six small pieces and perform the following activities. Develop the six pieces of film after performing the activities.

   a. Expose one piece of film to the white light in the room.

   b. Expose one piece of film to the safelights only.

   c. Expose one piece of film to a piece of black-and-white copy with the emulsion side of the film toward the copy.

   d. Expose one piece of film to a piece of black-and-white copy with the base side of the film toward the copy.

   e. Expose one piece of film to red-and-white copy with the emulsion side of the film toward the copy.

   f. Expose one piece of film to copy with blue, green, and yellow images.

   Examine the pieces of film on a light table and discuss the results.

3. Following the procedures given in Unit 54, try to identify and repair light leaks in the darkroom.

4. Establish the basic exposure for making line negatives with your camera. Find the best f–stop for your camera.

5. Calculate the camera setting for a 150% line exposure and make a negative. Make the calculations and exposure for a 50% exposure.

6. Using a contact screen, make a test exposure in your laboratory of the *Reflection Density Guide* for calibrating the *Graphic Arts Exposure Computer.* This can be done several times in small groups of three or four. The results of the groups can be compared after the test exposures are made.

7. Calibrate the computer for making half-tone negatives using the data from the test exposure.

8. Obtain several different pieces of continuous-tone copy and calculate the *main* and *flash* exposure for each. Calculate the exposure times for enlargements and reductions of some of the pieces of copy.

9. Visit a photoengraver or printing plant that has a process photography department. Discuss with the photographer the procedures that he follows to produce negatives. Learn about his work experience and his educational preparation for being a photographer. Prepare a comprehensive report on your findings and present it orally to the group.

Placing an image carrier on
a printing press. (Original Heidelberg)

UNIT 64

INTRODUCTION TO LETTERPRESS IMAGE CARRIERS

Letterpress image carriers are used on presses to reproduce multiple images. The principle of letterpress is *printing from a raised surface;* the image on a letterpress image carrier therefore stands out in relief. The image carrier must be of high quality to obtain good reproductions on paper or other receptors. Several different kinds of letterpress image carriers are used and each is designed for specific pruposes.

BASIC KINDS OF IMAGE CARRIERS

Letterpress image carriers are divided into two major divisions: (1) first-generation originals, and (2) second-generation duplicates.

First-generation originals are image carriers made directly from film negatives and positives which come from original copy (Fig. 64-1). Photoengravings and nonmetallic photosensitive image carriers are produced by using film negatives or positives.

Film negatives or positives are not needed when making electronic engravings. Original copy is scanned by a photographic cell that transposes light rays into electronic signals. This in turn operates a stylus that cuts away the nonreproducing area of the image carrier. This method is fast and economical and is rapidly gaining favor within the graphic arts industry.

Two first-generation original image carriers not shown in Fig. 64-1 are the linoleum and wood-block cuts. These two hand-cut or hand-carved relief image carriers have an important historic background. However, the modern letterpress has no place for hand-prepared image carriers. For the hobbyist or beginning student of graphic arts, though, these two economical materials offer excellent reproduction qualities. The procedure of preparing a linoleum block is outlined in Unit 72.

Second-generation duplicates (Fig. 64-2) include those made from molds or patterns of first-generation original image carriers. The four common duplicates are (1) stereo-

PHOTOENGRAVING

ELECTRONIC ENGRAVING

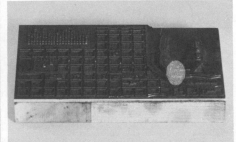
NONMETAL PHOTOSENSITIVE

Fig. 64-1. First-generation original letterpress image carriers.

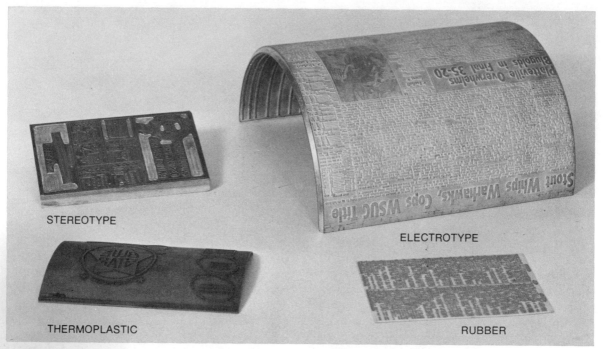

STEREOTYPE

ELECTROTYPE

THERMOPLASTIC

RUBBER

Fig. 64-2. Second-generation duplicate letterpress image carriers.

type, (2) electrotype, (3) rubber, and (4) thermoplastic. These are considered to be the workhorses of the letterpress graphic reproduction method.

Duplicate image carriers are used on presses to save the original image carriers from wear or possible damage. Several duplicates can be made from an original and placed on several presses to speed completion of a production run.

The molds or patterns used to make duplicates can be transported easily; therefore national advertisers mail or ship them to all parts of the country or world. The graphic arts company can then produce the required kind and number of duplicates for its situation.

MATERIALS USED

Several different materials, metallic and nonmetallic, are used to produce letterpress image carriers. The most common metallic materials are copper, zinc, and magnesium. Lead, tin, and antimony are combined to form an alloy for stereotype castings.

Research conducted by several United States and European companies has proven

that all-metal image carriers are not necessary. Nonmetallic and synthetic materials such as plastic and rubber are used successfully to produce original and duplicate image carriers.

Some of the latest image carriers are made with a combination of metallic and nonmetallic materials. A hard plastic reproduction surface laminated to a rubber base provides a cushioning effect for the entire image carrier. This combination of materials allows greater freedom in the receptors upon which graphic images can be reproduced. Other combinations of materials are being developed and will prove useful in the future.

SHAPES OF RELIEF IMAGE CARRIERS

Relief image carriers are prepared in three basic forms: (1) flat, (2) curved, and (3) wrap-around (Fig. 64-3). Nearly any of the metallic or nonmetallic materials can be used to prepare image carriers in these shapes.

The flat shape is the oldest and is still being used. Generally, flat image carriers

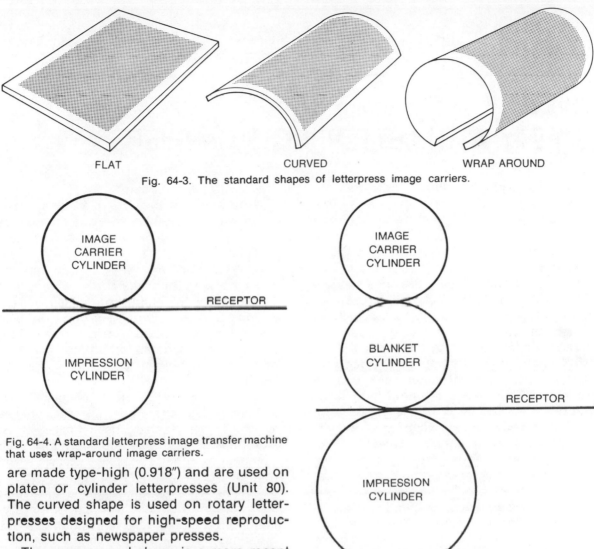

Fig. 64-3. The standard shapes of letterpress image carriers.

FLAT   CURVED   WRAP AROUND

Fig. 64-4. A standard letterpress image transfer machine that uses wrap-around image carriers.

Fig. 64-5. A letterset letterpress image transfer machine that uses wrap-around image carriers.

are made type-high (0.918″) and are used on platen or cylinder letterpresses (Unit 80). The curved shape is used on rotary letterpresses designed for high-speed reproduction, such as newspaper presses.

The wrap-around shape is a more recent development in the area of letterpress. These flexible carriers are used on both the letterpress and the letterset presses. Wrap-around letterpress image carriers print directly on receptors (Fig. 64-4). Wrap-around letterset image carriers print on a blanket, which in turn prints on the receptor (Fig. 64-5). The main difference in the two is that the image is wrong-reading on the letterpress image carrier and right-reading on the letterset image carrier.

HISTORICAL HIGHLIGHTS

Relief image carriers made of wood were used in the Orient during the eighth and ninth centuries, but the art of printing was not practiced in Europe until the fifteenth and sixteenth centuries. The first illustration reproduced for public dissemination was in the *Nuremberg Chronical* (Germany) in 1493.

Until 1880 it was necessary to hand-cut a wood block to reproduce an illustration or picture. At that time the photoengraving method of producing relief image carriers was developed. Today, wood blocks are cut only by the hobbyist or those interested in original graphic art.

UNIT 65
SAFETY WITH LETTERPRESS CARRIERS

Safety is a prime requisite for anyone involved in graphic arts just as in any other laboratory-type activity. Tools and machines with sharp cutting edges must be used with respect and caution. A basic knowledge of how they handle and operate is very important for efficient and safe use. The suggestions given are for your protection. Use your better judgment and common sense in all phases of laboratory activity.

Research conducted by the National Safety Council shows that most accidents in school industrial laboratories occur around 10:00 A.M. There are also more school laboratory accidents on Wednesdays than on any other day, with the exception of the day before and the day after a vacation.

Permission. Request permission from your instructor before operating any equipment.

Clothing and *jewelry.* Secure loose clothing and remove jewelry before operating any machine so that they will not become entangled in a machine.

Safety guards. Check to see that all guards are in place before turning on the power. Equipment with moving parts should always have protective guards.

Air vents. Start exhaust fans before working with chemicals or toxic metals.

Electrical connections. Be certain that all machines are properly grounded and that all electrical connections are in good repair.

Eye and face protection. Wear safety goggles and face shields when operating cutting machines and using chemical solutions.

Floor drain. Floor drains should be located near machines and tanks containing chemical or other solutions. Make certain that all drains are open.

Hand and arm protection. Wear suitable gloves when necessary to protect the hands and arms from cuts, abrasions, heat and chemical burns.

Body protection. Wear rubber aprons when working with chemicals. The aprons should cover the entire front of the body.

Good housekeeping. Keep good order in any laboratory or work area. Never allow waste materials, scrap, or junk to collect on the floor. An unkept laboratory invites an accident.

Materials storage. Store containers of chemical solutions near the floor. They should all be labeled. Place boxes, tools, and other items on storage shelves in such a manner that they are easily accessible and will not vibrate off the shelf.

Illumination. Adequate light is important for safety. An operator who can see everything well is usually able to avoid dangerous situations.

Noise. Excessive noise is a deterrant to safety. An unusually noisy machine should be repaired, replaced, or operated with special care.

Fire. Charged fire extinguishers must always be in operative condition. They should be located where they are easily seen in the laboratory. Be extremely careful when handling flammable materials.

Sharp objects. Handle and use sharp tools with care. Linoleum block cutting-tools are razor sharp and should be handled with special care. Follow all safety precautions when cutting a block. Look where you are walking and avoid bumping into heavy machinery or equipment having sharp corners.

UNIT 66
PHOTOENGRAVINGS

Photoengraving is the art and science of producing original relief image carriers by photographic, chemical, and mechanical means. The first commercial use of photoengravings took place in the United States about 1880. Before this time, illustrations were prepared in wood or metal by hand. The hot-type mechanical composing machine was developed around 1886. With these two inventions, the publishing industry was able to increase production and quality of books, newspapers, and all printed material.

Photoengraving changed little from the 1880s until the middle of the twentieth century. Much tedious and technical hand work was necessary to produce a high-quality image carrier. Modern methods and equipment can be used to produce a quality photoengraving in minutes instead of hours.

Fig. 66-1. A whirler used to distribute and dry the light-sensitive solution placed on photoengraving image carriers. (Master Sales and Service Corp.)

One-step etching has been the key to speed and quality. Before powderless etching, the photoengraver had to etch or cut away the metal several times to remove sufficient quantities of metal in the nonimage areas.

Photoengravings are made from zinc, copper, or magnesium. Zinc is probably the oldest of all photoengraving materials. Magnesium is the latest metal to be used. Copper, because of its fine-grained characteristic, is generally used for halftone engravings. Zinc and magnesium are commonly used for line engravings, but halftones with coarse screens are also suitable for these two metals.

PRODUCING A PHOTOENGRAVING

1. Obtain the illustrations and photographs. Illustrations of solid tones are considered line copy. Photographs are classed as halftone copy (Unit 43).
2. Photograph the copy with a process camera to obtain high-contrast negatives (Units 56, 58).
3. Strip the negatives in their proper position on a flat (Section 11). NOTE: The negatives are turned over to obtain the necessary *wrong-reading* image on the photoengraving.
4. Coat the piece of metal zinc, copper, or magnesium with a light-sensitive solution. This is done in a whirler shown in Fig. 66-1. The light-sensitive solution is poured onto the revolving metal. The turning or whirling action distributes the solution evenly (Fig. 66-2) and a heating element in the whirler dries the light-sensitive solution.

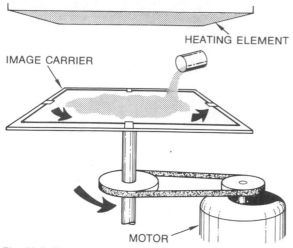

Fig. 66-2. The general operating mechanism of a whirler and the sensitizing procedure for an image carrier.

Fig. 66-3. Exposing the light-sensitive metal through the negatives which contain the images. (Horan Engraving Company, Inc.)

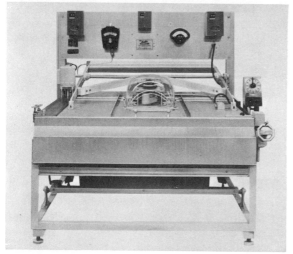

Fig. 66-4. An etching machine used for photoengravings.

Fig. 66-5. An etching machine shown in Fig. 66-4 with the the top open and two image carriers mounted. (Master Sales and Service Corp.)

Presensitized metal that eliminates having to apply the light-sensitive solution just prior to exposure is also available.

5. Place the high-contrast negatives in contact with the metal. Put both items in an exposure frame and subject them to bright light (Fig. 66-3). The light-sensitive solution hardens as the light rays pass through the transparent areas of the negatives.

6. The coated metal is developed after exposure with proper chemicals. Areas subjected to light are retained; the light-sensitive coating on the unexposed areas of metal is washed away. The image is further hardened by chemical means or by heat, which makes it etch-resistant.

7. The metal is now ready for etching. Place it into an etching machine (Fig. 66-4). Clamp it to a base in a horizontal position (Fig. 66-5).

8. Spray or splash the liquid etching solution against the surface of the metal. The nonimage area (that area which is not etch resistant) is washed away, leaving the image stand-out in relief.

9. The next step is to cut away, or rout, the larger nonimage areas of the metal. A radial-arm router (Fig. 66-6) is used for this. This step is necessary because

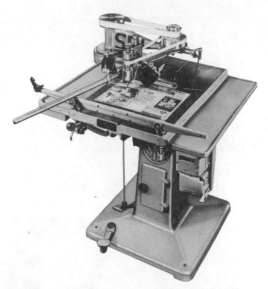

Fig. 66-6. A radial-arm router used to remove large nonimage areas of the photoengraving. (Master Sales and Service Corp.)

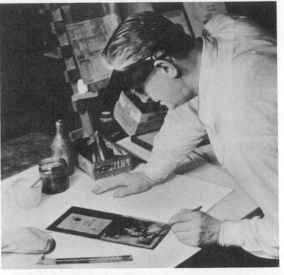

Fig. 66-7. A skilled engraver inspecting and spot etching the machine-made photoengraving. (Horan Engraving Company, Inc.)

larger nonimage areas may reproduce when proofing or printing.

10. The last phase of the production steps is called finishing. A highly skilled engraver inspects the image area. Hand tooling and spot etching improve the final reproduction (Fig. 66-7).

11. The metal, now a relief image carrier, is proofed in a reproduction proofpress. Simulated press conditions help provide for quality control during the press run to follow.

12. Blocking or mounting is done after the proofs have been approved. The metal is fastened to a block of wood or metal which makes it type-high. It is used directly on a press or to prepare duplicate image carriers (Fig. 66-8).

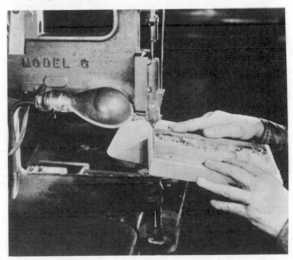

Fig. 66-8. Blocking or mounting the photoengraving to make it type-high. (Horan Engraving Company, Inc.)

UNIT 67
NONMETALLIC PHOTOSENSITIVE IMAGE CARRIERS

Nonmetallic photosensitive relief image carriers have been used commercially only since 1960. Several years of research were needed to perfect materials, primarily plastic, capable of being used to produce image carriers comparable to metal.

Two advantages of using plastic to make original image carriers are: (1) the time-saving factor, and (2) the cost of the material as compared to the cost of copper, zinc, or magnesium materials. An entire original plastic image carrier can be made in less than 20 minutes. This is considerably less time than that required to make metal carriers.

PROCESSING

1. The blank plate must be sensitized (Fig. 67-1). Some brands of plates are made light-sensitive when manufactured.
2. A high-contrast negative is placed in close contact with an unexposed light-sensitive plate (Fig. 67-2). A vacuum frame, a unit used to expose the negative and plate, is used to obtain perfect contact between negative and plate.
3. The plate is exposed through the negative to ultraviolet light (Fig. 67-3). The light striking intended image areas makes the photosensitive layer of the plastic plate insoluble.
4. Unexposed, or soluble, areas are then washed away by a spray of mild etch and water (Fig. 67-4). The etching solution is sprayed against the plastic plate through fine nozzles.

Fig. 67-1. The blank plastic plate must be sensitized in a carbon dioxide atmosphere. (E. I. DuPont de Nemours & Co.)

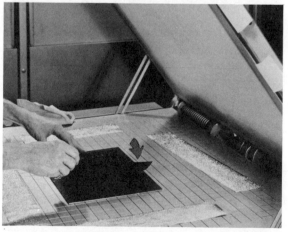

Fig. 67-2. Placing a film negative in contact with the light-sensitive plastic in a vacuum frame. (E. I. DuPont de Nemours & Co.)

5. The plate, now an image carrier, can be installed on a press and copies can be printed (Fig. 67-5).

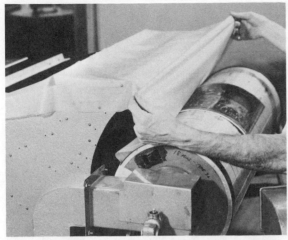

Fig. 67-3. A round plate being prepared for exposure to ultraviolet light. (E. I. DuPont de Nemours & Co.)

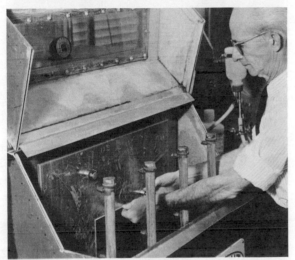

Fig. 67-4. Areas not exposed to light are washed away with a mild etch and water solution that is sprayed onto the plastic. (E. I. DuPont de Nemours & Co.)

THE BASIC LAYERS

There are three basic thicknesses or layers of a nonmetallic photosensitive image carrier (Fig. 67-6): (1) the emulsion or photosensitive layer, (2) the acetate or bonding layer, and (3) the base or support layer. A cross section view, as shown in Fig. 67-6, illustrates what happens in processing a photosensitive plastic image carrier. Notice that where the negative allows the light to strike the emulsion layer the emulsion is not removed. The unremoved emulsion becomes the printing or image transfer surface.

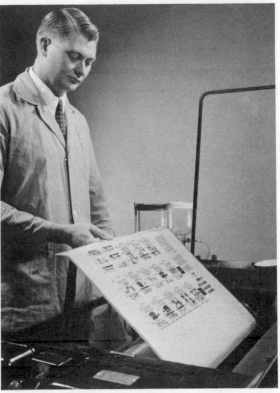

Fig. 67-5. Installing a flexible plastic plate on a press cylinder. (Eastman Kodak Co.)

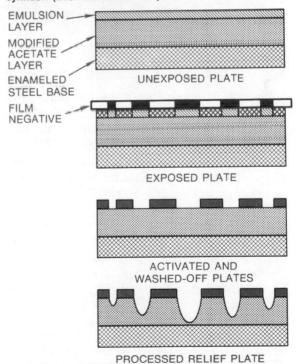

EMULSION LAYER

MODIFIED ACETATE LAYER

ENAMELED STEEL BASE

UNEXPOSED PLATE

FILM NEGATIVE

EXPOSED PLATE

ACTIVATED AND WASHED-OFF PLATES

PROCESSED RELIEF PLATE

Fig. 67-6. A cross-section of a plastic original image carrier. (Eastman Kodak Co.)

UNIT 68
ELECTRONIC ENGRAVINGS

Image carriers made by electronic engraving methods are used in the same manner as are photoengravings and photosensitive plastic. They can be flat-mounted, or attached to press cylinders and used to print directly on paper or other solid materials. These original image carriers are also used to make matrices for producing duplicate letterpress image carriers.

The main advantage of using electronic methods to produce relief image carriers is the speed with which an image carrier can be made. A typical newspaper photograph can be engraved in less than an hour and speed is important to the publishing industry.

EQUIPMENT

Several companies produce electronic engraving equipment for the graphic arts industry. Each machine manufactured has specific advantages in the kinds of work for which it is best suited. Two typical machines designed on a metal lathe principle are shown in Figs. 68-1 and 68-2.

The original copy (photograph or line drawing) is attached to the copy cylinder (Fig. 68-3). A photoelectric cell scans the copy and changes the reflected light into electrical signals. These are then transferred to the cutting head (Fig. 68-4), which activates a stylus. The stylus cuts away unwanted material, leaving the desired image in relief. As noted in Fig. 68-5, a background in electronics is needed to understand completely the principle of an electronic engraver.

Fig. 68-1. An electronic engraving machine that will produce relief image carriers. (Fairchild Graphic Equipment)

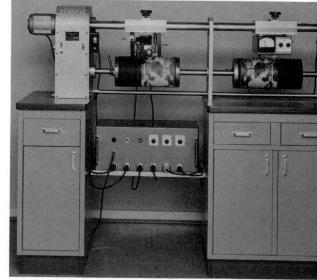

Fig. 68-2. An electronic engraving machine that will produce relief image carriers. (Jens Scheel-Mechanische Gerate)

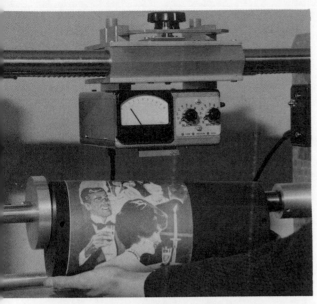

Fig. 68-3. The copy cylinder and scanner of an electronic engraver. (Jens Scheel-Mechanische Gerate)

Fig. 68-5. Some of the electronic components of an electronic engraver. (Jens Scheel-Mechanische Gerate)

Fig. 68-4. The cutting head and cylinder of an electronic engraver. (Jens Scheel-Mechanische Gerate)

Fig. 68-6. An electronic engraving machine that produces flat relief image carriers. (H.C.M. Corp.)

A machine that produces flat-relief image carriers (Fig. 68-6) operates in a different manner than the machines shown in Figs. 68-1 and 68-2. In this machine the system of transferring the image to the cutting edge by light reflection and electronic signals is similar, but the image carrier material is held flat and rigid. The engraving head, containing a stylus, moves back and forth and engraves the relief image. Flexible plastics and metals such as zinc, magnesium, and copper can be engraved.

UNIT 69
STEREOTYPES

Stereotypes are the oldest and most economical of the four basic duplicate image carriers. They date back to the mid-eighteenth century but did not become an important factor in the graphic arts industry until the early part of the nineteenth century. This process is widely used by magazine and newspaper publishers.

fibers, and a filler which is usually clay. This material is called matrix paper.

3. Remove the moisture after the matrix or mat is made. If molten metal is poured against a wet matrix, the metal will form improperly. Special heating units are often used to dry the mats thoroughly (Fig. 69-3).

TYPE TO BE
STEREOTYPED

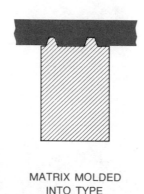

MATRIX MOLDED
INTO TYPE

METAL POURED
ON MATRIX

FINISHED
STEREOTYPE

Fig. 69-1. The basic stereotype process. (International Association of Electrotypers & Stereotypers, Inc.)

The process of making a stereotype is basically simple (Fig. 69-1) but much research has been conducted to perfect it to the present stage where: (1) type and original image carriers are assembled, (2) a matrix or mold is formed, (3) the metal is poured on the matrix, and (4) a finished stereotype emerges.

MAKING A STEREOTYPE

1. Lock up the type and original engravings, as outlined in Section 9. The engravings can be halftones or line illustrations. It is important that a good lockup be obtained before proceeding to the next step.
2. Make a matrix of the type, halftones, and illustrations (Fig. 69-2). The matrix material is made from wood pulp, rag

Fig. 69-2. A stereotype matrix or mat made by a heavy-duty roller. Mats are also made by direct pressure. (International Association of Electrotypers & Stereotypers, Inc.)

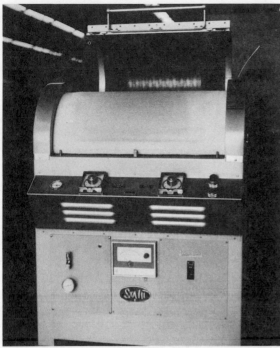

Fig. 69-3. A mat-drying and mat-forming machine used to preform mats for curved stereotypes. (Sta-Hi Corp.)

Fig. 69-4. Preparing to pour a flat stereotype casting. (International Association of Electrotypers & Stereotypers, Inc.)

4. Cast the stereotype image carrier (Fig. 69-4). The mat is fastened to a flat or curved casting box (Fig. 69-5) and molten metal is poured against it. The metal, primarily lead, solidifies immediately. The casting can be removed from the casting box after pouring.
5. After casting, cut the flat and curved stereotypes to size. Special saws are used to cut the metal (Fig. 69-6).

Fig. 69-5. A stereotype flat-casting machine (Nolan Corp.)

Fig. 69-6. A stereotype saw used on flat castings. (Nolan Corp.)

Fig. 69-7. A stereotype flat-plate shaver. (Hammon Machinery Builders, Inc.)

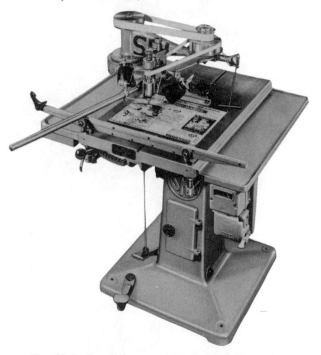

Fig. 69-8. A radial-arm router is used to remove unwanted metal from a flat stereotype casting. (Master Sales and Service Corp.)

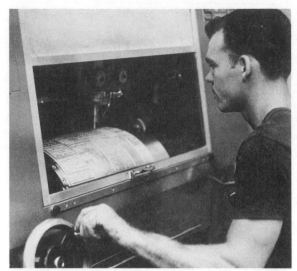

Fig. 69-9. A curved stereotype casting being routed on a completely enclosed unit. (Sta-Hi Corp.)

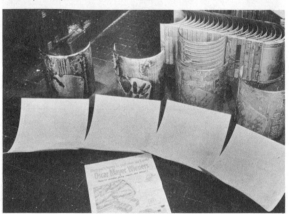

Fig. 69-10. Prepared stereotype casting ready to be used on a high-speed rotary press. A set of four-color castings (in the foreground) is press ready. (International Association of Electrotypers & Stereotypers, Inc.)

6. Shave the flat stereotype to a predetermined thickness on a plate shaver (Fig. 69-7). This is necessary to obtain an exact type-high image carrier.

7. Remove excess metal in the nonimage areas with a router (Figs. 69-8 and 69-9). If this step is not completed, portions of the nonimage areas will reproduce, causing poor reproductions.

After routing, the stereotype casting is ready for the press. Several curved castings are prepared for large rotary presses (Fig. 69-10).

UNIT 70
ELECTROTYPES

Electrotype image carriers are metal reproductions of type, photographs, and illustrations. Electrotypes are made by depositing or plating metal on a mold through the electrolysis or electrochemical process.

The basic process for making an electrotype is illustrated in Fig. 70-1. Graphic material that is to be electrotyped is molded in specially prepared material (Fig. 70-1, 1 through 4). Silver or graphite is then applied to the mold to make it conductive of electricity (Fig. 70-1, number 5). The mold is

hung in a tank of plating solution and the electrical connections are made.

Current is turned on and the process of electrolysis takes place, forming multilayers of copper on the mold (Fig. 70-1, number 6). The copper shell is stripped from the mold (Fig. 70-1, number 7).

A metal supporting material is applied to the back of the copper shell (Fig. 70-1, number 8), and is shaved to proper thickness. The result is an unmounted electrotype (Fig. 70-1, number 9), or a mounted one (Fig. 70-1, number 10).

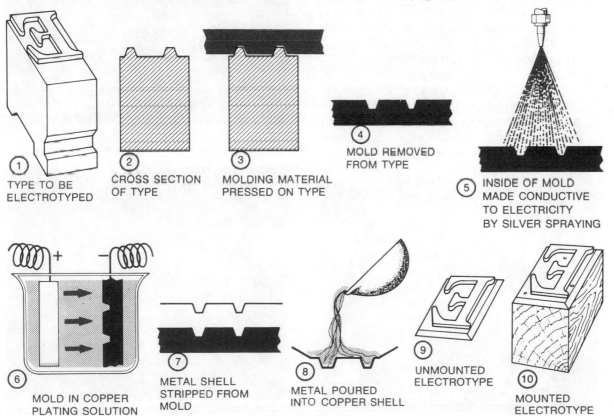

1 TYPE TO BE ELECTROTYPED
2 CROSS SECTION OF TYPE
3 MOLDING MATERIAL PRESSED ON TYPE
4 MOLD REMOVED FROM TYPE
5 INSIDE OF MOLD MADE CONDUCTIVE TO ELECTRICITY BY SILVER SPRAYING
6 MOLD IN COPPER PLATING SOLUTION
7 METAL SHELL STRIPPED FROM MOLD
8 METAL POURED INTO COPPER SHELL
9 UNMOUNTED ELECTROTYPE
10 MOUNTED ELECTROTYPE

Fig. 70-1. The basic electrotype process. (Electrotypers and Stereotypers Handbook)

MAKING AN ELECTROTYPE

1. Lock up the type and engravings as outlined in Section 9. The engravings could be either halftone photographs or line illustrations. It is important that a good lockup be obtained before proceeding with the preparation of an electrotype.

2. Make a mold of the type, photographs, and illustrations (Fig. 70-2). Lead, plastic, metal, or wax can be used to make the mold.

3. Make the mold conductive of electricity. Spray it with a thin film of silver (Fig. 70-3). Graphite can also be used, especially on wax molds.

4. Complete the preparation of the plating tank. Add electroplating solution and the copper anode to the tank (Fig. 70-4). The mold is then put in the plating tank and the electrical connections are made.

5. Turn on the direct-current electricity. Copper from the copper anode begins to flow through the electroplating solution to the electrically conductive mold. The voltage of the electricity is low, but the amperage is extremely high.

6. Remove the mold and electrotype shell from the plating tank after a predetermined period of time (Fig. 70-5). In the electrolytic action a copper thickness of approximately 0.012 inch has been deposited on the mold to form the electrotype shell.

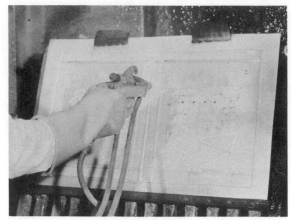

Fig. 70-3. Silver spraying the mold. (Electrotypers and Stereotypers Handbook)

Fig. 70-4. Placing the copper anode in the electroplating tank. (Electrotypers and Stereotypers Handbook)

Fig. 70-2. A plastic electrotype mold. (Electrotypers and Stereotypers Handbook)

Fig. 70-5. Removing the mold and electrotype shell from the electroplating tank. (Electrotypers and Stereotypers Handbook)

Fig. 70-6. Removing the completed electrotype shell from the mold. (Electrotypers and Stereotypers Handbook)

Fig. 70-7. Casting or backing an electrotype shell with lead. (Electrotypers and Stereotypers Handbook)

Fig. 70-8. Trimming surplus material from the edges of the stereotype casting. (Electrotypers and Stereotypers Handbook)

Fig. 70-9. Shaving the back of the electrotype casting to obtain the desired image-carrier thickness.

7. Apply tin to the back of the copper shell. This bonds the copper to the lead backing material.

8. Remove the completed shell from the mold (Fig. 70-6). At this point in the process the copper shell is a perfect duplicate of the original type, photographs, or illustrations.

9. Add lead to the back of the thin copper shell to help reinforce it (Fig. 70-7). The support metal is composed of approximately 94% lead, 3% tin, and 3% antimony.

10. Trim the surplus material from the edges after the backing material has solidified and cooled (Fig. 70-8). It is necessary to trim the edges of the casting with extreme accuracy.

11. Make the electrotype casting to the specified thickness. The excess material is shaved from the back with a milling machine (Fig. 70-9). An electrotype thickness must remain within a tolerance of 0.00025 of an inch.

12. With a router, remove the dead metal in the nonproducing areas of the electrotype image carrier (Fig. 70-10). If these areas are not removed they will reproduce when in the press.

13. Electrotype image carriers are either mounted on wood blocks (Fig. 70-11) or attached to the flat casting directly on a prepared base on a cylinder press (Fig. 70-12).

Fig. 70-10. A radial-arm router is used to remove the dead metal left in the nonreproducing areas of the electrotype. (Electrotypers and Stereotypers Handbook)

Fig. 70-11. Electrotypes being mounted on wood blocks to make them type-high. (Electrotypers and Stereotypers Handbook)

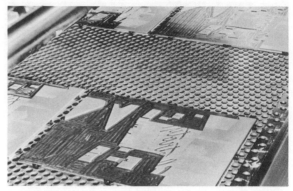

Fig. 70-12. Flat electrotypes attached to a cylinder press, ready for use. (Electrotypers and Stereotypers Handbook)

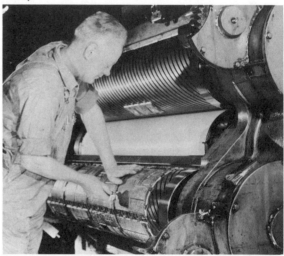

Fig. 70-13. Curved electrotypes being attached to a rotary press. (Electrotypers and Stereotypers Handbook)

Curved electrotype image carriers can also be produced to fit a high-speed rotary press. The same basic procedures are used to prepare a round casting as are used to prepare the flat one. Special equipment is needed to regulate the proper rounding, size, and thickness of the electrotype.

The pressman in Fig. 70-13 is attaching curved electrotypes to a high-speed rotary press. By using multiple electrotypes several pages will be printed with each revolution of the cylinder.

UNIT 71

RUBBER AND THERMOPLASTIC IMAGE CARRIERS

Rubber and *thermoplastic image carriers* are in the duplicate category. The same essential procedure is used to manufacture each; the specific materials needed are different. Each carrier requires a mold, heat, and pressure to obtain a relief image on the surface of either rubber or plastic.

COMMERCIAL RUBBER IMAGE CARRIERS

There are three common uses for rubber image carriers: (1) they are used on all standard letterpress machines, (2) they are used where flexibility is needed, and (3) they are used to print on various surfaces, even irregular ones.

Flexible rubber image carriers are used exclusively in the image-transfer process of flexography (Unit 81). It has been found

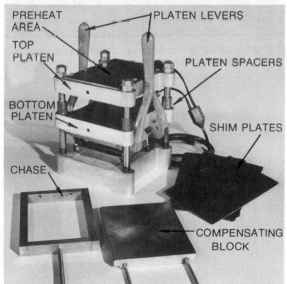

Fig. 71-1. A small rubber-stamp molding press. (American Evatype Corp.)

through research that the rubber surface will accept the special inks needed to print material by the flexography process. Rubber image carriers are used to print a multitude of packaging containers and materials.

The manufacture of rubber stamps is very similar to that of image carriers for standard letterpress and flexography presses. Rubber stamps are known to almost everyone because they are used in nearly every business establishment, as well as in homes. They transfer everyday messages such as **Rush, Do not drop,** and **Special handling.** The procedure for molding rubber stamps is outlined in this unit.

RUBBER STAMP PRESS

A rubber stamp press consists of two flat surfaces or platens parallel to each other, heating elements for each platen, and levers to force the two platens together (Fig. 71-1). Several companies manufacture small stamp presses. Consult the operator's manual for the specific procedure for operating each machine.

PARTS AND USES

Top and *bottom platens.* These are the heated working surfaces which close when forming the matrix and the rubber stamp.

Platen levers. The two levers raise the bottom platen. The top platen is stationary.

Platen spacers. These tubular devices allow the two platens to be closed precisely the same amount each time.

Chase. This rectangular device is used to hold the type securely while the matrix is being made.

Compensating block. This is a thick rectangular metal block used in place of the type when the rubber stamp is being formed from the matrix.

Shim plates. These are used to protect the face of the platens. The plastic matrix material and gum rubber will stick to the platens if these are not used. Shim plates are also used to add thickness when necessary.

Preheat area. The compensating block, chase, and type are placed on this area for preheating prior to making the matrix and rubber stamp.

MOLDING RUBBER STAMPS

1. Compose the typeform. If available, use special heat-resistant type when making a rubber stamp. Because of the heat, standard foundry type may become smashed when the matrix is being made. Remember to proof the typeform.
2. Plug in the press. Heat until the platens reach approximately 300° F.
3. Lock up the typeform in the chase (Fig. 71-2). Use the procedure outlined in Unit 77. Be sure to place type-high bearers on each side of the line of type. There should be a minimum of one pica between the type and each bearer. The bearers prevent the typeform from being smashed while making the matrix.
4. Cut a piece of matrix board ¼ inch larger on all four sides of the typeform, including the bearers.
5. Place the chase and locked-up type form on the hot compensating block. It should rest on the preheat area of the press (Fig. 71-3) for at least five minutes.
6. Place the cut-to-size matrix board on the locked-up typeform. Note the correct side of the matrix board.
7. Place a shim plate on the matrix board.
8. Open the platen of the hot press and insert a shim plate on the bottom platen.
9. Place the chase, matrix board, and shim plate between the platens (Fig. 71-4).

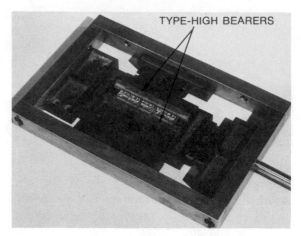

Fig. 71-2. A typeform properly locked in the rubber-stamp press chase (refer to Unit 77 for lock-up procedure).

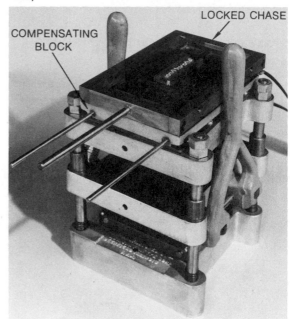

Fig. 71-3. Preheating the locked typeform.

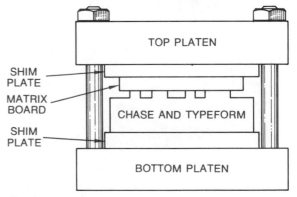

Fig. 71-4. Proper position for the matrix assembly.

Check the edges of the shim plates. They should be clear of the corner posts so they will not be clamped between the platen spacers and the platens.

10. Allow the typeform and matrix board to heat for two minutes. Do not close the platens.

11. After the two-minute period close the platens until the top platen contacts the shim plate. Allow the press to stay in this position for a few seconds.

12. Close the platens gently until they come in contact with the platen spacers (Fig. 71-5). Do not force the platen levers down. This could damage the type and result in a poor matrix. The press should remain in this position for ten minutes to allow the matrix board to cure completely.

13. Raise the platen levers after the ten-minute heating period.

14. Remove the entire contents from between the platens. Pry the finished matrix from the typeform with a screwdriver or similar instrument (Fig. 71-6). Be extremely careful not to damage the type or the newly formed matrix.

VULCANIZING THE RUBBER DIE

1. Remove all shim plates from between the platens.

2. Heat the press and compensating block, if necessary.

3. Cut a piece of gum rubber ¼ inch larger than the type area in the matrix.

4. Remove the holland cloth from the gum rubber. Powder the newly exposed side liberally with release powder.

5. Place the gum rubber, powdered side down, on the matrix.

6. Place the matrix and gum rubber on the compensating block.

7. Place the holland cloth and a shim plate on top of the gum rubber. The holland cloth prevents the rubber from sticking to the shim plate.

8. Open the platens and insert the materials in the press (Fig. 71-7).

Fig. 71-5. The platens in a closed position.

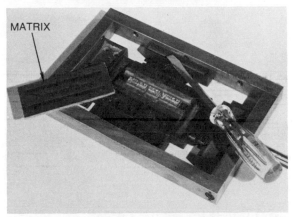

Fig. 71-6. The completed matrix after removal from the typeform.

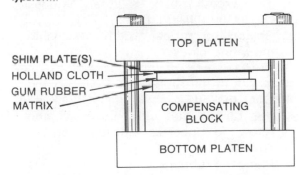

Fig. 71-7. The proper position for rubber vulcanizing assembly.

9. Close the platens until the top one contacts the shim plate. Allow the press to remain for a few seconds, then slowly close the platens completely. The rubber should vulcanize for eight minutes.

10. Open the platens. Remove the contents by carefully pulling the rubber stamp die from the matrix (Fig. 71-8).

11. Allow the rubber stamp die to cool.

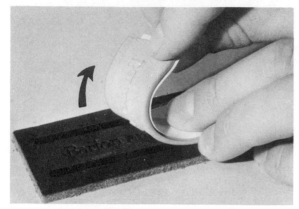

Fig. 71-8. Removing the rubber stamp die from the matrix.

Fig. 71-9. A completed rubber stamp and test print.

MOUNTING THE DIE

1. Trim excess rubber as closely as possible to the raised letters.
2. Select the proper width of cushion mounting block.
3. Cut a piece of mounting block the length of the rubber die.
4. Coat the cushion mounting block and the rubber die with rubber cement. Allow the rubber cement to dry on both surfaces.
5. Place the rubber die in the correct position on the cushion mounting. Press it firmly into place.
6. Test the rubber stamp (Fig. 71-9).
7. Place an identification label in the window area of the mounting block.

MOLDING COMMERCIAL RUBBER-IMAGE CARRIERS

Large rubber image carriers used for standard letterpresses and flexography presses are made in the same manner as

Fig. 71-10. A commercial molding press. (American Evatype Corp.)

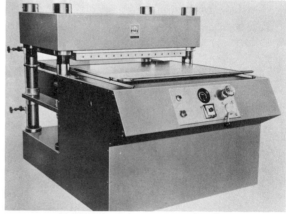

Fig. 71-11. An automatic molding press. (Pasadena Hydraulics, Inc.)

are rubber stamps. The primary difference in the manufacture of large image carriers and rubber stamps is the size of the equipment used. Motorized molding presses (Fig. 71-10) and hydraulic-operated molding presses with automatic controls (Fig. 71-11) are used instead of the small molding press used for rubber stamps.

A method of producing rubber image carriers which uses photosensitive glass is now in use. Comparison of the new photosensi-

CONVENTIONAL PROCESS

①	②	③	④	⑤
ORIGINAL ART WORK	FILM NEGATIVE	ENGRAVING	PLASTIC MOLD OR MATRIX	RUBBER IMAGE CARRIER

PHOTOSENSITIVE GLASS PROCESS

①	②	③	④
ORIGINAL ART WORK	FILM NEGATIVE	GLASS MOLD OR MATRIX	RUBBER IMAGE CARRIER

Fig. 71-12. A comparison of the conventional and photosensitive glass processes of molding rubber image carriers. (Corning Graphic Media Products)

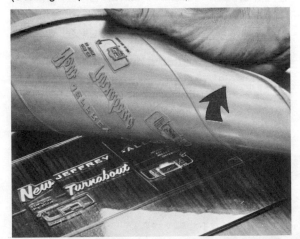

Fig. 71-13. A rubber image carrier being removed from a photosensitive glass matrix. (Corning Graphic Media Products)

tive-glass process with the conventional one in Fig. 71-12 indicates that one step can be eliminated. In the conventional process, an engraving (a relief-metal image carrier) or standard type is needed to form the plas-tic matrix. The photosensitive-glass process eliminates this step. It is possible to etch directly into a special photosensitive glass after it has received an exposure through a standard film negative. The advantages of this process are saved time and a higher-quality rubber image carrier (Fig. 71-13).

THERMOPLASTIC IMAGE CARRIERS

Image carriers from molded plastic are made in a manner similar to that just described for rubber image carriers. Type is composed, a matrix is made just as for rubber, and then plastic is used instead of rubber to obtain the final result.

Thermoplastic image carriers are used in the same way as are the metal ones and they are more economical to produce. The printability and wearability of thermoplastic image carriers compare favorably to that of metal.

UNIT 72
LINOLEUM BLOCKS

Wood blocks have served as image carriers for many centuries. Before movable type was invented, entire pages of words were hand carved into wood to form the image carrier. Pictures or illustrations were also carved into this material for reproduction purposes. Even after the invention of movable type, wood blocks were the only method that could be used to reproduce pictures.

The first peoples to experiment with block printing were the Chinese, Syrians, and Egyptians. They also attempted to use stone blocks. Actual block prints dating as early as the eighth and ninth centuries have been found in China and Japan. The earliest-known wood blocks used in Europe date back approximately to the fifteenth century.

Today, hand-cut block prints are seldom used because of the availability of sophisticated image carriers. These were discussed in previous units. Some hobbyists and craftsmen, though, prefer to cut their own blocks because of the economy and the personal pride of accomplishment.

Linoleum is the common material used today because it is easier to cut than wood. It is economical and has a smooth texture which provides excellent image-transfer properties. For students of graphic arts, linoleum blocks provide an economical means of gaining an understanding of relief image transfer.

ILLUSTRATIONS FOR LINOLEUM BLOCK

Illustrations must be kept simple because linoleum blocks are cut by hand. It is better for the beginner to attempt simple, basic designs, but after experience is gained, more detail can be added to the block cut.

The positive design (Fig. 72-1) shows the illustration as a solid print or a silhouette. Little attempt is made to show detail.

The negative design (Fig. 72-2) shows a different illustration reversed from the positive. The image area has been cut away. The background has been printed to form the outside edges of the illustration. The color

Fig. 72-1. A positive design.

Fig. 72-2. A negative design.

Fig. 72-3. A line-positive design.

Fig. 72-4. A line-negative design.

of the image is the same as the paper color, but the background could be reproduced in any desired tint.

The line-positive design (Fig. 72-3) shows the illustration as lines only. Narrow border lines and detail lines have been left in relief; all the background has been removed. This type of illustration has the disadvantage of possibly collapsing under pressure during printing operations.

The line-negative design (Fig. 72-4) shows the illustration as narrow white or paper-color lines. Narrow portions of the linoleum have been removed so that they cannot print. This type of design is sometimes more advantageous than the line-positive design because no problems are encountered with breakage or collapse of lines.

Detail and emphasis can be added to the illustration if a combination of all four basic methods of design are used (Fig. 72-5). A well-cut linoleum block reproduction is sometimes difficult to distinguish from a chemically or mechanically produced one.

Fig. 72-5. A linoleum block cut in which the four basic types of designs were used.

CUTTING

1. Select or develop an illustration.
2. Transfer the illustration to a plain sheet of white typing paper. Darken the area that will reproduce.
3. Reverse the illustration by placing the paper upside down on the light table. Trace the image. The illustration must be reversed before it is transferred to the linoleum block. If this step is not done, the illustration will reproduce backward. An exception to this step could be taken if the illustration were symmetrical.
4. Transfer the illustration to the linoleum block. Place a sheet of carbon paper on the linoleum block. Place the reversed illustration on top of the carbon paper,

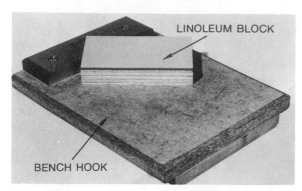

Fig. 72-6. A linoleum block properly positioned on a bench hook.

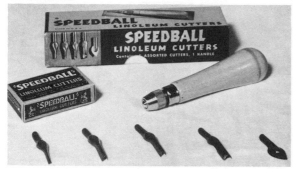

Fig. 72-7. A common set of linoleum-block cutting tools. (Hunt Manufacturing Co.)

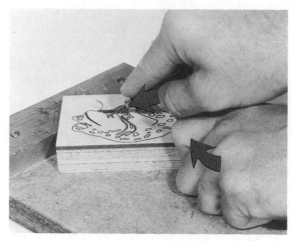

Fig. 72-8. Using a "liner" cutting tool to cut around the entire illustration.

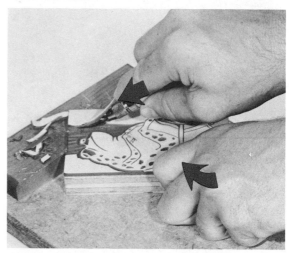

Fig. 72-9. Removing large nonimage areas with a U-shaped gouge.

Fig. 72-10. Using a type-high gauge to determine block height. Just as for foundry type, it must be 0.918 inch high.

then apply firm pressure on the pencil when transferring the illustration.

5. Place the linoleum block on a bench hook (Fig. 72-6). The two primary purposes of a bench hook are to insure safety and to provide firmness. Linoleum-block cutting tools are sharp and a slip of the hand could cause an injury. The bench hook also helps to hold the block while the design is being cut; it permits you to have your hand behind the sharp cutter tool. The block can be held firmly in place and more accurate cutting is accomplished.

6. Select the smallest V-shaped cutter (called a liner) from a set of common cutting tools (Fig. 72-7).

7. Cut around the illustration (Fig. 72-8). Do not attempt to cut too deeply with the liner. The purpose of this first cut is to make a clean edge around the image area. NOTE: keep the hands behind the cutting tool.

8. Use a V-shaped gouge to cut the lines deeper. Do not cut on the image side of the narrow (liner) cut.
9. Remove all nonimage areas with the appropriate size U-shaped gouge (Fig. 72-9). The farther from the image it is, the deeper the cut must be. The nonimage areas may print if the cuts are not sufficiently deep.
10. Make the block type-high (0.918 inch) before it is proofed. Use a type-high gauge (Fig. 72-10) to determine ac-

curately the proper backing needed. Use chip board and other papers of varying thicknesses to bring the block to the proper height.
11. Proof the linoleum block in a standard proofpress. Place the block in a galley, ink the image, and pull a proof just as if it were a standard typeform.
12. Make necessary corrections in the linoleum cut and reproof it. The linoleum block is now ready to be used on a platen or cylinder letterpress.

UNIT 73

LEARNING EXPERIENCES: LETTERPRESS IMAGE CARRIERS

DISCUSSION TOPICS

1. Name the two divisions of letterpress image carriers. Why has each division received the name given to it? List the several letterpress image carriers within each of the two major divisions.
2. Enumerate several materials, metallic and nonmetallic, that are used to produce letterpress image carriers. Cite an advantage of using a combination of metallic and nonmetallic materials in the same image carrier.
3. List the three basic forms of relief image carriers. Identify the materials that are used to make each of these image-carrier forms. Why is there a need for these three basic forms?
4. Describe a photoengraving. What means or methods are used to prepare photoengravings? List the metals commonly used to prepare photoengravings.
5. Briefly describe the steps in producing a photoengraving. Identify the special equipment needed in the production

stages. How are film negatives used in the process of preparing a photoengraving? Explain what happens when the liquid etching solution is sprayed or splashed against the metal surface.
6. Since when has plastic been used as a material for first-generation original relief image carriers? Why wasn't this material used before that date? Name the two advantages of using plastic over metal.
7. Compare and contrast the processing procedures for nonmetallic (plastic) photosensitive image carriers and for photoengravings. How are these two procedures alike? How are they different?
8. Explain the method or process of preparing electronic engravings. Cite the primary advantage of using electronic engravings over the other two first-generation relief image carriers. Name and describe the two different styles of machines that are used to prepare electronic engravings.

9. Compare the methods of producing stereotype and electrotype letterpress image carriers. What important ingredient is used in the preparation of an electrotype that is not used in the preparation of a stereotype? How does the mounting process vary between these two letterpress image carriers?

10. Name two materials that can be sprayed on the mold in the preparation of an electrotype to make the mold conductive of electricity. Describe the principle of electroplating. How is the thickness of the copper on the mold controlled during the electroplating action?

11. List the three common uses for rubber image carriers. Why is rubber sometimes used as an image-carrier material rather than the several metals and even plastic? Cite an everyday use of a rubber relief image carrier.

12. How does the procedure for preparing a small rubber stamp differ from that of preparing a large flexographic relief image carrier? Which of the normal steps necessary to prepare a rubber image carrier can be eliminated when using photosensitive glass as the matrix material? Why is it possible to eliminate this step? Does the production of thermoplastic image carriers differ greatly from that of rubber image carriers?

13. Identify the material that was used in the production of relief image carriers long before movable metal type was invented. Is this material still used to any great extent today? If so, where? What material is being used today as a substitute? What advantages does this material have over wood?

ACTIVITIES

1. Obtain a sample of each kind of letterpress image carrier. These samples can be obtained in local commercial graphic arts concerns if they are not available in the school graphic arts laboratory. Mount and build each image carrier to type-high. Proof each image carrier under the same proofing conditions. Using a magnifying glass, compare the results of each proof. Also carefully inspect the several image carriers and compare them to each other.

2. Visit several commercial graphic arts companies. Ask to see their production facilities for letterpress image carriers. Carefully observe the steps for producing each kind of first-generation and second-generation letterpress image carrier. Compare the methods used in each commercial concern and discuss them in class.

3. Prepare a rubber stamp. Compose the type, prepare the matrix, vulcanize the rubber, and mount the stamp. Carefully compare your stamp to a commercially made stamp. What qualities does a commercially made stamp have that your does not, and vice versa?

4. Cut a linoleum block. Obtain or draw an illustration, transfer it to the linoleum, cut away the nonimage areas, make the block type-high, and proof the image. Carefully study the proof and make needed corrections until the linoleum block proof is a close reproduction of the original illustration. Retain the linoleum block until after Section 10 has been studied. You then will produce copies from the linoleum block.

The printed page can live forever.

This is the marketing plan for the infant organization that later became known as the United States of America.

The Declaration of Independence is still as fresh and up-to-date today as it was the day John Hancock signed it.

A message in print is not like a message in time.

A message in time will last for 10, 20, 30 or 60 seconds. Like a stroke of lightning, a message in time lives gloriously for a moment and then dies.

A message in print can die just as fast. On the other hand, a message in print can be read for 10 minutes, can be taken to the store a week later or perhaps saved for several lifetimes.

If you have something important to say, your message will last longer if you put it in print.

Your message in print will live as long as it is relevant to the needs and interests of your marketplace.

Your message in print can live forever.

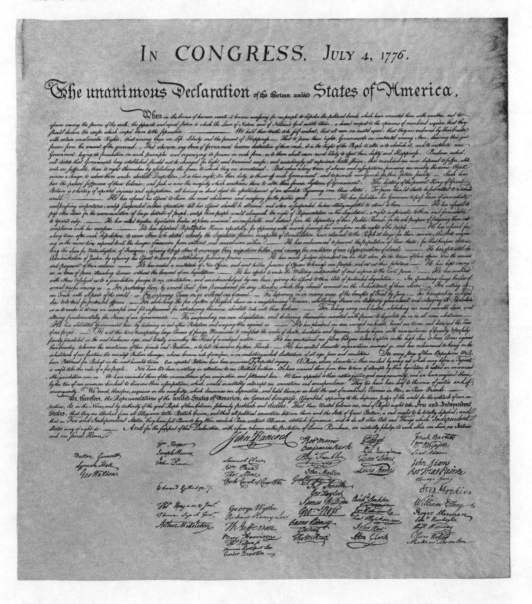

A stoneman is placing plates in place in a multi-page lockup. It will be used to print one side of a signature.

SECTION **9**

UNIT 74
INTRODUCTION TO LETTERPRESS LOCKUP AND IMPOSITION

Lockup and *imposition* are operations carried out after type has been composed, but before it is printed on the press. Their purpose is to hold the typeform securely and locate it properly within a metal frame called a *chase*. The chase, with the locked-up type, is then held in the press.

For many years lockup and imposition were done on a flat stone table, usually marble. That is why this work is called *stonework* even though a stone table is rarely used today. The person who does the operation is called a *stoneman*. He is a skilled craftsmen and a very important part of the production team in a printing plant. An error in his work could cause delay or failure In future operations.

Several different kinds and sizes of typeforms can be printed on the same letterpress printing press. One situation might require that only one typeform should be printed on a sheet of paper (Fig. 74-1). Another could necessitate printing two or more typeforms on the same sheet (Fig. 74-2).

The stoneman arranges the type so that It will print in the proper position on the press. He must be thoroughly familiar with the tools and procedures of stonework and with the operation of the presses on which the type will be printed.

Fig. 74-1. Locking up a single page for printing on the press.

Fig. 74-2. Locking up several pages of type that will all be printed on a single sheet of paper.

Typeforms also are locked up to make *stereotype* and *electrotype* plates (Figs. 73-3 and 74-4). These are made to duplicate original typeforms (Section 8). This section pertains only to methods of locking up type to be printed directly on a press. However, the procedures are essentially the same as those used for locking up typeforms for making duplicate plates.

Fig. 74-3. A page for a newspaper that has been locked up to make a stereotype mat.

Fig. 74-4. A lockup to be used for making an electrotype plate. (The Challenge Machinery Co.)

UNIT 75
TOOLS AND EQUIPMENT

The tools and equipment used for letterpress lockup and imposition are generally uniform in all printing establishments. The *stoneman* is responsible for insuring that the tools and equipment are in good working condition. He must also organize the tools and equipment so that they can be efficiently used when making a lockup.

IMPOSING STONE AND BASE

Modern *imposing stones* are metal surfaces on which the lockup process is done (Fig. 75-1). The top of the stone has been machined to be as accurate as the bed of the press on which the type will be printed. The stone has a babbeted edge on which the open side of a galley can rest while moving the typeform from the stone to a galley. For proper care the stone should periodically receive a light coating of oil to prevent rust.

Several styles of bases are used as supports for the imposing stone. While the main purpose of the base is to establish a satisfactory working height, it is also used for storage of furniture, reglets, chases, and galleys. Most bases also include a drawer and shelves to store quoins, quoin keys, type-wash containers, and planer blocks (Fig. 75-2).

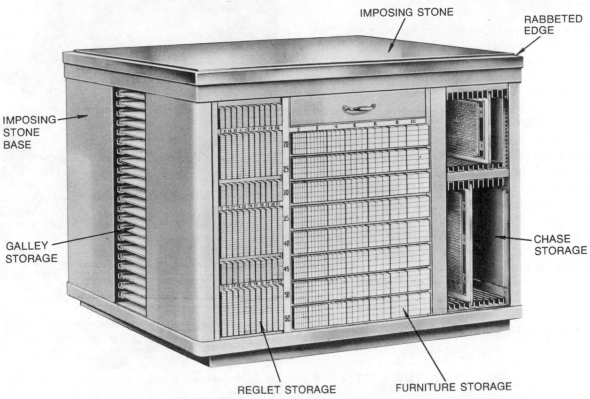

IMPOSING STONE

RABBETED EDGE

IMPOSING STONE BASE

GALLEY STORAGE

CHASE STORAGE

REGLET STORAGE

FURNITURE STORAGE

Fig. 75-1. An imposing stone and the front side of a typical imposing-stone base.

CHASE STORAGE

GALLEY STORAGE

Fig. 75-2. The back side of the base shown in Fig. 75-1.

CHASES

A *chase* is a rectangular frame made from cast iron or steel. It is clamped into a press after type has been locked into it (Fig. 75-3).

Different sizes of presses require different size chases. There are also several kinds of chases available for most presses. Figure 75-4 shows a *standard chase* for a platen press. It is used for most lockups. The standard chase often has handles at the top to facilitate handling. The *skeleton chase* in Fig. 75-5 has the same outside dimensions as the standard one, but has larger inside measurements. It is quite useful for locking up large amounts of type. The *spider chase* in Fig. 75-6 is a special kind used to lockup small typeforms.

The bottom of the chase must be flat. If it becomes warped, considerable difficulty will be encountered when locking up and printing with the typeform.

FURNITURE AND REGLETS

Wood and metal blocks, called *furniture,* are used to fill the space between the typeform and the inside edge of the chase. Fig. 75-7 shows an example of a lockup in which light-weight metal furniture is used to fill the space between the typeform and the chase.

Several sizes of wood and metal furniture are shown in Figs. 75-8 and 75-9. Furniture is stored in racks, according to standard pica lengths and widths (Figs. 75-1 and 75-10). These standard *widths* are 2, 3, 4, 5, 6, 8, and 10 picas. Standard *lengths* of furniture are 10, 15, 20, 25, 30, 35, 40, 45, 50, and 60 picas. Furniture can also be obtained in longer lengths when needed. The length of the furniture is stamped on one end of each piece.

Reglets are thin pieces of wood furniture. They are stored in racks similar to those used for regular furniture (Fig. 75-10). Reglets are 6 and 12 points thick and vary in length in single-pica units from 10 to 60. They are often used as line spacing as well as for the lockup procedure.

Fig. 75-3. Clamping a chase with a lockup into a small pilot press.

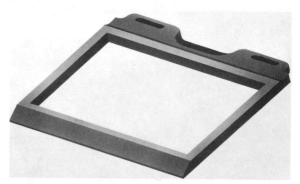

Fig. 75-4. A standard chase for a platen press. Not all chases have handles at the top.

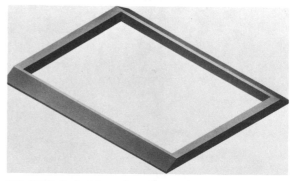

Fig. 75-5. A skeleton chase for a platen press.

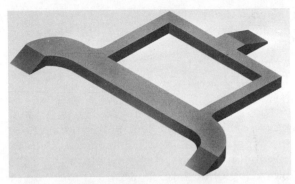
Fig. 75-6. A spider chase for a platen press.

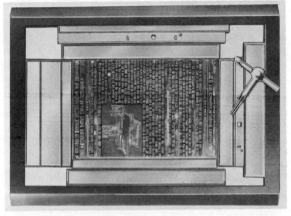
Fig. 75-7. A locked up typeform using metal furniture and high-speed quoins.

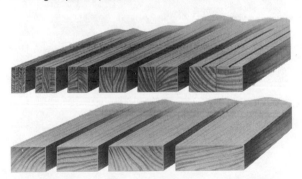
Fig. 75-8. End View of wood furniture and reglets.

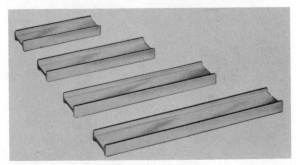
Fig. 75-9. Lightweight metal furniture.

Fig. 75-10. A furniture rack used to store and organize wood furniture. Similar racks are used for metal furniture.

QUOINS AND QUOIN KEYS

Quoins (pronounced coins) are metal devices that expand to tighten the furniture against the typeform and the chase. Wedge-shaped quoins (Fig. 75-11) and cam-type quoins (Fig. 75-12) are used primarily for small typeforms. High-speed quoins, shown in Fig. 75-13, are made in several sizes. They are extremely useful in locking up large forms and when a high degree of accuracy is required in *register* (positioning the typeform to print in a specific location or position on a piece of paper).

The scale located on top of the high-speed quoin (Fig. 75-13) permits the person using it to tighten the quoin to a specific tension. When the quoin must be loosened for corrections, it can be retightened so that the typeform is in precisely the same original position.

Fig. 75-11. A common wedge quoin.

Fig. 75-12. Cam quoins and a quoin key.

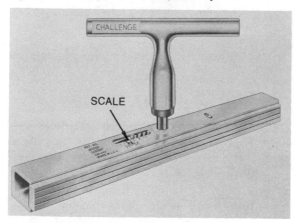

Fig. 75-13. High-speed quoin and key.

Quoin keys tighten (expand) or loosen quoins. Each kind of quoin has a specific key (Fig. 75-14).

PLANER BLOCK

The *planer block* (Fig. 75-15) is a solid block of wood with one flat surface. After the typeform has been locked up, the flat surface is placed on the typeform and the block is lightly tapped with a quoin key or mallet. This pushes the type characters in the typeform down so that the feet touch the stone and the faces are in the same plane and perfectly level across the top.

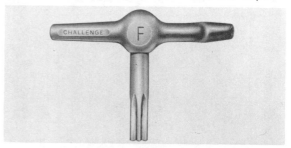

Fig. 75-14. A quoin key.

Fig. 75-15. A planer block.

UNIT 76
KINDS OF LOCKUPS

Nearly all typeforms, regardless of size or shape, are locked up by one of two lockup methods: the *chaser* method or the *furniture-within-furniture* method. The only difference between the two is in the placement of the first four pieces of furniture around the typeform.

CHASER METHOD

The most commonly used method of locking up a typeform is the chaser method. This is most appropriate for typeforms with dimensions that do not equal standard pica lengths of furniture.

To begin the chaser method of locking up:

1. Measure the typeform to determine its dimensions in picas. Fig. 76-1 shows a typeform of 22 x 33 picas.
2. Select four pieces of furniture. Two should be longer than the ends (top and bottom) of the typeform; two should be slightly longer than the sides. The lengths of the pieces of furniture that are placed around the typeform in Fig. 76-2 are 25 x 40 picas.
3. Place the furniture around the typeform. One end of each piece should be placed next to the corner of the typeform. The opposite end should extend past the other end of the typeform.

When all of the furniture is around the typeform, the edge of one piece should overlap the end of another one. The pieces of furniture appear to be chasing each other around the typeform (Fig. 76-2).

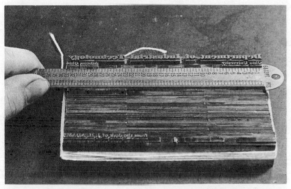

Fig. 76-1. Measuring a typeform to determine the proper length furniture for the chaser method of lockup.

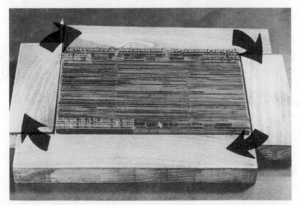

Fig. 76-2. The placement of the first four pieces of furniture around the typeform using the chaser method.

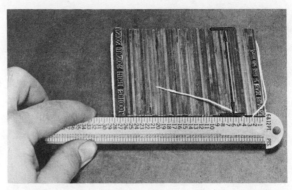

Fig. 76-3. Measuring a typeform for the furniture-within-furniture lockup method.

FURNITURE-WITHIN-FURNITURE METHOD

The furniture-within-furniture method is used with typeforms that have been composed to lengths that correspond to standard pica lengths of furniture (10, 15, 20, etc.). Some printers prefer this method because of its stability, However, it does not apply to as many situations as the chaser method.

To begin the furniture-within-furniture method of locking up:

1. Measure the typeform. The length of the ends of the typeform must equal standard pica length furniture before this method can be used. The dimensions of the typeform in Fig. 76-3 are 20 x 28 picas.
2. Select four pieces of furniture. Two should be equal to the length of the ends of the typeform. The other two should be slightly longer than the sides. The furniture lengths used for the typeform in Fig. 76-4 are 20 x 30 picas.
3. Locate the furniture around the typeform. The first two pieces should be placed at the ends so that the corners of the furniture are next to the corners of the typeform. The other two are placed next to the sides of the form so they overlap the ends of the furniture at the ends of the typeform as shown in Fig. 76-4.

Fig. 76-4. The first four pieces in place for the furniture-within-furniture lockup method.

PLANING THE LOCKED-UP TYPEFORM

A locked-up typeform should always be planed (made smooth and even across the top) before printing. The purpose of this planing operation is to push down all type

characters until all faces are in the same plane. Typeforms that have not been planed or have been improperly planed could cause press makeready problems or damage type.

Place the locked-up typeform in a flat position on the imposing stone and loosen the quoins until the furniture is snug against the type. Be sure that the quoins are not too tight or too loose. Place the planer block on the top of the typeform and tap the block lightly with a quoin key or mallet. Move the block over the typeform to be sure that all type characters have been covered by the block. Remember, type can be damaged if the block is hit too hard or if it is not absolutely flat on the typeform. Tighten the quoins after the typeform has been planed.

After the typeform has been locked up, store it for later printing or place it directly in the press for immediate printing. Take special care when handling the lock-up. Type can be damaged quite easily, and any sudden impact could pi (scramble) it.

UNIT 77
LOCK-UP PROCEDURE

Every typeform uses practically the same lock-up procedure. The only difference is in the placement of the first four pieces of furniture around the typeform, as discussed in Unit 76. Before starting to make the lock-up, all lines in the typeform must be justified. The typeform should be securely tied very carefully.

LOCK-UP

1. Clean the imposing stone. Even a small particle of dirt under any type character can cause *embossing* (a raised type character). Dirt also causes excessive wear on the type unit.

2. Move the typeform from the galley to the imposing stone (Fig. 77-1). Handle it very carefully, using both hands, so that you do not pi the typeform.

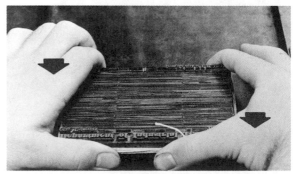

Fig. 77-1. Moving the typeform from the galley to the imposing stone.

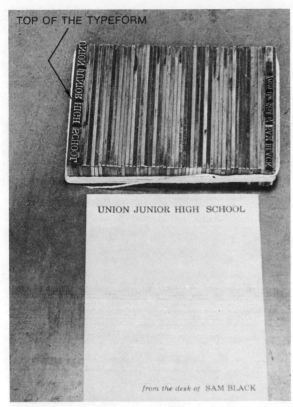

Fig. 77-2. If the typeform is to be printed parallel to the short edge of the paper, the top of the form should be to your left.

3. Position the typeform so that the head (top) is either to your left or nearest you. If the head is to be printed parallel to the short edge of the sheet of paper, place it to your *left* (Fig. 77-2). If the head is to be printed parallel to the long edge of the sheet, place it *nearest* you (Fig. 77-3).

4. Place the appropriate chase around the typeform (Fig. 77-4). One of the long edges should be nearest you. Designate the long edge of the chase that is farthest from you as the top of the chase.

5. Position the typeform in approximately the center of the chase. A smaller form can be positioned a little nearer the top of the chase to make feeding the press easier. When a typeform is to be printed at one end or on a corner of a piece of paper, position it so the paper will be in the center of the platen of the press.

6. Determine the kind of lockup that is appropriate for the typeform. The chaser

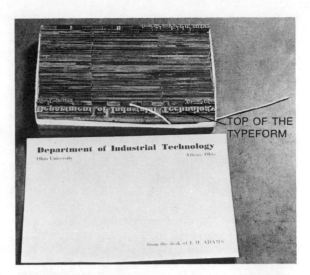

Fig. 77-3. If the typeform is to be printed parallel to the long edge of a sheet of paper, the top of the typeform should be nearest you.

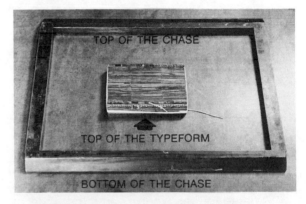

Fig. 77-4. A chase placed around the typeform.

Fig. 77-5. Placement of the first four pieces of furniture for the chaser method of lockup.

should be used for the typeform shown in Fig. 77-4.

7. Select the first four pieces of furniture.

8. Place the first four pieces of furniture around the typeform (Fig. 77-5).

Fig. 77-6. Furniture fills the space between the typeform, bottom of the chase and the left of the chase.

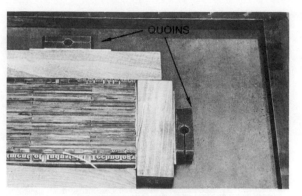

Fig. 77-8. Quoins are located at the top and right of the chase.

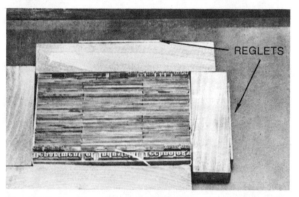

Fig. 77-7. Reglets placed between the furniture.

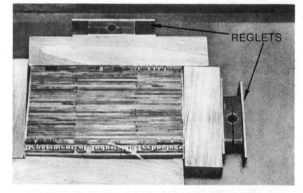

Fig. 77-9. Reglets in proper position between the quoins and the chase.

9. Fill with furniture the space between the bottom of the chase, the left of the chase, and the typeform (Fig. 77-6). Notice that the length of the furniture becomes longer when nearer the edge of the chase. This makes the lockup more stable.
10. Place reglets next to the furniture between the type, the right edge of the chase, and the top edge (Fig. 77-7).
11. Place quoins next to the reglets. The number of quoins required along the edge of a typeform will depend on the size of the type (Fig. 77-8). NOTE: Quoins should always be placed at the top and the right of the chase.
12. Place reglets next to the quoins (Fig. 77-9). Reglets prevent quoins from damaging the regular furniture.
13. Carefully remove the string from around the typeform (Fig. 77-11).
14. Fill the remaining space at the top and right of the chase with furniture (Fig. 77-10).

Fig. 77-10. Furniture that is properly placed around the typeform.

15. Use the quoin key to tighten the quoins until they are snug but not tight.
16. Carefully lay a planer block on the typeform and tap it gently with a mallet or quoin key.
17. Tighten the quoins (Fig. 77-12). Do this in stage. Tighten one quoin a little, then the next one a little. Continue to do this until all are tight. Take care not to tighten them too much. Excessive pressure could break the chase.

Fig. 77-11. Removing string from around the typeform.

Fig. 77-12. Tightening the quoins.

CHECKING THE LOCKUP FOR LOOSE LINES

After type has been locked up it should be examined for loose lines. If any lines or pieces of type are loose they could fall out when the locked-up form is lifted. If the type is loose, it could also be pulled out by the ink on the press when the typeform is printed. This must be avoided.

To check for looseness of type, place a quoin key under one corner of the chase to lift the chase off the imposing stone. With the corner of the chase off the imposing stone, tap all areas of the typeform to identify or test loose type-characters and lines of type (Fig. 77-14). After tapping the lines, remove the quoin key from under the corner of the chase and loosen the quoin. Correct any loose lines in the locked-up typeform while it is flat on the imposing stone.

Fig. 77-13. A locked up typeform resting on a quoin key before testing for loose lines.

Fig. 77-14. Testing a lockup for loose lines.

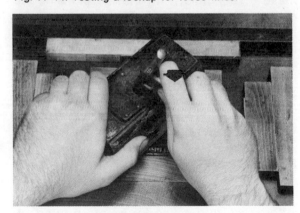

Fig. 77-15. Planing a typeform.

Figure 77-15 shows the process of planing the typeform. Once this final step has been completed, the typeform and chase are ready for the press. As outlined elsewhere, care must be taken when placing the chase in the press to prevent damage to the type.

The procedure for locking up more than one typeform in the chase is similar to that for locking up a single typeform.

UNIT 78
MULTIPLE-PAGE LOCKUP AND IMPOSITION

Several typeforms are frequently placed in the same chase. The entire contents of the chase are printed on a single sheet of paper and the page is then separated into several smaller sheets. This procedure reduces the amount of press time required to print an item and increases the efficiency of the finishing operations.

The procedure for locking up more than one typeform in the same chase is similar to that for locking up a single typeform. In each, the typeforms are arranged next to each other so that they will print in the proper position.

Locking up several forms is easier if the stoneman arranges the typeforms in a rectangular shape. In Fig. 78-1 the four forms make a rectangle, with the correct amount of space between them. The stoneman can treat the rectangle in the same manner as he does a single typeform.

The size of the press on which the printing will be done must be considered. The sheet size of the press must be sufficiently large to accommodate all of the typeforms, with ample margins between them.

DUPLICATE FORMS

When large quantities of items, such as letterheads and office forms are printed, it is sometimes more economical to print several identical items on a large sheet of paper. The sheet is cut to the correct size after the ink is dry. This procedure reduces the number of sheets to be fed through the press by the number of duplicate forms that are locked up. For example, if only 1 typeform were used for 30,000 copies, 30,000 sheets would have to be fed through the press. If 6 duplicate forms are locked up in

Fig. 78-1. Four typeforms locked into one chase.

a single chase, only 5,000 sheets have to be fed through. This is called printing *six-up.* If only 4 typeforms are used, it is printing *four-up.*

Instead of actually composing several forms of type, duplicate plates are often used to reduce the composition time. In other situations several typeforms are used. The cost of additional composition or plate preparation must be considered before using this method. The procedure is impractical if the cost exceeds the savings realized from reduced press time.

Fig. 78-2 shows a combination of duplicate plates being locked up. In this case two plates of four different items are locked up together and printed simultaneously. For this procedure to be economical all items must require the same kind of paper, require approximately the same number of copies be printed with the same color ink, and be about the same size and shape.

Fig. 78-2. Duplicate plates being locked up.

Fig. 78-3. A printed signature.

IMPOSITION OF SIGNATURES

Printed items such as books, booklets, magazines, pamphlets, and programs are printed with several different pages on both sides of a single sheet of paper (Fig. 78-3). The printed sheets are then folded so that the pages are in proper sequence (Fig. 78-4). This printed sheet is called a *signature*. A signature usually has 4, 8, 16, or 32 pages. This depends on the imposition.

The *saddle* or center of the signature is the side that will be stitched or stapled to hold it together after trimming (Fig. 78-5). The *head* is the top edge of the pages. A fold commonly occurs at the head; when folded it is called the *closed head*. The *closed edge* and *open edge* of a signature form the right edge of the finished book or booklet. The closed edge is so named because of the fold that occurs on that edge. On smaller signatures there is no closed edge, and it is termed only an edge.

Folio is the term given to the number of the page. The folio on the front page of a signature is the smallest number in the signature. When all signature are bound together the head and edges are trimmed so the pages can be turned. The bottom is also trimmed to produce an even, clean looking side.

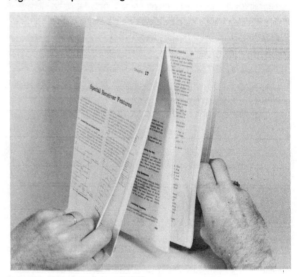

Fig. 78-4. A folded signature.

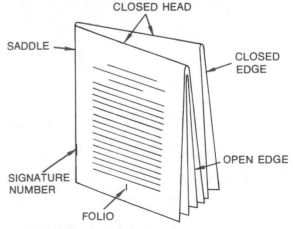

Fig. 78-5. Parts of a folded signature.

Imposition refers to the placement of the pages in proper sequence after the sheet is printed and folded. A complete *page layout* is made before arranging the pages. This is a sheet of paper on which fold lines, page numbers, and page heads (tops) have been accurately placed (Fig. 78-6). It determines the *stone layout*, which is a plan for placing the pages of type on a stone accurately. Notice that the stone layout in Fig. 78-7 is the exactly opposite of the page layout.

Space between typeforms must be established accurately. Allowance must be made for *margins, trimming,* and *creep* (Fig. 78-8). Margins are the spaces between the printed pages and the edges of the folded sheet. Trimming takes into consideration the amount of paper removed from the three outside edges after the signature is folded. Creep occurs when the signature is folded and the inside pages extend past the outside ones (Fig. 78-8). When the signature is trimmed, the inside pages will be slightly smaller than the outside ones and the inside margin (next to the center) of the inside pages will not line up with the inside margins of the outside pages. Creep is usually considered only when the signature is quite large.

CONSIDERATIONS

Before signature imposition is done, the following questions should be answered:

1. What is the exact size of the image area of the largest page included in the signature? (Image area means the outside dimension of the typeform).
2. What is the exact size of the margins for all four sides of the page?
3. How much will be trimmed from the three outside edges?
4. How much space should be allowed for creep? (This need be considered only for signatures of more than sixteen pages.)
5. What is the sheet-size capacity of the press on which the signature is to be printed? This determines the number of pages printed on a signature.

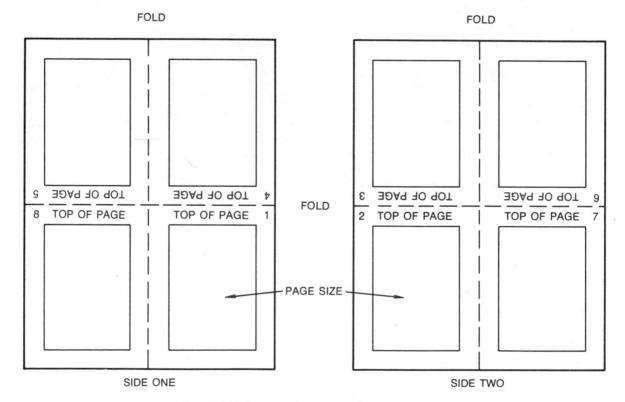

Fig. 78-6. Page layout for an eight-page signature.

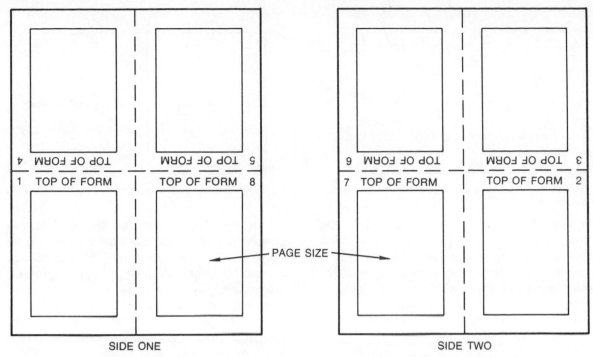

Fig. 78-7. Stone layout for an eight-page signature. It is opposite of a page layout.

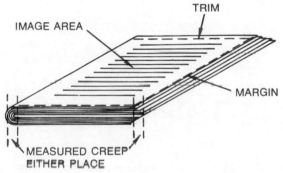

Fig. 78-8. Creep, trim, and margin.

The precise sheet size can be calculated when the above questions are answered. It is necessary to know the sheet size to make accurate page and stone layouts. In Fig. 78-7 the fold lines and image size of the pages have been identified. The head and page numbers have been clearly marked.

DETERMINING PAGE SEQUENCE

The *folding schedule* is determined before the actual page layout can be made. It refers to the location, sequence, and direction of each fold. Begin with the first page; number each one on both sides. This information is easily transferred to the stone lay. Remember that the stone layout is an *exact opposite* of the page layout.

SHEETWISE METHOD

Two impositions are required to print a signature by the *sheetwise method.* Fig. 78-6 shows a page layout of this method, sometimes called *work-and-back* method. Half of the pages are locked into a chase and printed on one side of the sheet. When the ink is sufficiently dry, the remaining half is printed on the opposite side of the sheet.

WORK-AND-TURN OR WORK-AND-TUMBLE METHODS

When a signature has a small number of pages or when the pages are small enough in size to be all locked into one chase, the *work-and-turn* or *work-and-tumble* methods of imposition are often used. In both cases, all the pages of the signature are

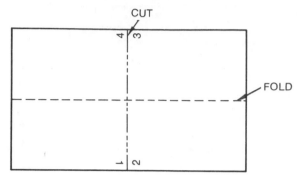

Fig. 78-9. Page layout of a four-page signature—work and turn.

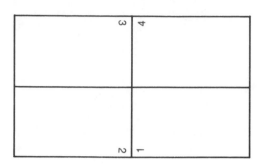

Fig. 78-10. Stone layout of a four-page signature—work and turn.

printed on both sides of the sheet; the sheets are later cut in half. They are folded after the cutting operation. The sheet size must be *twice* the size of the desired finished signature sheet size.

Fig. 78-9 shows a page layout for a signature to be printed by the *work-and-turn* method. Fig. 78-10 illustrates the stone layout for this signature. The sheets are printed on one side and then turned over from side-to-side, and all the pages are printed on the second printing. Lock-up procedure, paper size and shape, and press preparation are very important because the register edges (edges against the guides of the press) are changed for both methods.

UNIT 79
LEARNING EXPERIENCES: LETTERPRESS IMPOSITION

DISCUSSION TOPICS

1. What is the basic purpose of locking up a typeform? For what other reasons are lockups made? What is the person who makes the lockup called? Why is he called that?
2. What is the surface on which the lockup is made? How did the working surface get its name? What are modern surfaces made from? Why are the edges rabbeted? What are some uses of the base on which the working surface is placed?
3. Name the metal frame in which typeforms are locked up. Identify some of the different shapes of frames and list their purposes and tell how they are used.
4. What is the name of the pieces used to fill space between the typeform and the metal frame? From what materials are the pieces made? Give the standard widths and lengths.
5. Name the thin strips of wood used to fill space between the typeform and the metal frame. How are they measured?
6. Give the name of the metal devices used to tighten the typeform into the metal frame. Describe two different kinds. How are they tightened?
7. Explain the use of the planer block.

8. Name the lockup method used with typeforms that do not have standard pica lengths or widths. Describe the procedure of locking up a typeform with this method. Sketch the placement of the first four pieces of furniture in a typeform of 16 x 28 picas. Indicate their overall sizes.
9. Which kind of lockup is most appropriate for use with typeforms of standard pica lengths? Describe the procedure for the placement of the first four pieces of furniture around the typeform. Sketch the placement of the first four pieces of furniture in a typeform of 20 x 30 picas. Indicate the sizes.
10. Explain why it is important that all lines of the typeform be justified.
11. Draw complete lockups, illustrating both kinds of locking-up methods. Indicate the best location for the quoins.
12. How is the typeform checked for loose lines?
13. Describe the procedure used to plane a typeform.
14. What is meant by printing *six-up*? When would such a lockup be appropriate?
15. What is meant by the term *signature*? What is meant by *imposition of signatures*? How many pages do signatures usually contain?
16. Define the term *imposition*. What is a page layout? What is a stone layout? What kinds of allowance must be made between the typeforms? Describe them.
17. What considerations must be made to determine the exact sheet size for making signature impositions?
18. What is a folding schedule? How does it affect the signature imposition?
19. Describe the *sheetwise* method of imposition. What is another name for this method?
20. How do the work-and-turn and work-and-tumble methods differ? How does the sheetwise method of imposition differ from them?

ACTIVITIES

1. Obtain a photoengraving or wood block of standard pica length and width (25 x 40 picas). Lockup the block using both lockup methods. Have your practice lockup checked.
2. Get four or eight photoengravings, stereotypes, or electrotypes which have been mounted type-high. Make proofs and give each a page number. Lock them up as a sheetwise imposition; as a work-and-turn imposition; and as a work-and-tumble imposition. Linoleum blocks with numbers cut on them can be used if the suggested ones are not available.
3. Look at an old textbook and examine the back. Notice that it was assembled by placing signatures together. Count the number of pages in one of the signatures to determine the number of pages in the signature. Try to make an estimate of the size of the original sheet of paper on which the signature was printed.
4. Visit a local newspaper or printing plant. Observe a stoneman making lock-ups. Ask him about procedure, shortcuts, and problems which he encounters. Ask him what things he has to know and do to be a stoneman. Prepare a detailed report on your visit.

UNIT 80
INTRODUCTION TO LETTERPRESS IMAGE TRANSFER

Transfer of an image by letterpress is accomplished from a relief surface, as explained in Unit 5. There are three different press designs common to letterpress: (1) platen, (2) cylinder, and (3) rotary.

PLATEN

The platen-press operating principle is illustrated in Fig. 80-1. The impression (image transfer) is made at one time as the entire typeform is pressed against the paper.

Platen presses are hand-operated (Fig. 80-2), power-operated with hand feed (Fig.

Fig. 80-2. A hand-operated platen press. (Chandler & Price Co.)

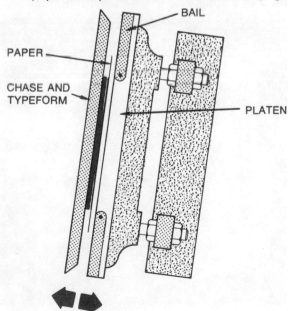

Fig. 80-1. The operating principle of the platen letterpress.

Fig. 80-3. A hand-fed, power-operated platen press. (Chandler & Price Co.)

Fig. 80-4. An automatic platen press. (Original Heidelberg)

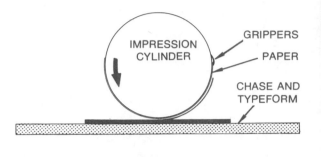

Fig. 80-5. The operating principle of the cylinder letterpress.

80-3), or automatic feed (Fig. 80-4). The size of a platen press is determined by the inside dimensions of the chase. Hand-operated platen presses generally have a maximum chase size of 6½ x 10 inches. Power-operated platen presses are commonly available in three sizes: 8 x 10, 10 x 15, and 12 x 18 inches. The top speed of an automatic platen press is approximately 5,000 iph (impressions per hour).

CYLINDER

The cylinder-press operating principle is shown in Fig. 80-5. Image transfer is made to the paper as the flat typeform moves against the impression cylinder. Only a small portion of the sheet receives the image at a given time.

Modern cylinder presses are designed for automatic feed and delivery of paper. The size of the press is determined by the maximum sheet size that can be run though it. Usual sheet sizes range from 15 x 23 to 31 x 44 inches. Press speeds go to a maximum of 5,000 iph. Two basic designs of cylinder presses are the horizontal (Fig. 80-6) and the vertical (Fig. 80-7).

Fig. 80-6. A standard horizontal cylinder letterpress that will print an 18" x 23" sheet. (Original Heidelberg)

Fig. 80-7. A cylinder letter press in which the typeform is placed in a vertical position. (The Miehle Co.)

ROTARY

The operating principle of the rotary press is illustrated in Fig. 80-8. Rotary presses can be sheet-fed or web-fed (by a continuous roll of paper). With many, two-image carriers can be attached to one image-carrier cylinder; one revolution of the cylinder therefore produces two complete impressions.

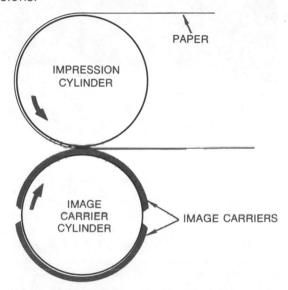

Fig. 80-8. The operating principle of the rotary letter-press.

Fig. 80-9. A two-color, sheet-fed rotary letterpress. (Original Heidelberg)

Rotary press designs vary greatly. A two-color sheet-fed rotary press (Fig. 80-9) must have a specific arrangement (Fig. 80-10) to accommodate the two image-carrier cylinders. It is possible to have only one impression cylinder and print in two colors. The speed of this press is 5,500 iph.

Large newspaper and magazine presses (Figs. 80-11 and 80-12) are designed for multiple pages, color, and high speed. Magazine and most high speed presses must contain a heating unit to dry the ink when printing on glossy paper. Both types of presses are equipped with folding units that

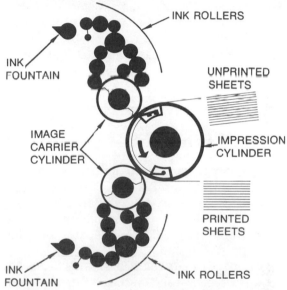

Fig. 80-10. The operating principle of the two-color letterpress shown in Fig. 80-9.

Fig. 80-11. A web multiple-printing newspaper letter-press. (The Goss Co.)

Fig. 80-12. A high-speed, multicolor magazine press. (The Goss Co.)

Fig. 80-13. A typical eighteenth century pressroom. (Diderot's Encyclopedia, Colonial Williamsburg)

cut and fold the web of paper to the desired finished size. The cylinders of a typical newspaper press turn at 35,000 revolutions per hour.

EARLY PRESSES

Gutenberg was compelled to develop a press to print from his movable-metal type. The press was crudely patterned after a wine press, but he succeeded in creating pressure which could transfer the ink from the type to the paper.

For many years, improvements in press design were few and in the eighteenth century American colonists were still using the same basic press as Gutenberg's. A typical pressroom of an eighteenth century printer is shown in Fig. 80-13. Note that the presses were constructed of wood. Bracing them to the roof helped make them secure.

Two men were required to operate these presses, and production was only a few hundred sheets per day. It has been said that two experienced pressmen could print an average of 200 sheets per hour.

The importance of the printing press is expressed in a legendary poem written by Robert H. Davis.

I am the printing press born of mother earth. My heart is of steel, my limbs are of iron, and my fingers are of brass.

I sing the songs of the world, the oratorios of history, the symphonies of all time. I am the voice of today, the herald of tomorrow. I weave into the warp of the past the woof of the future. I tell the stories of peace and war alike. I make the human heart beat with passion or tenderness. I stir the pulse of nations, and make brave men do braver deeds, and soldiers die.

I inspire the midnight toiler, weary at his loom, to lift his head again and gaze with fearlessness into the vast beyond, seeking the consolation of a hope eternal.

When I speak, a myriad people listen to my voice. The Saxon, the Latin, the Celt, the Hun, the Slav, the Hindu, all comprehend me. I am the tireless clarion of the news.

I cry your joys and sorrows every hour. I fill the dullard's mind with thoughts uplifting. I am light, knowledge, power. I epitomize the conquests of mind over matter. I am the record of all things mankind has achieved.

My offspring comes to you in the candle's glow, amid the dim lamps of poverty, the splendor of riches; at sunrise, at high noon, and in the waning evening. I am the laughter and tears of the world, and I shall never die until all things return to the immutable dust.

I am the printing press.

—*Robert H. Davis*

UNIT 81
FLEXOGRAPHY

Image transfer is made from a relief surface in flexography similar to that done in letterpress. The primary differences in these two image-transfer methods are in the kind of image carriers and the kind of inks used.

The first flexographic press was probably built in the year 1890 in England, but it was not until the middle 1920s that this process was brought into the United States. In recent years, dramatic improvements have been made to develop this method of reproducing images into one of the most important in the graphic arts industry.

USES

The primary growth of flexography has been synonymous with that of the packaging industry. Materials such as paper bags, polyethylene films, foils, gift wraps, and pressure sensitive tapes used to package manufactured goods are nearly all printed by the flexography process. It is also gaining prominence in printing books, business forms, folding boxes, and specialty items such as shower curtains and drinking straws.

IMAGE CARRIERS AND INK

Image carriers for flexographic reproduction are made of either natural or synthetic rubber laid in uncured form over a matrix. Heat and pressure are used to cure the rubber, after which it is shaved to a predetermined thickness. The completed image carrier is then fastened to the press cylinder by adhesives or mechanical anchorages for the printing operation. The process of producing relief, rubber flexography image carriers is discussed in Unit 71.

Ink is extremely important to this process. Because flexography is used to print packaging materials for food products, the food and drug laws are very strict regarding the contact of inks with food. Flexographic ink is thin and dries quickly. Much research has been conducted to develop ink with opacity, heat resistance, gloss, alkali and acid resistance, and permanency.

IMAGE TRANSFER DEVICES

Standard flexographic presses are of the rotary type and are designed to print in one or several colors. They range in size from 20 to 60 inches wide but they can be specially-built to accomodate a wider web. Unprinted rolls (webs) of stock are threaded into the press, printed, force dried, and rewound into rolls.

Press speeds are measured in feet per minute. Common speeds range from 200 to 800 fpm. Several variables determine press speeds: type of equipment, type of work, quality of work desired, kind of inks used, and kind of materials being printed.

Generally, flexographic presses are classified into two major groups, based on press design. The original press construction, similar to rotary letterpress, is called stack-type (Fig. 81-1). The image carrier cylinder of this machine (Fig. 81-2) can have several rubber plates attached to it to permit duplicate images and/or different ones to be printed at the same time.

Fig. 81-1. A four color, stack-type flexography press. (Wolverine Flexographic Manufacturing Co.)

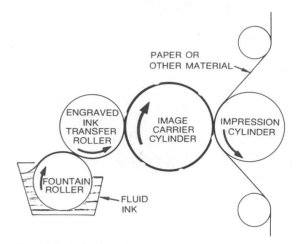

Fig. 81-2. A single-color image transfer unit of a stack-type flexography press.

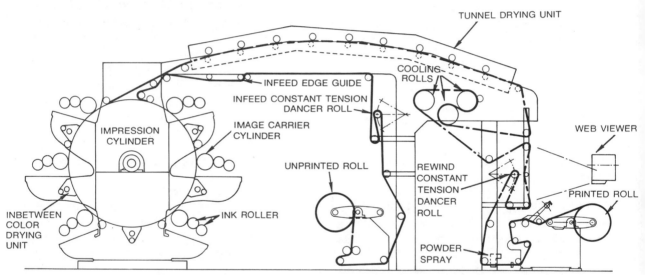

Fig. 81-3. A schematic of a six-color, single-impression cylinder flexography press.

The second kind, the single-impression cylinder flexography press contains an enlarged and centrally-located impression cylinder that serves all image transfer units. Assured fixation of the web is the most appealing advantage of this press over the stacked design. This type of press (Fig. 81-3) is very similar to the stack type except for the printing unit. The large impression cylinder must be machined accurately to within .003 inch to provide the printing surface needed for quality results. Many are water cooled to maintain exact cylinder diameter.

UNIT 82
SAFETY WITH PLATEN AND CYLINDER PRESSES

The following safety precautions make an efficient check list for safe operation practices of platen and cylinder presses.

Permission. Request permission from your instructor before operating the platen or cylinder press.

Clothing. Do not wear loose-fitting clothing. It can be dangerous. Remove ties, and roll up or button long sleeves.

Jewelry. Remove wrist watches, bracelets, and rings from wrists and fingers. These items can be caught on the press and pull you into moving parts.

Hands and fingers. Be cautious where you place your hands when a press is running. They could easily become caught in moving parts.

Adjustments. Make adjustments only when a press is stopped.

Guards. All safety guards should be in place and fastened securely before the press power is turned on. All belts, chains, gears, and shafts should be adequately covered.

Instruction manual. Read the instruction manual carefully before using the presses. Each manufacturer designs these machines differently; the operating controls and adjustments may therefore be located in positions other than those shown on the presses used in Units 83 through 87.

Press speed. Operate the hand-fed platen press at a slow speed until you develop the necessary rhythm for smooth feeding and delivery of sheets. The cylinder press should also be operated slowly until adequate skill is acquired to operate safely.

One operator. Only one person should operate a platen or cylinder press at a time. These machines are one-man machines and it becomes extremely dangerous when two or more persons attempt to run controls.

Stopping the press. Turn the power off and stop the press before leaving it.

Stance. Place your feet firmly when operating presses.

Clean floors. Keep the floor free of waste paper and oil. You could easily slip. Do not leave tools on the floor or on the press after making adjustments or repairs. Return them to their proper locations.

Lubricating a press. Stop the press before oiling or greasing it.

Safety switch. Use the safety switch or device properly for each press. Power presses should all contain electrical safety switches. Some also have mechanical devices that, when activated, will not allow the power to be turned on.

Carrying a locked chase. Carry the locked chase to the press with care, as a dropped one could easily injure your foot. Keep your back straight when removing a locked chase from the storage rack or press.

Feeding the press. Feed and remove sheets of paper from the hand-fed press cautiously but deliberately. Learn and remember the safe working areas of a press when hand feeding. Never attempt to retrieve a printed sheet that has been dropped into a moving press.

Makeready knife. Always know where you have placed your makeready knife. Use it with care when completing the makeready operation on the platen or cylinder press.

Ink solvents. Store the ink solvent in a safety can and use a solvent that is inflammable or has a low flash point. Do not strike matches in its vicinity. Do not use carbon tetrachloride.

Air circulation. There should always be adequate air circulation to carry away solvent fumes that could cause headaches and drowsiness.

UNIT 83
PLATEN PRESS PREPARATION

Proper preparation of the platen press (Fig. 83-1) is a necessity. Careful attention to preprinting details insures trouble-free operation and will result in a job well done. Follow the procedure as given to prepare the platen press for operation.

PARTS AND USES

Platen. The smooth metal casting that provides the impression surface.

Ink fountain. The ink reserve that automatically replenishes the ink rollers.

Ink disk. The ink rollers obtain ink from the disk on each revolution of the press.

Platen guard. A safety device designed to keep hands from between the platen and the typeform.

Feed board. Sheets to be printed are placed on the feed board.

Delivery board. After sheets have been printed, they are placed on the delivery board.

Impression lever. This lever controls whether an image is transferred. Pushing it forward does not allow the typeform to strike the paper. Pulling it backward permits impression.

Counter. This device records the number of sheets printed.

PRESS PREPARATION

1. Move the grippers to the outer edge of the platen (Fig. 83-2).
2. Tighten the gripper nuts. This prevents them from sliding between the typeform and platen while the press is being prepared.

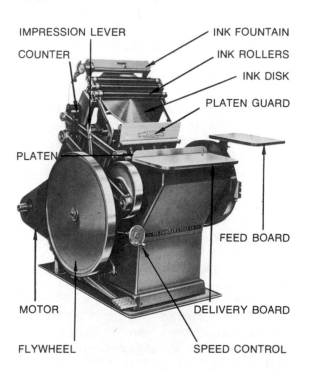

Fig. 83-1. A 10 x 15-inch hand-fed platen press. (Chandler and Price Co.)

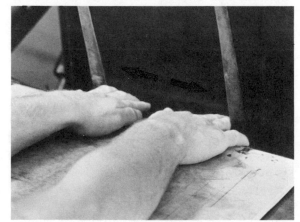

Fig. 83-2. Moving the grippers to the outer edge of the platen.

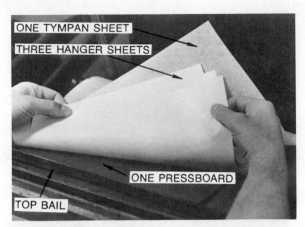

Fig. 83-3. Dressing the platen.

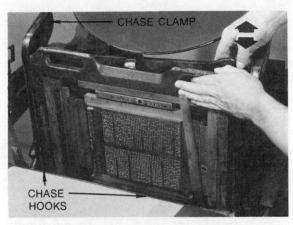

Fig. 83-5. Placing a locked chase in the press.

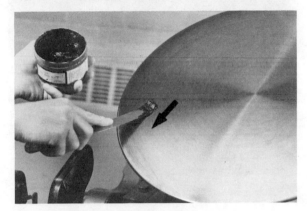

Fig. 83-4. Inking the platen press.

Fig. 83-6. An impression pulled on the tympan.

3. Dress the platen (Fig. 83-3). Use the following dressing materials in the order listed:
   a. one tympan sheet of 0.006 inch oiled manila paper
   b. three hanger sheets, each of 0.003 inch coated paper
   c. one pressboard of 0.020 inch smooth-finished hardboard.
   The total thickness of these three materials is 0.035 inch. The tympan and hanger sheets are clamped under the bottom and top bails. Do not place the pressboard under the bails.
4. Ink the press (Fig. 83-4). Do not use the ink fountain for short runs; place only a small amount of ink on the ink disk. The amount of ink will vary, depending on the press and typeform sizes. An amount equal to a thimbleful would be a good beginning. Additional ink can easily be added later if needed.

5. Turn on the power. Allow the press to run until the ink is distributed.
6. Turn off the press.
7. Wipe the bottom of the typeform to remove dirt particles. Then place the chase and typeform in the press (Fig. 83-5).
8. Set the bottom of the chase against the two chase hooks; secure the top with a chase clamp. The quoins should be positioned to the top and right sides of the press.
9. Pull an impression on the tympan (Fig. 83-6). Roll the press over by hand to print on the tympan. It is not necessary to obtain a high-quality print, but all parts of the typeform should be visible on the tympan.
10. Determine the paper position on the tympan:

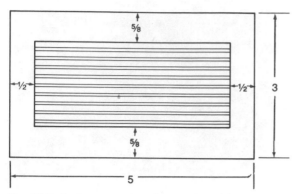

Fig. 83-7. An image centered on a sheet of paper.

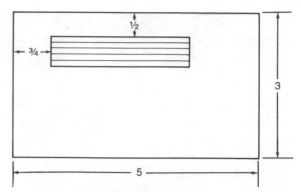

Fig. 83-8. Predetermined top and left margins.

a. To center the image on the paper, measure the image length and width; subtract the image size from the paper size and equally divide the marginal area on all four sides (Fig. 83-7).

b. A predetermined margin can be selected for any of the four sides (Fig. 83-8).

c. After determining margins, mark guidelines on the tympan for the side and top edges of the paper (Fig. 83-9).

11. Secure the gauge pins to the tympan. Gauge pins are devices that hold the paper in place on the platen while the sheet is being printed.

a. Two gauge pins are positioned at the top edge of the paper, approximately 1/6 the width of the paper from the ends (Fig. 83-10).

b. One gauge pin is positioned at the left edge of the paper, approximately 1/3 the height of the paper from the top edge (Fig. 83-10).

c. Insert the center prong under the tympan 1/8 inch outside the guideline.

d. Extend the prong under the tympan 1/2 inch and force it back through the surface.

e. Continue sliding the gauge pin until the guide edge is in line with the guideline (Fig. 83-11). Do not allow the prong to extend through the hanger sheets.

12. Check gauge pins and gauge-pin tongues to see that they clear the typeform. If not, the type will be damaged.

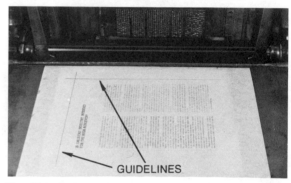

Fig. 83-9. Guidelines drawn on the tympan for the top and side edges of the paper.

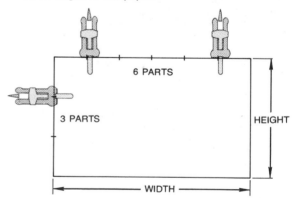

Fig. 83-10. The proper position of the gauge pins.

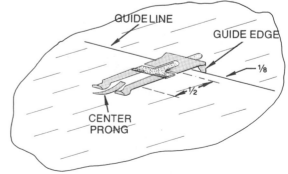

Fig. 83-11. A properly installed gauge pin.

Fig. 83-12. Pulling the trial impression.

Fig. 83-13. The gripper positioned over the margin of the printed sheet.

13. Wipe the inked image from the tympan. Use a clean cloth slightly dampened with ink solvent.
14. To pull a trial impression (Fig. 83-12):
    a. place a sheet of paper against the gauge pins;
    b. pull the impression lever;
    c. roll the press over by hand.
15. Measure the position of the image. If it is not correct, slide the gauge pins ac-cordingly. After obtaining the proper printing position, lightly tap the top of the gauge pins to secure them in the tympan sheet.
16. If necessary, move grippers into posi-tion over the margin of the sheet (Fig. 83-13). Be sure that they clear the type-form and gauge pins.
17. Proceed with the makeready in an or-derly manner.

UNIT 84
PLATEN PRESS MAKEREADY AND OPERATION

An important process called *makeready* must be completed after the preliminary steps of press preparation have been car-ried out. Makeready is the process of equal-izing the impression of all parts of the type-form as it prints on a sheet of paper. Perfect image transfer takes place with proper makeready.

Operation of a hand-fed platen press re-quires hand and eye coordination which can only be acquired with practice. Follow the procedure outlined to complete a print-ed job.

PRESS MAKEREADY

1. Obtain the proper printing position on the paper.
2. Check for punch-through (excessive type pressure) to the back of the sheet. Lay a printed sheet upside down on a smooth, hard surface. Feel for the raised areas caused by impressing the type-form too hard against the paper. If *punch* is detected, remove a hanger sheet and repeat inspection. If there is excessive punch, the height of the plat-en may need adjustment.
3. Identify image areas that are printing too lightly.
4. Circle the letters or areas on a printed sheet that need additional impression (Fig. 84-1).
5. Place makeready paste inside the cir-cled areas. Use the paste sparingly.
6. Lay a sheet of tissue paper over a cir-cled area. Cut the tissue with a make-

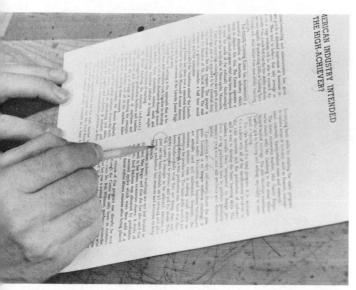

Fig. 84-1. Identifying and circling image areas that are printing too lightly.

Fig. 84-2. Adding tissue to the image areas that are printing too lightly.

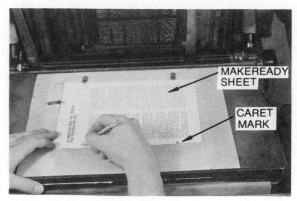

Fig. 84-3. Cutting caret marks.

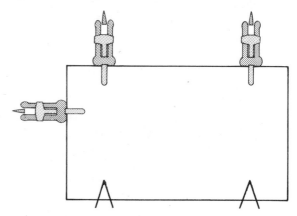

Fig. 84-4. The correct position of caret marks.

ready knife to conform with the lines (Fig. 84-2). Be careful to cut only through the tissue.

7. Place the pasted-up sheet (now called a makeready sheet) in the press against the gauge pins.

8. Cut two caret marks (inverted *V)* through the makeready sheet and tympan (Fig. 84-3). The position of the marks should be directly across from the two gauge pins (Fig. 84-4). The caret marks are used to align the makeready sheet under the tympan.

9. Remove the makeready sheet.

10. Raise the top bail only; fold back the tympan.

11. Paste the makeready sheet on the top hanger sheet (Fig. 84-5) by aligning the caret marks in the makeready sheet with those that were cut in the hanger sheet. Use paste sparingly.

12. Remove a hanger sheet to compensate for the additional thickness of the makeready sheet.

13. Remove the pressboard from the bottom of the platen dressing. Place it between the tympan and top hanger sheet. This smooths the different thicknesses of the makeready sheet.

14. Lower the tympan sheet and reclamp the platen dressing under the top bail.

15. Take a trial impression.

16. Inspect the image. If additional impression is required, add tissue to the needed areas on the makeready sheet. Repeat this step until perfect impressions are obtained.

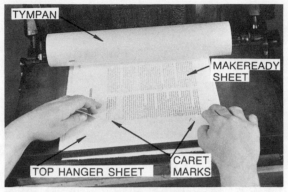

Fig. 84-5. Attaching the makeready sheet to the top hanger sheet.

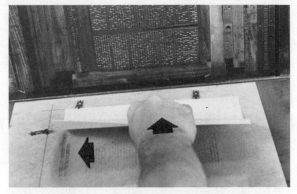

Fig. 84-6. Placing a sheet against the gauge pins.

PRESS OPERATION

1. Clear away all materials from the feed and delivery boards.
2. Place a pile of paper stock on the feed board.
3. Turn on the power and run the press at a slow speed.
4. With the right hand, place a sheet against the gauge pins when the platen is open (Fig. 84-6). Position the sheet against the bottom two pins. Slide the sheet over to the side pin.
5. Pull the impression lever back with the left hand.
6. Remove the printed sheet with the left hand.
7. Feed another sheet with the right hand (Fig. 84-7). These two operations must be completed during the few seconds that the platen is open.
8. Push the impression lever forward if the sheet is not being properly fed to the gauge pins.

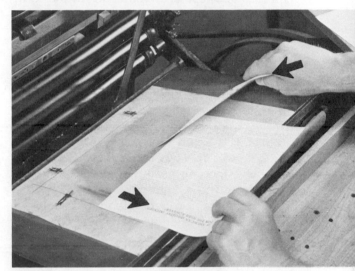

Fig. 84-7. Feeding the hand-fed platen press.

9. On the next revolution of the press, straighten the sheet, pull the impression lever, and begin feeding and delivering the sheets again.
10. Finish printing the desired number of copies.
11. Clean the press as outlined in Unit 87.

UNIT 85
CYLINDER PRESS PREPARATION

The automatic cylinder press prints flat typeforms. These are type either in the form of hot composition or foundry type or in the form of original or duplicate letterpress image carriers, or a combination of the two.

In this printing procedure the press is inked, the paper is loaded on the feed tray, and the locked chase is placed into the press. Suction delivers one sheet at a time to the impression cylinder grippers and guides. The sheet travels around the cylinder between the typeform and the cylinder to receive the impression or image. It is then taken from the cylinder grippers by the delivery grippers and deposited into a delivery tray. This is repeated as many times as there are sheets to be printed.

Proper preparation of the cylinder press (Fig. 85-1) is essential. Careful attention to preprinting details helps insure trouble-free operation and will always result in a job well done.

PARTS AND USES

Typeform and Chase Bed. Here the locked typeform is placed in the vertically designed cylinder press.

Feeder Unit. This unit automatically feeds single sheets of paper to the grippers on the impression cylinder.

Impression Cylinder. This is a cylinder with grippers that causes the paper to contact the typeform for the image transfer.

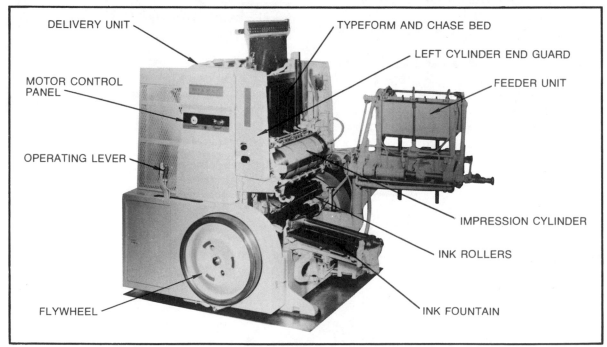

Fig. 85-1. A cylinder letterpress machine. (The Miehle Co.)

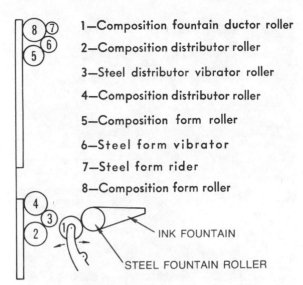

1—Composition fountain ductor roller

2—Composition distributor roller

3—Steel distributor vibrator roller

4—Composition distributor roller

5—Composition form roller

6—Steel form vibrator

7—Steel form rider

8—Composition form roller

Fig. 85-2. The arrangement of the ink rollers for the vertical cylinder press referred to in Units 85 and 86.

Ink Rollers. The several ink rollers deliver ink to the type after each impression.

Ink Fountain. The ink reserve automatically replenishes the ink rollers.

Operating Lever. Movement of this lever controls the starting and stopping of the press. It also acts as a brake.

Motor Control Panel. This contains the motor start-stop switches and the oil pressure gauge.

Left Cylinder End Guard. This guard encloses the left end of the cylinder. It protects the operator as the cylinder moves up and down. It also prevents the electric power switch from being turned on when the cylinder is open for making adjustments. The entire purpose of the guard is SAFETY.

Delivery Unit. In this unit the sheets are delivered and jogged or straightened after receiving the image.

CYLINDER PRESS PREPARATION

1. Lubricate the press. Many printing presses are equipped with an automatic lubrication system. This should be inspected to see that it is operating correctly. Keep the oil reservoir full. Use only oil that is recommended by the manufacturer of the press.

Fig. 85-3. Placing ink into the fountain.

Fig. 85-4. Using fountain screws to regulate the flow or distribution of ink from the fountain.

2. Install the ink rollers. Follow the roller schedule according to the manufacturer's press manual (Fig. 85-2).
3. Turn the flywheel by hand and roll the press through one entire cycle to determine whether the ink rollers have been installed correctly. Repeat this step each time an adjustment or an addition is made on the press.
4. Place ink into the fountain (Fig. 85-3). The amount of ink needed depends upon the job to be printed. Do not oversupply the fountain because air dries ink rapidly, causing ink to be wasted.
5. Close the ink fountain.
6. Ink the rollers. This is called *inking the press.*
   a. Roll the press by hand until the ductor roller contacts the fountain roller.
   b. Turn the fountain roller with the hand crank. Adjust the fountain screws (Fig. 85-4). Each screw or *key* regulates the amount of ink released from a specified area of the fountain. An even flow or distribution of ink is essential.

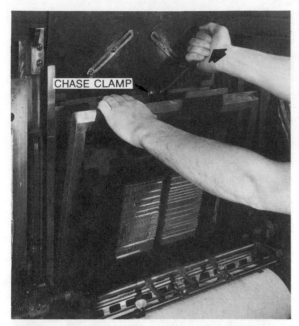

Fig. 85-5. Securing a locked chase in a cylinder press.

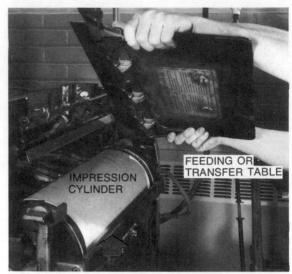

Fig. 85-6. Attaching the feeding, or transfer, table with the impression cylinder in the *up* position.

c. Engage the ratchet lever (see Fig. 85-4). This turns the fountain roller while the press is operating. Make the adjustment which allows the fountain roller to turn a specified distance at each revolution of the press.

d. Turn on the press motor. Engage the clutch (operating lever) to ink the press. Run the press until all rollers are thoroughly inked.

e. Stop the press at the bottom of its stroke and engage the safety control. All automatic presses have safety controls; locate and use them.

6. Place the chase and locked typeform in the press.

a. See that the form has been locked up correctly. Generally, chases for cylinder presses are designed for a specific installation. Vertical adjustment of the image on the page is made by repositioning the form; it is therefore essential that the form be locked in the correct position.

b. Position the chase in the press. Secure it firmly with the chase clamp (Fig. 85-5).

7. Attach the feeding, or transfer table (Fig. 85-6).

a. Rotate the press by hand until the impression cylinder is in the up position.

b. Attach the feeding, or transfer table. Lock it in place.

c. Rotate the press by hand until the impression cylinder is in the down position.

8. Set the side register guide so that the image will be printed in the correct position.

a. Measure the image area of the form according to the sheet size that will be printed. Mark it (Fig. 85-7).

b. Fold the total margin area in half to center the image on the sheet.

c. Set the side register guide to correspond to the desired position of the sheet (Fig. 85-8).

9. Prepare the feeder.

a. Swing the feeder from open position and lock it in operating position (Fig. 85-9).

b. Adjust the feeder front pile guides according to the sheet width and the position of the side register guide (see Fig. 85-10).

c. Load a supply of paper stock in the feeder.

d. Raise the feeder pile table to within ½ inch of the top of the front pile guides (Fig. 85-10).

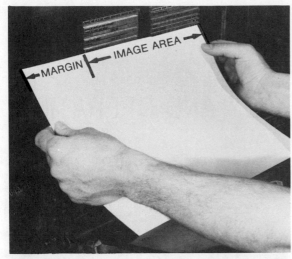

Fig. 85-7. Determining the amount of image or margin area of the sheet.

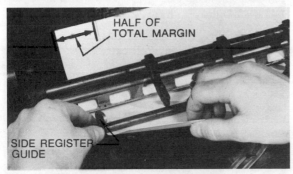

Fig. 85-8. Setting the side paper register guide.

e. Adjust the rear corner pile guides to correspond to the paper stock.

10. Prepare the feeder air suction and the blow nozzles.
   a. Install the correct air suction shoes for the paper to be printed.
   b. Position the air suction shoes 1 inch from the sides of the pile of paper (Fig. 85-10).
   c. Adjust the air-blow nozzles so the top few sheets of the pile are *floating on air.* This allows the air suction shoes to pick up one sheet at a time.

11. Adjust delivery jogging guides.
   a. Release the press safety and start the press.
   b. Feed one sheet through; then stop the press just before the sheet is released by the delivery grippers.
   c. Adjust the delivery side and rear joggers to accept the sheet (Fig. 85-11).

Fig. 85-9. Closing and locking the feeder in the operating position.

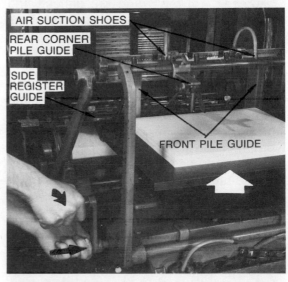

Fig. 85-10. Raising the feeder pile table to the proper feeding level.

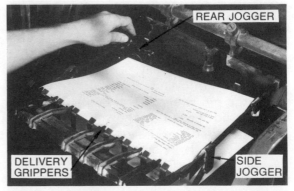

Fig. 85-11. Adjusting the delivery joggers to accept the sheet.

The preliminary press preparation is now completed. Press makeready and operation are presented in Unit 86.

UNIT 86
CYLINDER PRESS MAKEREADY AND OPERATION

The important process of *makeready* must be completed, as noted in the opening paragraph of Unit 84. This takes place after the preliminary steps of preparing a press for operation have been accomplished. Makeready is a rewarding but difficult and time-consuming phase of press operation. Equalization of impression on all parts of the typeform is a must if good results are to be obtained.

Repacking the impression cylinder is a part of the makeready process that normally is completed before a cylinder letterpress is set up for a specific job. Before a different typeform is positioned in the press, previous makeready sheets that would not be applicable must be removed. This operation is termed *packing the impression cylinder.*

PACKING THE IMPRESSION CYLINDER

1. Engage the safety by opening the left cylinder end guard (Unit 85).
2. Turn the press by hand until the cylinder is in a working position. Engage the brake.
3. If necessary, disengage the cylinder to revolve it manually.
4. Turn the cylinder, using the special large pin wrench (Fig. 86-2). Turn until it is positioned as shown in Fig. 86-1.
5. Turn the reel rod slightly with the small pin wrench; release the pawl from the ratchet wheel (Fig. 86-1).
6. Turn the cylinder until the gripper bar is exposed, and then loosen the gripper-bar clamp screws (Fig. 86-2). Remove the gripper bar.
7. Remove the packing sheets one by one. Discard unusable ones.

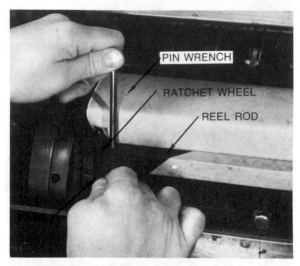

Fig. 86-1. Removing the cylinder packing.

Fig. 86-2. Removing the cylinder gripper bar.

8. Collect the packing sheets. The several kinds and sizes of presses require different amounts of packing. Consult the manufacturer's manual. Normally, three or four pieces of tympan paper and several hanger sheets are needed.
9. Fold over the gripper edge of each sheet approximately 1 inch.
10. Place each sheet so that the folded edge is on the cylinder gripper and spike it on the cylinder pins (Fig. 86-3).

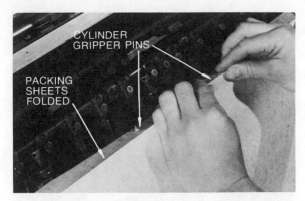

Fig. 86-3. Placing new packing sheets on the cylinder.

11. Replace the gripper bar. Tighten it in place.
12. Add two loose hanger sheets within the packing.
13. Turn the cylinder until the reel rod and ratchet are visible (Fig. 86-1). Keep the packing sheets smooth and snug.
14. Wrap the tympan sheet around the reel rod. Tighten the packing by turning the reel rod.
15. Engage the pawl into the ratchet wheel to secure the reel rod.
16. Turn the cylinder to inspect the packing, which must be tight and smooth.
17. Engage the cylinder if it was disengaged in Step 3.

The cylinder is now properly packed and the press can be prepared according to the information found in Unit 85.

MAKEREADY FOR A SPECIFIC FORM

1. Obtain the proper printing position on the paper (Unit 85).
2. Print a few sheets.
3. Check for punch-through to the back of the sheets. Lay a printed sheet upside down on a smooth, hard surface. Feel for raised areas caused by impressing the paper too hard against the typeform. If punch is detected, remove one or more hanger sheets from the impression cylinder packing.
4. Start the press.
5. Print one sheet, then stop the press just short of the delivery grippers.
6. Check to see that contact is not made.

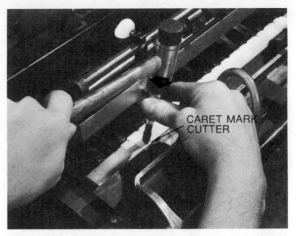

Fig. 86-4. Cutting caret marks through a printed sheet, through the tympan, and into the top hanger sheet.

7. Turn the press power off and engage the safety.
8. Cut two caret (line-up) marks through the printed sheet, through the tympan, and into the top hanger sheet (Fig. 86-4). The special tool used in this figure is available but a standard makeready knife can also be used.
9. Remove the sheet from the press.
10. Inspect the sheet. Add tissue paper to the light areas. Refer to Steps 3, 4, and 5 in Unit 84 for specific details on how to prepare the makeready sheet.
11. Open the packing of the impression cylinder.
12. Glue the makeready sheet to the top hanger sheet according to the caret marks (Fig. 86-5).

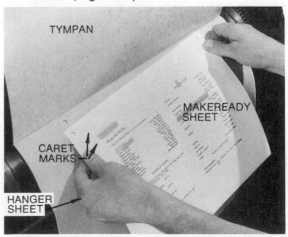

Fig. 86-5. Attaching the makeready sheet to a cylinder hanger sheet.

13. Remove the loose hanger sheet to compensate for the added thickness of the makeready sheet. Also place a loose hanger sheet between the makeready sheet and the tympan, then secure the cylinder packing again.
14. Print approximately 12 copies.
15. Stop the press. Examine the printed sheets. If additional impression is required, add tissue to the needed areas on the makeready sheet that is already attached to the impression cylinder packing.
16. Repeat Steps 15 and 16 until perfect impressions are obtained.

CYLINDER PRESS OPERATION

1. Clear away all tools and materials used to set up the press.
2. Recheck all adjustments to make sure that the press will operate properly.
3. Set the automatic counter.
4. Begin to print the desired number of copies.

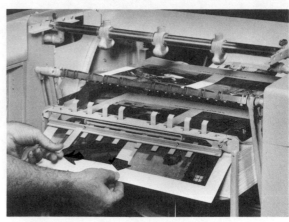

Fig. 86-6. Removing a sheet from the delivery to inspect the printing quality.

5. Check to see that the sheets are being printed properly during the press run (Fig. 86-6).
6. Regulate the ink fountain to obtain an even balance of ink across the printed sheet.
7. After printing the desired number of copies, stop the press and remove all printed and unprinted sheets.
8. Wash the press according to the procedure outlined in Unit 87.

UNIT 87
PRESS CLEANUP PROCEDURES

Cleaning a platen or cylinder letterpress is an easy but very important part of press operation. All ink must be removed from the ink rollers and press supply areas, such as the ink fountain, ink plate, and ink disk. This must be done after the press has been used because the ink dries and damages the press.

PLATEN PRESS CLEANUP

1. Remove the chase from the press.
2. Place it on the stone.
3. Wash the typeform.

4. Obtain two cloths, one clean and another previously used. Also get a can of solvent.
5. Pour solvent on the used cloth and wipe the ink disk and rollers (Fig. 87-1).
6. Pour solvent on the clean cloth. Again wipe the ink disk and rollers. No ink should remain on the press rollers or ink disk. NOTE: Do not pour solvent on the disk itself as it will run down the front of the press.
7. Replace all materials used in the printing operation.
8. Unlock the chase.
9. Replace all items.

Fig. 87-1. Washing the ink disk and rollers of a platen press.

CYLINDER PRESS CLEANUP

1. Remove the chase from the press.
2. Place it on the stone.
3. Wash the typeform.
4. Slowly run the press until the impression cylinder is positioned to expose all ink rollers and the ink plate.
5. Turn off the power, set the brake, and engage the safety.
6. Remove the excess ink from the ink fountain with an ink knife and put the ink back in the original can.
7. Clean the ink fountain blade, the fountain rollers, and the ductor roller (Fig. 87-2). Wipe the fountain clean with a cloth and solvent.
8. Remove each composition ink roller and wash it thoroughly (Fig. 87-3).
9. Place the clean rollers in a special roller rack to prevent them from getting flat on one side.
10. Wash each steel ink roller that is permanently mounted in the press.
11. Wipe the ink plate free of ink (Fig. 87-4). Ink allowed to dry on the plate causes inking problems the next time the press is used.
12. Wipe down the press, using a cloth dampened with solvent. This removes ink and oil build-up. The press is now ready for the next job.
13. Unlock the chase and replace all items.

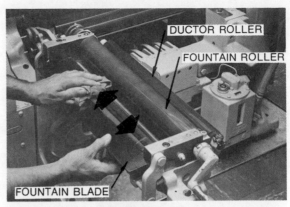

Fig. 87-2. Cleaning the ink fountain.

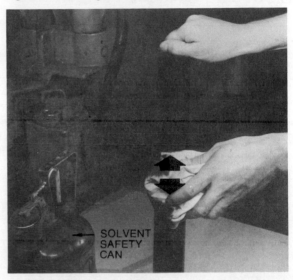

Fig. 87-3. Washing a composition ink roller that has been removed from the press.

Fig. 87-4. Washing the ink plate of a cylinder press.

UNIT 88
LEARNING EXPERIENCES: LETTERPRESS IMAGE TRANSFER

DISCUSSION TOPICS

1. List the three press designs common to the letterpress method of image transfer. Illustrate the operating principle for each design. Which is the oldest of these three designs?
2. How are the sizes of the presses generally designated? What is the maximum speed of each of the press designs? Name the several advantages of the rotary press over the other two letterpress presses.
3. Who has been given credit for developing the first press? Describe this press and others that followed. Explain how these presses were operated.
4. Explain the principle of flexography. How does it differ from the normal method of letterpress image transfer? When was this process first used? When was it first used in the United States?
5. Name the several uses of the flexographic method of image transfer. Enumerate the several qualities that flexographic inks must have. How has the federal government regulated flexographic inks?
6. Describe the flexographic press. Illustrate two press designs common to this method of image transfer. What kind of image carrier is used in flexography? Why is it used?
7. Identify the primary parts of the platen press. Which of these parts controls whether or not an image is transferred? Which part has the specific purpose of promoting safety?
8. Explain the procedure for dressing the platen on the platen press. Identify the material and purpose of each of the packing sheets. Which devices hold the dressing securely to the platen?
9. How much ink should be placed on the platen press? When should the ink fountain be used?
10. In what position should the locked chase be placed into the platen press? Which devices hold the chase in place?
11. Explain the procedure for securing the gauge pins to the tympan. Give the procedure for determining where the paper should be positioned on the platen so that the image is reproduced in the correct location. Give the purpose of the grippers on a platen press.
12. Define the term *makeready*. Cite the first step in the makeready process. What should be done if excessive punch is detected?
13. Explain the procedure for correcting image areas that are printing too light. Identify the sheet of paper that is positioned on the top hanger sheet that contains small pieces of tissue paper. Cite the purpose of the two caret marks.
14. Describe the operation procedure for the hand-fed power platen press. Where should the unprinted sheets be positioned? Where should the printed sheets be positioned? Which hand is used to remove the printed sheet from the press? What should be done if a sheet is not properly fed to the gauge pins?
15. Describe the manner in which the automatic cylinder press operates. How do

horizontal and vertical presses differ? Compare the impression surfaces on the platen and cylinder presses.

16. Identify the major parts of the vertical cylinder press. Give the primary purpose of the left cylinder end guard. How is the function of the left cylinder end guard activated?

17. Describe the procedure necessary to ink the vertical cylinder press. What adjustments are necessary to regulate the amount of ink added to the ink rollers during the press operations?

18. Why is it important to have a good lock-up before the chase is placed into the cylinder press? How is the vertical position of the image on the sheet altered? How is the chase secured in the chase-bed of the cylinder press?

19. Explain the procedure for preparing the feeder section of the cylinder press. Why is it necessary to install the correct air-suction shoes? How do the air-blow nozzles affect the feeding of the paper into the press? Identify the adjustments necessary in the delivery system of the cylinder press.

20. Why is it necessary to inspect and change the packing papers on the impression cylinder prior to printing a new job? Name the types or kinds of paper used as packing sheets. Why is it necessary that the cylinder packing be tight and smooth?

21. How does the makeready operation for a cylinder press differ from that for a platen press? After the makeready sheet has been placed within the packing of the impression cylinder, why is it a good idea to print several copies before stopping the press to examine the printed sheets? What is the correct procedure for altering the makeready sheets?

22. Why is it important to clean the platen and cylinder presses soon after use? Outline the steps necessary to clean a platen and a cylinder press. In the cleaning operation, what must be done to the cylinder press that is normally not necessary on the platen press?

ACTIVITIES

1. Research the history of each of the press designs and prepare a short paper on each design. Arrange an exhibit in one of your school display cabinets.

2. Obtain or prepare a rubber flexographic image carrier. Adhere the rubber image carrier to a metal can small enough to allow the image carrier to nearly encircle the circumference of the can. Ink the rubber image carrier with the hand brayer and transfer the image by rolling the cylinder (can) over a sheet of paper. If possible, attempt to prepare a working model of a flexographic press.

3. Plan a job that is to be printed on a platen press. Compose and lock up the form in the correct manner. Obtain or cut the paper that you will need for your job. Suggested jobs are name cards, book marks, stationery, and address cards. Print the desired number of items with the platen press. Set up, operate, and clean the press properly.

4. Plan a job that is to be printed on a cylinder press. Compose and lock up the form in the correct manner. Obtain or cut the paper that you will need for your job. Suggested jobs are stationery, pamphlets, handbills, business forms, and newspapers.

5. Lubricate a platen and/or a cylinder press. Obtain the press operator's manual and study the procedures for lubricating that particular press. Be certain to locate the several points that need lubrication with oil or grease. Using a cloth dampened with ink solvent, wipe the entire press free from ink, oil, and dirt accumulation.

A stripper examines a halftone positive on a light table. He will prepare the positive for making a lithographic image carrier.

UNIT 89
INTRODUCTION TO LITHOGRAPHIC IMPOSITION

Lithographic imposition is more commonly called *stripping.* The person who does the stripping is known as the stripper. His job is to make a *flat,* which is used to make a lithographic plate. The plate is used on the press to make the prints.

The flat consists of a negative (or negatives) which is attached to a masking sheet. It is usually orange or yellow in color and is often called *goldenrod paper.* This sheet prevents unwanted light from reaching the plate when the plate is exposed. After the negative is attached to the masking sheet,

that material which covers the image areas is removed. This permits light to pass through only the image areas of the negative.

The flat is then placed over a plate. Light passes through the negative to expose the light-sensitive plate (Fig. 89-1). This operation is usually done with a special plate-maker that causes the flat and the plate to be in tight contact. Fig. 89-2 shows a typical platemaker with the flat over the plate.

The flat is the negative master for making plates, and any number of plates can be made from one master. The flat is often stored or filed in a flat position so that it can be used at a later date. If the plate becomes warped or damaged, the flat can be used to make a new one. This plate will be an exact duplicate of the original one.

The basic functions of a stripper are to prepare the masking sheet so that it corre-

GOLDENROD

NEGATIVE LIGHT SENSITIVE   NEGATIVE   PLATE
          SURFACE   IMAGE AREA

Fig. 89-1. Flat and plate position when exposing a negative.

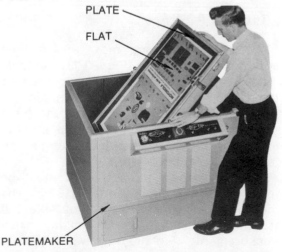

PLATE

FLAT

PLATEMAKER

Fig. 89-2. A platemaker with the flat and plate in position. (nuArc Co.)

sponds to the original layout, attach the negatives, cut windows in the masking paper to expose the image areas of the negative, and opaque clear unwanted areas on the negative. A stripper's work must be careful and precise. He must be sure not only that the negative is in the correct location on the masking sheet but also that the negative is properly aligned. Each page must lay back-to-back squarely when printed.

The stripper's jobs range from simple ones, such as accurately placing one negative on a masking sheet, to more complicated ones such as locating several negatives on a single masking sheet. His work becomes even more complicated when he prepares flats for color printing. Flats for color printing must be prepared so that when the plates are made and printed the colors will match up precisely.

UNIT 90
TOOLS AND MATERIALS OF THE STRIPPER

A stripper requires several pieces of equipment and materials that are different from those used for other jobs in a printing establishment. He must be thoroughly knowledgeable about each item to use them efficiently. Most strippers have their equipment and materials organized so that they are easily located when needed. They also take care to be sure that they have sufficient quantities of materials and that their equipment is in good condition.

LIGHT TABLE

The stripper spends most of his time working at a light table (Fig. 90-1). The table consist of a frame, a frosted glass top, and lights below the glass top which enable him to see adequately. The edges of the table are usually bordered by accurate straight edges so that a T-square and triangle can be used for accurate work.

When extremely precise work must be done, a line-up table is used (Fig. 90-2). The line-up table is similar to the light table, but has micrometer gauges for making exact measurements. Fig. 90-3 shows a line-up table on which a complicated layout has been assembled.

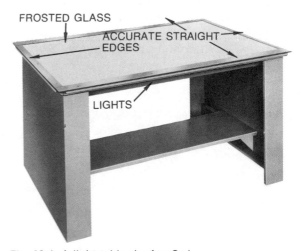

Fig. 90-1. A light table. (nuArc Co.)

T-SQUARE AND TRIANGLES

A T-square and triangles are needed to make layouts, align negatives, and cut negatives and masking paper. Those used most often have stainless steel construction which provide accurate guides when cutting along the edges with a knife. Stainless steel tools are not as easily damaged as are wood or plastic ones. Fig. 90-4 shows a stainless steel T-square, stainless steel triangles, and a standard bevel rule.

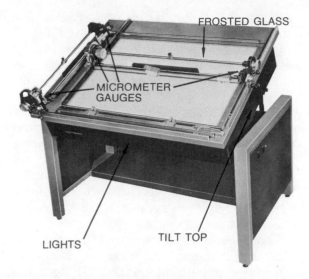

Fig. 90-2. A line-up table. (Craftsman Table Co.)

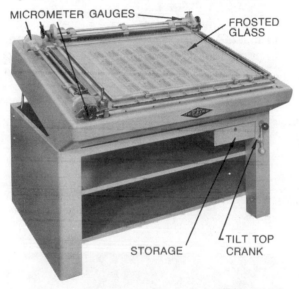

Fig. 90-3. A layout on the glass top of a line-up table.

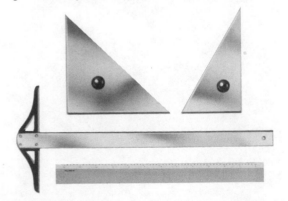

Fig. 90-4. Stainless steel T-square and triangles along with a beveled rule.

Fig. 90-5. A linen tester is used to examine negatives and a swing-base magnifier is used to identify defects.

RULES

Rules are used to make measurements on either the negatives or masking paper. Stainless steel rules are often preferred. In addition to making measurements, they are sometimes used as straightedges. A thin rule, or one with a beveled edge, is best because more accuracy is obtained in using it.

LINEN TESTER AND MAGNIFYING GLASS

Linen testers and magnifying glasses are used to examine negatives during stripping procedures. Magnification identifies tiny imperfections in negatives. Fig. 90-5 shows a linen tester and a swing-base magnifier.

OTHER SMALL TOOLS

There are many other small tools which aid the stripper in his work:

Knives. Knives are used by the stripper to cut negatives and masking material. A common frisket knife is popular. The knives should be kept very sharp. Knives with replaceable blades are often preferred by strippers because less time is required to replace a blade than to keep the blade sharpened. Single-edge razor blades are sometimes used as substitutes for knives.

Scissors. Scissors are used to trim negatives. Their cutting edges should be very sharp to make clean cuts.

Brushes. Artist's brushes are used to opaque (block out) negatives. Several sizes of brushes, from very fine to medium, should be available to the stripper. They should always be kept clean.

MATERIALS

Materials are those items used or consumed during the stripping operation. An ample supply should be maintained. They should be stored so that they are easily obtainable.

Masking Paper. This material is used as a support for negatives when making a flat. It is yellow or orange in color. The color is important because it prevents light, which could cause exposure, from reaching the plate.

Masking sheets are made from either paper or plastic. Paper is used for general-purpose work. Plastic is used when extreme accuracy is required and when expansion and contraction of paper masking material might cause errors.

Several sizes of masking paper are available. The size is determined by the size of the plate to be used on the printing press. It is the same size or slightly larger than the plate. Some masking sheets are available with guidelines printed on the sheet which makes it easier to align the negatives. Masking sheets made for larger presses do not usually have guidelines, and the stripper must put them on if they are necessary for accuracy.

Opaque Solution. This is a water-soluble material available in cake, paste, or liquid form. Pinholes and other clear areas on the negative that are not to be printed are blocked out with opaque. The stripper thins the opaque with water to form a creamy consistency before applying it to the negative with a brush or a pen.

Tape. Both lithographic and common clear pressure-sensitive tape are used during the stripping operation. Lithographic tape is red or brown, and is used to hold negatives to the masking sheet or to cover unwanted image areas on the negative. Like the masking material, it prevents light from reaching the plate. Tape should be placed in dispensers to be easily used when the stripper needs it.

UNIT 91
PREPARATION AND LAYOUT FOR STRIPPING

All stripping operations begin with the stripper planning or laying out and doing certain preparatory work. Most errors in stripping occur because of inadequate or improper layout. The location of the negatives on the masking sheet determines their appearance on the printing plate.

PREPARING FOR STRIPPING

The stripper first examines the negative or negatives which are to be attached to the masking sheet. Inspection can sometimes be done without the aid of magnification; however, magnification is needed when examining a halftone or extremely fine line work (Fig. 91-1).

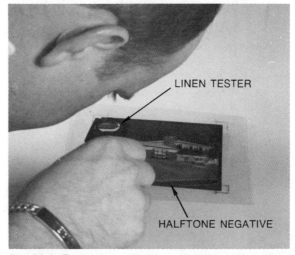

Fig. 91-1. Examining a halftone negative with a linen tester.

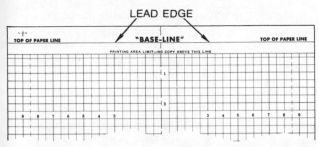

Fig. 91-2. Portion of the masking sheet that corresponds to the lead edge of a printed page.

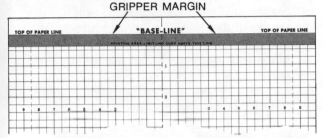

Fig. 91-3. The gripper margin is the space between the lead edge of the printed page and the place where the image will print.

Specifications, including the original layout, which accompany the negative should be carefully checked by the stripper. Before the stripper does the layout for the flat, he must know where the image will appear on the printed sheet, the size of the paper on which the image will be printed, the specific size of the margins, how the printed sheets will be treated after printing (trimmed, stitched, padded, etc.), and, if there are several negatives to be placed on one sheet of paper, their sequence and position on the masking sheet.

Location of the lead edge. The stripper must place the negative image on a masking sheet so that it will print in the correct position on the final printed sheet. To do this he determines which point, or edge, of the masking sheet corresponds to the lead edge of the sheet of paper being printed. The lead edge is that edge of the paper which feeds into the press first, the edge held by the press grippers. Some masking sheets are made with this information printed on them (Fig. 91-2). Others have no marking. The stripper makes measurements and marks the location of the lead edge. This is different for each press, and he gets this information from the pressman.

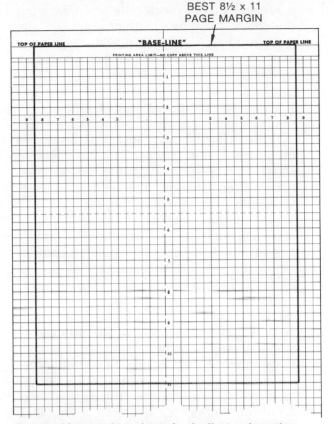

Fig. 91-4. Many masking sheets for duplicators have the best location for the sheet of paper marked by dotted lines.

Identifying the gripper margins. The gripper margin for each press must be known. This is the distance between the lead edge of the sheet of paper and the position where the first part of the image will be printed. This portion of the paper is held by the press grippers or the parts of the press that carry the paper through it. Fig. 91-3 shows the usual gripper margin of a masking sheet of ¼ to ⅜ inch. *No image prints above this line.* As with the lead edge, the stripper must locate and mark the gripper margin on the masking sheets that do not already contain this information.

Locating the sheet margins. Sheet margins show the exact place where the sheet will be represented on the masking material. There is usually a best location for sheet margins. Fig. 91-4 shows the best 8½ x 11-inch sheet margin for the masking sheet, and eventually for the press. Notice that the lead edge of the sheet is one of the margins.

It serves as a reference point for measuring the lower margins (margins opposite the lead edge). In Fig. 91-4 the side margins are located so that the sheet will be in the center of the masking sheet.

LAYOUT FOR STRIPPING

The stripper should lay out or draw and mark the sheet margins on the masking sheet. This shows the location of the negatives. Even though the masking sheet shown in Fig. 91-4 has the 8½ x 11-inch sheet margins marked, it is advisable to mark the lines so that no error will occur. It is essential that sheet margins be precisely marked on masking sheets that do not provide guidelines.

Marking the masking sheet for a single page. Printing jobs such as letterheads, posters, and office forms are printed on single sheets of paper. These jobs present the simplest kind of stripping operation because the stripper is concerned with the location of the negatives on only one page. A flat for a letterhead is shown in Fig. 91-5. The procedure for laying out this flat is to:

1. Examine the negative and determine the location on the sheet of paper.
2. Mark the sheet margins for the paper on which the negative will be printed. The sheet size in Fig. 91-5 is 8½ x 11-inch, and should be so marked (Fig. 91-6).

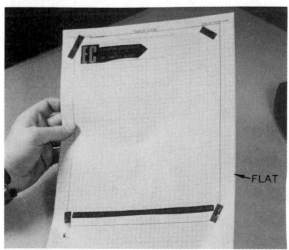

Fig. 91-5. A completed flat for a letterhead.

3. Mark the exact location of the negative within the sheet-size markings (Fig. 91-7). No part of the negative image should be in the area above the gripper margins (Fig. 91-3).

Marking the masking sheet for multiple pages on a sheet. Laying out the masking sheet for printing multiple pages on a single sheet of paper is similar to that for laying out for a single page. The primary difference is that the sheet margins must be subdivided to identify the pages which will appear on the sheet. The procedure is as follows:

1. Mark the masking sheet to locate the sheet sizes.

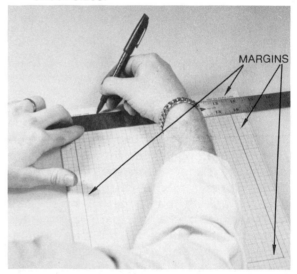

Fig. 91-6. A stripper marking the sheet margins for an 8½ x 11-inch sheet.

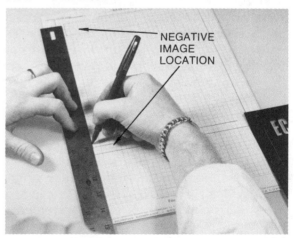

Fig. 91-7. Marking the image location within the page margins.

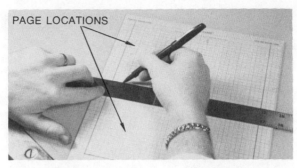

Fig. 91-8. Marking a masking sheet for stripping duplicate negatives.

2. Locate the page sizes (Fig. 91-8). This example requires that the two identical negatives (Fig. 91-9) be printed on the same 8½ x 11-inch sheet. After the sheets are printed, they are cut to form sheets of 5½ x 8½ inches.

3. Mark the location of each negative image in each of the parts of the 8½ x 11-inch sheet margins.

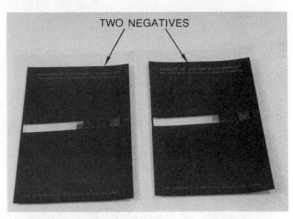

Fig. 91-9. Duplicate negatives to be stripped into the marked masking sheet.

This procedure is also followed to print more than two pages on a sheet. When printing publications, such as booklets, pamphlets, or books, preliminary layouts are also required so the stripper will know where to place the negatives on the flat.

UNIT 92
ATTACHING NEGATIVES TO THE MASKING SHEET

Negatives are attached to masking material with lithographer's tape. The tape holds the negatives securely to the masking sheets so that they will not move out of position when the flat is handled or used to make plates.

The following procedure is used by many strippers. It is especially recommended for making duplicator-size flats of up to 11 x 17-inch sheet size. During the stripping operation, the negatives are kept right-reading for convenience and simplicity. Strippers preparing flats for large presses generally do not use the method as outlined below. They place the negatives on the masking sheet upside-down.

ATTACHING THE NEGATIVES

This procedure must be carried out on a light table similar to the ones shown in Unit 90. The stripper should have a sharp stencil knife and supply of lithographer's tape in a heavy dispenser. A rule, T-square, and triangles are also needed to check the accuracy of the placement of the negatives on the masking sheet.

The stripper should have already marked the exact location of the images and page margins on the masking sheet. The surface of the light table must be clean and free of dust and dirt. Dirt can scratch the negative emulsion.

1. Place the negative on the glass surface of the light table, with the emulsion side of the negative down against the glass (Fig. 92-1). The stripper should be able to read the image on the negative. The image that represents the lead edge of the sheet to be printed should be placed farthest from the stripper on the table.

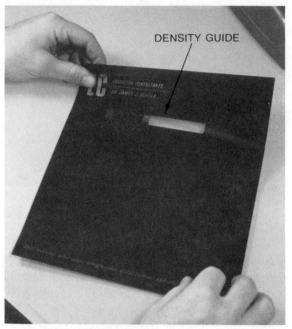

Fig. 92-1. Place the negative on the light-table glass with the emulsion side down.

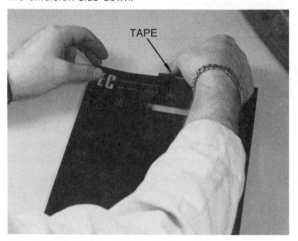

Fig. 92-2. Tape the negative to the glass.

2. Secure the negative to the light table with a small piece of tape (Fig. 92-2). This keeps it from moving.

3. Place the marked masking sheet over the negative. Move it into the proper position (Fig. 92-3). The masking sheet is translucent enough for the stripper to see the image in the negative when the light is on. The printed lines on the masking sheet should be up toward the stripper.

4. When the piece of masking sheet is in position, hold it firmly with one hand.

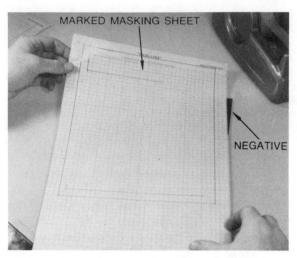

Fig. 92-3. Place the marked masking sheet over the negative.

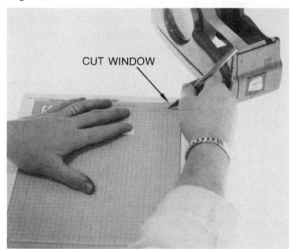

Fig. 92-4. Place the masking sheet over the negative and cut a small window.

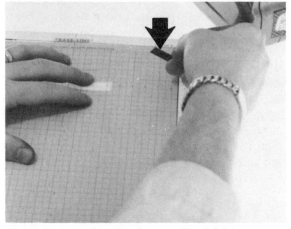

Fig. 92-5. Place tape over the small window. The tape will stick to the masking sheet and to the negative.

Cut a small window in it (Fig. 92-4). The cut should be over one of the corners of the negative. Take care not to cut through the negative.

5. Place a small piece of lithographer's tape over the entire window (Fig. 92-5). The tape holds the corner of the negative to the masking sheet.

6. Still holding the masking sheet in place, cut three more windows at the other corners of the negative and place tape over them. When this is done, the stripper will no longer have to hold the masking sheet in place.

7. Carefully remove the negative and masking sheet from the light table. Remove the tape used to hold the negative to the light table.

8. Turn the unit (negative and masking sheet) over.

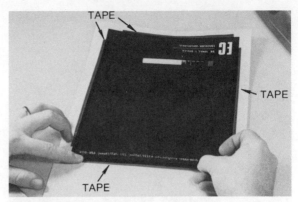

Fig. 92-6. When the negative is attached by the window, turn the unit over and tape the negative to the back of the masking sheet.

9. Place strips of tape along the edges of the negative to hold it securely to the back of the masking sheet (Fig. 92-6).

10. Check the unit to be sure that the negative is in the exact position required.

UNIT 93
CUTTING WINDOWS AND OPAQUING

Additional procedures must be carried out after the negative is attached to the masking sheet. These are: (1) cutting windows to expose negative image areas, (2) combining illustrations and halftones with other line negatives, and (3) opaquing. Each step is important to the completion of a satisfactory flat.

CUTTING WINDOWS

When the negative is attached to the masking sheet, it is still not possible to make a plate. The masking sheet covers the image on the negative and does not permit light to pass through the negative to expose the plate (Fig. 93-1). The stripper must cut away the masking sheet that covers the image on the negative.

To cut the windows to expose the negative image areas, place the flat on the light table so the masking sheet is toward the stripper. Cut around the negative image areas with a sharp knife as shown in Fig.

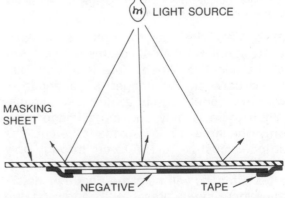

Fig. 93-1. Masking sheet prevents light from passing through the negative in certain areas.

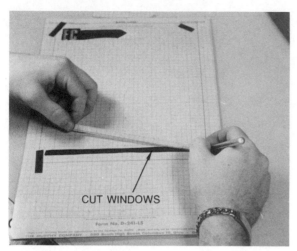

Fig. 93-2. Cut away the masking sheet to expose the open areas of the negative.

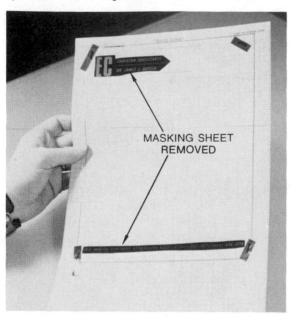

Fig. 93-3. Remove the masking material to expose the image areas of the negative.

93-2. Make the cuts through the masking sheet about ⅜ inch outside the image areas of the negative. When there is a large distance between the images on a negative, windows should be cut around each image. When there is only one large image area, only one large window needs to be cut. The stripper must be careful to cut through only the masking sheet and not through the negative. Practice will help the beginner determine how much pressure to apply on the knife.

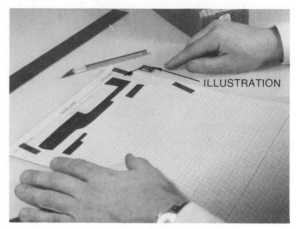

Fig. 93-4. Cut the illustration or halftone negative to size.

After the windows have been cut (Fig. 93-3), examine the flat to be sure that all of the masking sheet has been removed from the image area. When the masking sheet has not been completely cut, fuzzy edges sometimes remain and interfere with the image areas. The stripper should make an additional check of the flat by turning it upside down. This is an easy way to identify areas which have not been removed, as yellow or orange can be seen through the negative image areas where the sheet has not been removed.

COMBINING ILLUSTRATIONS AND HALFTONES WITH LINE NEGATIVES

It is frequently necessary to make negatives of illustrations and halftones separately from the main line negative. These must eventually be combined with the main line negative before making the plate. This procedure illustrates the method to combine negatives with no guidelines on them. It can be used with negatives which are attached to the masking sheet and with those that are not attached.

1. Cut the masking sheet away from the area where the illustration or halftone will be placed.
2. Cut the illustration or halftone to a size that is slightly larger than the image that will be printed (Fig. 93-4). Usually about

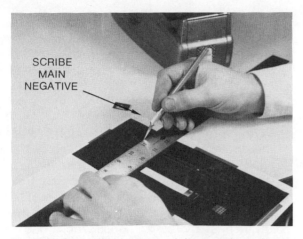

Fig. 93-5. Scribe the emulsion of the negative to locate the illustration on the main negative.

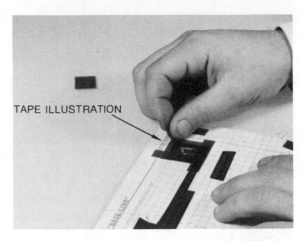

Fig. 93-7. Place the illustration in the hole and tape it to the main negative.

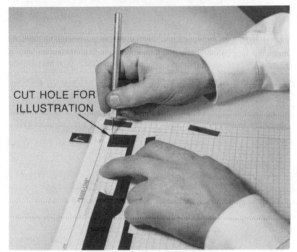

Fig. 93-6. Cut the main negative where it was scribed.

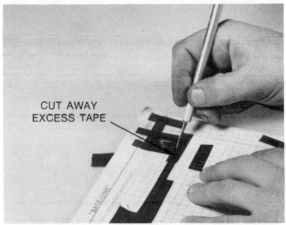

Fig. 93-8. Cut away excess tape so it will not cover image areas.

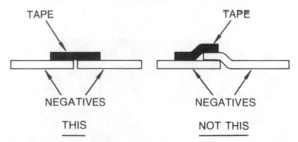

Fig. 93-9. Negatives should butt against each other, not overlap.

¼ to ⅜ inch larger on all sides is sufficient. It is best to cut the negatives with the aid of a straightedge.

3. Turn the flat over and mark the exact location of the negative to be added by scribing or scratching the emulsion of the main negative (Fig. 93-5).

4. Turn the flat over so the negative image is readable. Cut the main negative along the guidelines which were scribed on the reverse side (Fig. 93-6).

5. Place the illustration or halftone into the hole made by removing the part of the main negative. Be sure the emulsion side is toward the glass of the light table. Attach the two negatives with strips of lithographer's tape (Fig. 93-7).

6. Cut away the tape that covers the image area to be printed (Fig. 93-8).

The two negatives should not overlap. They should butt against each other as shown in Fig. 93-9. It is better to have a little space between the negatives than to have them overlap. The tape should always be placed on the base or shiny side of the film.

OPAQUING NEGATIVES

Small unwanted holes, called *pinholes,* are frequently found on line negatives. Unless these are covered on the negative, they will show up on the printing plate and be printed. In other situations it is necessary to block out certain portions of a negative to prevent them from printing. This process is called *opaquing* and sometimes *spotting.* It can be done on negatives before or after they are attached to the masking sheet, but it is better to opaque after they have been attached.

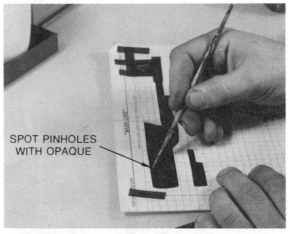

Fig. 93-10. Cover pinholes by applying opaque solution to the negative.

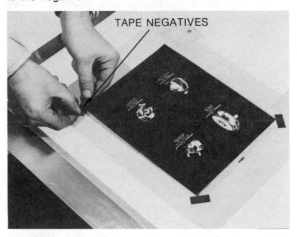

Fig. 93-11. Attach the negative to the glass of the light table.

Place the emulsion side of the flat or negative against the glass of the light table. The shiny side should face the stripper. Carefully examine the negative for pinholes. It is often helpful to start at the top of the negative and proceed down rather than try to randomly identify the pinholes.

When a pinhole is identified, touch the tip of the opaquing brush on the surface of the negative where the pinhole appears (Fig. 93-10). Be careful not to let any opaque material cover the negative image areas. The opaquing solution should be mixed until the solution has a creamy consistency. Use a very fine brush to do most opaquing jobs.

Large areas of a negative sometimes need to be blocked out or opaqued. Lithographer's tape, rather than opaquing solution, is often used on large areas. This is done by taping the negative on the light table with the base side of the negative toward the stripper as shown in Fig. 93-11. When negative is securely taped to the light table, the stripper should cover the entire image area with the strips of tape so that they overlap only slightly. The tape is cut away with a very sharp stencil knife to expose the areas that are to be printed (Fig. 93-12).

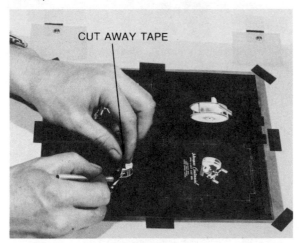

Fig. 93-12. After covering the image areas of the negative with tape, cut away the tape and expose only the desired images.

UNIT 94
MULTIPLE STRIPPING

Multiple stripping is often necessary when several pages are to be printed on a single sheet of paper. A signature for a book or several duplicate pages, such as business forms, are examples of the need and uses of multiple stripping. The primary advantage of printing multiple pages on a single sheet of paper is that it conserves press time. It takes ten times longer to print ten individual sheets than it does to print ten pages on a single sheet.

The procedure for stripping duplicate pages is essentially the same as for stripping the pages of a signature. The main difference is that when stripping pages for a signature the stripper must arrange them into a page layout similar to those shown in Unit 78. The following procedure deals with stripping duplicate pages to be printed on a single sheet of paper:

1. Mark the location of the sheet on the masking sheet as shown in Unit 91.

2. Divide and mark the location of the individual pages within the sheet markings on the masking sheet (Fig. 91-8).
3. Mark the location of the image of each negative within the page areas as shown in Fig. 94-1.
4. Attach the negatives to the masking sheet as was done for a single page as shown in Fig. 94-2.

This procedure requires a negative for each duplicate page. All of the pages are exposed to the plate at the same time. When numerous duplicate pages (for example, twenty) are to be printed on a single sheet, considerable care is needed in making

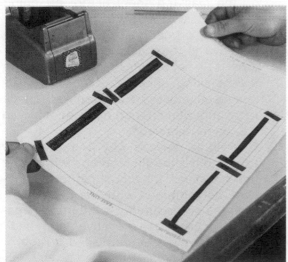

Fig. 94-1. Mark image locations on the masking sheet.

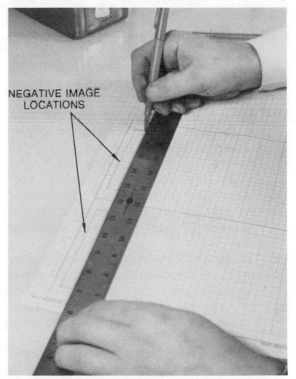

NEGATIVE IMAGE LOCATIONS

Fig. 94-2. Attach the negatives.

Fig. 94-3. A photocomposing machine. (Consolidated International Equipment and Supply Co.)

duplicate negatives to insure high quality. Great care is also needed when stripping the negatives into place. Any variation in negatives and an inaccuracy in stripping could cause inferior plates.

Some companies have *step-and-repeat* machines. This machine uses a single negative to produce several images on the plate. The individual negative is held in the film holder. The plate is placed behind the negative. The negative is then precisely moved to different spots on the plate. The light source is placed behind the negative to expose the plate. The photocomposing machine shown in Fig. 94-3 exposes a single plate, or two simultaneously.

UNIT 95
LEARNING EXPERIENCES: LITHOGRAPHIC IMPOSITION

DISCUSSION TOPICS

1. Give another name for lithographic imposition. What is the person who makes the flat called?
2. Describe the masking sheet. Describe the *flat*. How is the flat used in the lithographic printing process?
3. List the basic operations which the stripper must complete in making a flat.
4. How is the light table used by the stripper? Identify the differences between a conventional light table and a line-up table.
5. Name the tools and materials needed by a stripper to prepare a flat. Give the function of each item.
6. What are some of the items of information which a stripper must know before he begins to make a flat?
7. Define the term *lead edge*. How does the stripper identify the lead edge on a masking sheet?
8. Why must the gripper margin be identified and accounted for when making a flat? About how much space is required for the gripper margin on a flat?
9. What kinds of markings should be made on the masking sheet before attaching the negative to it?
10. Give the procedure for attaching the negative to the masking sheet.
11. Why is it necessary to cut windows in the masking sheet to expose the attached negatives? How can you check to be sure that enough masking material has been removed?
12. Give some reasons why it is necessary to combine line illustrations with other line negatives. Why must halftone negatives be combined with line negatives?
13. Give the procedure for combining negatives. How are the negatives attached? Why must the tape be placed on top or on the base side of the negatives?
14. How are pinholes covered on negatives?

What is the name of the material applied to the negatives? Which side of the negative should this material be applied? Why?

15. Explain the procedure for opaquing large areas from negatives.

ACTIVITIES

1. Obtain a masking sheet and mark it to identify the lead edge, gripper margin, and sheet size for an 8½ x 11-inch sheet of paper.
2. Secure the negative or negatives to be printed on an 8½ x 11-inch sheet of paper. Mark the masking sheet to indicate the exact positions for the negatives.
3. Attach the negatives from step 2 to the masking sheet and cut the windows. Examine the negatives and opaque any pinholes.
4. Lay out a masking sheet for the placement of four 4¼ x 5¼-inch duplicate images on an 8½ x 11-inch sheet of paper.
5. Make the appropriate layouts for producing a four-page signature using the sheetwise method of printing (work-and-back).

The platemakers are preparing a large 35-image plate which will be used to print labels for fruit cans.

UNIT 96
INTRODUCTION TO LITHOGRAPHIC IMAGE CARRIERS

A plate or image carrier is used in the offset lithographic process to produce the image or print. The plate can be a thin piece of paper, plastic, or metal that is wrapped around the plate cylinder of the offset-lithography press (Fig. 96-1). The plate is dampened and inked on the press, and the ink from the plate is transferred to the blanket cylinder of the press. The image on the blanket is transferred to the paper during the printing process.

There are several methods used to produce plates that can be printed on an offset-lithography press. Each method has advantages and disadvantages. The *platemaker* determines the method most suitable to yield the desired quality of print. His job has traditionally been to make plates from flats, but recently several methods have been developed which do not require flats. This has changed the platemaker's role somewhat.

The platemaker is an essential person in the process of producing a print by the offset lithographic printing method. He provides the *pressman* with plates which will print with the quality required by the customer. If the platemaker sends an inaccurate or poorly made plate to the pressman, production schedules will be delayed and materials wasted. The result is a reduction in the profit made from the printing job.

Manufacturers of platemaking equipment and materials are developing new methods of producing better-quality plates more efficiently and economically. There are many kinds of plates; this section examines three common types.

1. *Direct image plates.* The image is drawn or typed directly on a specially coated plate.
2. *Presensitized plates.* The plate has a light-sensitive surface which is exposed by using a flat.
3. *One-step photographic plates.* The plates are produced directly from the copy without using a negative.

The *photochemical plastic plate* is another plate that is quite popular. This is the same kind of plate that was discussed in Unit 67, but is different in that it is thinner and the image is a readable one. The image on the photochemical plate used for letterpress printing is a mirror (reverse) image.

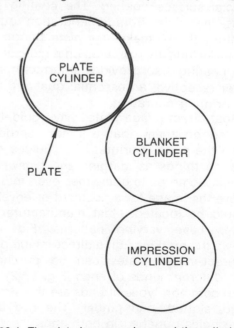

Fig. 96-1. The plate is wrapped around the cylinder.

UNIT 97
DIRECT-IMAGE PLATES

Direct-image plates are so designated because the image to be printed is applied directly to the surface of the plate. The image is placed on the plate with anything that is greasy, such as ball-point pens, grease pencils, or typewriter ribbons. When the image is completed it can be immediately printed on the press. It is almost as easy to work with direct-image plates as it is to manipulate a piece of paper.

PLATES

Direct-image plates are made primarily for offset-lithography duplicators of 11 x 17-inch printing size, or smaller. The plate consists of a base, usually paper, which has a special surface coating. The coating protects the plate from deterioration during printing. It also makes the plate smooth, so that drawings are executed on it quite easily. The coating also provides a surface that is water receptive, an essential quality during the printing operation.

Most direct-image plates have guidelines printed on them that will not reproduce when the plate is printed. The guides refer to such things as margins and typewriting scales. Some plate guidelines even indicate where the image for a postcard or envelope should be located. Most manufacturers of plates have varying patterns. Fig. 97-1 shows the markings on a direct-image plate.

Direct-image plates can be purchased with different kinds of ends (Fig. 97-2). The most common types of ends are the straight edge, slotted, and pinbar. The two latter have holes punched in both ends.

METHODS OF PRODUCING IMAGES

The usual methods of placing images on direct-image plates are to type or draw them directly on the plate. A special ribbon must be used for typing. Special pencils or pens will produce an image when used to draw on the plate. The typewriter ribbon and pencils must be greasy to produce an image that will repel water.

Typewriter ribbons. Lithographic typewriter ribbons look like the conventional ones and can be used for regular typing. However, regular ribbons cannot be used to prepare direct-image masters or plates because they do not have ink that is water repellent. Lithographic ribbons are filled with a greasy ink which repels water and accepts ink. Cloth ribbons are satisfactory for only about eight to ten typings. After that the image is unsatisfactory. *Carbon* ribbons, used on electric typewriters, yield a better image than do cloth ones, but they are good for only one typing.

Pencils and pens. Pencils used to produce images on direct-image plates are grouped as (1) nonreproducing, and (2) reproducing. The nonreproducing type are used to place guidelines on the plate and do not print when the plate is printed. Lines made with a nonreproducing pencil come off when the plate is washed with press fountain solution prior to printing. This pencil is used with very little pressure so that the plate is not scored.

Reproducing pencils place an ink-recep-

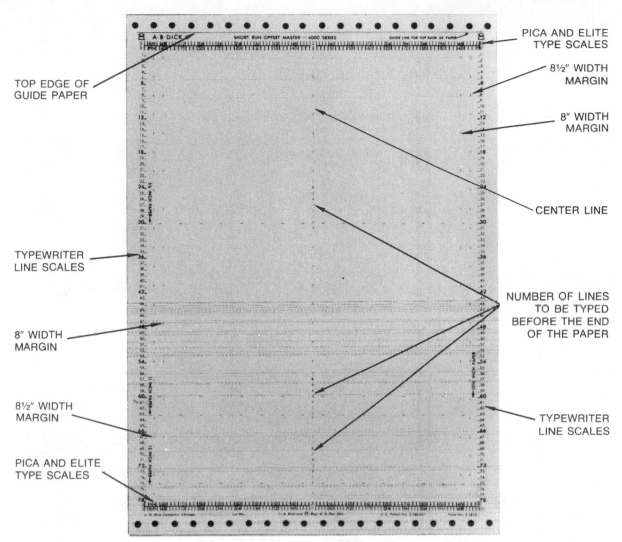

Fig. 97-1. A direct-image plate with markings.

TOP EDGE OF GUIDE PAPER

PICA AND ELITE TYPE SCALES

8½" WIDTH MARGIN

8" WIDTH MARGIN

CENTER LINE

TYPEWRITER LINE SCALES

NUMBER OF LINES TO BE TYPED BEFORE THE END OF THE PAPER

8" WIDTH MARGIN

8½" WIDTH MARGIN

TYPEWRITER LINE SCALES

PICA AND ELITE TYPE SCALES

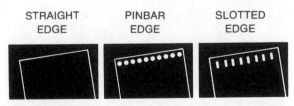

STRAIGHT EDGE   PINBAR EDGE   SLOTTED EDGE

Fig. 97-2. Plates that have different kinds of ends. (A.B. Dick Co.)

tive and water-repellent image on the plate. *Grease crayons* can be used to draw on the plate, but they do not yield as sharp an image or as fine a line on the master. They are satisfactory for making large printing lines or areas.

Ball-point pens with special ink have become one of the best and most widely used instruments to draw images on direct-image plates. They give a very even line and a sharp image. They do have a tendency to smear, however, and the image is often difficult to erase. Fig. 97-3 shows writing done with three different types of instruments.

Drawing fluid which produces an appropriate image is available. It can be applied with a ruling pen, brush, or artist's pen. *Special carbon paper* is also obtainable and is used for producing images on direct-image plates.

Erasers. A soft eraser can remove errors made on the direct-image plate. The eraser should contain very little abrasive because it will damage the coating on the plate.

John Carlson   *John Carlson*   *John Carlson*

REPRODUCING PENCIL   BALL-POINT PEN   CRAYON

Fig. 97-3. Different results are obtained by using pencils, ball-point pens, or crayons.

TYPING ON A DIRECT-IMAGE PLATE

Typing on a direct-image plate is nearly as easy as typing on paper. The same procedures are used, but the typist must take special care when handling the plate and making erasures.

Preparing the typewriter. The typewriter must be kept clean. Dirt in it can get on the plate and require extra cleaning time when the plate is printed. The type should also be cleaned frequently to produce a sharp and clean image.

Placing the ribbon in the typewriter. Use the ribbon suitable to make direct-image plates. Place the ribbon in the typewriter when there is no plate in the machine. This prevents smearing the plate.

Placing the plate in the typewriter. Handle the plate as you would a piece of paper. Avoid excessive fingerprints by not handling it any more than necessary. Fingerprints are greasy and will print if not completely cleaned off. Some typists even wear gloves when handling direct-image plates. Adjust the plate in the typewriter so that the material to be printed is in the correct location, as shown in Fig. 97-4.

Typing on the plate. Both manual and electric typewriters are suitable for typing on direct-image plates. Pressure must be even to produce an even image, and should be just sufficient to make a clear, sharp impression. Too much pressure causes embossing which creates hollow spots as shown in Fig. 97-5. The low-pressure setting is necessary on an electric machine which produces a much more even impression.

DRAWING ON A DIRECT-IMAGE PLATE

Drawing is done on a direct-image plate with special pencils or pens which produce a greasy image. The person making the drawing should not handle the plate more than necessary. Both free-hand and mechanical drawings can be made. Guidelines are first placed on the plate with a nonreproducing pencil.

THIS TOUCH IS TOO HEAVY.

THIS TOUCH IS CORRECT.

Fig. 97-5. Correct typing pressure is essential for a good image on a direct-image plate.

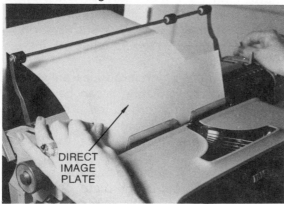

Fig. 97-4. A direct-image plate used in a typewriter.

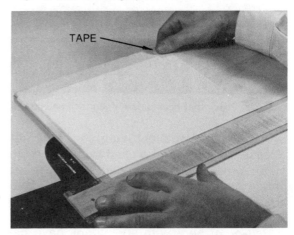

Fig. 97-6. A direct-image plate on a drawing board.

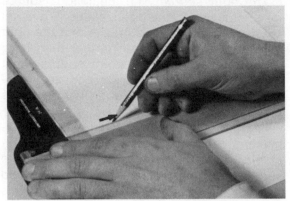

Fig. 97-7. Drawing with a nonreproducing pencil.

Procedure:

1. Place the direct-image plate on a drawing board. Tape it down like a regular piece of drawing paper (Fig. 97-6).
2. Make guidelines on the plate, using a nonreproducing pencil. Make them very light so that they can be removed easily (Fig. 97-7). Place a piece of paper over the part of the plate not being drawn on to prevent fingerprints or dirt from getting on it.

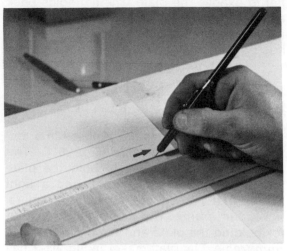

Fig. 97-8. Drawing with a reproducing pencil or pen.

3. With the guidelines in place, make the drawing using a reproducing pencil or ball-point pen (Fig. 97-8).
4. Make free-hand drawings in exactly the same way but without using drawing instruments. Take extra care to keep dirt and fingerprints off the direct-image plate.

UNIT 98
EXPOSING PRESENSITIZED PLATES

One of the reasons for the popularity of offset lithographic printing is the development of presensitized plates. Prior to the development of these plates, platemakers had to sensitize their own plates by applying a light-sensitive material to metal plates. This was time consuming and often produced unsatisfactory plates. Today most printers purchase and use presensitized ones.

Presensitized plates consist of a base and a light-sensitive coating. Bases are made of paper, plastic, or metal. Aluminum metal-base plates are the most widely used. The quality of the light-sensitive coating on the plate permits it to be handled for a short period of time in subdued light. Some plates are produced with light-sensitive coatings on both sides of the base.

Presensitized plates are made to fit specific press sizes. They also have varying degrees of durability. A printer can buy short-run plates that are good for about 2,000 copies, or he can obtain ones that will yield hundreds of thousands of copies.

Flats are placed over plates to cover the entire surface. When the flat and plate are in tight contact, light is passed through the flat to expose the plate. The flat holds back all light, except where there are clear areas, in the negatives. After the plate is exposed, it is processed and is ready to be printed.

EQUIPMENT FOR EXPOSING PRESENSITIZED PLATES

Presensitized plates are exposed in a machine called a *platemaker* (Fig. 98-1). The platemaker has a frame to hold the plate and the flat in tight contact, and a light source that is adequate to expose the plate.

Vacuum frame. The most efficient frame for holding the plate and the flat is the *vacuum frame.* The platemaker in Fig. 98-2 has a vacuum frame. It consists of a rubber blanket and a glass cover. The blanket is attached to a vacuum pump. The plate is placed in the frame and the flat is put over it so that the light passes through the negatives and expose the plate. When the plate and flat are in position, the glass cover is replaced (Fig. 98-3). The vacuum blanket compresses the plate and the flat to produce a perfect and tight contact (Fig. 98-4).

The light source. The ideal light source for exposing presensitized plates is a *point source* (Fig. 98-5). This means that the light comes from a single point rather than from a multiple source. The point source must produce *ultraviolet* light. Carbon arc, mercury vapor, and pulsed xenon light sources are commonly used.

Lights not specifically designed for platemaking can cause serious problems. Examples of inadequate light sources are the sun, flood lamps, filament-type bulbs, and fluorescent bulbs. Some of the problems caused by these sources are overheating, sticky tape on the flat, and underexposed plates.

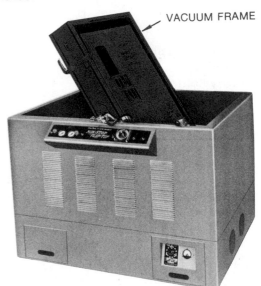
VACUUM FRAME

Fig. 98-2. Vacuum frame on a plate maker.

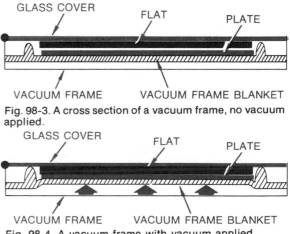
GLASS COVER   FLAT   PLATE

VACUUM FRAME   VACUUM FRAME BLANKET

Fig. 98-3. A cross section of a vacuum frame, no vacuum applied.

GLASS COVER   FLAT   PLATE

VACUUM FRAME   VACUUM FRAME BLANKET

Fig. 98-4. A vacuum frame with vacuum applied.

Fig. 98-1. A typical plate maker.

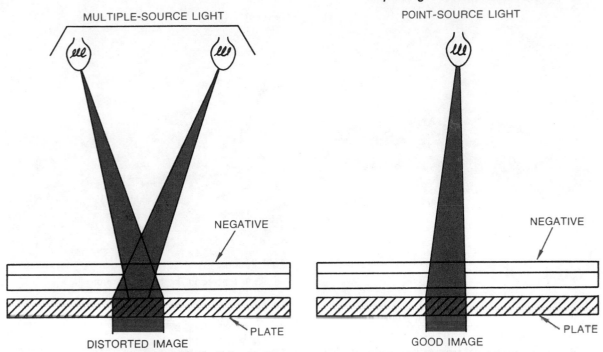

Fig. 98-5. The effects of multiple-source and point-source lights.

DETERMINING PLATE EXPOSURE

Presensitized plates are exposed when intense ultraviolet light strikes them. The flat is placed between the plate and the light source to permit the light to strike the plate only where there are clear areas in the negative. Like film, plates can be either underexposed or overexposed. Underexposure causes poor, or short, press life in which the image leaves the plate after only a few copies have been printed. Overexposure will not harm the plate, but is a waste of time.

A *platemaker's transparent gray scale* is used to determine the proper exposure time. This is a piece of film with several different densities of gray, ranging from clear to completely black. Each density is referred to as a *step*. A gray scale is shown in Fig. 98-6.

The gray scale is attached to the flat (Fig. 98-7). The flat, with the gray scale in position, is then exposed. After the plate has been processed and is still wet, the photographer rubs over the gray scale area vigorously with his fingers. If the plate has

Fig. 98-6. A platemaker's sensitivity guide (gray scale).

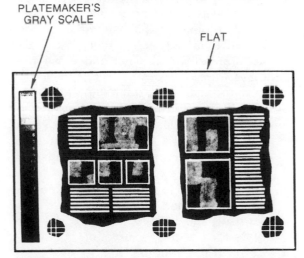

Fig. 98-7. A flat with a gray scale stripped into the margin.

been sufficiently exposed, the number 6 step will remain as shown in Fig. 98-8. The number 6 step should be as dark as the number 1 step. If the gray scale reading is less than number 6, increase the plate exposure time. If it is greater, reduce the time.

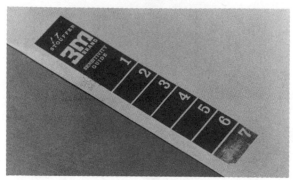

Fig. 98-8. A platemaker's gray scale developed on a plate.

PLATE EXPOSURE PROCEDURE

The following procedure is a guide in exposing most plates with a platemaker. The person using the platemaker should be familiar with the exposure specifications for the specific plate he uses. He should also be thoroughly knowledgeable about the use of his equipment.

1. Load the plate and the flat into the platemaker (Fig. 98-9). Place the sensitive side of the plate toward the glass of the vacuum frame. Place the flat over the plate so that the image on the negative is readable. Align the plate accurately with the flat and close the glass frame.

2. Turn on the vacuum pump. Pressure should make firm contact between the plate and the flat. Be sure the flat stays aligned with the plate.

3. Move the vacuum frame into position so that light can expose the plate.

4. Set the timer for the correct exposure time determined by the gray scale.

5. Turn on the light source. Expose the plate for the proper amount of time.

6. Turn off the vacuum pump.

7. Remove the plate and the flat from the vacuum frame and process the plate as outlined in Unit 99.

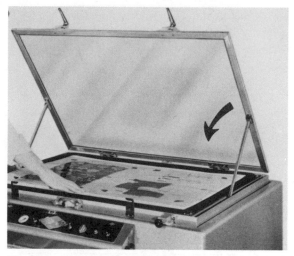

Fig. 98-9. Plate and flat being loaded.

Fig. 98-10. Vacuum frame being moved into position.

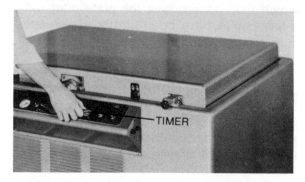

Fig. 98-11. Setting the timer for correct exposure.

UNIT 99
PROCESSING PRESENSITIZED PLATES

After exposure, presensitized plates must be processed before they can be used on the printing press. *Processing* is often termed rubbing up a plate. The purposes of processing are (1) to remove the unexposed light-sensitive coating from the plate, (2) to add a lacquer-type material to the image areas to produce a visible image, and (3) to prevent the plate from oxidizing.

PROCESSING EQUIPMENT

Plates are processed on a clean, flat surface. Special plate processing tables are not absolutely necessary but are available and can be very helpful. Fig. 99-1 shows a plate developing sink, used when a supply of water is required. The plate finishing table (Fig. 99-2) has a heater for drying plates rapidly. Clamps are used to hold the plate in position on the table.

PROCESSING THE PLATE

Many types of presensitized plates are available for nearly any size of press. Each requires a special processing technique developed by the manufacturer. The platemaker should follow the instructions carefully for the particular plate he is using. Following is a typical procedure for processing conventional presensitized plates.

1. Collect the materials needed to process the plate (Fig. 99-3). They should be organized close to the processing area.
2. Pour some process gum solution onto the plate. This solution is called a desensitizer by some manufacturers.

Fig. 99-1. Plate developing sink. (nuArc Co.)

Fig. 99-2. Plate finishing table. (nuArc Co.)

Fig. 99-3. Materials used to process presensitized plates. (3M Co.)

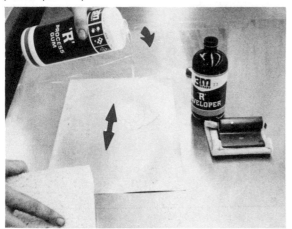

Fig. 99-4. Applying process gum to remove light-sensitive coating. (3M Co.)

Fig. 99-5. Developing the plate. (3M Co.)

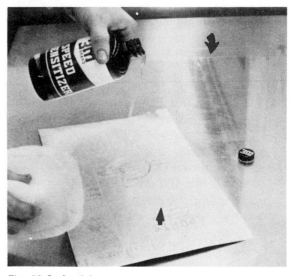

Fig. 99-6. Applying process gum after developing the plate. (3M Co.)

3. Wipe the entire plate with a sponge (Fig. 99-4).
4. Pour developer onto the plate. This liquid is called a lacquer by some manufacturers.
5. Rub the developer over the entire surface of the plate until a uniform medium color is obtained (Fig. 99-5). Wash the excess developer from the plate with water.
6. Pour some process gum onto the plate.
7. Polish the plate until it is dry, using a cloth pad or clean cheesecloth as shown in Fig. 99-6.

Steps 6 and 7 can be omitted if the plate is used immediately on the press. The plate can also be used without performing Steps 4 and 5, but it is difficult to see the image on it.

UNIT 100

CORRECTING, PRESERVING, AND STORING PLATES

Plates are quite sensitive to oxidation and scratches and must be handled with care to give satisfactory results when used on the press. But problems occur even when the most careful precautions are taken to protect the plates. The following procedures are similar to those suggested by plate manufacturers for correcting, preserving, and storing presensitized plates.

MAKING CORRECTIONS

Plates are made to reproduce exactly what is on the negative of the flat. Once the plate is made, it is difficult and at times impossible to make any changes. It is much easier and less costly to prevent errors than to correct them. However, two kinds of corrections can be made on the presensitized plate. They are deletions and additions.

Deletions. Deletions are the removal of unwanted areas from the plate. Small areas, such as spots from pinholes on the negative, can be removed by rubbing lightly with a clean, soft rubber eraser which has been moistened with water or fountain solution from the press. This is often done after the plate has been attached to the press. Be extremely careful not to damage or scratch the plate with the eraser.

Large areas are removed with a special *deletion fluid* provided by the manufacturer of the plate. It must be applied when the plate is dry, using a clean cotton swab or pad. After the image has been removed from the plate, the deletion fluid is flushed away with water.

Additions. It is often possible to repair broken lines, damaged letters, or holes in solid areas of a plate. Broken lines are repaired and minor additions made by scratching the surface with a sharp needle or knife held at a slight angle. The plate should be dry for this repair.

Holes in solid areas are repaired with *plate tusche,* available from the plate manufacturer. The *tusche* (a form of greasy lithographic ink) is applied while the plate is dry, but before it is gummed (preserved). It is rubbed on the area with a cotton swab for about 30 seconds. Neutralize the tusche with water and dry the plate immediately. Rub ink into the dry area where the tusche was applied; then gum the plate.

Correcting is not as satisfactory as producing an initially correct plate, and the procedures for correcting should be used only when it is not practical to make a new plate.

PRESERVING PLATES

Plates are preserved to prevent oxidation and minor abrasions and scratches. Most plates are preserved before and after they are printed. Plates are kept after printing when it is likely that they will be used again. A protective coating is applied to the surface. One common material used as a protective coating is *gum arabic.* The platemaker should follow the manufacturer's instructions because some plates require a special solution.

The same procedure outlined in Unit 99 for gumming the plate is usually suitable for preserving it. It is important to prevent air bubbles by polishing the gum dry. If the air bubbles break, oxidation occurs in that spot. The result is a plate that will print little specks. Before the plate is printed, the gum is removed with water or fountain solution from the press.

STORING PLATES

Plates are sometimes prepared several days before they are printed. They can be damaged during this time unless special care is taken with them. Costly delays in production will result.

It is always best to *hang* plates rather than stack them on top of each other. If they must be stacked, place protective paper between them. Take care that both sides are completely dry. Moisture attacks the protective gum coating and causes oxidation. Some platemakers prefer to store plates in large envelopes which protect them from abrasion and makes handling easier.

Fig. 100-1 shows a storage cabinet used to organize and store or hang plates. It should be placed in an area of the plant away from moisture and excessive heat.

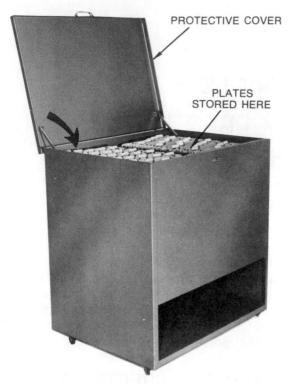

Fig. 100-1. A plate storage cabinet. (Foster Manufacturing Co.)

UNIT 101
ONE-STEP PHOTOGRAPHIC PLATES

One-step photographic plates are unique because the press-ready plate is obtained directly from the camera or direct platemaking machine (Fig. 101-1). Considerable time is saved because it is not necessary to make negatives or strip a flat to obtain the photographic plate.

Special equipment is required to produce this type of plate (Fig. 101-2). The equipment is essentially like a process camera that is used to make negatives. The primary difference is that in this process the image is placed directly on a plate rather than on a piece of film. The plate is developed like a presensitized one and is ready to be placed on a press for printing.

The equipment produces a readable image on the plate (Fig. 101-3), unlike a conventional process camera which produces a reverse image. There is an attachment for the process camera which enables it to be used for exposing plates.

Some machines are built for exposing the plates only. These plates must be developed after they are removed from the exposure machine (see Fig. 101-4). Other machines both expose and develop the plates.

One-step photographic plates are used primarily on duplicator-size printing presses. Their main advantage is that they produce a press-ready plate quickly. They are used extensively where rapid production

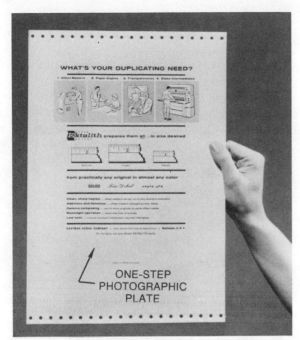

Fig. 101-1. A photographic plate produced without the aid of a flat. (Eastman Kodak Co.)

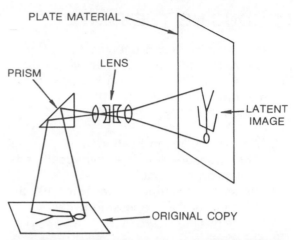

Fig. 101-3. The camera produces a readable image.

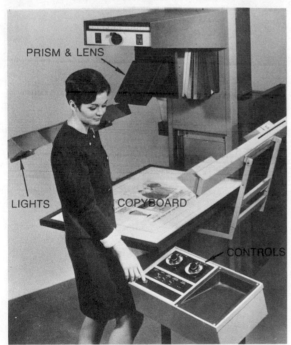

Fig. 101-2. A machine for making one-step plates. (Itek Business Products)

Fig. 101-4. A machine used to expose plates. (Eastman Kodak Co.)

Fig. 101-5. A machine capable of screening continuous-tone copy on plates. (A-M Corp.)

is required. Most machines produce plates from line copy only, but a few, such as the one shown in Fig. 101-5, are capable of screening continuous-tone copy to produce halftones.

PRODUCING THE PLATE

Each machine has a specific operational procedure for efficient and effective production of plates. The following is suitable for the machine shown in Fig. 101-6.

1. Place the copy on the copyboard (Fig. 101-7).
2. Adjust the magnification (Fig. 101-8). The exposure time is automatically adjusted on this machine.
3. Press the operation lever (Fig. 101-9). This starts the processing cycle.
4. Press the start button (Fig. 101-10). The plate is automatically exposed and processed.
5. The processed plate comes from the machine (Fig. 101-11).

The exposure lights are enclosed in this machine (Fig. 101-12). This particular model also makes regular process negatives by using the vacuum-back attachment (Fig. 101-13). It produces enlargements (Fig. 101-14) or reductions (Fig. 101-15), as well as same-size reproductions.

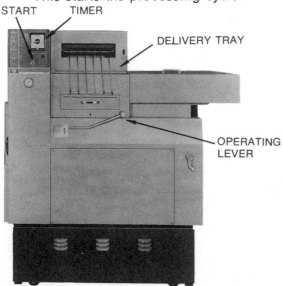

Fig. 101-6. A typical machine used to make one-step photographic plates. (A-M Corp.)

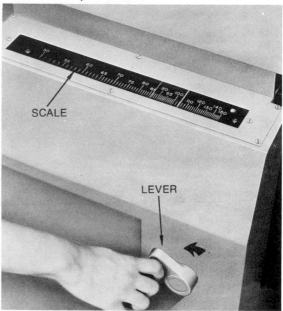

Fig. 101-8. Adjusting the magnification. (A-M Corp.)

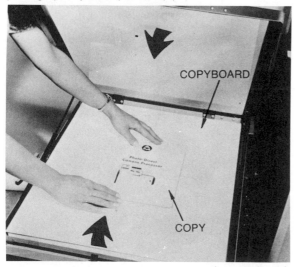

Fig. 101-7. Operator placing copy on the copyboard. (A-M Corp.)

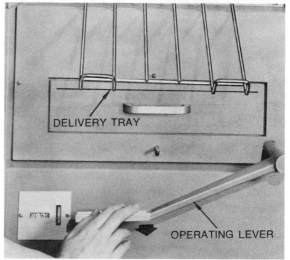

Fig. 101-9. Engagement of the operating lever. (A-M Corp.)

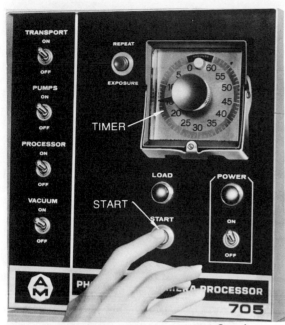

Fig. 101-10. Press the start button. (A-M Corp.)

Fig. 101-11. The process plate is delivered to the tray. (A-M Corp.)

Fig. 101-12. Exposure lights enclosed in the machine. (A-M Corp.)

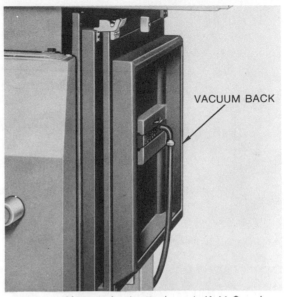

Fig. 101-13. Vacuum-back attachment. (A-M Corp.)

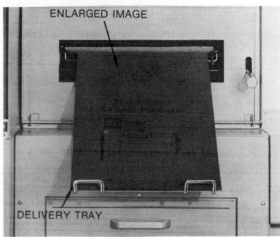

Fig. 101-14. Enlarged image on the plate. (A-M Corp.)

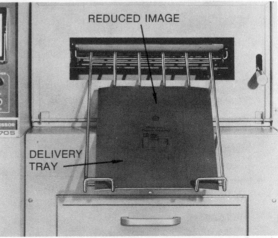

Fig. 101-15. Reduced image on the plate. (A-M Corp.)

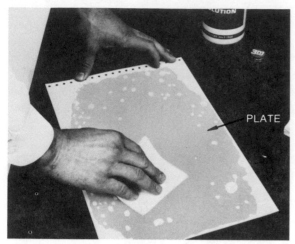

Fig. 101-16. Preparing a plate for the press. (3M Co.)

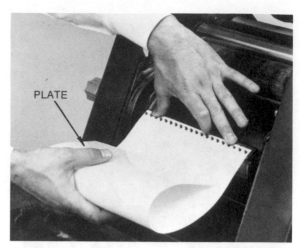

Fig. 101-17. Placing a plate on the press. (3M Co.)

PREPARING THE PLATE FOR PRINTING

Most of these plates require additional chemical processing before being placed on the printing press. This varies from man-ufacturer to manufacturer. Fig. 101-16 shows a pressman preparing a plate for printing. When the plate is ready, it is placed on the press like other plates (Fig. 101-17). The quality of the print should be as good as one from a presensitized plate.

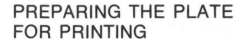

UNIT 102

LEARNING EXPERIENCES: LITHOGRAPHIC IMAGE CARRIERS

DISCUSSION TOPICS

1. What is the person called who makes plates?
2. Give four kinds of plates that are made for use on lithographic presses. Briefly describe each.
3. How does the direct-image plate get its name? What is the base most commonly made from? Describe the purposes of the surface coating on direct-image plates. List some of the different guide markings on a direct-image plate. Show the three common kinds of edges on direct-image plates.
4. Give two methods of producing images on direct-image plates. What is unique about the images placed on direct-image plates?
5. Describe two kinds of typewriter ribbons used to type on direct-image plates. Give the names of two kinds of pencils which are used to make drawings on direct-image plates and explain the purpose of each. Name other methods of making drawings on direct-image plates.
6. What is the procedure for typing on direct-image plates? Give some of the precautions that should be observed when typing on direct-image plates.

7. List the procedure for making drawings on direct-image plates. Identify some of the problems that can be encountered while drawing on direct-image plates.
8. How does a presensitized plate differ from a direct-image plate? Name some of the materials used for the bases of presensitized plates.
9. Describe the platemaker used to expose presensitized plates. Tell how the vacuum frame operates. What kind of light source is most desirable for exposing presensitized plates? Give some examples of satisfactory and unsatisfactory light sources used for exposing presensitized plates.
10. What is the result of underexposing a presensitized plate? Give the effects of overexposure.
11. Name the device used to determine the proper exposure time for presensitized plates. How is it used to determine the best exposure time?
12. List the procedure for exposing a presensitized plate. Give the exact position of the flat in relation to the plate during the platemaking procedure.
13. What is another name for processing presensitized plates? List the three primary purposes of processing presensitized plates.
14. Give the procedure for processing a presensitized plate. Identify differences in procedure for processing plates intended for different uses.
15. List two methods of making deletions on presensitized plates. How are additions made on presensitized plates after the plates have been processed?
16. Describe the procedure for preserving presensitized plates. Why is it necessary to preserve the plates? What precautions must be observed when preserving a plate?
17. What is the most serious problem that can occur in storing presensitized plates?
18. How do one-step photographic plates differ from presensitized plates? Describe the procedure used to make a one-step photographic plate.

ACTIVITIES

1. Secure a presensitized plate and examine the markings on the plate. List the purpose of each of the markings.
2. Using several different tools, try to produce images on the direct-image plate. Examples of tools are listed below.
   a. Nonreproducing pencil
   b. Reproducing pencil
   c. Regular graphite pencil
   d. Regular ball-point pen
   e. Ball-point pen made for drawing on direct-image plates
   f. Grease pencil (Crayon)
   g. Typewriters with a regular ribbon
   h. Typewriter with a reproducing ribbon
   i. Typewriter with a carbon ribbon
   In addition to using different tools to produce images on direct-image plates, apply various pressures when making the images.
3. Print the plate from Item 2 and examine the printed sheets to determine the best methods for preparing a direct-image plate.
4. Obtain a masking sheet and a platemaker's sensitivity guide. Cut several windows in the masking sheet. Make them the same size as the sensitivity guide. Tape the sensitivity guide into one of the windows. Place the flat, with the sensitivity guide, over a plate in the platemaker and cover up the additional windows. Make an exposure of slightly less time than that presently being used in the laboratory. After the exposure, remove the sensitivity guide and place it in another window. Cover the window from the first exposure and make another exposure of the sensitivity guide, using a little more time. Continue this procedure until all of the windows have been used. Process the plate to determine the best exposure as recommended by the manufacturer.
5. Visit a printing plant which has the equipment for making one-step photographic plates. Ask the operator to explain the process of making a one-step photographic plate. Prepare a detailed report on your visit and interviews.

Operating a small offset-lithography press. (Addressograph-Multigraph Corp.)

UNIT 103
INTRODUCTION TO OFFSET-LITHOGRAPHY PRESSWORK

The lithographic principle of image transfer is that grease and water do not readily mix. This principle allows an image to be transferred from one smooth surface to another smooth surface (Fig. 5-2). Large and small offset-lithography presses are designed on this principle.

OFFSET-LITHOGRAPHY PRESS SYSTEMS

Offset-lithography presses (large or small, sheet- or web-fed, single- or multiple-color) contain five major systems (Fig. 103-1). These are (1) the feeding, (2) the cylinder, (3) the dampening, (4) the inking, and (5) the delivery systems. The operator must understand each system thoroughly. Different brands and models of presses contain controls in various locations, but if each of the systems is understood it is possible to determine the location of the controls and adjustments needed.

Feeding system. The feeding system includes the area of the press from the pile of single sheets or the roll of paper through the line-up mechanism, and into the blanket and impression cylinders. This system must be adjusted to feed and line up one sheet of paper at a time.

Cylinder system. The cylinder system contains the plate, blanket, and impression cylinders. The plate cylinder secures the thin lithographic plate, which when inked transfers the image to the blanket (offset-

ting); the blanket in turn transfers the image to the paper. The impression cylinder holds the paper in contact with the blanket.

Dampening system. The dampening system sometimes called the water system contains a supply fountain and a few rollers which transfer a thin coating of ink-repellent solution to the plate as it revolves around the plate cylinder. The solution is basically water, but it contains some special additives to repel ink. With the development and use of the *driography plate* this system can be eliminated from duplicators and presses. Such a plate has a special dry surface that transfers an inked image without the need of a water solution.

Inking system. As it revolves around the plate cylinder, the inking system containing several rollers carries and distributes a sup-

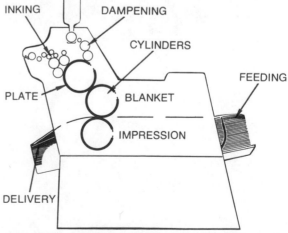

Fig. 103-1. The five systems of an offset-lithography duplicator or press.

ply of ink to the image of the plate. Several ink rollers are needed to carry the proper supply of ink necessary to cover fully the image during each revolution of the press.

Delivery system. After being printed, the sheets must be delivered from the cylinders to a collection area. This system can hold several hundred printed sheets.

THREE-CYLINDER PRESS DESIGN

The *three-cylinder* press design (Fig. 103-2) contains plate, blanket, and impression cylinders. A thin metal, plastic, or paper plate is fastened to the plate cylinder with specially designed clamps. As the cylinder revolves, the plate receives a thin coating of water in the nonimage areas and a coating of ink within the image area. The plate rolls against the blanket cylinder and the image is offset onto the blanket. As the blanket and the impression cylinders roll together with paper in between them, the image is offset from the blanket onto the paper. Most offset-lithography presses, large and small, (Fig. 103-3) incorporate the three-cylinder press design.

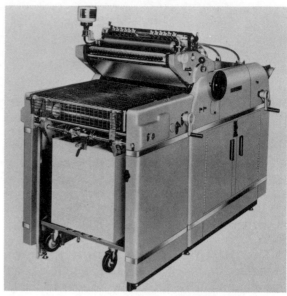

Fig. 103-3. An offset-lithography press that incorporates the three-cylinder design. (A-M Corp.)

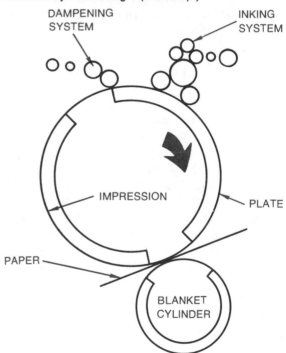

Fig. 103-4. A two-cylinder press design.

TWO-CYLINDER PRESS DESIGN

The *two-cylinder* press design (Fig. 103-4) incorporates an over-sized upper cylinder that includes the plate and the impression segment. The lower, smaller cylinder con-

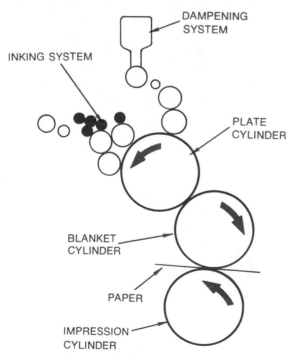

Fig. 103-2. A three-cylinder press design.

Fig. 103-5. An offset-lithography press that incorporates the two-cylinder design. (Fairchild Camera and Instrument Corp.)

tains the blanket. When no paper is traveling between the upper and blanket cylinders, the plate is *offsetting* the image onto the blanket.

When the plate area of the upper cylinder completes a one-half revolution, a sheet of paper begins to pass through the two cylinders. The impression segment of the cylinder forces the paper against the blanket cylinder, causing the image to offset to the paper. During this time the plate is again receiving a new supply of water and ink, in readiness to complete another printing cycle. The offset-lithography press in Fig. 103-5 employs the two-cylinder press design. These presses are commonly used for office and in-plant reproduction needs.

FOUR-CYLINDER PRESS DESIGN

The four-cylinder press-design (Fig. 103-6) incorporates plate, blanket, impression, and delivery cylinders. The delivery cylinder, added to the typical three-cylinder press design, aids in precision delivery of the printed sheet. It is used on nearly all commercial

heavy-duty offset-lithography presses (Fig. 103-7). Another addition to this press design is the two dampening form rollers that roll against the plate to insure proper application of the dampening solution. There are also four ink-form rollers for thorough application of ink to the image area of the plate.

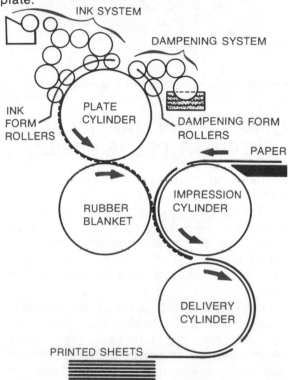

Fig. 103-6. The ink, dampening, and cylinder systems typical of a large offset-lithography press.

Fig. 103-7. A commercial heavy-duty offset-lithography press incorporating the press schematic in Fig. 103-6. (The Miehle Co.)

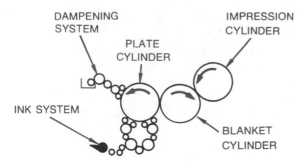 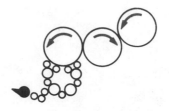

Fig. 103-8. Schematics of an offset-lithography and letterset press. Left schematic: dampening system in place, making is an offset-lithography press. Right schematic: dampening system removed, making it a letterset press.

OFFSET-LITHOGRAPHY AND LETTERSET PRESS DESIGN

The offset-lithography and letterset press design incorporates the features of both offset-lithography and letterpress into one single unit. A schematic (Fig. 103-8) indicates how these two principles of image transfer are used. The normal three cylinders (plate, blanket, and impression) are used with this press design.

When the press is used for offset-lithography, the dampening and ink systems are in place (left schematic Fig. 103-8). When used as an offset-letterpress (letterset) press, the water-dampening system is removed (right schematic Fig. 103-8). Shadow-relief image carriers are attached to the plate cylinder, which needs to receive ink only on the raised image areas. As the cylinder revolves, the ink is transferred (offset) to the blanket cylinder. It, in turn, off-

Fig. 103-9. An offset-lithography and letterset press incorporating the press schematics in Fig. 103-8. (Heidelberg Eastern, Inc.)

sets the image onto the paper as it passes between the impression and blanket cylinders. This offset adaptation is used in several commercial presses (Fig. 103-9).

UNIT 104

OFFEST-LITHOGRAPHY DUPLICATORS AND PRESSES

Offset-lithography machines are designated as either *duplicators* or *presses.* A duplicator is not generally designed to reproduce high-quality work. The adjustment and controls in the various systems are not as precise as are those of a large, heavy-duty commercial press. There is a minimum of ink rollers, limiting the image area of the plate that can receive the proper amount of ink. There is also a limited set of dampening rollers.

Offset-lithography machines that are considered to be presses are precision pieces of equipment. A press contains all of the controls needed to produce high-quality printed products.

Several manufacturers produce offset-lithography duplicators and presses. Each manufacturer has many models and sizes. The different sizes and designs allow the person buying duplicators and presses to make a variety of selections. Some presses are designed for general uses; others are made specifically for a certain category of printed products.

OFFICE DUPLICATORS

Offset-lithography duplicators are designed for simple but fast operation. Persons with minimum instruction can operate small table-top models (Fig. 104-1). Larger offset-lithography duplicators, such as those designed to handle sheets 14 x 20 inch (Fig. 104-2), can print large-and small-sized sheets. These duplicators require more skill to operate than do the table-top models, but a person can learn this skill in a reasonable amount of time.

Fig. 104-1. A table-top offset-lithography duplicator. (A. B. Dick Co.)

Fig. 104-2. A 14 x 20-inch offset-lithography duplicator. (Royal Zenith Corp.)

Attachments that increase speed of production are available for offset-lithography duplicators. The duplicator shown in Fig. 104-3 contains a *roll-sheet feeder,* which cuts the paper from the roll in the size needed for a specific job. The single sheets are fed into the duplicator. A *program control* allows the operator to select the number of sheets desired. The machine turns off when this number is reached. Also available is a *chain delivery* which carries duplicated sheets from the cylinder to a stacking area. This eliminates jam-ups which are common to an ejection-type delivery.

FORM AND JOB DUPLICATORS

Several makes and models of offset-lithography duplicators and presses are designed to produce specialty items. Needs in the business world have dictated the design. *Web-fed* multiple-unit duplicators (Fig. 104-4) print several colors on one or both sides of the sheet. These presses can perforate, punch, trim, number, and insert carbon paper during one pass. They are limited as to width of paper, but have a very high printing speed.

COMMERCIAL PRESSES

Presses used to produce high-quality single- and multiple-color printed materials are precision-built pieces of equipment. They are used to print products ranging from advertising brochures to magazines, books, and newspapers. They can be either sheet fed (Fig. 104-5) or web fed (Fig. 104-6). They are also designed as single-, two-, four-, five-, and six-color presses.

Large-publication web-fed presses (Fig. 104-6) include a *printing unit,* a *drying section,* and a *folding unit.* The web of paper enters the machine and is printed with four colors. The web is dried as it passes through the drying oven, and is then folded into signatures that make up a book or magazine. The press shown in Fig. 104-6 produces high-quality printing at speeds of 1,500 feet per minute.

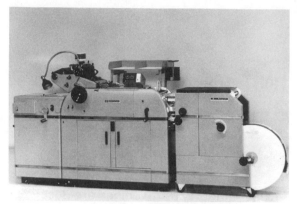

Fig. 104-3. A high-speed office offset-lithography duplicator equipped with a roll-sheet feeder, program sheet control, and chain delivery. (A-M Corp.)

Fig. 104-4. A multiple-unit web press designed for specialty work. (Didde-Glaser, Inc.)

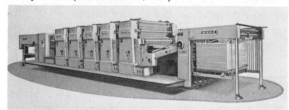

Fig. 104-5. A five-color sheet-fed commercial offset-lithography press. (The Miehle Co.)

Fig. 104-6. A four-color, web-fed, signature-offset-lithography press. (John C. Motter Printing Press Co.)

UNIT 105
OFFSET-LITHOGRAPHY PRESS SAFETY

The offset-lithography press or duplicator is a machine which requires safety in operation. Observation of the following basic safety rules will produce more effective results and assist in the maintenance of this precision-built type of equipment.

Permission. Request permission before beginning work with the offset-lithography press.

Clothing and jewelry. Wear suitable clothing and remove jewelry. Loose clothing, long hair, or bulky jewelry may become entangled in the press.

Safety guards. Power equipment should have the proper safety guards placed over moving parts. Inspect the press to see that all guards are in place before using it.

Air circulation. Make sure there is adequate air circulation. If necessary, start exhaust fans or open windows or doors before working on the press. Ink solvent fumes must be removed from the press area.

Electrical connections. Be certain that all electrical connections on the press are in good condition and that the press is properly grounded. Arrange the cords so that no one will trip and fall.

Good housekeeping. Keep the laboratory neat, clean, and orderly. Never allow waste materials to collect around the press working area. An unkept work area invites accidents or fires.

Materials storage. Store containers of water-fountain solution, ink cans or tubes, and ink solvents on shelves within easy reach.

Illumination. Adequate lighting is important for safety. Turn on all overhead and press lights while operating the machines.

Noise. Excessive noise causes distraction and is a deterrent to safety. Keep talking and laughter to a minimum.

Fire. Keep fire extinguishers in charged condition and located in conspicuous places in the laboratory. Handle with care all flammable materials.

Ink and solvent-soaked rags. Place all such rags in a metal safety-can containing a tight metal lid. Spontaneous combustion is an ever-present threat.

Hands and fingers. Be careful where you place your hands when a press is running. They can easily become caught in moving parts.

Adjustments. Do not make any adjustments while a press is running.

Instruction manual. Read the instruction manual carefully before you use any offset-lithography duplicator or press. Each manufacturer designs presses differently; the operating controls and adjustments may therefore be located in positions other than those shown in Units 106 through 108 and Unit 111.

Press speed. Operate the offset-lithography press at a slow speed until enough skill is acquired to increase the speed safely.

One operator. Only one person should operate the offset-lithography press at a given time. Small presses are one-man machines and the situation becomes dangerous when two or more persons attempt to operate the controls.

Stopping the press. Turn off the power and stop the press before leaving it. A press running without an operator near is dangerous to other persons who might be working in the area.

Lubricating the press. Do not oil or grease the press parts while the press is running. Use the oil can or grease gun only on a nonoperating piece of machinery, any printing press.

UNIT 106
THE OFFSET-LITHOGRAPHY PRESS

All brands and models of offset-lithography presses have control levers, wheels, and knobs. It is necessary to know the function of these devices before efficient press operation can be accomplished. The controls of the feeding, cylinder, and dampening systems and additional running controls for the press/duplicator shown in Units 107, 108, 109, and 111 are shown in Fig. 106-1. The ink and delivery systems controls are pictured in Fig. 106-2.

FEEDING SYSTEM CONTROLS

R. Speed-control lever. This 10-position speed control is adjustable from 4200 to 9000 iph (impressions per hour).

S. Left and right jogger control knobs. These control knobs move the side jogger, ball race, and tapes all at one time.

T. Air-blow control. This control regulates the amount of air delivered to center and side air-blow paper separators.

U. Vacuum control. This control regulates the suction delivered to the suction feet.

V. Back paper feed control. The paper feed control located at the paper feeder end is in the *off* position when at the extreme left. It is in the *on* position at the extreme right.

W. Paper platform handwheel. The paper platform is raised or lowered by this device.

Y. Left and right paper stack side guides. These flip-up side guides are adjustable horizontally for varying widths of stock.

Z. Paper stack back guide. This is adjustable for varying lengths of stock as well as for horizontal positioning. The paper stack

back guide is also a flip-up guide to facilitate loading.

CYLINDER SYSTEM CONTROLS

O. Handwheel. The handwheel can be used to manually turn the press through its full cycle.

AA. Manual plate-to-blanket impression control. Turning this control to the left or towards the delivery end places the plate and blanket cylinders on impression if preinking of the blanket is desired.

CC. Vertical positioning control knob. This control is used for vertical positioning of the image on the paper being run.

DAMPENING SYSTEM CONTROLS

L. Dampener fountain roller control knob. This control allows the operator to turn the dampener fountain roller by hand.

M. Dampener volume control. This 11-position control regulates the amount of fountain solution delivered to the dampening system.

N. Form roller control lever. This is a 3-position operating lever. Off is to the extreme left. In the center position, the dampener form roller is placed in contact with the plate. The third position drops the ink-form rollers and is the operating position.

DD. Auxiliary dampener form roller control knob. This control has three functions: (1) when the position indicator is up the dampener-form roller is taken out of contact with the plate; (2) turning this control one position to the right will place it in its

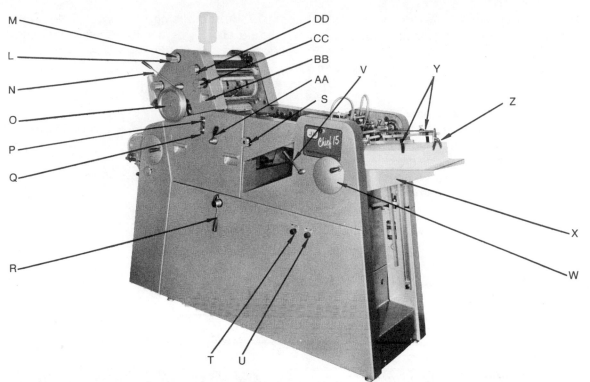

Fig. 106-1. The feeding, cylinder, and dampening system controls for an offset-lithography press. (American Type Founders Co., Inc.)

normal operating position; and (3) turning the control to the extreme right releases the retaining arms, permitting the dampening form roller to be easily removed.

INK SYSTEM CONTROLS

A. Ink fountain roller control knob. When filling the ink fountain, a twist of this control knob will carry ink down into the fountain.

B. Ink volume control. This 7-position control regulates the amount of ink being delivered to the system.

C. Ink-fountain manual-control lever. The ink-fountain roller turns only when paper is being fed; when it is necessary to supply ink to the entire ink system without feeding paper, as when first inking up, simply depress this lever.

DELIVERY SYSTEM CONTROLS

F. Delivery sheet stop. Paper is jogged from the rear against the sheet stop.

Fig. 106-2. The delivery and ink system controls for an offset-lithography press. (American Type Founders Co., Inc.)

H. Delivery lock release. When depressed, this control allows the paper pile to be raised manually.

I. Delivery paper feed control. This lever is used to control the feed of paper from the delivery end.

J. Delivery pile handwheel. This can be used to lower and raise the paper pile.

K. Delivery rate lowering control. This control is used to determine the rate at which the delivery board will drop to maintain the top of the pile at a constant height.

BB. Automatic copy counter. The counter should always be set to 00000 before starting a run. It usually counts to 99999.

MISCELLANEOUS

D. Delivery light.
E. Delivery side-guide control knobs.
G. Delivery board.
P. Drive motor switch.
Q. Air-vacuum pump switch.
X. Paper platform.

UNIT 107
PREPARING THE PRESS

Several preoperating preparations must be completed before printed copies are obtained. The four press systems that must receive attention are the (1) feeding, (2) delivery, (3) inking, and (4) dampening systems.

FEEDING SYSTEM PROCEDURE

1. Lower the paper platform by pushing in on the paper platform handwheel. Then turn it counterclockwise.
2. Set the inside of the left paper stack side guide on the scale marking for the size sheet to be run (Fig. 107-1).
3. Lay a sheet of the size paper stock to be run in position; set the right paper stack side guide so that it will be about $\frac{1}{16}$ away from the edge of the paper.
4. Set the front guides to a line representing $\frac{1}{4}$ of the front edge of the paper (Fig. 107-2).
5. Center the suction feet on the front guides directly above the thin metal sheet separators (Fig. 107-1).
6. Position the front air-blower in the center of the sheet edge (Figs. 107-1 and 107-2).

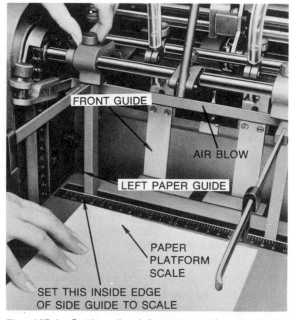

Fig. 107-1. Setting the left-paper-stack side guide. (American Type Founders Co., Inc.)

7. Load the paper platform and raise the paper stack to within ¼ inch of the sheet separators.
8. Set the paper stack back guide so that the front wings are on top and the back wings are behind and up to the stack (Fig. 107-3).

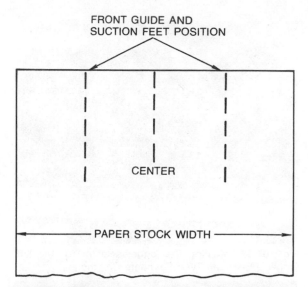

Fig. 107-2. Positions for front guides, suction feet, and front air blow.

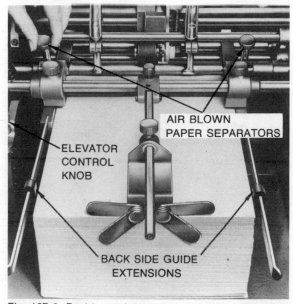

Fig. 107-3. Positions of paper stack-guides. (American Type Founders Co., Inc.)

9. Set the back side guide extensions so that they are about ½ inch from the back of the sheet, or at their extreme when running larger-size stock (Fig. 107-3).

10. Set the side air blow paper separators to blow about ⅔ of the way back and across the paper. The second hole in the air blower tube should be in line with the top of the paper when the paper is ¼ inch below the metal sheet separators (Fig. 107-4).

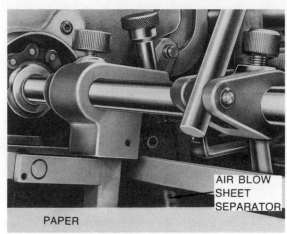

Fig. 107-4. Correct position of the side air blow paper separator. (American Type Founders Co., Inc.)

11. Lower the paper platform to one inch. Turn on the drive motor switch. Allow the paper platform to raise automatically. Adjust the elevator control knob (Fig. 107-3) so that the paper stack stops about ¼ inch below the metal sheet separators. (Turning the knob clockwise lowers; turning it counterclockwise raises the height of the stack of paper).

12. Set the feedboard joggers. The paper is picked up from the paper stack, moved to the paper pull-out roll by the sucker feet, and then delivered to the paper feedboard. It travels down the feedboard via the conveyor tapes to the paper stop bar and joggers. It is then jogged into correct feeding position.

Paper may be jogged from either the left- or the right-hand side. The latter is used only when running copy on *both sides* of the paper, in which case for good printing use the left-hand jogger the first time through and the right-hand one for the second time through the backup. This uses the same paper edge for jogging during each printing cycle. For work printed on *one side only,* use the left-hand jogger. Moving the jogger selector to center position sets both joggers in motion while the press is running. The center position is often used when printing small-sized jobs.

Left-hand jogger. Hold the right jogger with your left hand; pull it toward you while you move the jogger selector back toward the feedboard (Fig. 107-5). This sets the left jogger in motion.

Right-hand jogger. Hold the left jogger with the left hand; push it away from you while you move the jogger selector into forward position, toward the front of the press. This sets the right jogger in motion.

13. Set the feathers (Fig. 107-6). Lower the feather on the idle jogger by pressing down on the front end of the feather retainer. The feather on the jogger being used should be raised by pressing down on the back end of the feather retainer. The feather on the idle jogger should be depressed no more than $\frac{1}{16}$ inch when the active jogger moves a sheet for lineup.

DELIVERY SYSTEM

The paper is picked up from the paper stop bar by the tumbler grippers. It is carried through the impression phase and then transferred to the delivery grippers where it is delivered to the stack.

14. Raise the delivery board to the uppermost position by depressing the delivery lock release. Then turn the delivery pile handwheel clockwise.

15. Feed a sheet of paper through the machine, allowing it to drop into normal delivery position on the delivery board.

16. Loosen the delivery side guide control knobs (Fig. 107-7). Bring the stationary side guide against the sheet of paper. Tighten the control knob. Turn the press handwheel until the automatic side-jogging guide is in the extreme inward position. Slide it to within $\frac{1}{16}$ inch from the paper when the paper is against the stationary guide. Tighten its control knob.

17. With the paper against the front guide, turn the handwheel until the back jogging guide is in extreme inward position (Fig. 107-7). Loosen the guide setscrew, slide the guide to the paper, and retighten the setscrew.

18. Run several sheets through the press to check all adjustments. Turn on the drive motor switch; slow the press to slowest

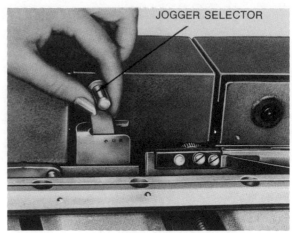

Fig. 107-5. Adjusting the jogger selector for the left jogger. (American Type Founders Co., Inc.)

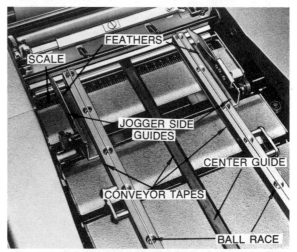

Fig. 107-6. The paper feedboard. (American Type Founders Co., Inc.)

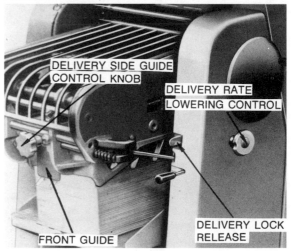

Fig. 107-7. The chain and delivery controls. (American Type Founders, Co., Inc.)

speed; turn on the air-vacuum pump switch; and engage the paper feed control lever. Carefully inspect the sheets as they pass through the machine and make necessary adjustments. It is imperative that the paper feeds through the machine efficiently and smoothly to insure maximum quality of reproduction.

INKING SYSTEM

19. Before filling the ink fountain inspect the ink rollers to see that they are clean of all lint, dust, and glaze, especially if the press has been idle for several days. Clean if necessary.
20. Fill the ink fountain at least half full with a suitable ink for the image content and the kind of paper (Fig. 107-8).
21. Turn the ink fountain roller control knob counterclockwise; turn the ink fountain adjusting screws until a thin film of ink is evenly distributed over the fountain roller (Fig. 107-9).
22. Place the ink-feed volume control (Fig. 106-2) on the third notch. Turn on the power switch. Depress the ink-fountain manual-control lever. Run the machine until all ink rollers are covered with a thin film of ink.
23. Raise the manual control lever. Turn the press off. The inking system is now ready to transfer ink to the plate image.

DAMPENING SYSTEM

24. Inspect the dampener fountain roller. It should be free of dirt and ink. Clean if necessary.
25. Fill the dampener fountain bottle with the proper mixture of fountain solution and water for the plate to be run.
26. Invert the bottle with the spout down over a sink or wastebasket. Be sure that the float valve does not leak. Bring the bottle over the side of the machine, being careful not to spill any solution on the ink rollers, and insert it in its holder.

Fig. 107-8. Filling the ink fountain. (American Type Founders Co., Inc.)

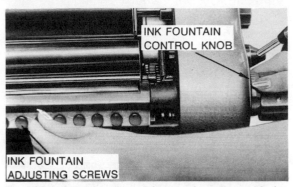

Fig. 107-9. Adjusting the ink flow to the rollers with the fountain adjusting screws. (American Type Founders Co., Inc.)

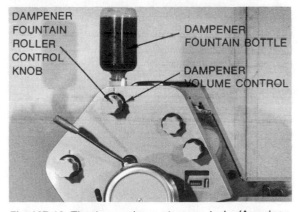

Fig. 107-10. The dampening system controls. (American Type Founders Co., Inc.)

27. Moisten a cotton pad with fountain solution. Wipe the entire surface of the dampening rollers until each is thoroughly moistened but not wet.
28. Set the dampener volume control (Fig. 107-10) on the second notch. Run the press for approximately twenty revolutions. The dampener system is now ready to use.

UNIT 108
RUNNING THE PRESS

It is important to follow a prescribed sequential procedure when running an offset-lithography press. Quality printing results from following a standard operating technique.

PRINTING COPIES

1. Check all systems of the press in accordance with the information given in Unit 107.
2. Get the prepared plate (image carrier) and inspect it for flaws. Quality printing cannot result from a poorly prepared plate.
3. Inspect and clean the plate cylinder. It must be thoroughly clean before the plate is attached. A small particle of dirt under a plate can ruin it in a few revolutions of the press.
4. Turn the press with the handwheel until the plate cylinder lead plate clamp is in the proper position (Fig. 108-1).
5. Attach the lead edge of the plate to the lead plate cylinder clamp (Fig. 108-1). Start at the far side or right side of the plate and place each clamp hook in a plate hole. Hook each hole securely while holding the tail or bottom edge of the plate taut with the right hand.
6. Hold the tail of the plate with the right hand and turn the press clockwise with the handwheel until the tail clamp is in view (Fig. 108-2).
7. Bring the tail clamp up with spring tension and attach the trailing edge of the plate to the clamp (Fig. 108-2). Hook each hole securely in the plate.
8. Tighten the plate clamp by turning the plate clamp vernier wheel clockwise

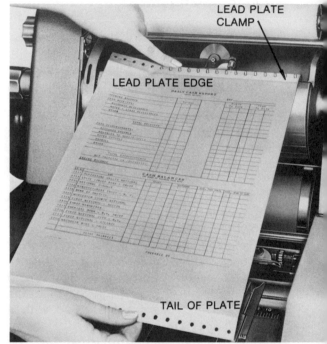

Fig. 108-1. Attaching the lead plate edge to the lead clamp of the plate cylinder. (American Type Founders Co., Inc.)

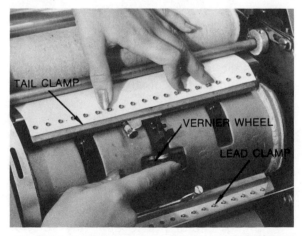

Fig. 108-2. Tightening the plate around the cylinder with the vernier wheel. (American Type Founders Co., Inc.)

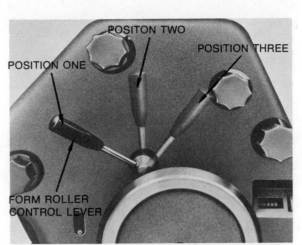

Fig. 108-3. The three positions of the form roller control lever. (American Type Founders Co., Inc.)

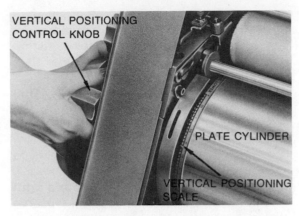

Fig. 108-4. Vertical image position adjustments. (American Type Founders Co., Inc.)

(Fig. 108-2). Secure the lock nut to prevent the plate from loosening on extremely long press runs.

9. If a metal plate is used, moisten it thoroughly with a cotton pad that has been dipped into the dampening fountain solution. This removes the gum protective coating.

When using a plate made of paper, pre-etch it with the recommended plate brand solution before placing it on the plate cylinder. This prevents ink from the ink rollers being placed accidentally on the unprotected plate during installation.

10. Turn on the press power switch.
11. Turn the form roller control lever to the second position (Fig. 108-3). This places the dampening form roller against the plate. Allow the press to make several revolutions. This places an even layer of dampening solution over the nonimage area of the plate.
12. Turn the form roller control lever to the third position (Fig. 108-3). This places the inkform rollers against the plate along with the dampening form roller. Allow the press to make several revolutions to place an even layer of ink on the image areas of the plate.
13. Turn on the air-vacuum pump switch. Run three or four sheets through the press.
14. Return the form roller control lever to position one and turn off the press.

15. Inspect a printed sheet for proper image position. Adjustments may be necessary for (1) vertical positioning, (2) horizontal positioning, or (3) crooked copy.

Vertical adjustment:
   a. Turn the press with the handwheel until the vertical positioning control knob is aligned with the plate-cylinder lock nut located at the end of the plate cylinder (Fig. 108-4).
   b. Engage or mesh both by pushing and holding in the vertical positioning control knob.
   c. Turn the control knob to the left to unlock the cylinder. By turning the handwheel the image can be either raised or lowered to the desired position.
   d. Turn the control knob to the right. Relock the plate cylinder. *Note:* Never attempt a vertical adjustment while the press is running.

Horizontal adjustment:
   a. Move the paper to the left or right. This adjustment is made by moving the right and left jogger control knobs simultaneously in the desired direction (Fig. 106-1).
   b. When the copy has been centered correctly, adjust the paper stack accordingly.

Adjustment of crooked copy:
   a. Square the crooked copy on the plate to the paper by using the paper-stop bar-straightening adjustment (Fig. 108-5).

b. Loosen the binder screw allowing the bar to be tilted in either direction. This eliminates the need for adjusting the angle of the plate on the plate cylinder.

16. Repeat Steps 11 through 15. Continue this until the image is printing in the correct position on the sheet.

17. Check for adequate ink coverage. Increase or decrease the supply of ink to the rollers.

18. Set the copy counter to 00000 and print the desired number of copies. Observe the quality of the printed sheets as the press runs. Make necessary adjustments (Unit 110).

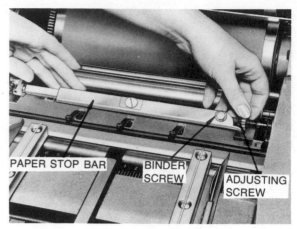

Fig. 108-5. Crooked image position adjustments. (American Type Founders Co., Inc.)

UNIT 109
OPERATING ADJUSTMENTS

Special adjustments are necessary during the preparation stage (Unit 107) and the running stage (Unit 108) of press operation. Some are preventive maintenance; others are normal operating requirements. They are categorized according to the press systems.

FEEDING SYSTEM

Double sheet eliminator. This unit should be positioned in the center of the paper (Fig. 109-1) whenever possible.

1. To move the unit, loosen the retaining screw, depress the release lever, and slide the unit to the desired position.

2. Obtain a strip of paper approximately two inches wide that will be used for printing. Fold it end-to-end but do not match the edges closer than one inch. This gives a paper strip of one-sheet thickness in one area and of double-sheet thickness in another area.

3. Turn on the press and the vacuum.

4. Place the single and then the double areas of the paper strip under the thickness control.

5. Adjust the double-sheet eliminator thumbscrew until the ejection mechanism does not engage with a single thickness but will take hold with the double sheet.

Elevator control knob. The elevator control knob (Fig. 109-2) regulates the maximum height to which the top of the paper pile will be elevated automatically. Turn the elevator control knob clockwise to lower the pile; counterclockwise to raise it.

Printing speed. The press speed can be either increased or decreased by a speed-control lever (see Fig. 106-1). The handle is moved down to increase the speed; up to decrease it. Speed changes should be made gradually and then only while the press is running.

Fig. 109-1. The double sheet eliminator unit. (American Type Founders Co., Inc.) .

Fig. 109-2. The location of the elevator control knob. (American Type Founders Co., Inc.)

DELIVERY SYSTEM

Delivery rate lowering control. This control (Fig. 109-3) determines the rate of descent of the delivery board. It is graduated to compensate for the entire range of stock that can be accommodated. A general rule of thumb governing correct adjustment of this control is that if the top of the paper stack remains at a point about halfway up on the side guide, the control is in correct adjustment.

Fig. 109-3. The delivery system and rate lowering control. (American Type Founders Co., Inc.)

Fig. 109-4. Identical ink strips 3/16 inch wide on the plate indicate properly adjusted inkform rollers. (American Type Founders Co., Inc.)

If the top of the paper stack climbs higher than halfway up, turn the control clockwise to increase the rate of descent. If the top sinks below this halfway point, turn the control counterclockwise to decrease the rate of descent.

INKING SYSTEM

Form rollers adjustment:
1. Attach a clean, dry plate to the plate cylinder.
2. Turn the handwheel until the plate clamps face the feeder. This leaves the plate facing the inkform rollers.
3. Drop the inkform rollers momentarily by placing the form roller control lever in the third position.
4. Lift the inkform rollers.
5. Revolve the plate cylinder until the two strips of ink are in view (Fig. 109-4).

6. Both strips should be nearly identical and approximately 3/16 inch wide. If they do not meet these requirements, make adjustments. Check the press operator's manual.

DAMPENING SYSTEM

Form roller
1. Attach a plate on the plate cylinder.
2. Tear two strips of 16-pound paper to one-inch widths.
3. Insert one strip on the right side; insert the other on the left between the plate and dampener form roller (Fig. 109-5).
4. Drop the form roller onto the plate by placing the form roller control lever in second position. Make sure that the auxiliary dampener roller control (Fig. 106-1) is in the on position.
5. Pull on the paper strips. Each should have a slight but equal amount of resistance. If they do not, make adjustments. Check the press operator's manual.

Oscillator roller
1. Place the two strips of 16-pound paper between the oscillator roller and the form roller (Fig. 109-6).
2. Make the same check for resistance as was done on the form roller and plate.
3. Adjust if necessary.

Ductor roller
1. Turn the handwheel until the ductor roller contacts the oscillator roller.

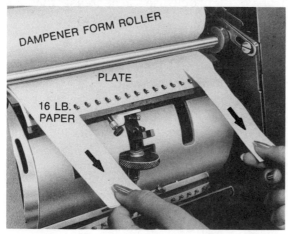

Fig. 109-5. Testing dampener form roller pressure against the plate. (American Type Founders Co., Inc.)

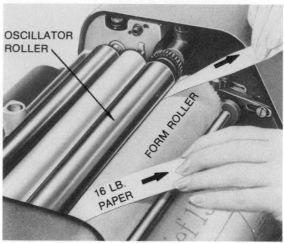

Fig. 109-6. Testing the pressure between the dampener oscillator roller and the form roller. (American Type Founders Co., Inc.)

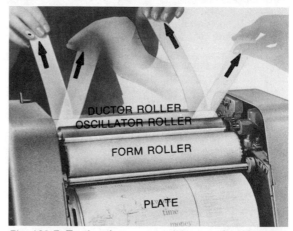

Fig. 109-7. Testing the pressure between the dampener ductor roller and the oscillator roller. (American Type Founders Co., Inc.)

2. Place two strips of 16-pound paper between these two rollers (Fig. 109-7).
3. Make the same resistance check and adjust if necessary.

CYLINDER SYSTEM

Plate-to-blanket impression
1. Attach a plate to the plate cylinder.
2. With the auxiliary dampener form roller control to the *off* position, drop the form roller control lever into third position until the plate is solidly inked.
3. Turn the handwheel until the plate is in position to contact the blanket about halfway around.

4. Place the impression between the plate and blanket cylinder to *on* and release the impression immediately.
5. Revolve the blanket cylinder until the ink strip is visible. It should be even and about ³⁄₁₆ inch wide (Fig. 109-4). If the ink strip does not meet these requirements, make adjustments. See the press operator's manual.

Blanket-to-paper impression

1. Attach a plate to the plate cylinder.
2. With the auxiliary dampener form-roller control to the *off* position, drop the ink-form-roller control lever into the third position until the plate is solidly inked.
3. To get an impression between the plate and blanket cylinder turn the pressure control to *on*; turn on the press and completely ink the blanket.
4. Turn the handwheel until the inked surface of the blanket is next to the impression cylinder.
5. Insert a sheet of the paper stock to be run between the impression cylinder and the blanket.
6. Place the blanket and impression cylinders on *impression* and release.

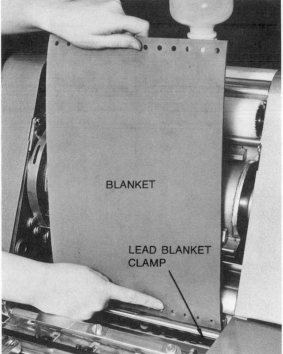

Fig. 109-8. Hooking the blanket to the lead blanket clamp. (American Type Founders Co., Inc.)

7. Remove the paper. If this adjustment is accurate, there will be a strip of ink about ³⁄₁₆ inch wide on the paper. If the strip is wider or narrower, make the needed adjustments.

BLANKET INSTALLATION

Although the blanket is constructed of high-quality material, it must be replaced periodically because of the chemicals and ink which soak into the surface making the blanket brittle. Dirt and dust particles also impregnate the blanket.

1. Turn the handwheel until the lead blanket clamp is in position (Fig. 109-8).
2. Hook the blanket onto the lead blanket clamp (Fig. 109-8). Be certain that all hooks penetrate the holes in the blanket.
3. Hold the blanket tight using the right hand. Turn the handwheel with the left hand until the blanket tail clamp comes into view.
4. Hook the tail end of the blanket onto the blanket tail clamp (Fig. 109-9).
5. Turn the vernier wheel counterclockwise until tight.
6. Check to see that all hooks are correctly positioned in the holes punched into the blanket.
7. Run approximately fifteen sheets of paper through the press. Stop and retighten the vernier wheel. Secure it with the locknut.

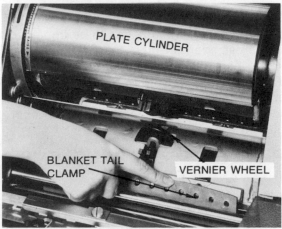

Fig. 109-9. Hooking the tail end of the blanket to the blanket tail clamp. (American Type Founders Co., Inc.)

BLANKET CONSTRUCTION

Since the early part of the twentieth century, when rubber was accidentally discovered to be an excellent transfer medium in lithography, almost all lithographic blankets have had a top surface of natural rubber. Modern construction, however, uses synthetic rubber.

A lithographic blanket has two, three, or four plies of cotton fabric laminated by means of thin layers of rubber. This laminated structure is covered with an approximate 0.020-inch thick top layer of rubber compound.

BLANKET PRESERVATION

The most important part of blanket maintenance is *wash-up*. Never permit ink to dry on it. As a general guide, the blanket should be washed at the following times:

1. Before being used for the first time.
2. After every 3,000 to 4,000 impressions or if the printing quality deteriorates.
3. During a paper load change.
4. At quitting time.
5. When the press is stopped for any length of time.

Soak a good lint-free rag with blanket solvent. Wipe the entire surface of the blanket evenly with the rag. Wipe it again until it is dry, using a completely dry rag. Do not use too much blanket-wash solvent because it could seep under the blanket and swell the edges.

A blanket should rest; after being used for a period of time, remove it from the press cylinder. Clean it thoroughly and hang it up to dry and rest for several days. During this period the blanket will be restored as swelled edges or smashes disappear. Two blankets should be used alternately on press runs.

If a blanket is left on the press over a weekend or during other extended periods when the press is not running, blanket tension should be released. Also, the blanket should be covered to protect it from sunlight and dust.

UNIT 110
PRINTING PROBLEMS[1]

Many times the reproduction quality of the job being printed needs to be improved. The press operator must then diagnose and solve the problem to the best of his ability. The following examples of printed results and ink-related problems, causes, and remedies may help the inexperienced operator to solve the problem quickly.

PRINTED SHEET PROBLEMS AND CAUSES

A Good Image (Fig. 110-1). Good copy has crisp, dark lines and solids, a clean background, clear halftones, screens and

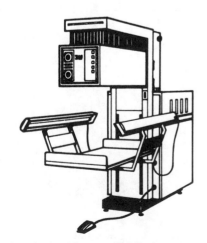

Fig. 110-1. A good image. (3M Co.)

[1]Adapted from A-M Corporation Publication.

reverses, good registration, and completely dry sheets.

Background Dirty, Scumming (Fig. 110-2). Dirty copy could be caused by too much ink, not enough moisture, dirty dampener-roll covers, or dampener covers tied too tightly on ends.

Gray, Washed Out, Dirty Background (Fig. 110-3). This problem could be caused by glazed ink rollers, glazed blanket, too much inkform roller pressure, or too much dampener form roller pressure.

Too Dark (Fig. 110-4). Excessive darkness, where halftones and fine reverses fill in, or sheet dries slowly, could be caused by too much ink, too much impression-to-blanket pressure, or not enough plate-to-blanket pressure.

Weak Spots (Fig. 110-5). Weak spots may be caused by incorrect plate-to-blanket pressure, incorrect impression-to-blanket pressure, low spots in the blanket, "blind" image on plate caused by dried gum or too strong a fountain solution, or a glazed blanket.

NonImage Area Filling (Fig. 110-6). This may be caused by a poor or old plate, a plate fogged from room light, or improper plate development.

Image Breaks Down While Plate Is Running (Fig. 110-7). Image breakdown may be the result of too much dampener form roller pressure, too much inkform roller pressure, too much plate-to-blanket pressure, a fountain solution which is too strong, or end play in the form rollers.

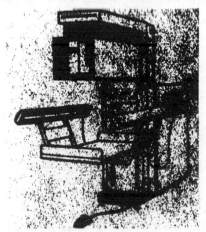
Fig. 110-2. The background is dirty. (3M Co.)

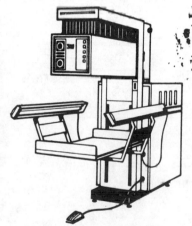
Fig. 110-3. A gray, washed-out background, plus dirt. (3M Co.)

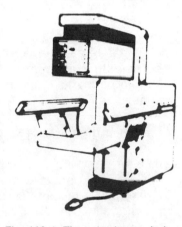
Fig. 110-4. The print is too dark. (3M Co.)

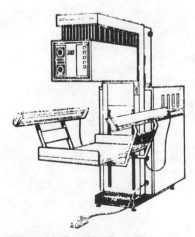
Fig. 110-5. Weak spots, throughout. (3M Co.)

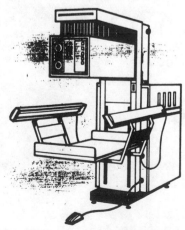
Fig. 110-6. Nonimage area filling. (3M Co.)

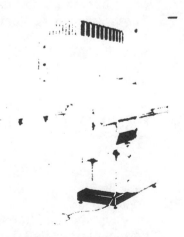
Fig. 110-7. The image breaks down. (3M Co.)

UNIT 111
CLEANING THE PRESS

It is essential to clean the press thoroughly after finishing a unit of work. The three press systems that require attention are (1) the ink, (2) the dampening, and (3) the cylinder systems.

CLEANING THE DAMPENING SYSTEM

1. Remove the fountain supply bottle. Discard the remaining solution. Rinse the bottle with plain water. A new solution should be made when the press is used again.
2. Remove the water from the dampening system trough by soaking it out with a cotton pad.
3. Inspect the dampener fountain roller. If any ink has collected on the roller, remove it with a cloth and a soft bristle brush soaked in ink solvent.
4. Inspect the ductor and form rollers. Replace covers, if necessary and read the press operator's manual.
5. Turn the auxiliary dampener form roller control knob to the extreme left position (Fig. 106-1). This removes the dampener form roller from contact with the plate.

CLEANING THE INKING SYSTEM

1. Remove the ink from the ink fountain with an ink knife. Save unused ink, if possible.
2. Remove the ink fountain; lay it on a newspaper-covered table and clean it thoroughly. The fountain is removed by tilting it up toward the ink rollers (90 degrees), and then lifting it upward (Fig. 111-1).
3. Clean the ink fountain roller with a solvent-soaked rag.
4. Attach a cleanup sheet (made of blotter stock) to the plate cylinder. The cleanup sheet is attached just like a plate. NOTE: It is assumed that after the printed copies are completed the plate is removed from the press and properly cared for.
5. Turn on the press.
6. Place an amount of solvent across the large ink roller (Fig. 111-2). Use an oil can or plastic squeeze-bottle. Allow the press to run for several revolutions.
7. Drop the ink rollers on the cleanup sheet by moving the form roller control lever to the third position (Fig. 108-3). Be certain that the auxiliary dampener form-roller control knob is in the extreme left position. See Step 5 under Cleaning the Dampening System.

Fig. 111-1. Removing the ink fountain from the press.

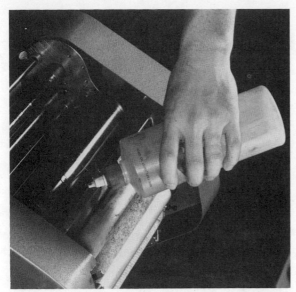

Fig. 111-2. Placing solvent on the large ink roller during the cleaning operation.

8. Add an additional amount of solvent to the large ink roller as the cleanup sheet absorbs the ink and solvent from the rollers.
9. Stop the press. Replace the cleanup sheet with a new one. Repeat Steps 6 through 8. Do this until the ink rollers are completely clean.

10. Remove the cleanup sheet. Save the sheets until the next press cleanup and use the reverse sides.

CLEANING THE CYLINDER SYSTEM

1. Using a rag dampened with ink solvent, wipe the three cylinders (plate, blanket, and impression) free of ink. Dry the cylinders with a dry rag.
2. Remove glaze from the blanket with a special glaze remover.
3. Inspect the impression cylinder for hardened ink buildup and remove it with ink solvent or a special cylinder cleaner.

SECURING THE TOTAL PRESS

1. Wipe down the entire press.
2. Lubricate needed parts in preparation for the next printing job.
3. Turn off all electrical power to the press.
4. Cover the press with a dust-protector cloth.

UNIT 112
LEARNING EXPERIENCES: LITHOGRAPHIC IMAGE TRANSFER

DISCUSSION TOPICS

1. Identify the five major systems of offset-lithography presses. Note the basic purpose of each system.
2. Name the cylinders in a press of the three-cylinder design; of the two-cylinder design; of the four-cylinder design. Describe the principle of each press design.

3. Compare the offset-lithography duplicator and the offset-lithography press. Cite the primary difference between the two types of machines. Describe a forms duplicator.
4. Describe the dual designed press-offset-lithography and offset-letterpress (letterset). What style of image carriers does this press use? Are all five press

systems used during the printing operation on this press?

5. What capabilities does a commercial offset-lithography sheet-fed press possess? Identify the special capabilities of the offset-lithography web-fed press. What are the advantages in using a sheet-fed press over a web-fed press? The disadvantages?

6. Identify the four press systems that must receive attention prior to operating the offset-lithography press. Which of these systems should be checked first, second, third and fourth? Must these four systems be checked before printing any job on the press?

7. Describe the procedure necessary to attach a plate or image carrier to the plate cylinder. Why must the plate cylinder be thoroughly cleaned before attaching the plate? Give the purposes of the vernier wheel and the locknut on the cylinder that holds the plate.

8. List the steps necessary to obtain printed copies once the plate has been attached to the plate cylinder. Give the three position changes of the image that are possible on the press.

9. Enumerate the several operating adjustments that must be attended to for each of the press systems. Cite the special importance of the double-sheet eliminator that is part of the feeding system. When should speed changes be made on most presses?

10. Explain the method used to check for proper pressure between the inkform rollers and the plate cylinder; between the plate cylinder and blanket cylinder; between the blanket cylinder and the impression cylinder. Also explain how dampening system roller pressures are checked.

11. Why is the blanket an important part of the offset-lithography press? Enumerate the steps necessary to install a blanket on the press.

12. Describe the construction of an offset-lithography blanket. How can the surface and body of the blanket be preserved? When should the surface of the blanket be washed? Why does a blanket need a rest?

13. Identify several problems and causes of poorly printed sheets from the offset-lithography press. List the remedies that can overcome these several problems.

14. Name the three offset-lithography press systems that require a thorough cleaning after a job is finished or at the end of the day. Which of these press systems should receive attention first during the cleanup operation?

15. Outline the procedure for cleaning the ink system. What special adjustment is necessary in the dampening system before the cleanup operation of the inking system begins? Why should the electrical power to the press be turned off as one of the final steps in securing the total press?

ACTIVITIES

1. Obtain 100 sheets each of three different sizes of 20-pound bond paper. These sheets should vary in width as well as length. Make the necessary adjustments on the feeder and delivery systems on the offset-lithography press for each of the three paper sizes. Adjust the press accurately enough so that all 100 sheets of each size go flawlessly through the press.

2. Prepare the dampening and inking systems of the press. Make the necessary checks of the dampening system rollers, the inking system rollers, and the cylinder system pressure. If any of these checks show a need for press adjustments, get proper supervision and make the adjustments.

3. Obtain a prepared lithographic plate. It can be either a direct image or a photosensitive plate. Also obtain 300 to 400 scrap sheets of paper which are cut to a size suitable for the image on the plate as well as for the press. Set the press up and practice running the press by printing the scrap sheets. Make all necessary press adjustments and reproduce the job to the best of your ability.

4. Start from the beginning and print a job by using the offset-lithography press. Plan, compose, complete the photography work, prepare the photosensitive image carrier, and print the job. Suggested jobs are personal stationery, business forms, pamphlets, and small newspapers. Use ink other than black if you wish. Remember to clean the press thoroughly when you have finished printing the job.

5. Visit a commercial printing plant that has offset-lithography presses. Ask to observe these presses in action. Carefully watch the skilled operator as he prepares, operates, and cleans the press. Take special note of the operator's skill and knowledge in making the necessary adjustments to obtain a quality printed job. Interview an operator about his job, skills, and training and prepare a detailed report.

A gravure laboratory-model press used for research and education.

UNIT 113
INTRODUCTION TO THE GRAVURE PRINTING PROCESS

The *gravure printing process* is one of the major graphic reproduction methods. It is also known as the rotogravure process. It differs from the other graphic reproduction methods in several significant production areas, but one important point is very similar. Like other processes, the gravure process is used to reproduce images for the purpose of visual communication. It has advantages and disadvantages; it is important therefore that the limitations are understood by the persons who need printed materials.

Graphic materials are reproduced by the gravure process from image areas that are sunken below the nonimage area of the image carrier (Unit 5). Intaglio, a method which reproduces images from a sunken surface, differs from gravure in that intaglio uses lines produced either by hand or mechanical means. Gravure uses shallow, minute ink wells or dots of ink.

Intaglio is the origin of this type of image transfer. Gravure which uses a screened-dot pattern is a specific adaptation of the original intaglio. *All* image material is screened to produce dots in the gravure process. This image material includes photographs, artist's renderings, illustrations, and type matter. The dots produced by the screen are so small that they cannot be noticed except with the use of a magnifying glass.

PRODUCTS PRODUCED BY GRAVURE

The gravure process is used to produce materials such as newspaper supplements and magazines, packaging, wrappers, advertising brochures, trading stamps, and magazines (Fig. 113-1). Other items include mail order catalogues, gift wrappings, food-package labels, floor covering, automobile upholstery material, handbags, table and counter top high-pressure laminate, and wood-grain coverings for furniture (Fig. 113-2). The number of products is unlimited and more appear constantly as the result of

Fig. 113-1. Some of the many printed products produced by the gravure process.

Fig. 113-2. Specialty products printed with the gravure process.

this process. Approximately 56% of gravure materials is used for publication work, 27% for packaging, and 17% for specialty items.

A recently developed technique permits rolls of completely seamless material to be printed with absolute uniformity of design. This makes possible authentic reproduction of wood and leather grains, marble patterns, linen weaves, and similar effects.

The United States Bureau of Engraving and Printing uses the intaglio process to produce paper currency and postage stamps. It recently installed a press that produces postage stamps at a record speed of 1,700,000 per hour.

PRODUCTION STEPS

The production steps of the gravure process follow the normal pattern of all graphic reproduction processes (Unit 3). Within each phase, however, special considerations and treatment are necessary. The design and layout, composition, and photoconversion phases are similar, so no specific discussion is made of them in this section.

A notable exception within the photoconversion phase is that continuous-tone film negatives and positives are used *instead* of the halftone ones common to letterpress and lithography reproduction processes. The production of gravure image carriers (Unit 114) and the image transfer presses (Unit 115) are significantly different and are treated in detail in these units.

ADVANTAGES AND DISADVANTAGES

There are several advantages and disadvantages in gravure reproduction methods. They are important considerations in the production of printed products.

Advantages
1. Color that looks almost like continuous-tone printing. This is similar to color photographic prints.
2. Long image life of the image carriers.
3. Capacity to produce images on a great variety of materials.
4. High reproduction results on inexpensive printing substitutes such as newsprint paper.
5. Fast-drying ink.
6. Exceptionally high press speed.

Disadvantages
1. Initial high cost of producing image carriers like wrap-around plates and cylinders.
2. Limited type size and styles. Type smaller than 8 point should not be used unless necessary and the type-face cannot contain hairline strokes. The type should be medium-to-bold style which lacks fine detail.
3. Inability to make quick and easy image carrier plate changes. If one part of the total image needs to be changed, the entire image carrier must be re-etched. This takes time and is quite expensive.
4. More precision required to obtain quality results.

HISTORICAL HIGHLIGHTS

Authorities do not agree on the exact origin of gravure, but it is generally conceded that the process was developed in Italy as a method of engraving gold and silver plates. This artistic development of hand intaglio engraving passed through successive stages, each leaving techniques that have continued through the centuries. Today intaglio is still considered an art process of definite value. Etching and/or dry point is basic to this process (Unit 117).

The invention of photography gave impetus to the gravure reproduction method. During the 1880s and 1890s Karl Kleitsch (Klic) of Vienna, Austria, successfully applied photographic methods to produce the gravure image carrier and a press having cylinders (rotogravure). He used a carbon-tissue process invented in 1864 by Joseph Swan, an Englishman.

The first large-scale commercial use of gravure took place in 1914 when the *New York Times* newspaper established its own rotogravure facility. The process has been somewhat slow in developing because of some secrecy surrounding the methods of making the image-carrier cylinders and the actual printing presses. However, great progress has been made in refining and perfecting this image-transfer method. It is used throughout the world and its future is limited only by the creative minds of the technicians and artists.

UNIT 114
GRAVURE IMAGE CARRIERS

The three main types of gravure image carriers are the (1) flat plate, (2) wrap-around plate, and (3) cylinder. *Flat plates* are used on special sheet-fed presses that produce stock certificates and other high-grade limited-copy materials.

Wrap-around plates are used to print art reproductions, books, mail order booklets, calendars, and packaging materials. The wrap-around plate is thin and flexible and attaches to a cylinder similar to one on an offset-lithography press. They can be used economically only on short runs (30,000 copies or less). They cannot produce a continuous design or pattern because of the area needed to clamp the plate to the cylinder.

Cylinder image carriers are the most common within the industry; the conventional method of preparing cylinders for printing is therefore presented in this unit. Preparation of a gravure cylinder is a most critical process and each step in its production must be done with exacting care if quality results are expected. Many products that require a wood grain, some packaging designs, floor and wall coverings, textiles, and some newspaper printing have continuous patterns. To print these continuous patterns the never-ending-cylinder type of production is used.

PREPARING CYLINDER FILM POSITIVES

It is necessary to prepare film positives for gravure production.
1. Prepare photographs, artwork, and type composition as discussed in Section 4, and Section 16.
2. The type and artwork are photographed in a process camera to obtain the film negative (Section 7).
3. The continuous-tone film negatives (those that contain no dots) are prepared from photographs that contain varying shades of gray.
4. The film negatives are then carefully retouched by the engraver to correct imperfections.
5. The retouched negatives are set up in proper position and a one-piece film positive, combining all elements of the image, is made (Unit 60).

Fig. 114-1. Stripping film positives in preparation for exposing the image. (Roto Cylinders)

Fig. 114-2. Inspecting preproofs of the film positives. (Roto Cylinders)

6. The engraver carefully inspects the film positive and retouches it to make final corrections and adjustments.
7. Several film positives are stripped together for the image to cover the entire cylinder (Fig. 114-1).
8. Photographic proofs are made of the film positives and the engraver closely inspects them for needed corrections (Fig. 114-2).

READYING THE CYLINDER

During the time that the film positives are being prepared, the surface of the gravure cylinder is prepared to accept the image. The cylinder must be carefully prepared before the etched image is placed onto it.

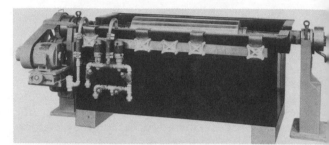

Fig. 114-3. A cylinder copper plating tank. (Standard Process Corp.)

Fig. 114-4. Using a high-precision lathe to remove part of the copper coating. (Roto Cylinders)

9. The thin coating of copper, containing the image used on the previous printing job, is removed. This is done on a special gravure cutting lathe.
10. A new coating of copper must be placed on the cylinder surface. To do this the cylinder is placed into an electroplating tank and coated with copper to approximately 0.005 inch over the specified finished diameter (Fig. 114-3).
11. The cylinder is accurately centered in a high-precision lathe and is cut to a fine finish with a diamond tool to within 0.002 inch (Fig. 114-4).
12. The cylinder is placed on a special grinder and super-finished to the exact specified diameter and smoothness (Fig. 114-5). It is now ready to receive the image.

EXPOSING THE IMAGE

The entire image is screened with the gravure process. This includes the type, artwork, and photographs. Special gravure screens (Fig. 114-6) containing 150 to 300

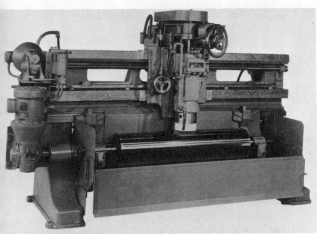

Fig. 114-5. A machine which grinds and polishes the cylinder to an exact specified diameter and smoothness. (Standard Process Corp.)

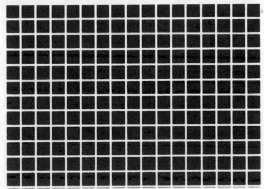

Fig. 114-6. A magnified view of a gravure screen. Note the transparent lines.

Fig. 114-7. Exposing the carbon tissue through the film positives with a carbon-arc lamp. (Roto Cylinders)

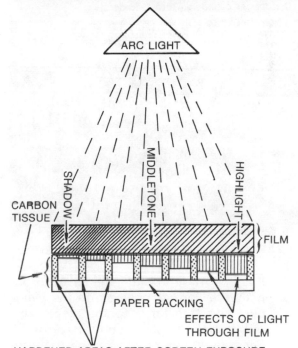

Fig. 114-8. Effects of the light on the carbon tissue during exposure.

lines to the inch are used. Note that the lines are transparent, unlike those of the normal halftone screen. A sheet of carbon tissue, coated with a layer of orange-colored light-sensitive gelatin on a paper backing sheet, is placed in contact with a gravure screen. Both items are placed in a vacuum frame.

13. The carbon tissue is exposed to strong arc lamps through the screen. The transparent lines of the screen allow light to strike the carbon tissue, hardening it and making it insoluble to the etching solution which will later be placed upon it.

14. The screen is removed from the carbon tissue and the film positive is placed over the tissue. The tissue is again exposed to carbon arc lamps through the film positive (Fig. 114-7). The gelatin-sensitized coating of the carbon tissue hardens in proportion to the amount of light that passes through the positive (Fig. 114-8). In highlight or lightest areas the gelatin is hardened to the greatest amount; in shadow areas (darkest) it is hardened to the least.

15. The exposed carbon tissue, containing the complete image, is transferred carefully to the copper cylinder (Fig. 114-9).

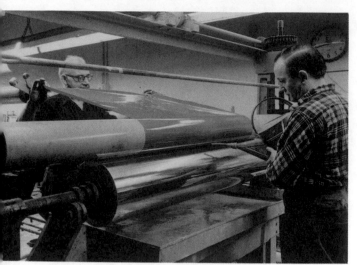

Fig. 114-9. Transferring the exposed carbon tissue to the copper cylinder. (Roto Cylinders)

Fig. 114-10. A semiautomatic carbon tissue transfer machine. (The John C. Motter Printing Press Co.)

It is important to place the tissue in exactly the correct position on the cylinder. The transfer machine places approximately 1,300 pounds of pressure per square inch on the carbon tissue to make it adhere properly to the copper cylinder (Fig. 114-10).

16. After the carbon tissue has been adhered to the cylinder, the paper backing (See Fig. 114-8) is removed and hot water is used to wash away the unhardened gelatin remaining where the light did not penetrate. Large nonimage areas of the cylinder are "staged out" (hand painted with asphaltum) to resist the action of the etching solution. The cylinder is now ready for etching.

ETCHING THE CYLINDER

17. The cylinder is carefully removed from the transfer machine to the etching trough. The etching solution can be either poured onto the rotating copper cylinder or placed in an etching machine that allows the cylinder to rotate constantly in a bath of acid (Fig. 114-11). The etching solution penetrates the gelatin and attacks the copper.

The etching depth of the copper is determined by the thickness of gelatin in each rectangular dot. Because the gelatin is thickest within the highlight area of the image, it takes a longer period of time before the etch penetrates it. The depth of the etching within that area is therefore very slight (Fig. 114-12). Within the shadow area of the image there is only a small amount of gelatin to protect the cylinder, and the etching solution quickly attacks the copper and etches to greater depth. Compare Figs. 114-8 and 114-12 for a thorough understanding of the preparation and use of the carbon tissue. The shadow cells are etched to approximately 38 microns in depth; highlight

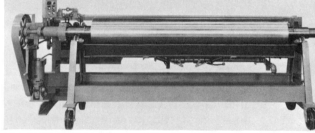

Fig. 114-11. An etching machine that rotates the cylinder in a trough containing etching solution. (Standard Process Corp.)

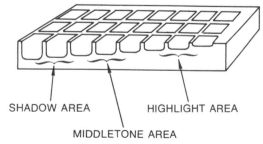

SHADOW AREA   HIGHLIGHT AREA

MIDDLETONE AREA

Fig. 114-12. The action of the etching solution through the carbon tissue to the copper.

Fig. 114-13. Inspecting the cylinder after it has been etched. (Roto Cylinders)

Fig. 114-14. Hand-correcting flaws in the etched cylinder. (Roto Cylinders)

cells to 3 or 4 microns. Cells of depth between these extremes represent the middle tones. 25 microns = 0.001 inch.

18. The cylinder is carefully inspected microscopically (Fig. 114-13) after it has been etched for a period of time. If any flaws appear it is possible to re-etch to correct the defect (Fig. 114-14).

PROOFING AND FINISHING THE CYLINDER

19. The cylinder is proofed on a special gravure press (Fig. 114-15) after inspection. The proof results are compared with the original copy. If flaws are found in the cylinder, it is possible for the finisher to hand-correct them as shown in Fig. 114-14.

20. A thin chrome plating is placed over the copper cylinder surface (Fig. 114-16) after it is considered to be perfect. The chrome is much harder than the copper and provides better wear for many more copies. The cylinder is now completely prepared and is ready to be placed on the printing press.

CONVENTIONAL CYLINDER PREPARATIONS

Conventional methods of cylinder preparation date back to the nineteenth century when the first commercial application of the intaglio-mechanical principles took place. This early effort took into ac-

Fig. 114-15. Proofing the cylinder on a gravure proof press. (Roto Cylinders)

Fig. 114-16. Chrome plating the cylinder for better wear. (Roto Cylinders)

count the concept of a pattern of square dots, all the same size, laterally arranged. The etched cells in highlight areas are very shallow, with the depth increasing in direct ratio to the increase in tone. Tones are thus determined by the thickness of the ink film in the cells, rather than by the size of the dots. The foregoing paragraphs describe the conventional method of cylinder preparation. Principles of this method form the basis for virtually all other gravure processes.

UNCONVENTIONAL CYLINDER PREPARATIONS

Several variations in methods of preparing the gravure cylinder are now practiced. Each method or special technique has special advantages, and also disadvantages. The major difference between these processes and the conventional gravure process is that in the former the square dots vary in size as well as depth. This allows a wider range of tonal values.

ELECTRONIC ENGRAVING OF CYLINDERS

Present procedures for producing gravure cylinders are time consuming and demand several skilled personnel. Electronic engraving machines reduce the amount of production time and labor. The engraving machine (Fig. 114-17) is equipped with two synchronized rotating cylinders. One is the copy cylinder; the other is the actual cylinder that will be placed upon the press.

The continuous-tone original copy to be reproduced is attached on the copy cylinder. During rotation of the copy cylinder, the image is scanned by means of a light beam and a photo-optical system. The quantity of reflected light is converted into

an electrical impulse which acts as a control signal for the engraving chisel.

The engraving chisel cuts pyramid-shaped cells (Fig. 114-18) out of the gravure printing cylinder. The up-and-down movement of the chisel determines the depth of the cells, and consequently the amount of ink each cell can hold. This in turn controls the tonal values.

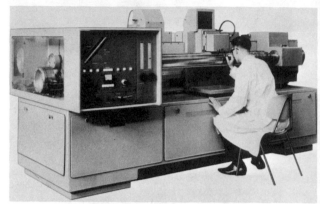

Fig. 114-17. An electronic gravure cylinder engraving machine. (Stork Inter-American Corp.)

DIRECTION OF ENGRAVING

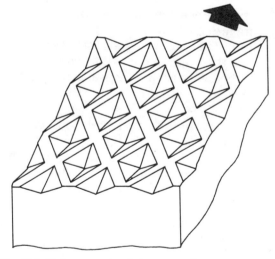

Fig. 114-18. An example of electronically engraved cells. (Stork Inter-American Corp.)

UNIT 115
GRAVURE PRINTING PRESSES

Modern, efficient gravure presses and equipment evolved from the first ones developed in England late in the nineteenth century. In 1924 the *New York World* newspaper printed the first four-color newspaper gravure supplement. The press was of German design and was equipped with a folder, a flat sheet delivery, and a reel for accepting a web of paper. Shortly after that, several other four-color gravure presses began operation in both the United States and in Canada.

The early gravure presses ran 8,000 to 10,000 impressions per hour, (iph), but production was quickly increased to 12,000 to 15,000 iph. The maximum width of web was 60 to 66 inches. Presses now print webs up to 100 inches wide at a speed of 18,000 feet per minute.

Electrostatic assist is a recent development in the gravure image transfer process. An electronic charge is imposed between the copper and impression cylinders, which causes ink to transfer to the receptor (surface being printed) much more efficiently. This has improved gravure printing quality.

Computers have been integrated into the press control systems to make possible many prepress run adjustments and settings. With the computer it is possible to preregister and keep in register the multicolor images.

The basic operating principle of a gravure press, whether sheet fed or web fed, remains the same (Fig. 115-1). The image carrier cylinder, or flat plate, must be covered with a thin ink. The ink is removed by the doctor blade from nonimage areas, and the plate or cylinder is pressed against the receptor (usually paper) to transfer the image.

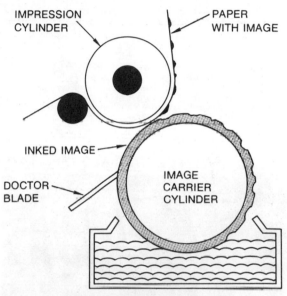

Fig. 115-1. The operating principle of a gravure press.

All gravure presses, large or small, use this reproduction principle. Rotogravure is the name stemming from *roto* meaning web or roll-fed presses.

THE GRAVURE PRESS

The gravure process reproduces fine color printing; it is therefore common to see multiunit presses (Fig. 115-2). The paper web is fed from rolls that are sometimes below the first floor, and enters up through the floor to the press. A five-unit color press prints on one side of the paper (unit A), then turns the paper over and prints four colors on the second side (units B, C, D, and E). See Fig. 115-2. With one pass through the press, therefore, both sides of a sheet are printed and four-color reproductions appear on one of the sides.

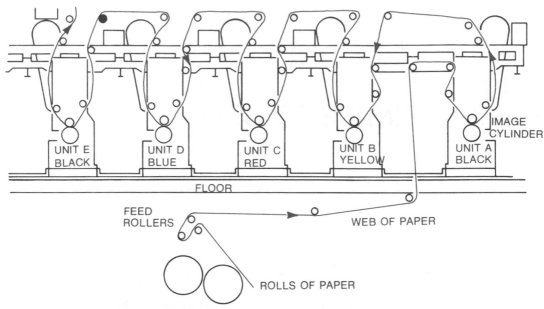

Fig. 115-2. A schematic view of a rotogravure press indicating color units and paper feed. (The Denver Press)

Fig. 115-3. A four-color compact gravure press that prints a web 26 inches wide. (Holweg Corp.)

Fig. 115-4. A six-station rotogravure press in operation. It handles a web 43½ inches wide. (Regar World Corp.)

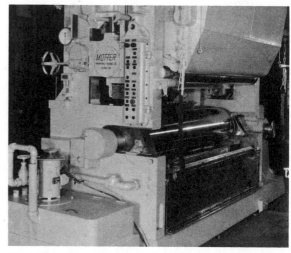

Fig. 115-5. A close-up view of a heavy-duty rotogravure press printing station. (John C. Motter Printing Press Co.)

The usual gravure presses print webs from approximately 20 to 50 inches wide. These presses can have from one (Fig. 115-3) to six (Fig. 115-4) color units for printing each of four colors placed in the line. As the width of the web increases, the construction of the press becomes heavier and more massive. A close-up view of a heavy-duty rotogravure press (Fig. 115-5) shows castings and bearings. A rotogravure press is a precision machine weighing many tons.

THE DOCTOR BLADE

The *doctor blade,* made of fine steel, 0.006-inch thick, wipes ink from the non-image area of the cylinder. This blade is the key to quality reproduction. If it fails to remove ink from unwanted areas, these areas will print and the quality of the reproduction will thus be reduced. The blade is held in firm contact with the cylinder and oscillates (moves) back and forth to eliminate possibility of grooves forming in either it or the cylinder.

Doctor blades are reground after continued use to insure a precision scraping edge. Special grinders (Fig. 115-6) smooth the scraping edge with utmost accuracy.

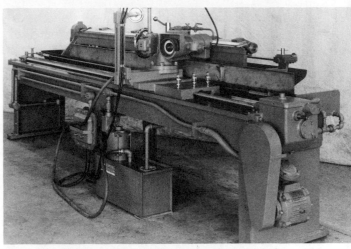

Fig. 115-6. A doctor blade being reground on a precision grinder. (John C. Motter Printing Press Co.)

UNIT 116
SAFETY WHEN ETCHING AND ENGRAVING

Etching and engraving entail the use of equipment and solutions. The precautions listed below will assist in producing quality work while protecting the worker.

Permission. Request permission from competent authority before beginning either etching or engraving.

Clothing and jewelry. Secure loose clothing and remove jewelry and wrist watches. Loose clothing and long hair can become entangled in moving equipment.

Safety guards. Have the safety guards installed over moving parts of both the plate-whirler and the thermography machine. Hand-operated machines such as the etching and engraving press must also have the proper safety guards over moving parts.

Air vents. Start exhaust fans before working with chemicals, acids, or solvents. Check to see that the exhaust system is working properly. If a power exhaust system is not installed, open windows and/or doors.

Eye and face protection. Wear safety glasses and/or a face shield when working with etching solutions and when making a hand engraving.

Body protection. Wear rubber gloves and an apron when using etching solutions. Gloves should extend to the elbows, and the apron should be large enough to cover the entire front of the body.

Good housekeeping. Keep the laboratory orderly. Never allow waste materials to collect on the floor because of fire. Accidents are more likely to occur in confused situations and environment.

Floor drain. Floor drains should be located near sinks and containers holding liquid etching solutions. Check all drains and remove any obstructions.

Illumination. Have adequate lighting. Seeing well insures safety; not being able to see the work clearly can be dangerous.

Materials storage. Store containers of etching solutions and ink solvents near the floor. Place boxes, tools, and other items on storage shelves in such a manner that they are easily accessible and will not vibrate from the shelf.

Noise. Excessive noise is a deterrent to safety; talk and laughter should therefore be kept to a minimum.

Fire. Fire extinguishers *must* always be in a charged condition and located in conspicuous places in the laboratory. Be careful when using the hotplate or thermography machine. Do not leave these units unattended when they are turned on. These two units are capable of starting fires.

Sharp objects. Handle and use sharp tools with care. Engraving tools must be used with utmost precaution. Do not carry them in your pocket unless protective caps are in place.

Ink- and solvent-soaked rags. Place all rags containing ink or solvents in a metal safety can having a tight, metal lid. Spontaneous combustion could occur if these rags are not placed in this style of container.

Burns. Electrical burns are painful. Be careful when using the hotplate and when operating the thermography machine.

Safety shower. Whenever chemicals are used in any laboratory, a safety shower must be near. Persons who spill caustic chemicals or solutions on their bodies or in their eyes will need to immediately flush the affected areas with large volumes of cool water.

UNIT 117
FLAT-PLATE GRAVURE ETCHING

Flat-plate gravure etching can be done in most small laboratories The method described here is not foolproof but it will provide some direction in the procedures and problems of making gravure cylinders.

Aluminum is the suggested metal to use because it is plentiful and easy to etch. A distinct disadvantage, however, is its softness. This is most noticeable during the proofing operations.

MAKING THE PLATE

1. Obtain a piece of aluminum. A size of 4 x 5 inches is sufficient.
2. Clean one side very thoroughly with water and pumice. Use a soft cotton pad to scrub the metal with the pumice. Use plenty of water as it is very important that the metal be clean. Keep fingerprints from the metal surface.
3. Dry the metal with forced air from an air hose, or use the heat of two 250-watt infrared heat bulbs.

4. Apply a photoresist solution formulated for aluminum. Pour the liquid resist on the plate; distribute it by tilting the plate from side to side. NOTE: Room illumination must be *low* when working with photoresist.
5. Place the plate in a whirler (Fig. 117-1). Allow it to whirl for five minutes *without* heat.

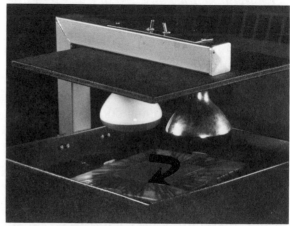

Fig. 117-1. Whirling a plate to distribute the photoresist.

6. Dry the photoresist while in the whirler. Allow the whirler to continue turning, and turn on the heating element. Two 250-watt infrared heat bulbs will work well. Ten minutes are generally sufficient for drying.

7. Expose the plate. Position the halftone film positive emulsion-side-up, on the plate. Any good exposure unit can be used and the length of exposure depends upon the light source and the speed of the photoresist. It will be necessary to conduct exposure tests with available equipment.

8. Develop the exposed plate in the appropriate developer that is compatible with the aluminum photoresist. The developer softens the image area of the plate that was not struck by the light.

9. Wash away the softened photoresist with a bath of warm water.

10. Etch the plate in the appropriate aluminum etch (Fig. 117-2). Allow the etch to bite into the plate approximately 0.002 to 0.003 inch. NOTE: The halftone film positive contains various dot sizes and when the plate is etched the wells will all be the same depth. This is unlike conventional gravure cylinder methods (Unit 114).

11. Flush the plate with cold water to remove the etching bath.

Fig. 117-2. Etching an aluminum gravure flat-plate.

12. Immerse the plate into the developer again. This softens the remaining photoresist. Flush with water.

13. Dry the plate with compressed air. Inspect the final etching with a magnifying glass.

PROOFING THE PLATE

Proofing procedures are similar to printing a dry-point engraving (Unit 118). It is possible, however, to remove the ink from the nonimage area with either a hard rubber, squeegee, or plastic straight edge. This would then simulate the press doctor blade action.

UNIT 118
HAND ENGRAVING AND PRINTING

There are several methods of hand engraving and etching. These terms are used interchangeably, but actually should not be. To *engrave* is to cut an object with a tool and to *etch* is to remove by chemical-acid means.

Both engravings and etchings are true intaglio methods of reproducing images.

Lines are cut or etched below the nonimage surface of the image carrier. The image carrier, made of copper, steel, or plastic, is then inked over the entire surface. The ink is wiped from the nonimage high portion, leaving the lines filled with ink. The image carrier is then pressed against a paper receptor to transfer the image.

COPPER AND STEEL HAND ENGRAVINGS

Copper and steel image carriers are used in making commercial hand engravings. Both types are made in the same basic manner. Copper, a relatively soft metal, can be engraved more easily than steel, but it is limited to fewer copies. Steel can print almost unlimited copies if it has been hardened after the engraving process.

An engraver is a highly skilled person. He must be able to engrave the image in the metal image carrier in reverse (Fig. 118-1). He uses several engraving tools, called *gravers,* having different cutting edges that produce many different widths and shapes of lines. The small images require the use of a magnifying glass while working with the gravers.

The engraved plate is mounted in a die-stamping press and printed copies are produced (Fig. 118-2). The press automatically inks the plate and presses it to the paper with great pressure. The pressure causes the ink to transfer and also causes a raised image on the paper. This gives the final product a look of distinction.

Ten thousand copies can be printed from copper engravings; 250,000 from steel ones. With special hardening and plating it is possible to produce several thousand more copies from each kind of metal plate. Automatic feed die-stamping presses (Fig. 118-3) print and emboss at speeds of 3,600 iph.

Fig. 118-1. A skilled engraver cuts the image into a copper plate. (Josten's)

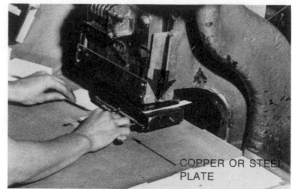

Fig. 118-2. Carefully hand-feeding a die-stamping press. (Josten's)

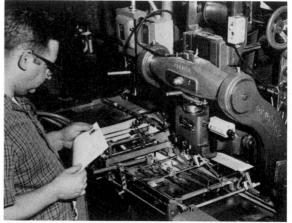

Fig. 118-3. An operator tends a high-speed automatic-feed die-stamping press. (Josten's)

Embossing is producing an image in relief without ink. Stationery, business cards, announcements, and invitations are examples of hand engraving and embossing. United States paper currency is printed from steel engravings, as are negotiable stock and bond certificates.

DRY-POINT ENGRAVING AND PRINTING

Dry-point engravings are produced by scratching lines in a piece of plastic, inking the plate, and pressing paper against it to make the print. Dry-point engravings are composed entirely of lines and can be very intricate (Fig. 118-4). With practice it is possible to prepare high-quality prints at an economical price. Greeting cards, bookplates, bookmarks, artwork, and many other items are produced by this intaglio process.

Fig. 118-4. A reproduction of a dry-point engraving.

Fig. 118-5. Using a sharp-pointed engraving tool to prepare a dry-point engraving.

SELECTING THE COPY

It is important to select an illustration that is suitable to be produced by lines only. Landscapes, people, and animals are excellent illustration sources, although many more topics can be reproduced. It is impossible to reproduce complete solid-image areas, although near-solid ones can be achieved by crosshatching or drawing the lines close together.

PREPARING THE PLATE

1. Prepare the copy of the illustration on white bond paper. It must be made the same size as the desired final print. Use black ink when preparing the copy illustration.

2. Tape the copy upsidedown on the glass of a light table. The plate is prepared in reverse so that the final prints are right-reading.

3. Place a transparent plastic sheet 0.15 to 0.040-inch thick over the copy. Tape it securely in place. The image is visible through the paper and plastic because of the light from the light table.

4. Obtain a dry-point engraving tool and scratch the lines of the copy (Fig. 118-5). The sharp-pointed tool can be a sheet metal scriber, a sharpened nail imbedded in the end of a ⅜ inch dowel, a large sewing needle, or the metal point of a bow compass.

5. Scratch or engrave the entire illustration on the plastic plate. Dark and heavy lines must be engraved more deeply than thin, light ones. A burr must develop on each line to produce a good reproduction.

REPRODUCING THE PRINTS

1. Prepare the paper. Select a soft-surfaced paper such as uncoated book paper or mimeograph stock. Dampen the paper slightly. Stack it and allow it to stand under a weight for 24 hours.

2. Mix the ink. Use letterpress or lithography all-purpose ink. Mix a drop of reducing varnish with a thimbleful amount of ink. Use a glass ink plate and ink knife to prepare it.

3. Using a cloth dauber, work the ink into the engraved lines on the plate. It is better to get too much ink on the plate than not enough.

4. Remove the ink from the nonreproducing area of the plate by wiping it with a cotton cloth (Fig. 118-6). The heel of the hand may also be used to polish the nonreproducing surface completely clean.

5. Place the inked plate on the bed of the engraving and etching press (Fig. 118-7), engraved side up.

6. Lay a predampened sheet of paper stock over the plate. Also place two felt blankets over the paper and plate.

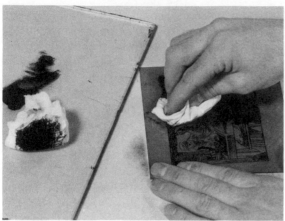

Fig. 118-6. Removing ink from a dry-point engraving with a cotton wiping-cloth.

7. Adjust the press impression roller with the adjusting screws so that a high amount of pressure in pounds per square inch will be exerted on the paper and plate as they pass between the roller and the bed.

8. Turn the wheel of the press to move the bed under the impression roller. This causes the ink to transfer from the engraved lines of the plate to the paper.

9. Remove the felt blankets and the printed sheet carefully (Fig. 118-8). Inspect the sheet for flaws and diagnose any imaging or inking problems. Additional lines can be added and existing ones made deeper.

10. Make corrections or alterations if necessary.

11. Make additional prints. Repeat steps 3 through 9.

12. Multicolor prints are made by inking different portions of the illustration with several colors of ink. Remove the ink and print the plate in the usual manner.

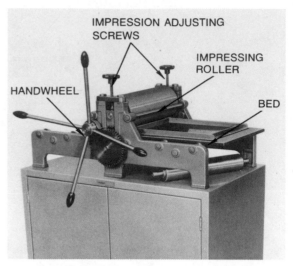

Fig. 118-7. A hand-operated engraving and etching press. (The Craftool Co.)

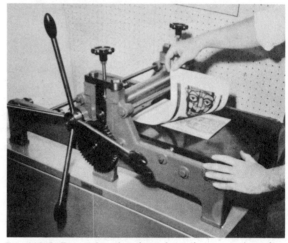

Fig. 118-8. Removing the sheet from the engraving after it has been printed. (The Craftool Co.)

13. Clean the plate. Remove all ink from the engraved lines with ink solvent. The plate can be stored and used again at a later date.

UNIT 119
THERMOGRAPHY

Thermography is a raised printing process used to produce varied effects on printed materials. The word thermography is a combination of the words *thermo* meaning heat and *graphy* to write and is defined as *heat writing.* It has been used for years and has served to add aesthetic qualities to printed materials.

The raised printing result is obtained by sprinkling special rosin powder over a freshly printed sheet. Excess powder is removed from the noninked areas and the powder that adheres to the wet ink is subjected to heat. The heat melts the powder, and, after cooling, a raised effect results.

Several models of commercial thermographic equipment are available. A hand-fed model is shown in Fig. 119-1. Fig. 119-2 pictures a model placed in-line with a printing press. Hand-fed models require that the operator powder the sheet prior to placing it in the machine. Automatic in-line machines

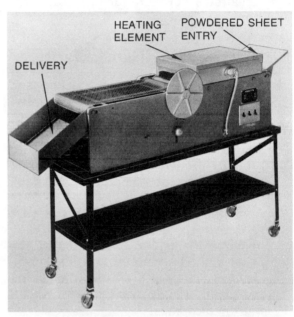

Fig. 119-1. A hand-fed thermography machine containing a heating element and wire belt. (Virkotype Corp.)

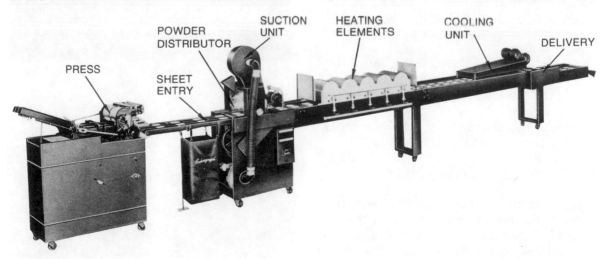

Fig. 119-2. An automatic thermography machine which has been placed in-line with a printing press.

that accept freshly printed sheets from nearly any kind of a press, powder the sheet, remove excess powder, heat the sheet and powder, and cool the sheet to complete the process. A commercial plant installation is shown in Fig. 119-3.

Thermography products include greeting cards, stationery, business cards, and formal announcements. Thermography also enhances package design, ceiling tile, hardboard panels, wall coverings, metal containers, children's furniture and accessories, and home appliances.

PRODUCTION PROCEDURE

1. Complete the necessary design and layout, composition, photography, plates, and printing steps. Letterpress, offset-lithography, or screen-printing image-transfer methods can be used to produce printed sheets. It is important to do a good job of printing the image on the receptor sheet.
2. Apply the special thermography powder to the sheets while the ink is still wet. Immerse the entire image area of the sheet in the pan of powder (Fig. 119-4).
3. Remove the excess powder by tapping the sheets sharply over the pan containing the powder.
4. Heat the sheet to melt the powder and fuse it with ink by:
   a. Putting the sheets through a hand-fed thermography machine (Fig. 119-5), or
   b. Holding the sheets over the heat of a standard hotplate (Fig. 119-6) until the powder melts and fuses to the ink.
5. Allow the sheets to cool before stacking and packaging.

DESIGN LIMITATIONS

Type, halftone reproductions, and pen-and-ink illustrations are suitable for thermography. Exceptionally fine detail is usually not suitable, but with care and the use of correct ink and powder, fine detailed illustrations can result.

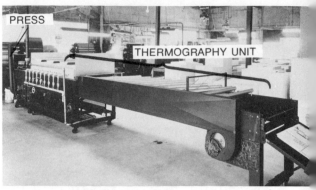

Fig. 119-3. A commercial installation of a thermography unit in-line with a press. (Virkotype Corp.)

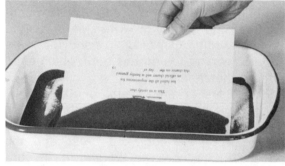

Fig. 119-4. Immersing freshly printed sheets in the thermography powder.

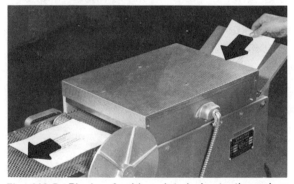

Fig. 119-5. Placing freshly printed sheets through a hand-fed thermography machine.

Fig. 119-6. Holding the freshly powdered sheet over a hot-plate to melt the thermography powder.

Generally, type less than 6 point in size should not be used; although 5 point can be satisfactory provided it is open face and in the sans-serif family. Delicately-serifed letters, particularly in small sizes, should be avoided as they tend to fill in with powder after heating.

POWDERS AND INKS

Neutral powders permit the color of the base ink to show through; opaque colors have complete hiding power. Opaque colors come in white, orange, red, yellow, pink, and green. Metallic and fluorescent colors are also available.

The powders have granulation ranging from coarse to very fine. The choice depends upon the image; if it contains fine lines, use a fine powder. A coarse powder causes fine lines to fill in and lose their individual detail.

Almost all inks can be used in the thermography process, because ink serves only as an adhesive for the powder. Special inks having little or no dryer in them should be used for high-quality work.

UNIT 120
LEARNING EXPERIENCES: GRAVURE PRINTING PROCESS

DISCUSSION TOPICS

1. Illustrate the image-transfer principle of the gravure process. How does this principle differ from the letterpress, lithography, and screen printing principles?
2. Give another name besides gravure for this graphic reproduction process. What special significance does this name have? How does it differ from the term gravure?
3. List several of the products that are printed with the gravure method.
4. Cite the advantages and disadvantages of the gravure reproduction method. Specifically identify the typeface requirements for the gravure process.
5. Describe the early beginnings of the gravure process. Who has been given credit for first applying photographic methods to the production of a gravure image carrier?
6. Name the three types of gravure image carriers. What are the advantages and disadvantages of each type? Name products that are produced with each image carrier.
7. Identify the major steps in the production of a gravure cylinder. Cite the similarities in methods of producing letterpress and lithographic image carriers.
8. Identify the method used to remove the copper from an already-used cylinder. How is new copper applied to the cylinder? What methods are used to finish the cylinder prior to exposing the image?
9. List the steps in exposing and etching the cylinder. Explain the purpose of the carbon tissue. In what areas of the cylinder does the etching solution attack the copper cylinder?
10. Compare the conventional, unconventional, and electronic engraving methods of preparing gravure cylinders. Cite the advantages and disadvantages of the electronic engraving method of preparing gravure cylinders.
11. Describe the operating principle of the

gravure press. Why are multiunit, multicolor gravure presses common? Cite the common sizes and speeds of gravure presses.

12. Define doctor blade. Why must the doctor blade be a precision piece of equipment?

13. When were the first gravure presses installed in the United States? In commercial concerns? What company was responsible for first introducing color gravure printing to the United States? What have the recent developments of electrostatic assist and computers done for the gravure method of image transfer?

14. What is the purpose of the photoresist in the preparation of flat-plate gravure etchings? Explain what is happening when the aluminum flat plate is placed into the whirler. Give the purpose of the developer that is used on the aluminum plate.

15. Compare engraving and etching. How are these two methods of preparing image carriers alike and unlike? Are these methods still used commercially today?

16. Briefly identify the steps necessary to produce a dry-point engraving. Also identify the steps necessary to reproduce copies from the dry-point engraving. Why are better reproduction results obtained through the printing operation when the sheets of paper have been predampened?

17. Define thermography. What are the advantages of this process? Disadvantages?

18. Describe the equipment necessary to accomplish the process of thermography. Identify products that can be or are produced by the thermography method. Cite design limitations.

ACTIVITIES

1. Visit a gravure printing plant. Carefully observe the methods used to prepare the flat-plate or cylinder gravure image carriers. Carefully observe the gravure printing press. Are these presses sheet-fed or web-fed? How fast can they produce printed products? Obtain example products that the company produces, especially gravure products. Inspect these products carefully with a magnifying glass and observe their quality. Analyze your observations.

2. Prepare a flat-plate gravure etching. Obtain the necessary materials, prepare the film positive, and make the etching. Proof the finished plate and compare the proof with the original copy that was used to prepare the film positive. Carefully inspect the plate with a magnifying glass to observe the depth of the ink wells.

3. Prepare a dry-point engraving and reproduce several copies from it. Use different engraving tools to discover which tool does the best job and is easiest to use. During the printing operation try reproducing prints on dry paper as well as on dampened paper. Also experiment with different kinds, consistencies, and colors of ink.

4. Plan, compose, and print items such as personal stationery, announcements, or invitations suitable for thermography. Complete the procedures that are necessary to produce raised printing (thermography). If possible, experiment by using different kinds and sizes of type, by using different kinds and colors of ink, and by using different colors and grades of thermography powder. Compare the results of each of these several experiments.

The printed page can live forever.

This advertisement appeared in the January 2, 1915 Saturday Evening Post.

Contrary to popular belief, the ad ran just once, yet hardly a week goes by that Cadillac or its agency, MacManus, John & Adams, do not get requests for copies.

A message in print is not like a message in time.

A message in time will last for 10, 20, 30 or 60 seconds. Like a stroke of lightning, a message in time lives gloriously for a moment and then dies.

A message in print can die just as fast. On the other hand, a message in print can be read for 10 minutes, can be taken to the store a week later or perhaps saved for several lifetimes.

If you have something important to say, your message will last longer if you put it in print.

Your message in print will live as long as it is relevant to the needs and interests of your marketplace.

Your message in print can live forever.

The PENALTY OF LEADERSHIP

IN every field of human endeavor, he that is first must perpetually live in the white light of publicity. ¶Whether the leadership be vested in a man or in a manufactured product, emulation and envy are ever at work. ¶In art, in literature, in music, in industry, the reward and the punishment are always the same. ¶The reward is widespread recognition; the punishment, fierce denial and detraction. ¶When a man's work becomes a standard for the whole world, it also becomes a target for the shafts of the envious few. ¶If his work be merely mediocre, he will be left severely alone—if he achieve a masterpiece, it will set a million tongues a-wagging. ¶Jealousy does not protrude its forked tongue at the artist who produces a commonplace painting. ¶Whatsoever you write, or paint, or play, or sing, or build, no one will strive to surpass, or to slander you, unless your work be stamped with the seal of genius. ¶Long, long after a great work or a good work has been done, those who are disappointed or envious continue to cry out that it can not be done. ¶Spiteful little voices in the domain of art were raised against our own Whistler as a mountebank, long after the big world had acclaimed him its greatest artistic genius. ¶Multitudes flocked to Bayreuth to worship at the musical shrine of Wagner, while the little group of those whom he had dethroned and displaced argued angrily that he was no musician at all. ¶The little world continued to protest that Fulton could never build a steamboat, while the big world flocked to the river banks to see his boat steam by. ¶The leader is assailed because he is a leader, and the effort to equal him is merely added proof of that leadership. ¶Failing to equal or to excel, the follower seeks to depreciate and to destroy—but only confirms once more the superiority of that which he strives to supplant. ¶There is nothing new in this. ¶It is as old as the world and as old as the human passions—envy, fear, greed, ambition, and the desire to surpass. ¶And it all avails nothing. ¶If the leader truly leads, he remains—the leader. ¶Master-poet, master-painter, master-workman, each in his turn is assailed, and each holds his laurels through the ages. ¶That which is good or great makes itself known, no matter how loud the clamor of denial. ¶That which deserves to live—lives.

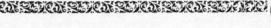

Cadillac Motor Car Co. Detroit, Mich.

Attaching the squeegee to a semi-automatic screen process press.

UNIT 121
INTRODUCTION TO SCREEN PRINTING

Screen printing, also termed silk screen printing, stencil printing, mitography, fabritecture, or screen process printing, is different from other methods of reproduction. Whereas letterpress, lithography, and gravure printing transfer ink *from* an image carrier, the screen printing method prints *through* it. Heavy-bodied inks are forced through a fine-mesh screen for direct printing on any type of product, whether flat or three-dimensional.

Among the components necessary for screen printing are (1) the screen fabric prepared as a stencil, (2) a frame to hold the screen fabric, (3) the squeegee, and (4) ink (Fig. 121-1). The sheet is positioned on the printing base, the screen frame is lowered, the squeegee is pulled to force ink through the mesh to make the print, the frame is raised, and the stock is removed. On some presses, the screen is stationary and the squeegee moves to make the print; on others the squeegee is stationary and the screen frame and bed underneath both move.

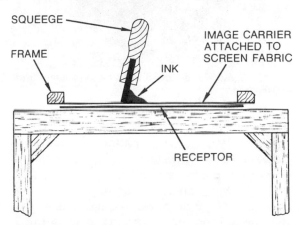

Fig. 121-1. The basic components of a screen-printing unit.

Fig. 121-2. Screen printing as done by the ancient Japanese.

HISTORICAL HIGHLIGHTS

The stencil principle used in screen printing has been traced back to ancient times. It is known that the Chinese, Egyptians, and Japanese pounded colored pigments through stencil woven from human hair onto a variety of objects, including pottery, fabrics, and decorative screens (Fig. 121-2).

During the Middle Ages the art spread throughout Europe for making such diverse items as religious images and playing cards.

In the seventeenth century, stencils were used in England to make wallpaper decorations. Early American Colonists used the technique to place designs directly on walls, furniture, and textiles.

The first commercial screen printing plant in the United States was founded on the west coast in 1906. This process remained largely a hand-art craft until the middle of the twentieth century. No individual or in-

Fig. 121-3. A few products printed by the screen-printing method.

Fig. 121-4. Additional products printed by the screen printing method.

vention can be credited with the rapid rise of screen printing which began in 1940. It resulted from a combination of many improvements in presses, drying equipment, screen materials, and inks.

World War II created a demand for permanent identification of huge quantities of military equipment and supplies. A wide range of materials and shapes, from small ampules to tanks, were successfully marked by screen printing. Wartime requirements for fluorescent and phosphorescent coatings and markings were satisfied most efficiently by screen printing. This led to the postwar boom in the display industry.

As late as 1953, screen printing was described as the least industrialized of all graphic arts. Today it is a mechanized industry, having recently moved from an industrially restricted hand operation to a process having a considerable degree of mechanization. The U. S. Census Bureau recently reported that screen printing is one of the fastest growing segments of the graphic arts.

PRODUCTS

Mechanization of equipment, versatility of the process, and flexibility of production make possible many uses for screen printing. Fig. 121-3 shows a few examples of printing on flat, curved, cylindrical, and

other fabricated shapes made from materials such as paper, wood, metal, glass, cloth, rigid and nonrigid plastics, rubber, and fiberglass. Fig. 121-4 illustrates additional printing of advertising displays, designs on dishes and decorative china, and decals of any type, including reflective decorations, bolt fabrics, wallpaper, packages of every kind and surface composition.

Other products include braille dots on thin paper for lightweight books for the blind and electrical circuits for portable radios, TV, hearing aids, and other small electronic equipment. Color dots on the inside of color TV picture tubes, and capacitors for micro-miniature circuitry are also products made with the aid of screen printing. The majority of the circuits in missiles and spacecraft are printed by the screen printing method.

An important feature of screen printing is its ability to use a wide range of inks or paints. The present range of ink bases includes alkyd-type enamels, oleo resinous-base colors, vinyls, acrylics, nitrocellulose lacquers, ethyl-cellulose, and daylight fluorescent.

Drying time of ink is a limiting factor in screen printing. The quick-drying kinds have a drying range from fifteen seconds to fifteen minutes. So-called slow-drying inks require from thirty minutes to as much as twenty-four hours. Drying is accelerated with aid of heat, large volumes of moving air, or both.

PREPARING IMAGE CARRIERS

Three basic methods are used to prepare screen printing image carriers: (1) knife-cut film (2) photographic, and (3) washout (tusche). Knife-cut paper is also used, but it is not a common process within the industry.

Knife-cut films. A greatly used technique is the knife-cut method (Units 127 and 128). A coating of transparent colored film is bonded to a piece of transparent plastic or backing paper. Image areas are only cut through the top layer of the film and removed. Solvent is used to seal the stripped film to the bottom of the screen. After minor additional preparations, the backing paper is removed and the screen is printed.

Photographic methods. Photographic methods employ the same principles used in other photomechanical processes. Light-sensitive emulsions harden when exposed to intense light. Emulsions may be applied directly to the printing screen or coated on a semipermanent carrying support such as paper or transparent film.

Film positives are made from original copy and placed in a vacuum frame in contact with either the sensitized emulsion-coated screen in the direct process or with the photographic film. They are then exposed to light. After exposure, soft or unexposed areas are developed or washed away while the nonprinting hardened areas remain to form a stencil.

Washout (tusche) method. This method is primarily an art technique that requires the desired image first be outlined on the screen. The image area is then coated with tusche block-out material. Liquid glue is applied to both the nonimage and image areas of the screen. The tusched image areas are then washed away with a solvent, leaving a clear-screen image area.

UNIT 122
INDUSTRIAL EQUIPMENT AND PRODUCTION METHODS

During the past several years many attempts have been made to mechanize screen printing. A great deal of money has been spent in experimental work, but until recently no single press was recognized as the most suitable equipment for this versatile process. The various screen principles can be grouped for clarity.

Rotary screen. In machines of this type, the printing screen is attached to a cylinder or drum which has a stationary squeegee in the center. As the drum rotates, paper is fed onto a cylinder and brought into contact with the drum at the point where the squeegee is located.

Rocker-type machines. The *Selectasine* machine is an example of the oldest type of screen press. An oscillating curved platen carries the stock to a stationary squeegee. The ink is forced through the screen which is attached to a reciprocating frame sliding under the squeegee.

Bottle-printing machines. In these the squeegee is stationary; a flat screen makes a reciprocating movement; and the stock is fed to a rotating drum.

Flatbed type machines. These resemble the setup used in hand-letterpress printing. The flatbed is a much larger motor-driven operation than hand printing.

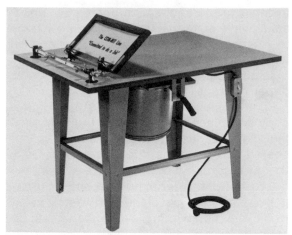

Fig. 122-1. A hand-operated screen printing unit containing a vacuum table. (Atlas Silk Screen Supply Co.)

Fig. 122-2. A one-armed hand-operated screen printing unit. (Atlas Silk Screen Supply Co.)

COMMERCIAL HAND-OPERATED PRESSES

Automatic screen printing presses print on a variety of products, but possibly will never completely replace hand-screen printing. Hand-screen printing has many variables which require special adjustments and equipment.

The typical screen printing unit is still used commercially, but has given way to simple improvements that increase quality and speed. Vacuum table units (Fig. 122-1) improve register and printing quality. Adaptations of bars and handles to the squeegee (Fig. 122-2) increase the printing speed. Other adaptations which may be built to order are available from commercial sources or are self-designed.

THE FLATBED SCREEN PRINTING PRESS

The *flatbed* screen press was developed in the 1930's. This simple clam-shell press is capable of screen printing posters, cardboard displays, metal signs, and decals. It mechanized the hand action of the squeegee and the raising and lowering the screen. Feeding and take-off still remain manual operations (Fig. 122-3).

The flatbed press now incorporates many refinements, such as automatic feed and delivery, vacuum stock holding beds, micrometer adjustments, and automatic timers (Fig. 122-4). Speed has increased from a few hundred impressions per hour to as many as 2,000. Size has increased from small 12 x 18-inch presses to popular 52 x 60-inch ones; special large ones of 66 x 144 inches are also available.

THE CYLINDER SCREEN PRINTING PRESS

A major development in the design of screen printing presses occurred in 1949 when a press that used the cylindrical platen principle (Fig. 122-5) was perfected. Because the flat screen travels on top of the cylinder (Fig. 122-6), the cylinder-screen frame arrangement resembles a flatbed cylinder press turned upside down. The revolving vacuum cylinder is perforated so that suction can keep the sheet from moving.

The squeegee is stationary during the printing cycle. The chase and cylinder are reciprocal in action so that the stock is moved forward at the same speed as the screen frame. Sheets are fed, printed, and delivered flat. The squeegee raises and the cylinder and screen frame move back to starting position after each impression.

Cylinder press operation includes high-speed press refinements utilized in letterpress and lithography. With the development of this press it was possible for the first time to feed, print, and deliver automatically. Cylinder presses make up to 6,000 iph, and sizes go as high as 52 x 76 inches.

Fig. 122-3. A semiautomatic hand-fed screen-printing press. (Advance Process Supply Co.)

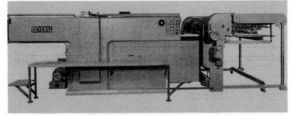

Fig. 122-4. A large-size screen-printing press equipped with automatic feed and delivery. (General Research, Inc.)

Fig. 122-5. A cylinder-type screen-printing press with automatic feed and delivery. (General Research, Inc.)

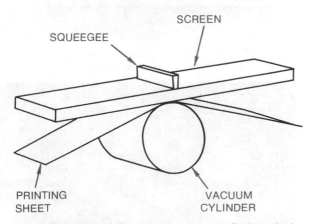

Fig. 122-6. The mechanical impression-cylinder principle of the screen-printing press shown in Fig. 122-5. (General Research, Inc.)

SPECIALTY SCREEN PRINTING PRESSES

Screen printing is a versatile method of reproducing graphic images, as discussed in Unit 123. To print on the many different shapes and kinds of objects special presses must be built. Many round, cylindrical, and flat objects are printed. Several press designs have evolved to handle this situation. Some use hand-operating principles with special object holders (Fig. 122-7). A significant difference from the flatbed press is apparent in the cylindrical one, where the squeegee is stationary except for up-and-down movement, and the frame moves back and forth as the object revolves during the printing.

Fig. 122-8 shows a large commercial packaging facility with a completely automatic screen printing line. It includes a product unscrambler unit, a flame treater, a cleaning and destaticizing unit, a screen printer, and a heat-drying unit. Production speeds of 3,600 iph are possible.

Manufacturers producing products that require printed images often have screen printing facilities within their plant. Textile-garment (Fig. 122-9) and playground equipment (Fig. 122-10) manufacturers are typical examples.

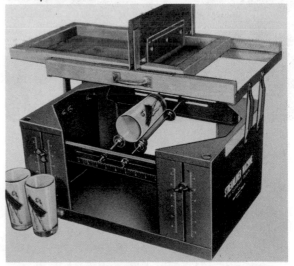

Fig. 122-7. A hand-operated screen-printing press designed for cylindrical objects. (Atlas Silk Screen Supply Co.)

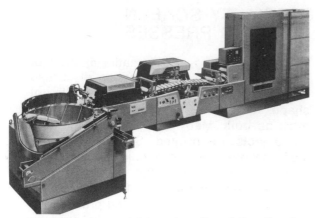

Fig. 122-8. A completely automatic printing line for one-color screen printing of plastic containers. (American Screen Process Equipment Co.)

Fig. 122-9. A textile-garment screen-printing unit. (Vastex Machine Co.)

Fig. 122-10. A screen printing unit for printing multicolor spiral patterns around the circumference of a long cylindrical object. (Turco Manufacturing Co.)

DRYING EQUIPMENT

Freshly printed sheets directly from the screen printing press cannot be laid on each other as are those from letterpress and lithography presses. The deposit of ink is too heavy for it to set and dry immediately, although the improved inks now dry more quickly.

Wood or metal drying racks (Fig. 122-11) are commonly used in small commercial screen printing plants. They are raised, the printed sheets are placed on each rack beginning from the bottom, and the rack is lowered to make the next one available.

Wicket dryers are used when increased production is required. They contain an endless belt of lightweight metal racks that hold the printed sheet as it travels over the drying distance (Fig. 122-12). Circulating air dries the sheets. Wicket dryers can be equipped with forced-air heating units to shorten the drying time. These units are usually placed in-line (Fig. 122-13).

Fig. 122-11. A multishelf wooden drying rack. (Cincinnati Printing and Drying Systems, Inc.)

Fig. 122-12. A screen-printing wicket dryer with an enclosed heating unit. (General Research, Inc.)

Fig. 122-13. A semiautomatic screen printing press with an attached wicket dryer. (M & M Research Engineering Co.)

Fig. 122-14. A screen-printing drying oven. (Cincinnati Printing and Drying Systems, Inc.)

Drying ovens hold portable drying racks (Fig. 122-14). The freshly printed sheets are placed on the racks, rolled into the oven, and completely dried within a short time. Continuous conveyor-belt dryers (Fig. 122-15) are placed in-line with a high-speed screen press. Heated air constantly circulates around the printed sheet which therefore dries very rapidly. These drying units are equipped to remove gas fumes coming from the ink and to cool the sheets after being heated. There are also ovens or kilns for firing ceramic screen-printed products.

Fig. 122-15. A forced-air, high-speed drying screen-printing unit. (American Screen Process Equipment Co.)

UNIT 123

SCREEN PRINTING EQUIPMENT FOR HAND PRODUCTION

Screen printing equipment for hand production includes a frame, some screen fabric, a squeegee, filmcutting tools, and drying equipment. There are several expendable supplies such as film and chemicals for the image carriers, ink, solvent, and plenty of wiping cloths. The cost is minimal compared to cost for the letterpress and lithography printing methods. Some of the equipment can easily be made in the home or school laboratory.

SCREEN PRINTING FRAMES

Screen frames suitable for hand production can be constructed as in Unit 125, or purchased from commercial supply houses. The frame can be of a size needed for general work, or designed for specific jobs. A screen printing unit contains a frame stretched with fabric, a baseboard, hinges, and the hinge lock.

SCREEN FABRIC

Many kinds of materials are used as *screen fabric.* The first use of silk fabric as a screen to hold the image carrier generally is credited to early screen printers in the United States, who began to use silk of the bolting cloth variety. Samuel Simon of Manchester, England obtained a patent relating to screen printing in 1907. Other materials used besides silk include organdy, nylon, dacron, vinyon, perforated stainless steel, and bronze.

Screen fabrics, such as silk, viewed with a magnifying glass appear as finely woven mesh strands with openings which allow liquid ink to pass through. Silk is graded by the number of openings per linear inch between the strands. These openings, called meshes, determine the fineness and coarseness of the silk. Mesh count is identified by number; the larger the number, the finer the silk. Typical mesh counts are listed.

NUMBER	MESH COUNT
6xx	74
8xx	86
10xx	109
12xx	125
14xx	139
16xx	157
18xx	166
20xx	173
25xx	200

Numbers 6xx and 8xx are considered *coarse;* 12xx and 14xx are *medium* and should be used for most work; and 18XX and 20xx are *fine,* with 25xx rated *very fine.*

Organdy is an inexpensive substitute for silk. Disadvantages are that it does not have the strength or the uniform weave of silk, nor is it possible to obtain in varying mesh counts. Organdy is available only in one mesh count of approximately 10xx to 12xx.

Fig. 123-1. A typical hand screen-printing frame and base. (Dick Blick)

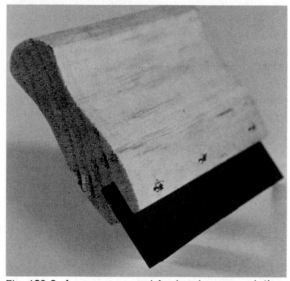

Fig. 123-2. A squeegee used for hand screen printing.

It can be used for relatively short runs of large detail work, where extremely accurate register may not be important. Nylon, polyester and metal fabric are used industrially for more precise printing, and they are available in coarse and very fine meshes.

SQUEEGEE

The squeegee (Fig. 123-2) is used to draw the ink across the screen, causing it to penetrate the openings of the image carrier.

Fig. 123-3. Squeegee blade angles, each designed for a specific purpose.

Fig. 123-4. A fixed-blade film knife.

Fig. 123-5. A swivel-blade film knife.

This penetration produces the print. Squeegees for hand use consist of a smoothly fashioned strip of wood with a hard rubber blade fastened to it. The blades are usually ³⁄₁₆ to ½ inch thick, and project from the wooden handle ¾ to 1¼ inches. They must be kept clean and free of blade nicks. Quality printing on different materials requires the blade edge to be shaped in specific ways (Fig. 123-3). The general shapes and uses for each squeegee blade angle are:

A. *Square-edged.* For flat objects and all general use.

B. *Square-edged with rounded corners.* For extra-heavy ink deposits, for printing light colors on dark backgrounds, and for printing with fluorescent inks.

C. *Rounded edge.* For textile printing with heavy ink deposits.

D. *Single-sided bevel edge.* For glass and nameplates.

E. *Double-sided bevel edge, flat point.* For ceramic printing.

F. *Double-sided bevel edge.* For direct printing on uneven surfaces such as bottles and containers. Also for delicate textile designs.

FILM-CUTTING TOOLS

A sharp cutting instrument is needed to prepare hand-cut lacquer film or water-soluble film (Units 127 and 128). A single-edged razor blade will serve this purpose but a standard *film knife* (Fig. 123-4) contains a fixed blade with an aluminum handle and is ideal. The blade can be replaced when it becomes dull. *Swivel-blade knives* (Fig. 123-5) are used when a great number of curves or irregular lines are contained in the illustration to be used. The blade rotates freely within the handle to allow cutting irregular lines without twisting the handle.

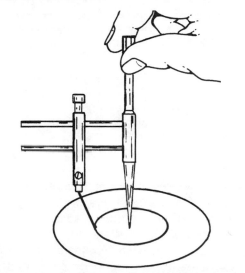

Fig. 123-6. An adjustable circle cutter capable of making circle diameters of from ⅛ to 3⅞ inches.

Fig. 123-7. A beam circle cutter to make diameters of from ⅞ to 26½ inches.

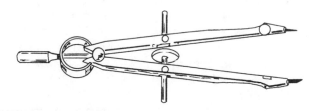

Fig. 123-8. A draftsman's bow compass outfitted with a knife blade.

Small *circle cutters* (Fig. 123-6) and large *beam cutters* (Fig. 123-7) are available. A draftsman's *bow compass* (Fig. 123-8) can be adapted to cut circles in film.

Fig. 123-9. A loop-knife film-line cutter.

Fig. 123-10. Dual-knife parallel-line cutters.

Fig. 123-11. An adjustable dual-knife parallel-line cutter.

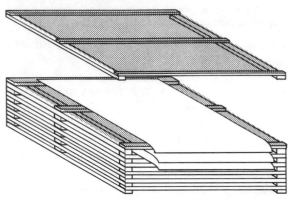

Fig. 123-12. Drying frames that can be constructed easily.

There are cutting knives designed to cut various width lines. A *loop-knife film-line cutter* (Fig. 123-9) is designed with the cutting edge in a circle. When this knife is drawn along the film it removes a specific width of the lacquer or water-soluble film. It comes in three sizes. *Dual-knife parallel-line cutters* produce several widths of lines. A *fixed-width parallel-line cutter* (Fig. 123-10) contains four cutters. *Adjustable dual-knife parallel-line cutters* (Fig. 123-11) are convenient tools also. The same amount of pressure must be placed on each of these blades during the cutting operation.

DRYING EQUIPMENT

There is need for some kind of drying arrangement because screen printing inks do not dry rapidly enough to allow the freshly printed sheets to be stacked immediately after printing. A rack arrangement for flat objects is pictured in Fig. 123-12. These individual racks can be stacked very easily and allow the air to circulate freely among the printed sheets to dry the ink rapidly. Commercial drying racks that contain individual racks that are hinged to a framework are also available.

Fig. 123-13. A hanger-clothesline method of drying garments.

Garments such as T-shirts and sweatshirts can be dried after printing by placing them on a hanger on a clothes line (Fig. 123-13). Other textile items can be dried in a similar manner.

UNIT 124
SAFETY WITH SCREEN PRINTING EQUIPMENT AND MATERIALS

Screen printing is a very safe graphic arts area in which to experiment. Definite cautions, however, must be observed to produce an acceptable quality product. Following the precautions listed below will insure safety while working in this phase of graphic arts.

Permission. Request permission from competent authority before beginning work with screen process.

Clothing and jewelry. Secure loose clothing and remove jewelry before working in the screen process area.

Safety guards. Work with care when constructing a screen process press. Use safety guards where applicable.

Air vents. Start exhaust fans before working with chemicals or solvents. If a power-exhaust system is not in effect, open the windows and or doors.

Electrical connections. Be certain that all electrical connections on power equipment used for the screen process press are in good repair and properly grounded.

Eye and face protection. Wear safety glasses and face shields when operating power equipment and when mixing the necessary photographic chemicals.

Floor drains. Floor drains should be located near sinks and tanks containing photographic chemical solutions. A safety shower should be nearby. The drain will remove the safety shower water.

Body protection. Wear a rubber apron when working with photographic chemicals and ink solvents.

Good housekeeping. Never allow waste materials to collect on the floor or shelves.

Materials storage. Store containers of photographic chemical solutions, lacquer thinner, and ink solvents near the floor. Place boxes, tools, and other items carefully on storage shelves.

Illumination. Have adequate lighting. Being able to see well can eliminate a dangerous situation.

Fire. Fire extinguishers must always be in a charged condition and placed in conspicuous locations. Be extremely careful when handling flammable materials such as lacquer, adhering liquid, lacquer thinner, and ink solvents.

Sharp objects. Handle and use sharp objects with care. Razor blades and knives, used to prepare hand-cut water and lacquer films, are extremely sharp.

Hand-skin protection. Check to see whether the lacquer-adhering liquid and lacquer thinner irritates your skin or respiratory system.

Hot water. The hot water used to remove photographic film from the screen fabric should be used carefully.

Ink and solvent-soaked rags. Place all rags containing ink or solvents in a metal safety can having a tight metal lid.

UNIT 125
SCREEN PRINTING PRESS CONSTRUCTION

Constructing screen printing press units is not difficult. With some basic woodworking skills and access to power equipment, building the units takes only a short time. Woods for the frame are usually either white pine or poplar. White pine, fir plywood, or masonite are suitable for the base.

FRAME CONSTRUCTION

The frames can be any size, but a two-by-three proportion is a common shape for the screen. The inside dimensions of the frame should be approximately three inches longer and wider than the material to be printed. The dimensions (width and thickness) of the wood for the frame must increase as the overall frame size increases, because strength is an important consideration. If the frame is weak or poorly constructed, the printing results will also be of poor quality. Observe the following steps in building the press units.

1. Select the screen size from Table 125-1. This is the inside frame dimensions based upon the planned maximum image area to be printed.

Table 125-1. Screen and Image Size Ratio (Inches)		
Suggested Maximum Image Size	**Inside Screen Dimensions**	**Frame Wood Dimensions**
3 x 6	6 x 9	¾ x 1¼
6 x 9	9 x 12	1 x 1½
9 x 15	12 x 18	1¼ x 1½
12 x 20	15 x 23	1¼ x 1¾
15 x 24	18 x 27	1¼ x 2

Suggested inside screen dimensions for desired maximum image sizes.

2. Select and cut the framing stock to length. Use one of three corner joints: miter, end-lap, or miter-spline as shown in Fig. 125-1.
3. Cut the groove for the cord in the bottom side of the framing stock (Fig. 125-2.) The cord tightens and holds the screen fabric over the frame.
4. Assemble the frame, using glue, nails, or corrugated fasteners. The frame must be very secure.

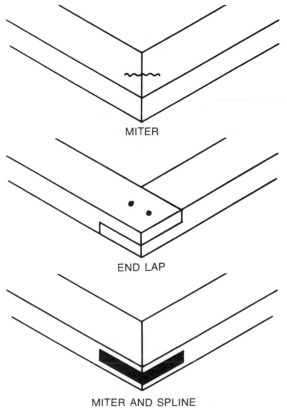

MITER

END LAP

MITER AND SPLINE

Fig. 125-1. The three common screen frame corner joints.

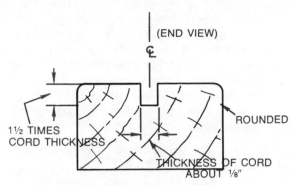

(END VIEW)

1½ TIMES CORD THICKNESS

ROUNDED

THICKNESS OF CORD ABOUT ⅛"

Fig. 125-2. The size, depth, and position of the groove for the cord in the framing stock. Note the rounded edges on the groove side of the stock.

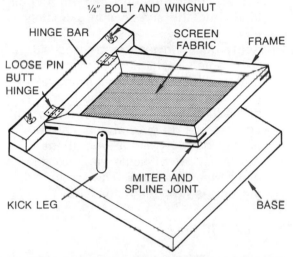

¼" BOLT AND WINGNUT

HINGE BAR

SCREEN FABRIC

FRAME

LOOSE PIN BUTT HINGE

MITER AND SPLINE JOINT

KICK LEG

BASE

Fig. 125-3. A typical home/school screen-printing unit.

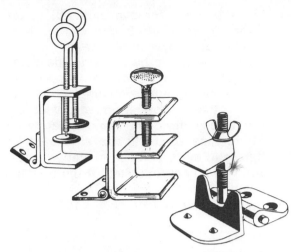

Fig. 125-4. Three types of commercial hinges used to hinge the screen frame to the base.

8. Center the screen frame from side-to-side on the base board and place it in contact with the hinge bar.
9. Fasten the frame to the hinge bar with loose pin-butt hinges (Fig. 125-3).
10. Fasten a kick-leg to the side of the frame. This keeps the screen up while a printed sheet is being removed and a new one inserted.
11. Apply two coats of sealer to the frame and base. The sealer makes it easier to remove the ink from the frame and base after completing the printing operation.

Commercial hinges eliminate the need for a hinge bar (Fig. 125-4). Commercial hinges are used when several screen changes are needed throughout a work period. The hinges attach directly to the base, and the screen screen frame is held in place by turning down the clamp bolt or wing nut.

BASE CONSTRUCTION

The base is used as a hinging support for the frame. Plywood or masonite ¼ to ¾ inch thick works well. The larger the screen frame, the thicker the plywood or masonite should be. The base is also used as a surface to locate and hold the paper or other material to be printed.

5. Cut the base. It should be approximately two inches larger on each side than the outside dimensions of the frame.
6. Cut a piece of stock the same as that used for the frame (Fig. 125-3). This will be the hinge bar.
7. Fasten the hinge bar flush or even with the end of the base board (Fig. 125-3). Use ¼-inch carriage bolts and wing nuts.

ATTACHING THE SCREEN FABRIC

12. Cut a piece of screen fabric (either organdy, silk, nylon, or dacron) approximately two inches larger on each side than the groove in the frame.
13. Cut four pieces of cord to fit the grooves in the frame. They should be slightly shorter than the actual groove lengths to eliminate overlap at the corners when the screen is attached.

14. Lay the frame, groove side up, on a table or workbench and center the screen fabric over the frame.
15. Fasten the fabric by pressing the cord and fabric into the grooves (Fig. 125-5). Use a bookbinder's folding bone or some other narrow, rounded object, or a specially designed commercial tool. Stretch the screen fabric so that it is tight and even. A loose screen will result in poor reproduction of the printed copies.
16. Using a razor blade, cut and remove

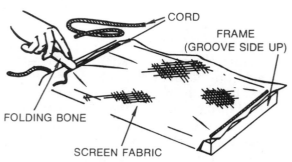

Fig. 125-5. Attaching the screen fabric to the screen frame by the cord-and-groove method.

excess fabric from beyond the grooves. Leave approximately ¼ inch of the fabric extending beyond the grooves.
17. Apply a coat of finish sealer around the groove side of the frame and allow it to dry thoroughly. This adheres the fabric to the frame and assists in holding the screen taut.

TAPING THE FRAME

18. Apply gummed tape to the bottom grooved side of the frame. The tape should cover the entire bottom and extend onto the screen approximately ½ inch.
19. Apply gummed tape to the top side of the frame. Position it evenly with the bottom tape on the screen and extend it up the inside walls of the frame. This procedure keeps the ink from the corners and grooves and is therefore of benefit during cleanup operations.
20. Apply a coat of sealer to the tape to make cleanup easier. The screen printing unit is now ready for use.

UNIT 126
ARTWORK FOR SCREEN PRINTING

The screen printing method of graphic reproduction is very versatile (Unit 121). The design and layout artist has a great deal of freedom in preparing the artwork. The artwork depends much on the method that is used to prepare the screen image carrier or the printing screen.

ARTWORK FOR HAND-CUT FILMS

Hand-cut films require artwork of high quality. They are used to produce large let-

tering for posters and basic illustrations that do not contain a great amount of detail. Exactness in artwork will produce quality work; it is difficult, for example, to cut perfect letters from sketchy artwork.

ARTWORK FOR DIRECT PHOTOSENSITIVE SCREENS

Artwork for direct *photosensitive screens* can be prepared by several methods (Unit 129). The image to be printed must be prepared on translucent or transparent paper or plastic. If *type* is to be used, five composition methods can be employed. These are: (1) foundry type, Unit 28; (2) hot metal, Unit 29; (3) impact, Unit 30; (4) dry transfer, Unit 31; and (5) hand mechanical, Unit 31.

The *silhouette method* is another way to prepare artwork for direct photosensitive screens (Fig. 126-1). The image, an actual object or one cut from black paper, is laid on the photosensitive screen and the light exposure is made. The important consideration is that the image be very dense. Light must not pass through the image while the photographic exposure is being made.

ARTWORK FOR PHOTOGRAPHIC SCREEN FILM

Whether hand-drawn illustrations or mechanically composed type, artwork for *photographic screen film* should be prepared by exacting methods (Unit 130). Because this type of reproduction produces high-quality work, it should be used only to obtain such results. The artwork must therefore be very well done.

All methods of composition can be used. After the type and illustrations are prepared by an artist, a paste-up is made and a film positive is then produced. The film positive is used to expose the photographic screen film.

ARTWORK FOR PAPER STENCIL AND WASHOUT SCREENS

These two screen-preparation methods do not require exacting artwork (Unit 134). Rough sketches are sufficient because much of the lettering and illustrations can be done during the screen image-carrier preparation.

DIVIDING FOR COLOR

In all graphic reproduction methods, it is necessary to select those areas of the il-

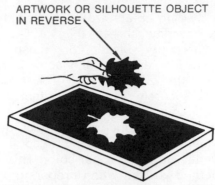

Fig. 126-1. Silhouette artwork can be used to prepare direct photosensitive screens.

lustration or full page that are to be reproduced in specific colors. Three methods can be used for the screen-process reproduction method.

1. *Artwork with an overlay sheet.* This method is the simplest and can be used with hand-cut films, paper stencil, and washout screens. The artwork is prepared either by hand or mechanical means on one sheet, in black and white.

A tissue overlay sheet similar to a comprehensive overlay sheet is placed over the artwork (Unit 24). The colors and other pertinent information are indicated on this sheet. During the preparation of the image carriers careful attention must be given to the sheet for proper preparation of *each* color.

2. *Artwork with full color.* When two or more colors are to be used on a screen printing reproduction, it is often convenient to prepare the artwork in full color, just as it will appear upon completion. This eliminates the need for imagining what the final result will be. It also gives additional practice in selecting and handling several colors on one reproduction.

A set of colored pencils will generally provide the necessary colors, although pencil colors do not usually correspond with accuracy of hue to screen printing ink colors. Artwork with full color can be used for hand-cut cut films, paper stencil, and washout screens.

3. *Artwork with overlays.* This method is most exacting and time consuming. The basic color or key area of the copy is prepared on a base paper or plastic sheet.

The succeeding colors are each placed on separate overlay sheets (Fig. 126-2) of translucent paper, plastic, or transparent plastic. The content for each color is also placed on the overlay sheet. The overlay sheets are securely fastened together. Note the register marks (Fig. 126-2), as it is essential that these be included on each overlay, including the base sheet. Also, mark each overlay with the proper color. This artwork method is used when preparing multiple-color work for direct photosensitive screens and photographic screen film. Stripping film is available commercially for use in preparing each overlay.

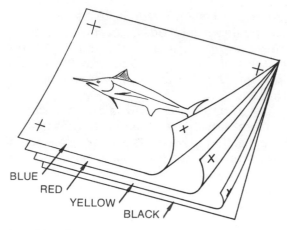

Fig. 126-2. The overlay method used for color division.

UNIT 127
LACQUER-SOLUBLE HAND-PREPARED FILM

Hand-cut films with a lacquer base revolutionized the screen printing industry around 1930. Until that time, several crude methods of preparing the screen stencil or printing screen were used. The film made possible intricate and higher-quality screen reproduction.

Lacquer film has two layers (Fig. 127-1). The *film* and the *backing* are held together with a special cement that releases when the backing must be removed prior to printing. The backing sheet makes the film stable and holds film elements in place until it is attached to the screen.

CUTTING THE FILM

1. Prepare the artwork, including illustrations and words.
2. Fasten the artwork securely to a hard, flat surface by using small pieces of masking tape. A drawing board, table top, or piece of glass is suitable.

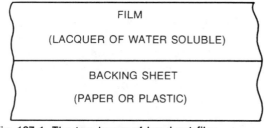

Fig. 127-1. The two layers of hand-cut film.

3. Obtain a piece of lacquer film; fasten it down over the artwork. The film should be at least one inch larger on each side than the image area of the artwork.
4. Begin cutting the film (Fig. 127-2). Cut the curved areas freehand or use the necessary special tools. Be certain to use a sharp knife and penetrate only the lacquer film. Use a T-square and triangle to help guide the knife on straight cuts. NOTE: The backing sheet should not be cut, but no damage will result if this happens once or twice in isolated areas.

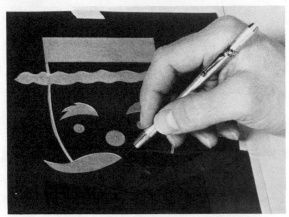

Fig. 127-2. Hand cutting lacquer film.

Fig. 127-3. Removing the lacquer film from the image areas after it has been cut.

5. Lift the lacquer film from the image areas by using a special stripping blade or the knife blade and a finger as shown in Fig. 127-3.

6. Remove all loose pieces of film from the lacquer film image carrier. A piece of masking tape wrapped around a finger, adhesive side out, will assist in picking up small pieces. NOTE: If pieces of film from the nonimage areas are accidentally removed during the cutting operation, they may be reattached to the backing sheet with rubber cement.

7. Carefully remove the film (now an image carrier) and illustration from the board or glass after cutting. Preserve the cut film until it is to be adhered to the screen.

ADHERING THE FILM

1. Check the screen. Make certain the screen material (silk, organdy, nylon, dacron, or wire) is perfectly clean. Also be certain the screen is stretched tight over the frame.

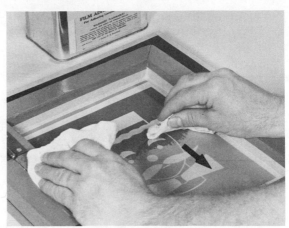

Fig. 127-4. Adhering the cut lacquer film to the screen.

2. Lay the cut film (film side up) on the hard, flat surface of either a table or the base board of the screen printing unit.

3. Place the clean screen (fabric side down) over the film. Visually position the screen and film so that the material to be printed can fit under the frame without touching the hinges.

4. Obtain a four-to-five-inch square piece of cotton cloth and fold it into a pad about two inches square. It will be used to apply the film-adhering liquid.

5. Fold a cotton cloth approximately 12 to 16 inches into a square and use it as a loose pad to fit the hand.

6. Saturate the small, neatly folded pad with adhering liquid suitable for the film being used. Wipe over a small four-to-six-inch square area of the film.

7. Wipe this area immediately, using the larger dry cloth (Fig. 127-4). Continue this action until the entire cut film is adhered. The adhering liquid softens or dissolves the film slightly to adhere to the screen. If the adhering liquid is allowed to stand on the film it will dissolve it too much, thus making ragged edges along the image. CAUTION: Begin adhering *one* side of the film, and continue across until all is adhered. This tends to eliminate most wrinkles and air bubbles.

8. Revolve the drying cloth constantly so a dry surface is always used to wipe the film. Keep the adhering pad well saturated with adhering liquid.

9. Examine the entire surface of the cut film. Properly adhered areas will turn darker when the adhering liquid is applied. If light spots remain, touch them up carefully by wiping with the adhering pad; then wipe immediately with the drying cloth.

10. Allow the adhered film to dry for approximately five to ten minutes. Stand the frame up so that air can reach both sides.

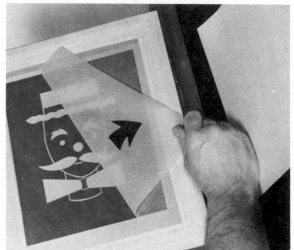

Fig. 127-5. Removing the backing sheet from the cut film.

11. Remove the backing sheet (Fig. 127-5). Grasp a corner and pull as parallel as possible to the screen. This prevents excessive stretching of the screen.

12. If an area of the film pulls away from the screen, STOP. Allow the backing sheet to resume its original position, and lay the frame back down on the flat surface. Adhere the area again, allow to dry, then continue removing the backing sheet.

13. The film is now properly adhered. Continue the screen printing procedure given in Unit 131.

REMOVING FILM FROM THE SCREEN

1. Place several newspapers under the screen and pour lacquer thinner over the lacquer film. Thoroughly saturate it and allow to soak for two or three minutes.

2. Lift the screen, leaving the dissolved lacquer film on the newsprint.

3. Repeat Steps 14, 15, and 16 if any lacquer film remains in the screen. It should be perfectly clean.

UNIT 128
WATER-SOLUBLE HAND-PREPARED FILM

The two main classes of knife-cut stencil-forming materials are (1) that composed of a thin film of *lacquer-type material* supported by a plastic or paper backing sheet, and (2) a *water-type film* material supported by translucent plastic. Both are cut and stripped with the material to print removed in an identical manner. When this is completed they are adhered to the stretched fabric to form the printing screen.

Water-soluble hand-cut films do not require the use of flammable lacquer thinner. Water is far less expensive than lacquer thinner which is used for adhering and cleaning, and the final printing quality of water-soluble film compares favorably with that of lacquer-type film.

CUTTING THE FILM

Water-soluble film is cut the same way as lacquer-soluble film. Use a sharp knife for quality results. During the cutting, if the film is accidently lifted off in a nonimage area it can be replaced with a thin layer of rubber cement.

This type of film picks up moisture during high humidity conditions, and becomes softer. It is suggested that film be kept in the original container or tube in an air-conditioned room. A piece of sheet plastic is often used under the hands while cutting. This helps prevent excessive perspiration from getting on the film.

ADHERING THE FILM

1. Remove old ink and dust from the screen.
2. Moisten the stretched screen material thoroughly with a wet cloth. Wipe the material lightly with a dry, absorbent cloth, leaving the screen fabric damp.
3. Place the cut film on a hard, smooth surface, film side up (right reading) as shown in Fig. 128-1. A surface of glass

Fig. 128-2. The screen positioned over the film.

or metal the same size as the inside of the screen frame is the best surface for this. This procedure is called a *build-up*.
4. Place the stretched screen over the cut film.
5. Position the frame, making sure there is perfect contact between the screen and film (Fig. 128-2).
6. Adhere the film to the screen according to the procedures outlined in Unit 127, Steps 4 through 14. Remember to substitute cold water for the lacquer-adhering liquid.

Fig. 128-1. The hand-cut water-soluble film is properly positioned on the glass build-up.

REMOVING FILM FROM THE SCREEN

1. Brush both sides of the screen with cold water. Use a stiff-bristled brush to insure thorough wetting of the film.
2. Allow the wet screen film to soak for four to ten minutes, then place the screen in a sink and flush away the film with either cold or hot water (Fig. 130-4).

UNIT 129
DIRECT PHOTOSENSITIVE SCREENS

Photographic screens are prepared by (1) the direct photosensitive screen method, as explained in this unit, and by (2) the photographic screen printing film method in Unit 130. Both methods require knowledge of basic photographic principles and a few pieces of special equipment. Greater detail results with photographic screen methods than with hand-prepared ones. Photographic-prepared screens, therefore have a wider variety of uses.

Direct photosensitive screens are so-called because a light-sensitive liquid emulsion is coated directly into the screen fabric. Following exposure to light and using some specially prepared artwork and developing with water, the screen becomes the screen printing image carrier. This durable printing screen produces thousands of impressions without deterioration.

The *direct method* of making printing screens is widely used in textile, electronic, ceramic, and chemical industries. It is popular in the general areas of point-of-purchase display, decal, and pressure-sensitive fields.

SENSITIZING THE SCREEN

It is necessary to observe certain light-safe conditions when working with photosensitive materials. Most direct-sensitizing compounds are not light-fast. Too much light during screen preparation will ruin the light-sensitiveness of the screen, but sufficient indirect light with which to see and work comfortably may fall upon the working area. A 15-watt frosted bulb placed eight feet from the working area will provide sufficient light and will not damage the emulsion.

Materials needed:
1. A screen printing frame stretched with fabric.
2. Direct photo-screen sensitizer in either liquid or powder form. (The powder form is referred to throughout this unit).
3. One mixing jar with a screw cap, large enough to hold the needed amount of liquid sensitizer.
4. One small cup or formula vessel to hold the prepared sensitizer solution.
5. A heat source and a container for boiling water.
6. One small piece of silk or nylon stocking for straining the sensitizer solution.
7. One soft bristle brush, ½ inch or larger.
8. One piece of chipboard approximately 2 x 4 inches to serve as a squeegee.

PREPARING THE EMULSION

1. Warm the formula vessel in a pan of hot water to remove the chill.
2. Pour the specified amount of manufacturer's photoscreen sensitizer and boiling water into the mixing jar. Screw the cap on firmly and shake the jar for four to five minutes. NOTE: Be careful because the jar may be hot due to the boiling water.
3. Strain the mixture by holding a piece of the nylon or silk fabric tightly over the mouth of the jar. Pour the prepared emulsion through the fabric into the formula vessel. Keep the formula vessel containing the newly mixed emulsion in a pan of hot water until the screen-sensitizing process has been completed. Use the solution as soon after mixing as possible.

COATING THE SCREEN

1. Clean the screen fabric with a cleaner and water. Do this before the emulsion is prepared.
2. Hold the screen at a 45° angle.
3. Using a brush, apply the liquid photo emulsion liberally to the bottom side of the screen (Fig. 129-1).
4. Use a chipboard squeegee to smooth the emulsion before it dries, working on both sides of the screen. This helps remove air bubbles which could later chip off during the printing procedure.
5. Dry the screen thoroughly. This step should be carried out in the dark. A fan will shorten the drying time.
6. Apply a second light-sensitive emulsion under very subdued light. Lay the screen flat on a table, bottom side up, and apply emulsion liberally with the brush.
7. Smooth out the excess emulsion with the squeegee. After the second coat has dried the screen is ready for exposure.

STORING SENSITIZED DRY SCREENS

Generally, sensitized screens should be exposed on the same day they are coated. However, some sensitized screens can be stored for use at a later time. The storage location must be a completely light-safe or light-proof such as an envelope or a cabinet. Screens can be stored for several days or even up to six weeks, depending upon the recommendation of the manufacturer. Thus several may be sensitized at the same time, stored, and then used as needed.

EXPOSING THE SCREEN

Materials needed:
1. A light exposure source. A #2 photo flood or a 200-watt frosted bulb with reflector will work, but a carbon arc unit works best.
2. One piece of clean window glass as large as the screen or artwork (copy).

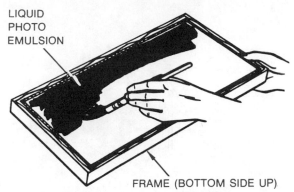

Fig. 129-1. The liquid photo emulsion is applied to the bottom side of the screen. (Dick Blick)

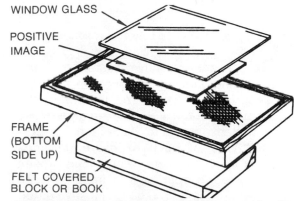

Fig. 129-2. The correct arrangement prior to making the exposure on a photo-screen. (Dick Blick)

3. The prepared copy.
4. A wood block or thick book covered with black felt of approximately the same size as the screen, but thicker than the screen frame.

Exposing:
1. Place the felt-covered block or book directly under the light source.
2. Place the screen, bottom side up, in position over the block or book. The block or book must be thicker than the frame to provide needed pressure on the screen.
3. Place the prepared positive transparency (copy) over the screen. The right-reading side must be in contact with the bottom side of the screen.
4. Position the piece of clear glass over the positive transparency, pressing it into perfect contact with the sensitive screen. This completes the proper arrangement of materials prior to exposure (Fig. 129-2).

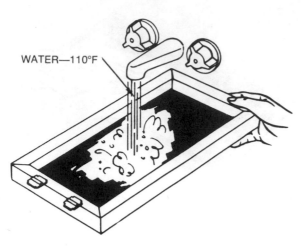

WATER—110°F

Fig. 129-3. Washing out the unexposed photo emulsion. (Dick Blick)

5. Expose the sensitive screen to light. The time involved depends on the light source, distance of the light from the screen, and the size of the screen. Make a trial exposure to determine the correct time of each exposure for each condition. If the copy has been prepared properly, it is impossible to over-expose it. The light-sensitive emulsion is hardened when struck by light; the need for positive copy on a transparent or translucent sheet is therefore apparent.

Developing:

1. Hold the screen at a 45° angle and allow a moderately strong stream of tap water at 110° F. to strike the image area (Fig. 129-3).

2. Wash the screen until the image or unexposed area is completely free of emulsion. NOTE: At this point the regular room lights may be turned on. If the nonimage area of the light-sensitive emulsion washes away, the exposure length should be increased.

3. Remove the screen from under the water tap and blot excess water by laying the screen (top side up) on a few sheets of newsprint. Lay folded sheets of newsprint inside the frame and press down with the hands.

4. Inspect the screen against a light. Check to see whether all unexposed emulsion is washed out. If some remains, repeat the washing and drying steps.

5. After the screen image appears completely clean, allow it to dry. The screen is now ready for masking as shown in Unit 131.

RECLAIMING THE SCREEN

Materials needed:

1. Powder stencil remover.
2. Warm water.
3. A pan large enough for the screen and frame to be placed inside.
4. Paper towels or newsprint paper.

Procedure:

1. Be certain that all ink is removed from the screen and frame as shown in Unit 133.
2. Mix the powder stencil remover with water, following the manufacturer's specifications.
3. Place the screen top side up inside the pan.
4. Pour the liquid stencil remover inside the screen.
5. Allow the screen to soak for two to six hours. Leave it overnight if desired.
6. Rinse the screen thoroughly with water when the stencil remover has liquified the emulsion.
7. Blot with paper towels or newsprint.
8. Allow the screen to dry. It is now ready for reuse.

UNIT 130
PHOTOGRAPHIC SCREEN PRINTING FILM

Photographic film for screen printing contains two layers consisting of a support sheet of thin plastic, and a light-sensitive emulsion, usually gelatin. The film is generally water soluble, making it rather easy to use. Some film is presensitized at the factory with a light-sensitive coating, while others must be sensitized by the user. The presensitized type is referred to in this unit. The use of photographic film for screen printing is also called *indirect photoscreen.*

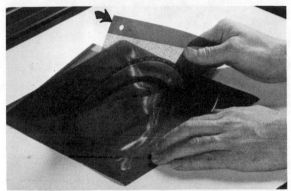

Fig. 130-1. The film positive is positioned over a presensitized piece of photographic screen film prior to exposure in a vacuum frame.

PREPARING THE COPY

The *copy,* a positive transparency, can be prepared either by the hand-mechanical method as outlined in Unit 129 or by the following mechanical-photographic method:
1. Complete the necessary design and layout work, and compose the type by one of the several methods outlined in Section 4.
2. Obtain or prepare the necessary illustrations and photographs, and prepare the paste-up as in Unit 46. For review purposes, study Section 6.
3. Make a film positive, using thin-base film (Unit 60).

EXPOSING THE PRESENSITIZED FILM

A darkroom is not needed with most presensitized photoscreen films, but the film must be kept away from sunlight and bright fluorescent lights.
1. Open the glass frame of the carbon arc (or other light source) exposure unit and thoroughly clean the glass on both sides. Place the presensitized screen film in the vacuum frame with the plastic support side up.
2. Place the film positive over the screen film with the emulsion up (wrong reading) as in Fig. 130-1. Close the frame, turn on the vacuum pump, and make the exposure. The length of exposure varies, depending upon the light source and the distance the light is from the film. A 35-amp arc placed 30 inches from the film should provide the proper exposure in three minutes.

The longer the exposure, the thicker the film; the shorter the exposure, the thinner the film. To find the best exposure, make a set of test strips ranging from thin to thick.

DEVELOPING THE FILM

1. Mix solutions A and B with water to make up the developer, and pour it into a photographic tray large enough to accommodate the photoscreen film.

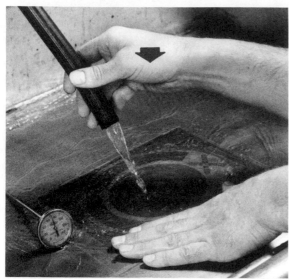

Fig. 130-2. Washing the developed photo-screen film.

2. Immerse the photoscreen film in the developer (emulsion side up). Develop the film for 1½ minutes. The time may vary, depending upon local conditions.
3. Place the film in a plate-developing sink containing a cold-and-hot water mixing arrangement and a hose (Fig. 130-2). Wash the film with warm water until the image is completely clear. Be certain that the water temperature is correct for the type of film; check the manufacturer's specifications.
4. Finish washing the film with cold tap water from 30 seconds to one minute after the image is clear.

ADHERING THE FILM TO THE SCREEN

Be certain that the screen material (silk, wire, nylon, or dacron) is clean. Prepare a clean screen by first wetting it and sprinkling it with a powder cleanser, and then rubbing a brush lightly in a circular motion over the entire surface. Flush the entire screen with water, making sure that all cleanser particles are removed. NOTE: Wash the screen before exposing and developing the photoscreen film; then dry the screen fabric throughly.

1. Obtain a piece of glass that is larger than the film but smaller than the inside of the screen frame. This will be used as the build-up (Unit 128).
2. Place the wet film on the build-up glass (emulsion side up), and place the clean screen frame in position over the film. Press lightly.
3. Blot the screen and film with unprinted newsprint paper to remove water from the film (Fig. 130-3). A photographic print roller or ink brayer can be used to insure good contact. Use several changes of the newsprint paper.

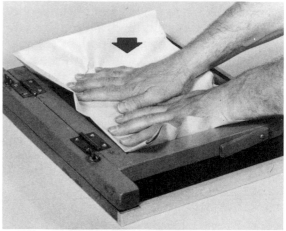

Fig. 130-3. Newsprint paper is used to blot excess water from the photographic screen film during the adhering phase.

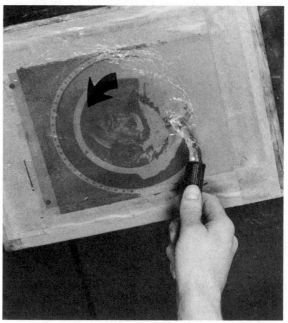

Fig. 130-4. The water-soluble photographic film is flushed from the screen with hot water.

4. Stand the frame up and allow the screen and film to dry thoroughly. A fan can be used to shorten the drying time.
5. Peel off the thin plastic support sheet after the film is dry. This is done by the same method used with the lacquer and water-soluble hand-cut films (see Units 127 and 128).
6. Wash off the adhesive residue from the film with naphtha or benzene after the plastic support sheet has been removed. The screen is now ready to be masked for printing.

REMOVING THE FILM

1. Flush the screen with hot water, the hotter the better (Fig. 130-4). The film will dissolve and come off quickly. Use a small amount of enzymes on the screen if any haze is left.
2. Wash the screen with vinegar to stop the action of the enzymes, then throughly flush it with water. The screen is now ready for the next piece of film.

UNIT 131
MASKING THE NONPRINTING AREAS

It is necessary to mask or block out the nonprinting areas around the perimeter of the screen after the film (stencil) has been attached to it. This essential step must be done with care if quality printing is to be accomplished. Select the most appropriate masking from the several of the materials available.

PAPER MASKING

Paper masking can be used when approximately 100 or fewer copies will be printed. The ink used in the printing operation will eventually penetrate the masking paper and permit spots to leak onto the finished prints. It is suggested that a minimum number of prints be made using this masking method. Bond paper, 16 or 20 pound, is suitable. The masking paper can be applied to either the top or bottom sides of the screen.

TOP-PAPER MASKING

1. Lay the screen frame on a flat surface, top side up.
2. Obtain four sheets of paper; two sheets for the width of the inside of the frame and two for the length. All four sheets should be wide enough to cover the unused screen and the frame on each side.
3. Tape the four sheets in place around the image (Fig. 131-1). Leave a minimum of ¼ inch of space between the image and the tape. Masking tape ¾ inch wide works best.

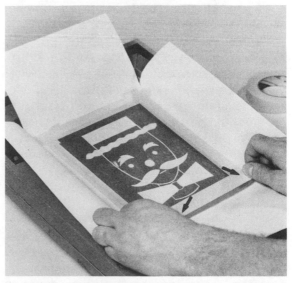

Fig. 131-1. A screen masked with paper from the top of the frame.

Fig. 131-2. Marking the paper masking where the opening is to be made for the image.

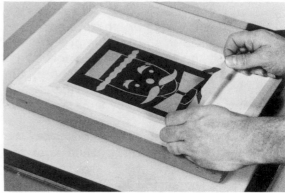

Fig. 131-3. A properly positioned and fastened masking sheet on the underside of the screen.

4. Tape the sheets at the corners and any other places where ink may leak through to the material being printed.

BOTTOM-PAPER MASKING

1. Lay the screen frame on a light table, bottom side up.
2. Obtain a sheet of paper as large as or larger than the outside dimensions of the screen frame.
3. Lay the sheet over the screen. Use a *pencil* to mark the opening needed for the image (Fig. 131-2). The opening should be at least one inch *larger* than the image area. Also mark the maximum sheet size one inch *smaller* than the frame on all four sides.
4. Remove the sheet and cut it to the outside dimensions. Also cut the opening for the image. A single-edge razor blade works satisfactorily.
5. Attach the masking sheet to the underside of the screen by taping all inside and outside edges with masking tape (Fig. 131-3). During printing the ink will adhere the masking sheet very securely to the screen fabric.

LIQUID MASKING

Two main types of liquid masking materials are lacquer-base and water-base. Both are applied to the screen in the same manner. The use of one or the other depends upon the ink to be used; for example, if

water-base ink is to be used, a lacquer block-out is necessary.

Transparent and opaque masking liquids are available in both water- and lacquer-base materials. Because of the convenience in seeing what is to be printed, transparent block-out is preferred. Liquid block-out can be used to patch open areas or pinholes in the screen film (image carrier).

BRUSH APPLICATION

1. Lean the screen, back or bottom side up, against a support.
2. Using a one-inch brush, apply a thin coat of block-out to all open nonprinting screen areas (Fig. 131-4). Allow the block-out to dry.
3. Apply another thin coat and allow it to thoroughly dry. Two coats generally are sufficient.
4. Inspect the screen for pinholes and apply additional liquid mask if needed.

PAPERBOARD SQUEEGEE APPLICATION

1. Lean the screen, back or bottom side up, against a support.
2. Obtain a piece of paperboard approximately 2 x 4 inches in size. A piece of chipboard similar to the back of a writing tablet works well.
3. Place this paperboard squeegee against the screen near the bottom and pour a small amount of block-out on the screen (Fig. 131-5).

Fig. 131-4. Applying liquid masking with a brush to nonprinting areas of the screen.

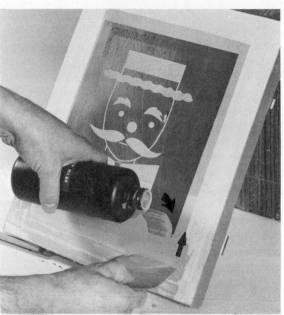

Fig. 131-5. Using a chipboard squeegee to apply liquid masking to nonprinting areas of the screen.

4. Draw the squeegee upward, distributing the block-out throughout the nonprinting areas of the screen. Continue until the screen has been covered and allow the block-out to dry.
5. Apply a second coat to cover any areas not filled during the first application.
6. Inspect the screen for pinholes and apply additional liquid mask or opaque if necessary.

TAPE MASKING

If small areas of open screen remain between the film and the frame, masking tape or gummed paper tape may be used to mask out the ink. Apply the tape to the underside of the screen and overlap sufficiently to insure that the ink will not penetrate and spoil the material being printed.

UNIT 132
THE PRINTING OPERATION

The printing operation is done after all preliminary work of preparing the image carrier and masking the nonprinting areas have been completed. The basic operation is not difficult and excellent results can be achieved with limited practice.

SCREEN PRINTING INK

It is important to select the proper ink for the material to be printed. Many types of inks are available for screen printing work. They are needed because of the extremely wide variety of surfaces on which screen printing is possible.

In addition to color and gloss characteristics, screen printing ink considerations involve: ease of printing, length of time to air dry, length of time to force dry under heat, weather resistance, durability, thickness after printing, and penetration into the material.

There are four principle categories of screen printing inks. An additional special group makes five. Each category has identifying characteristics, purposes, handling methods, and solvents. Before a material is screen printed, special thought must be given to the proper selection of ink.

Water-base inks. These inks are subdivided into two main classes: those for indoor work on paper, and those for printing on textiles. The inks in the first type mix readily with water, are easily printed, dry quickly after printing, and are easily cleaned from the screen during cleanup. The textile inks are very complex in chemical formulation and they can be used on cotton, silk, linen, and other textiles.

Oil-base inks. These are commonly termed poster inks. They have a higher degree of scuff-and-wear resistance than do the water-base ones and are available in a very wide range of colors. They dry somewhat more slowly than water-base inks, but generally can be force-dried in a very few minutes or even seconds. The average air-drying time is 30 minutes.

Synthetic enamel inks. This type of ink presents an appearance resembling glossy enamel. The vehicle or base consists of synthetic varnishes and resins. Synthetic enamel inks are used to print decals and outdoor signs and on sheet metal, plastics, wood, glass, and previously painted surfaces. Drying time is longer than for oil-base inks, but force-drying methods will often shorten it considerably.

Lacquer-base inks. Lacquer-base inks are slightly more volatile· than the previous three categories and present certain fire hazards. When printed they are quite flexible, tending not to crack or break. These inks are very fast drying, which makes them useful in printing packaging containers within a production line.

Special formulations. Several special materials are used in screen printing. Among them are flock adhesive, printed circuit formulations, cloth decorating mediums, and materials within the ceramic family. Each has special application methods and must be treated carefully for successful results.

PRINTING PROCEDURE

1. Attach the prepared screen frame to the base unit according to one of the methods presented in Unit 125.
2. Place a sheet of paper or other material to be printed under the screen. Position it according to the image in the screen.
3. Carefully raise the screen, leaving the paper in the correct location on the baseboard.
4. Obtain or cut three chipboard guides approximately ¾ x 1 inch.
5. Fasten the guides to the baseboard with masking tape. Place two guides on the long side of the sheet and one on the short side (Fig. 132-1). Lower the screen and obtain a squeegee slightly longer than the image width.
6. Spread newspapers on the table under and around the screen printing unit. The newspapers speed up cleanup. Prepare the ink and follow the manufacturer's specifications carefully to obtain good results.
7. Place a sheet to be printed against the guides.
8. Pour a bead of ink the width of the image on the hinge side of the screen (Fig. 132-2).

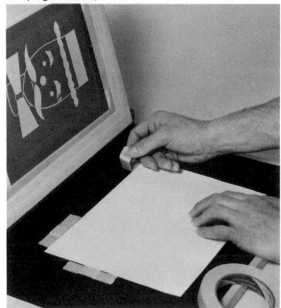

Fig. 132-1. Guides properly positioned and fastened to the screen-printing baseboard.

9. Grip the squeegee securely and pull the ink across the image to be printed (Fig. 132-3). Firm pressure on the squeegee removes excess ink from the top of the screen. Hold the squeegee at approximately 60° forward and make only one pull per print.

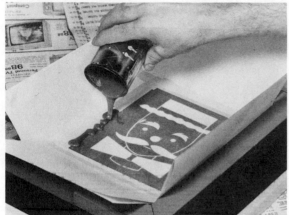

Fig. 132-2. Pouring a bead of ink on the hinge side of the screen in readiness for printing.

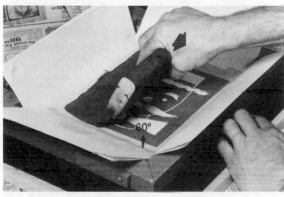

Fig. 132-3. Making a printed copy.

10. Lift the squeegee with the excess ink and replace it on the hinge side of the screen. Lift the screen and remove the print and inspect for flaws and make needed corrections.
11. Repeat Steps 9 and 10 for additional printed copies. Add ink when necessary.
12. Place the freshly printed sheets on drying racks until they are completely dry.

PRINTING ON SPECIAL MATERIALS

Screen printing can be used to print on various kinds and shapes of materials. Printing on these materials requires adaptation of standard printing units to the material and even specially designed units to accept the product to be printed.

Thick, flat objects. Objects up to ⅛ inch can generally be printed with the screen mounted flat on the baseboard. The screen and baseboard must be separated for thicker objects (Fig. 132-4). It is also possible to print on boxes by building up the screen to accommodate the existing thickness.

Cylindrical objects. Bottles, cans, and other cylindrical objects can be printed on a special screen press. Commercial cylindrical screen printers are available, but units can also be made in the school laboratory (Fig. 132-5). When printing on cylindrical objects, the screen moves horizontally, the squeegee remains stationary (permanent), and the object being printed generally revolves under the screen.

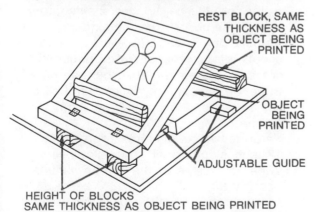

Fig. 132-4. A method for preparing the screen-printing unit when printing thick objects.

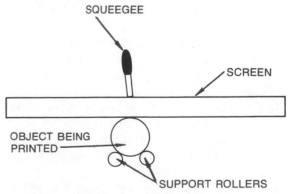

Fig. 132-5. A cylindrical screen-printing unit.

UNIT 133
SCREEN CLEANUP PROCEDURES

Cleaning the screen printing unit immediately following the printing operation is essential. If the ink is not removed soon after the printing has been done, it will dry, cake in the fabric, and the screen will have to be discarded. This would be expensive and certainly not practical, considering the time required to prepare a frame with a new piece of screen fabric.

All screens are cleaned in the same basic manner, even though different image carriers and inks are involved. The correct solvent for each kind of material to be removed must be used. Check the manufacturer's recommendations for suggested solvents for the various image carriers and inks.

The cleanup operation can be messy, but with care and consideration for the other person a neat, final job can result. Have plenty of newspapers available and wrap all ink-soaked materials except rags in clean newspaper before discarding into the wastebasket. Place soiled solvent-soaked rags in a metal safety can.

Fig. 133-1. Using a chipboard spatula during the cleanup operation to remove excess ink from the screen.

REMOVING THE INK

1. Place several sheets of newspapers under the screen as soon as the printing operation is completed.
2. Remove excess ink from the screen and squeegee, using a piece of chipboard of approximately 3 x 4 inches as a spatula (Fig. 133-1).
3. Replace the ink in the original can if no drier or other material was added to it for the printing operation.
4. Discard the chipboard spatula by wrapping it in newspaper.
5. If a top or bottom paper mask was used, it should now be removed. Carefully re-move the tape, holding the paper so as not to place undue stress on the screen fabric.
6. Pour some ink solvent on the screen. Be certain to use the correct solvent for the type of ink. Use water for water-base ink, mineral spirits for oil-base ink, and lacquer thinner for lacquer-base ink. Allow the solvent to soak briefly.
7. Wipe the inked area of the screen with a medium-sized cloth approximately 12 inches square. The cloth absorbs much of the ink; the newspaper sheets under the screen absorb the remainder.
8. Remove one or two of the top saturated sheets of newspaper from under the screen to renew the absorbent surface.
9. Repeat the cleaning process until all of the ink has been removed from the screen.
10. Saturate two clean cloths approximately 12 inches square with the ink solvent.
11. Wipe both sides of the screen simultaneously (Fig. 133-2).
12. Store the screen after all traces of ink have been removed. It can be used for future additional copies, or the emul-

sion or coating making up the image carrier can be removed to free the screen for another job.

REMOVING THE IMAGE CARRIER

The image carrier, which may be screen printing film or coating, can be taken off after all ink has been removed. It is impossible to remove it intact from the screen; if future printing needs are planned, the image carrier must, therefore, be preserved in the screen.

Follow the procedure for removing image carriers of each kind. If a liquid mask was used to block out the nonprinting areas of the screen, it must also be removed. Use the correct solvent and repeat Steps 6 through 11 under Removing the Ink.

STORAGE OF THE SCREEN

It is essential that screens be stored properly to preserve them. Stacking several frames on top of one another on a bench is unsatisfactory; frames placed in a vertical position within a rack helps protect the screen fabric (Fig. 133-3).

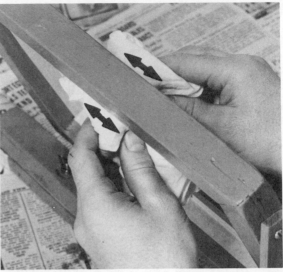

Fig. 133-2. Wiping both sides of the screen to remove ink and foreign material.

The storage rack should be constructed with all sides enclosed except the front. This helps prevent heavy deposits of dust and other foreign material from gathering on the screens. It also protects them from being punctured and ruined for future use.

Screens handled with care will give much service. One screen is capable of accepting several image carriers and making several thousand impressions.

Fig. 133-3. A screen storage rack containing thirty frames.

UNIT 134
PAPER STENCIL AND WASHOUT SCREENS

The paper stencil and the washout, tusche and glue, are two of the earliest and most economical methods of preparing screen printing image carriers. *Tusche* is a substance like lithographic ink in crayon form that is used as a resist in screen work. These two screen preparation mediums will produce excellent results, although they are not widely used commercially.

PAPER STENCIL IMAGE CARRIERS

One of the most simple screen preparation methods is to construct a *paper stencil* image carrier. A paper mask or stencil is adhered to the screen fabric with the ink used to print the copies. The image is cut out of the paper with a razor blade or an artist's knife. Copies are printed in the usual manner. The paper stencil method should be used for work involving simple illustrations or large lettering. It is possible to print up to 200 copies with this method.

PREPARING THE STENCIL

1. Select the copy; remember to keep it simple.
2. Obtain a piece of white bond paper (20-pound is best). It should be slightly smaller than the outside dimensions of the frame.
3. Place the copy on a light table. Tape it down and then tape the white bond sheet over the copy (Fig. 134-1).
4. Cut out the image, using a razor blade or an artist's knife (Fig. 134-1). If letters or parts of the illustration contain

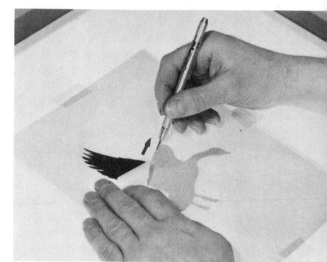

Fig. 134-1. Preparing a paper stencil by cutting out the image to be printed.

centers it will be necessary to leave connecting links. Avoid these if at all possible.

5. Obtain a clean screen printing frame and base. Place a sheet of clear newsprint paper on the base and place the cut stencil sheet on the newsprint paper. Lower the screen and position it if necessary.
6. Complete the printing operation as outlined in Unit 132. The ink will adhere the paper stencil sheet to the screen fabric.
7. Remove the paper after printing the desired number of copies and clean the screen as outlined in Unit 133.

THE WASHOUT SCREEN

The *washout method* is sometimes called the tusche and glue method because originally glue was used as the masking or block-out material. Commercial water- and lacquer-base block-out materials are now available.

This method of preparing the screen image carrier utilizes a liquid or crayon tusche material. The image areas of the screen are filled with the tusche material and a liquid is used to fill the remaining areas of the screen. The tusche is then removed to form the image carrier.

The washout screen method is commonly used for the reproduction of fine-art compositions, which generally are produced in limited editions. These compositions can be reproduced to look much like the original. Cost of this method is less than that of most graphic reproduction methods.

PREPARING THE WASHOUT SCREEN

1. Select the copy. Landscapes and artist's renditions are best for this method.
2. Thoroughly clean the screen fabric with cleanser and water.
3. Tape the copy to a flat table top and lay the screen over the copy.
4. Trace the image onto the screen, using a soft pencil. Accuracy is important.
5. Lift the screen and prop it against a support at a slight angle.
6. Apply liquid tusche to the image area of the screen, using a lettering or art brush (Fig. 134-2). Allow the tusche to dry thoroughly.
7. If a crayon tusche stick is used, lay the screen on a flat, hard surface when applying the tusche. Interesting texture patterns can be obtained by laying heavily grained wood or other porous material under the screen and rubbing over the screen with the tusche stick. The tusche will stick to the screen only in the high areas of the underlying material.
8. Apply the masking or block-out after the tusche is completely dry. Use water-base or lacquer-base liquid block-out, depending upon the ink to be used.
9. Apply the liquid block-out with a brush or a chipboard squeegee, as outlined in

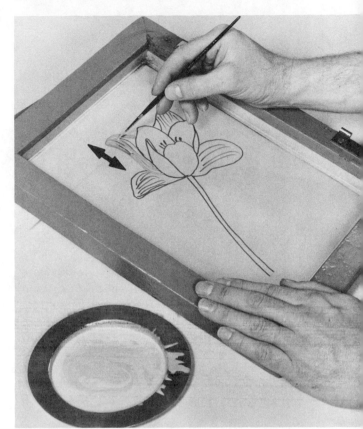

Fig. 134-2. Applying liquid tusche to the image area of the screen.

Unit 131. Apply the block-out to the top side of the screen, including the tusche covered areas. If this is not done, it will be more difficult to remove the tusche material.

10. Remove the tusche after the liquid block-out is dry. To do this, saturate two cloths with solvent. Work from both sides of the screen and wash out the tusche (Fig. 133-2). Use the correct solvent (usually turpentine, benzene, or naphtha) to dissolve the tusche.
11. Mask out the screen around the edges of the frame with paper or tape (Unit 131).
12. Print the copies as outlined in Unit 132. Several hundred copies can be reproduced before the block-out material begins to deteriorate.
13. Clean the screen according to the information contained in Unit 133. Remove the block-out with water or lacquer thinner.

UNIT 135
MULTICOLOR SCREEN PRODUCTION

One of the attractive features of screen printing is the ease with which colors are introduced into the reproduction. Several mechanical methods are possible by which colors are registered or positioned and printed. Only one method will be discussed in this unit. With ingenuity and planning, however, other register and printing methods can be developed. The use of register marks, though, is common to all multicolor screen production.

COPY PREPARATION

The correct preparation of the copy for multicolor work is essential to quality reproduction. The number of colors to be printed is not important, although the reproduction of two colors requires the same basic procedural steps as the reproduction of three or more.

The following procedure should be followed for hand-cut (lacquer or water-base) films:

1. Obtain the multiple-color copy that is appropriate for hand cutting.
2. Divide the color. Each color area should be shaded with a corresponding colored pencil or should be appropriately marked indicating the proper colors (Fig. 135-1).
3. Place two register marks on the copy. They should be placed at opposite corners a minimum of one inch from the nearest copy. Use an ink ruling pen and make the lines ½ inch long and at 90° to each other. Preprinted register marks that include an adhesive backing can be conveniently used too.

4. Cut one piece of film for each color. If colors are next to each other take extreme care when cutting the film. Carefully cut the register marks in each piece of film.
5. Adhere the film to the screen. It is more convenient to have one screen per color, although this is not necessary. If only one screen printing unit is available, print the first color, clean up the screen, adhere the film, and then print the second color.
6. Mask the screen or screens as outlined in Unit 131. If multiple pages are being printed, check the imposition carefully.

Fig. 135-1. Multicolor copy suitable for screen printing hand-cut film. Note the register marks.

7. Print the first color. Normally, the lightest color is printed first, although this is not necessary. Print approximately six copies with the register marks, then cover the marks from the underside with masking tape. Also print approximately 10% more per color than the number of final copies needed. These extra prints are necessary because of normal spoilage during the operation.
8. After the first color has dried, the second color can be printed. Prepare the screen in the usual manner. To register the second color, place one of the first prints containing the register under the screen. Move it around until the printed register marks of the first color and the register marks cut into the film of the second color align. Raise the screen carefully and position the guides.
9. Make one or two trial prints of the second color which has the register marks. Inspect for the correct position and make guide adjustments if necessary. Cover the register marks and complete the second color printing.
10. Complete additional colors.
11. Clean the screens thoroughly.

UNIT 136
LEARNING EXPERIENCES: SCREEN PRINTING

DISCUSSION TOPICS

1. List other names by which screen printing is identified. How does screen printing differ from letterpress, lithography, and gravure image-transfer methods?
2. Who were the first people to use screen printing? Was this method of reproducing images readily accepted in the United States? Identify some of the many products that can be printed by the screen printing method.
3. Name the four principles that have been tried in the development of screen printing presses. Name the principle press designs that are in common use today. Briefly describe the operating principle of each type.
4. Describe the several different commercial drying systems that are available. Cite the methods and pieces of equipment that are used for drying purposes in small commercial plants or in school laboratories.
5. Identify the several items that are needed for hand screen printing production. Compare the cost of hand equipment to that of commercial automatic equipment.
6. What are the different kinds of screen fabrics that can be used? Name the system that is used to identify the different grades of silk. Explain 12xx.
7. Why is the squeegee an important screen printing tool? How is the squeegee constructed? In what condition must it be kept for quality printing results?
8. List the several film cutting tools. Why is it wise not to use a single-edge razor blade to prepare hand cut films? How can a draftsman's bow compass be used to prepare hand-cut films?
9. What kind and size of material is appropriate for screen frame construction? Illustrate the groove method of fastening the screen fabric to the frame. Why is gummed tape applied to both sides of

the frame? Give the purpose of the sealer.

10. Explain the artwork requirements for the different methods of preparing the screen printing image carriers. Compare the requirements of each.

11. Describe hand-cut lacquer film. Briefly explain the procedure used in preparing a lacquer hand-cut image carrier. What procedure is used to fasten the lacquer film to the screen fabric?

12. Compare the water-soluble and lacquer-soluble hand-prepared films. List the advantages and disadvantages of each. How does the adhering procedure for water-soluble film differ from that of lacquer-soluble film?

13. Name the two methods of photographically preparing screen printing image carriers. What advantages do the photographic methods have over the hand-prepared image carriers?

14. Explain the general procedure for sensitizing and exposing the direct photosensitive screen. Is it possible to store a presensitized direct photosensitive screen? What is the purpose of the window glass?

15. Describe the conditions in which the presensitized photographic screen film can be used. Under what conditions is it possible to use direct photosensitive screen materials?

16. Explain what takes place during the exposure of photographic screen film through the positive. Cite the purpose of the liquid developer. Give the purpose of the warm water wash after the film has been exposed and developed.

17. Cite the primary purpose of masking the nonprinting areas of the screen. Enumerate and describe the methods that can be used for masking. Give the advantages and disadvantages of each method.

18. List the categories of screen printing inks. Identify the uses of each. Why is it important to select the correct ink for the material being printed?

19. Explain how to position the paper stock under the screen frame so that the image is reproduced in the correct position. What material can be used for the paper guides? Where should these guides be placed?

20. Explain how it is possible to print on thick, flat objects and cylindrical objects with the screen printing method. How is it possible to print on textile material such as sweatshirts, T-shirts, and tablecloths? Illustrate some jigs that may be helpful.

21. Why is it necessary to remove the ink from the screen soon after the printing operation has been completed? Describe the procedure for removing it. How are the several kinds of image carriers removed from the screen?

22. Identify some materials or products that could be printed by using the paper-stencil method. Cite the limitations of this method.

23. Explain the general procedure for preparing a washout screen. What types of finished products are generally suited to this method? Give another name that is used to identify the washout method of preparing the screen.

24. Why are register marks important when producing multiple-color reproductions? Where should the register marks be placed on the original copy? Why don't the register marks appear on the printed copies?

ACTIVITIES

1. Obtain as many products as possible that have been printed by the screen printing method. Carefully examine the quality of the images. Cite the improvements that could have been made to obtain a higher-quality product. If possible, determine the kind or category of ink that was used on each printed example.

2. Construct a screen printing unit. Prepare a unit for flat materials and/or for cylindrical objects. Carefully design the unit for high-quality printing results and maximum efficiency.

3. Plan, prepare, and print a product suitable for screen printing. Select the most appropriate image carrier for the particular job. Remember to use the correct ink.

4. Compare the several methods of preparing the screen printing image carriers. Select an illustration for a particular product and attempt to prepare an image carrier by each of the several methods. Print and critically analyze the results from each of these image carriers. Repeat this experiment with a different type of illustration for another product.

5. Produce a four-color poster advertising a future event in your school. Use a different method of preparing the image carrier for each color. Remember to choose the appropriate image carrier for each color element. Have friends or fellow students critique your work.

The photographer is developing a photograph in a darkroom.

UNIT 137
INTRODUCTION TO PHOTOGRAPHY

For thousands of years man attempted to capture and preserve what he saw with his eyes. This can be seen by the attempts of the caveman to draw pictures of hunting exploits on the walls of his caves. Until relatively recent times paintings and drawings were the only means that man had of keeping visual records.

It was not until the mid-eighteenth century that the first process for producing permanent photographic images was developed. This was done by the French painter, Daguerre. An American, George Eastman, was the person who first made photography practical for everyone by producing roll film and standardizing camera sizes in which the film would fit. Since Eastman's developments in the late 1800s, rapid and important technological advances have taken place in photographic equipment, materials, and processes.

Photography influences each day of a person's life. The photographs in books, newspapers, and many other forms of printed materials help you understand and feel more a part of the scene. Photographs in catalogs and on advertisements permit you to see what you are buying. Photographs assist scientists with exploration of the unknown; help doctors cure patients; assist engineers with design and construction of buildings, roads, and bridges; help law enforcement officers solve crimes; and make it possible for people to remember past experiences.

Nearly everyone can own a camera and take pictures. Even the most modestly priced cameras produce excellent photographs, if handled correctly. The develop-ment of highly automated processing equipment has made it possible for a person to have black-and-white film developed and photographs made very economically. The automated processing procedures permit a person to have film developed within twenty-four hours.

A photograph is produced by exposing film in a camera, developing the film to make a negative, and making a positive print on photographic paper from the negative. The positive print is the *photograph* (Fig. 137-1).

Many people enjoy making their own photographs rather than taking their film to a commercial processor. This section explains the procedures for taking and processing photographs.

Fig. 137-1. A photograph is the end result of taking a picture.

385

UNIT 138
KINDS OF CAMERAS

A camera is used to expose film to make a negative for a photograph. The primary purpose of a camera is to hold the film so that light will not reach the film until the photographer takes the picture. The characteristics which nearly all cameras have in common are: a light-tight box, a lens, and a means of controlling the amount of light that enters the camera. Some cameras are more sophisticated than others and have more devices to increase versatility in taking pictures.

The parts of cameras have already been discussed in Unit 51. Cameras used for general photography are much the same as those used for process photography, except that the latter usually are much larger.

BOX CAMERAS

Box cameras (Fig. 138-1) are the simplest type of camera and many different models are manufactured. Basic cameras can be purchased for a few dollars; more sophisticated ones can cost several hundred dollars. Nearly all box cameras have only one or two shutter speeds and a lens with the focus in a fixed position.

Box or small cartridge cameras are quite easy to operate and many models yield excellent snapshots. Enlargements are not usually as sharp as those made from negatives by more expensive cameras because of the poorer quality of the lens.

TWIN-LENS REFLEX CAMERAS

A twin-lens reflex camera, as the name suggests, has two lenses (Fig. 139-2). The two lenses are usually identical. The top lens permits the photographer to view the subject very nearly as it will appear on the film. The lower lens is used to make the actual exposure on the film.

It should be understood that the image that passes through the top lens is a little higher than the image that passes through the lower lens. This situation creates a problem when close-up exposures are made. When making close-up photographs with a twin-lens reflex camera, aim the camera so that the image viewed through the top lens and as seen in the view finder is

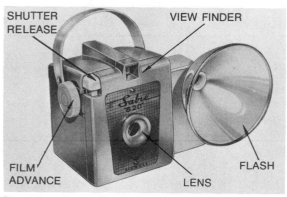

Fig. 138-1. A box camera. (Brumbarger Co., Inc.)

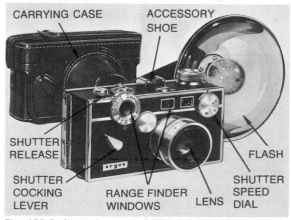

Fig. 138-2. An early range-finder camera. (Argus, Inc.)

a little above the picture that you actually want to take.

Twin-lens reflex cameras are the choice of many professional photographers because of their relatively small size and because many models are made with extremely high-quality lenses. Most twin-lens reflex cameras use 120-size film, which produces a negative size of 2¼ x 2¼ inches.

MINIATURE CAMERAS

Miniature cameras are small and compact. The most popular one is the 35mm. The name originated from the size of film which is 35 millimeters wide.

Figs. 138-2 and 138-3 show two *range finder* 35mm cameras. The range finder is a mechanism that permits the photographer to sight what he is photographing and to determine when he has the object in focus.

Fig. 138-3. A range finder camera with light meter. (E. Leitz, Inc.)

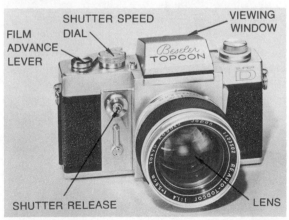

Fig. 138-4. A 35mm single-lens reflex camera. (Charles Beseler Co.)

The miniature-type camera has become popular because it is easy to carry and use. Increased quality of film and the development of color film for slides have also contributed to this popularity. Film for 35mm cameras is purchased in rolls large enough to make 20 or 36 exposures. The 26mm camera, recently developed, is becoming quite popular because the film is packaged in cartridge form for easy loading and handling. The pocket camera, 16mm film size, is a late addition to the wide range of miniature cameras.

SINGLE-LENS REFLEX CAMERA

Single-lens reflex cameras are unique because the photographer views the image, focuses the camera, and makes the exposure through the same lens. Even though this is done with the view camera discussed later, the single-lens reflex camera permits more flexibility than does the view camera because it is more mobile. Most single-lens reflex cameras have lenses that can be removed and replaced with other lenses or attachments.

The most common single-lens reflex cameras use 35mm and 120-size film. Fig. 138-4 shows a 35mm single-lens reflex camera, Fig. 138-5 pictures one which uses 120-film.

Fig. 138-5. A single-lens camera that uses 120-size film. (Paillard, Inc.)

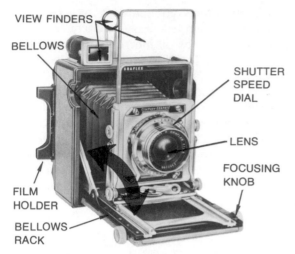

Fig. 138-6. A typical press camera. (Graflex, Inc.)

Fig. 138-7. A press camera with attachments for easy handling. (Graflex, Inc.)

Fig. 138-8. A view camera. (Calumet Mfg. Co.)

Fig. 138-9. A view camera that has been adjusted to compensate for image distortion. (Calumet Mfg. Co.)

PRESS CAMERAS

Press cameras similar to the one shown in Figs. 138-6 and 138-7 became popular because they were used by newspaper photographers. They are bulky and cumbersome but are built to withstand rough treatment. Most press cameras use 4 x 5-inch film, which yields a large negative when detail is required. This type camera has given way, to a great extent, to the more popular and compact twin-lens and single-lens reflex cameras for press photography.

VIEW CAMERAS

Ground glass at the back of the view camera enables the photographer to view what he is photographing (Fig. 138-8). Studio photographers use this type of camera because it yields large 4 x 5-inch and 8 x 10 inch negatives and the photographer can correct for distortion of the image (Fig. 138-9). Because of the size and the view-focus mechanism with ground glass and bellows, this camera is generally used for photographing subjects that are not moving. The film must be loaded into film holders in a darkroom and then put in the camera.

Several other cameras are available for special purposes. *Subminiature* ones use film as small as 9mm wide. *Aerial* cameras are used to photograph large land areas. *Underwater* cameras take pictures below the surface of water. A camera for nearly any purpose can be purchased.

UNIT 139
DETERMINING THE PROPER EXPOSURE

Film is exposed when light strikes the film in the camera. If the proper amount of light enters the camera, the resulting photograph will have maximum detail in all areas. When too much light enters, the negative will become too dark and there will be a loss of detail in the highlight (lightest) areas of the positive print. A negative that has been underexposed with not enough light will be too light and there will be a loss of detail in shadow (dark) areas.

The main factors which must be considered to achieve a properly exposed negative are film speed, amount of light, lens aperture opening (f-stop), and shutter speed. These are interrelated and a change in one requires that the photographer reconsider the others.

FILM SPEED

Film speed indicates the sensitivity of the film to light. Fast film is very sensitive to light and requires less light to make exposures. Slow film is not as sensitive to light as fast film.

The relative speed of film (fast, medium, slow) is indicated by the *ASA* (American Standards Association) numbers listed on the package or on the instruction leaflet that accompanies the film. A fast film will have an ASA number of around 300 or greater; medium-speed film 125 to 200; and slow-speed 100 and less.

Slower film has smaller grain structure than fast film. It tends to produce photographs having more detail than do the fast films with larger grain structure. Select a film with the lowest possible ASA number that will permit the proper exposure, especially when negatives are to be enlarged by several times. An outdoor exposure in bright sun requires a slower film than an exposure made inside a building with little available light.

AMOUNT OF LIGHT

The amount of light needed for an exposure is of prime importance. If too much light enters the camera the negative will be overexposed. It will be too dark and the positive print will be too light. If too little light enters the camera the negative will be underexposed and too light. The final print will, therefore, be too dark.

Light for making exposures can come from either natural or artificial sources. Natural light is produced by the sun. Sources of artificial light are constant ones like flood lights or flash lights. Two common flash sources are the flash gun (Fig. 139-1), and the electronic flash (Fig. 139-2). The flash gun consists of a reflector and a bulb. The

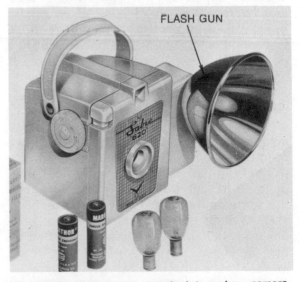

Fig. 139-1. A flash gun attached to a box camera. (Brumberger Co., Inc.)

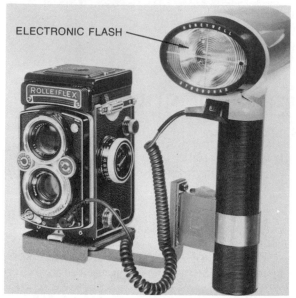

Fig. 139-2. An electronic flash attached to a twin-lens reflex camera. (Honeywell, Inc.)

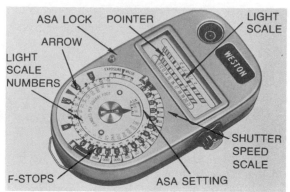

Fig. 139-3. A typical light meter. (Weston Instruments)

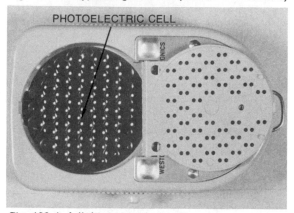

Fig. 139-4. A light meter photocell.

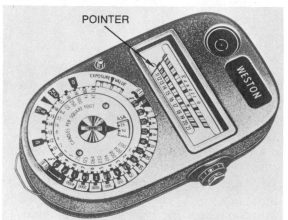

Fig. 139-5. The pointer indicates the amount of light that enters the camera. (Weston Instruments)

bulb is ruined after each exposure and must be replaced with a new one. Electronic flash devices consist of a reflector and bulb, but the bulb can be used several thousand times. A recent development is the *flash cube* having four bulbs. It automatically turns ¼ of a turn each time an exposure is made. Each side has a new bulb. The cube can be used only on cameras built for it.

Measuring light for exposures. Natural light and constant light can be measured by a device called a light meter (Fig. 139-3). Light enters a photoelectric cell as shown in Fig. 139-4 and causes a pointer to move to a number on the scale (Fig. 139-5). The number indicates the *relative* amount of light available for making the exposure.

Measuring light from flashes. Many different sizes and kinds of flash bulbs are manufactured. Each produces a different amount of light, but a particular size always produces a consistent amount of light. For example, a 25B bulb gives more light than does an AG-1B, but all 25B bulbs produce the same amount, as do all AG-1B bulbs.

Flash bulbs have a *guide number* for each film and shutter speed. These are printed on the packages. The guide number determines the exposure values. Electronic flashes used a guide number system similar to the one used for flash bulbs.

LENS APERTURE

The *lens aperture* or iris refers to the size of the opening where light passes through the lens. This was discussed in Unit 50 and should be reviewed. Some cameras have only one lens opening while others have variable lens openings.

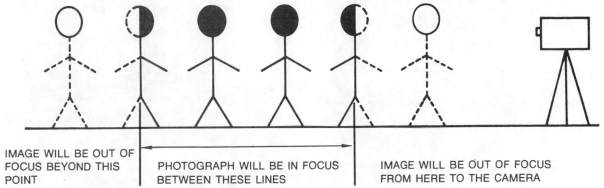

IMAGE WILL BE OUT OF FOCUS BEYOND THIS POINT

PHOTOGRAPH WILL BE IN FOCUS BETWEEN THESE LINES

IMAGE WILL BE OUT OF FOCUS FROM HERE TO THE CAMERA

· Fig. 139-6. Only a certain part of the image in a photograph will be in focus. This is known as the depth of field.

The lens aperture determines the *depth of field* as well as the size of the lens opening. Depth of field is the amount of the photographic subject which will be in focus for a specific lens opening. The distance from the closest part of the photograph to the farthest part in focus is the depth of field. Fig. 139-6 illustrates this. Small lens openings produce a greater depth of field than do larger ones.

SHUTTER

A camera *shutter* permits the photographer to regulate the amount of *time* that light enters the camera. The shutter remains closed to prevent light from entering the camera until the photographer makes the exposure. Different cameras have varying shutter speeds. Common shutter speeds range from one second to 1/500 of a second. Some have speeds of 1/1000 of a second or more. Most cameras also have a *B* shutter setting which permits the photographer to open the shutter for a time period longer than one second. Most inexpensive cameras have a nonadjustable fixed shutter speed.

SELECTING APERTURE AND SHUTTER SPEED

The photographer must control the amount of light which enters the camera to expose the film. This is done by using both the aperture and shutter speed. Several

combinations permit the same amount of light to enter the camera. For example, a correct exposure might require an aperture of f/8 with a shutter speed of 1/100 of a second.

The photographer can also have the same amount of light enter the camera if he uses any of the following combinations:

1. f/11—1/50 of a second
2. f/16—1/25 of a second
3. f/5.6—1/200 of a second
4. f/4—1/400 of a second

Notice that when the f-stop is changed the shutter speed is either doubled or halved.

The photographer must determine which combination of aperture and shutter speed is best for the photograph being taken. If he wants a long depth of field, he will select a combination with a smaller aperture (larger f-number). A very fast-moving subject would need a fast shutter speed and a larger aperture to prevent the image from blurring.

DETERMINING EXPOSURES WITH A LIGHT METER

Several different varieties and qualities of light meters are available to photographers. The photographer must select the light meter which will perform according to his needs. In most cases a photographer selects a light meter which will permit him to make measurements of light that correspond to the cameras he uses. Many newer

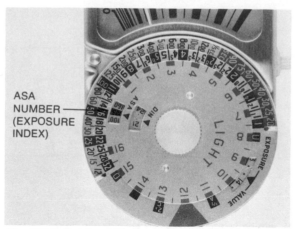

Fig. 139-7. Set the ASA number on the light meter.

Fig. 139-8. Read the number near the pointer. This indicates 11½.

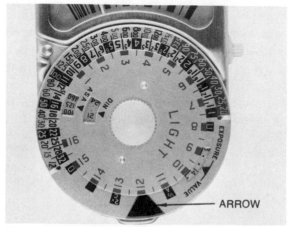

Fig. 139-9. Rotate the dial until the arrow is next to the proper number. Here, it is 12.

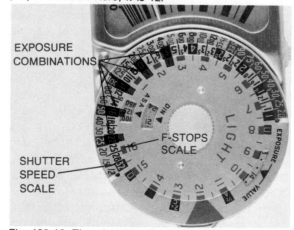

Fig. 139-10. The photographer must select the combination of *f*-stop and shutter speed that fits the situation.

cameras have built-in light meters. Nearly all light meters have slightly different faces and the photographer should be familiar with the markings on his meter. He should also become familiar with the instructions which accompany a light meter when it is purchased.

Regardless of the light meter markings or the arrangement of the parts of the meter, a similar procedure is followed to determine the correct lens opening and shutter speed. The photographer should set the exposure index or ASA number first (Fig. 139-7). The ASA number can be found on the film instruction sheet or on the film package. When the ASA number has been accurately set, point the photoelectric cell of the meter toward the subject. A more accurate reading can be obtained by tilting the meter slightly downward to prevent strong light from directly overhead entering the cell. The light should cause the pointer to move to a number on the scale of the meter (Fig. 139-8). Rotate the dial until the arrow is next to the number indicated on the scale, as shown in Fig. 139-9. The lens openings and shutter speed which will yield a correct exposure will be next to each other on the scale. Fig. 139-10 illustrates that several possibilities are usually available to the photographer. The photographer must select the lens opening and shutter speed which will produce the best exposure for a particular situation. Beginning photographers should experiment to determine the kinds of results which can be obtained.

Light meters can be used for a great number of situations. The procedure given above is used for making conventional exposures. As a photographer attempts to gain special effects he should learn how to make use of the light meter for those situations.

DETERMINING FLASH EXPOSURES

The flash unit on a camera requires a specific size of flash bulb. Each kind of flash bulb has a *guide number* for a particular film and shutter speed. For example, 160 is the guide number for a 25B flash bulb when the bulb is used with film which has an ASA number of 125 and a shutter speed of 1/125 of a second. To obtain the proper lens opening, the number is divided by the distance from the flash to the subject being photographed. If the distance is eight feet from the flash to the subject, the lens opening closest to f/20 would be appropriate. Guide numbers and instructions for various flash bulbs are usually shown on the flash bulb package.

Electronic flash units, while different from flash bulb units, are used in much the same way as flash bulbs. That is, an electronic flash unit has a guide number which is divided by the distance from the flash to the subject. Many photographers tape the appropriate guide number for different film speed on the flash unit as a reminder. Other reminders are also used.

UNIT 140
PHOTOGRAPHIC FILMS AND PAPERS

The two materials on which photographic images are produced are *films* and *papers.* Film is exposed in the camera and produces a negative when developed. The negative is used to expose photographic paper to produce a positive print as shown in Fig. 140-1. The skill which the photographer demonstrates in exposing and developing these materials determines the quality and effect of the final photographic print. In fact, many photographers can be identified by the techniques they use in exposing and processing these materials.

PHOTOGRAPHIC FILM

Photographic films were discussed in Unit 52. While that unit deals primarily with films used for process photography, students should study it again before proceeding with this unit. Many of the characteristics of film such as film bases which are common to film used for both process photography and general photography will not be repeated in this unit.

Fig. 140-1. A photographic positive print.

Films used for general photography are designed to produce a continuous-tone negative. Prints made from continuous-tone negatives yield a full range of tones or grays from white to black. *Panchromatic* film that is sensitive to all colors of light is the film which is most commonly used, but some photographers prefer *orthochromatic* film for special purposes. Orthochromatic film is sensitive to all colors of light but red.

Film speed. Films used for general photography are usually much faster thus more sensitive to light than films for process photography. The speed of film is determined by the size of the silver grains suspended in the emulsion. The larger the grain size, the faster the film. Film speed is indicated by ASA numbers which appear on the package or on the instruction sheet or leaflet which accompanies the film. A slow film has a low ASA number, such as 50; a fast film has a higher number, such as 300.

Before selecting the type of film, consideration should be given as to where it will be used. If pictures are to be taken in minimum light, a fast film is advisable; in bright sunlight, a slow one is best. To achieve consistency many photographers select one or two kinds of films: a slow film for outside and a fast or medium film for inside photographs. By using only one or two kinds of film, the photographer has the opportunity to become extremely familiar as to how the film reacts to specific situations.

Film graininess. Some films produce prints in which the grain is more apparent than in others. Fast films have larger grains suspended in the emulsions and are more likely to yield prints in which the grain is more visible.

Any enlarged negative has a tendency to show grain. For this reason it is desirable to use large rather than small-size film. For example, when enlargements must be made, a 2¼ x 2¼-inch negative will have to be enlarged about five times to yield an 8 x 10-inch print, but a 4 x 5-inch negative must be enlarged only about two times to produce an 8 x 10-inch print.

Fine-grain film should be used when it is necessary to enlarge the negative to obtain

the correct size of print. The grains in fine-grain film are smaller, seem to blend together, and are less noticeable when enlargements are made. The grain structure on fast film with coarse grain structure is usually very noticeable on even small enlargements. The method and procedures used to develop film also affects grainy appearance of a print. Fig. 140-4 shows an enlargement with a grainy appearance.

Film sizes. Camera and film manufacturers have generally agreed on a few standard sizes of film and also on the method of packaging a particular size. They build their cameras so that one of the standard film sizes will fit into them. Some common

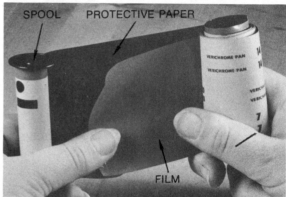

Fig. 140-2. A roll of 120 film and its contents.

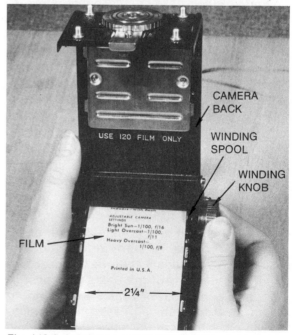

Fig. 140-3. Loading a roll of 120 film into a camera.

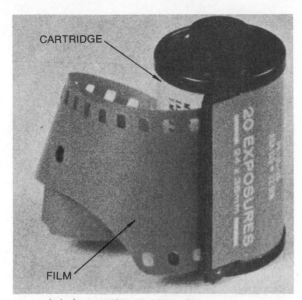

Fig. 140-4. A magazine of 35mm film

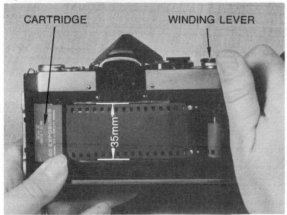

Fig. 140-5. Loading 35mm film.

sizes of films are 35mm (135 magazines), 120 film, 620 film, and 4 x 5-inch film. A recently developed product is 26mm film, packaged in easy-to-load cartridges.

Films are packaged in rolls, magazines, cartridges, or sheets. Roll film comes on a spool and is held on by a paper cover (Fig. 140-2). It is loaded in the camera as shown in Fig. 140-3.

Film 35mm in size is packaged in magazines or cartridges. There are 20 or 36 exposures (Fig. 140-4). Fig. 140-5 shows 35mm film being loaded into a camera.

Sheet film is loaded into film holders which are placed into the camera to make exposures. A different film holder must be placed into the camera for each exposure.

PHOTOGRAPHIC PAPERS

There are many varieties of photographic papers for making positive prints. A piece of photographic paper consists of a base and an emulsion. The photographer should be familiar with all types in order to choose the one best suited for specific needs.

Bases. Photographic base papers must be of high quality. They are white in color and free of all impurities, and are sufficiently substantial to withstand development chemicals, water, rapid drying, and age.

The bases are made in varying weights. Two of the most commonly used are single weight (SW) and double weight (DW). Single-weight papers are more economical and are used when prints will have only slight abuse. Double-weight papers take longer to dry. They are used to make large prints and ones which will receive considerable handling. Photographs for display, such as portraits, are often printed on this heavier paper.

Emulsions. The emulsion on photographic printing papers, as on film, consists of light-sensitive crystals suspended in a gelatin. The emulsion is coated on the base which is usually paper. Emulsions are made of either silver chloride, silver bromide, and chlorobromide which is a combination of chloride and bromide salts.

Silver chloride emulsions are least sensitive to light and are referred to as slow emulsions. Chloride papers are used primarily for contact printing because the light source is relatively close to the paper and therefore more intense.

Silver bromide emulsions are used in enlarging and for projection printing papers. They are much more sensitive to light.

Chlorobromide emulsions yield a medium-speed paper. It can be used for either contact or projection printing.

Emulsions on paper are considerably slower than those on film. They also are not sensitive to some colors of light. Because of this, certain papers can be handled in a darkroom with particular safelights. Instructions of manufacturers usually indicate the appropriate safelight for a specific printing paper.

Emulsion contrasts. Printing papers are manufactured in several grades of contrast to help the photographer adjust for negative-contrast variations. Contact papers are usually made in six grades or contrasts. Each has a number ranging from 0 to 5. A *flat* negative with very little contrast should be printed on number 3, 4, or 5 paper.

Projection papers are also graded by number, but manufacturers do not have complete agreement on the range. Like contact papers, projection papers of a low number such as 1 can be used to print negatives with high contrast, or hard negatives. The larger numbers 3, 4, or 5 should be used with negatives of little contrast. Normal negatives are printed with average-contrast paper.

Another type of printing paper has only a single grade but produces a complete range of contrasts in negatives. Adjustment for the various contrasts is accomplished by using filters on the enlarger. By using this type of paper the photographer does not have to purchase several packages of paper with different contrast numbers.

Printing paper finishes. Photographic printing papers are available in several finishes. The most common one is called *glossy* and has a very shiny surface. Other finishes are termed *semimatte, matte, silk,* and *rough.*

Papers are also manufactured with varying degrees of whiteness. Colors include cream white, white, snow white, and old ivory. They are designed to induce psychological effects. Dealers usually have available samples of all finishes and colors.

UNIT 141
FILM DEVELOPMENT

When film is exposed, a latent image is produced on the film. A *latent image* consists of silver salt in the film emulsion which has been exposed to light. It cannot be seen until the actual image on the film has been developed. The image on the developed negative is an opposite of the original subject which was photographed. Where the subject was light, the negative will be dark and the lighter the area of the subject, the darker the corresponding negative area. The areas of the subject which are dark and reflect very little light will appear to be clear on the developed negative. There usually are some areas of the subject which are somewhere between light and dark. The in-between areas will appear to be gray on the negative after development.

DEVELOPMENT CHEMICALS

Continuous-tone film is processed in four different solutions—They are developer, stop bath, fixer, and water. The photographer should be careful to select chemicals which will be compatible. Most photographers select a specific kind or brand of the various chemicals and use them exclusively. By doing this they learn precisely what kinds of results will be obtained when film is developed.

Developer. The developer transforms the exposed silver halide crystals to metallic silver. Developers are known as *reducers* because they divide the chemical compound silver halide to a basic part which is metallic silver. Several developers are available for film development. Each is designed for a specific purpose. Some help produce extremely fine-grain negatives; others yield a coarse grain. Those which produce a fine-grain negative usually work slower than developers which produce medium or coarse grain. The beginning photographer should select the developer recommended by the film manufacturer in order to get acceptable results.

Stop baths. Stop baths which are used for continuous-tone film are similar to those used for developing process negatives. Many photographers use a mild acetic acid solution and others prefer clean water. Film should remain in a water-stop bath longer than in the acetic acid one. The purpose of a stop bath is to *stop* the developing action of the developer and to reduce the amount of contamination of the fixer.

Fixers. The fixers used in continuous-tone film processing are the same as those used in making process negatives. They remove the unexposed and undeveloped silver crystals and harden the emulsion of the film. After fixing has occurred, the negatives are safe in room light.

Water. Washing with water is a necessary function because the fixing solution and all other chemicals must be washed from the film with it.

Wetting agent. Many photographers like to place the film, after it has been developed, into a wetting agent or solution. This should be done after the film has been washed. This solution reduces the number of water spots on the film after it dries.

DEVELOPING FILM

Continuous-tone film must be developed in total darkness. Even the smallest amount of any kind of light will ruin the film. Two techniques used for this process are tray development and tank development. Even sheet film is frequently developed by the tank method which is popular for roll-type films.

Equipment. Many pieces of the equipment used to develop process negatives are also used for continuous-tone film. The pho-

tographer, in addition to having the required chemicals, should have an appropriate developing tank, thermometer, graduate, funnel, and timer.

Developing tanks. Several kinds of developing tanks are available for developing both roll and sheet film. Tanks are made of plastic, stainless steel, or hard rubber. Some are adjustable for several different sizes of film and others are made for a specific size of film only. Fig. 141 shows a typical plastic developing tank used to develop various sizes of roll film. Fig. 141-2 pictures a stainless steel tank used for developing one size of film only.

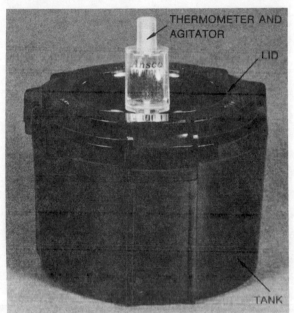

Fig. 141-1. An adjustable plastic developing tank.

Fig. 141-2. A stainless steel developing tank for 35mm film.

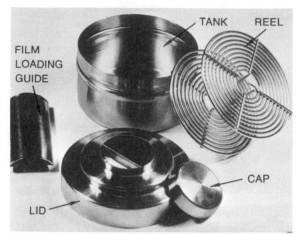

Fig. 141-3. The parts of the tank in Fig. 141-2.

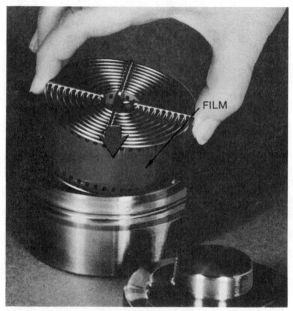

Fig. 141-4. Placing a reel into a developing tank.

Fig. 141-5. Pouring chemicals into a tank.

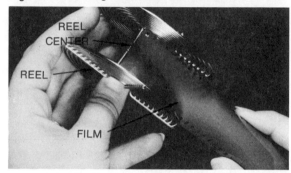

Fig. 141-6. The film is loaded from the center toward the outside of the reel.

Developing tanks simplify the development process. Once the tanks are loaded with film, they are light-tight and the film can be developed in a lighted room. Fig. 141-3 pictures the parts of a stainless steel developing tank used only for 35mm film. The film is loaded into the reel and placed in the tank (Fig. 141-4). After the film is loaded and the lid is in place, the chemicals are poured in and out of the holes on the top of the lid (Fig. 141-5).

Loading roll film. A major difference between types of tanks used for roll film is in the kind of reel on which the film is loaded. Regardless of the kind of reel in the tank,

the film must be loaded in total darkness. The photographer should practice loading the reel, using a dummy roll of film, until he can do it efficiently with his eyes closed.

The photographer in Fig. 141-6 is loading a reel in which the film is started at the *center* of the reel. The film is fitted into the grooves of the reel by bending the film slightly.

Fig. 141-7 shows the photographer loading a reel on which the film is fed into the reel from the *outside* toward the center of the reel. In this case, the reel works like a ratchet and automatically feeds the film into the reel. All that has to be done is feed the end of the film into the slots on the reel, as shown in Fig. 141-7. When this is done the sides of the reel are turned back and forth until the film is loaded (Fig. 141-8). The reel in this tank must be completely dry before loading the film, or the film will stick and thus not feed into the reel properly. Be-

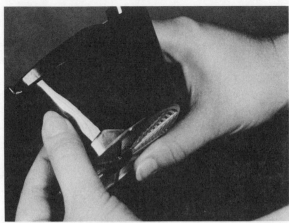

Fig. 141-7. The film is started at the outside edge of the reel and is fed toward the center.

Fig. 141-8. Feeding the film using a ratchet action.

Fig. 141-9. Arranging tank parts for easy location in the dark.

cause the tank must be loaded in total darkness, the photographer must organize the tank parts before starting to load the film (Fig. 141-9).

Processing the film. The following factors are of prime importance when developing film. They are development time, temperature of the chemicals, and agitation of the film during development. The photographer should follow the recommendations of the film or developer manufacturer with reference to these factors.

All of the chemicals should be collected and prepared by the photographer before loading the film into the tank. Developer, stop bath, fixer, and wetting agent must be brought to very nearly the same tempera-

ture. An easy way to accomplish this is to place all of the chemicals into containers. The containers can be placed in running water of the desired development temperature for a period of time until the chemicals are the same temperature as the water. This will also establish the correct water temperature for washing the film after it has been developed.

When the film has been loaded into the tank, the tank should be filled with water of the same temperature as the temperature of the chemicals. Agitate the tank while the water is in it to prevent air bubbles from forming when the developer is poured into the tank. Once the film is completely wet, pour the water out of the tank. Be sure that all of the water is gone so that the developer will not be diluted.

Fill the tank with *developer* as quickly as possible. If the developer is poured into the tank too slowly, the lower edge of the film will develop more than the upper edge. The film should remain in the tank for the time specified by the manufacturer. Be sure to agitate the film in the developer as recommended. Correct agitation causes new developer to come into contact with the film in the tank. Too much agitation will cause overdevelopment, and streaks will occur if the film is not agitated enough. Pour the developer out of the tank when the film has been developed for the correct amount of time. Some developers are re-used and may be returned to the container while other developers are discarded after use. Check the recommendations of the manufacturer or information about the correct procedure.

Stop bath should be poured into the tank *immediately* after development. If this is not done, the action of the developer will continue and the result will be overdevelopment of the film.

Many photographers prefer to use clear water as a stop bath instead of an acetic acid solution. When water is used, the tank can be placed under running water. The stop bath should be poured out of the tank when it has sufficiently stopped the action of the developer. Some photographers like to wash out the tank with clear water to eliminate the acetic acid stop bath before fixing the film.

When the developing action has been stopped, the fixer should be poured into the tank. Be sure to fix the film long enough to remove the undeveloped silver salts. Most manufacturers recommend a specific amount of time for fixing film. The fixer should be poured back into the container for reuse after the fixing is complete.

After the film has been fixed, the tank lid can be removed. Place the tank under running water of the same temperature as the other solutions. The washing will remove all of the processing chemicals from the film very easily.

The film should be placed in a *wetting agent* to prevent water spots from forming on the film. This should be done after the film has been removed from the reel.

Clips should be attached to both ends of the film and it should be hung in a dust-free location until it is dry. Extreme care should be used to prevent dust and finger prints from forming on the film surfaces. This can be partially accomplished by placing the dry negatives in envelopes and handling the film only by the edges.

It is very important that the developing tank be thoroughly cleaned after use. It should be washed completely in running water, especially in all the corners and ridges to eliminate all of the chemicals from these parts. Be sure to dry all parts of the tank so that it will not collect dust. The tank should also be stored in a good dust-free location.

CONTACT PRINTING

Photographs are made by passing light through a negative onto photographic paper. This process which produces a picture exactly like the original subject is known as photographic printing. The two most common methods of making photographic prints are *contact* printing and *projection* printing.

A photograph or positive print is obtained because of the various densities from opaque to clear in the negative. More light passes through the clear areas than through the dark, opaque densities. Places where light strikes the photographic paper turn dark after development. If only a little light strikes the paper as in the gray areas of the negative, the photographic paper turns gray. When no light strikes the paper, the paper will be white when developed.

Contact printing produces a photograph that is the same size as the image on the negative. Several prominent photographers perfer to make contact prints because of the detail and lack of observable grain in the print. Contact printing, however, is not appropriate for small-size negatives.

Contact printing is the simplest method of making a photographic print. The negative is placed in contact with photographic paper with the emulsion side of the film next to the emulsion side of the paper (Fig. 142-1). Light passes through the negative and strikes the paper. It is then processed in a developer, stop bath, fixer, and water.

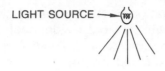

LIGHT SOURCE

NEGATIVE BASE — NEGATIVE — PAPER EMULSION — EMULSION — PHOTOGRAPHIC PAPER — BASE

Fig. 142-1. Contact prints are made with the negative emulsion pressed tightly against the photographic paper emulsion.

GLASS
BACK
FRAME

Fig. 142-2. A crude contact printing frame.

CONTACT PRINTING DEVICES

The two devices used to make contact prints are the contact printing frame (Fig. 142-2) and the *contact printer* (Fig. 142-3). When the frame is used, the negative is placed with the base or shiny side against the glass. The printing paper is placed over the negative with the emulsion side against the negative. The pressure plate back is then placed over both (Fig. 142-4). The frame is placed in front of a light source to expose the paper. The printing frame must be loaded in a darkroom with only the safelight on.

The contact printer is usually more elaborate and easy to use than the printing frame. It is a box with a glass plate on top. A light source is located in the base and a platen holds the film and paper tightly together. Most contact printers have a safelight in the base which helps the photographer to lo-

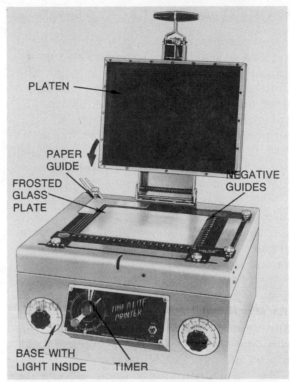

PLATEN
PAPER GUIDE
FROSTED GLASS PLATE
NEGATIVE GUIDES
BASE WITH LIGHT INSIDE
TIMER

Fig. 142-3. A contact printer. (Industrial Timer Corp.)

Fig. 142-4. Assembling a contact printing frame.

cate the film and paper. Many contact printers have a timer to control the exposure time accurately.

The base side of the negative is placed on the glass plate of the printer. The photographic paper is positioned on top of the negative with the emulsion side down. The platen is closed and the light is turned on to make the exposure.

MAKING A CONTACT PRINT

The process of making a contact print consists of making an exposure and developing the exposed photographic paper. The photographer must select the exposure technique appropriate for his situation. The discussion which follows will relate to making prints with a contact printing frame.

All of the negatives should be examined and grouped according to the relative contrast of the negatives. Negatives which have a high degree of contrast will appear to have many areas that are clear or opaque. Normal contrast negatives will have several shades of gray as well as clear and dark areas. Flat negatives will consist primarily of shades of gray with almost no clear or dark areas. The negatives should be examined and stored in a dust-free location and the photographer should handle the negatives with care to prevent fingerprints from getting on the negative surfaces.

The contact printing frame should be thoroughly cleaned to eliminate dust, dirt, lint, and fingerprints. Any dirt on either the negative or the printing frame could ruin the print. The frame should be handled to prevent dirt and fingerprints from reaching the frame after it has been cleaned.

Development solutions can be prepared after the frame is ready but before it is loaded. Trays slightly larger than the largest print to be made should be filled with the appropriate developer, stop bath, and fixer. The temperature of the chemicals should be between 68° and 75° F. as recommended by the manufacturer. In addition to the three trays for the chemicals, one large tray should be prepared with running water.

Place the negative on the glass of the printing frame with the base side against the glass of the frame. Several small negatives can be positioned on the glass of a large printing frame, provided they have the same relative contrasts. All of this can be done in normal room light.

At this point the darkroom door should be closed and the white lights turned off. Safelights, as specified by the manufacturer of the printing paper, should be turned on. With the safelights on, place a piece of contact paper over the negative with the emulsion side of the paper against the negative.

Make a test exposure to determine the best exposure. This is done by placing a piece of opaque paper over all but a small strip of the negative. The exposure is made by turning on the light for a certain number of seconds. After the first exposure is made, move the piece of opaque paper to expose a little more of the negative and make the second exposure for the same length of time as the first exposure. Repeat this procedure until the entire negative is exposed. The beginning photographer should use number 2 paper until he learns to distinguish negative contrasts more accurately.

The test strip should be developed using *precisely* the same technique that will be used to develop the final prints. Process the photographic print by placing it in the developer tray until the image is visible. Remove the print, place it in the stop bath for 30 seconds, then into the fixer solution for 5 minutes. Then wash and dry thoroughly. When the negative has been processed, examine it to select the strip which has the most normal contrast (Fig. 142-5). If none of

OVEREXPOSURE   CORRECT EXPOSURE   UNDEREXPOSURE

12 SEC   10 SEC   8 SEC   6 SEC   4 SEC   2 SEC

Fig. 142-5. A test strip made to determine the proper exposure time.

the strips is good, repeat the procedure until a good test strip is obtained. The procedure should be repeated for all negatives having significantly different contrasts.

After the correct exposure time has been established, place another piece of paper in the frame and expose it for the correct amount of time. This exposure should be developed exactly like the test exposure. If the procedure is accurate, the resulting photograph should look like the one in Fig. 142-6.

WASHING AND DRYING PRINTS

A photographic print must be thoroughly washed and dried after it has been fixed. Many photographers tend to ignore proper practice and the result is an inferior print.

Washing. Wash prints for at least one hour in clean, running water. A special tray which allows frequent changes of water should be used. If the prints are not completely washed they will discolor quickly.

Drying. A print is dried according to the finish desired on the print. Use a *ferrotype*

Fig. 142-6. A contact print made by using the test exposure time from Fig. 142-5.

plate for a glossy finish. This is a plate of metal with a highly polished surface. Place the print on the plate with the emulsion side down. Roll with a roller to remove the excess water and to produce good contact. There are print dryers available with a polished, heated plate to speed the drying process. If a rough, or matte, finish is desired, the print is placed between photo blotters and permitted to remain there until completely dry.

UNIT 143
PROJECTION PRINTING

Projection printing or enlarging is another method of producing photographic prints. Where the contact printing method discussed in Unit 142 yields a photographic print that is the same size as the image on the negative, projection printing permits the photographer to make prints which are larger than the negative. Prints are enlarged by using a device called an *enlarger* (Fig. 143-1).

Projection printing provides several advantages over contact printing. The main advantage is that it is possible to secure prints which are much larger than those ob-

tained from contact printing. It is easier to use only a portion of the negative to make a print. The photographer can also control the contrast and distortion in certain areas of the print better than he can in contact printing. The primary disadvantage of projection printing is that by enlarging the image of the negative, the grain structure of the negative is also enlarged and is much more visible on the final print. With the current popularity of smaller cameras, such as the 35mm, enlarging is essential to obtain a print large enough to be useful. When it is known that a negative is to be enlarged,

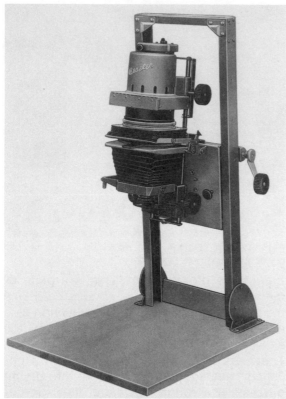

Fig. 143-1. A typical enlarger. (Charles Beseler Co.)

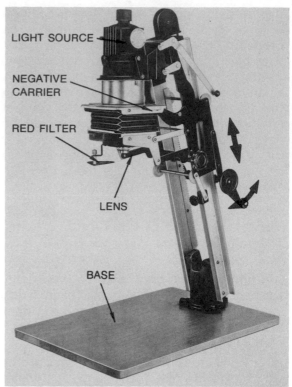

Fig. 143-2. The essential parts of an enlarger. (Simmon-Omega)

it is very important that the photographer use every precaution to keep the grain structure of the negative at a minimum.

ENLARGERS

Enlargers are used to make projection prints or enlargements. Enlargers are available in several qualities and sizes. There is also a large variety of attachments which can be used with the enlarger.

The primary parts of an enlarger are the light source, negative carrier, lens, and base. These parts, plus a *red filter,* are shown in Fig. 143-2. The light source is located in the top of the enlarger so that it will shine through the negative. Different light sources are available for certain enlargers. The negative carrier is a frame that is used to hold the negative in a flat position parallel to the enlarger base. Most enlargers have several film carriers for different sizes of film. Lenses are possibly the most important and costly part of the enlarger. The lens, in addition to being a major element

in determining the print quality, is used to control the amount of light that reaches the print paper. The base is used to hold the projection paper when making an enlargement.

The negative is held in the enlarger between the light source and the base where the projection paper is held. As the light passes through the negative and lens, the image spreads out (Fig. 143-3). The farther the negative is from the base, the larger the projected image. The image is *focused* by varying the distance between the negative and the lens.

MAKING A PROJECTION PRINT

The primary differences between contact printing and projection are the methods used to expose the paper and the kind of paper used to make the print. Processing of the exposed print paper is the same as was described in Unit 142. The photographer should consult the manufacturer's recom-

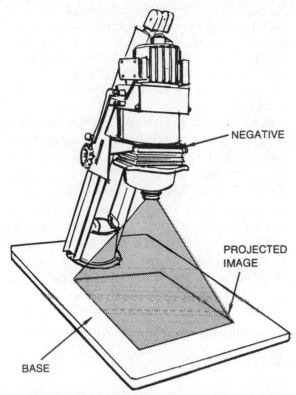

Fig. 143-3. the projected image spreads out as the negative moves farther away from the base of the enlarger.

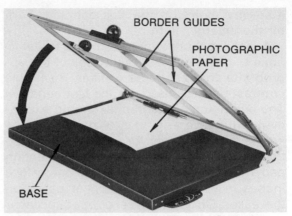

Fig. 143-4. An enlarging easel. (Simmon-Omega)

mendations regarding the kind of developer to use with the projection paper. The trays can be arranged in the same manner as for contact printing. Be sure to use trays which are larger than the size of the paper being used to make the prints.

Like all other photographic activities, special care must be taken to eliminate all dust and dirt from the activity area. The enlarger should be cleaned before beginning to make prints. If possible the inside of the enlarger should be vacuumed frequently to remove dust and dirt which normally collect. Keeping the enlarger covered when it is not in use keeps dirt to a minimum. The lens should also be cleaned to remove dirt and fingerprints. The negative carrier and easel are areas which tend to collect dirt.

The negatives should be examined and dust should be cleaned from them. Care must be taken to keep from damaging the negative. Many photographers use a fine brush or blow the dust and dirt from the negatives. Dirt remaining on the negative

will be magnified and will be quite visible on the final print.

Place the negative into the negative carrier. The emulsion side should be toward the lens. Be very careful not to scratch the negative or get fingerprints on it while placing the negative in the carrier or while placing the carrier into the enlarger. The negative carrier, including the negative, should be placed in the correct position in the enlarger.

Adjust the *easel* to the desired print size and place it on the base of the enlarger. Easels are used to hold the print paper flat while making an enlargement. An example of an easel is shown in Fig. 143-4. Place a piece of white paper in the easel where the print paper will be held.

Turn on the darkroom safelights and turn off the white light. The darkroom must be dark to enable accurate adjustments on the enlarger. When the darkroom is dark, turn on the enlarger light and adjust the lens so that maximum light reaches the easel. Adjust the location of the easel and enlarger head (light source, negative carrier, and lens) until the correct size image is obtained on the easel.

The image should be focused by adjusting the lens. This adjustment sometimes changes the size of the image and will cause the need for the head to be readjusted. When the image is in focus, reduce the lens opening until the extremely fine detail of the negative is gone. Then open the lens until the detail is first visible. This provides a starting point on the lens opening. Turn off the enlarger light.

A test exposure should be made to determine the best exposure time. Select the appropriate contrast paper or filter, if variable contrast paper is used, for the test negative. The beginning photographer should experiment with several grades of paper until he knows the best paper for negatives of a particular contrast. Cut the piece of projection paper into several strips of about one or two inches in width. Place a strip of paper on the easel. Obtain a piece of opaque paper and place it over the entire strip except for a small portion at one end. Turn on the enlarger for about two seconds. This time varies for different kinds of paper. Move the opaque paper a small distance to expose a little more of the strip and make another two-second exposure. Continue this procedure until the entire test strip is exposed.

Process the test strip as described in Unit 142. The test exposure should appear much like the one shown in Fig. 142-5. Examine the test to determine the best exposure time. More than one test strip might have to be made if a good exposure cannot be identified.

After the best exposure time has been determined, place a piece of print paper in the easel. The photographer should be sure that his hands are clean and dry before handling the print paper. Make the exposure by using the same exposure time determined by the test exposure. The procedure used to develop the print must be precisely the same as the procedure used to develop the test strip. Be sure that the prints are permitted to wash long enough to remove all of the chemicals. Use the drying technique that will yield the desired print finish.

UNIT 144
FINISHING AND MOUNTING PRINTS

After the photographic prints have been processed in chemicals and thoroughly washed, they must receive additional attention before they are ready for use. Finishing operations usually consist of drying, applying a finish, and mounting. The finishing techniques and mounting methods used with photographs are determined by the kind of paper used and the preference of the photographer or customer.

Finishing is the process of applying an appropriate surface to the photographic print. While several kinds of surfaces are available on papers such as glass, matte, and linen, they are usually finished with a gloss or dull surface.

Photographs which are to be used for reproduction (printed) should be finished with a gloss surface. The gloss surface increases the quality of the black areas and lengthens the *tonal range.* Tonal range is the difference between the highlight areas and the shadow areas.

When photographs are to be used for decoration, the photographer selects a paper with a finish suitable for the situation. For example, portraits are often printed on matte surface papers to produce a *soft* effect. Billfold prints are sometimes printed on linen surface paper with a semigloss surface because this surface does not become soiled as easily as a matte surface paper.

DRYING

Photographic prints absorb large quantities of liquid during the development and washing process. By the time a print is ready to dry the only liquid that should be contained in the print is clear water. If any of the development chemicals remain in the print paper, there is a chance that the print will be discolored after drying.

Prints can be either air dried or dried by applying heat from a drying device. Air drying is much slower and most photographers use commercial drying machines. The results, however, are the same whether prints are air dried or heat dried.

APPLYING GLOSS SURFACES

Gloss surface prints are dried with the surface of the print against the surface of a *ferrotype* plate. A ferrotype plate is a thin sheet of metal with a highly polished, shiny finish on the surface. The quality of the surface of the ferrotype plate determines the quality of the finish on the print. Photographers take special precautions to protect the surface of the ferrotype plate from scratches, surface pits, fingerprints, dust, and dirt. Commercial print dryers have large drums with ferrotype surfaces.

The ferrotype plate should be thoroughly cleaned before applying a print to the surface of it. Flush the surface of the plate with clean water first to remove loose dust and dirt. Dry the plate with a soft cloth.

After the print has been thoroughly washed but before it is removed from the water, rub your hand over the surface of the paper. This removes the air bubbles that have collected on the surface of the print during washing. Lift the print from the wash tray by holding two adjacent corners of the print.

Hold the print over the ferrotype plate and slowly lower it onto the plate. Place the print so that it *rolls* onto the surface of the plate. This prevents air bubbles from forming between the print and the plate. Use a squeegee or roller to smooth the print on the plate and to remove excess water. A window washer blade works as well as a squeegee. Be sure to press the print into firm contact with the plate (Fig. 144-1).

Place a photographic blotter sheet over the back of the print and roll it with a roller (Fig. 144-2). Permit the print to dry on the plate until it pops off of the plate by itself.

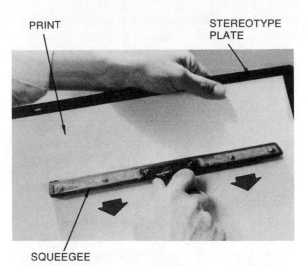

Fig. 144-1. Press the photographic print firmly against the ferrotype plate with a squeegee.

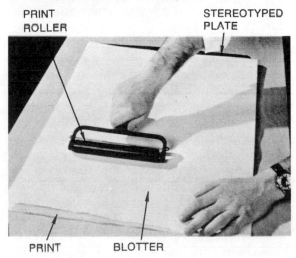

Fig. 144-2. Place a photographic blotter over the back of the print and roll it with a roller.

Drying speed can be increased by placing the plate near a heater or by using a print dryer.

APPLYING DULL FINISHES

Similar procedures to those used to dry gloss prints are used to dry prints which require dull or matte finishes. Prints should be placed between two pieces of photographic blotter paper. The rough surface of the blotter paper gives the prints their surface texture. When heated dryers are used, carefully place the back of the print against the ferrotype plate. Blotters can be obtained from most photographic supply stores.

MOUNTING PHOTOGRAPHS

Many situations require that photographs be mounted by attaching the print to a heavier piece of material. This is usually done when the print will be handled frequently or displayed. A good mounting enhances the appearance of a photograph because it prevents the surroundings from detracting from the image on the print.

Photographs are mounted on heavy material called *mounting board.* It is available in colors and with several different kinds of surfaces from most art supply stores. The more frequently used boards are white and gray but other colors are appropriate for other circumstances.

The most satisfactory method of mounting photographs is to use *dry mounting tissue.* This material is heat-sensitive and is placed between the print and mounting board. The heat causes the dry mounting tissue to bond to both the back of the print and the front of mounting board.

To mount a photograph attach a piece of dry mounting tissue about the same size as the print to the center of the back of the print. Use a *tacking iron* as shown in Fig. 144-3, or a household iron. When the household iron is used, set the control at a temperature appropriate for silk or wool. The dry mounting tissue should then be trimmed to the same size as the print. The tissue should not be visible.

After the dry mounting tissue has been applied to the print, mark the exact location of the print on the mounting board. Make the marks light enough to be removed if necessary. Place the print on the board and attach the mounting tissue on three corners with the tacking iron (Fig. 144-3).

When the print is tacked to the mounting board, place the print into a *dry mounting press* for about one minute. The press temperature should range from 200° to 275°F. If a dry mounting press is not available, a household iron can be used quite effectively. Place a double thickness of paper over

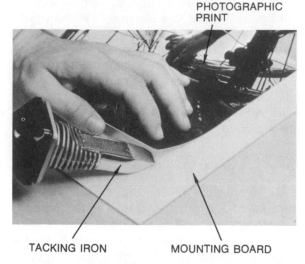

PHOTOGRAPHIC PRINT

TACKING IRON   MOUNTING BOARD

Fig. 144-3. Attach three corners of the dry mounting tissue to the mounting board.

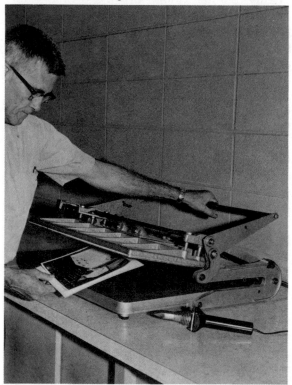

Fig. 144-4. The dry mounting operation.

the print and apply the iron to the surface with the temperature set between silk and wool. Be sure to keep the iron moving so that the heat will be evenly distributed. Work from the center of the print to the edges.

UNIT 145
LEARNING EXPERIENCES: PHOTOGRAPHY

DISCUSSION TOPICS

1. Name the three main steps necessary to make a photograph.
2. List the three essential characteristics of cameras. Explain each.
3. Describe the six kinds of cameras discussed in this section. Give some advantages and disadvantages of each. Identify some special kinds of cameras used for specific photographic jobs.
4. What are the four main factors which must be considered when determining exposures? Give the result of permitting too much light to enter the camera. What is the result of not enough light entering the camera?
5. Give another name used to describe the act of taking a picture.
6. Explain what is meant by the term *film speed.* How is the photographer able to determine whether a particular film has a fast, medium, or slow film speed? Give an example of an ASA number for a fast, medium, and slow speed film.
7. How does the grain structure relate to film speed? To what extent will this affect the kind of film a photographer selects for taking pictures?
8. If too much light enters the camera, how will the negative appear? How will the positive print appear? Describe the appearance of the negatives and positives when too little light has entered the camera. What is the name of the problem which occurs as the result of too much light? Too little light?
9. Give the two main sources of light available for making exposures and give examples of each.

10. What is the name of the device used to measure natural and constant artifical light? Which part causes the pointer to move?
11. Give another name for the lens aperature of a camera. What is the primary purpose of it? Identify another effect of the lens aperature.
12. Explain the purpose of the shutter on a camera. Give some of the common speeds of shutters. What does the *B* setting on a shutter mean?
13. List the procedure for determining the shutter speed for a camera when using a constant light source. How does a change in the aperature opening affect the shutter speed?
14. How does the photographer determine the exposure setting when using a flash?
15. Explain the difference between panchromatic film and orthochromatic film. Why is panchromatic film more useful for general photography than orthochromatic film?
16. List some common film sizes. Name some different methods of packaging film.
17. What is the purpose of photographic paper? Describe some of the differences in bases and emulsions used to make photographic papers.
18. Explain what is meant by *emulsion contrasts.* How does the photographer use paper contrasts in his work? Describe some different finishes used on photographic papers.
19. How does a latent image differ from a

visible one? Explain how the visible image of a negative compares with the original subject that was photographed.

20. Name the solutions required to process film. Describe and explain the purpose of each.
21. List the procedures used to process film. What equipment is required for effective film development?
22. Give two methods used to make positive prints. What is the main difference between the two methods?
23. Identify the two devices used to make contact prints. How does the size of the print compare to the size of the negative used to make the print?
24. Give the procedure for making a contact print. How is the proper exposure time determined?
25. What is the unique advantage of projection printing? Give another name for this technique.
26. Describe the enlarger and its primary parts. How is the size of the positive print determined? Tell how the photographer focuses the negative image on the printing paper. What is the name of the device used to hold the projection paper flat and in the proper position for making a print?
27. Give the procedure for making a projection print. Explain how the proper exposure time is determined for making a projection print.
28. What is the purpose of ferrotyping? How does the finished print appear? Describe the ferrotype plate. Give the procedure for ferrotyping a positive print.
29. When is it necessary to mount a print? Give the name and describe the material commonly used to mount prints. List the procedure for mounting a print.

ACTIVITIES

1. Obtain and examine several different kinds of cameras. Compare them by identifying differences with respect to the essential parts.
2. Secure an exposure meter and determine the possible lens aperature and shutter speeds for a film with an ASA number of 125. Compare your results with those of another person. If there are differences, try to determine why they occurred.
3. Expose a roll of film using the following procedure. The procedure is designed for a roll of film with twelve exposures, but could be done with more or less exposures on the roll.
   a. Expose the first frame three f-stops greater than a normal exposure.
   b. Expose the second frame two f-stops greater than a normal exposure.
   c. Expose the third frame one f-stop greater than a normal exposure.
   c. Make a normal exposure for the fourth frame.
   e. Expose the fifth frame one f-stop smaller than a normal exposure.
   f. Expose the sixth frame two f-stops smaller than a normal exposure.
   g. Expose the seventh frame three f-stops smaller.
   h. Record the settings and expose the next five frames varying the f-stop and shutter speed to obtain a normal exposure.
   Process the film to obtain normal negatives. Examine the negatives and identify the differences among them. Make projection prints from the negatives using normal contrast paper and process the prints to obtain good prints from the normal negatives.
4. Visit your photographic retail store and identify the kinds of equipment available for black-and-white photography. Learn the cost of equipment and supplies.
5. Visit your local professional photographer and ask him about some of the techniques he uses to produce his photographs. What kinds of equipment does he use in his work? Prepare a detailed report on your visit.
6. If there is a company which specializes in general fast photographic service in your community, visit it. Try to identify differences between the company's procedure and that of a professional photographer.

The Story of My Life in the Printing Industry

By DR. BENJAMIN FRANKLIN

Philadelphia—I was born in Boston, New England, on January 17, 1706. My father had seven children by his first wife and by a second wife ten more. I was the youngest son and the youngest child.

My elder brothers were all put apprentices to different trades. I was put to the grammar-school at eight years of age, my father intending to devote me, as the tithe of his sons, to the service of the Church. My early readiness in learning to read and the opinion of all his friends, that I should certainly make a good scholar, encouraged him in this purpose of his.

I continued at the grammar-school not quite one year until my father, from a view of the expense, took me from the grammar-school and sent me to a school for writing and arithmetic. I acquired fair writing pretty soon, but I failed in the arithmetic and at ten years old I was taken home to assist my father in his business of a tallow-chandler and sope-boiler. I disliked the trade.

My bookish inclination, at length, determined my father to make me a printer, though he had already one son (James) of that profession. In 1717 James returned from England with a press and letters to set up his business in Boston. I signed the indentures when I was yet but twelve years old, to serve as an apprentice till I was twenty-one.

In 1720 or 1721, James begun to print a newspaper, the New England Courant, the second that appeared in America. I remember his being disuaded by some friends from the undertaking, as not likely to succeed, one newspaper being, in their judgment, enough for America. Not long later, some problems at the printinghouse and action by the Assembly came to the return of my old indenture to me, and when a difference arose between my brother and me, I took upon me to assert my freedom, presuming that he would not venture to produce new indentures.

When he found I would leave him, he took care to prevent me getting employment in any other printinghouse of the town by going round and speaking to every master. By selling some of my books for passage I went to New York on a sloop. I was then a boy of but 17.

I could find no employment in New York, but was sent on by a gentleman to one Keimer's printinghouse in Philadelphia. Keimer asked me a few questions, put a composing stick in my hand to see how I worked and then said he would employ me.

The printers at Philadelphia were wretched ones, and I, appearing a young man of promising parts, was asked by the governor to have my own business he would set up. I would first go to London to improve myself so that on my return to America I could set up to greater advantage.

In England, I immediately got into work at Palmer's, then in a famous printing-house in Bartholomew Close, and here I continu'd near a year, before I went to work at Watt's, an even greater printing-house, near Lincoln's Inn Fields, where I continued all the rest of my stay in London. At my first admission into Watt's, I took to working on a press, later going to the composing-room. We sail'd from Gravesend on the 23rd of July, 1726, and landed in Philadelphia on the 11th of October. I was then only 20 years old.

In my own Philadelphia printing-house in 1726, my partner was Hugh Meredith, 30 years of age, who had worked at press with Keimer. From the Quakers we procured the printing of forty sheets of their history, the rest being to be done by Keimer. It was a folio, pro patria size, in pica, with long primer notes. I composed of it a sheet a day, and Meridith worked it off at press.

It was often eleven at night, and sometimes later, before I had finished my distribution for the next day's work, for the little jobbs sent in by our other friends now and then put us back. But so determined I was to continue doing a sheet a day of the folio, that one night, when, having imposed my forms, I thought my day's work over, one of them by accident was broken, and two pages reduced to pi. I immediately distributed and compos'd it over again before I went to bed; and this industry, visible to our neighbors, began to give us character and credit.

Our partnership was dissolved about 1729, and soon after I obtained through a friend, the printing of the Newcastle paper money, another profitable jobb as I then thought it. He procured for me, also, the printing of the laws and votes of that government, which continued in my hands as long as I followed the business. In 1729, I purchased the Pennsylvania Gazette from Keimer.

In 1737, I was offered and accepted the commission of deputy at Philadelphia to the postmaster-general. I found it of great advantage, for it facilitated the correspondence that improved my newspaper, increased the number demanded, as well as the advertisements to be inserted, so that it came to afford me a considerable income.

My partnership with printers at Carolina having succeeded, I was encouraged to engage in others, and to promote several of my workmen, by establishing them with printing-houses in different colonies. Most of them did well, being enabled at the end of our term, six years, to purchase the types of me and go on working for themselves. I had, on the whole, abundant reason to be satisfied with my being established in Pennsylvania.

The rest of my story and my services to my country the reader already knows.

(Courtesy of *Printing Impressions*)

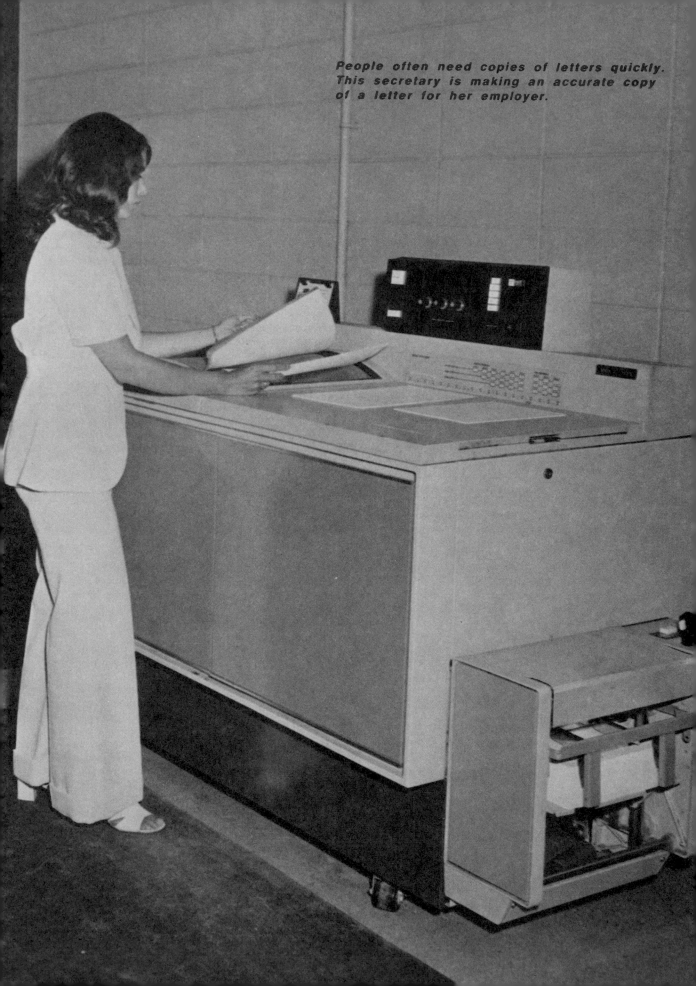

People often need copies of letters quickly. This secretary is making an accurate copy of a letter for her employer.

UNIT 146
INTRODUCTION TO DUPLICATION METHODS

It is frequently necessary to transmit information more rapidly and economically than is possible by using those printing methods discussed in previous sections of this book. The quality of the print is sometimes not as important as is the time required to pass the information on. Examples of such situations are numerous. Many industries require daily inventory records, production schedules, and production output reports for distribution to a limited number of persons. A real estate broker may need to make copies of official documents. School officials need daily records of students to distribute to teachers.

The area of limited-copy duplication is so important to business and industry that extensive research has developed new processes and machines. There are so many different kinds of machines and processes on the market that it is impossible to discuss all of them in this section. In fact, many of the office copying methods and machines became obsolete quickly. Processes like spirit duplication and mimeograph duplication are simple and economical and the basic process will remain functional and practical for many years. However, improvements are continually making them more versatile and efficient.

For the purposes of this section, a distinction will be made between duplication and copying. The decision to use a particular duplication method or an office copier depends on several factors. Some of the main considerations are how rapidly the information must be distributed, the kind of equipment that is available, which method is most economical (including labor), the number of copies that must be made, and the preciseness with which the original must be reproduced.

DUPLICATION

Duplication methods consist of several processes which produce copies from an image carrier that has been made for the particular process. An example is offset (lithographic) duplication, in which a direct image offset master (the image carrier) is prepared, placed on the printing press (duplicator), and copies are duplicated. The copies look exactly like the image on the master. Other commonly used duplication methods are spirit and mimeograph. The photocopy method of duplication is not an offset or lithographic process.

COPYING

Copying methods are different from those of duplication because they produce accurate prints from the original. No additional image carrier is needed. Copiers are usually of most advantage when only a few copies are required.

Nearly every business has at least one copying machine in its office. Some have several different methods and machines available. Each has certain advantages and disadvantages.

413

UNIT 147
SPIRIT DUPLICATING

Spirit duplicating uses a duplication fluid to dissolve the carbon or aniline dye on the master (image carrier). The dissolved carbon is what is seen on the printed sheet. Because the image eventually disappears completely from the master, the spirit duplicating process produces only about 100 to 300 good copies.

The duplicator consists of a master cylinder, an impression cylinder, a fluid container and a fluid applicator as shown in Fig. 147-1. The sheets are fed into the duplicator or press and pass against the applicator (Fig. 147-2). The paper absorbs a small amount of the duplicating fluid from the applicator. It then passes between the master and the impression cylinders (Fig. 147-3). The sheet of paper, still damp from the fluid, is pressed by the impression cylinder against the master on the master cylinder. The damp sheet dissolves a very small portion of the carbon from the master each time an image is printed. When the carbon is gone, the master is discarded.

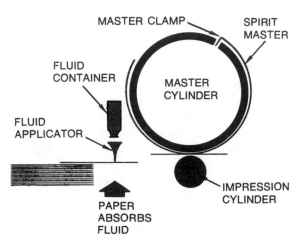

Fig. 147-2. The paper moves against the fluid applicator.

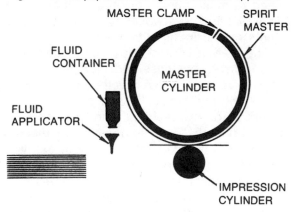

Fig. 147-3. The image is created because of pressure between the master cylinder and impression cylinder.

SPIRIT DUPLICATOR MASTER UNIT

The two main parts of a spirit duplication *master unit* are a piece of specially prepared paper called the master sheet and the carbon sheet. The aniline dye sheet is universally called the *carbon* sheet. Howev-

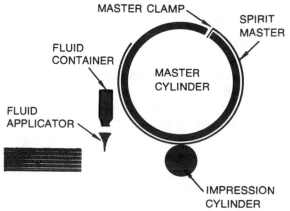

Fig. 147-1. Fundamental parts of a typical office spirit duplicator.

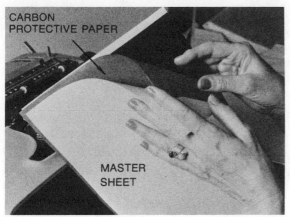

Fig. 147-4. The master unit.

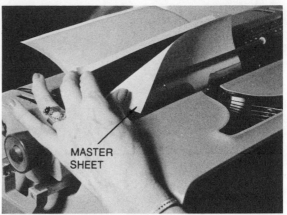

Fig. 147-5. Insert the master sheet with the open part up.

er, use of the word carbon is not technically correct since there is no carbon present.

The two parts of the master are often attached to each other, with the carbon against the back of the master sheet. There is usually a plain protective sheet of paper between the sheets of the master unit to prevent carbon from transferring to the master sheet until desired (Fig. 147-4). The carbon paper is detached and the master sheet on which the image has been deposited is placed on the duplicator.

Master sheets and carbon sheets can be purchased separately. Masters come in several colors, such as red, green, black, blue and purple. The most common color in use is purple because the dye is capable of producing many more copies than the other colors.

PREPARING THE MASTER

Spirit duplicator masters are prepared by applying pressure to the front side of the master sheet with the carbon below it. The carbon image on the back side of the master sheet is nonreadable in reverse. It must be in reverse because the image on the master sheet is again reversed when it is printed.

Typing on the master. Spirit masters are usually prepared either by typing or drawing on them. Regardless of the method used, the work is done on the front side of the master sheet.

Before typing on the spirit master, the

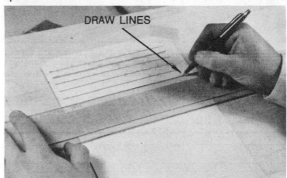

Fig. 147-6. Draw lines on the master sheet.

typist should thoroughly clean the typewriter keys so that there will be a clean, sharp image on the master. The protective sheets between the sheets of the master unit must be removed before inserting the master unit into the typewriter. The master unit should be placed in the typewriter so that the front part of the master sheet will face toward the typist. It is easier to make corrections on the master sheet if the open end of the master unit is placed into the typewriter first (Fig. 147-5). Once the master unit has been rolled into place, typing on it is very similar to typing on a regular sheet of paper. It is extremely important that the keys strike the master with an even pressure and not cut through it.

Drawing on the master unit. One of the advantages of the spirit duplicating process is its ability to duplicate drawings. Drawing should be done by placing the master on a hard surface to attain clean, sharp lines. It is sometimes easier to leave the protective

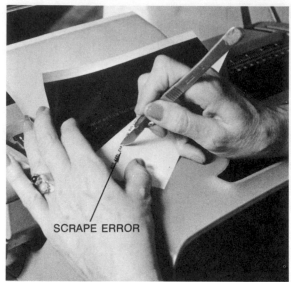

Fig. 147-7. Scrape carbon off the back of the master sheet.

sheet between the sheets of the master unit when sketching guidelines. When the guidelines are complete, remove the protective sheet and draw over the lines with either a pencil or ball-point pen (Fig. 147-6). The protective sheet should be replaced to prevent unwanted marks or scratches being made on the master.

Multiple colors can be easily produced by interchanging the carbon sheets when making a master. All colors are duplicated at the same time on the spirit duplicating machine with colorful results.

MAKING CORRECTIONS

Corrections are made on spirit masters by scraping the carbon off carefully with a sharp knife or razor blade. A small segment of new carbon paper should be placed where the error was corrected and a new image placed on the master sheet.

This is done by rolling the master up in the cylinder until the error is seen. Pull the master sheet back toward you and scrape off the carbon involving the error (Fig. 147-7). Then place a small piece of new carbon paper behind the area where the error was corrected. Be sure the carbon side of the

new piece of carbon paper is against the back of the master sheet. The master unit is rolled back into place in the typewriter and the correction made by striking the correct typewriter key. Be sure to remove the piece of carbon paper used to make the corrections.

PRINTING THE SPIRIT MASTER

Spirit masters are printed on duplicators similar to the hand-operated one shown in Fig. 147-8. The master is attached to the master cylinder (Fig. 147-9). The sheets are fed into the duplicator. When the desired number of copies is printed the master sheet is removed and discarded, or placed in a folder for future use.

Fig. 147-8. A hand-operated spirit duplicator. (Bell & Howell, Ditto Division)

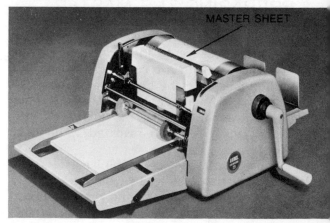

Fig. 147-9. A spirit duplicator with a spirit master attached to the master cylinder. (A.B. Dick Co.)

UNIT 148
MIMEOGRAPH DUPLICATING

The mimeograph duplicating process, sometimes called *stencil duplicating,* is an inexpensive and efficient communication method. A greater number of copies can be obtained from a mimeograph stencil or image carrier than from a spirit duplication master. The four major elements required for mimeograph duplicating are the stencil, ink, paper, and a mimeograph duplicator.

MIMEOGRAPH STENCIL

The *stencil* is an essential element of the mimeograph process. The quality of the print, as with other printing processes, depends on how well the stencil or image carrier is prepared. A mimeograph print is obtained by passing ink through open spots or areas in the stencil (Fig. 148-1).

A stencil is made from a fibrous, porous tissue (Fig. 148-2) to permit ink penetration (Fig. 148-3). The fibrous tissue is coated on both sides with a wax material that does not permit ink to pass through (Fig. 148-4). The coating is such that nearly any pressure applied to the surface will push the coating to the side, leaving the fibrous material exposed (Fig. 148-5). Ink may then be squeezed

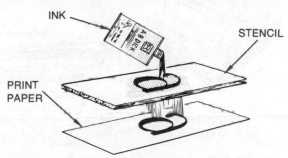

Fig. 148-1. Ink passes through spots on a stencil to produce an image on paper. (A.B. Dick Co.)

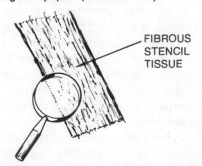

Fig. 148-2. The core of a stencil is made from a fibrous material. (A.B. Dick Co.)

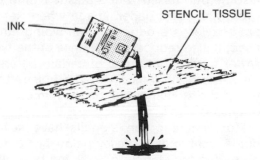

Fig. 148-3. Ink passes through the fibrous material. (A.B. Dick Co.)

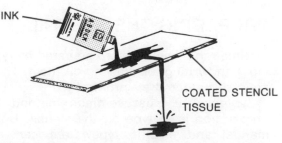

Fig. 148-4. The coating on both sides of the stencil prevents the ink from passing through. (A.B. Dick Co.)

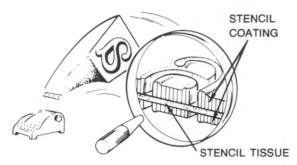

Fig. 148-5. Pressure on the stencil causes the coating to be moved aside. (A.B. Dick Co.)

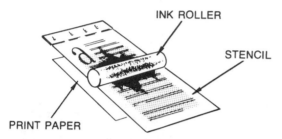

Fig. 148-6. Ink is forced through openings in the stencil. (A.B. Dick Co.)

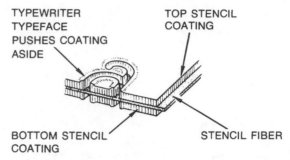

Fig. 148-7. A typewriter letter strikes the stencil and pushes the coating aside. (A. B. Dick Co.)

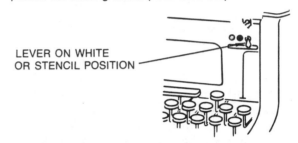

Fig. 148-8. Stencils are typed best when the ribbon indicator is set on white or stencil setting. (A.B. Dick Co.)

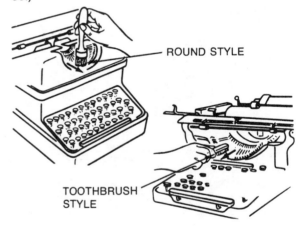

Fig. 148-9. Clean the typefaces with a brush to obtain a sharp image on the stencil. (A. B. Dick Co.)

through the stencil onto the paper below the stencil (Fig. 148-6).

A basic stencil has a stencil sheet, typing cushion, and a backing sheet. Stencils can also be purchased with a plastic typing film over them. A broader image where letters are heavier is produced when typing film is used. It also reduces the chance of the typewriter cutting out areas of certain letters in the stencil, such as an *o*. The holes at the top of the stencil hold it on the mimeograph duplicator.

Most mimeograph stencils have several guide markings. These help the person preparing the stencil to know the best place to put the image and to see the duplicating area limit or boundaries.

PREPARING THE STENCIL

Mimeograph stencils are prepared by typing, handwriting, or drawing on them. They are also prepared electronically.

Typing. The most common method of preparation is to type on the stencil. Both manual and electric typewriters can be used. The latter produces a more uniform image because the pressure is more even.

When the typewriter typeface strikes the stencil, the wax coating is pushed aside to expose the porous, fibrous material (Fig. 148-7). For best results the typewriter ribbon setting should be set on white or stencil (Fig. 148-8). The typewriter produces a sharper image if the typefaces are kept clean (Fig. 148-9).

Typing on a mimeograph stencil is similar to typing on regular paper. The stencil should be inserted into the typewriter with the stencil sheet toward the typist and the

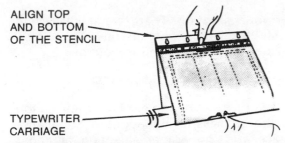

Fig. 148-10. Align the top and bottom of the stencil in the typewriter. (A. B. Dick Co.)

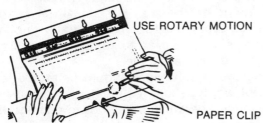

Fig. 148-11. Rub over errors with the round end of a paper clip. (A. B. Dick Co.)

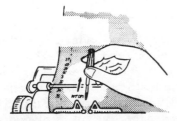

Fig. 148-12. Brush correction fluid over the error. (A. B. Dick Co.)

holes at the top. When the stencil is in place, release the carriage pressure and align the top and bottom of the stencil as shown in Fig. 148-10. The stencil can now be rolled into position for typing.

When it is necessary to correct an error, roll the stencil up in the typewriter until the error is exposed. Rub or burnish over the error with a paper clip in a circular motion (Fig. 148-11). Paint over the burnished error in a vertical stroke with correction fluid (Fig. 148-12). The stencil can then be rolled back into place to correct the error. When using a typewriter, apply less pressure to make the correction than to make the original image.

Handwriting. Handwriting is done on a stencil with a stylus, which is similar to a ball-point pen. A *writing sheet* (smooth, heavy, hard-surface paper or matte-surface plastic sheet) is placed between the stencil

Fig. 148-13. Hold the stencil firmly while writing. (A. B. Dick Co.)

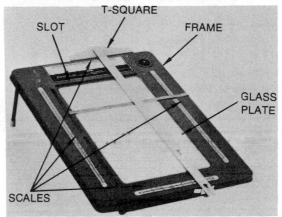

Fig. 148-14. An illustrated stencil drawing board. (A. B. Dick Co.)

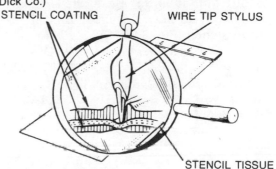

Fig. 148-15. The stylus is used to make drawings. (A. B. Dick Co.)

sheet and the typing cushion. The stylus is used like a ball-point pen on paper. For best results roll the stylus between the fingers while writing (Fig. 148-13).

Drawing. An illuminated drawing board (Fig. 148-14) is used for making drawings on stencils. It consists of a frame, a translucent glass plate, and a light below the glass plate which illuminates it. Rules are located at the top, bottom, and sides of the frame. A slot near the top of the drawing board takes the backing sheet. A T-square is used

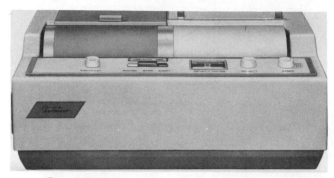

Fig. 148-16. An electronic stencil-making machine. (Gestetner Corp.)

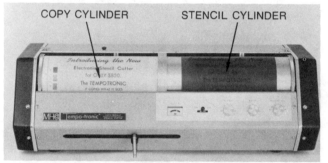

Fig. 148-17. Copy is placed on one cylinder and the stencil is placed on the other. (Milo Harding Co.)

as a straight edge to make drawings. A stylus is used to draw an image on a mimeograph stencil (Fig. 148-15).

Electronically prepared stencils. One of the newer machines for preparing stencils for mimeograph duplication is the *electronic stencil maker* (Fig. 148-16). This instrument produces a stencil which looks exactly like the original sheet of copy. Copy is prepared like that for photomechanical reproduction. Once ready, the copy is placed on one of the cylinders of the electronic stencil maker. The mimeograph stencil is put on the other cylinder. The stencil maker scans the image and reproduces it on the stencil (Fig. 148-17).

MIMEOGRAPH INKS

Mimeograph inks are more fluid than most printing inks. Many inks are available for mimeograph duplication and final selection depends on the duplication requirements and the kind of equipment used. It is a good policy to consult your duplicator dealer to determine the correct kind of ink

for your situation. There are quick drying, paste, emulsion, and oil base inks. Most inks come in black and in colors.

MIMEOGRAPH PAPER

One of the single most important factors in the successful mimeograph duplication process is the proper selection of paper. Mimeograph paper is available from almost any paper dealer. The paper should be absorbent or the ink will smear or set-off. Bond paper used for mimeograph duplication is very similar to regular bond. Card stock is also available.

Mimeograph paper should be stored in a cool, dry location. It should be stacked flat. Handle it carefully so as not to damage the corners.

THE MIMEOGRAPH DUPLICATOR

The mimeograph duplicator is the machine used to print the stencil. The essential parts are the cylinder, impression roll, and ink pad. Duplicators also have mechanisms which feed the paper between the cylinder and the impression roll. Ink is placed inside the cylinder and passes through the holes in the cylinder onto the pad when pressure is created between the cylinder and the impression roll (Fig. 148-18). Ink is placed inside the cylinder and passes through the holes in the cylinder onto the pad, which absorbs it. The stencil is applied against the pad and when pressure is created between the cylinder and the impression roll the ink

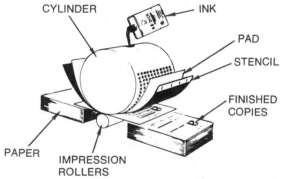

Fig. 148-18. The paper is pressed against the stencil by pressure from the stencil cylinder and impression rollers. (A. B. Dick Co.)

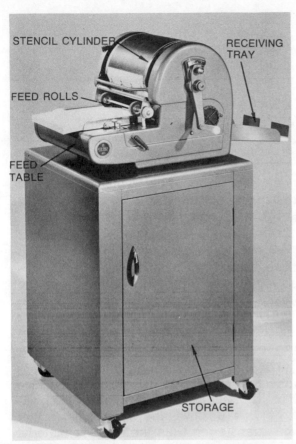

Fig. 148-19. A hand-operated mimeograph duplicator. (A . B. Dick Co.)

passes through the open parts of the stencil onto the paper.

Mimeograph duplicators which operate by hand or electrically are equally efficient if operated correctly. Fig. 148-19 shows a hand-operated one. In Fig. 148-20 an electrically operated one is pictured. The following procedure is used to duplicate copies:

1. Clamp the stencil to the cylinder using the head clamp. The stencil is placed on the cylinder so that the image is *not* readable.
2. Load the paper in the feed table.
3. Lower the feed rolls to touch the paper.
4. Turn on the duplicator. The sheets are fed through the machine between the cylinder and the impression rolls and into the receiving tray.
5. When the desired number of copies has been duplicated, stop the duplicator.
6. Remove the stencil and place it in an absorbant storage folder for future use.
7. Cover the cylinder with the protective cover sheet. This is necessary as the cover sheet prevents ink from drying on the pad. It is also wise to keep the entire duplicator covered to protect it from dust and dirt.

Fig. 148-20. An electrically operated mimeograph duplicator. (A. B. Dick Co.)

UNIT 149
OFFICE COPYING METHODS

Office copying methods have revolutionized practices in both large and small businesses. They are a tremendous time saver and, therefore, save money. Many different office copiers are manufactured. Each has certain advantages and disadvantages. The copier that most nearly fills the needs of a particular office is the one that should be used. Copiers are usually classified according to the way copies are made. One way to classify copiers is according to whether or not the copiers use silver halides in the process.

SILVER HALIDE COPIERS

Copiers using *silver halides* (usually silver chloride or silver bromide) require several steps and produce a wet copy. It requires more time to produce a copy by this method than by the more widely used non-silver halide technique. All silver halide copiers operate in essentially the same way, but there are slight differences in procedure. The operator should learn the specific procedure required for each type.

Two different chemically treated sheets of paper are used with most silver halide copiers. One of the sheets is the *negative.* It is coated with a silver halide and other chemicals to form a light-sensitive emulsion. The second sheet is called the *positive* and has a gelatin layer not sensitive to light.

The original copy is placed so that the face is against the emulsion of the negative sheet. The copy and the negative sheet are placed in the machine. Light passes through the negative sheet, striking the copy below. The light striking the dark image areas of the copy is absorbed and does not reflect. That which strikes the nonimage areas reflects to the negative sheet above and exposes it (Fig. 149-1).

The exposed negative sheet is separated from the copy. It is placed in contact with the positive sheet. The emulsion of the negative materials is placed in contact with the gelatin layer of the positive sheet (Fig. 149-2). The two sheets are placed in a *developer* which turns the exposed silver halide latent image areas to metallic silver.

The unexposed silver halide from the negative transfers to the gelatin of the positive material. Because of a chemical in the gelatin of the positive, the silver halides that were transferred from the negative material are turned to metallic silver by the developer (Fig. 149-3). The two sheets are then placed between rollers to press out the excess developing solution. They are pulled apart and a black-on-white image results on the positive material. The negative material is discarded after each print has been made. This process in rarely used anymore.

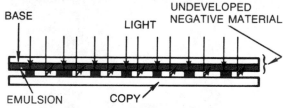

Fig. 149-1. Exposure of a silver halide master.

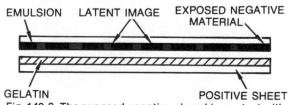

Fig. 149-2. The exposed negative placed in contact with the positive sheet.

Office Copying Methods 423

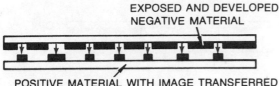

EXPOSED AND DEVELOPED
NEGATIVE MATERIAL

POSITIVE MATERIAL WITH IMAGE TRANSFERRED
FROM NEGATIVE AND DEVELOPED

Fig. 149-3. The unexposed silver salts are transferred to the positive sheet.

MODERN COPIERS

The three most widely used non-silver halide copying processes are the *thermographic,* the *transfer-electrostatic,* and the *direct-electrostatic.* All three produce copies directly from the original, using only one sheet of paper. Because of this, copies are made more rapidly and are usually far less expensive.

Thermographic process. The thermographic process produces an image by a heat reaction. The image of the original copy must contain carbon black or a metallic compound in order to produce an image on the print paper. A specially treated paper is used that is coated with compounds that form a colored substance when heated.

The treated sheet of paper is placed over the original copy, with the treated side up. Infrared radiation passes through it and strikes the original. The infrared radiation that strikes the image of the copy below is absorbed and becomes heated (provided the image is carbon black or metallic). The heat that comes from the image areas of the original copy is transmitted to the heat-sensitive paper. This causes the compound to form a colored image that corresponds to the image areas of the original copy (Fig. 149-4). Fig. 149-5 shows a thermographic copier.

Transfer-electrostatic process. The transfer-electrostatic process uses the photoconductive property of a selenium plate or drum. This plate or drum has the ability to hold electric charges in darkness. Selenium is a material which when combined with metal has variable electrical conductivity. The electrical conductivity varies with the intensity of illumination or light.

The first step in making a copy by this process is to coat the selenium drum with

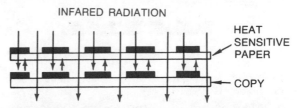

INFARED RADIATION

HEAT SENSITIVE PAPER

COPY

Fig. 149-4. Infrared radiation produces an image on heat-sensitive paper.

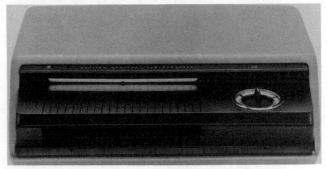

Fig. 149-5. A common thermographic copier. (3M Co.)

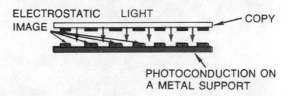

ELECTROSTATIC IMAGE   LIGHT   COPY

PHOTOCONDUCTION ON A METAL SUPPORT

Fig. 149-6. Light reflected from the nonimage areas of the copy cause the electrostatic charges to leave the drum in those areas.

a uniform positive electrostatic charge. This is done in total darkness. As long as the selenium drum remains in darkness the electrostatic charges will remain on it.

After the drum is charged it is exposed to the original copy through a lens system much like that in a process camera. Where light is reflected from the copy nonimage areas and hits the drum, the electrostatic charge leaves the drum. The dark areas of the copy reflect little or no light. The areas on the selenium drum which correspond to the dark areas of the copy will retain the positive electrostatic charge. No image is seen on the drum at this time, but it has an *electrostatic image.* (Fig. 149-6). For illustrative purposes, a flat plate has been used instead of a curved drum.

When the electrostatic image has been placed on the drum, *toner* is cascaded or poured over the drum. Toner has a pigment

POWDER ADHERES TO
CHARGED AREAS

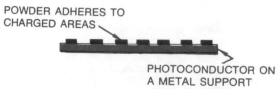

PHOTOCONDUCTOR ON
A METAL SUPPORT

Fig. 149-7. Toner adheres to the electrostatic charge on the drum.

POWDER IS
TRANSFERRED
TO PAPER
AND FUSED
WITH HEAT

UNTREATED DUPLICATION
PAPER

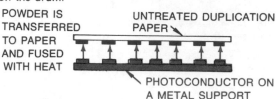

PHOTOCONDUCTOR ON
A METAL SUPPORT

Fig. 149-8. Toner is transferred to the paper to form the final print.

Fig. 149-9. A modern transfer-electrostatic copier.

or color and is negatively charged. The negatively charged toner is attracted to the positively charged selenium drum. This forms a visible powder image in reverse on the drum (Fig. 149-7).

A sheet of regular, untreated paper is placed over the powder image on the drum. The paper is given a positive electrostatic charge. The toner transfers from the drum to the paper (Fig. 149-8).

The toner is only lightly attracted to the sheet of paper and could be removed easily by brushing the image. To make the image permanent the toner is fused by heating the paper. The toner powder melts and bonds to the paper.

The last step in the process is for the machine to clean the drum to make it ready for the next copy. This is not part of the copy-

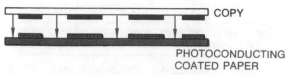

COPY

PHOTOCONDUCTING
COATED PAPER

Fig. 149-10. Direct electrostatic process.

PHOTOCONDUCTING
COATED PAPER

Fig. 149-11. Powder adheres to the electrostatic charges that remain on the paper.

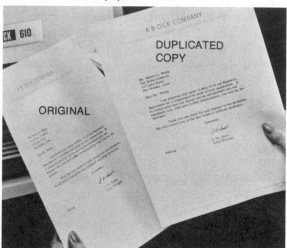

Fig. 149-12. A direct electrostatic copier. (A. B. Dick Co.)

making process but is necessary before another copy can be made. Fig. 149-9 shows a modern transfer-electrostatic copier.

Direct-electrostatic process. This process is similar to the transfer process. The primary difference is that the electrostatic image is produced directly on the print paper and, therefore, is not transferred to the paper from a drum. Zinc oxide treated paper is used. The coating placed on it makes the paper heavier than regular sheets used with the transfer-electrostatic process.

The special paper is first given a negative electrostatic charge in total darkness. It is then exposed to the original copy with a lens system similar to that in a process camera. Light from the nonimage areas of the copy causes the negative charges on the treated paper to leave those areas. The areas on the special paper that correspond to the image areas of the original copy retain the electrostatic pattern to form the electrostatic image that is a duplicate of the original copy (Fig. 149-10).

The image is made visible by a developer similar to the toner. The powder is positively charged and adheres to the paper when it is applied (Fig. 149-11). As in the transfer-electrostatic process, the paper is heated to make the developer bond to the paper.

Fig. 149-12 shows a direct electrostatic copier. When the original is fed into the copier, the copy that comes out will look exactly like the original.

UNIT 150
LEARNING EXPERIENCES: LIMITED COPY DUPLICATION METHODS

DISCUSSION TOPICS

1. Distinguish between duplicating and copying.
2. Identify some common duplication methods. What are some things that must be considered when selecting a duplicating or copying method?
3. Explain the basic principle of spirit duplication. How did the name *spirit duplication* originate? Why does the master wear out in a comparatively short time?
4. Describe the parts of the master unit. Give the purpose of each part. What is the most common color of prints from spirit duplication? Give other colors.
5. Describe briefly how the spirit duplication master is prepared. Give some common methods used to prepare it. How should the image appear on the master?
6. Explain the procedure for typing on a spirit duplication master. What is the procedure for drawing on a master?
7. How are corrections made on spirit duplication masters? List the details.
8. Which side of the spirit master should be attached to the duplicator? What is the name of the part of the duplicator to which the master is attached?
9. Give another name for the mimeograph duplication process. What is the main advantage of mimeograph duplication over spirit duplication?
10. Describe the mimeograph stencil. What is the process which permits a print to be made from mimeograph stencils?
11. Identify the basic parts of a mimeograph stencil. What are some of the markings on a mimeograph stencil?
12. What is the most common method used to prepare a mimeograph stencil? List two other methods of preparing stencils.
13. List the procedure for typing on a mimeograph stencil. How are corrections made?
14. How does the procedure for writing and drawing on stencils differ from the procedure for typing on them?
15. Briefly describe the procedure for making an electronic mimeograph stencil.
16. Describe how mimeograph ink differs from conventional printing inks. List several kinds of inks available for mimeograph duplicators.
17. What is an essential quality of mimeograph duplicator paper? How should paper be stored?
18. List the essential parts of a mimeograph stencil. How should the stencil be attached to the duplicator?

19. Name two categories used to classify office copiers. What is the primary difference between the two categories?
20. Explain the fundamental procedure required to make copies with a silver halide copier.
21. Give the three primary kinds of non-silver halide copiers.
22. Describe the thermographic process of making copies.
23. How does the transfer-electrostatic method of making copies differ from the direct-electrostatic method? Explain each.

ACTIVITIES

1. Obtain a spirit duplication master and identify the parts of the master. With the protective sheet in place, sketch a drawing on the master sheet. Remove the protective sheet and complete the drawing on the master by using several different writing instruments, such as wide, medium, and fine pencils and ball-point pens. Examine the completed master to see what kind of image is produced by the various writing instruments.

2. Remove the protective sheet from a master unit and place the master in a typewriter. Using different pressures on the typewriter keys, type on the master. Remove the master from the typewriter and examine the images produced.
3. Place the master from activity number 1 on the spirit duplicator and print several copies using different impression roller pressures. How do the copies differ from each other? Use the same procedure for the master prepared in activity number 2.
4. Prepare a mimeograph stencil by typing and drawing on the master or stencil. Use both a ball-point pen and a stylus to make the drawings, and use different typewriter pressures. When the stencil is prepared, hold the sheet up to the light and identify the parts of the image that are not completely clear. Print the master on the duplicator to determine which images produce the best print.
5. Visit several duplicator distributors and request demonstrations and explanations of the machines and their basic principles of operation. Prepare a detailed report on your visit.

A N
INQUIRY
INTO THE
RIGHTS of the BRITISH Colonies,

Intended as an Anſwer to

The Regulations lately made concerning the Colonies, and the Taxes impoſed upon them conſidered.

In a Letter addreſſed to the Author of that Pamphlet.

By *RICHARD BLAND*, of VIRGINIA.

Dedit omnibus Deus pro virili portione ſapientiam, ut et inaudita inveſtigare poſſent et audita perpendere.
LACTANTIUS.

WILLIAMSBURG:
Printed by ALEXANDER PURDIE, & Cº.
MDCCLXVI.

Title page of AN INQUIRY . . . , printed by Alexander Purdie. Written in the midst of the Stamp Act controversy, this influential pamphlet presented a reasoned view of the colonists' position. It appeared before Purdie formed a partnership with John Dixon.

(Courtesy, *Colonial Williamsburg*)

A highly mechanized, modern book-binding plant. (The Smyth Manufacturing Co.)

UNIT 151
INTRODUCTION TO FINISHING AND BINDING

Finishing and binding procedures are used to complete the products of the design and layout personnel, compositors, camera operators, platemakers, and pressmen. Without these two procedures, quantities of printed materials produced every day would never reach the public in usable form.

Books have played an important part in the progress of our modern world. The oldest books were baked clay tablets used in Asia Minor approximately 5,500 years ago. Another form of early books was the scroll, made from a roll of animal skins or crude paper. These were used by the Egyptians, Chinese, Greeks, and Romans.

The art of hand bookbinding rapidly developed after the invention of movable metal type by Johann Gutenberg in 1450. After the development of machines which produced hundreds and thousands of printed sheets per hour it became necessary to place these sheets in usable form. The book form used today appears to be the answer and has proved its value.

Early bookbinders performed all operations by hand. Most of the equipment and hand tools were made by the bookbinder and it was necessary for him and his assistants to work long hours to put printed sheets in a usable and aesthetic form for those persons anxiously waiting to read and learn.

Fig. 151-1 shows a typical eighteenth-century American bookbindery. Note that all

Fig. 151-1. A typical eighteenth-century bookbindery. Several important binding operations can be seen: Left (a) beating folded sections of a book so that they will lie flat, (b) stitching folded sections to the heavy cords that hold the book together, (c) trimming the edges of a freshly sewn book on a ploughing press, and (d) pressing freshly bound books in a large standing press. Right: (1-3) the blocks and hammer used by the binder, (4) the sewing frame, (5-6) twine, (7-12) parts of the sewing frame, and (13-14) wood or bond folders. (Diderot's Encyclopedia, Courtesy, Colonial Williamsburg)

operations are done by hand. Modern binding methods and equipment have improved book construction quality beyond the dreams of the early bookbinders. Thousands of high-quality books are produced in a single day by using automated equipment.

Not all printed sheets are bound into books. Some need only to be cut to size, folded, or perforated to be of value. These several operations are commonly referred to as *finishing the sheets.* Several things can be done to a printed sheet of paper to make it more valuable without binding it into a book. These specific items and many others are discussed in detail in Unit 153, *Finishing Methods.*

UNIT 152
SAFETY IN FINISHING AND BINDING

Finishing and binding tools and equipment must be handled and operated with care. Read and follow these safety suggestions very closely to protect yourself and fellow students.

Permission. Always secure permission from competent authority before using the paper cutter, hot stamp press, wire stitcher, and other power equipment.

Jewelry. Remove rings, bracelets, and wrist watches before operating machines with moving parts such as those mentioned above.

Paper cutter knife. Keep fingers from touching the razor-sharp cutter-knife edge. Always keep the clamp below the knife.

Paper cutter knife lever. Be certain that the knife lever is in *up* position and securely locked with the knife safety button, pin, or lever after each cut. If it is not properly locked it could fall and strike the operator on the head, causing serious injury.

Hands. Keep both hands on the lever or control buttons when cutting. Observe caution when using the hot stamp machine to prevent burning your hands. Keep hands and fingers from under the head of the wire stitcher.

Hand shears. Use hand shears with care. Never point them in the direction of fellow classmates or workers because eyes could be easily injured if hand shears are used carelessly.

Electrical wire. Keep electrical wire from touching the heated portion of the hot stamp machine. If the insulated covering of the wire shows wear, repair or replace it.

Wire stitcher head. Be certain to have nothing under the stitching head when the power is turned on. Sometimes the trip pedal is activated accidently while the machine is turned off. Check this.

Safety glasses. Wear safety glasses when operating the wire stitcher.

Removing staples. Use a special puller to remove staples, not your fingernails. Staple ends are sharp.

Binder's knife. Handle the binder's knife carefully. Keep it sharp for easier use.

Hot glue pot. Keep the glue pot clean. Set it in a spot where it will not be knocked over or accidently touched.

Sewing needle. Always know where the sewing needle is located. Use it with care and protect your fingers while sewing.

Backing press. The clamping pressure of the backing press is tremendous. Keep fingers and hands from between its jaws.

Back or dovetail saw. Handle the saw carefully when cutting the sewing opening in the binding edge of the signatures. Keep it sharp.

Machine operation. Only one person at a time should operate a machine. Unsafe conditions often result when two or more persons try to use the same machine at the same time.

UNIT 153
FINISHING METHODS

Several finishing operations can be performed after sheets of paper have been printed to make them more valuable. It is not always necessary to bind two-dimensional graphic materials into a book. Study the following operations to understand the finishing methods.

CUTTING

Several different types of machines may be used to cut and trim sheets of paper. They vary from the office-style bar cutter in Fig. 153-1 to the single-knife hydraulic cutter in Fig. 153-2 and the fully automatic hydraulic three-knife book trimmer shown in Fig. 153-3.

Each of these machines is designed to perform *cutting* and *trimming* functions with accuracy and speed. The action of a hand-operated paper cutter is given in Unit 154. Cutting is probably the most common finishing operation regardless of the binding used.

Fig. 153-2. A single-knife hydraulic paper cutter. (The Challenge Machinery Co.)

Fig. 153-1. A table-top bar paper cutter. (Michael Lith Sales Corp.)

Fig. 153-3. A fully automatic three-knife book trimmer. (Consolidated International Corp.)

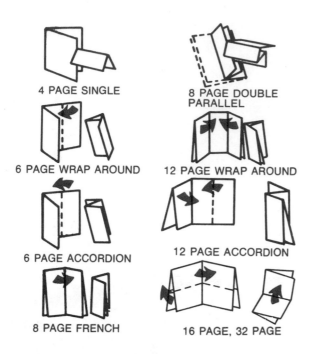

4 PAGE SINGLE

8 PAGE DOUBLE PARALLEL

6 PAGE WRAP AROUND

12 PAGE WRAP AROUND

6 PAGE ACCORDION

12 PAGE ACCORDION

8 PAGE FRENCH

16 PAGE, 32 PAGE

Fig. 153-4. Several common ways of folding paper.

FOLDING

Folding is the act of doubling over a sheet of paper to make creases or folds. Paper can be doubled over several times parallel or at right angles to form several pages. Many attractive folders and brochures are prepared by creatively folding paper. Fig. 153-4 illustrates some common paper folds.

Sizes and designs of paper-folding machines vary from light-duty office types (Fig. 153-5) to heavy-duty types (Fig. 153-6). Large complex folding machines which cut and fold the printed web of paper into a book or magazine signatures can also be attached directly to roll-fed presses.

SCORING

Scoring places a crease in a sheet of paper to facilitate folding (Fig. 153-8). Creasing or scoring the paper in a narrow line weakens paper fibers and causes the sheet to fold easily.

Two methods are commonly used to score. The oldest uses a type-high, round-face scoring rule. A straight piece of rule is

Fig. 153-5. A typical office letter-folding machine. (The Challenge Machinery Co.)

Fig. 153-6. An industrial folder capable of folding a 32-page signature. (Bell and Howell Business Equipment Group)

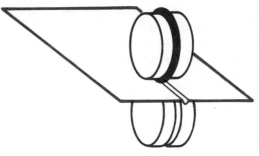

Fig. 153-7. A tongue-and-groove set of scoring rollers.

locked in a chase and placed in a platen press or in a special scoring machine. The paper is creased when the rule strikes it.

The second method of scoring is done by the rotary principle. A special set of tongue-and-groove rollers (Fig. 153-7) can be attached to many presses and folding machines. Special perforating machines also score by this principle (Fig. 153-10).

Generally, heavy or thick papers must all be scored before folding. This is done on the paper folder during the folding operation. It is good practice to score the sheet on the inside of the fold (Fig. 153-8).

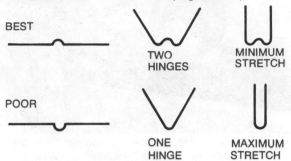

BEST

TWO HINGES

MINIMUM STRETCH

POOR

ONE HINGE

MAXIMUM STRETCH

Fig. 153-8. The proper and improper way to fold a sheet of paper after scoring.

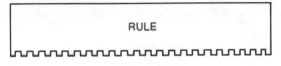

RULE

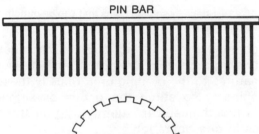

PIN BAR

WHEEL

Fig. 153-9. Three common ways to perforate sheets of paper.

Fig. 153-10. A high-speed scoring and perforating machine. (F. P. Rosback Co.)

PERFORATING

Perforating is the process of cutting a series of slits or punching a series of holes in a sheet of paper to facilitate tearing. There are three common methods of perforating (Fig. 153-9).

1. The perforating rule used on a platen or cylinder press.
2. The pin bar used on a special machine which punches holes in a sheet.
3. A perforating wheel attached to the ejector section of a press or to the delivery end of a paper folder.

Also, specially designed equipment is capable of scoring and perforating at a high rate of speed (Fig. 153-10). This machine utilizes the scoring and perforating wheel arrangement. Commercial graphic arts plants having a large volume of perforating and scoring use machines of this type. The small community printer, however, relies on his platen press, pin-bar punch perforator, or folding machine.

GATHERING

Gathering is the assembling of single sheets or signatures (large sheets folded to form pages) in the correct order prior to binding. It is done either by hand or machine. Most people have collected several sheets of paper together and then stapled them to form a booklet at one time or another. By doing this an important phase in the completion of a published work has been carried out.

Collating is a term often confused with gathering. To *collate* means to examine a gathered group of signatures which will form a book to verify their order and number. Collating marks are printed in different positions on the binding fold of signatures. After the publication has been folded and gathered a distinct pattern is formed by the collating marks; errors can, therefore, be detected easily.

Page-gathering equipment varies from the desk-top, semi-hand-operated type in Fig. 153-11 to the programmed automatic sorter shown in Fig. 153-12. The latter is

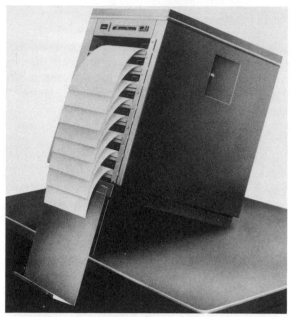

Fig. 153-11. A desk-top semiautomated gathering machine. (Pitney-Bowes, Inc.)

Fig. 153-12. An automatic sorting machine used in conjunction with a duplicator to gather sheets. (Pitney-Bowes, Inc.)

positioned at the delivery end of a duplicator or lithographic offset press. It delivers the sheets to individual bins. After the several pages of a booklet have been graphically reproduced, the gathered ones are bound and the job is completed.

Large binderies use equipment capable of gathering single sheets or folded signatures. An eighteen-station, side-gathering

Fig. 153-13. An 18-station gathering machine for single sheets or signatures. (Consolidated International Corp.)

PAPER EDGE

Fig. 153-14. Specially shaped holes that can be punched in sheets of paper.

machine is shown in Fig. 153-13. Machines of this type gather, straighten, and deliver signatures to the binding unit. Usually these machines also stitch the pages or signatures together and frequently trim all three sides in one operation.

PUNCHING AND DRILLING

These are the necessary operations when holes are desired for inserting pages in ring binders. The hand paper punch or the three-hole notebook punch are commonly used in offices. Heavy-duty *punching* equipment is needed by graphic arts binderies to produce holes in large-volume work. Specially shaped holes can be punched in a sheet of paper (Fig. 153-14) with the same equipment that is used to punch standard round holes from ⅛ to ½ inch.

Drilling machines are used primarily for round holes, but with special attachments some different shapes can be obtained. Also cornering of sheets can be done. The advantage of drilling is that several hundred sheets can be drilled at one time, whereas

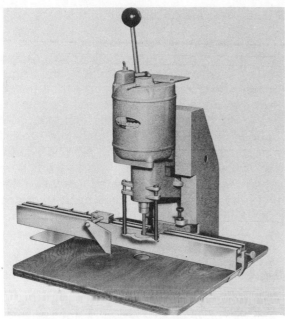

Fig. 153-15. A single-head bench-model paper drill. (The Challenge Machinery Co.)

Fig. 153-16. A multiple-head floor-model paper drill. (The Challenge Machinery Co.)

only a few sheets can be punched at one time. Drilling machines vary from the single-head bench model in Fig. 153-15 to the multiple-head floor model shown in Fig. 153-16.

Fig. 153-17. A heavy-duty automatic die-cutting and embossing press. (Chandler and Price)

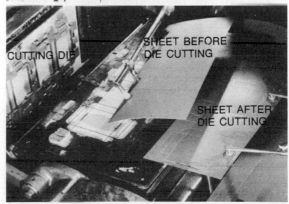

Fig. 153-18. Die-cutting boxes on an automatic die-cutting press. (Chandler and Price)

DIE CUTTING

Die cutting is the process of cutting paper or other sheet materials into special shapes. The cutting die is prepared by sawing into a piece of ¾-inch plywood the shape that is to be die cut. The cutting rule is then inserted into the space made by the saw blade. Cork or rubber squares are fastened to the wood near the die. They force the stock from the die after an impression is made.

Standard platen and cylinder letterpresses can be used if rollers are removed, but special heavy-duty die-cutting machines are used for a high volume of work (Fig. 153-17). Almost any desired shape can be die cut as shown in Fig. 153-18.

Fig. 153-19. A table-model hot-stamping machine (Halvorfold-Kwikprint Co.)

Fig. 153-20. A heavy-duty hydraulic hot-stamping machine. (Wynn Manufacturing Co.)

HOT STAMPING

Hot stamping is used to place images of type or illustrations on covers of casebound books. Basically, hot stamping is an image-transfer process. It is commonly thought of, however, as a finishing process because it is directly concerned with the completion of bound books. Gold, silver, or colored foil is placed between the type and the book cloth, and through the use of heat and pressure a permanent image is formed. Machines for this process vary from small hand-operated ones in Fig. 153-19 to heavy-duty hydraulic-operated types shown in Fig. 153-20.

LAMINATING

Laminating is commonly thought of as a bonding of several layers of a substance to

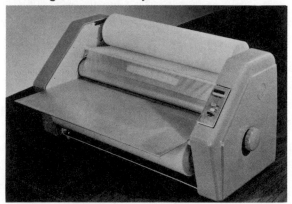

Fig. 153-21. A table-model laminating machine. (General Binding Corp.)

Fig. 153-22. An automatic rotary laminating machine. (General Binding Corp.)

form a homogeneous solid such as plywood. In the graphic arts, however, laminating is the process of placing a thin layer of transparent film, polyester or polyethylene, on both sides of a printed sheet. The printed materials are protected from damage resulting from rough use, water, oil, and chemical materials. Laminating also enhances the beauty of materials printed in color by bringing out the full brilliance.

Methods of applying the transparent film range from using hand-operated devices (Fig. 153-21) to completely automatic laminators (Fig. 153-22). Heat and pressure are required for all methods of transparent-film lamination.

UNIT 154
PAPER-CUTTING PROCEDURES

Paper cutting is an important phase in the preparation and completion of printed materials. Paper must frequently be cut to size before it can be printed. Printed material coming from a press generally needs to be cut or retrimmed; the paper cutter is, therefore, an important machine in the graphic arts industry.

Hand- and power-operated paper cutters are operated in essentially the same manner. The primary rule with all paper cutters must be *Think* and *Practice Safety*. A machine containing a razor-sharp blade is not a toy.

Planning the best cut is important. Many hundreds of dollars could be wasted quickly if one or more cuts are improperly made. An operator of a paper cutter should prepare a cutting chart before making the first cut. The operator must figure how many smaller press sheets are obtainable from one large stock sheet, the number of stock sheets needed, the amount of waste that should be expected, and the best order for making cuts.

PLANNING FOR CUTTING

1. Determine the number of copies and the sheet size for printing. This is called a *press sheet*.
2. Select the kind of paper to be used.
3. Measure the large stock sheet size.
4. Calculate the number of press sheets that can be obtained from the stock sheet. Figs. 154-1 and 154-2 illustrate methods of determining this information. Study the illustrations closely to understand how each method is accomplished.
5. Figure the number of stock sheets needed. After you know the maximum press sheets obtainable from a stock sheets, use simple division to find how many stock sheets are necessary, A 10% press spoilage is commonly figured for average press runs of a few hundred to a few thousand copies.

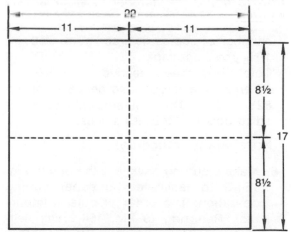

Fig. 154-1. A drawing method of calculating the number of press sheets obtainable from one stock sheet: stock sheet 17 x 22 inches; press sheet 8½ x 11 inches; four press sheets obtained

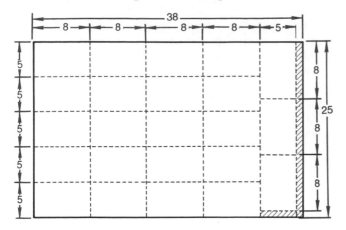

Fig. 154-2. A second drawing method of calculating the number of press sheets obtainable from one stock sheet: stock sheet 25 x 28 inches; press sheet 5 x 8 inches; 23 press sheets obtained.

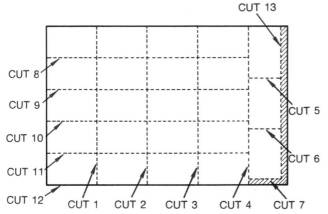

Fig. 154-3. Cutting chart to determine the order of cuts.

How to figure the number of stock sheets needed.

Number of copies desired   = 750
10% press spoilage   = 75
Total press sheets needed   = 825
17 press sheets obtained per stock sheet.
$825 ÷ 17 = 48\frac{9}{17} = 49$ stock sheets needed to obtain 825 press sheets.

NOTE: Always round up.

6. Make a cutting chart like the one in Fig. 154-3 to facilitate the paper cutting operation. The order of cuts is important. Referring to Fig. 154-2 will help prevent making a wrong cut. Prepare a cutting chart in such a way that the least number of paper cutter settings is required.

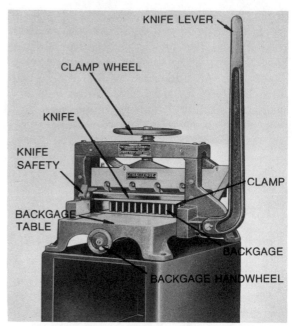

Fig. 154-4. A bench-model, lever-operated paper cutter. (The Challenge Machinery Co.)

PARTS AND PURPOSES

Learn the parts and the purposes of the paper cutter (Fig. 154-4). In this way one can better become a careful, safe, and efficient operator.

Table. The flat, smooth horizontal surface on which the paper is placed while being cut.

Backgage. An adjustable part against which paper is placed to cut the desired size.

Backgage Handwheel. The wheel which adjusts the depth of the backgage from the cutting knife. Turning the wheel clockwise moves the backgage back for a larger-cut sheet. Turning it counterclockwise makes the sheet smaller.

Clamp. A pressure bar which is lowered on the paper to keep it from moving while being cut.

Clamp Wheel. The clamp wheel raises and lowers the clamp.

Knife. The knife should always be razor-sharp. It is the heart of a paper cutter.

Knife Lever. The lever operates the cutting knife. Pressure applied to the lever forces the knife to cut through a stack of paper.

Knife Safety. This is a very important safety device which is a part of most paper cutters. It locks the knife in an *up* position and must be released before the knife can be lowered to cut paper. It is designed so that both hands must be used.

PAPER-CUTTER OPERATION

1. Move the backgage to the desired cutting size by turning the backgage hand wheel (Fig. 154-5). Most cutters have a backgage position indicator which shows the depth of cut to be made (Fig. 154-6).

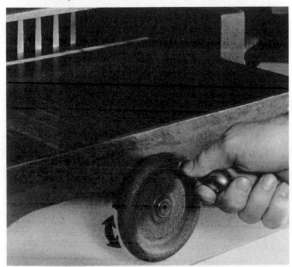

Fig. 154-5. Turning the backgage handwheel to position the backgage before inserting the paper.

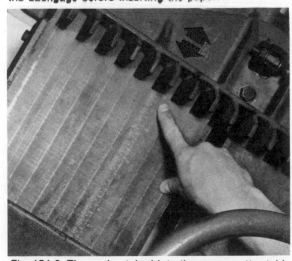

Fig. 154-6. The scale etched into the paper-cutter table helps in setting the backgage correctly.

2. Tighten the locking screw for the backgage wheel when the desired position is attained.
3. Jog the paper.
4. Place the paper in position on the table against the backgage and the left side of the paper cutter (Fig. 154-7).
5. Place a protective piece of chipboard or thin cardboard on top of the paper immediately behind the path of the blade. This protects the top sheets of paper from possible clamp damage (Fig. 154-8). The chipboard protective sheet is not necessary if the cutter is equipped with a solid plate on the clamp.
6. Lower the clamp by turning the clamp wheel to the right. The clamp should be tight against the paper.
7. Grasp the knife lever with the right hand. Pull the knife safety with the left hand. Lower the knife slightly (Fig. 154-9).

Fig. 154-7. Placing the paper against the backgage and left side of the paper cutter.

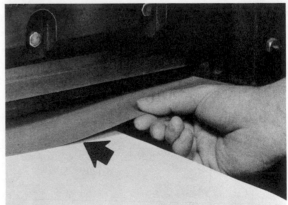

Fig. 154-8. Protective chipboard (thin cardboard) placed under the clamp.

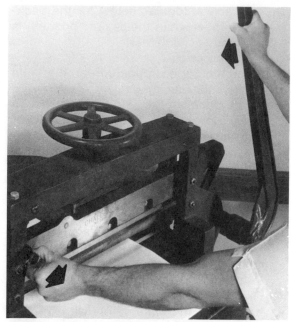

Fig. 154-9. Pull the knife safety while holding the knife lever.

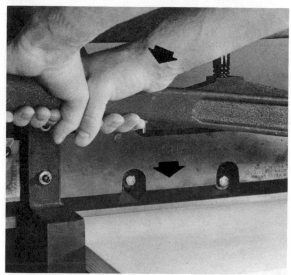

Fig. 154-10. The knife and knife lever in the lowest position after the cut has been made.

8. Move the left hand to the knife lever and pull the lever with *both hands.* Cut the paper (Fig. 154-10), but do not slam the blade to the paper. A better cut results if the knife is brought to the paper and then pulled through it firmly.

   Fig. 154-10 also illustrates the action of the knife. The knife has a slicing movement to the left through the paper.

9. Raise the knife after the cut has been made. *Caution:* Be certain that the safety catch has caught before you remove your hands from the knife lever. If it does not catch, the knife may fall and possibly cause a serious injury to you.
10. Raise the clamp by turning the clamp wheel counterclockwise and position the bottom of the clamp approximately ⅛ inch below the knife. This protects the operator from hand injuries while removing and inserting paper.
11. Remove the cut paper. If additional cuts are to be made, set the backgage for the new size desired. Follow the instructions outlined in this unit.

SPECIAL CUTS

Paper cutters are used not only to cut plain and printed flat paper. Booklets must also be trimmed. Fig. 154-11 shows saddle

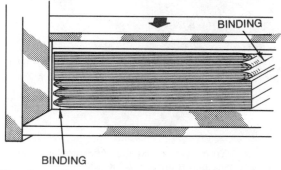

Fig. 154-11. Trimming saddle-stitched books. Note the slicing action of the knife.

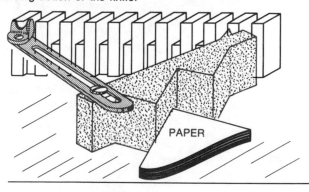

Fig. 154-12. Paper stock guide for cutting paper at any angle.

stitched booklets properly positioned in the paper cutter. Note that half of the books should be turned with the bound edge to the left side, and half to the right. This helps to level the books and to equalize the pressure so the clamp will hold all sheets securely.

Angle cuts can be made by using a jig that attaches to the backgage (Fig. 154-12). This device can be adjusted to any angle. The paper to be cut is placed against it before the clamp is lowered. Normal cutting/trimming procedure is then followed in making these special cuts.

UNIT 155
BASIC BINDING METHODS

Sheets of paper, folded or unfolded, are bound together in several different ways. Evidence of this is visible in almost any place we look. Books of various sizes, thicknesses, and methods of binding (Fig. 155-1) are common and are used throughout the world.

Methods of binding, or holding, the sheets of paper together are important to the use and life of the book. Some binding methods are designed for low cost and

short life; others for a long life of hard use. Most persons who use a book are unaware of the binding method that holds the sheets together. They are aware only of the graphic information contained on the sheets.

BINDING METHODS

Mechanical. The two common mechanical bindings are *spiral wire* and *plastic cylinder.* Spiral wire binding (Fig. 155-2) is fre-

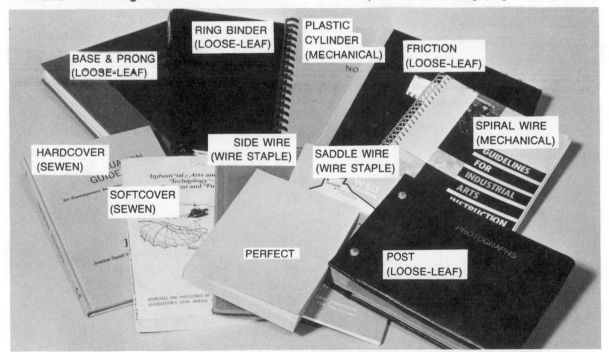

Fig. 155-1. Books of various sizes and thicknesses bound by common binding methods.

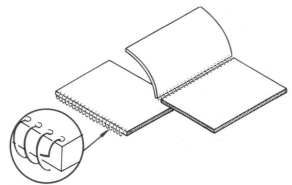

Fig. 155-2. Spiral-wire binding.

Fig. 155-6. Base-and-prong binding.

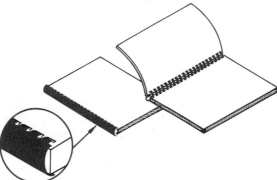

Fig. 155-3. Plastic-cylinder binding.

Fig. 155-7. Friction binding.

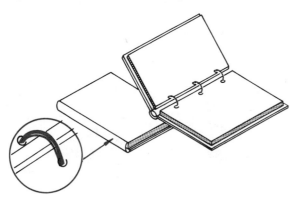

Fig. 155-4. A ring binder.

Fig. 155-8. Saddle-wire binding.

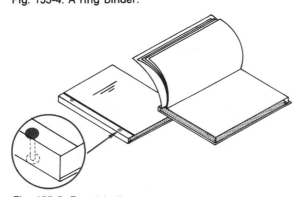

Fig. 155-5. Post binding.

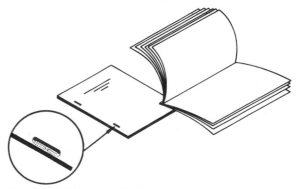

Fig. 155-9. Side-wire binding.

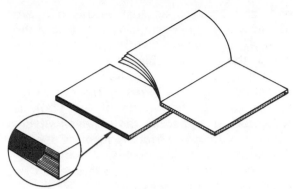

Fig. 155-10. Perfect binding.

Fig. 155-12. Sewn hard-cover or case-bound binding.

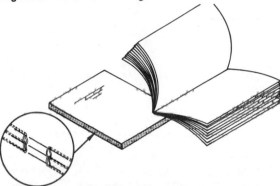

Fig. 155-11. Sewn soft-cover binding.

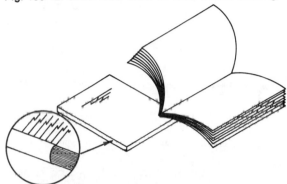

Fig. 155-13. Ultrasonic (welding) binding.

quently used for school notebooks. Plastic-cylinder binding (Fig. 155-3) takes care of business reports and books such as monographs.

Mechanical bindings are not considered highly permanent, but they do withstand some rough use. The sheets do not need to be of a uniform size and the bound book lies flat when opened.

Loose-leaf. This style of binding permits ease in adding or removing sheets. The *ring binder,* usually three-ring, (Fig. 155-4) is the most popular. The *post-binding* method (Fig. 155-5) is suitable for photograph albums and catalogs.

The *Base-and-prong* method (Fig. 155-6) is similar to post binding. Both methods can be used to bind single sheets of uneven size into thicknesses of up to three or four inches. *Friction binding* (Fig. 155-7) is rapidly becoming popular. A plastic U-shaped strip is slid on the binding edge, clamping the paper edges. Booklets of a few pages are suited to this binding method.

Wire staple. Two common binding methods use wire staples. The *saddle-wire* meth-od (Fig. 155-8) is used to bind magazines and small booklets. The *side-wire* type (Fig. 155-9) is used for binding thicker magazines and books. Staples are placed through the fold in saddle-wire binding and in side-wire binding the staples hold sheets together on the left margin. Both methods are economical and materials can be rapidly bound by hand or with automatic equipment.

Perfect. Perfect binding (Fig. 155-10) was developed because a need existed for a binding method that did not require sewing and hard covers. Sheets of paper are held together by a flexible adhesive. Pocket-size books are almost exclusively bound in this manner and with automated equipment. It is fast, economical, and results in an attractive product.

Sewn. Sewn bindings are the most permanent way to hold sheets of paper together. Strong thread is placed through the binding edge of each sheet and securely holds all sheets in place between the covers of a book.

Sewn bindings with soft covers (Fig. 155-11) will withstand hard use for a limited time. Technical information is often bound in this manner because the book will pass through many hands during its brief but valuable life. Chances of individual sheets or signatures falling from an inexpensively bound book with technical material cannot be tolerated.

Sewn bindings with hard covers (Fig. 155-12) are used when hard use and long wear are expected. *Case bound,* and *case binding* are other names given to this common bookbinding method. Most library books and school textbooks, just as this one, are bound with hard covers or cases. This is the most expensive bookbinding method but it is also the most durable.

Welding. Binding by welding is the most recent development in fastening a book together. The binding edge of the book is subjected to ultrasonic radio waves which, because of heat and friction, fuse the sheets. The sheets may then be bound with either a soft or hard cover. This has proven to be a very effective process.

UNIT 156
SOFT-COVER BINDING

Soft-cover binding is a popular and practical method of holding sheets of paper together. Economy, binding speed, and versatility are prominent advantages of this type of binding. The procedures for several of the soft-cover methods are presented.

PLASTIC-CYLINDER BINDING

Materials
  Printed sheets
  2 Covers
  1 Plastic cylinder

Tools and Equipment
  Paper cutter
  Special multiple-hole punch
  Plastic-cylinder binding machine
  Hand shears

1. Gather the sheets and the covers in correct order, either by hand or by machine.
2. Trim the gathered sheets to the desired size. Paper measuring 8½ x 11 inches is not usually trimmed because it is a common booklet size.
3. Punch holes in the binding edge with the special multiple-hole punch (Fig. 156-1). Adjust the punch accurately.

Plastic cylinders are available in several diameters; different punching positions are, therefore, required. Punching specifications are listed on the machine. Note that the holes are rectangular.

4. Attach the plastic cylinder to the punched sheets. A special machine opens and holds open the several tongues on the cylinder while the sheets are positioned (Fig. 156-2). The diameter of the cylinder should be slightly larger than the thickness of the booklet.

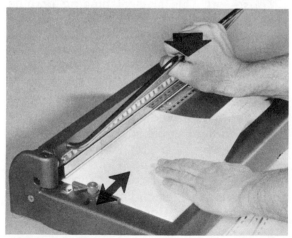

Fig. 156-1. Punching holes in the binding edge of a booklet with a multiple-hole punch.

Fig. 156-2. Attaching the plastic cylinder to the punched sheets.

5. Trim the plastic cylinder with a pair of shears to correspond to the height of the booklet. Plastic cylinders are usually 11 inches long to conform to the standard 8½ x 11-inch sheet of paper.

POST BINDING (LOOSE-LEAF)

Materials
   Printed sheets
   2 Binder's board covers
   2 Binder's board strips
   2 Binding cloth coverpieces
   2 Binding cloth end sheet pieces
   Glue
   Hot stamping foil
   2 Binding posts

Tools and Equipment
   Board shears
   Rule
   Glue brush
   Folding bone
   Hand shears
   Paper cutter
   Hot-stamp press
   Type
   Paper punch

1. Gather the sheets of paper and trim them to the specified size. NOTE: The following information is given for the front cover only. All steps should be followed for the back cover, omit Step 16.
2. Cut the heavy binder's board material used for the stiff cover. Use board shears (Fig. 156-3). This piece should be ⅛-inch wider and ¼-inch higher than the sheets of paper.

Fig. 156-3. Cutting binder's board with a board shears.

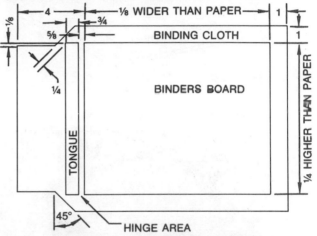

Fig. 156-4. *Post* tongue and cover construction.

3. Cut a binder's board strip ¾-inch wide and the same length as the binder's board cover height. This piece will be used for the tongue.
4. Cut the binding cloth which will cover the binder's board. It should be 5 inches larger than the cover width and 2 inches larger than cover height.
5. Apply glue to the binder's board cover. Hot or cold bookbinder's glue should be used.
6. Place the cover, glued side down, on the binding cloth. Position this piece one inch from each of three sides of the binding cloth (Fig. 156-4). Rub the glued area with a folding bone to remove wrinkles and air pockets.
7. Apply glue to the binder's board strip. Position it ⁵⁄₁₆ inch from the cover board (Fig. 156-4). This strip forms the tongue of the book cover.
8. Trim the corners of the binding cloth to the left of the tongue (Fig. 156-4).

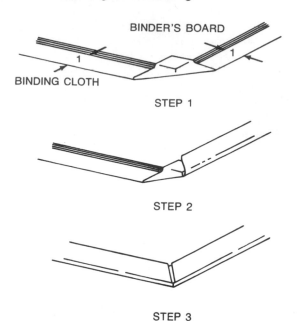

STEP 1

STEP 2

STEP 3

Fig. 156-5. Steps in making the library corner.

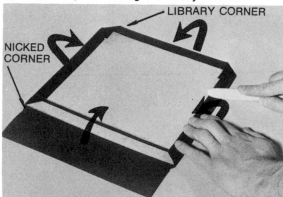

Fig. 156-6. Gluing the binding cloth over the edges of the binder's board.

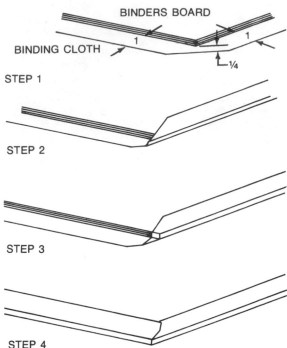

STEP 1

STEP 2

STEP 3

STEP 4

Fig. 156-7. Steps in making the nicked corner.

9. Glue and fold over the binding cloth on the front corners (opposite the tongue side) at 45°. This begins a library corner (Fig. 156-5).
10. Glue and fold the top and bottom pieces of binding cloth over the binder's board (Fig. 156-6).
11. Glue and fold the binding cloth at the two remaining corners over the tongue to form nicked corners (Fig. 156-7).
12. Glue and fold the remaining binding cloth over the binder's board cover and tongue (Fig. 156-6). Firmly rub the area between the tongue and binder's board with a folding bone. This area is the hinge.

13. Cut a piece of binding cloth or end sheet ¼-inch smaller than the width and ¼-inch smaller than the height of the binder's board cover.
14. Apply glue. Position the piece on the inside of the cover. Allow a ⅛-inch margin on all four sides. This conceals the binding cloth edges and makes an attractive cover both inside and out.
15. Press the cover in a bookpress or under heavy weights for 24 hours.
16. Hot stamp the book title and other desired information on the front cover (Fig. 156-8).
17. Punch holes in the sheets and the cover tongues.
18. Assemble the book with binding posts. These are bolt-like devices available in ½-inch to several-inch lengths.

SADDLE-WIRE STITCHING

Materials
  Pamphlet content (printed pages)
  1 Cover
Tools and Equipment
  Wire stitcher
  Paper cutter

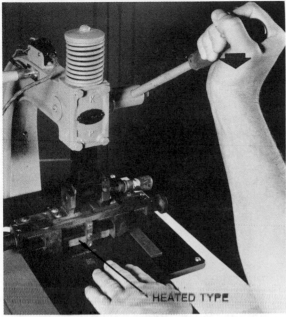

Fig. 156-8. Hot stamping the loose-leaf cover with gold leaf foil.

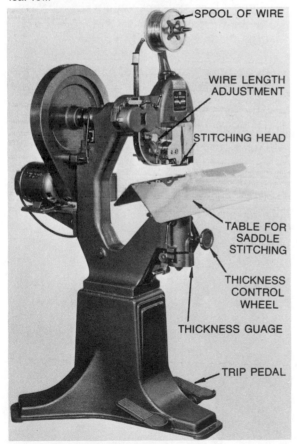

SPOOL OF WIRE

WIRE LENGTH ADJUSTMENT

STITCHING HEAD

TABLE FOR SADDLE STITCHING

THICKNESS CONTROL WHEEL

THICKNESS GUAGE

TRIP PEDAL

Fig. 156-9. A wire-stitching machine ready for saddle stitching. (Interlake Steel Corp.)

1. Fold the printed sheets into signatures. This can be done either by hand or by using a folding machine (Fig. 153-6).
2. Gather the signatures and the cover. Make certain all pages are in correct order. Gathering is done either by hand or by a mechanical gathering device (Fig. 153-13).
3. Prepare the stitcher for saddle stitching (Fig. 156-9). Stitchers are used to make wire-staple bindings—saddle-wire and side-wire.
   a. Place the saddle-stitching table on the stitching machine.
   b. Adjust the thickness control by placing the pamphlet (the signatures and cover) in the thickness gauge. Remember to open the pamphlet before inserting it into the gauge.
   c. Adjust the wire for length. The number on the wire-length adjustment lever should correspond to the number indicated on the thickness gauge.
   d. Check to see that the wire on the machine will be appropriate for the pamphlet thickness being stitched.
   e. Check the maintenance manual for additional specific adjustments.
4. On a practice pamphlet, make several staples to determine if all machine settings are correct. Step on the trip pedal and release it immediately to obtain one staple. If the trip pedal is held down, the stitcher will continue to operate. Make the necessary adjustments.

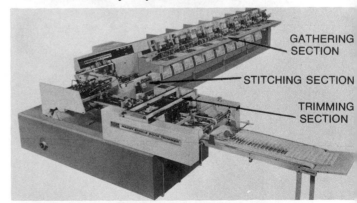

GATHERING SECTION

STITCHING SECTION

TRIMMING SECTION

Fig. 156-10. A machine that gathers, stitches, and trims saddle-stitched pamphlets, magazines, and books. (Harris-Seybold Co.)

5. Place staples evenly (two or three, depending on pamphlet height) in the fold of the pamphlets. See Fig. 155-8 for the specific locations.
6. Trim the three unbound edges to give the pamphlet a neat appearance. Follow the cutting procedure outlined in Unit 154.

The machine in Fig. 156-10 gathers, stitches, and trims several thousand pamphlets per hour when on a mass-production basis.

SIDE-WIRE STITCHING

Materials
Book or pamphlet content
2 Book covers
1 Binding tape

Tools and Equipment
Wire stitcher
Folding bone
Paper cutter

1. Fold the printed sheets into signatures.

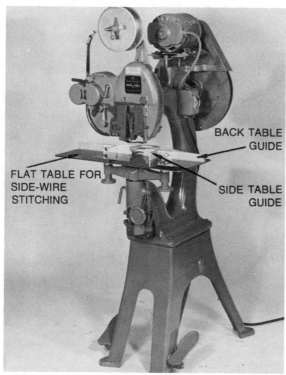

FLAT TABLE FOR SIDE-WIRE STITCHING

BACK TABLE GUIDE

SIDE TABLE GUIDE

Fig. 156-11. A wire-stitching machine ready for side-wire stitching. (Interlake Steel Corp.)

2. Gather the signatures or the single sheets.· Side-wire binding permits the use of single sheets.
3. Prepare the stitcher for side-wire stitching (Fig. 156-11).
   a. Place the flat table on the stitching machine.
   b. Attach the back and side guides to the table. Adjust the guides to the approximate stitching positions.
   c. Finish preparing the stitcher according to Step 3a, b, c, d, and e under *Saddle-Wire Stitching*.
4. Use a practice pamphlet or book. Make several stitches to determine if all machine settings are correct. If not, make the needed adjustments.
5. Place two or three staples evenly along the binding edge of the booklet (Fig. 155-9). Make final adjustments of the back and side guides at this time.
6. Place binding tape, which has colorful paper or cloth with an adhesive backing, around the binding edge (Fig. 156-12). This covers the staples and binding edge to improve the appearance of the book. Smooth this tape with a folding bone.
7. Trim the three unbound edges to give the book an attractive appearance. Follow the cutting procedure outlined in Unit 154.

A bookstitcher or side-wire stitcher used in industry is shown in Fig. 156-13. It contains six stitching heads.

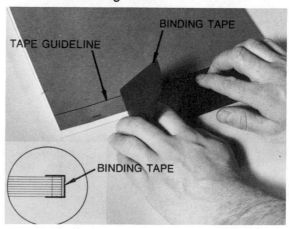

TAPE GUIDELINE

BINDING TAPE

BINDING TAPE

Fig. 156-12. Placing binding tape around the binding edge of a side-stitched book.

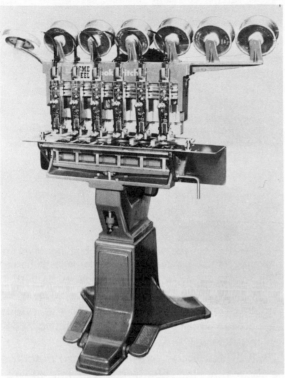

Fig. 156-13. A bookstitcher or side-wire stitcher with six stitching heads. (Interlake Steel Corp.)

PERFECT BINDING (HAND METHOD)

Materials
Book content
1 Super (gauze-like material)
2 End sheets
Adhesive

Tools and Equipment
Glue brush
Rule
Binder's knife
Shears
Paper cutter

1. Gather the printed signatures or single sheets. Place an end sheet on the top and bottom of the signatures or sheets.
2. If signatures, trim the binding edge. This exposes the edges of all the sheets and allows the adhesive to contact each one.
3. Place scrap divider sheets between each book.
4. Jog the sheets and place in a perfect binding (padding) press (Fig. 156-14).

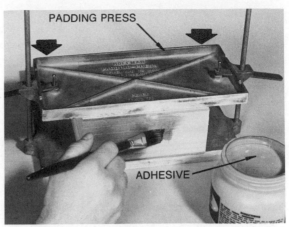

Fig. 156-14. Applying adhesive to the binding edge of several book piles that are being perfect-bound.

Pieces of binder's board on the top and bottom of the book pile help to make the stack firm. This assists in handling the books before and after gluing.

Several books may be glued at one time. The number depends upon the thickness of each and the capacity of the perfect binding press.

5. Apply adhesive to the binding edges of the books (Fig. 156-14). The adhesive, sometimes called padding compound, is a dairy-product glue having excellent penetrating and elasticity qualities.

The first coat of adhesive should penetrate the edges of the sheets $\frac{1}{16}$ inch, so brush it into the sheets well. Allow to dry for approximately 10 to 15 minutes without moving.
6. Apply the second coat of adhesive.
7. Place a strip of super over the wet glue. With a folding bone, press the super into the wet adhesive. Allow to dry. The super greatly increases the binding strength.
8. Remove the top clamp from the perfect binding press, then remove the stack of book bodies. Use a binder's knife to cut the super and glue and separate each book body.
9. Cut the cover to wrap around the front, binding edge, and back of the book body.
10. Score or mark the wrap-around cover to correspond with the book thickness. Scoring makes folding the paper easier

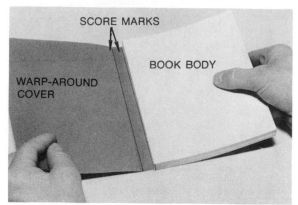

SCORE MARKS

BOOK BODY

WARP-AROUND COVER

Fig. 156-15. Attaching the wrap-around cover to a perfect-bound book.

Fig. 156-16. An automatic perfect binding machine equipped with a signautre and single-page gathering unit.

at the binding edges. It can be done by hand, but is commonly performed as described in Unit 153.

11. Apply a coat of glue to the binding edge of the book body.

12. Attach the wrap-around cover as shown in (Fig. 156-15).

13. Press the cover of the binding edge, now called a backbone, with a folding bone. Allow it to dry for several hours.

14. Trim the three unbound edges of the perfect-bound book. Do not place ex-

cessive pressure on the backbone of the book with the clamp of the paper cutter while trimming as excessive pressure tends to crush it.

A fully automatic perfect binding machine is shown in Fig. 156-16. It is capable of producing more than 6,000 perfect-bound books per hour.

UNIT 157
CASE BINDING

Case binding is the most durable method of binding. A *case,* sometimes called a hard cover, is wrapped around the book to protect the pages from damage. Several materials are combined to form a case-bound book (Fig. 157-1).

PARTS OF A BOOK

Body. This is the part of the book which contains graphic information in the form of pages.

Case. The covers of a hardbound book.

End sheets. The blank sheets of paper placed at the front and back of a book.

Their purpose is to help hold the body in the case and to protect the first and last printed pages.

Backbone. The back, or binding, edge of any bound book. Spine is a synonymous term.

Super. This is the gauze-like fabric glued to the backbone and case. It provides a permanent link between them.

Binder's board. A thick, gray, rigid paper board used to make the case.

Book cloth. A fabric made either from synthetic or natural materials. It is used to cover the two pieces of binder's board that form the case.

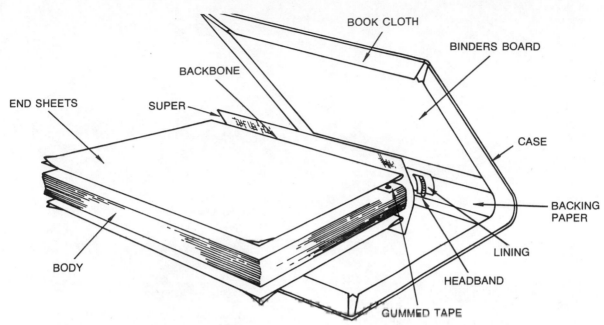

BOOK CLOTH

BINDERS BOARD

BACKBONE

END SHEETS

SUPER

CASE

BACKING PAPER

LINING

HEADBAND

BODY

GUMMED TAPE

Fig. 157-1. Parts of a case-bound book.

Backing paper. A stiff but flexible paper strip placed between the two binder's boards. It gives the book cloth stability around the backbone.

Lining. A heavy kraft paper glued to the backbone to provide a smooth, even surface.

Headbands. Colorful beads of thread placed for decoration at the top and bottom of the backbone.

Gummed tape. Strong reinforcement tape glued to the edges of the end sheets.

Thread. This is usually linen thread used to sew the book signatures together.

CASE BINDING

There are several distinct steps in case binding a book. By studying these the graphic arts student should understand the basic manufacturing procedures.

1. Large printed sheets of paper (the pages for the book) are folded into signatures. Special paper-folding machines perform this function (Fig. 153-6).
2. End sheets are cut to size, taped, folded, and glued to the first and last signatures of the book. Generally, an end sheet is placed on the front and at the back of the book.
3. The several signatures necessary for one book are then gathered in their proper order. Machines designed to collect signatures into the proper groupings are used (Fig. 153-13).
4. The signatures are then sewed together. One of three methods is used, depending upon the style, intended use, and thickness of the book.
   a. *Saddle sewn.* Signatures are sewn through the fold (Fig. 157-2) with a heavy-duty sewing machine. This method is used for notebooks, stamp collection books, and account books.
   b. *Flat sewn.* Two to several signatures or single sheets up to 1 inch in

Fig. 157-2. A saddle-sewn book.

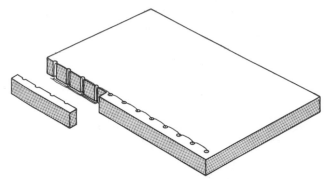

Fig. 157-3. A side-sewn book.

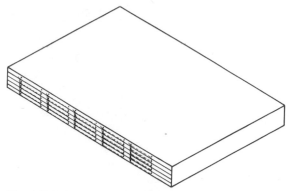

Fig. 157-5. A signature-to-signature sewn book.

Fig. 157-4. A high-speed side-sewing machine. (The Dexter Co.)

Fig. 157-6. An automatic signature-to-signature book-sewing machine. (The Smyth Manufacturing Co.)

thickness are sewn through the side of the sheets (Fig. 157-3). Side-sewing machines can sew more than 1,000 books per hour (Fig. 157-4). This method is used for school textbooks where hard use is expected.

c. *Signature-to-signature sewn.* Two to any number signatures can be sewn together. The thickness of the book is not limited by machine capacity but only by the feasibility of handling the bound edition. In this method of sewing the books have an individual hinge at each signature because the signatures are sewed one to another (Fig. 157-5).

Sewing machines used for this method are either hand-fed or completely automatic (Fig. 157-6). An au-

tomatic machine sews up to eighty-five signatures per minute.

Signature-to-signature sewing is the most expensive. Advantages lie in the strength of the book, which opens and stays open easily and the fact that only a small binding margin is needed.

5. After the body has been sewn together it must be prepared to receive the hard cover. Several operations make it ready for the cover. All of these together are called *forwarding.*

a. *Nipping and smashing.* During the sewing operation the binding edge of the book body has gained additional thickness because of the thread. To make the finished book more attractive and easier to handle, the binding edge and the total book body are pressed under a great amount of pressure. This makes it the same exact thickness throughout.

The nipping operation places heat and pressure only on the sewing or binding edge of the body. Metal bars under hydraulic pressure are forced against each side of the book to press the sewn edges firmly (Fig. 157-7).

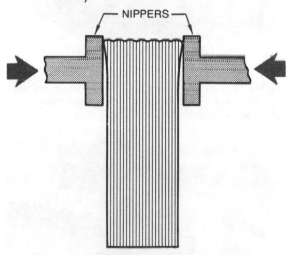

Fig. 157-7. Nipping a sewn book body. Heat and pressure force the binding edge together.

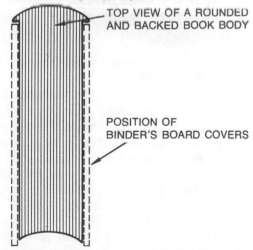

TOP VIEW OF A ROUNDED AND BACKED BOOK BODY

POSITION OF BINDER'S BOARD COVERS

Fig. 157-8. The shape of book body after it has been rounded and backed.

Immediately after the book has been nipped, the body moves to the next station in the machine and the entire unit is smashed. Metal plates are forced against both sides of the book body under pressure. This makes the body the same thickness. During nipping and smashing procedures, glue is applied mechanically to the binding edge of the book body. The glue dries rapidly and assists in holding the book body in its compressed position.

b. *Trimming.* Once the book has been nipped and smashed it receives final trimming. In most large book binderies an automatic three-knife book trimmer is used (Fig. 153-3).

c. *Rounding and backing.* The final bound book is rounded and backed to make it more attractive and usable. The backbone will actually receive a convex shape; the front edge a concave form (Fig. 157-8).

After the book is rounded, it is backed. This is the process of flaring the binding edge (Fig. 157-8). The binding edge, or backbone, is flared or backed to a thickness of the binder's board used to make the cover.

Both operations are done not only to improve appearance but also to aid the reader to open, keep open, and close the book. An automatic machine that rounds and backs a book body is shown in Fig. 157-9.

Fig. 157-9. An industrial rounding and backing machine. (The Smyth Manufacturing Co.)

Fig. 157-10. An automatic lining and headbanding machine. (The Smyth Manufacturing Co.)

Fig. 157-11. An automatic casemaker for hard-cover construction. (The Smyth Manufacturing Co.)

Fig. 157-12. A casing-in machine. This is where the body and cover are joined to form a complete book. (The Smyth Manufacturing Co.)

Fig. 157-13. A book-forming and pressing machine. (The Smyth Manufacturing Co.)

d. *Attaching super, headbands, and lining.* A lining and headbanding machine (Fig. 157-10) attaches the three backbone materials. A coating of glue is applied to the backbone. The next operation is to attach the super or gauze-like material. Another coating of glue is then applied and the headbands and lining are attached. The super serves as the bridging agent between the book body and the book case. Headbands are only decorative. The lining of a heavy kraft paper gives the backbone a smoother surface.

Book bodies travel from the rounding and backing machine directly to the lining and headbanding machine. When ejected they are completely forwarded and are ready to receive the hard book covers.

6. During the time that the book bodies are being prepared the covers are also constructed and stamped. It is very important that the cover fit the book body; it must, therefore, be made with great care. Ingredients such as book cloth, binder's board, and backing strip are cut and handled with accuracy. A case-making machine (Fig. 157-11) combines these three cover materials by gluing, positioning, pressing, and folding them into a usable book case.

After being completed each case is stamped with the book title, author, publishing company, and any additional information. Standard automatic printing presses are specially equipped to accept the thick covers and to use heat and foil to produce images on them. The platen press produces the image just as does the hot-stamping machine (Fig. 153-19).

7. The book bodies and book cases are now ready to be united. This is called *casing in*. Glue is applied to the front and back end sheets of the body; the case is properly positioned on the body. These operations are done simultaneously on a casing-in machine (Fig. 157-12). It is extremely important that the body be properly positioned within the case.

8. The cased-in books travel to a book forming and pressing machine (Fig. 157-13). They receive heat and pressure to adhere the end sheets to the cover and to form the hinges on the front and back.

9. The books are now complete and can be used. Publishers often place a book

Fig. 157-14. A book-jacketing machine. (The Smyth Manufacturing Co.)

jacket around the book to protect the cover and to provide a place for additional promotional information. These are attached by hand or by a book-jacketing machine (Fig. 157-14).

10. The books are ready for distribution. Corrugated cardboard cartons are constructed to a specific size to accept certain sizes of books. The books are carefully packed and are shipped for distribution.

UNIT 158
HAND CASE BINDING

Hand case binding can be done in the school laboratory with a minimum amount of equipment. The same procedure is carried out in hand case binding as is done in commercial case binding. The student, therefore, after completing a hand case binding job should understand basic industrial book-binding procedures.

For illustration purposes, a year's volume of professional journals or any magazine will be hand case bound. The signature-to-signature sewing method is used to bind them. A single issue of a journal could be saddle sewn or several could be flat sewn. All other basic hand case bound operations would be performed in the same manner.

Materials
  Issues of journals
  Transparent mending tape
  2 Binder's boards
  1 Piece binding cloth
  4 End sheets
  2 Pieces lining paper
  2 Headbands
  3 Sewing tapes
  1 Piece super
  Sewing thread
  Hot stamping foil
  Binding glue (hot or cold)

Tools and Equipment
  Board shears
  Paper cutter
  Hand shears
  Folding bone
  Pressing boards
  Book clamp
  Sewing frame
  Backing press
  Backing hammer
  Back saw
  Hot-stamping machine
  Glue brush
  Glue pot
  Rule
  Sewing needles

BINDING

1. Arrange the journals in chronological order. Place the December issue index in the back. NOTE: For this binding procedure, the term *signature* will be used instead of journal.
2. Remove the staples from each signature. Be careful not to tear the pages.
3. Repair torn pages with transparent mending tape. Each signature may need tape over the staple holes on the inside of the center. Remove advertising inserts. They will be of little value because they become obsolete.
4. Prepare the four end sheets:
    a. Using heavy-weight book paper, cut two end sheets ¾-inch wider than the signatures, but the same height. Fold the extra ¾-inch over and lay these two sheets aside.
    b. Cut two end sheets the same size as the signatures.
    c. Cut two binding cloth strips 2½ inches wide and the same height as the signatures.
    d. Glue each of these two end sheets to the binding cloth strips with a ½ inch overlap.
    e. Fold a ¾-inch strip of binding cloth over, good side up. Study Fig. 158-1.
5. Attach the end sheets to the first (top) and last (bottom) signatures:
    a. Apply glue inside the ¾-inch folded flaps, using the all-paper end sheets.
    b. Place one of the end sheets on the front of the first signature, with the ¾-inch flap folded around the back of the signature.
    c. Place the second all-paper end sheet on the back of the last signature, with the flap around the front of the signature (Fig. 158-2).

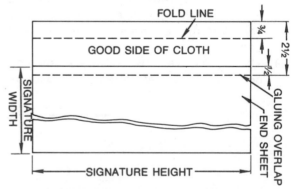

Fig. 158-1. The dimensions for preparing end sheets.

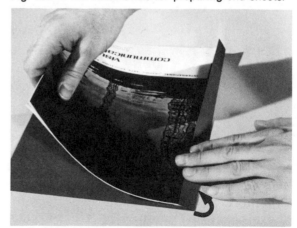

Fig. 158-2. Placing an end sheet on the last or bottom signature.

d. Apply glue to the ¾-inch folded flaps of the other paper-and-cloth end sheets.

e. Attach them directly over the all-paper ones in the same manner.

f. Place the two signatures in a book press.

g. Allow the glue to dry thoroughly. Place waxed paper above, between, and below the signatures to prevent them from sticking together.

h. Replace the signatures in their correct chronological order when they are dry.

SEWING SIGNATURES TOGETHER

6. Jog the signatures and place saw-guide boards on each side. Put the assembly in a clamp: two 1 x 4's with two bolts; two wood handscrew clamps; or a standard backing press will serve clamping needs.

7. Mark lines for the saw cuts on the binding edge of the signatures (Fig. 158-3). The lines must be square across the binding edge of the signatures. They must also conform to the width of the sewing tape that is used.

8. Cut into the saw-guide boards and the binding edge with a backing or dovetail saw according to the lines marked. See Figs. 158-3 and 158-4. Saw approximately ¼-inch deep to pierce the inside center pages of the signatures. The saw cuts provide openings for the sewing operation. The saw-board guides can be used many times as they save the time necessary to measure and mark the binding edge each time a new group of the same-size signatures is bound.

9. Unclamp the signatures and position them on a sewing frame.

10. Fasten the sewing tape to the front edge of the sewing frame according to the saw cuts (Fig. 158-5).

11. Prepare the needle and thread. The approximate length of thread needed is determined by multiplying the signature height by the number of signatures.

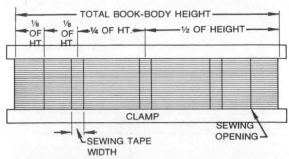

Fig. 158-3. Suggested position for the sewing tapes and end sewing openings. All eight lines represent saw cuts and sewing openings in the signatures.

Fig. 158-4. Sawing the binding edge of the signatures to provide openings for sewing.

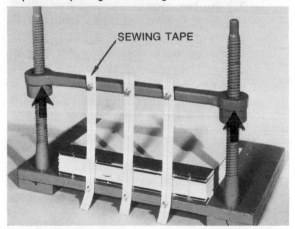

Fig. 158-5. The signatures and sewing tape properly positioned on the sewing frame.

Begin the sewing operation with the last signature:

a. Open the signature to the center. From the outside, insert the needle through the sewing opening on the right side.

b. Bring the needle back out at the first opening or saw cut to the left.

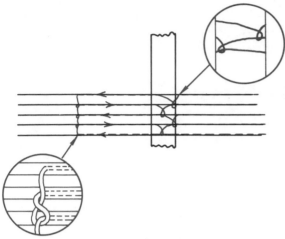

Fig. 158-6. The sewing techniques around the sewing tapes and at the end sewing openings.

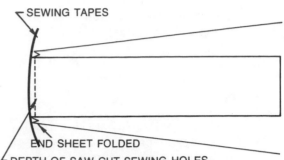

Fig. 158-7. Binding cloth of top and bottom end sheets folded to cover saw cuts or sewing holes.

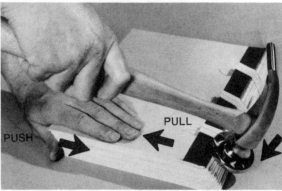

Fig. 158-8. Rounding a book body by the hand method. Note the position of the thumb and fingers on the book body.

c. Go around the sewing tape, back into the signature, out, around the tape. Continue until the left sewing opening is reached.

12. Lay the next signature in position:

a. Begin sewing from left to right. After reaching the first tape (left one), loop the thread of the first signature. Continue sewing (Fig. 158-6).

b. Tie the two signatures together when the right end of the second is reached.

c. Continue with the remaining signatures. The sewing technique at the end-sewing openings is shown in Fig. 158-6. When the last signature has been sewn, take several of these end stitches to secure it firmly. This sewing technique gives a tightly sewn one-unit book body.

13. Release the sewing tapes from the sewing frame. Cut them to extend one inch on each side of the book body.

FORWARDING THE BOOK BODY

14. Nip and smash the book body (see Step 5, Unit 157). Use the backing press for nipping and the book press for smashing.

15. Apply a coating of glue to the backbone and allow it to dry thoroughly while under pressure.

16. Fold the binding cloth on the top and bottom end sheets to cover saw cuts (Fig. 158-7).

17. Trim the three unbound sides with a standard paper cutter (Unit 154). Trim the front first; the bottom second; and the top last.

18. Round the back of the book body (refer to Unit 157-9).

a. Rounding by the hand method involves holding the front edge with one hand and hitting the binding edge with a bookbinder's hammer (Fig. 158-8). Push on the center pages and pull on the front and back pages while hitting the binding edge.

b. Backing the book body involves placing it in a backing press with the binding edge extending ⅛-inch above the jaws. Use a bookbinder's hammer to hit the backbone with light, glancing blows (Fig. 158-9). Strike the backbone from the center toward the edges.

Fig. 158-9. Backing a book body by the hand method. The backbone should extend 1/8 inch above the backing press jaws.

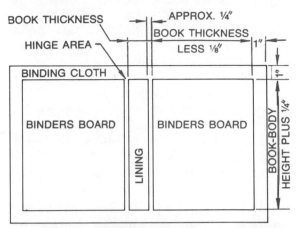

Fig. 158-10. Parts, sizes, and positions of a book case.

Fig. 158-11. Pulling the binding cloth over the second or top binder's board.

19. Attaching the super, headbands, and lining:
    a. Cut a piece of super ½-inch less than the body height and 3 inches greater than the body thickness.
    b. Apply glue to the book backbone.
    c. Attach and center the super.
    d. Cut two headbands ½-inch longer than the body thickness.
    e. Apply glue to the ends of the backbone.
    f. Position the headbands with the bead edge toward the body.
    g. Trim them to exact body thickness with hand shears.
    h. Cut a piece of heavy kraft paper the same size as the backbone and glue it to the backbone. This strip (called lining) helps smooth the backbone.

PREPARING THE CASE

20. Cut binder's boards and binding cloth (Fig. 158-10) as follows:
    a. Cut two binder's boards (Fig. 156-3). Determine the size by increasing the body height by ¼-inch; decrease body width by ⅛-inch.
    b. Cut a piece of binding cloth 2-inches larger than the binding board height and 3-inches larger than the two combined board widths, plus the body thickness.
    c. Apply glue to one binder's board.
    d. Press it to the reverse or inside of the binding cloth. Allow the binding cloth to protrude 1 inch beyond the board on three sides.
    e. Position the book body on the glued binder's board. Allow the board to extend ⅛-inch beyond the top, front, and bottom.
    f. Spread glue on the second binder's board.
    g. Place it on the book body with the glued side up. It must be in perfect alignment with the bottom binder's board.
    h. Pull the binding cloth over the second binder's board (Fig. 158-11) and smooth down. Make sure the boards do not move.

i. Remove the book body and thoroughly press the binding cloth to the boards, using a folding bone. NOTE: Be sure that the two binder's boards are parallel.
21. Cut and attach the cover lining strip (Fig. 158-10) as follows:
    a. Cut a piece of heavy kraft paper the same size as the backbone.
    b. Glue the lining strip midway between the binder's boards. Make certain it is parallel with the top and bottom of the boards (Fig. 158-10).
22. Fold the binding cloth over the binder's boards as follows:
    a. Make nicked or library corners (refer to Figs. 156-5 and 156-7).
    b. Glue and fold the binding cloth over the four edges.
    c. Place the case in a book press for several hours. Be sure two pressing boards are in place with flanges to form the book hinges.
    d. Allow the case to dry thoroughly.
23. Hot stamp the desired lettering on the case as follows:
    a. Compose the type with special hot stamp type.
    b. Heat the stamping unit.
    c. Place the type in the pallet.
    d. Align the case, clamp, and stamp (see Fig. 156-8).
24. Hang the volume into the case. This is called *casing-in.*
    a. Place the book body into the case in the correct position.

b. Open the top cover. Place a sheet of scrap paper between the sewing tapes and the end sheet.
c. Apply glue to the super and tapes.
d. Remove the scrap paper; replace it with a sheet of waxed paper.
e. Close the top cover. Turn the volume over.
f. Repeat Steps b, c, d, and e for the back cover.
g. Place the book between two pressing boards.
h. Clamp in a book press for eight hours. The pressing boards, along with pressure, help form the cover hinge (Fig. 158-12). Note the flange on the pressing board and how it forms the hinge.
25. Complete casing-in the book as follows:
    a. Open the top cover and place a sheet of scrap paper between the two end sheets.
    b. Apply glue to the outside end sheet.
    c. Replace the scrap paper with a sheet of waxed paper.
    d. Close the cover and turn the book over.
    e. Repeat Steps a, b, c, and d for the back cover.
    f. Place the volume between two pressing boards (also called pressing plates). Clamp in a book press for another eight hours (Fig. 158-13). Book completed.

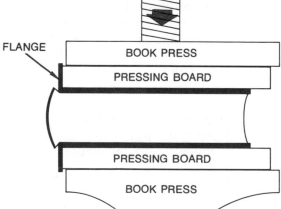

Fig. 158-12. The order and arrangement of the book and pressing boards in the book press.

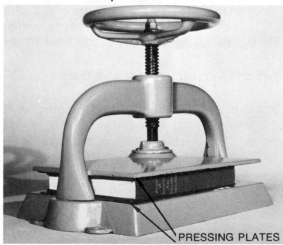

Fig. 158-13. A bound volume between two pressing plates in a book press.

UNIT 159
MICROSTORAGE AND RETRIEVAL SYSTEMS

Microstorage and retrieval systems are commonly categorized as microform, which is a general term for all very small (micro) images. Most of the forms use photographic film in rolls, strips, or small pieces (Fig. 159-1). There are seven basic steps followed with all methods of microform (Fig. 159-2): (1) The original document is exposed, (2) the film is processed, (3) the form is coded, (4) duplicated, (5) stored, (6) retrieved at some later date, and (7) images are produced on screen or on paper copies for use.

The present value and future development of microform systems cannot be overestimated. Primarily, microform systems are designed and used to preserve original documents and to save space in their storage.

Fig. 159-1. The several forms of microform. (Eastman Kodak Co.)

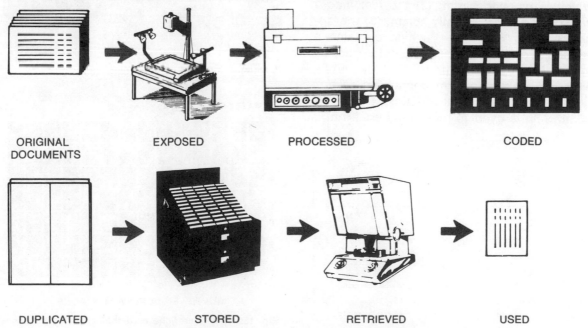

ORIGINAL DOCUMENTS   EXPOSED   PROCESSED   CODED

DUPLICATED   STORED   RETRIEVED   USED

Fig. 159-2. Microform storage and retrieval system.

Paper becomes yellow and deteriorates with age, but film retains its original condition for many years.

The space-saving factor is probably the most important feature of the systems. It is now possible to record the entire Bible on one microfilm card less than two inches square. If books were published in micro-image form, an encyclopedia could be carried in a person's pocket; a book could be mailed in a small envelope for the price of first-class postage. The several million volumes of books in the Library of Congress could be reduced to be contained in less than ten small filing cabinets. The Apollo astronauts took thousands of pages of reference material on their missions. This material was contained in one small unit.

The greatest uses of microform are for reference and for transmitting or carrying graphic information from one location to another. Libraries use microform to relay information to people located in other geographical areas by copying the original document on a microform.

MICROFORM STORAGE

Four common microform storage methods in use (Fig. 159-3) are (1) the *roll film* which is usually 35mm; (2) the *film magazine* or cartridge, usually 16mm; (3) the *aperture card* (Fig. 159-4) which contains a small clip of film attached to a data processing card; and (4) the *microfiche* (Fig. 159-5), which is a sheet of film containing several pages of the original document. Usually 35mm film is used to record material that is

not often required. The magazine cartridge is used to record company or industry documents and customer records. The aperture card is used to record the microimages of large engineering drawings and the microfiche system is used to record company documents and entire books, magazines, and even libraries. Most daily newspapers use microimaging to record their daily newspaper on film for storage in file cabinets instead of keeping the original newspapers in large storage areas.

With all microform storage systems, special equipment is needed to (1) reduce the original document to microimage form, (2) to process the microfilm, (3) to duplicate the microimages, and (4) to retrieve the information. The major piece of equipment to begin the microimaging process is a camera (Fig. 159-6). Several are available and most reduce the original document by 16 to 20 times or more. Some cameras are designed to only photograph the image; others photograph and develop the film.

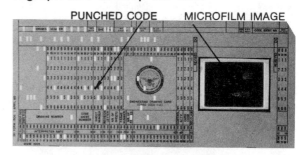

PUNCHED CODE   MICROFILM IMAGE

Fig. 159-4. A coded aperture card. (3M Co.)

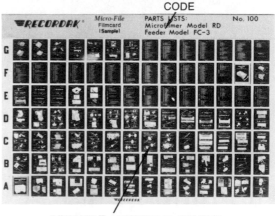

CODE

MULTIPLE MICROFILM IMAGES

Fig. 159-5. A microfiche card that contains 98 pages. (Eastman Kodak Co.)

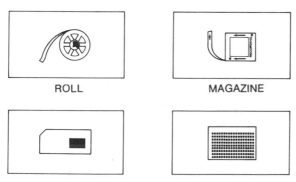

ROLL   MAGAZINE

APERTURE CARD   MICROFICHE

Fig. 159-3. The several microform storage methods.

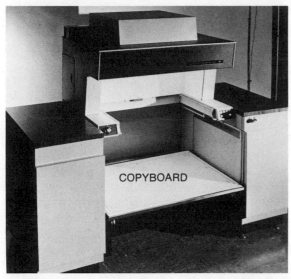

Fig. 159-6. A compact microform camera and film processor unit. (3M Co.)

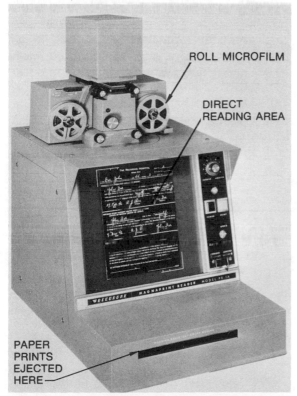

Fig. 159-7. A reader-printer designed to accept 16mm and 35mm microfilm in roll form. (Eastman Kodak Co.)

MICROFORM RETRIEVAL

There must be a retrieval system available for each of the four microform storage methods. Most machines are designed for

Fig. 159-8. A high-speed retrieval system that uses a magazine containing 16mm film. (Eastman Kodak Co.)

Fig. 159-9. A reader-printer designed to accept aperture cards. (3M Co.)

only one storage method, but some are capable of accepting more than one. The reel film can be retrieved by using a machine similar to that pictured in Fig. 159-7. The unit enlarges the microimage to the original size and projects it on a screen or reading area. It also has the capability of producing hard-copy paper prints.

The magazine microimage system, as noted earlier, is used to store company or industry records. A sophisticated retrieval system has been designed for quick recovery of desired information (Fig. 159-8). It locates information in seconds.

Aperture cards, because of their punched

coding system, can also be located quickly, inserted into a reader-printer (Fig. 159-9), and the information enlarged to a size that is very readable. If a print is desired a simple

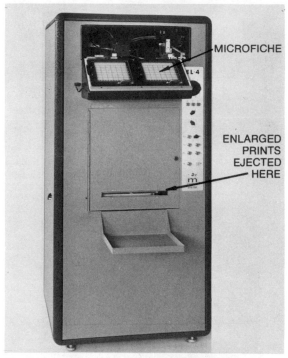

MICROFICHE

ENLARGED
PRINTS
EJECTED
HERE

Fig. 159-10. An automatic microfiche enlarger-printer. (The National Cash Register Co.)

turn of the dial produces in seconds a hard copy at small cost.

The microfiche system uses an enlarger printer (Fig. 159-10). It produces prints of the entire microfiche card or of one or more selected pages within the microfiche.

A BRIEF HISTORY

Microfilm dates back to the late nineteenth century. An enterprising Frenchman, Rene-Prudent-Dragon, photographed 1,000 telegrams on a film strip two inches wide. He attached the film to the leg of a pigeon to send it on a communications mission. It was not until World War II, however, when the military made great use of microform images, that the trend to microfilm began. Following that war there seemed to be little use for microforms, but because of forward-looking business people uses for this system were developed and promoted. It has only been in recent years that the full potential of microform systems has been realized. The future of microform storage and retrieval systems will be expanded greatly through the imagination of executives in business, industry, government, publishing, and education.

UNIT 160
LEARNING EXPERIENCES: FINISHING AND BINDING

DISCUSSION TOPICS

1. Give the purpose of finishing and binding. Identify some of the early book forms. Explain why binding improvements have paralleled the development of books.
2. List ten common finishing methods. Give the purpose of each.
3. Why is it important to make proper plans before cutting a large amount of paper? List the considerations to observe before cutting.
4. What is the primary rule that must be observed by the operator who is cutting paper? What parts of the paper cutter are especially involved with this rule?
5. Why is there a need for a clamp on the paper cutter? Describe the cutting action of the paper-cutter knife.
6. Enumerate the basic binding methods. Identify the specific kinds or ways of holding the sheets of paper together within each binding method. Which of

these bindings is the most permanent?

7. Name the most recent development in fastening sheets of paper together to form a book. Give the principle of this binding method.

8. Why is it essential that a special binding machine be used when attaching the punched sheets to the cylinder in plastic-cylinder binding? Why is there a large number of tongues on the plastic cylinder?

9. With the post or loose-leaf binding method, how much larger should the binder's board cover material be cut than the book pages? Why should the cover be larger than the pages?

10. Illustrate the different kinds of corners that are used when preparing the covers for books. Cite the advantages and disadvantages of each.

11. Give the difference between a stapling machine and a stitching machine. What is the primary advantage of a stitching machine as compared to a stapling machine in producing saddle-wire and side-wire bound books?

12. Describe saddle-wire binding and side-wire binding. When is each used? What disadvantage does side-wire binding have?

13. Name the binding medium used in perfect binding. Name some common materials that are bound by this method. Explain the purpose of the *super*.

14. Enumerate the parts of a case-bound book. What are the purposes of the backing paper and the headbands?

15. List and describe the three methods of sewing signatures together. Identify the type of publications that is sewn by each method.

16. Define *nipping* and *smashing*. What would be the result if a book body does not receive either of these two operations?

17. Name the process, or binding stage, whereby the book bodies and the book cases are united in the case-binding method. Why is it essential that the machine that does this operation be adjusted with precise care?

18. Give the purpose of the saw cuts on the binding edge of the signatures when doing hand-case binding. How many of these saw cuts are needed?

19. With which signature should the sewing operation begin in hand-case binding? Cite the purpose of the sewing tape.

20. Describe the method of preparing the case in hand case binding. Why should the binding cloth protrude approximately one inch beyond the edges of the binder's board?

21. What is the primary advantage of microstorage and retrieval systems? How has this method helped with the problem of the ever-increasing attainment of information?

22. List the four common microform storage methods. Which methods are normally used to record company documents, books magazines and even the entire contents of libraries?

23. Describe the retrieval systems used for each one of the four microform storage methods. How is it possible to locate information that has been stored on one of the microform methods?

ACTIVITIES

1. Visit a commercial bookbinding plant. If possible, also visit a large graphic arts printing plant that has a bindery department. Observe the methods of binding and the procedures by which each commercial plant operates its bindery. Prepare a detailed report on your visit.

2. As a class project, plan and produce from 50 to 100 copies of a booklet. Complete the necessary paper cutting, trimming, folding, scoring, and binding operations. Use either the side-wire or saddle-wire method of binding.

3. Bind five books by each of the methods described in Unit 156.

An aerial view of a large paper manufacturing plant along the Mississippi River. (U. S. Forest Service)

SECTION

UNIT 161
INTRODUCTION TO PULP AND PAPER MANUFACTURING

Paper manufacturing is a basic industry which had its beginning approximately 2,000 years ago. Today it is increasingly a part of the present era of technological change and dynamic industrial growth.

There are over 5,000 manufacturing plants for pulp, paper, and paper products. Practically all of the fifty states have manufacturing plants in over 1,200 cities and towns and the number of employees in the paper industry approaches one million. The per capita consumption of paper is expected to average 580 pounds per year.

PAPER PRODUCTS

Paper has many forms other than the common sheet. Some of these include paper bags, paper for cigarettes, gun cartridges, diapers, drinking cups, filters of all kinds, and polishing cloths. Others include roofing materials, soda straws, towels, signs, wallpaper, sandpaper, building paper, and food wrappers. The fashion world designs and manufactures some paper clothing.

Fig. 161-1. A paper house that can be used as a summer beach house or a winter ski chalet. Then, if desired, it can be collapsed for storage. (American Paper Institute)

Permanent houses of the future may be constructed almost entirely of paper. Today, paper houses that can be used for temporary living are available for summer or winter sports (Fig. 161-1).

PAPER AND THE LIVING INDEX

The relationship between the living index of the United States and the production and consumption of paper products is closely parallel. For comparison, it is noted that in Sweden and Canada the annual per capita consumption of paper is approximately two-thirds that of the United States. Russia uses about one tenth as much paper per person as does the United States. In China, where the original discovery of paper was made nearly 2,000 years ago, the average consumption is estimated at no more than a few pounds of paper per person each year.

HISTORICAL HIGHLIGHTS

Thousands of years ago man expressed himself laboriously by etching pictures and symbols on stones, walls of caves, and bones. Later he used other surfaces such as beeswaxed boards, palm leaves, bronze, silk, and clay tablets. The ancient Greeks used a parchment made from animal skins. Four thousand years ago the Egyptians discovered the more receptive writing surface of the papyrus plant, which they made into a cross-woven mat of reeds and pounded it into a hard, thin sheet. The word *papyrus* is the origin of our word *paper*.

Paper as we know it today was invented

in 105 A.D. by Ts'ai Lun, a Chinese court official. In all likelihood, Ts'ai mixed mulberry bark, hemp, and rags with water, mashed them into a pulp, pressed out the liquid, and hung the thin mat to dry in the sun. This basic wood mixture set off mankind's greatest revolution in communications. In China one emperor had a library of 50 thousand books at a time when most of the great leaders of Europe could not even write their names.

Nearly one thousand years passed before the Chinese technique of paper making was brought into Europe by the Moors of North Africa. Ironically, along the route from the Orient the method of making paper from wood was lost. It took civilization nearly two thousand more years to find the way back to the most practical and plentiful of all raw materials for paper, *wood*.

Until the early 1800s the Western world made paper from rags and cloth. Each sheet was individually turned out by dipping a screen into a vat of water-suspended fibers and then filtering the water away from them. A skilled worker could produce about 750 sheets of paper a day. It was an expensive, tedious process that did not answer the urgent demand for paper.

During the Revolutionary War, the colonists literally did without paper. Soldiers tore up old books to make wadding for their guns. Washington's generals sent him messages on mere scraps of paper. John Adams, in a letter to his wife, wrote, "I send you now and then a few sheets of paper; this article is as scarce here as with you." In desperation, General Washington ordered the discharge of some paper makers from military service and sent them back to the mills.

In 1798 paper production went from hand to machine production. Nicholas-Louis Robert, a clerk at a paper-making mill in Essenay, France, devised a plan for a machine that replaced hand dipping and which produced paper in a continuous roll. It was a large, endless wire screen turned by hand to filter the pulp.

Robert could not get backing for his idea in France, so he sold the patent to the Fourdrinier Brothers in England. They built a practical machine, but failed to provide inexpensive, plentiful paper. The embryonic industry was restricted by the lack of raw materials, as rags were expensive and limited in quantity.

In 1850, Friedrich Gottlob Keller of Germany read a treatise by Rene de Reaumur, a French scientist who lived 100 years earlier. Reaumur noted that wasps used a minute amount of wood fiber to make nests, the texture of which resembled paper. He wrote, "The wasp invites us to try to make fine and good paper from the use of certain woods." Keller developed a machine for grinding wood into fibers. In a few years Hugh Burgess, an Englishman, advanced mechanized paper making another step by inventing a chemical pulping process.

In 1865, C. B. Tilghman, an American scientist, solved a major chemical problem with his invention of the sulphite process for dissolving unwanted resins in wood. Two years later a pulp-grinding machine was imported from Germany to Stockbridge, Massachusetts, and the age of economical mass production of paper in America was launched.

Newspapers increased; more and less expensive magazines were published. The small slate used by students gave way to notebooks and lined paper. Boston mills produced 75 million paper shirt collars a year. Between 1889 and 1900 the production of paper doubled to about 2½ million tons a year.

TREES, THE RAW MATERIAL

The American Tree Farm System was instituted May 21, 1941 on the Clemons Tree Farm at Montesano, Washington. From the 120 thousand acres of this first tree farm, the system has grown to include more than 67 million acres of forest land in 29 thousand certified tree farms.

The impact of tree farming is dramatically illustrated by a tall stand of timber shown in Fig. 161-2. It takes several years for a tree to develop to maturity, and replanting is essential.

Trees are the basic raw material for paper. For illustration, a Douglas fir must be between thirty and forty years of age before it is usable for pulp. This points up the fact that careful, long-range management of this important raw material for paper is essential to economic growth.

Fig. 161-2. A tall stand of tree-farm timber to be used in making paper. (Nekoosa-Edwards Paper Co.)

Fig. 161-3. Wood is one of the basic ingredients in paper manufacture. (Nekoosa-Edwards Paper Co.)

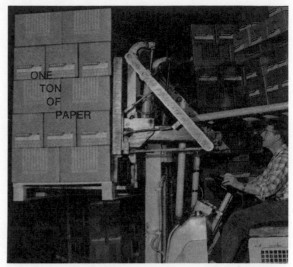

Fig. 161-4. Many elements make up a ton of paper. (Nekoosa-Edwards Paper Co.)

Fig. 161-5. A fresh water supply is essential when making paper. (Nekoosa-Edwards Paper Co.)

Fig. 161-6. Alum, clay, rosin, dye, and pigments must be mixed in proper proportions. (Nekoosa-Edwards Paper Co.)

WHAT GOES INTO A TON OF PAPER

Many other ingredients (Fig. 161-3) besides wood are needed to produce a ton of paper (Fig. 161-4). A supply of fresh water is essential (Fig. 161-5). Other elements and power sources required are indicated in Figs. 161-6 through 161-11.

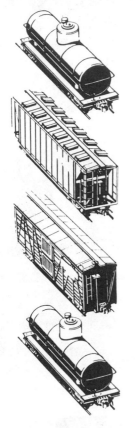

SULFUR
70 POUNDS

MAGNESIUM HYDROXIDE
83 POUNDS

QUICK LIME
360 POUNDS

SALT CAKE
91 POUNDS

CAUSTIC
59 POUNDS

CHLORINE
123 POUNDS

STARCH
105 POUNDS

Fig. 161-7. Many pounds of sulfur, magnesium hydroxide, lime, salt cake, caustic, chlorine, and starch must be used in the production of paper products. (Nekoosa-Edwards Paper Co.)

Fig. 161-8. Skill and know-how required of paper makers cannot be measured by the ton. (Nekoosa-Edwards Paper Co.)

Fig. 161-9. Coal is often used to produce the heat for paper making. (Nekoosa-Edwards Paper Co.)

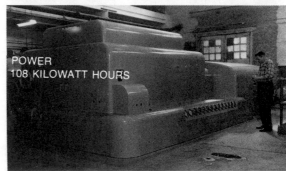

Fig. 161-10. Electric power operates paper-making machinery. (Nekoosa-Edwards Paper Co.)

Fig. 161-11. The most modern plants and equipment for manufacturing paper products are costly. (Nekoosa-Edwards Paper Co.)

UNIT 162
PULP MANUFACTURING

Wood fiber was first used in 1844 and now constitutes 95% of all the papermaking fiber in the world. Wood fibers are obtained from deciduous, or hardwood, trees that have short-length fibers and whose leaves fall each year. Other fiber-bearing woods come from coniferous or cone-bearing, soft-wood trees having fibers that are long, thick, and strong.

WOOD SOURCES

Over 490 million acres of forests in the United States are sources, in part, for papermaking. A program of continued re-planting is necessary (Fig. 162-1) even with this amount of available acreage. Although paper companies purchase more and more timberland, the majority of mills are supplied by the small woodlot farmers.

Better means of transportation and improved highways have resulted in an increase in the trucking of logs (Fig. 162-2), in addition to moving them by rail. In certain areas the logs are brought to the mills by water. After the wood is weighed and purchased, it is placed in storage piles (Fig. 162-3).

Fig. 162-2. Loading pulpwood onto a truck with a fork-lift. (U. S. Forest Service)

Fig. 162-1. Seedlings are planted to replenish the nation's pulp and timber lands. (Nekoosa-Edwards Paper Co.)

Fig. 162-3. Pulpwood is stacked neatly in piles or dropped to form stacks. (U. S. Forest Service)

DEBARKING

From the piles, stacks, or lagoons, the logs are placed either on a conveyor or in a flume (a flowing trough of water) to go to the debarkers. There are both mechanical and hydraulic types of debarkers. The mechanical one shown in Fig. 162-4 is the oldest and most widely used. A drum with vertical slotted plates rubs the logs clean, and if they are not completely debarked the first pass through, they are sent through the drum a second time (Fig. 162-5). It takes less than 30 minutes to debark tons of logs.

Hydraulic debarkers strip the bark from the log by means of water jets. The log is placed in a revolving stand and jets of water under 1500-2000 psi pressure peel the bark from it.

CHIPPING

After the debarking process the logs travel to a chipper, which is a disk fitted with knives that radiate from the hub to the circumference of the disk. The log drops into this swirling disk at about a 45° angle and in seconds a five-foot log is reduced to a jumble of chips of a suitable one-inch size or less.

The chips go over a series of screens and the oversized ones are sorted out and sent to a rechipper. The sawdust and undersized ones are used for fuel or some other profitable purpose. The correct-sized chips then go to a storage area.

PULPING

The three broad classifications of pulping methods are (1) chemical, (2) mechanical (groundwood), and (3) a combination of chemical and mechanical. The object of all pulping processes is to release the fibers from the log. This is done in the chemical method by chemically removing the non-cellulose material which cements the fibers together. In the mechanical process, the fibers are ripped from the log by friction. The chemical-mechanical method employs

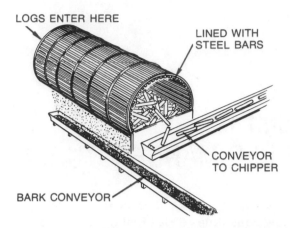

Fig. 162-4. A debarking drum can be operated either dry or partially submerged in water. (The Mead Corp.)

Fig. 162-5. Pulp logs are sorted after leaving the debarker. Those not fully debarked are returned to the machine. (Nekoosa-Edwards Paper Co.)

both chemical action to loosen the fibers and mechanical action to tear them apart.

Chemical pulping. The wood chips are reduced to fibers, not by ripping as in the groundwood process, but by separating each individual fiber from its bonding material. A slab, chip, log, or any wood substance is composed of fibers held together by a glue-like material called *lignin*. Chemical pulping dissolves the lignin binding agent, freeing the fibers. The primary chemical pulping processes use soda, sulfate, and sulfite in the cooking liquors. The chips are conveyed from a storage area to the digesters (Fig. 162-6) which contain the chemicals in which they are cooked.

The mixture is heated in one of two ways

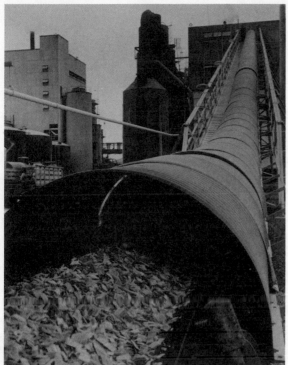

Fig. 162-6. Chips are moved from the storage bins to the giant digesters by covered conveyor. (U. S. Forest Service)

Fig. 162-7. Workmen secure the lid of a digester prior to cooking the chips. (Nekoosa-Edwards Paper Co.)

(Fig. 162-7). Direct heating involves live steam being added directly into the digester. In the alternate method the liquor is pumped through a heat exchanger which is heated.

When the cooking is completed, the pressure is released and the chips (almost in pulp form) are sent into a blow tank. They next go to a washer which removes as much as possible of the cooking chemicals and the dissolved noncellulose. The pulp, now called *brown stock,* is ready for the next operation. In the case of printing paper, this is called *bleaching.*

In recent years there has been a great deal of interest in a continuous digester

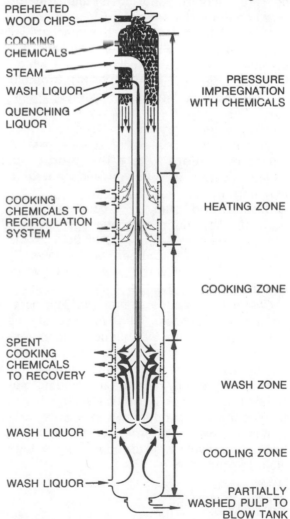

PREHEATED WOOD CHIPS

COOKING CHEMICALS

STEAM

WASH LIQUOR

QUENCHING LIQUOR

PRESSURE IMPREGNATION WITH CHEMICALS

COOKING CHEMICALS TO RECIRCULATION SYSTEM

HEATING ZONE

COOKING ZONE

SPENT COOKING CHEMICALS TO RECOVERY

WASH ZONE

WASH LIQUOR

COOLING ZONE

WASH LIQUOR

PARTIALLY WASHED PULP TO BLOW TANK

Fig. 162-8. A continuous digester over 200 feet tall can produce 700 tons of pulp per day. (American Paper Institute)

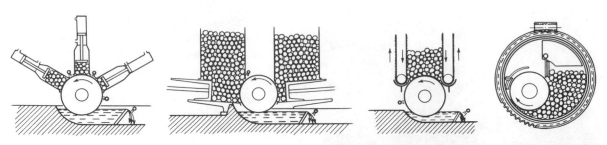

A—THREE POCKET GRINDER   B—MAGAZINE GRINDER   C—CHAIN GRINDER   D—RING GRINDER

Fig. 162-9. The four types of mechanical pulpers. (The Mead Corp.)

(Fig. 162-8), which has a steady in-flow of chips and a constant output of pulp. This equipment is readily adapted to automation, is cheaper to install, has less operating costs (particularly labor costs) and is therefore economically sound.

Mechanical pulping. In the mechanical pulping process (Fig. 162-9), the logs are taken from the debarker to a grinder which tears the fibers from the logs. Logs are held against the grindstone by hydraulic pressure. The ground-off fibers mix with the cooling water spray on the stone to form a slurry of pulp. The slurry passes over a series of screens where the good pulp, called accepts, is removed and sent to a cleaning unit.

Groundwood pulp is a combination of both superior and inferior qualities. It is very efficient because from 90% to 95% of the wood is turned into fiber. Much power is required to grind wood and unless hydroelectric power is available, the cost is high.

Chemical-mechanical pulping. This is a combination process. The wood substance is reduced partially by chemicals, then separated completely mechanically. In the michemical process the chips are lightly cooked to partially dissolve the binding material. The half-cooked chips are next sent to mechanical grinders where the separation is completed. An intermediate pulp with both a relatively high strength and a high yield is produced.

BLEACHING

Bleaching is essentially an extension of the pulping process (Fig. 162-10). The pur-

Fig. 162-10. The pulp is bleached to remove lignin stains and produce a bright white material. (Nekoosa-Edwards Paper Co.)

pose is to remove stains and produce a bright white pulp. Main bleaching agents are chlorine gas, calcium hypochlorite, hydrogen peroxide, and chlorine dioxide. These chemicals react with the color-bearing materials to place them in solution or to release oxygen which destroys them.

Groundwood is bleached by peroxide under controlled conditions. After bleaching has taken place the bleaching agent is neutralized and the pulp is ready for use with no washing required.

BEATING AND REFINING

Beating and refining are important steps in the sequence of operations called stock preparation. The pulp is carried from the pulping and bleaching operations to beaters and refiners.

Beating. A modern beater (Fig. 162-11) performs two functions: (1) it insures completely separated fibers so they will not form

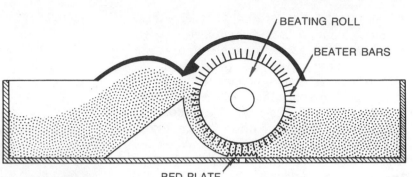

Fig. 162-11. The side view of a typical beater. (The Mead Corp.)

Fig. 162-12. A battery of disc refiners. (The Mead Corp.)

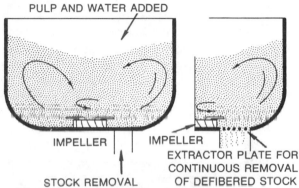

Fig. 162-13. A batch hydrapulper is shown on the left. The continuous hydrapulper (detail on the right) uses a screened outlet to permit properly defibered pulp to be continously withdrawn. (The Mead Corp.)

shives, or lumps, when formed into a sheet, and (2) it modifies the individual fibers so that the papermaker can *felt* them into a uniform sheet with certain desirable mechanical, optical, and chemical properties.

Refining. The refiner (Fig. 162-12) has a bar-studded rotating element which fits closely together. The water-suspended pulp is pumped through the refiner continuously. The fibers are cut and shortened to produce a more uniform pulp.

Pulping. Pulping, or more accurately, repulping, resuspends dried pulp or paper in water. No attempt is made to develop any fiber property. The purpose is to break the pulp or paper down to individual fibers prior to further processing. There are many types of pulpers, all of which can be classified as *batch* and *continuous* (Fig. 162-13).

ADDITIVES

Many noncellulose items are added to the *fiber furnish* before it is carried to the paper machine. They can be added at almost any point in the stock-flow system, but the majority are added at the beaters because that is the least expensive and most convenient place, and no special equipment is needed. At this point the additives are absorbed into the fiber before bonding takes place, and they also result in a uniform distribution.

The four categories of additives used before the pulp goes to the paper machine are (1) material to change inter-fiber bonding, (2) materials to improve optical and physical properties, (3) internal sizing to improve liquid resistance of the paper, and (4) dyestuffs and pigments to impart color to the paper.

CLEANING

The final step in pulp preparation prior to the paper machine is cleaning. The two basic methods of cleaning stock are by screening and by pressure drop cleaners.

Screening. The stock must be screened for uniform fiber dispersion until it is free of fiber clumps, dirt, and other foreign matter. Stock clumps are formed from undercooked wood chips, wastepaper, slime growth, and similar hard-to-break-up materials.

Centricleaner. The pressure drop, or cyclone-type, cleaner (Fig. 162-14) operates on the principle that dirt, fiber bundles, uncooked pulp, and other unwanted materials are heavier than acceptable fiber. When the pulp is spiraled at high velocity, the heavier foreign matter moves to the outside of the spiraling flow.

The cyclone cleaner generally consists of a tapering tube into which the stock is introduced at the side and near the top. The spiraling pulp moves downward toward the small end of the shaft. At the same time an inner spiraling column, or vortex, moves to the top of the shaft where the acceptable stock is removed. The dirt, fiber bundles, and other materials are heavier and cannot make the up-turn and are rejected at the bottom of the shaft.

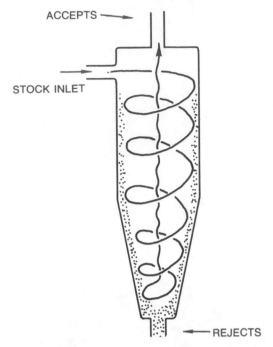

Fig. 162-14. A centricleaner used to clean pulp. (The Mead Corp.)

UNIT 163
PAPER MANUFACTURING

Paper-making machines are monsters of modern mechanization. Some of the larger ones are as long as a football field and are among the largest machines in industry (Fig. 163-1). They are capable of producing paper over 200 inches wide at more than 2,000 feet-per-minute. Today, many processes are controlled by computers; however, operator skill is one of the best controls for paper quality.

FORMING PAPER

Paper pulp is delivered to the continuously moving *Fourdrinier* wire through the head box. The mixture is 99% water to pulp at the wet end (Fig. 163-1). As the pulp trav-

Fig. 163-1. The wet end of a giant paper-making machine. (Kimberly-Clark Corp.)

els the length of the wire, water is removed by gravity and vacuum, and the remaining solids form a mat of paper. At the end the pulp passes through a first set of press rolls. It continues through the drying, sizing, and finishing stages of the *Fourdrinier* paper machine.

WATERMARKS

Watermarks are designs that are placed into the paper without using ink. A watermarked paper is often considered to be of high quality. Good grades of bond paper are used for letterheads, envelopes, and other business uses. A watermark often serves to advertise the company that produced the paper or the business concern that uses it.

Two means of producing watermarks are (1) the dandy roll method (Fig. 163-2) and (2) the rubber stamp roll method (Fig. 163-3). The *dandy roll* produces the true watermark. A cylindrical frame, wrapped with wire cloth, rides on top of the *Fourdrinier*

wire near the end where the pulp leaves the screen to enter the first press drying section. The dandy roll may have either a recessed design or raised letters. As the wire watermark form comes in contact with the still-fluid paper, it displaces some of the fibers to produce a specific pattern.

When the *rubber stamp roll* is used it is located in the wet press section of the paper machine and is generally used on lower-cost papers which are produced at higher speeds. Rubber stamp watermarking produces a sheet that is slightly embossed because of the raised images upon the rubber.

WATER REMOVAL AND DRYING

The wet press section of the paper machine is located immediately behind the *Fourdrinier* wire. The wet sheet, still over 80% water, passes between rolls covered with wool and other rollers made of granite, brass, or hard rubber. The thickness or cali-

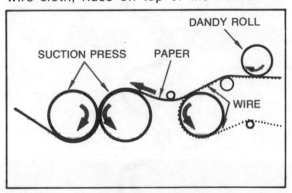

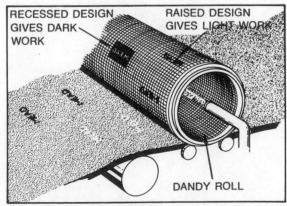

Fig. 163-2. A watermark produced by the dandy-roll method. (The Mead Corp.)

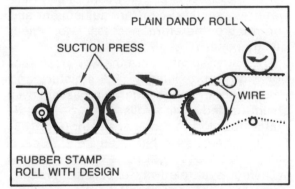

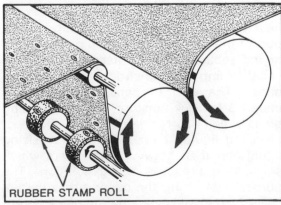

Fig. 163-3. A watermark that is produced by the rubber stamp roll method. (The Mead Corp.)

Fig. 163-4. Two operators, the machine tender and the back tender, make adjustments in the wet-press section of a paper-making machine (The Mead Corp.)

Fig. 163-5. An operator checks the adjustments of a pocket ventilating roll within the drying section of the paper-making machine. (The Mead Corp.)

ber of the sheet is partially controlled at the wet press section; constant adjustment and control are therefore necessary to obtain quality paper (Fig. 163-4).

The paper sheet leaves the wet press section with approximately 60% moisture and enters the drying section. It passes over steam-heated drying rolls that are approximately four to five feet in diameter (Fig. 163-5). The paper is heated alternately on each side as it passes from roll to roll.

Drying is a relatively expensive process because of the large capital outlay required to install and maintain the many steam-heated rollers. The cost is generally a large part of the cost of the finished paper. In the drying section a sizing press is usually located to improve the surface quality of the paper. The web of paper, now approximately 5 to 10% moisture, enters the sizing press which has two large rollers and a vat of sizing liquid. It runs through the sizing liquid and then between two rollers which squeeze out excess sizing solution. The purposes of sizing the paper are to harden its surface to resist penetration of ink, to enable it to resist the effect of handling, and

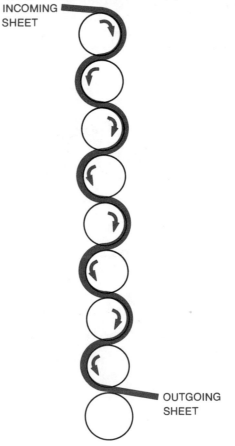

INCOMING SHEET

OUTGOING SHEET

Fig. 163-6. A calender stack of nine polished steel rolls.

Fig. 163-7. The dry end of a paper-making machine. (Nekoosa-Edwards Paper Co.)

to fasten the loose surface fibers to the base sheet. The paper leaves the sizing press containing approximately 25% water.

The paper goes to another drying section similar to the previous one; it then leaves and enters a calender stack (Fig. 163-6) which has eight or nine highly polished steel rolls 16 to 24 inches in diameter. The paper passes over and around each roll to improve smoothness and gain a more uniform thickness. The felt and wire marks that were in the paper from the *Fourdrinier* wire and the drying cylinders are smoothed.

The paper leaves the calender section and is taken up on a reel located at the dry end of the paper-making machine (Fig. 163-7). On the larger machines it is possible to wind paper in rolls having diameters of up to 88 inches.

METHODS OF MANUFACTURING PAPER AND PAPERBOARD

Three principle methods of manufacturing paper and paperboard are (1) the *Fourdrinier,* (2) the cylinder, and (3) the inverform. These are illustrated in Fig. 163-8.

Fourdrinier. Much of the paper made in the United States is manufactured on this type of machine. The pulp mixture, forced from the head box (Fig. 163-8A), travels approximately 30 feet along an endless wire. It then mats semidry as the water drops away. The matted fibers are thrown off the wire and proceed through press rolls and a set of dryers. If the paper is to receive a slick, shiny surface, this coating step precedes the drying process. If a smooth, hard surface is desired, the paper goes through a calender stack before being wound onto a core or reel.

Cylinder. This method is used to manufacture paperboard and building paper. The advantage of this unit is that successive layers of fibers and other stock preparations can be formed to produce packaging materials. A series of vats contain the various mixtures which are fed into the top liner, filler, and back liner (Fig. 163-8B). For example, a board can have a good printed surface, a filler of inexpensive pulp, and another surface with protective qualities. The machine is also used to manufacture tissue and other absorbent papers.

Inverform. This is a relatively new machine (Fig. 163-8C). It is used to produce several types of board. It uses an endless wire similar to that in the *Fourdrinier* but has mounted over the top of it a number of head boxes and forming-wire units, each for a different type of stock. Advantages include high-operating speeds and more economical manufacture of some special boards.

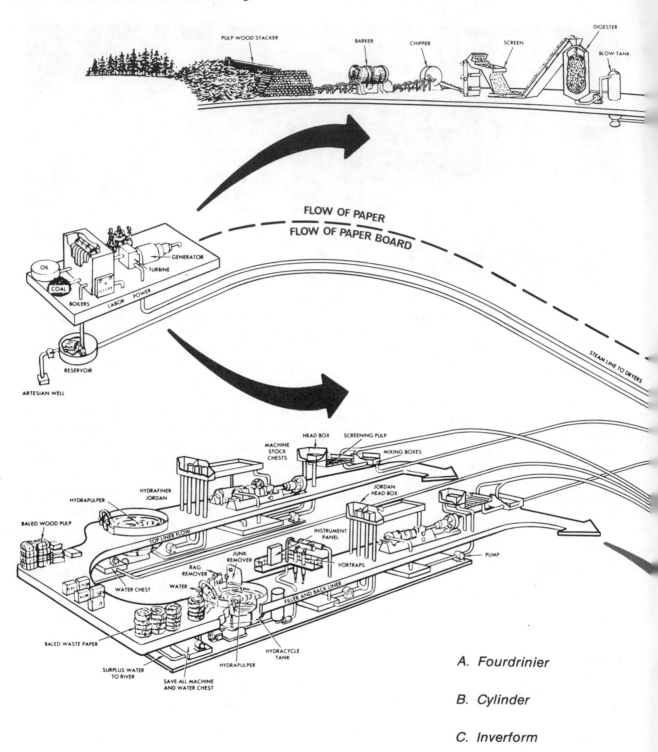

A. *Fourdrinier*

B. *Cylinder*

C. *Inverform*

Fig. 163-8. The three principle methods of manufacturing

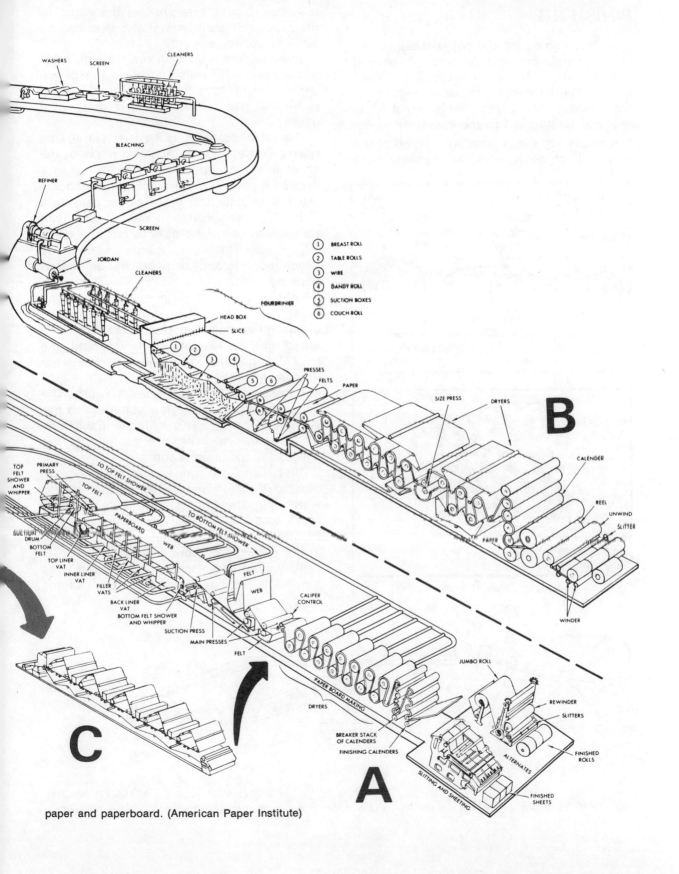

WASHERS
SCREEN
CLEANERS
BLEACHING
REFINER
SCREEN
JORDAN
CLEANERS

FOURDRINIER
HEAD BOX
SLICE

1. BREAST ROLL
2. TABLE ROLLS
3. WIRE
4. DANDY ROLL
5. SUCTION BOXES
6. COUCH ROLL

PRESSES
FELTS
PAPER
SIZE PRESS
DRYERS

B

CALENDER
REEL
UNWIND
SLITTER
PAPER
WINDER

TOP FELT SHOWER AND WHIPPER
PRIMARY PRESS
TO TOP FELT SHOWER
TOP FELT
PAPERBOARD
TO BOTTOM FELT SHOWER
SUCTION DRUM
BOTTOM FELT
WEB
TOP LINER VAT
INNER LINER VAT
FILLER VATS
BACK LINER VAT
BOTTOM FELT SHOWER AND WHIPPER
SUCTION PRESS
MAIN PRESSES
FELT
WEB
FELT
CALIPER CONTROL

JUMBO ROLL
REWINDER
SLITTERS
FINISHED ROLLS

C

PAPER BOARD MAKING
DRYERS
BREAKER STACK OF CALENDERS
FINISHING CALENDERS
ALTERNATES
SLITTING AND SHEETING
FINISHED SHEETS

A

paper and paperboard. (American Paper Institute)

FINISHING

After it comes off the paper-making machine the paper must go through several finishing steps. These are inspecting, sheeting, special finishing, and packaging. When these steps are completed the paper is ready to be shipped to the customer.

A necessary step following removal of the large roll of paper from the machine is to rewind it. During this process the edges of the paper roll are trimmed and then can be cut into desirable widths.

Some papers are again run through a set of calender steel rolls and are super-calendered. This places special finishes on the paper that has been designated for specific uses.

The art of fashioning a paper surface by raising or depressing localized areas of the sheet through application of pressure in a desired repetitive pattern is termed *embossing.* It is usually accomplished by passing a web of paper through a pair of engraved rolls which press the pattern into the sheet (Fig. 163-9). There are a number of methods which result in one- or two-sided embossed patterns.

Rolls of paper to be cut into sheets can come directly from the rewinder or from any of the other finishing processes. The rolls are placed on reel stands which hold one to a dozen rolls. From the reel the paper passes through *slitters* (Fig. 163-10) which cut the paper into the correct width. The paper then goes through a *cutter* which has a knife revolving on a cylinder. Each time the cylinder revolves, the knife cuts the sheet to a specified length.

After being cut, the sheets are taken on moving belts to machines called *layboys* which jog the sheets into uniform piles. Most modern layboys are equipped with counters that automatically insert a marker at the required number of sheets.

Skilled workers inspect, count, and wrap the sheets into specified quantity packaging

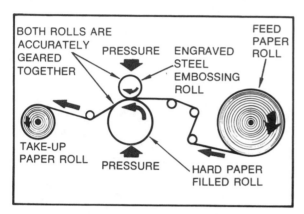

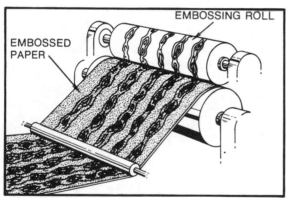

Fig. 163-9. Embossing paper. (The Mead Corp.)

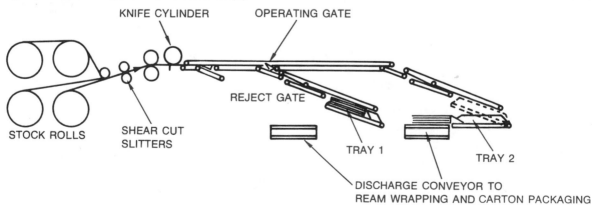

Fig. 163-10 Schematic of a cutter used to cut rolls of paper into individual sheets. (Nekoosa-Edwards Paper Co.)

(Fig. 163-11). Hand sorting or inspecting is usually done on high-grade paper, but machines have been developed to complete all of the necessary operations from cutting through wrapping without human help. Large rolls of paper are handled with great care while being wrapped (Fig. 163-12). These rolls will be used on large presses designed for a continuous web of paper, and if the rolls are mishandled, hundreds of dollars worth of fine paper could easily be ruined. The boxed and wrapped paper is shipped to customers via truck, railroad, airplane, and ship. Some of the paper made in the United States is exported to other countries.

PAPER RESEARCH

The paper industry stresses research in many ways. Research specialists are involved in laboratory test tube work, prelogging, tree-thinning procedures, tree farming, and soil conservation. Many firms in the pulp and paper industry have research laboratories that employ chemists, chemical engineers, physicists, biologists, and foresters. Projects include investigation of improved processes and products, more scientific uses of wood and other raw materials, and development of by-products from waste materials. The paper industry has jointly established the Institute of Paper Chemistry at Appleton, Wisconsin, to deal with broad research problems.

Research is not only conducted on finding improved products, but also on the equipment and power needed to complete specific operations within the paper-making process (Fig. 163-13). Millions of dollars are spent annually by the paper industry to continue the research program that has proved so successful.

Fig. 163-11 The inspecting, counting, and wrapping room of a paper mill. (Nekoosa-Edwards Paper Co.)

Fig. 163-12 A paper roll conveying system and packing operation in a paper mill. (The Mead Corp)

Fig. 163-13 Research being conducted in a university paper laboratory to study the power consumption in chipping operations. (U. S. Forest Service)

UNIT 164

KINDS, WEIGHTS, AND SIZES OF PAPER

There are many kinds, weights, and sizes of paper. One could not discuss them all in this unit because there are too many. A list of all the available varieties would be impossible to remember.

Basic papers used by the commercial printer are bond, book, bristol, cover, ledger offset, text, newsprint, duplicator, and mimeograph. Each is discussed briefly in this unit. Other papers, such as onionskin, tracing vellum, kraft wrapping, and paperboard are also available. Special ones for specific uses have been and will continue to be developed.

WEIGHTS AND SIZES

Papers are referred to as having a *specific weight* and a *basic size.* Weight generally refers to thickness, but this statement is not always true. It is most logical that in seeking a unit on which to compute bond weights, manufacturers chose the most frequently used 8½ x 11-inch sheet as one of the constants. The other constant is the quantity, which is always one ream of 500 sheets.

When a paper is said to be 24-pound bond it is meant that 500, 17 x 22-inch sheets of that paper weigh 24 pounds. This is called the *basis weight.* Even if this same paper were available in 34 x 44-inch sheets (four times the size) it would still be a 24-pound bond, although 500 sheets would weigh 96 pounds (four times as much).

Book papers generally do not have the same end use as the bonds, and therefore they do not have the same weights. Many books and papers, but by no means all, are printed from 25 x 38-inch sheets, and so the paper mills have settled on this basic size as the yardstick for computing weights of book papers.

One could expect a 24-pound bond paper and a 24-pound book paper to be the same weight and thickness, but since the book sheet is over twice as large as the bond sheet, it is somewhat less than half as thick. A 60-pound book paper would be the equivalent of a 24-pound bond paper.

BASIC PAPERS

Bond

The very many bond papers come in as many different varieties as there are applications for them.

Common Uses. Stationery, letterhead, business forms, direct-mail advertising, announcements, price lists, office systems, invoices, etc.

Requirements. Strength, permanence, good appearance and a crisp "snap," ink-receptive surface, good erasing qualities, freedom from fuzz.

Characteristics. Bond papers in a wide range of qualities are manufactured from rag fiber, cotton fiber, or chemical wood pulps. Rag content bonds may be 25, 50, 75, or 100% rag, with the balance of material in the first three grades consisting of bleached chemical wood pulp made from various combinations of bleached sulfite, sulfate, soda, and semichemical wood fibers. Bond papers have a hard, even finish on both sides of the sheet and are sized to prevent their absorbing writing or printing ink into the body of the paper. Size may be added in three different ways: (1) engine, or beater, sizing in which size is added while the paper is in the beater, (2) tub sizing, in which paper is dipped or immersed in the sizing solution, and (3) surface sizing, in which size is sprayed on both sides of the paper as it comes off the paper-making machine and before final drying. Rag bonds are generally watermarked and, like chemical wood bonds, have either a laid or wove formation and are produced in a variety of finishes.

Weights. Basis 17 x 22/500: 9, 13, 16, 20, 24 pounds

Sheet Sizes. 17 x 22, 17 x 28, 19 x 24, 22 x 34, 24 x 38, 28 x 34, 34 x 44 inches

Cut Sizes. 8½ x 11, 8½ x 13, 8½ x 14 inches

Book

Versatile book papers may be coated or uncoated and are adaptable to any printing process.

Common Uses. Books, pamphlets, folders, brochures, catalogs, direct-mail advertising.

Requirements. Variable, depending on end use of the printed product. Appearance, strength, opacity, permanency, and, with coated papers, good bond between paper and coating are factors to be considered.

Characteristics. Book papers are formed from such raw materials as mechanical and chemical wood pulps, straw, and reclaimed wastepaper. Usually two or more of these are mixed to form the basic solution, then mineral filler, size, and dye are added. Book papers may or may not be surface sized. Five different finishes are standard for the uncoated variety: antique, eggshell, machine, English, and supercalendered. Antique offers the roughest surface, with eggshell closely allied to it. Smoothest of the uncoated book papers is the supercalendered, which is rolled or ironed down under pressure to make a smooth printing surface. Base stock for coated book papers is the same as for uncoated, but is faced with mineral pigments mixed with adhesives and sometimes also a wax or soap to enhance the finish, or feel. Coating may be either dull or glossy on one or both sides of the paper.

Weights. Basis 25 x 38/500: Uncoated, 35, 40, 45, 50, 60, 70, 80, 100 pounds; Coated One Side, 50, 60, 70, 80 pounds; Coated Both Sides, 50, 60, 70, 80, 90, 100, 120 pounds.

Standard Sizes. 20 x 26, 22½ x 35, 24 x 36, 25 x 38, 28 x 42, 28 x 44, 32 x 44, 35 x 45, 36 x 48, 38 x 50, 41 x 54 inches.

Bristol

Bristols are a group of stiff, heavy papers in thicknesses from 0.006 inch up to and including index and postcards. Two or more plies of the same kind of paper may be pasted together for greater durability.

Common Uses. Records and filing, identification and time cards, business and commercial cards, self-mailers, programs, menus, announcements, file folders, booklet covers, and many more.

Requirements. Smooth, hard, uniform surface, free from lint, sturdy enough to withstand extensive handling.

Characteristics. A bristol is usually made from sulfite or sulfate pulp, or both, but may also include rag pulp. Index bristols are thoroughly sized to make them suitable for writing and printing, have good wearing and recording qualities, and are primarily used for card files of all kinds. A variety known as printing bristol is somewhat stiffer and less durable under heavy-use conditions than index. Postcard bristols may be either uncoated or coated in dull or glossy finish on one or both sides. Both types are used for postal and return cards. Cast-coated postcard stock has the best printing quality and is suitable for picture postcards, menu covers, and others. There is also a class known as folding bristol, which has long, flexible fibers, allowing the paper to be folded more easily.

Weights. Index (Basis 25½ x 30½/500), 90, 110, 140, 170, 220 pounds; Postcard (Basis 22½ x 28½/500), 94, 100, 105 pounds; Printing and Folding (Basis 23 x 35/500), 110, 125, 150, 175, 200, 250 pounds.

Standard Sizes. Index, 20½ x 23¾, 22½ x 28½, 22½ x 35, 25½ x 30½, 25½ x 35½, 8½ x 11 (cut size); Postcard, 22 x 28, 22½ x 28½; Printing and Folding, 17 x 22½, 22½ x 28½, 22½ x 35, 23 x 29, 23 x 35, 35 x 46 inches.

Cover

Cover paper is a term applied to a great variety of papers used for the outside covers of catalogs and brochures to enhance appearance and provide complete protection for the contents.

Common Uses. Booklet and manual covers,

binders, programs, directories, self-mailers, broadsides, announcements.

Requirements. Resistance to handling and abrasion, good appearance, permanence of color, ability to accept standard types of printing, plus such others as screen printing and embossing, foldability, holding to binding glue.

Characteristics. Cover papers are usually made from rag pulp, chemical wood pulp, or a mixture of the two, but may also contain mechanical pulp. Cover papers may be uncoated or coated on one or both sides. Most have a wove formation; some have a laid finish and are watermarked or deckle-edged. Many of the uncoated papers are given a textured finish to simulate linen, leather, corduroy, and other specialties. Others are calendered to accept halftone printing, cloth lined (by a lamination process), or pasted back-to-back to provide a cover material with extra strength, or with a different color on each side. Coated papers may be cast coated for smoothness and gloss, metallic coated for special effect, surface sized for offset printing, or plastic coated with a transparent film. There are also plain-coated covers with either dull or glossy finishes which are similar to coated book paper except that they are made in heavier weights.

Weights. Basis 20 x 26/500: Uncoated, 40, 50, 65, 80, 90, 100, 130 pounds; Plain Coated, 50, 60, 65, 80 pounds.

Standard Sizes. 20 x 26, 23 x 29, 23 x 35, 26 x 40, 35 x 46 inches.

Ledger

Ledger papers are similar to bonds, but are generally somewhat smoother, harder, heavier.

Common Uses. Primarily for bookkeeping and records, but also for statements, legal documents, and other forms.

Requirements. Strength, tear resistance, water and ink resistance, erasability, smooth, nonglare surface, adaptability to binding, resistance to splitting, flexibility.

Characteristics. Ledger papers are commonly made from rag pulp, bleached chemical wood pulp, or a mixture of the two, and are

available in several grades. Due to longer length of fiber, they are stronger than equivalent weight bonds. Most are sized, calendered.

Weights. Basis 17 x 22/500: 24, 28, 32, 36 pounds.

Standard Sizes. 17 x 22, 17 x 28, 19 x 24, 22 x 34, 24 x 38, 28 x 34, 22½ x 22½, 22½ x 34½, 24½ x 24½ inches.

Offset

Offset papers are essentially book papers, specially formulated to meet offset-lithography requirements.

Common Uses. Reports, proposals, manuals, form letters, advertising and promotional material, forms, etc.

Requirements. Proper moisture content and *pH* value, freedom from lint and paper dust, good pick strength.

Characteristics. Some grades of offset paper are made from rag pulp and bleached chemical wood pulp, others from a combination of bleached chemical and mechanical pulps. All offset paper is engine sized and often tub sized as well. Papers may be uncoated or clay coated on one or both sides. All are processed to eliminate distortion.

Weights. Basis 25 x 38/500: 50, 60, 70, 80, 100, 120, 150 pounds.

Sheet Sizes. 25 x 38, 22½ x 35, 28 x 42, 28 x 44, 32 x 44, 35 x 45, 36 x 48, 38 x 50, 38 x 52, 41 x 54, 44 x 64 inches.

Cut Sizes. 8½ x 11, 10 x 14, 11 x 17 inches.

Text

Text papers were originally used in the manufacture of books and textbooks, but now have much broader application.

Common Uses. Booklets, brochures, pamphlets, manuals, portfolios, menus, announcements, letterheads, self-mailers, annual reports, catalogs, surveys, promotional material.

Requirements. Appearance, opacity, strength, pick resistance, foldability.

Characteristics. Text papers come in many decorative colors and a variety of finishes, including antique, vellum, smooth, felt-marked, patterned and laid, and often have a deckle edge. Some are made from rag pulp, but most from chemical wood pulps or a combination of rag and wood pulps. Fillers are added for opacity.

Weights. Basis 25 x 38/500: 60, 70, 80 pounds.

Standard Sizes. 23 x 29, 23 x 35, 25 x 38, 26 x 40, 35 x 45, 38 x 50 inches.

Newsprint

Newsprint is the lowest grade of paper used for quantity printing.

Common Uses. Newspapers, handbills, telephone directories.

Requirements. Low permanence and strength, low light glare which helps to reduce eye strain.

Characteristics. Grayish in color. Newsprint is produced by the ground-wood or mechanical method; therefore, the fibers are very short. Because of the short fibers it will fold easily either direction. It will yellow and become brittle after a period of time. Very absorbent to ink which means that little or no dryer needs to be used in the ink.

Weights. Sheet Basis 24 x 36/500: 34 pounds; Roll Basis 24 x 36/500; 32 pounds.

Standard Sizes. Sheets: 8½ x 15⅛, 22 x 30, 22 x 32, 22 x 35, 24 x 35, 24 x 36, 26 x 40, 28 x 42, 30 x 44, 32 x 44, 35 x 44, 36 x 48 inches. Rolls: 35, 52½, 70 inches.

Duplicator

In this category are all those papers for use as either masters or copies in the gelatin, spirit, *Azograph,* and *Chemograph* duplicating processes.

Common Uses. Office systems, form letters, notices, bulletins, announcements, manuals, menus, news and publicity releases, production schedules, and many other applications where inexpensive, limited volume duplication is required.

Requirements. Master papers: Freedom from lint, ability to accept carbon image and release readily for duplication, imperviousness (in spirit masters) to solvent. Copy papers: Smooth surface, good strength, freedom from lint.

Characteristics. Coated and uncoated book papers are used for both masters and copies. Master paper for the gelatin process is hard sized, has a smooth surface with a slight tooth. For the spirit process, master paper

is specially coated or enameled to conform with the requirements of the process. *Azograph* and *Chemograph* master paper has a firm surface which prevents typewriter keys from cutting too deeply into the paper. Copy papers may be coated but generally are uncoated, have smooth surfaces and good strength.

Weights. Basis 17 x 22/500: Gelatin Process Masters, 16, 20, 24 pounds; Other Master Papers, 24, 28 pounds; Copy Papers, 16, 20, 24 pounds.

Sheet Sizes. 17 x 22, 17 x 28, 19 x 24, 22 x 34, 24 x 38, 28 x 34 inches.

Cut Sizes. 8½ x 11, 8½ x 13, 8½ x 14 inches.

Mimeograph

Mimeograph paper is similar to bond but has a rougher finish.

Common Uses. Reports, announcements, notices, manuals, form letters, schedules.

Requirements. Opacity, rapid ink absorption, strength, lint-free surface.

Characteristics. Toothy surface minimizes the amount of ink received from the stencil and aids in setting ink.

Weights. Basis 17 x 22/500: 16, 20, 24 pounds.

Sheet Sizes. 17 x 22, 17 x 28, 19 x 24, 22 x 34, 24 x 38, 28 x 34 inches.

Cut Sizes. 8 x 10½, 8½ x 11, 8½ x 13, 8½ x 14 inches.

RECYCLED PAPER

Recycling is not a new idea in our society, but it has a new importance resulting from the constantly increasing amount of solid waste generated by industry, business, and the general population. Recycling is simply the reuse of resources and materials of all kinds which have been outworn or discarded in their original manufactured form. Recycling is reclaiming and reprocessing of previously wasted used products and raw materials to make them into useful products again. Metals and glass and water are recyclable, for example. Even land can be recycled through reforestation.

Perhaps more than any other material, paper is recycleable. A principal source of waste paper for recycling is the waste of business, industry, and the general waste of America's cities. New York alone produces thousands of tons per hour of solid waste, 40 to 60% of which is paper and paperboard. Recycled paper is defined by the federal government as follows:

> The various paper stocks shall contain minimum specified percentages, by weight, of fibers reclaimed from solid waste or waste collected as a result of a manufacturing process but shall not include those materials generated from and reused within a plant as part of the paper making process.

There are 46 grades of waste paper as defined by the Paper Stock Institute. In addition, there are several hundred specialty grades of waste paper that do not clearly fit into the 46 grades. These are frequently referred to as high grades and low grades. *High grades* is a term used in the trade for waste that can be recycled into fine printing papers. *Low grades* can be recycled into folding cartons, building board, and/or roofing materials. Furthermore, old newspapers can be recycled into new newsprint.[1]

CALIPERS AND WEIGHTS

Different kinds and weights of paper have varying thicknesses. It is customary to designate paper according to pounds, but this also

[1] Bergstrom Paper Company.

Table 164-1. Calipers and Weights

The calipers listed are approximate averages. Variations will be found from one mill run to another, either to the light or heavy side of the basis weight, within trade custom tolerances. One point equals 1/1000 of an inch.

BOND, MIMEO, DUPLICATOR

bs. 17 x 22	13#	16#	20#	24#
Sulphite Bond	.003	.0035	.004	.0045
Cotton Fiber Bond				
Cockle Finish	.003	.0035	.004	.0045
Smooth Finish	.0025	.003	.0035	.004
Mimeo		.004	.005	.0055
Duplicator		.0025	.003	.0035

LEDGER

bs. 17 x 22	24#	28#	32#	36#
Smooth Finish	.0045	.005	.0055	.006
Posting Finish	.005	.0055	.006	.0065

BOOK PAPERS

bs. 25 x 38	45#	50#	60#	70#
Offset				
Regular	.0035	.004	.0045	.005
Antique	.004	.0045	.005	.006
Bulking		.0055	.0066	.0077
English Finish	.0032	.0035	.004	.0045
Supercalendered	.0022	.0025	.003	.0035
Gloss Coated		.0025	.003	.0035
Dull Coated		.003	.0035	.004
Coated 1 Side			.0032	.0037

bs. 25 x 38	80#	100#	120#	150#
Offset				
Regular	.006	.0075	.009	.011
Antique	.007	.009	.011	.013
Bulking	.0088	.011	.0135	
Gloss Coated	.004	.0055		
Dull Coated	.0045	.006		
Coated 1 Side	.004			

COVER PAPERS

bs. 20 x 26	50#	60#	65#	80#	90#	100#	130#
Uncoated							
Smooth			.0065		.011		.013
Antique	.007		.010				.020
Coated	.005	.0055	.006	.008	.009	.010	

bs. 20 x 26	50#	65#	80#	94#	110#
Lusterkote	.0055	.0065	.008	.010	.012

INDEX BRISTOL

bs. 25½ x 30½	90#	110#	140#	170#
Smooth Finish	.007/.0075	.008/.009	.0105/.0115	.013/.014

means that the sheet has a specific thickness. There are many times when a pressman must know the thickness of paper he is printing or needs to purchase. Tables have been prepared to save him time (Table 164-1). Note the thickness similarities among the several papers and the differences in weight.

WEIGHTS OF SPECIAL SIZES

The Constant Factor Schedule (Table 164-2) offers a quick way to find the 1,000-sheet weights of special-size sheets. First, find the number of square inches in the proposed size. Then, multiply the number of square inches by the constant factor. The answer is the 1,000-sheet weight of the special size.

Example: The proposed size is 46 x 58 inches. Substance weight is 80 pounds, 46 x 58 is 2,668 square inches.

Under the heading of book paper in Table 164-2, locate 80 lbs. and the corresponding factor of 0.1684. Multiply 2,668 sq. in. x 0.1684 = 449.2912. This rounds out to 449 lbs. per 1,000 sheets in size 46 x 58 inches. The factors in Table 164-2 represent the WEIGHT OF 1,000 SHEETS ONE INCH SQUARE.

The *MM* system of basis-weight determination refers to the weight of 1,000 sheets, size 25 x 40 inches. Therefore, the *MM Basis Weight* of any basis weight listed is obtained by moving the decimal point of the factor three places to the right.

Example: The MM Basis weight of 70-pound book paper is 147.4 pounds. The MM basis weight of 140-pound Index Bristol is 360 pounds.

Table 164-2. Constant Factor Schedule

BOOK PAPER		NEWSPRINT, TAG AND CRAFT		BRISTOL	
Basis wt. 25x38/500	1000 Sheet Factor	Basis wt. 25x36/500	1000 Sheet Factor	Basis wt. 22½x28½/500	1000 Sheet Factor
25	.0526	32	.0741	67	.2090
30	.0632	34	.0787	80	.2489
35	.0737	35	.0810	82½	.2573
40	.0842	40	.0926	90	.2807
45	.0947	50	.1157	100	.3119
50	.1053	60	.1389	120	.3743
60	.1263	100	.2315	140	.4366
70	.1474	125	.2894	160	.4990
80	.1684	150	.3472	180	.5614
100	.2105	175	.4051	200	.6238
120	.2526	200	.4630		
140	.2947	250	.5787		
150	.3158				

BRISTOL		COVER PAPER		BONDS, WRITINGS AND LEDGER	
Basis wt. 23x35/500	1000 Sheet Factor	Basis wt. 20x26/500	1000 Sheet Factor	Basis wt. 17x22/500	1000 Sheet Factor
100	.2484	50	.1923	8	.0428
125	.3106	60	.2308	9	.0481
150	.3727	65	.2500	11	.0588
175	.4348	80	.3077	12	.0642
200	.4969	90	.3462	13	.0695
250	.6211	100	.3846	16	.0856
		130	.5000	20	.1070
				24	.1283
				28	.1497
				32	.1711
				36	.1925

INDEX BRISTOL	
Basis wt. 25½x30½/500	1000 Sheet Factor
90	.2314
110	.2829
140	.3600
170	.4372
220	.5657

Leslie Paper Co.

UNIT 165
PURCHASING AND DETERMINING COST OF PAPER

Basically, paper can be purchased in either sheet form or roll form. With each of these two useful paper forms several different amounts of stock can be purchased from the paper supply company. Rolls of paper are packaged and sold by weight; whereas sheets of paper are normally packaged and sold according to the number of sheets.

Individual sheets of paper are commonly sold by the package, carton, or bundle. The number of sheets contained in each of these three packaging media varies according to the kind of paper. For example, a package of bond paper normally contains one ream, or 500 sheets, whereas a package of index bristol paper contains normally only 100 sheets. The purpose of the different amounts is for handling convenience. Five hundred sheets of index bristol paper would be too heavy and clumsy for one person to handle; convenience factors therefore have been considered.

PURCHASING PAPER

Paper can be purchased by the package, the carton or bundle, the four carton or four bundle, and the sixteen carton or sixteen bundle (Table 165-1). The same paper will have different prices depending upon how it is packaged or the amount of paper that is purchased at one time. The price difference of the varying amounts of paper is basically dependent upon the labor cost. It is obvious that it takes much time to handle and distribute one package of paper that contains from 100 to 500 sheets in comparison to handling and shipping sixteen cartons of paper that could contain 64,000 sheets. The labor charge per sheet is there-fore much less when handling larger quantities of paper.

In most cases, paper supply houses will not require that sixteen cartons of one specific weight and color be purchased to obtain the sixteen-carton price. They will allow an assortment of full packages to make up a complete carton.

Some materials are difficult to categorize by the package, carton or bundle; these items are called wrapped goods and are sold according to poundage which in turn is equal to so many cartons. For example, 500 pounds normally equals 4 cartons and 2,000 pounds equals 16 cartons.

Table 165-2 indicates the number of sheets that can be purchased in broken package quantity before paying the equal amount for a full package. If only 312 sheets of bond paper were needed to produce a specific commercial printing job, it would

---

Table 165-1. Packaging and Pricing

Package Price applies only on orders for not less than an original package of one item.

Carton or Bundle Price applies only on orders for not less than an original carton or bundle of an item.

4 Carton or 4 Bundle Price applies only on orders for not less than 4 original cartons or bundles. May be assorted so long as each item assorted is an even carton or a multiple thereof.

16 Carton or 16 Bundle Price applies only on orders for not less than 16 original cartons or bundles. May be assorted so long as each item assorted is an even carton or a multiple thereof.

Carton Assortments - Full packages of sealed goods may be assorted for a carton multiple under 4 or 16 carton assortment privilege.

This assortment privilege applies only to printed papers listed from page 11 through page 122.

Wrapped Goods Equivalents:
500 lbs. = 4 cartons
2000 lbs. = 16 cartons

Leslie Paper Co.

be unwise to purchase that amount of paper from the paper supplier. It would be more economical to purchase an entire package containing 500 sheets and actually receive 188 sheets free. Upon studying the chart it is obvious that the commercial printer should be well aware of the breaking point when purchasing paper.

DETERMINING COST OF PAPER

Upon selecting a specific kind, size, and weight of paper it is easy to determine the cost of the paper. Paper supply catalogs list several items for each kind of paper. These items include the color, sizes, weight, packaging, and pricing information (Table 165-3). From this price schedule, note that a 17 x 22-inch sheet will weigh 40 pounds per thousand sheets. The basis weight is 20 pounds and is packaged 3,000 sheets per

Table 165-2. Paper Breaking Points

	Shts. to Full Pkg.	Breaking Point
Blanks—100 Sht. Pkg.	100	63
50 Sht. Pkg.	50	32
Blotting—250 Sht. Ctns.	250	156
Bond Papers	500	312
Bristols	100	63
Cardboards	100	63
Cardboards	50	32
Carbon Paper	500	312
Cover Papers—Sulphite	250	156
Cover Papers—Fancy	100	63
Duplicator Papers	500	312
Flat Writing	500	312
Gummed Papers	500	312
Index Bristol	100	63
Label Papers, Plated	500	312
Ledger Papers—100 lb. weight	250	156
Under 100 lb. weight	500	156
Mimeograph Paper	500	312
Post Card	100	63
Press Board	100	78
Safety Papers	500	312
Text Papers	250	156
Text Paper Cover	100	63

Leslie Paper Co.

Table 165-3. Typical Price Schedule

JET STREAM BOND — 0207
Economy Bond (Sulphite)
Unwatermarked
Trimmed Four Sides
500 Sheets to the Package

WHITE

Basis 17x22 — 16 lbs.
Basis 17x22 — 20 lbs.

	Pkg.	Ctn.	4 Ctn.	16 Ctn.	Bkn. Pkg.
	Price Per 100 Pounds				
	$31.50	$26.00	$22.70	$21.10	$59.00
	30.30	25.00	21.80	20.30	57.00

Size	Wt. Per M	Basis Wt. 17x22	Shts. to Ctn.	Pkg.	Ctn.	4 Ctn.	16 Ctn.	Bkn. Pkg.
				Price Per 1000 Sheets				
17½x22½	34	16	4000	$10.71	$ 8.82	$ 7.71	$ 7.18	$19.82
17x28	41	16	3000	12.92	10.66	9.31	8.65	24.19
19x24	39	16	3000	12.29	10.14	8.85	8.23	23.01
22x34	64	16	2000	20.16	16.64	14.53	13.50	37.76
24x38	78	16	1500	24.57	20.28	17.71	16.46	46.02
28x34	82	16	1500	25.83	21.32	18.61	17.30	48.38
17x22	40	20	3000	12.12	10.00	8.72	8.12	22.80
17½x22½	42	20	3000	12.73	10.50	9.16	8.53	23.55
17x28	51	20	3000	15.45	12.75	11.12	10.35	29.07
19x24	49	20	3000	14.85	12.25	10.68	9.95	27.93
22x34	80	20	1500	24.24	20.00	17.44	16.24	45.60
24x38	98	20	1500	29.69	24.50	21.36	19.89	55.86
28x34	102	20	1500	30.91	25.50	22.24	20.71	58.14

COLORS — Canary, Pink, Blue, Green

Basis 17x22 — 16 lbs.
Basis 17x22 — 20 lbs.

	Pkg.	Ctn.	4 Ctn.	16 Ctn.	Bkn. Pkg.
	Price Per 100 Pounds				
	$34.00	$28.05	$24.50	$22.80	$63.00
	32.80	27.05	23.60	21.95	61.00

Size	Wt. Per M	Basis Wt. 17x22	Shts. to Ctn.	Pkg.	Ctn.	4 Ctn.	16 Ctn.	Bkn. Pkg.
				Price Per 1000 Sheets				
17x22	32	16	4000	$10.88	$ 8.98	$ 7.84	$ 7.30	$20.16
17½x22½	34	16	4000	11.56	9.54	8.32	7.75	21.39
17x22	40	20	3000	13.12	10.82	9.44	8.80	24.40
17½x22½	42	20	3000	13.78	11.37	9.92	9.23	25.49
17x28	51	20	3000	16.73	13.80	12.04	11.19	31.11
28x34	102	20	1500	33.46	27.59	24.07	22.44	62.22

carton. The cost of the paper is designated according to 1,000 sheets and varies according to how the paper is purchased, such as the package quantities of carton, four carton, sixteen carton, or broken package. It is obvious that the cost per 1,000 sheets becomes less as the quantity of paper increases. Take note that the broken package price is nearly twice as much as the full package price.

It is easy to determine the cost per sheet. This is done by moving the decimal three places to the left. For example if the package price for 1,000 sheets was $12.12, one sheet would cost $0.012, or slightly more than one cent.

Information concerning the pricing per 100 pounds of paper is also given in paper catalogs. Prior to the pricing of paper per 1,000 sheets all paper stock was sold by the pound. It was found that this pricing system was cumbersome and confusing. In recent years the pricing system has been changed to the present price per 1,000 sheets.

UNIT 166
MAKING PAPER BY HAND

The manufacture of paper may be more readily understood through the actual process of making paper by hand. The American Paper Institute has provided the following easy-to-follow instructions.

EQUIPMENT

1. A fine-meshed wire screen.
2. A metal pan such as an old biscuit pan, refrigerator tray, aluminum frozen food container, or some similar shape.
3. A forming rack or mold. This can be made from a second pan that will fit inside the first. Cut out the entire bottom, leaving only the sides.
4. A basin that will hold at least 10 quarts of water.
5. Thirty sheets of facial tissue, not the *wet strength* kind.
6. Two sheets of blotting paper, pan size.
7. Laundry starch. One tablespoon of instant starch to two cups of water provides what commercial paper makers call *size*.
8. An egg beater or blender and a rolling pin.
9. A household electric iron.

PROCEDURE

1. Tear sheets of tissue and place them in the basin.
2. Pour in the starch sizing and add additional water to make about 10 quarts.
3. Beat until thoroughly mixed (Fig. 166-1). This forms the pulp.
4. Prepare the paper machine which is the combination of the pan, screen, and forming rack (Fig. 166-2). The pan and rack shown came from an old refrigerator tray.
5. Hold the forming rack firmly on the screen and dip it sideways into the pulp mixture (Fig. 166-3).
6. Clean off the excess pulp that is outside the forming rack.
7. Lift out the screen on which the pulp has formed (Fig. 166-4).
8. Dry the screen and wet sheet of pulp between two pieces of blotting paper (Fig. 166-5). The sheet will stick to the blotting paper.
9. Press out excess water with a rolling pin.
10. Iron dry (not too hot) the sheet which is still between the blotters (Fig. 166-6).
11. Trim the edges with scissors. You now have a sheet of handmade paper.

Fig. 166-1. Beating the tissue sizing mixture to make the pulp. (American Paper Institute)

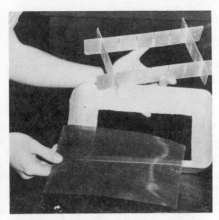

Fig. 166-2. Preparing the paper machine. (American Paper Institute)

Fig. 166-3. Dipping out the pulp mixture. (American Paper Institute)

Fig. 166-4. Lifting out the screen on which pulp is deposited. (American Paper Institute)

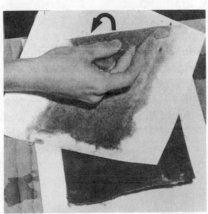

Fig. 166-5. Blotting the wet sheet of pulp between two pieces of blotting paper. (American Paper Institute)

Fig. 166-6. Drying out the sheet of pulp between blotters. (American Paper Institute)

UNIT 167

LEARNING EXPERIENCES: PULP AND PAPER MANUFACTURING

DISCUSSION TOPICS

1. What evidence is there to uphold the statement, " . . . paper manufacture is one of the world's largest basic industries?" Provide the data for the following: number of manufacturing plants for pulp, paper, paperboard, and paper converters; number of states containing paper manufacturing plants; number of cities and towns containing paper manufacturing plants; and number of employees in the paper industry. Use reference books.

2. List some of the many paper products, other than paper, that are produced for

printing purposes. Which of these paper products do you have in your personal possession or use often?

3. Describe the relationship between paper and the living index in the United States. How does paper usage in the United States compare with that in many other countries?

4. Name some of the materials that were used to record thoughts and events prior to the development of paper. What nation has been given credit for making the first paper? Identify the materials that were used to prepare it.

5. Describe the early development and the importance of paper. How long did it take the paper-making process to find the way to Europe from China?

6. When was the first paper-making machine devised? Name the person who is given credit for this invention. Who promoted the development of the machine and also attached their name to it? What was the major obstacle in the development of the paper-making machine?

7. Describe the tree-farm concept. When was this system first instituted? Cite the primary benefit of this system.

8. Enumerate the ingredients necessary to produce paper. Why is fresh water such an essential factor in the production of paper?

9. Name the two categories of wood that are used for paper making. Cite the advantages and disadvantages of each kind. Why is a combination of these two wood categories generally used in paper production?

10. Who owns the majority of the pulp wood acreage? How is pulp wood transported to the paper mills? How are the logs handled once they reach the paper mill?

11. Explain the process of debarking the logs. Why is it essential that the logs be fully debarked prior to the chipping operation?

12. Why is it important that the chip size be uniform? How is the uniform size of the chips assured?

13. Compare the three methods of pulping. Why is there a need for the different pulping methods? Identify the uses of the paper made from each pulping method.

14. Why is it essential to bleach the pulp? Name the binding material that produces brownish-black fiber stain. Identify the materials that are used as bleaching agents.

15. Describe the beating, refining, and cleaning operations that are necessary in preparing paper pulp. Name the two methods of cleaning the pulp.

16. Describe a paper-making machine. Identify the various sections or divisions. Give the production rate of some of the large paper-making machines.

17. Explain how a sheet of paper is formed. Why is it necessary that the paper pulp contain so much water when it enters the paper-making machine?

18. Give the purpose of a watermark. Describe the two methods that are used to place watermarks on paper.

19. Name the three principal methods of manufacturing paper and paperboard. Compare these three methods.

20. Identify the different ways of finishing paper after it has been delivered from the paper-making machines. Why is some of the paper left in roll form and not cut into sheets? How is paper packaged for shipment?

21. Why is there need for paper research? Identify some of the areas of research that are being conducted in the paper industry.

22. List the several kinds of paper. Give the use or uses of each kind.

23. Explain the relationship between paper weight and size. How is paper weight determined? What is meant by the *basic size* of paper?

24. List the several packaged amounts by which paper can be purchased. Why is there an advantage in purchasing larger amounts of paper at one time? Cite the disadvantage in purchasing broken package amounts of paper.

25. How are paper prices listed in paper supply catalogs? Give the main advantage of this system.

26. Name the raw material that can be used to make handmade paper. What device is used to dry the freshly made sheets of paper?

ACTIVITIES

1. Visit a paper manufacturing facility. Carefully observe the pulping and paper-forming stages in the paper manufacturing process. Also take special notice of the finishing and shipping departments. Prepare a detailed report of your visit.
2. Obtain as many different kinds of paper products as you can. Examine the paper used in each product and attempt to determine the special treatment that the raw paper has received to make it useful for each particular use. Which pulping process was used to prepare the basic paper for each product? Report in detail your investigations.
3. Obtain samples of each of the several basic papers that are used for producing printed products. Examine each. Compare the surface finish of each paper, the thickness, the opacity, the strength, and the general quality. Use instruments such as a magnifying glass, microscope, and densitometer.
4. Compare the printability of each of the several kinds of papers. Make the comparisons by using the letterpress, lithography, and screen-printing image-transfer methods.
5. Determine the paper cost for one issue of your school newspaper or yearbook. Determine the cost of the paper used in a midterm test for an entire class. Do these costs surprise you? Is paper cheap or expensive? Defend your answer.
6. Prepare a batch of paper according to the information given in Unit 166. Make several sheets; after the sheets are fully dry, attempt to write with a pencil, ball-point pen, and an ink pen. Also print on the sheets by using a platen press. Compare the writing and printing results on handmade paper with commercially made paper.

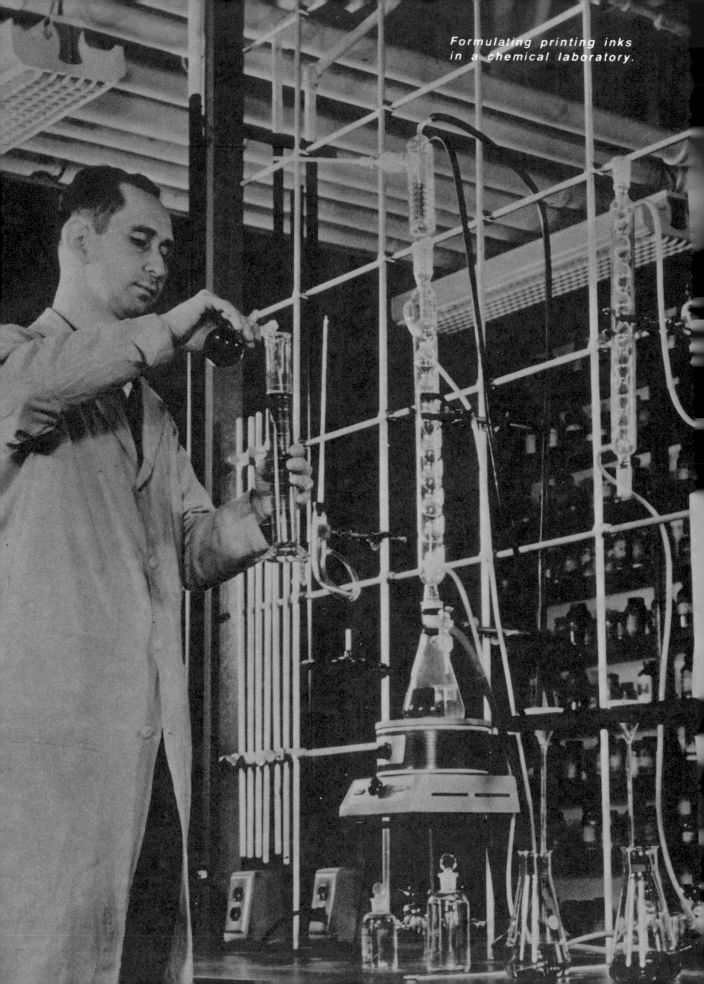

Formulating printing inks
in a chemical laboratory.

UNIT 168

INTRODUCTION TO PRINTING INKS

The printing process coats one material onto another. *Ink* is the most predominant coating material. *Substrate* is the material on which the ink is coated or printed. The problem of coating would be rather simple if all substrates had the same properties. This is, however, not the situation. There are thousands of different materials or substrates that must be coated. These include paper, glass, wood, metal, and plastic. Many new materials are constantly developed and require special inks.

The different printing processes also complicate the situation. Each requires a special kind of ink developed exclusively for that process. In addition, each printing process has several kinds of inks available. Water-base ink, oil-base ink, enamels, lacquers, textile, and epoxy inks are a few available for screen printing.

Inks are designed to withstand the effects of heat, abrasion, acids, alkalines, and other chemicals. The new speeds which the printing industry is attaining are also a challenge to the ink manufacturers. It is estimated that nearly one million new ink formulas are developed each year in the United States.

Ink was manufactured and used by the Chinese during the third century B.C. to print with blocks. Fig. 168-1 shows an early Chinese signature hand stamp. The manufacture of ink was well established in China several hundred years before the invention of movable type by Johann Gutenberg in 1450.

The ink manufacturing industry has made rapid and dynamic advances since the early Chinese developments. Today it is one of the fastest-growing parts of the chemical industry. The annual investment in printing inks in the United States is approximately 300 million dollars.

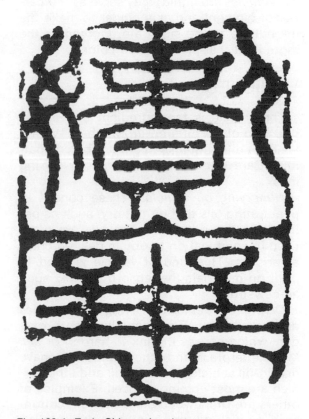

Fig. 168-1. Early Chinese hand stamp.

UNIT 169
COMPOSITION OF PRINTING INKS

The composition of printing inks varies considerably, depending on the printing process, the substrate or material on which the printing will be done, and the system required to dry the ink. Letterpress inks are quite different from gravure inks because of the different requirements of these printing processes. The ingredients contained in two different inks for a single printing process, such as letterpress, might be different and have varying drying requirements.

Ingredients in printing ink can be divided into three groups: vehicles, pigments, and others, such as driers and waxes (Fig. 169-1). *Vehicles* are liquid; they serve as the carrier of pigment and as a binder to make the ink adhere to the substrate. *Pigment* is the ingredient that provides the color.

VEHICLES

The vehicle is the ingredient that makes one kind of ink different from others. Vehicles from different inks might not be compatible. Care should be observed in mixing inks.

Nondrying oil vehicles. These consist of penetrating oils that do not dry, such as petroleum oils and resins. The oils are often used in combination to obtain desired characteristics. This kind of vehicle is used to print on materials that absorb the ink, such as newsprint.

Drying-oil vehicles. Drying-oil vehicles dry by oxidation. They actually absorb oxygen, which causes the ink to harden or *set*. Most letterpress and lithographic inks have drying-oil vehicles. Linseed oil and litho varnish are most commonly used. Examples of others are Chinawood oil, castor oil, cottonseed oil, fish oil, and synthetic drying oils.

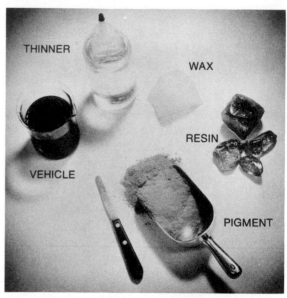

Fig. 169-1. Ingredients of printing ink. (National Association of Printing Ink Manufacturers)

Linseed-oil varnishes distribute well on the printing type or plates and transfer and adhere well to the substrate. Litho varnishes are designated by numbers. The numbers refer to the viscosity of the varnish. Litho varnish numbered 00000 is very thin, 00 and #1 are medium, #5 and #6 are heavy, and #9 and #10 are very heavy (sometimes called body gum).

Solvent-resin vehicles. Resin-oil vehicles consist of resin, oil, and a solvent. When ink is printed, the solvent is absorbed into the substrate almost immediately. Only a fairly dry coating of oil and resin remains on the surface, which dries by oxidation. Some kinds of letterpress and lithographic inks are made with resin-oil vehicles. They are called *quick-setting* inks.

Other kinds of vehicles. These include glycol, resin-wax, and water-soluble vehicles.

PIGMENTS

Pigments are an essential ingredient in inks, they are visible when the ink is printed. They are mixed with vehicles to use for specific printing processes.

Black pigments. These are primarily carbon, produced by burning gas or oil. Some common black pigments are channel black, furnace black, and lamp black. Some minerals are also used to produce black pigments for special printing purposes.

White pigments. White pigments are classified in two groups: opaque whites and transparent whites. Printed opaque whites cover the substrate like any other pigment. Materials used are titanium dioxide, zinc sulfide, and zinc oxides. The kinds of ink considered to be opaque whites are cover white and mixing whites. They can be used directly or mixed with other inks.

Transparent whites permit light to pass through the pigment so that the color below the ink can be seen. Some of the materials used to produce transparent white pigments are aluminum hydrate, magnesium carbonate, calcium carbonate, and clays.

OTHER INGREDIENTS

Special ink characteristics are obtained by adding such ingredients as driers, waxes, lubricants, gums, starches, and wetting agents. These usually are added at different times during the manufacture of ink. When any one is added after manufacture, it is necessary that it will mix satisfactorily with that particular type of ink.

Driers. The purpose of driers is to speed the oxidation and drying of the varnish or vehicle. Care should be used when adding driers to inks. Be certain the drier is the right kind for the particular ink.

Do not use too much drier because other problems will occur, such as drying on the press, fill-in of the halftones, and excessive sticking. As a general rule, one ounce of drier for each pound of ink will permit the ink to dry in four to eight hours.

Waxes. Waxes are used to combat setoff which is the transfer of ink from a printed sheet to the back of the sheet above. They also improve abrasion resistance. Waxes are added either during the cooking of the varnish or after the ink is prepared. Paraffin wax, beeswax, and carnauba wax are kinds used frequently.

Greases and lubricants. Greases and lubricants are used to help lubricate ink, reduce stickiness, and increase setting and drying. Cup grease, wool grease, and petroleum jelly are some types of lubricants. Too much lubricant will cause ink to print poorly; care should therefore be taken to use only enough to obtain the desired result.

UNIT 170
MANUFACTURE OF PRINTING INKS

The manufacture of printing inks consists of mixing pigments and other compounds with a vehicle sometimes called varnish. Mixing solid ingredients like pigments and compounds in the liquid varnish is called *wetting down.* Most inks are made by the *batch* method. This means that one quantity is made, then everything is cleaned up. Only standardized inks, like news ink, are produced by a continuous process.

Inks are ground after mixing. Grinding reduces the size of the solid particles and helps distribute the pigment and compounds into the varnish. The three-roll mill

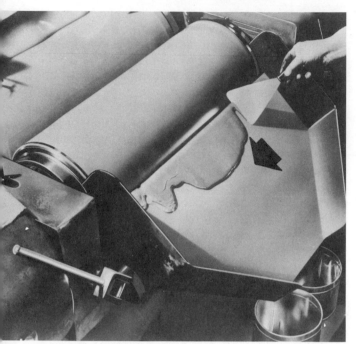

Fig. 170-1. A three-roll mill. (National Association of Printing Ink Manufacturers)

(Fig. 170-1) is effective, even though it is one of the old means of grinding inks. The three rolls of the mill are adjusted until there is only a small distance between them. The center cylinder turns at a different speed than the other two. The combination of the extremely small clearance between the cylinders or rolls and different speeds grinds the ink to extreme fineness after several passes through the mill.

Other methods of grinding inks use ball mills, colloid mills, sand grinders, and turbine mixers. Fig. 170-2 shows a ball grinder consisting of a rotating horizontal drum. The ingredients and steel balls are placed in it, and as it turns the balls fall on the mixture and exert a grinding action. The longer the drum turns, the finer the ink will be.

The fineness of the ink is measured to determine whether it has been ground sufficiently for the quality desired. Fig. 170-3 illustrates a test being made to determine fineness.

Fig. 170-2. A ball grinder. (National Association of Printing Ink Manufacturers)

Fig. 170-3. Testing the fineness of grind of an ink. (National Association of Printing Ink Manufacturers)

UNIT 171

PRINTING INKS

New kinds of printing inks are being developed constantly to cope with the demands of industry. Some major considerations in the need for new inks are the kinds of printing processes, the speeds of the printing processes, the eventual uses of the printed items, and the kinds of substrates.

PRINTING PROCESSES

Inks are made to fit the requirements of various printing processes. Often several of them are developed for use in a single printing operation.

Letterpress. Inks for letterpress printing must distribute well on raised surfaces like type, line plates, or halftone plates. Letterpress inks have moderate tack or stickiness and flow. Flow is the characteristic that causes ink to level out (Fig. 171-1).

The kind of printing press must be considered. Inks for platen presses are rather *short* and tacky and lack good flow ability. Cylinder press inks must have less tack and more *length*. This is the ability to stretch out to a long fine thread without breaking. Inks for rotary presses must have even less tack and more length. They should be able to dry quite rapidly.

Lithography. Lithographic inks are made to cover a flat surface smoothly. These inks are longer and more *viscous*. They have more body than letterpress inks. Lithographic inks must be resistant to water and to the mild acids contained in the dampening systems of offset lithography presses.

Gravure. Gravure, or intaglio, printing inks must have sufficient body to be pulled from the printing plate. Hand gravure printing requires a short ink; high-speed presses re-

Fig. 171-1. Testing the flow characteristics of ink. (National Association of Printing Ink Manufacturers)

quire longer ones. Drying speed is not as important a consideration for hand gravure printing as for rotogravure. Inks for hand printing can dry by oxidation. Rotogravure ink must dry by absorption or evaporation.

Screen Printing. Probably more inks or paints are available for screen printing than for any other type. Inks for screen printing must pass through small openings in the screen without clogging the screen. They must not damage the stencil or dry in the screen when being printed, should be appropriate for the substrate, and should dry rapidly on the substrate. Manufacturer's specifications and recommendations should be consulted before using a screen-printing ink. In general, screen-printing inks are thinner and more fluid than others.

USE OF PRINTED ITEMS

The eventual use of the printed item should be considered when ink is selected for a specific job. For example, packages used to hold foods must be printed with an odorless ink. Those used outdoors should use inks that are weather resistant. Books require ink that withstands aging. Bottles handled frequently must be printed with inks that withstand abrasion.

SUBSTRATE

Inks should fit the material, or substrate, as well as the printing process. Many problems are eliminated when the printer uses the correct ink for a specific kind of material or substrate.

Paper

When inking problems arise with papers, consult the manufacturer of the specific product. Paper is the most common material used as a substrate.

Newsprint. This is the least expensive paper, having coarse, open fibers. It contains no sizing and is quite absorbent. Inks commonly used for newsprint are very thin and dry by absorption. They contain little or no binder, leaving only pigment on the surface of the paper.

Uncoated papers. Bond, offset, and vellum papers usually use inks that dry by oxidation. They should have medium viscosity.

Coated papers. These types have surfaces that resist any ink penetration. Quick-setting inks are usually used. The inks are fluid and the pigments are extremely well dispersed because coated papers are used primarily for fine printing calling for extreme detail. Heat-set inks that dry by evaporation are also used. Many other papers, such as cardboard, parchment, glassine, and kraft require inks that meet the needs of both the material and the process used.

Nonpaper

Nonpaper materials include glass, fabrics, plastics, metals, woods, and ceramics. Many of these materials must be printed by either the screen-printing method or by flexography, due to the irregular surfaces and the nature of the substance being printed.

Nearly all nonpaper materials require rapid drying. In some situations, instantaneous drying is necessary. It is best to have inks specially formulated for these specific materials by the ink manufacturer. For example, a manufacturer of screen-printing inks will not recommend one of his inks for plastics until he tests the material and knows what it will be used for after printing. Many ink manufacturers will test their inks on the consumer's material.

TYPES OF INKS

Some common types of inks used graphic arts are listed. No attempt is made to identify all inks available. The best source of detailed information on inks is that provided by the manufacturer.

Heat-set inks. These are used on high-speed presses. The vehicle or bonding agent in heat-set inks must evaporate rapidly when heat is applied to the printed material. Resins and pigment remain on the surface of the paper. Presses using this type of ink must be equipped with a heating device and an exhaust system.

Quick-set oil inks. These inks have vehicles that are combinations of oil and resin. When the ink is printed, the oil penetrates the surface of the substrate and the film of resin and pigment dries by oxidation. They are used in both letterpress and offset printing processes.

Gloss inks. High gloss is obtinted in printing by using inks having a minimum penetration into the paper. Several paper characteristics, such as porosity, surface sizing, and coatings affect the gloss. The vehicle must be one that does not penetrate the paper rapidly.

News inks. News inks are made to dry by absorption. They are generally very thin and fluid, consisting of mineral oil and carbon black. News inks are designed for presses that run at high speed.

Metallic inks. These are inks having metal powders suspended in a vehicle. Aluminum powders are used to simulate silver. Bronze powder makes the inks appear to be gold.

The powders usually are added to the vehicle just before printing. The powders must be mixed thoroughly into the vehicle.

Magnetic inks. Magnetic inks have pigments that can be magnetized. They are used to print forms and checks when electronic recognition of characters is required.

The inks must be precisely formulated. They are usually used in lighographic printing.

Most ink manufacturers provide samples of their inks on different kinds of paper or other materials. The printer can then identify the kind of ink needed for a particular job.

UNIT 172
PRINTING INK DIFFICULTIES

Many difficulties encountered in the printing industry are unjustly attributed to the poor quality of ink. Other factors can cause poor results. These difficulties could be inaccurate matching of substrate to ink, poor press conditions, and the use of the wrong additives. It is often necessary to adjust or compensate for changes in the conditions of the substrate by changing the characteristics of the ink. Changes are made after consulting the recommendations of the manufacturer. Following are some of the common problems.

OFF COLOR

Variation in color can occur because of many reasons. Probably the most frequent cause is dirtiness of the press. The same ink (color) printed on two kinds of material will not have identical results. The thickness of the film of ink also produces color variation.

The ink formulator should have a sample of the color to be matched, paper on which the ink will print, and as much other information as possible. When he has formulated the ink, he makes a *draw-down*. Fig. 172-1 shows a draw-down being made to

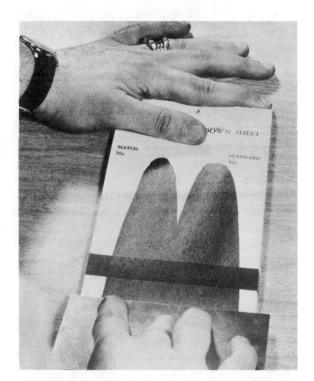

Fig. 172-1. Draw down test. (National Association of Printing Ink Manufacturers)

check new ink to the standard one for color, strength, and tone. The draw-down is made on a pad on which both the sample and the formulated ink are deposited with a thin blade.

SETOFF

Setoff occurs because the ink from the printed sheet transfers to the back of a sheet placed on top (Fig. 172-2). This usually happens on the delivery section of a printing press. Some common causes are static electricity, excessive heaviness of the ink film, slow penetration of ink into the paper, and improper handling of the printed material.

Take precautions to eliminate setoff as soon as possible. It often occurs when printing large areas like solids and halftones. Setoff can be reduced or eliminated by depositing only a minimum amount of ink on the substrate, adding some static elimination device to the press, making sure that the appropriate ink is being used, not pressing down on the top of freshly printed material, and not permitting the paper stacks to get too high.

IMPROPER DRYING

Improper drying results when ink does not harden or dry as rapidly as expected. Causes may be improper substrate, old ink that has lost its drier, or temperature and humidity. If the ink is old, the addition of a drier may eliminate the problem. Caution should be observed in using the correct driers and an accurate amount.

If the paper or substrate has a high moisture content or is not porous, poor drying can result. Low temperature and high humidity also cause insufficient drying of ink; the atmospheric conditions in the printing area should therefore be controlled when possible. The addition of a drier may help correct temperature and humidity problems.

STICKING

Sticking is the condition of two pieces of paper held together by an ink film. The primary causes are the same as for setoff and

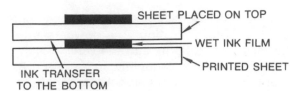

Fig. 172-2. Setoff occurs when one sheet is placed on top of another printed sheet.

improper drying. Many remedies used to reduce setoff and increase drying also eliminate sticking.

Too much drier inhibits penetration of ink into the paper, so do not use an excessive amount. The most effective solution is to print the thinnest possible ink film, which results in better drying and more rapid penetration.

CHALKING

Chalking is the result of inadequate binding. Binding is the property that holds the pigment to the substrate. The ink film in this situation is dry and is easily removed from the substrate by abrasive action. Smearing results from both chalking and inadequate drying.

The addition of a varnish which does not readily penetrate the paper surface is one solution to the problem of chalking. Probably the most satisfactory solution, however, is to select a more appropriate ink for the particular job. It is often necessary to print a clear protective coating over ink if chalking occurs on a completed job.

SPECKING

The term specking designates the appearance of small dots between the dots on halftones or in the nonprinted areas between line work. The cause may be contamination of the ink by dust, lint, setoff spray, and paper fibers. Other causes are heavy ink film, excessive impression, and poor makeready. Ink that is not properly ground can also cause specking.

STRIKE-THROUGH

Strike-through is the problem of ink going through the sheet of paper to the reverse side. Either the ink dries too slowly or excessive use has been made of nondrying oils. This occurs frequently on absorbent paper.

Strike-through is often confused with *set-off,* and *show-through.* The latter is the result of printing on thin or not very opaque paper so that the image can be seen on the reverse side. The ink in this case has not penetrated the paper.

PLATE WEAR

Inks that are not properly ground can cause excessive wear to printing plates. Other causes are inks that contain too much pigment and pigment that is too abrasive. Excessive roller pressure or papers containing abrasives may also contribute wear.

UNIT 173
MIXING PRINTING INKS

The purpose of mixing printing inks is to obtain new or different colors or to adjust the characteristic of a certain ink. Mixing inks is done both in the printing plant and at the ink manufacturing plant. Achieving a desired color requires that two or more different color inks with the same characteristics be blended. Adjusting inks to obtain satisfactory results involves essentially the same procedure and tools used for color mixing.

Inks mixed at the ink manufacturing plant are generally more satisfactory than those mixed at the printing plant. If inks are mixed by the printer, care should be taken that the mixture is thoroughly worked for uniformity of blend and quality.

TOOLS

The tools required for mixing inks are a slab, knife or spatula, and a set of scales.

The *slab* should be of nonporous material because porous ones retain ink from previous mixings and could ruin new mixtures. Heavy plate glass with ground edges makes a good, safe slab. Glass with excessive scratches should not be used because ink retained in them can contaminate new mixes.

Knives or *spatulas* are used to blend the ingredients on the slab and to remove ink from containers. Stiff, straight-edged knives, similar to putty knives, may be used to remove ink from containers. Because these knives can easily scratch the slab, use long flexible ones with rounded ends. They work more effectively in blending the ingredients. This type of knife is commonly called a spatula.

Scales are used to measure precise weight quantities of ingredients. Scales with a capacity of five pounds are usually sufficient for most jobs. Scales are most effective when the ink formulator or the person who mixes the ink must make more than one batch of a particular kind or color at any one time.

When an ink is mixed only once, scales are not always required. The ingredients are usually placed on materials such as plastic or other nonabsorbent matter so that the scales can be kept clean and ready for other jobs. The plastic material must be weighed and then this figure subtracted from the combined weight of the ingredients for an accurate weight.

INGREDIENTS

Ingredients required to mix inks or to make adjustments in ink characteristics should be carefully selected according to the needs of the particular situation. When possible, inks should be formulated in advance by the ink manufacturer, but the time required to print most jobs does not always permit such a service.

Materials can be grouped into (1) ingredients for adjusting characteristics of inks, and (2) colored inks for developing new colors. It is a good policy to obtain inks and additives, including driers and varnishes, that have the same characteristics and come from the same manufacturer.

The following is a minimum list of in-mixing and formulating ingredients for printing plants that are primarily concerned with using conventional oil ink for letterpress and lithographic printing.

1. Several grades of litho varnish: 00, 1, 4, and body gum
2. Driers
3. Waxes and compounds
4. Two or more kinds of black ink
5. Gray ink
6. Transparent and mixing white inks
7. Several strong colors, including blue, yellow, red, green, brown, and purple

MIXING

Two different situations require ink to be mixed. The first is the need to match an existing color or adjust its characteristics to meet a specific need. The second is the need to duplicate a previously determined formula. Ink is more frequently mixed than duplicated. Mixing inks according to a formula requires only that the formulator measure accurate amounts of certain ingredients and then blend them (Fig. 173-1).

When mixing inks, *hue, value,* and *chroma* must be considered. Hue is the shade, or characteristic, of a color that makes it different from another one. Value refers to the lightness or darkness. Chroma is the strength (brightness or purity) or grayness of a color.

It is helpful to refer to a color chart before starting the mixing process. The chart helps in obtaining certain desired colors. For example, the primary colors of yellow, red, and blue can be used to obtain many other ones. If yellow is mixed with red, orange is

Fig. 173-1. Mixing printing ink in a printing plant. (National Association of Printing Ink Manufacturers)

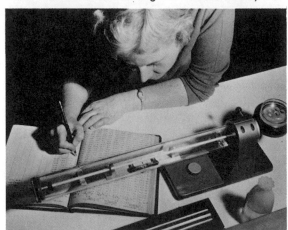

Fig. 173-2. Testing for ink penetration.

obtained. Greens result from mixing blues and yellows. Red and blue make violet.

Before mixing colors, all tools must be thoroughly cleaned to be sure that the mixture will not be contaminated. Use a color chart to select the proper hues for making the new color ink. Always place the lighter color ink on the slab first; then add the darker color to it. It is easier to make a light color ink dark than to make a dark color light. Add only a little dark color to the light color at a time. The color should be blended together until all streaks are eliminated. It is best to use a separate spatula for each ink color and a different spatula for blending the inks. Be sure to mix enough ink to print the entire job, as it is very difficult to duplicate a color.

Inks should be tested after mixing. Manufacturers make many tests for flow and fineness of grind. Fig. 173-2 shows a test made to determine ink penetration into the substrate. The technician in Fig. 173-3 is testing inks under ultraviolet light for fading and weathering tendencies.

Such tests are not usually made in a printing plant. Many times the only real test is to print with the ink on the press. Prints made with the finger, or the draw-down test, are useful methods to judge color qualities. Penetration and drying qualities can only be tested by permitting a print made on an appropriate substrate to dry under normal conditions.

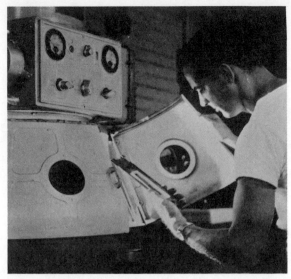

Fig. 173-3. Testing for ink fading and weathering tendencies under ultraviolet light.

UNIT 174.
LEARNING EXPERIENCES: PRINTING INKS

DISCUSSION TOPICS

1. What are the three main ingredients in printing inks? Describe each. Define the term substrate.
2. List the different kinds of vehicles. Give the specific uses of each.
3. Name some of the materials used to produce pigments. Give the difference between *opaque* white and *transparent* white and tell where each is used.
4. Identify some of the special ingredients in inks. Give the purpose of these special ingredients.
5. What is meant by the term wetting down? Give the difference between batch processing and continuous processing.
6. Describe the purpose of grinding inks. Explain the operation of the three-roll mill. List some other methods of grinding inks. Describe the grinding process of the ball grinder.
7. Name some of the considerations that an ink manufacturer must have in mind when formulating a new ink.
8. Describe the characteristics of letterpress ink.
9. Define the terms *tack, flow, length,* and *viscous.*
10. Give the characteristics of lithographic inks. Name some of the special problems that must be considered with lithographic inks.
11. Describe the unique requirements for gravure inks.

12. How do screen-printing inks differ from other inks? Explain some of the requirements of screen-printing inks.
13. List some printed items that might require special kinds of ink.
14. Identify some common substrates and identify the special ink requirements for each.
15. Name and describe some common types of inks and give the special uses of each.
16. What is meant by *off-color*? Name some of the causes of off-color. How does the ink formulator check a new ink for color?
17. Define the term setoff. Give the causes of setoff. How can setoff be reduced?
18. List some of the causes of improper drying. How can improper drying be corrected?
19. Define the term *sticking*. Give some ways to prevent sticking.
20. What is the cause of chalking? Identify ways to eliminate chalking before and after printing.
21. Describe the condition called *specking*. Give some of the causes of specking.
22. Define the term called *strike-through*. What is the cause? Explain how strike-through is confused with *show-through* and setoff.
23. Explain how inks can cause plate wear. What are some additional causes of plate wear?

24. List and describe the tools required to mix inks in the graphic arts laboratory or printing plant.
25. Give the two groups of materials required for mixing inks. What precautions should be observed? List some of the materials required for mixing and formulating inks.
26. Define the terms *hue, value,* and *chroma.* What is a color chart? Give the primary colors. How can orange, green, and purple be mixed using primary color inks?
27. Give the procedure for mixing inks in a printing plant or graphic arts laboratory. List the ingredients.

ACTIVITIES

1. List all of the different kinds of inks in your laboratory and tell the printing processes with which they would be used. What are some of the materials on which they could be printed?
2. Collect several different printed items. Identify the printing process used to print the items and try to establish what kind of ink was used to print the item.
3. Mix some inks to achieve different colors. Keep a record of the quantities of ingredients and try to match the ink with a second mix. Then try to match the ink a few days later.

Pressmen's Crossword Puzzle

By William C. Curr
New York, School of Printing

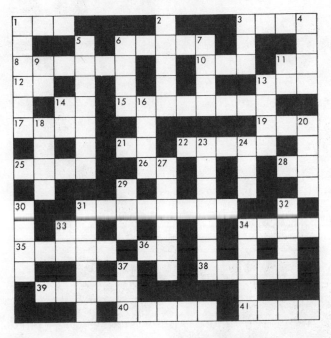

ACROSS:
1. Opposite side guide of near.
3. If feeder misses a sheet the press should ....
6. Gravure is known for its fine reproduc-tion of ....
8. When on impression the cylinder must ride on the ....
10. Electric .... control.
11. Type of electric current.
12. Square of type body.
13. An excess of .... will cause setoff.
14. Printing Pressmen (abbr.).
15. Highest skilled craftsman in the graphic arts.
17. Will cause a slur.
19. A wheel containing a high and low spot.
21. Pressman's parent.
22. Requires careful setting to eliminate a wrinkle.
25. Solids should be .... type high.
26. 1,000,000 impressions.
28. Printing unit of measure (abbr.).
31. Newsprint is made from ....
33. Reducing varnish.
34. Right side of paper.
35. For folding against the grain it is some-times necessary to .... a job.
36. Pressman's other parent.
38. A means of preventing setoff.
39. Result of over packing.
40. Strong brown paper.
41. Halftones are composed of various sized..............

DOWN:
1. Product of wood and rags for paper making.
2. Used to cut tissue.
3. To bundle.
4. Term used when coating pulls off a sheet.
5. Holds a sheet to packing.
6. When overprinting, second down Ink must .... on the first down.
7. An Ink .... before It dries.
9. Type measure.
11. Indefinite article.
13. Moving a press showly.
14. Jumbled type.
16. 500 sheets of a standard size.
18. A form that has not yet been printed.
20. What stereotypes are cast from.
23. Used to distribute ink.
24. Sized and super-calendered.
27. World's largest international printing trade union (abbr.).
29. Another name for a platen press.
30. An interlay is put between the plate and
31. Results of a bowed form.
32. Used for coating paper.
33. Reducing varnish.
34. Reward for spoiling job.
37. When it is doubtful it is advisable to

See page 531 for answers.

JUSTICE represents the administration of
that which is just and also merited reward
or punishment. (Shelburne, Vermont Museum)

UNIT 175
LEGAL RESTRICTIONS OF PRINTED MATERIALS PRODUCTION

Printers and publishers of all graphic materials in the United States must be on guard at all times to prevent becoming involved in legal matters relating to counterfeiting, pornography, and widely known legal violations dealing with copyrighting.

Copyright is the legal right of an author, artist, composer, or anyone to protect his writing, art, or music against copying. The first Federal Copyright Act was initiated in the United States in 1790. The present copyright law was enacted in 1947 and later amended. This grants statutory copyrights (authorized by law) for 28 years, after which time owners may extend it for another similar period of time.

Essentially, a copyrighted work is a message. A legal privilege of a copyright is to attempt to control part of a communication system. A copyright carries with it an exclusive right. Since the copyrighted item is basically a message, the exclusive right is that of making certain the message is correct by prohibiting anyone from reproducing it. It is also the right to try to insure it from being propagated for immoral purposes, or against the interest of the public, or even against the owner of the copyright. The main right of a copyright is to obtain economic benefit from the sale of the message, partly due to the scarcity of the uniqueness of it.

UNIT 176
HOW TO OBTAIN A COPYRIGHT

A *copyright* is a form of protection given by the law of the United States. The owner of a copyright is granted, by law, certain exclusive rights of his work. In addition to the exclusive right to copy his work, there are rights which include: (1) the right to sell or distribute copies of the work, (2) the right to transform or revise the work, and (3) the right to perform and record the work.

COPYRIGHTING

The Copyright Law lists thirteen broad classes of work in which copyright may be claimed. Within the classes are the following kinds of work: (1) books, (2) periodicals, (3) lectures or similar productions for oral delivery, (4) dramatic musical compositions, (5) musical compositions, (6) maps, (7)

511

works of art, (8) reproductions of works of art, (9) drawings of a scientific or technical character, (10) photographs, (11) prints, pictorial illustrations, and commercial prints and labels, (12) motion picture photoplays, and (13) motion pictures other than photoplays.

COPYRIGHT CLAIMS

Only the author or those deriving their rights through him can rightfully claim copyright. Mere possession of a work does not give the possessor the right to copyright.

STATUTORY COPYRIGHT FOR A PUBLISHED WORK

Three steps should be taken to secure and maintain statutory copyright in a published work: (1) produce copies with a copyright notice printed therein, (2) publish the work, and (3) register your claim in the U.S. Copyright Office. Under item (1) one must first produce the work in copies by printing or other means of reproduction. It is essential that all copies bear a copyright notice in the required form and position. Com-

munications should be addressed to the Register of Copyrights, Library of Congress, Washington, D. C. 20540.

Promptly after publication the following material should be sent to the above address: (1) application form (this form may be requested from the Copyright Office), (2) two copies of the best edition of the work as published, and (3) the registration fee for a published work.

COPYRIGHT NOTICE

The copyright notice, as a general rule, should consist of one of the three forms as shown in Fig. 176-1. For a book or other publication printed in book form, the copyright notice should appear on the title page, or on the page immediately following. The page immediately following is normally the reverse side of the page bearing the title. Note the copyright in this book.

Copyright
John Doe
1900

Copr., John Doe, 1900

©John Doe, 1900

Fig. 176-1. The three forms of displaying the copyright notice.

UNIT 177
COPYRIGHT INFRINGEMENT

When the United States was founded, the interest people had in protecting creations of an intellectual nature was great enough that a principle was written into the Constitution (Art. 1, Sec. 8 [8]):

The Congress shall have the power to promote the Progress of Science and the useful arts, by securing for limited times to authors and inventors the exclusive right to their respective writings and discoveries.

The concept of *writings* has been extended to include," . . . . original works of authorship fixed in any tangible medium of expression from which they can be perceived, reproduced, or communicated either directly or with the aid of a machine."

In early days the only means of reproducing writings was by the printing press. Infringement and unlawful printing were almost synonymous. Now reproduction of writings can include many different means and copying machines.

BREAKING THE LAW

What will you do when someone from another department or area comes to you for three copies of a page from a magazine? You usually go to the office copier in your room and run them off. It probably will never occur to you that this is most illegal. In many libraries, schools, and business establishments people are doing this every day, even though the work is copyrighted. Schools and libraries are among the most serious violators of this law and many have been taken to court because of it. Judgements against copyright violators are harsh.

It is not always easy to say whether a reproduction is an infringement. The copyright statute is elusive in application. The copyright owner may sue for damages and the court can award almost any amount of damage. It is a rather difficult task to catch the offender. The only solution at this time seems to be an honor system. Picture in your own mind the number of times you have seen the copyright law broken by other people.

UNIT 178
PORNOGRAPHY

Pornography is obscene or licentious writing or painting. Any discussion relating to the rights of freedom of the press or of speech must begin with the First Amendment of the United States Constitution which prohibits Congress from abridging freedom of press or speech. In a complex society It would be naive to believe that there can be no restriction on anything one may write or say.

An effective law Is one that Is sound and enforceable. It must meet the test of constitutional acceptability. It should provide realistic penalties and should receive the genuine support of an alert citizenry.

The role of the printer concerning the laws of obscenity is much clearer than that of the publisher. The printer is technically vulnerable at only two points: (1) by accepting the copy, and (2) on delivery of the completed product. To explain further, when a printer gives the copy to his typesetter and pressman, he has distributed obscene literature. He also distributes obscene literature when he delivers the finished product to the customer. In between these two activities he is doing nothing illegal since he only possesses the literature. In a few cases, printers have turned questionable material over to authorities, but not often. The printer should strive to make objective judgments as to what is or is not obscene. His reputation is often at stake.

The publisher is more vulnerable to the laws of obscenity due to the fact that he actually distributes the material directly for sale or supplies a vendor with the material to sell. The laws are a bit clearer concerning the sale and distribution of pornography than they are regarding the printing of it.

The U.S. Supreme Court, by a decision in the 1960's, enabled pornography to run rampant and virtually uncontrolled for almost 10 years. It declared that to be obscene any printed matter must be totally without *social redeeming* value. Some printing firms openly engaged in printing hard-core pornography without fear of prosecution because they could prove that practically anything has *some* social redeeming value. However, in 1973 the U.S. Supreme Court ruled that standards for obscene material could be set by the local citizenry. This resulted in many local court actions in which publishers and distributors of hard-core pornography lost.

UNIT 179
COUNTERFEITING

Counterfeiting (imitating with intent to deceive) of money is one of the oldest crimes in history. In some periods it was considered treasonous and punishable by death. During the American Revolution the British counterfeited American currency in such large amounts that the Continental currency soon became worthless. During the Civil War it was estimated that about one-third of the currency in circulation was counterfeit.

The late Robert H. Jackson, Associate Justice of the United States Supreme Court, described counterfeiting by saying, "Counterfeiting is an offense never committed by accident, nor by ignorance, nor in the heat of passion, nor in extremity of poverty. It is a crime expertly designed by one who possesses technical skill, and lays out substantial sums for equipment." See Fig. 179-1.

Counterfeiting is again on the rise because of the ease and speed with which large quantities of counterfeit currency can be produced and transported. Modern photographic and printing equipment is available and used by criminals as well as by legitimate establishments.

FACTS ABOUT UNITED STATES CURRENCY

1. Genuine currency is printed on special paper, manufactured under strict government control.
2. The paper contains many small red and blue fibers invisible to the naked eye.
3. Genuine notes are printed from engraved plates by master craftsmen who use the most sophisticated equipment.

Fig. 179-1. The procedure and result of counterfeiting.

4. There are eleven positions of important features of paper currency (Fig. 179-2).

Genuine paper money looks good because of the above-listed items. It is made by experts, made on costly machines designed solely for that purpose, printed from steel plates produced by expert engravers who produce clear lines (Fig. 179-3), and printed on distinctive paper.

Counterfeit paper money looks bad because it is usually a product of inferior workmanship; it is usually made with equipment designed for other purposes; it is printed from a plate which is made by a photomechanical process, causing loss of detail (Fig. 179-4); and it is printed on paper which does not contain the distinctive red and blue threads.

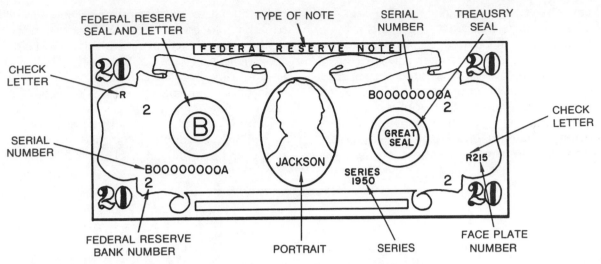

Fig. 179-2. Eleven positions of important features of paper currency.

PENALTIES

Counterfeiting and forgery are Federal offenses and carry heavy penalties. Making, possessing, or passing counterfeit bills can result in a $5,000 fine and up to 15 years in prison.

It is recognized that United States currency is so well protected with security features incorporated in its paper, printing, and engraving that it is without question among the world's most difficult currency to counterfeit.

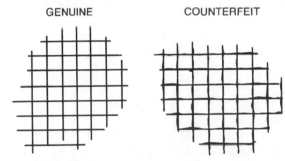

GENUINE

COUNTERFEIT

Fig. 179-3. Clear lines shown in genuine paper currency.

Fig. 179-4. Nonsharp lines of counterfeit paper currency.

UNIT 180
MORAL AND ETHICAL CONSIDERATIONS

Printers and publishers, no matter how large or small their establishments, must have a code of ethics regarding what they print. Book, newspaper, and magazine publishers, and also the ordinary printing firm must be aware of the values of the materials they print. Some of the items have a great deal of merit; some have no significant value. Others should never have been printed at all.

Many people accept the printed word as substantial truth. This is not because they are naive, but they know that one cannot print a completely false statement without risking libel. Thus the very daring involved in printing a misrepresentation establishes belief. The greater the exaggeration, the more believable it may become.

Especially when dealing with copyright, it is often difficult to prove that material has been stolen. It can easily develop into an embarrassing situation for both the printer and owner of the copyright. An example of this would be if a customer asked to have an advertising brochure printed. The printer would start from scratch, which would include doing design and layout work, composition, camera work, platemaking, and printing. The next time the customer wanted more of the same brochures printed, he might take it to another printer. The second printer could do it much cheaper, because all the preliminary work would heve been done. This is not illegal, but ethics certainly would be involved. A company, especially a small one, could be forced out of business due to irregular actions on the part of its customers. Much more than just good quality finished products must be considered before any printing or publishing is done.

UNIT 181

LEARNING EXPERIENCES: LEGAL CONSIDERATIONS FOR THE PRINTER

DISCUSSION TOPICS

1. Define the term copyright. When was the copyright law first enacted? When were the present copyright laws enacted in the United States?
2. Why should an author or writer obtain a copyright? List the several categories or classes of material that can be copyrighted. Who can claim copyright?
3. Explain the basic steps in obtaining the copyright for a published work. Where should the request for a copyright be addressed?
4. Illustrate the three methods of displaying the copyright notice. Where should the copyright notice for a published book be located?
5. How does the constitution of the United States protect authors and writers? Originally, why were copyright infringement and unlawful printing considered to be almost synonymous? Explain why that is now untrue.
6. Describe the role of the printer and publisher concerning the laws of obscenity (pornography). Why is a publisher more vulnerable to the laws of obscenity than the printer?
7. Define counterfeiting. Explain how counterfeiting can be a detriment to the economy of a country.
8. Enumerate the points that make good paper money look good; bad paper money look bad. What penalties can be enacted for counterfeiting?
9. How do morals and ethics enter into the graphic arts industry? What could happen if an untruth were printed about an individual or a group?

ACTIVITIES

1. Search through several different kinds of published materials. Observe the location of the copyright notice in each of the publications. Also note the styles or method of displaying the copyright notice. Which positions and methods of display are found most often?
2. Watch the local newspapers for accounts of counterfeiting offenses. Note the amounts of money involved in the counterfeiting situations and the penal-

ties given to those persons involved. Talk with local law enforcement authorites to obtain additional information about counterfeiting problems that occur in your city, county, or area of the country. How do counterfeiting problems in your geographical area compare to those of the total United States? Prepare a detailed report on your visit.

3. Write to the Copyright Office for information and forms and report on your findings and information.

4. Discuss copyright violations with your parents, friends, teachers, and librarians. Get their opinions regarding copying activities and compare their attitudes and opinions.

5. Research and discuss recent court decisions on the publication of pornographic materials. Discuss your local standards on obscene materials.

6. Discuss and defend the various moral and ethical considerations for the printer and publisher.

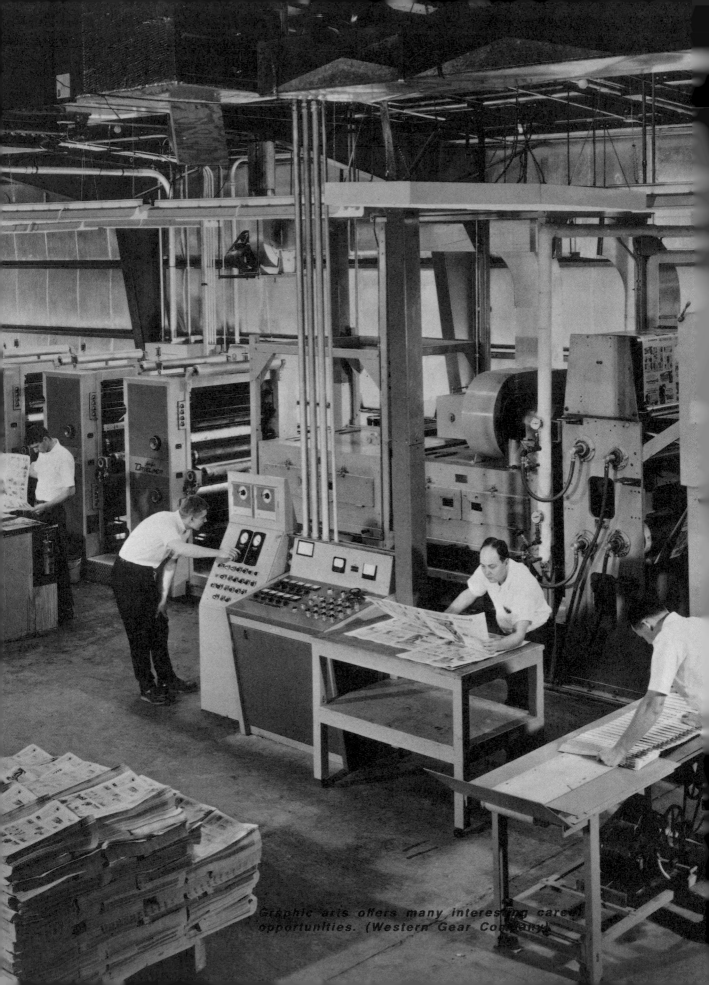

Graphic arts offers many interesting career opportunities. (Western Gear Company)

UNIT 182
INTRODUCTION TO CAREERS IN GRAPHIC ARTS

The graphic arts industry is involved in the economic growth and explosive expansion of this country and the world. This industry constantly needs people who are qualified. It will offer professional advancement for those interested in developing their future. Graphic arts offers many opportunities ranging from minimum-skill jobs to top management positions. Creative expression and functional craftsmanship are essential attributes of people interested in working in this dynamic field.

CHALLENGES

The challenges of the graphic arts industry are the result of technological developments in such areas as computers, copy and duplicating devices, microimage, electronic transmission methods, and the constant development and refinement of present processes. Other challenges deal more specifically with people who are interested in developing and promoting graphic arts. People must have the realization that they are making a contribution to our industrial society.

QUALIFICATIONS

Apprenticeship is a common method of entry into the skilled areas of graphic arts. In some instances it is the only means by which one may be trained to become a *journeyman* (skilled worker) in a unionized commercial plant. Formal apprenticeship is also required for journeyman status in many large establishments not covered by union contracts.

A registered apprentice is an employee who, under an expressed or implied agreement, receives instruction in an occupation for a stipulated period of time. He must also be employed in an apprenticeship program that is registered with a state apprenticeship agency or with the U. S. Department of Labor, Bureau of Apprenticeship and Training.

Apprenticeship within the graphic arts usually extends from four to six years, depending on the area of skill and the geographic location of the commercial plant. It covers all phases of the particular trade and generally includes classroom or correspondence study in related technical subjects which is in addition to training on the job. Applicants are usually between 18 and 35 years of age and must pass a physical examination.

One may also become qualified through formal education. A knowledge of graphic arts can be obtained through such courses in industrial arts and vocational-industrial education. Post-high school education includes vocational-technical institutes, trade schools, and college-university programs. Several technological and managerial graphic arts programs are being offered throughout the many higher education institutions within the United States. These four-year programs, which lead to a bachelor's degree, qualify the person to enter the industry in the mid-management categories. Graduate programs are offered that lead to the master's degree, qualifying one for higher management positions.

Fig. 182-1. Printing presses are being assembled in a manufacturing plant. (Heidelberg)

EARNING AND WORKING CONDITIONS

Earnings of production workers in the graphic arts industry are among the highest in the manufacturing field. These include the unskilled, semiskilled, and craftsmen. Recent statistics indicate that workers in all three categories are paid more per hour than other production workers. The wage varies from one classification in this occupation to another, and it is usually higher in cities than in smaller communities. It also varies with the type of commercial printing establishment.

The standard workweek is between thirty-five and forty hours, depending on the labor-management contract and also on the geographical location of the plant. Time and a half is generally paid for overtime and for work on Sundays and holidays. In newspaper plants, however, the craftsman's workweek often includes Sunday; there is therefore no additional rate of pay. Night-shift workers generally receive pay differentials above the standard day rate.

Annual earnings of craftsmen depend not only on the hourly rate of pay but also on how regularly they are employed. The graphic arts industry has fewer seasonal fluctuations than do many other industries.

Fig. 182-2. Preparing a printing press for operation.

This is one of the reasons it offers steadier employment and higher average annual earnings.

Working conditions within the industry, in general, are quite good. Many of the larger plants are air conditioned to insure quality control.

EMPLOYMENT OUTLOOK

Opportunities of many types exist. These range from the production and installation of equipment (Fig. 182-1), working with raw materials, production phases (Fig. 182-2), service, sales, and management. These opportunities are due to the continued rise in the volume of printed materials. They are based on population growth, the increasing high level of education, the expansion of American industry, and the trend toward greater use of printed materials for information, packaging, advertising, and various industrial and commercial purposes.

A PERSONAL BUSINESS

Young people often inquire as to how they can start a business of their own. This is a difficult effort because of the large capital outlay necessary to begin almost any private business. It is possible, however, to enter into the graphic arts production industry without a tremendous amount of money. Small business loans have helped many persons start their own shops.

It is interesting to know that of the approximately 40,000 graphic arts production establishments in this nation, about one-third are considered one-man operations. This means that the concern is owned and operated by one person employing, possibly, a few workers.

UNIT 183
PRODUCTION PREPARATION

Preparing material to be printed is an important aspect of the completed printed work. *Production* involves design and layout, composition, photography, and image carriers. Each of these specific areas is important to the completed product.

Fig. 183-1. Design and layout personnel prepare materials for publication. (M. Korn Packaging Co.)

DESIGN AND LAYOUT

The person involved in the area of *design* and *layout* originates the graphic product. With the imaginative planning and development of the original ideas, the completed item results.

Design and layout people must have definite artistic talent. They should enjoy working on drawing tables (Fig. 183-1) and arranging type and illustrations into usable form. The designer must have a good knowledge of color and how it affects people psychologically, since the final result must have visual impact.

COMPOSITION

A *compositor* is a person who assembles letters, words, sentences, and paragraphs into a form that can be duplicated many times. Several methods of composition exist, as mentioned earlier in this book. The person involved in composition must enjoy

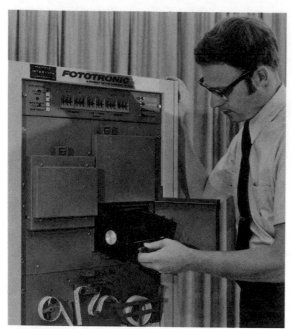

Fig. 183-2. This operator is preparing a high-speed tape-operated photographic composition machine. (Intertype Co.)

Fig. 183-3. A skilled photographer uses an industrial copy camera. (Ehrenreich Photo-Optical Industries, Inc.)

working with small materials and with delicate mechanical equipment.

In recent years, sophisticated procedures and equipment within the composition phase of the graphic arts industry have reached a high level. Computers and photographic techniques have entered into this area, making it complicated. Persons working in composition generally perform their work on the latest types of equipment (Fig. 183-2). It may be necessary to attend an industrial or technical night school to obtain sufficient knowledge for productive printing operations.

PHOTOGRAPHY

Photography plays an important role in the graphic arts. It deals with the production of the common photograph, usage of this medium in the composition area, production of photographic film negatives and positives, and preparation of finished printed material.

One who is interested in photography has many outlets for his talents. He may work for a daily newspaper, an advertising firm, or possibly even function as a free-lance

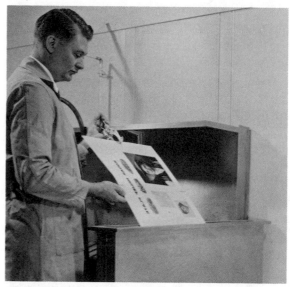

Fig. 183-4. A plate-maker prepares a relief image carrier. (Eastman Kodak Co.)

photographer. He not only takes photographs but may also develop and print the final pictures.

Other technicians may use enlargers to prepare prints or operate special copying cameras (Fig. 183-3) to make prints of an artist's rendition of outer space. Many persons may be involved with process cameras and normal darkroom activities, as discussed in earlier units in this text. People with a flair for photography have no problem obtaining work. In fact, the problem will be selecting the phase of graphic arts photography that they most prefer.

IMAGE CARRIERS

The ever-changing area of image carriers deals with preparing printing plates. Several new developments have required that many people be retrained and that new persons be trained with the background to do this type of work. A knowledge of chemistry is often desirable.

The tools of the image carrier specialist are the many different kinds of plate-making materials. These range from metal to plastic, rubber, and glass. Other new materials for this activity are being experimented with and perfected yearly. People in the image carriers area (Fig. 183-4) work in surroundings of chemicals, sinks, and etching tanks. Other items of equipment are exposure units, etching machines, and light-sensitive emulsion applicating machines.

UNIT 184
PRODUCTION OF PRINTED MATERIALS

The two main production phases are those of image transfer (press operations) and finishing and binding (where the materials are made into the final usable form). The pressmen and binders work directly with the printed products which are eventually distributed to consumers.

IMAGE TRANSFER

The actual *image transfer* or printing operation is performed on a press. Pressmen have the responsibility of making certain that the type, photographs, and illustrations are reproduced correctly. They must see that the necessary amount of ink is applied in all areas of each page. It is also their job to see that the total image is positioned properly on the page.

A pressman may work on large, web-fed presses (Fig. 184-1) or on large sheet-fed presses (Fig. 184-2) which require several men to operate. They may work on smaller machines requiring two or three persons or on a small machine where only one operator is required. The techniques of operating several styles and brands of presses vary, but basically all function in much the same general way.

Fig. 184-1. Operators prepare a web offset-lithography press for production. (The Cottrell Co.)

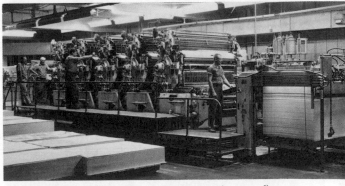

Fig. 184-2. Pressmen keep constant watch on a five-color sheet-fed press. (Western Printing and Lithographing Co.)

FINISHING AND BINDING

Finishing operations include cutting, folding, punching holes, and several other operations which make the printed materials usable. Special skills are needed to prepare the several different finishing machines for operation, such as the high-speed die cutter and creaser (Fig. 184-3).

Binding involves several different methods of fastening sheets of paper together to make the final product complete. Books, magazines, pamphlets, business forms, and advertising literature are bound together. Several different machines help to complete the many phases of binding, and skilled operators are in demand (Fig. 184-4). Binding machines and all graphic arts equipment require constant servicing to insure a high rate of production. Much of the work is done by hand.

Two types of binderies are *edition* and *pamphlet,* which bind books, magazines, and pamphlets. Job binderies do binding on contract for printers, publishers, or other customers. They can be operated as separate commercial establishments or as large commercial plants.

One who wishes to become a *journeyman binder* finds it generally necessary to complete a four- to five-year apprenticeship program. As in other areas of graphic arts, it

Fig. 184-3. A specialist prepares a high-speed die cutter and creaser for operation. (Consolidated International Corp.)

Fig. 184-4. Three women and one man are needed to an 18-pocket automatic gathering machine operating at peak capacity. (Consolidated International Corp.)

is possible to reduce this period of time if a person has had graphic arts training in a high school or a technical and vocational school, or other formal graphic arts work.

UNIT 185
MANAGEMENT AND SALES OPPORTUNITIES

Management and sales are two essential ingredients of all business enterprises, including the graphic arts industry. An executive vice-president of a large commercial graphic arts establishment has said, "The goal is to instruct the managers of tomorrow in the newer business tools such as computers, operations, and research. The aim is to turn out graduates who are specialists in change; men who are able to cope with the still-newer tools and machinery of tomorrow."

MANAGEMENT

Motivation of people to perform at a productive level is the key concept in management. The general climate that a manager creates for all of his personnel to work in is a more important factor than what he attempts to do with each individual.

A manager should:

1. Know how to utilize others around him.
2. Know where to look for experts who can strengthen weak areas.
3. Be creative and not be afraid to be different in actions and thought.
4. Have maturity.
5. Have a good personality.
6. Be willing to admit the need for help in understanding himself, his personnel, and their job responsibilities.
7. Develop the ability to rely on objectivity or facts rather than on opinions about certain business operations.
8. Be constantly concerned with developing his own motivation which, in turn, must motivate others.
9. Care about the successful operation of the company almost more than anyone else.

Management personnel must constantly be on the job (Fig. 185-1). They must want to devote more time to it than the average 8-to-5 shift. Special evening and weekend conferences and out-of-town trips are factors of self-improvement.

Young people interested in management opportunities will have the opportunity to develop their potential and obtain positions in this area. Management personnel is scarce and will become more so as business needs rise and the complexity of management increases.

SELLING

The sales phase of graphic arts is a most exciting challenge. A salesman must be a person dedicated to informing as many people as possible about the product. Graphic arts sales opportunities range from demonstrating and selling equipment (Fig. 185-2) to selling the printed product.

Profit is the prime motivation of almost all endeavors in business. A successful company makes a profit. This in turn means a good balance between sales and production. One of the key persons who maintains this proper balance is the salesman. The more he sells, the more the company can produce. Increased production, in most cases, helps to increase the profit margin.

The following are some necessary qualities for a salesman in the graphic arts:

1. An interest in the industry.
2. A desire to learn as much about the industry as possible.
3. A desire to work closely with people.
4. Devoting long hours to his work.
5. Good intelligence.
6. A desire to be constantly on the move.
7. Good grooming.
8. A sense of humor.
9. A good personality.

Fig. 185-1. Management personnel at work. (M. Korn Packaging Co.)

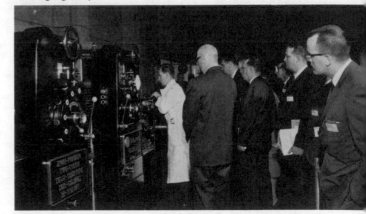

Fig. 185-2. A sales promotion demonstration of a new piece of equipment by a highly skilled operator. (Heidelberg)

UNIT 186
TEACHING OPPORTUNITIES

Teaching is a field in which career prospects are excellent. According to the Bureau of Labor Statistics of the United States Department of Labor, it is one of the largest of all professions, having over two million men and women employed full time.

Graphic arts presents many opportunities to persons who are interested in a teaching career and who especially like the graphic arts technical area. Over 4,000 schools in the United States offer courses and programs dealing with it. There is also an untold number of courses and seminars that are organized by industry.

GRAPHIC ARTS TEACHING OPPORTUNITIES

Teaching positions are available at almost any level in which a prospective graphic arts teacher would be interested. Industrial arts-graphic arts curricula are offered in secondary schools (grades 7-12) throughout the United States (Fig. 186-1). New programs which require more qualified teachers are being offered each school year.

Many vocational high schools offer courses which deal directly with teaching the skills needed to work in skilled-operator jobs in commercial graphic arts plants. Students who complete these technical-vocational programs can begin work immediately following high school. Such instruction requires teachers with knowledge and skills in many areas. An example would be the work done with process cameras and darkroom techniques.

Technical institutes and terminal technical programs in junior colleges provide instruction in skills. Teachers for these types

Fig. 186-1. A high school teacher demonstrates the operating procedure of an offset-lithography press.

of programs must be highly qualified in the knowledge of graphic arts production. Universities and colleges offering graphic arts management and technical curricula are in constant need of professors for this technical area (Fig. 186-2). Industry requires people with special graphic arts skills who can teach employees the techniques necessary to maintain current technical competency. Because industry in our society changes constantly, quite often on-the-job training can only be given directly in an industrial plant.

TEACHER QUALIFICATIONS

Teacher competencies vary with the individuals, but those considering teaching as a career should have the following attributes:

1. A personality acceptable to the people with whom they will work.
2. Above-average intelligence.

Fig. 186-2. A college professor lectures and discusses a technical graphic arts topic with his class.

3. A desire to teach a specific subject.
4. An attitude which permits the person to generate interest and reaction.
5. Ability to motivate the student.
6. Patience.
7. Ability to work long and hard with people until the educational objectives have been reached.

8. The ability to organize informational content.
9. The ability to demonstrate specific knowledge in a technical field.

A bachelor's degree is the usual requirement for teaching in secondary schools, most technical-vocational high schools, and technical institute positions. However, this is not always true in many trade and vocational schools where skilled graphic arts tradesmen are teaching and providing very effective instruction. The minimum requirement to teach in colleges and universities is usually a master's degree. The doctoral degree is becoming more desirable and is often necessary for teaching at the college-university level.

Industry does not always require formal education as a major requirement for the teaching-training programs, but people with formal education seem to have a better opportunity to fill these positions. It therefore behooves the person who wishes a career in this specific teaching field to acquire as much technical and general knowledge about graphic arts as possible.

UNIT 187
PULP AND PAPER MANUFACTURING OPPORTUNITIES

The pulp and paper manufacturing industry has many career possibilities. It uses many kinds of talent drawn from scientific, engineering, and liberal arts fields to fill a variety of technical, operating, and commercial positions.

Paper is made or marketed in all of the United States and in many foreign countries. The industry offers its employees an extremely wide choice of working locations and living environments.

ENGINEERING OPPORTUNITIES

Those persons having a degree in *industrial, civil,* or *mechanical* engineering have five possible areas of employment in the pulp and paper manufacturing industry:

1. Industrial engineers improve and maintain operating performance, reduce waste, prevent delays, achieve cost re-

ductions, and maintain a high level of production efficiency.

2. Power plant engineers and their employees are concerned with the design, supervision of construction, and operation of generating plants which furnish power.

3. Production, planning, and control employees help establish schedules to insure maximum use of available equipment, labor, tools, and capacity. They also coordinate production operations to meet delivery dates.

4. Quality control and production engineers and employees with a bachelor of science degree in either chemistry, chemical, or industrial engineering and who have from three to five years experience work in mill or plant production. Responsibilities include installation of product-inspecting and testing procedures gauged to establish quality standards. Professional advancement may lead to the office of quality control executive or manager.

5. Production time-and-motion employees are responsible for maintaining efficient plant operation for maximum production with minimum loss of effort by machine operators.

SCIENTIFIC OPPORTUNITIES

Persons having an advanced degree in *organic chemistry, physical chemistry,* or *biochemistry* and experience in *paper engineering* perform the following basic chemical research:

1. Conduct independent investigations to develop new products or processes.

2. Contribute to the solution of technical problems.

3. Solve problems of high-output production and manufacture.

4. Aim at extending product usefulness.

5. Work closely with the chemist.

RESEARCH OPPORTUNITIES

Two other areas of basic research carried on by mills dealing with products from their own forests are (1) basic research in *timberland management* which deals with the acquisition, culture, harvesting, and continued use of forest stands and, (2) basic research in *wood technology.* Both require degrees from a college of forestry, with additional education in botany, chemistry, geology, zoology, physics, environmental protection, and some general courses in economics and government.

Most members of the paper industry maintain their own established research facilities to improve existing products and develop new ones. Personnel working in research include skilled engineers, chemists, physicists, and foresters. College graduates with degrees in forestry analysis find varied positions in timber management, forestry and genetic research, and many other specialized fields.

MANAGEMENT, BUSINESS, AND LEGAL OPPORTUNITIES

Mill management and legal administrative requirements necessitate:

1. Lawyers in corporate, patent, tax, and real estate law.

2. Specialists on exports.

3. Engineers skilled in the operation of the entire plant.

4. Experts on labor, industrial, community, and employee relations.

5. Administrative heads to direct large staffs of office workers.

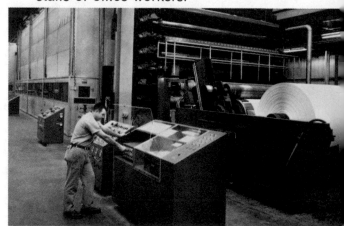

Fig. 187-1. A highly skilled paper machine operator feeds production information to a computer. (The Mead Corp.)

6. Traffic consultants.
7. Purchasing agents for materials and equipment.
8. Public relations, advertising, sales, and sales-service staffs.

PLANT OCCUPATIONS

Pulp and paper mill workers employed in plant jobs generally are divided into the three major occupational groups of (1) production workers who operate the various machines and equipment, (2) maintenance workers (Fig. 187-1) who maintain, install, and repair physical equipment, and (3) workers such as material handlers and stock clerks. Additional staff people include checkers and sorters for quality control, laboratory chemists, and packing and shipping operators.

OPPORTUNITIES FOR WOMEN

In a recent year, according to Federal Government figures, one out of every five workers in the paper industry was a woman. Some areas in which they have been particularly proficient are laboratory work, chemical testing, personnel, office management, secretarial, research, and finishing. In the future, opportunities for women are likely to be available in all areas of the paper industry.

UNIT 188
LEARNING EXPERIENCES: GRAPHIC ARTS CAREER OPPORTUNITIES

DISCUSSION TOPICS

1. Why is there and will there continue to be a need for graphic arts products? Identify some of the challenges that are being presented to the graphic arts industry. What makes a printed product successful?
2. Name the common method of entering the work force within the skilled areas of the graphic arts industry. Describe the qualifications necessary and the training programs.
3. How can a formal education help qualify people to enter the graphic arts industry? Where are formal education programs available? Is it possible to qualify for management positions upon entry into the industry?

4. Compare the earning power and working conditions within the graphic arts industry with those of manufacturing industries in general. Name the two factors influencing the annual earnings of craftsmen.
5. Describe the employment outlook within the graphic arts industry. Why does there appear to be a continued need for qualified personnel? Is it possible to start and operate one-man operations within this industry?
6. List the qualifications necessary for the four areas of work within the production-preparation phase of graphic arts. Why will it be necessary for people in the area of composition to be involved constantly in training programs? Cite the reason for a good knowledge of

chemistry for people who work or plan to work in the area of image carriers.

7. Describe the qualifications of people who work in the two areas of the production of printed materials. Name the general responsibilities of people within the image transfer and binding-finishing areas. Why do you think it is advisable for people in this area to have a high mechanical aptitude?

8. Cite the key concept in management. Why must a manager be adept in the art of communication? List the several qualifications for managers.

9. Give the range of sales opportunities in the graphic arts. Why must a salesman be dedicated to his or her work? What do each of the listed qualities for a salesman have to do with success?

10. Describe the teaching opportunities that are available in the graphic arts. Identify the qualifications necessary for teachers within the several levels or phases of graphic arts formal education.

11. List the five areas within the paper industry that people holding industrial, civil, or mechanical engineering degrees are qualified to enter. Briefly describe the responsibilities of personnel in each one of these areas.

12. Identify the opportunities in the paper industry for people who have an interest and competence in chemistry or law. What is the status of unskilled people? What reception do women find in the work force of the paper industry?

ACTIVITIES

1. Obtain career booklets describing opportunities within the graphic arts. These booklets are available from private industry as well as from local, state, and national graphic arts organizations. Talk with your school librarian and public librarian concerning materials that are available about careers in the manufacturing industries of which graphic arts is a part. Talk with your school vocational counselor, who should be knowledgeable of careers in several fields. One good source of information is the *Occupational Outlook Handbook* available from the U. S. Government Printing Office.

2. Visit a commercial graphic arts printing firm and talk with people in the areas of production, management, and sales concerning the opportunities in the graphic arts industry in your own geographical area. Talk with as many people as you possibly can so that a representative sampling of ideas and opinions is obtained. Visit more than one commercial plant if possible. Prepare a detailed report of your visit and findings.

3. Talk with your graphic arts teacher and other teachers concerning the opportunities and rewards of the teaching profession. Obtain information from the school vocational counselor, who should be able to give you information on the teaching profession on a national basis. Ask your graphic arts teacher what specific opportunities are available in the teaching of this technical area. Ask him to give you the opportunity to experience teaching by giving a short demonstration to fellow class members.

4. Visit a pulp and paper mill and talk with some of the production workers and management personnel. Obtain as much information as possible concerning the opportunities in the paper industry within your own geographical area as well as in the entire United States and possibly other countries. Observe closely all of the people on the job to see if the things that they are doing might interest you.

5. After obtaining all of the information from the four previous activities, sit down and thoroughly analyze your findings. Ask yourself the following questions: What would I like to do? Am I interested in the graphic arts as a possible career? If so, what specific area might I be interested in? If at this time I cannot decide, where should I attempt to collect more information?

Solution for crossword puzzle on page 509

INDEX

D

E

G

H

Q

R